PaperArt

Die Publikation erscheint aus Anlaß der PaperArt 5

5. Internationale Biennale der Papierkunst 1994 im Leopold-Hoesch-Museum und Papiermuseum Düren, 12. Juni – 25. September 1994

This book has been published on the occasion of PaperArt 5

5th International Biennale of Paper Art 1994 in the Leopold Hoesch Museum and the Papiermuseum Düren, 12th June – 25th September 1994

Dorothea Eimert

PaperArt

Geschichte der Papierkunst · History of Paper Art

Wienand Verlag

Schirmherr: Dr. hc. Johannes Rau, Ministerpräsident des Landes Nordrhein-Westfalen
Under the patronage of Dr. hc. Johannes Rau, Governor of the Land North Rhine-Westphalia

Sponsoren Sponsors:

Anker-Teppichfabrik Gebr. Schoeller GmbH & Co. KG, Düren
Getränkefachgroßhandel Willy Bongartz GmbH & Co. KG, Jülich
Canadian Pulp and Paper Association, Brüssel Brussels
Deutsche Bank, Mannheim und and Bonn
Dresdner Bank, Düren
Thomas Josef Heimbach GmbH & Co., Düren
Gebrüder Hoesch & Co. KG, Kreuzau
Initiative Umwelt und Papier – Info-Zentrum Papier, Karton und Pappe GmbH, Bonn
Jagenberg AG, Düsseldorf
Kultur- und Naturstiftung der Kreissparkasse Düren
GKD-Gebr. Kufferath GmbH & Co. KG, Düren
May + Spiess Papierverarbeitungswerk, Düren
Nordland Papier AG, Dörpen
Günther-Peill-Stiftung, Düren
PKL Verpackungssysteme GmbH, Linnich
Renker & Söhne Zerkall, Hürtgenwald-Zerkall
Papierfabrik Scheufelen, Lenningen
Sieger Wellpappe, Brühl
Papierfabrik Schoellershammer, Düren
Wellpappenfabrik Lamersorf, Inden
Westdeutsche Landesbank, Münster
Zewawell AG & Co. KG, Mannheim

Das Buch entstand mit besonderer Unterstützung der ZANDERS Feinpapiere AG
The book has been published with the special support of ZANDERS Feinpapiere AG

Leihgeber Loans by:

Staatliche Museen zu Berlin – Preußischer Kulturbesitz Berlin / Kupferstichkabinett – Sammlung der Zeichnungen und Druckgraphik
Galerie d'Art Contemporain Blancpain Stepczynski, Genf Geneva
Wolfgang Feelisch, Remscheid
Galerie Klaus Fischer, Berlin
John Gerard, Rheinbach-Hilberath
Edition Gutsch, Berlin
Galerie Lelong Zürich
Museum Ludwig, Köln Cologne
Axel-Hinrich und Christa Murken, Herzogenrath
Alfred Renker, Hürtgenwald-Zerkall
Holger Runge, Meerbusch
Tyler Graphics Ltd., Mount Kisco, New York
Galerie Andreas Weiss, Berlin
Städtische Galerie Villa Zanders, Bergisch Gladbach

Inhalt Contents

Papier – Medium der Kunst im 20. Jahrhundert

Paper – A medium for art in the 20th century

Kulturgeschichte aus dem Blickwinkel von Papier[1]: Das ist auch die Geschichte entscheidender Veränderungen in gesellschaftlicher und künstlerischer Hinsicht. Das Aussehen und die Materialität eines Papiers sowie seine Produktpalette für die Bereiche Handel, Wissenschaft und Kunst geben Aufschluß über zeitspezifische Bedürfnisse und strukturelle Wandlungen. Die hochentwickelten Kulturen der islamischen und morgenländischen Welt nutzten Papiere unterschiedlichster Qualitäten im Alltag und im Kunsthandwerk mehrere 100 Jahre früher als Kommunikationsmittel als das Abendland. Papier ist vor allem seit der Erfindung von Buch- und Bilddruck im 15. Jahrhundert der Kulturträger schlechthin. Künstler wählten und wählen für ihre Grafiken und Zeichnungen Papiere mit Bedacht, je nach Technik und künstlerischer Intention; ebenso wählerisch verhielten sich Drucker und Schriftsteller. Bis ins lesefreudige 18. Jahrhundert erfreute Papier sich allgemein in Europa hoher Wertschätzung. Papiermachen galt als Kunst. 1664 beschrieb ein Zeitgenosse 60 verschiedene Arbeitsschritte und zehn Berufstätigkeiten zur Fertigung eines Blattes Papier. Die heutigen riesigen, computergesteuerten Papiermaschinen bedürfen lediglich der Kontrolleure. Eine mittlere Papiermühle zu Ende des 18. Jahrhunderts produzierte am Tag 3000 bis 4000 Bogen. Die derzeit schnell-

Cultural history from a paper's eye view:[1]
This is a story of decisive changes socially and artistically. The way paper looks and feels as well as its line of products meant for commerce, science and art reflect the needs and the structural transformations of the times. The highly developed cultures of the Islamic and oriental world used paper of very varying quality as a means of communication in everyday life and in the crafts 100 years earlier than the occident did. Paper has, above all since the invention of book printing and picture reproduction in the 15th century, been the bearer of culture per se. Artists once chose, and still choose, paper with the deliberation necessary for implementing their graphic technique and their artistic intention. Printers and writers were no less discriminating. Far into the 18th century paper was a generally valued commodity among Europe's reading public. Making paper was considered an art. In 1664 a contemporary reported that 60 different steps of procedure and ten workers were needed to make one sheet of paper. Today giant, computer-run paper machines only require minimal supervision. A middle-sized papermill at the end of the 18th century produced 3000 to 4000 sheets of paper. Today's fastest paper machine production of much lower quality newspaper is up to 800 tons a day, which is 16.4 million square meters. The

ste Papiermaschine – für Zeitungsdruckpapier – kann an einem Tag bis zu 800 Tonnen erzeugen; das sind rund 16,4 Millionen Quadratmeter. Der bereits im 18. Jahrhundert beklagte als selbstverständlich betrachtete Gebrauch des kostbaren Stoffes Papier ist seit seiner uneingeschränkten Verfügbarkeit heute Normalität. Dies ist ein Ansatzpunkt für Künstler, die Schönheiten und Vorzüge des unendlich flexiblen und gestaltvariablen Materials Papier wieder gezielt ins Bewußtsein zu bringen. Papier kann flüssig sein wie Farbe, grafisch wie eine Zeichnung, leicht wie Luft, beweglich und dennoch stabil und jede beliebige Form annehmen.

Papier in seiner stark differierenden Beschaffenheit hat Künstler im 20. Jahrhundert zu wegweisenden Neuerungen angeregt. Die explosionsartige Wandlung des Weltbildes durch Forschung und neue Wissenschaften demontierte auch den traditionellen Kunstbegriff. Im Hinblick auf Papier bedeutet dies die allmähliche Entwicklung aus der dienenden Unmündigkeit für Bild und Schrift zu einem autonomen künstlerischen Sprachmittel.

Die vorliegende ‚Geschichte der Papierkunst' skizziert an markanten Stellen der Kunstentwicklung die Rolle des Papiers. Pablo Picasso und Georges Braque stellten radikal die tradierte Auffassung von Kunst in Frage. 1912 bauten sie aus dem bis dahin nur für Grafik und Zeichnung relevanten Material Papier erste Plastiken und fügten ihren Gemälden Tapetenfetzen und farbige Papiere als abstrakte gleichwertige Farbfelder ein. In der Folge erlebte die Collage aus bedruckten und unbedruckten Papieren vielgestaltige Variationen im Futurismus und Dadaismus, bei Kurt Schwitters und Max Ernst. Josef Albers untersuchte zusammen mit seinen Schülern am Bauhaus anhand des flexiblen, maschinell gefertigten Endlospapiers den materialgerechten Umgang, der zur natürlichen Form führt und manches Bildhauerwerk beeinflußte.

In den 40er Jahren sind es zunächst Jean Fautrier und Jean Dubuffet, die Papier und Papiermaché als formbare Masse nutzten, um Materialität und Stoff-

careless use of this precious material was already a reason for lamentation in the 18th century, but today has become normal in our age of unrestricted availability. This is a starting point for artists, who make us pointedly aware of the infinite flexibility and variability of the material, paper. Paper can be as liquid as paint, as graphic as a drawing, light as air, mobile and yet stable, and take on any shape or form.

Paper with its very differentiated properties has inspired artists in the 20th century to pioneering innovation. The explosive transformation of our cosmic view through research and the new sciences had dismantled the traditional definition of art as well. In relation to paper this has meant that picture and script have gradually become emancipated from mere functional servitude to become themselves autonomous artistic means of expression.

This present 'History of Paper Art' outlines the artistic development of the role of paper at crucial points in its career. Pablo Picasso and Georges Braque radically questioned the traditional conception of art. In 1912 they made their first sculptures out of paper, a material till then only relevant for graphic art and drawing, and incorporated scraps of wallpaper and colored papers into these pictures as abstract color-fields with equal rights. The collage made up of printed and non-printed papers subsequently took on varied shapes and forms in Futurism and Dadaism and with Kurt Schwitters and Max Ernst. Josef Albers and his students at the Bauhaus studied how best to deal legitimately with the material of flexible and mechanically produced continuous paper, all of which led to natural forms and influenced many subsequent works of sculpture.

In the 40s it was Jean Fautrier and Jean Dubuffet who first used paper and papier-maché as a formable mass, taking physical structure and texture as their theme. The French Nouveaux Réalistes carried these thoughts further in the 50s with their "cultivation of waste products". Everyday

lichkeit zu thematisieren. Die französischen Nouveaux Réalistes führten gegen Ende der 50er Jahre diesen Gedanken fort zu einer „Kultur des Mülls". Gebrauchsgüter wie Kannen, Flaschen, Briefumschläge und Plakatabrisse wurden zum Kunstwerk arrangiert. In den USA finden sich ähnliche Tendenzen bei Robert Rauschenberg, für den ebenfalls das Banale und Gewöhnliche ästhetische Möglichkeiten eröffnete. In den ersten Combine paintings verwandte er Postkarten und Zeitungsfotos. Yves Klein verweist auf eine transzendentale Immaterialität und führt die Monochromie ein. Absolute Reduktion der Sprachmittel in Farbe und individueller Handschrift wird Thema für viele Gruppierungen in Europa rund um die Düsseldorfer Gruppe ZERO. Papier in seiner Weiße und Reinheit veranschaulicht reduzierte Sprachmittel, minimale Farb- und Bewegungsveränderungen durch Licht und Schatten. Otto Piene, Günther Uecker und Jan Schoonhoven thematisieren dies. Eine Verwandlung in die Dreidimensionalität erfährt Papier durch Schneiden, Falten, Konstruieren und Prägen. Die weiterführenden Versuche von Franz Erhard Walther und Dieter Roth eröffnen den Bezug zur Natur und zu natürlichen Prozessen. Eigengesetzliche Vorgänge im Papier werden zum Kunstwerk: einsickernde Tinkturen, Schimmelbefall, allmählicher Zerfall durch Wasser, Luft oder Erde, Verfärbung durch Lichteinwirkung.
Dieser für Europa bis um 1980 typischen Papierkunst aus maschinell gefertigtem, makellos glattem Papier steht ein in den 60er Jahren in den USA entwickelter revolutionärer neuer Umgang mit flüssigem Papierstoff, mit Pulp, entgegen. Vorausgegangen war die Wiederentdeckung des handgeschöpften Papiers für die Grafik und als Basismaterial für Malerei durch Künstler wie Jackson Pollock, Willem de Kooning oder Robert Motherwell sowie die experimentelle Erweiterung der grafischen Techniken in die haptische Materialität.
Mit Robert Rauschenberg, der in den frühen 70er Jahren in der historischen Papiermühle Richard de Bas in Südfrankreich seine ersten Papierkunstwerke schuf, wurde der neue malerische Umgang

articles like pitchers, bottles, envelopes and torn-off billboard posters were transformed into works of art. In the US there were similar tendencies to be seen; Robert Rauschenberg likewise propagated new aesthetic possibilities for the banal and the everyday. In his first combines he used postcards and newspaper photos. Yves Klein proclaimed the spirit of transcendental immateriality and introduced monochromism. The absolute reduction of any kind of expressive color or individual gesture became a theme for many European groups in and around the Düsseldorf ZERO artists. The whiteness and purity of paper is able to embody this reduction in expression, as light and shadow is deployed to produce minimal changes in color and in movement. Otto Piene, Günther Uecker and Jan Schoonhoven made this the object of their study. Paper is transformed into three-dimensionality by cutting, folding, engineering and embossing. The on-going experiments of Franz Erhard Walther and Dieter Roth reveal the relationship to nature and to natural processes. The inherent laws that govern these processes on and with paper become themselves the work of art: the seeping of tinctures, the growth of mildew, the gradual dissolution through water, air or soil, discoloration through light. What is in the 1980s the typical European paper art of mechanically produced and perfectly smooth paper stands in stark contrast to the revolutionary treatment of fluid paper stock, or pulp, that began in the 1960s in America. What preceded it was the rediscovery of handmade paper as a basic material for the graphic arts and for painting by artists like Jackson Pollock, Willem de Kooning or Robert Motherwell as well as the experimental expansion of graphic techniques towards more tactile materiality.
In the person of Robert Rauschenberg, who in the early 70s created his first artworks out of paper in the historic Richard de Bas papermill in the south of France, the new artistic way with paperpulp became celebrated at one strike. The initiator of this whole undertaking was the lithograph printer,

mit Pulp schlagartig bekannt. Initiator des Unternehmens war der Drucker Kenneth Tyler, der heute das wichtigste experimentelle Zentrum für Papierkunst, Tyler Graphics in Mount Kisco, New York, führt. Er gewann bereits arrivierte Künstler wie Kenneth Noland, David Hockney, Ellsworth Kelly, Frank Stella und Anthony Caro für die neue innovative Technik der Papiermalerei und Papierskulptur.
Die Papierkunst aus Pulp zeigt seit den 70er Jahren in den USA, seit der Zeit um 1980 in Korea und Japan und kurze Zeit später in Europa vielgestaltige Facetten. In Europa vor allem bleibt auch die Tradition im Umgang mit vorgefertigtem Papier und mit Karton neben der neuen Vorliebe für Papierpulp erhalten. Dadurch ergibt sich eine variationsreiche Bandbreite von Papierkunst, auffallend intensiv vor allem in Deutschland, Belgien und den Niederlanden. Aus der Fülle qualitätvoller Papierkunst und der vielen Künstlerinnen und Künstler, die es verdient haben, in einer Geschichte der Papierkunst benannt zu werden, können hier jedoch nur wenige mit besonders markanten und typischen Werken herausgestellt werden.
Die traditionsreiche Papierstadt Düren mit ihren vielen Papierfabriken und papierzuliefernden und -verarbeitenden Betrieben hat die Kunst mit Papier und aus Papier zum turnusmäßigen Ausstellungsthema gemacht. 1981 zeigte das Leopold-Hoesch-Museum Düren eine Papierkunstausstellung, die erstmals für Europa die europäische Papierkunst aus vorgefertigtem Papier und die amerikanische Papierkunst aus Pulp in einer Ausstellung zusammenführte. Seit 1986 wird im Kunstmuseum und im benachbarten Papiermuseum unter jeweils wechselnder Thematik die Internationale Biennale der Papierkunst durchgeführt. Die Künstler der ‚PaperArt 5', der ‚5. Internationalen Biennale der Papierkunst', sind mit Bedacht auch im Hinblick auf die Thematik des vorliegenden Buches ‚Geschichte der Papierkunst' ausgewählt. 14 Künstler inszenieren 14 Räume. Sechs Künstler demonstrieren in Einzelarbeiten den neuen Umgang mit Pulp und handgeschöpftem Papier.

Kenneth Tyler, who runs the most important experimental center for paper art, Tyler Graphics in Mount Kisco, New York. It was his significant achievement to have won over already well-known artists like Kenneth Noland, David Hockney, Ellsworth Kelly, Frank Stella and Anthony Caro to the new innovative techniques for making paintings and sculpture with paper.
Since the 70s in the US and since approximately 1980 in Korea and Japan and somewhat later in Europe, paper art made out of pulp has displayed its numerous facets. Especially in Europe the tradition of using prefabricated paper and cardboard has remained in place alongside of the new-found love for paperpulp. This has resulted in a highly varied range of paper art, markedly so in Germany, Belgium and the Netherlands.
Of the great quantity of prestigious works and of artists who deserve mention in a history of paper art, only very few can be named, i.e., those with especially striking and/or especially typical works.
The paper city, Düren, with its long tradition of papermaking factories and their subcontractors and of paper processing industries, has made art with and of paper a theme for regular exhibitions. In 1981 one of these was held in the Leopold Hoesch Museum in Düren that for the first time in Europe brought together European paper art made of prefabricated paper and American paper art made of pulp. Since 1986 the International Biennale of PaperArt has been presented in the art museum and the neighboring paper museum, each time under a different thematic aspect.
The artists of 'PaperArt 5', the '5th International Biennale of PaperArt', have been carefully selected to coincide with the theme of the present book 'The History of Paper Art'. Fourteen artists have installed fourteen rooms. Six artists are demonstrating the new treatment of pulp and handmade paper with single works.
Otto Piene is showing five light ballets, two early ones from around 1960 and three new ones. Joel Fisher, one of the pioneers of American pulp paper

Otto Piene zeigt fünf Lichtballette, zwei frühe aus der Zeit um 1960 und drei neue. Joel Fisher, einer der Pioniere der amerikanischen Papierkunst mit Pulp, schafft einen meditativen Raum aus kleinen recycleten Papieren. James Rosenquist vertritt die farbenfreudige, großdimensionierte Malerei mit Pulp, kombiniert mit grafischen Elementen, und Anthony Caro die neue Skulptur aus handgeschöpftem Papier. A. R. Penck stellt eine neue Werkgruppe farbiger Papiergußarbeiten vor. Frank Badur und Kuno Gonschior zeigen stille Malereien mit Pulp. Felix Droese erstellte erstmals eine Mappe mit Wasserzeichnungen. Die Erhebung in die Immaterialität durch Abformung macht Andreas von Weizsäcker zum Thema.

Timm Ulrichs erarbeitet den Bereich der Totalkunst und des Prozeßvorgangs. Die Japanerin Takako Saito setzt sich mit Papier aus der Sicht von Fluxus auseinander und bezieht Zufall und Musik ins Papierkunstwerk ein. Die Koreanerin Eun Nim Ro inszeniert einen rituellen Raum, in dem sie den ursprünglichen Zusammenklang von Natur und Papier thematisiert. Der junge Chinese Huang Yong Ping versucht auf philosophische Weise chinesische und westliche Kultur im Papier zu verbinden. Der Russe Dmitri Prigov wählt Zeitungspapier, die Sprache des Alltags, zur intellektuellen, spirituellen Kommunikation. Der Franzose Jean-Luc Parant komponiert einen Raum von visueller Poesie. Reviva Regev formt eine Raumskulptur zur Thematik von Werden und Vergehen. Der junge Bulgare Milko Pavlov baut eine labyrinthische Skulptur aus Wellpappe. Tony Cragg, dessen Werk den Umgang mit Papier an sich schon vermuten läßt, nutzt hier erstmals Papier als Ausdrucksmittel. Michael Petry transponiert Papier in die Videokunst. Der junge Amerikaner A. Harold Barreiro komponiert Papiermusik und führt diese zur Eröffnung und zum Abschluß der Ausstellung auf. Die Polin Maria Orzel-Hercka zeigt „Bewegliche Bilder“ mit Papierkostümen und Papierbildern. Der Ausstellungsraum im Papiermuseum stellt historische Werke der Papierkunst der späten 50er bis frühen 70er Jahre exemplarisch vor.

art, has created a meditative room out of small bits of recycled paper. James Rosenquist represents bright-colored, large-scale pulp painting combined with graphic elements, and Anthony Caro the new sculpture made of handmade paper. A. R. Penck presents a new series of paper works of poured colored pulp. Frank Badur and Kuno Gonschior show meditative pulp paintings. Felix Droese has for the first time put together a portfolio of watermarks. Andreas von Weizsäcker takes as his theme the creation of immateriality by a process of moulding.

Timm Ulrichs does his work in the field of a total art system, pinpointing the process per se. The Japanese, Takako Saito, treats paper from a Fluxus standpoint and incorporates chance and music into paper art. The Korean, Eun Nim Ro, has installed a ritual room in which she thematizes the primeval harmony of nature and paper. The young Chinese, Huang Yong Ping, has tried to link Chinese and Western culture philosophically in paper. The Russian, Dmitri Prigov, has chosen newspaper, its everyday language, for intellectual and spiritual communication. The Frenchman, Jean-Luc Parant, has composed a room of visual poetry. Reviva Regev has created a sculpture in space on the theme of growth and decay. The young Bulgarian, Milko Pavlov, has built a labyrinth sculpture out of corrugated cardboard. Tony Cragg, whose work has always hinted at an association with paper, has here for the first time used paper as a medium of expression. Michael Petry transposed paper to videoart. The young American, A. Harold Barreiro, has composed paper music to be performed at the opening and the close of the exhibition. The Pole, Maria Orzel-Hercka, shows 'Moving Pictures' with paper costumes and paper scenes. The show room in the paper museum has put some historical and exemplary paper artworks from the late 50s to the early 70s on exhibit.

I wish to thank all the artists for their collaboration in preparing this book and the exhibition, above all Otto Piene, Dmitri Prigov, A. R. Penck, Tony

Für die Mitarbeit zur Vorbereitung des Buches und der Ausstellung möchte ich ganz herzlich allen Künstlern danken, vor allem den Herren Otto Piene, Dmitri Prigov, A. R. Penck, Tony Cragg und Timm Ulrichs, die durch ihre spontane Begeisterung für das Unternehmen schon in frühem Stadium zum Gelingen beitrugen. Horst Gläsker, der den schwierigsten Part der Ausstellung zu bestehen hatte, nämlich den Kampf mit der dominanten Architektur und der technisch schwierigen Situation der Treppenhauskuppel, gilt es besonders hervorzuheben.

Für die stets hilfreiche Unterstützung danke ich ganz herzlich Frau Marabeth Cohen-Tyler, Herrn Hubertus Schoeller, Herrn Alfred Renker und Herrn Bogislav von Wentzel, ebenso Frau Eva Nüsser M.A. vom Museum Abteiberg in Mönchengladbach, Frau Stephanie Schüssler M.A. und Frau Irmgard Gerhards. Danken möchte ich auch den Herren Wolfgang Feelisch, John Gerard, Jochen vom Berg, Frank Wollny, Dirk Olbertz, den Galeristen Horst Dietrich, Klaus Fischer, Herbert Gutsch und Michael Schulz sowie ganz besonders der Galerie Krings-Ernst und dem Direktor des Institut Français Cologne, Herrn Jean-Michel Phéline. Den Brüdern Aust von Televisor gilt mein Dank für gute Medienarbeit, Herrn Dr. Hans-Dieter Weger für die Unterstützung beim Sponsoring. Danken möchte ich allen Unternehmen und den Stiftungen, die Ausstellung und Publikation mit Geld- und Sachspenden unterstützt haben.

Ohne das tragende Engagement der Initiative Umwelt und Papier (IUP) und die Unterstützung des Verbandes deutscher Papierfabriken (VdP) hätte das Unternehmen ‚PaperArt – 5. Internationale Biennale der Papierkunst' nicht gelingen können. Ich sage Dank dem Geschäftsführer der IUP, Herrn Uwe Leesemann, und Frau Cornelia Trauschke M.A. sowie dem Präsidenten des VdP, Herrn Christoph Sieber-Rilke, und dem Geschäftsführenden Präsidialmitglied Herrn Dr. Peter Otzen.

Cragg and Timm Ulrichs who by their spontaneous enthusiasm at a very early stage in this undertaking helped it to succeed. I would like to give special mention to Horst Gläsker who had to deal with one of the greatest difficulty in mounting the exhibit, namely the struggle with the dominating architecture and the technically problematic site of the stairwell cupola.

For their ever helpful support I wish to thank very cordially Ms. Marabeth Cohen-Tyler, Mr. Hubertus Schoeller, Mr. Alfred Renker and Mr. Bogislav von Wentzel, as well as Ms. Eva Nüsser, M.A., from the Museum Abteiberg in Mönchengladbach, Ms. Stephanie Schüssler, M.A., and Ms. Irmgard Gerhards. I would also like to thank Messrs. Wolfgang Feelisch, John Gerard, Jochen vom Berg, Frank Wollny, Dirk Olbertz, the gallery owners Horst Dietrich, Klaus Fischer, Herbert Gutsch and Michael Schulz, and especially the Krings-Ernst Gallery as well as the director of the Institut Français Cologne, Mr. Jean-Michel Phéline. The Aust brothers from Televisor deserve thanks for good media work and Dr. Hans-Dieter Weger for his assistance in sponsoring. I would also like to thank all the companies and foundations that have supported the exhibition and this publication with donations in the form of money and/or goods.

The whole enterprise of 'PaperArt – 5th International Biennale of Paper Art' would never have been realized without the engagement of the 'Initiative Umwelt und Papier' (IUP), and the support of the Verband deutscher Papierfabriken (VdP). I also extend my thanks to the director of the IUP, Mr. Uwe Leesemann, and Ms. Cornelia Trauschke, M.A., as well as to the president of the VdP, Mr. Christoph Sieber-Rilke, and the chairman of its board, Dr. Peter Otzen.

I. Kulturfaktor Papier I. Paper as a cultural factor

Gäbe es unsere Kultur und die heutige Wissenschaft ohne Papier? Hätte Gutenberg einen anderen, ähnlich variablen Beschreibstoff gefunden, um ihn zu bedrucken? Künstler hätten auf anderen Materialien arbeiten können, aber ist es nicht das gedruckte Bild, das, vervielfältigt auf Papier, seit etwa 1400 mindestens ebenso einflußreich das Leben und die Geschichte bestimmt wie seit etwa 1450 das gedruckte Wort? Wie wäre der Handel, der Alltag ohne Papier?

Vor einigen Jahren zirkulierte das Gerücht vom Tod des Papiers, weil Computer und Bildschirm Papier angeblich überflüssig machen. Aber wird nicht eigentlich seit Einführung der neuen Datenverarbeitungsmöglichkeiten mehr Papier verbraucht?

Sicher ist, daß unsere Geschichte und Kultur untrennbar mit Papier verknüpft sind. Dokumente, Briefe, Manuskripte, Bücher, Landkarten, Zeichnungen und Grafiken sind ohne Papier kaum denkbar. Papier ist Trägermaterial von Informationen und Erkenntnissen, von Dichtung, Musik und bildender Kunst. Ohne Papier hätte eine Vermittlung und Überlieferung von Geschichte und Kultur nicht so umfassend stattgefunden.

Gesellschaften, die sich differenziert entwickeln, genügt eine mündliche Kommunikation nicht mehr. So bildeten sich im Laufe der Menschheitsgeschichte Bild- und Schriftsprachen. Diese bedurften

Would our culture and today's science even exist without paper? Would Gutenberg have found another similarly variable material for print? Artists could have worked on other materials, but is it not the printed image that, reproduced on paper since at least 1400, has influenced and determined life and history as much as has the printed word since 1440? What would trade be like, our everyday life, without paper?

Some years ago a rumor was circulated to the effect that paper was dead, because the computer and the screen made it superfluous. But is it not actually the case that even more paper has been used since the introduction of the new data processing?

It is certain that our history and culture are inseparably linked to paper. Documents, letters, manuscripts, books, maps, drawings, graphic works: all these are almost inconceivable without paper. Paper is the material that transmits information and knowledge, literature, music and the visual arts. Without paper the transmission and dissemination of history and culture would never have taken place so comprehensively.

Societies that develop in very differentiated ways are no longer satisfied with solely oral communication. So in the course of human history, ideogrammic and scriptal languages evolved. These needed inscribable surfaces. Those used were: rock

der Beschreibstoffe, wie Felswände, Steine, Baumrinden, Holz- und Tontafeln. In den polynesischen und amerikanischen Regionen um den Äquator nutzte man Tapa, im Orient und im Mittelmeerraum Papyrus, im Mittelmeerraum und in Europa das Pergament. Erst zwischen dem 13. und 15. Jahrhundert wurde dieses in Europa vom Papier verdrängt.
Von allen Beschreibmaterialien, die der Mensch je erfand, ist Papier am weitesten verbreitet. Sein Name leitet sich ab vom Papyrus, einem pflanzlichen Beschreibstoff, den Ägypter bereits um 3000 v. Chr. und später auch Griechen und Römer benutzten.

Die ältesten Papierfragmente, auf denen eine Landkarte gezeichnet ist, stammen aus Gräbern in China. Der in den 1970er Jahren erstellte Bericht des archäologischen Instituts der Provinz Gansu datiert sie in die westliche Han-Dynastie (202 v. Chr. – 8 n. Chr.). Die als Geheimnis gehütete chinesische Papiermachertechnik gelangte erst im 6. Jahrhundert nach Korea und im Verlauf des 7. Jahrhunderts nach Japan. In beiden Ländern wird noch heute nach alter Tradition von Hand in großen Mengen Papier geschöpft. Die Kenntnis des Papiermachens verbreitete sich früh nach Zentralasien, Tibet, Indien, Persien und Ägypten. Die Kultur der fernöstlichen und morgenländischen Welt kannte bereits im 9. Jahrhundert viele Sorten von Papier. Von den Feinstpapieren waren das samarkantische und das chinesische beliebt. Papiere konnten bereits antikisiert werden durch Safran und durch Sykomorensaft. Buntpapiere erzeugte man durch Auftragen von Farben, vermischt mit Stärke. Auch Papierformate waren bereits festgeschrieben.[2] Im Abendland gab es erst im 13. Jahrhundert die ersten Papiermühlen in Italien und zwar in Fabriano und Amalfi. In Fabriano wurden erstmals 1282 Papiere mit Wasserzeichen als Markenzeichen gekennzeichnet.
Der rasante Aufschwung des Handels im späten Mittelalter erforderte auch größere Mengen und eine reichere Palette an Papieren, zunächst als Bild- und Schriftträger, später auch als Ver-

walls, stones, tree bark, wood and clay tiles. In the regions close to the equator, Polynesia and America, it was tapa, in the Orient and the Mediterranean papyrus, also in the Mediterranean and in Europe parchment. It was not till somewhere between the 13th and 14th centuries that these materials were superseded in Europe by paper.
Of all the inscribable materials that man has invented, paper is the most widespread. Its name is derived from the papyrus plant, which provides an inscribable material that the Egyptians used as long ago as 3000 B.C. and the Greeks and Romans somewhat later.
The oldest paper fragments, found in graves in China, had a map drawn on them. The report put together in the 1970s by the Archeological Institute of the province of Gansu dated them back to the western Han Dynasty (202 B.C. to 8 A.D.). The Chinese technique of making paper was a well-kept secret and did not reach Korea till the 6th century and Japan till the 7th. In both countries large quantities of paper are still today made traditionally by hand. The knowledge of how to make paper then spread very soon to central Asia, Tibet, India, Persia and Egypt. The cultures of the Far East and the West in the 9th century were already acquainted with many kinds of paper. The paper from China and from Samarkand was the most popular among the finer kinds. Paper could already be made to look antique by an application of saffron or sycamore juice. Paper could be colored by applying colors mixed with paste. The paper sizes were already standardized.[2] In the west the first papermills were established in the 13th century: in the Italian cities of Fabriano and Amalfi. In the year 1282 in Fabriano the first watermarks were impressed on paper to serve as trademarks.
The boom in trade in the late Middle Ages brought with it greater quantities and a wider range of paper, in the beginning to bear images and writing, later also as wrapping material. The first papermills sprang up along the chief trade routes, the first in Germany (Nuremberg) in 1390, in Switzerland (Marly) in 1400,

packungsmaterial. Entlang der Fernhandelsstraßen etablierten sich die ersten Papiermühlen, 1390 die erste in Deutschland (Nürnberg), 1400 in der Schweiz (Marly), 1411 in Portugal, 1428 in Holland (Gennep), 1490 in England (Herefordshire).[3]

Der „Wissensträger" Papier wurde in Europa im Spätmittelalter zum wesentlichen Kommunikationsmittel. Der Wandel durch die technische und gewerbliche Revolution im 15. Jahrhundert führte zur Nachfragesteigerung. Durch den Bilddruck und den neuen Buchdruck kam es zu einer Mechanisierung des Abbildens und Schreibens, bildliche und schriftliche Erzeugnisse konnten durch Vervielfältigung in größeren Mengen verbreitet werden.

In China war bereits im 4. Jahrhundert n. Chr. die Möglichkeit der Bildervervielfältigung bekannt; Inschriftsteine färbte man mit Tusche und rieb die Zeichen auf Papier ab. Im Abendland nutzte man zur selben Zeit den Druck von Holzmodeln auf Stoffe. Der frühe Bilddruck auf Papier war die konsequente Fortführung dieser Technik. Schon vor 1400 wurden in manchen Klöstern und Wallfahrtsstätten auf Papier gedruckte Heiligenbilder verteilt. Die neue, unmittelbare Mitteilungskraft des Bildes glich einer Art Magie. Es war nun möglich, den Gläubigen das Erlösungswerk unmittelbar und auf individuelle Weise sichtbar zu machen. Glaubenserlebnisse waren nicht mehr primär an die Gemeinschaft gebunden, die private Andacht trat in den Vordergrund.

Um 1440 erfand Johannes Gutenberg den Druck mit beweglichen Metallettern, eine Technik, die in Korea bereits seit 1403 existierte. Mit der Erfindung des Bilddrucks und des Buchdrucks begann in Europa der Siegeszug des Papiers. Um 1500 zählte man in Europa bereits in 260 Orten mehr als 1100 Druckereien, die bis dahin etwa 40 000 Werke mit einer geschätzten Auflage von zehn Millionen Exemplaren gedruckt hatten, darunter alle wichtigen Werke der Antike und des Mittelalters, illustriert mit vielen Bilddrucken.[4]

Das Bedürfnis nach Bildern ging einher mit dem Drang nach persönlicher Entfaltung mit Hilfe von

in Portugal in 1411, in Holland (Gennep) in 1428, in England (Herefordshire) in 1490.[3]

Paper as a "conveyor of knowledge" proceeded to become an essential means of communication in Europe in the late Middle Ages. The changes wrought by the technical and trade revolution in the 15th century led to a rise in demand. Brought on by a growing need for picture and book prints, a mechanization in picture and script reproduction took place, and written products could now be copied and circulated on a larger scale.

The Chinese knew how to reproduce pictures as early as the 4th century; inscribed stone was stained with ink and the image rubbed onto paper. While at the same time in the West, wooden models were used to print fabric. The earliest printing of images on paper was the natural continuation of this technique. At some cloisters and pilgrimage sites even before 1400, pictures of saints printed on paper were handed out. The new direct power of communication seemed like magic. It was now possible to make a work of salvation visible to the believer in a direct and individual way. Experiences of faith were no longer primarily bound up with the community; private devotion became more prominent. Around 1440 Johannes Gutenberg invented printing with movable type, a technique that had existed in Korea since 1403. With the invention of picture and book printing, the triumphal advance of paper began in Europe. Around the year 1500 in 260 towns in Europe there were more than 1100 printing shops, which had printed approximately 40,000 works with an estimated edition of 10 million copies, among which were all the important works of antiquity and the Middle Ages containing numerous illustrations.[4]

The desire for images went hand in hand with the pursuit of personal development by means of knowledge. "The heavens have been studied, the earth explored, and everything found in the four corners of the world has come to light in art",[5] the humanist Konrad Celtis wrote in 1487 to Emperor Friedrich III.

Wissen. „Der Himmel ist erschlossen, die Erde durchforscht, und was in den vier Weltgegenden besteht, kommt ans Licht durch die Kunst“[5], schrieb der Humanist Konrad Celtis 1487 an Kaiser Friedrich III.

Mit dem Humanismus, der Reformation und dem Aufblühen der Naturwissenschaften etablierten sich Bilddruck, Buchdruck, Verwaltung und Wissenschaft. Papier wurde notwendig für die bildkünstlerischen und schriftlichen Systeme und für den Alltag. Der Beitrag des vervielfältigten Bilddrucks auf Papier für die Verbreitung von Wissen, Kulturgut, Religion, Geschichte, Kunst ist wesentlich. Das Bild ist immer von Wirkung. Vervielfältigt als Flugblatt, als eilige Information, als Pamphlet wurde es bereits an der Wende zur Reformation zum willkommenen Mittel für Einflußnahme und zur Ausübung von Macht.[6]

What also became established – together with Humanism, the Reformation and the flourishing of the natural sciences – was picture and book reproduction, administration, and science. Paper was necessary for all the systems of illustrative art and script as well as for everyday life. The contribution made by illustrations reproduced on paper has been crucial to the circulation of knowledge, culture, religion, history and art. Pictures always work. Duplicated in flyers, on sheets of last-minute information, in pamphlets, they were, on the eve of the Reformation, a welcome means of exercising influence and power.[6]

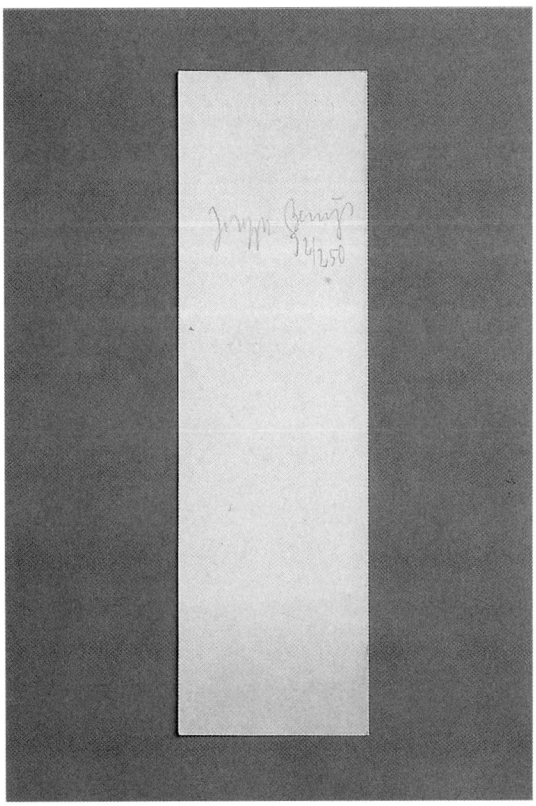

Joseph Beuys. From Olivestone, 1984. Löschblatt. 29,5 x 8,5 cm / Joseph Beuys: From Olivestone, 1984. Blotting paper. 29.5 x 8.5 cm

II. Innovationen für die Kunst – Experimente mit Materialien
II. Innovations in art – Experimentation with materials

II. 1. Papier, seine Qualität und Wertschätzung

Die Druckgrafik entwickelte sich im 15. Jahrhundert zum bildkünstlerischen Medium, zunächst im Holzschnitt, dann im Kupferstich und schließlich in der Radierung.
Immer wieder maßen namhafte Künstler der Druckgrafik besondere Bedeutung bei wie z. B. Dürer, Rembrandt oder Piranesi. Goya und vor allem Daumier führten das damals neue lithographische Verfahren zur ersten Blüte. Seit Toulouse-Lautrec und Munch verlor die Grafik niemals mehr an Gewicht und Anziehungskraft. Gerade im 20. Jahrhundert entwickelte sie eine eigenständige Ausdruckssprache, wie beispielsweise im Expressionismus, bei den Surrealisten oder den Künstlern am Bauhaus. Seit den ausgehenden 1950er Jahren nahm Grafik in den USA und in Europa eine immer stärkere Stellung ein. Die vertrauten Grenzen allerdings wurden in vielerlei Hinsicht überschritten. Ungewöhnlich große Formate entstanden, neue Druckträger wurden neben Papier eingesetzt.
Für die Papierkunst ist vor allem die in den USA bekannt gemachte neue Form von Papierarbeiten aus Pulp, aus gefärbter und gepreßter Papiermasse, von Interesse. Diese Papierbilder treten oft aus der Zweidimensionalität heraus und werden mit Colla-

II.1. Paper, its quality and esteem

Graphic print reproduction developed in the 15th century into a medium for art illustration, at first for the woodcut, then for copperplate engraving and finally for the etching.
Again and again well-known artists came to esteem graphic art as specially significant for their own work, for example Dürer, Rembrandt or Piranesi. Above all Goya and Daumier brought what was then the new technique of lithography to first fruition. Ever since Toulouse-Lautrec and Munch, the graphic arts have never lost their importance and their attraction. Especially in the 20th century they developed their own individual language, as seen in the case of Expressionism, the Surrealists or the artists of the Bauhaus. Since the end of the 50s, graphic art has established an ever stronger position in the United States and in Europe. The familiar boundary lines, however, have been overcome in many ways. Unusually large formats have been adopted and new surfaces other than paper used for printing.
What is of special interest for paper art is above all the new form made known in the US of works made of pulp, of dyed and pressed paper stock. These paper pictures often spring forward beyond two-

geelementen oder druckgrafischen Verfahren kombiniert. Die Sprache des Materials und der Weg in die dritte Dimension charakterisieren auch die Papierbilder, in denen Papier geprägt, gefaltet, durchbohrt, aufgerissen wird.

Jedes druckgrafische Verfahren, jede Zeichnung und jedes Aquarell kann erst dann zur optimalen Wirkung gelangen, wenn der Künstler „sein" Papier für das Kunstwerk findet und nutzt.[7] Ein guter Druck hängt auch entscheidend von der Wahl des richtigen Papiers ab; sie beeinflußt die Zeichnung und das Aquarell. Die Stärke des Papiers, seine Saugfähigkeit, seine Tonigkeit, Farbe und Struktur, seine Rauheit oder Glätte sind von Bedeutung und werden schließlich Teil der Komposition.

Die Eigenschaften einer jeden Papierqualität, die optische und haptische Erscheinung sind für Künstler zu allen Zeiten ein Kriterium für ihre Komposition gewesen. Frühe europäische Papiere des 15. Jahrhunderts zeigen Besonderheiten der Textur. Nicht nur die Struktur des Schöpfsiebes ist ziemlich klar sichtbar, sondern auch kleine gebogene oder gerade Linien. Es sind Rückstände des Filzes, zwischen denen das Blatt getrocknet wurde. Solche Merkmale finden sich in Papieren früher Holzschnitte, in feineren Papieren der Kupferstiche, z. B. bei Albrecht Dürer, und in vielen Büchern dieser Zeit. Dürer wählte seine Papiere mit Bedacht. Aus einem Brief von 1506 aus Venedig an Willibald Pirckheimer in Nürnberg geht hervor, daß er die Qualität des deutschen Papiers schätze: „Laßt mich wissen, was Papiers Ihr meint, das ich kaufen soll, denn ich weiß kein subtileres, als wir daheim gekauft haben."[8] Tiepolo verwandte für seine Holzschnitte ein sehr grobes, dickes Papier, für seine Drucke ein feineres Papier, auf dem die breitstehende Rippung des Siebes sichtbar ist.[9] Von den farbigen Papieren – sie standen in der Tradition der arabischen Papiere – wurde vor allem das blaue venezianische Papier bevorzugt. Seit den italienischen Frühdrucken des Aldus Manutius verwandte man seit dem 16. Jahrhundert farbige Papiere und farbigen Druck, um unterschiedliche Stimmungen

dimensionality and are combined with elements of collage or with graphic techniques. A new vocabulary is found for the material and the path to three-dimensionality is taken by those pictures in which the paper is stamped, folded, bored through or torn.

Every technique for graphic printing, also each drawing and each water color, cannot achieve its optimal effect until the artist finds and uses the right paper for "his" artwork.[7] A good print depends decisively on the choice of the right paper; it affects the drawing and the aquarelle. The thickness of the paper, its absorbency, but also its finish, color and texture, its rough or smoothness, are of significance and, in the end, become part of the composition.

The quality of each type of paper, its optical and tactile property, have been for artists of all ages a criterium for their compositions. Early European paper from the 15th century has a certain texture. Not only is the surface of the handpaper mould clearly visible, but also those small curved or straight lines of residues left by the felt layers between which the sheet was dried. These are characteristics found in the paper of early woodcuts, in the fine paper of copperplate engravings, e. g., those of Albrecht Dürer, and in many books of the time. Dürer chose his paper with great deliberation. A letter he wrote from Venice in 1506 to Willibald Pirckheimer in Nuremberg shows how much he valued the quality of German paper: "Let me know which paper you think I should buy, because I know none more subtle than that we purchased at home."[8] Tiepolo, for his woodcuts, used a very coarse and thick paper and for his engravings a finer one on which the laid surface of the mould was visible.[9] As to the colored papers in the tradition of the Arabian product, the blue Venetian paper was the favorite. Since the early Italian engravings of Aldus Manutius, colored paper and colored engravings were in use from the 16th century on to express different moods.[10] Rembrandt used oriental paper, so-called Japan paper, from 1640 to 1645. It had a

auszudrücken.[10] Rembrandt nutzte in den Jahren 1640 bis 1645 orientalisches Papier, Japanpapier genannt. Es hat eine weiche, seidige Oberfläche und saugt Farbe weniger stark auf als das damalige europäische weiße Papier. Ein Vergleich seiner Radierungen auf Japanpapier und europäischem Papier macht die Bedeutung dieses Mediums als Trägermaterial für die Komposition deutlich. Die Radierung auf Japanpapier zeigt eine lichtdurchflutete, sehr plastische Darstellung der Körper. Die Linien der Radiernadel, die Höhen und Tiefen der Kupferplatte sind klar und deutlich sichtbar. Auch die Schwärzen im Blatt wirken noch strukturiert und zeigen ein lebendiges Hell-Dunkel-Spiel. Das europäische Papier war saugfähiger, dadurch gingen die Brillanz der Darstellung und der offene Strich verloren. Die Schwärzen sind schwächer modelliert. Die Darstellung wirkt weniger „belichtet", weniger plastisch.[11]

Eine entscheidende Erfindung wurde in der Mitte des 18. Jahrhunderts gemacht: Mit einem gewebten Metalltuch konnten nun feine Spezialpapiere hergestellt werden. Die ungerippten Papiere (Velinpapier) mit glatter, makelloser Oberfläche ohne Schatten und Sicht der Stege, ohne Drahtnähte des alten Schöpfersiebes erfreuten sich großer Nachfrage. Schiller z. B. und sein Verleger Cotta stellten besondere Ansprüche an das Papier; ein Teil der schöngeistigen Literatur wurde auf dem neuen, schönen und kostbaren Velinpapier gedruckt.[12] Auch Goethe war Papierliebhaber und wählte die Papiere für seine Publikationen sorgfältig aus. Selbst in seinen Briefen achtete er auf die Verschiedenartigkeit des Schreibmaterials, das dem Briefinhalt entprechen sollte. „Es sind großenteils Oktav-, auch Halboktavblättchen, mit gedruckten Rändern eingefaßt... dann wieder Blätter ziemlich gewöhnlichen oder groben Schreibpapiers, einmal ein grünes Glanzbildchen, von des Herzogs Tische gerafft, einmal ein weißes Blatt mit farbiger Randbeblumung, aber auch Zettel von grobem blauem Papier."[13]

Gegenüber anderen Beschreibstoffen zeichnet sich Papier durch eine weitgefächerte Anspas-

soft, silky surface and absorbed less color than the white European paper made at the time. A comparison of his engravings on Japan paper and European paper makes the significance of this medium as the support for the composition clear. The engraving on Japan paper shows a translucent and very plastic representation of the figures. The lines made by the engraving tool, the heights and depths in the copperplate, are clearly visible. Even the different blacks on the print still look structured and show a distinct variation in light and dark. The European paper was more absorbent; the brilliance of the depiction and the open lines are lost. The blacks are less modulated. The depiction seems less "lit up", less plastic.[11]

A crucial invention was made in the middle of the 18th century: a wove screen could now produce fine grades of paper. The wove or vellum paper with smooth finish (with no visible shadows of the laid lines of the older type mould) was in great demand. Schiller, for example, and his publisher Cotta required certain grades of paper; some belletristic writing of the time was printed on the new, handsome and precious vellum.[12] Goethe was also an admirer of good paper and selected the paper for his publications very carefully, and even for his letters he made sure that the type of writing paper corresponded with the contents. "These are for the most part octave sheets, also halfoctaves, with borderwork ... then again quite common or coarse sheets of writing paper, once there was a brilliant green sheet snatched from the Duke's table, once a white sheet with a floral border in color, but also coarse, blue notepaper."[13]

In comparison to other inscribable material, paper is characterized by a wide-ranging adaptability to innumerable uses. Along with paper for writing, printing, drawing, there was a constant demand for commercial paper like colored wrapping paper. The differentiation between papers and products for further processing did not only depend on the state of the production methods but also on the taste then fashionable, commercial demand and everyday

sungsfähigkeit für unzählige Verwendungszwecke aus. Neben Schreib-, Druck-, und Zeichenpapier war stets das gewerbliche Papier wie buntes Packpapier gefragt. Die Differenzierung von Papieren und Weiterverarbeitungsprodukten hing nicht nur vom Stand der Produktionstechnik ab, sondern außerdem vom Zeitgeschmack, vom Gewerbebedarf und vom Alltagsanspruch. Ein Kaufmannslexikon aus der Mitte des 18. Jahrhunderts gibt Aufschluß über die damalige Vielfalt von Papieren: „Des Papiers gibt es verschiedene Gattungen, so wie sie der Gebrauch dessen erfordert. Nach solchem wird es sonderlich in Schreib-, Druck-Pack-Lösch-Papier oder Schrenz, eingetheilet: die sich wiederum nach ihrer Größe und Form; nach ihrer Feinheit, Stärke oder Schwäche; nach ihrer Farbe in fein, weiß, mittel und halbweiß, blau, braun und grau ec. sehr mannichfaltig unterscheiden und darnach Royal- Regal- Median- Post- Canzeley- Register- Cavalier ordinär und Concept-Papier; auch nach ihrem Formzeichen... Nicht viel anders verhält es sich auch mit dem gefärbten, besprengten, illuminierten, bunten, beblumten, wellenartigen, marmorirten, und sogenannten türkischen Papieren. Imgleichen mit den Gold-Silber- und Brocat-Papieren."[14]

In der zweiten Hälfte des 18. Jahrhunderts werden aufgrund neuer Moden weitere Farbpapiere, Tapetenpapiere, Pappe, Pappdeckel und Papiermaché gefertigt.[15]

Ein besonderes Papier verlangten Künstler für den Kupferstich. Führend für die Herstellung dieses feinkörnigen Papiers mit makelloser, seidenartiger Oberfläche und lockerer Beschaffenheit waren Frankreich und Basel. Die Kunstakademie Berlin schrieb 1806 einen Wettbewerb für die Herstellung von Kupferdruckpapier im Inland aus. Alle eingereichten Papierproben erwiesen sich jedoch als untauglich und zu teuer. Die Gutachter der Akademie vermißten die seidenartige Weichheit des Papier und die gelbliche Farbe, die das französische Kupferdruckpapier hatte und die den Druck gut hervortreten ließ. So schildert Goethe in seiner

requirements. A sales manual from the middle of the 18th century throws a light on the diversity of paper from that time: "There are different species of paper dictated by use, according to which they are divided into printing, wrapping, blotting paper or thin cardboard: these in turn differ greatly according to size and form, to fineness (strength or fragility), to color of fine, white, medium and off-white, blue, brown and gray, etc. and subsequently according to royal, regal, median, post, canzeley, register, ordinary cavalier and scratch paper [names of traditional German formats]; also according to their watermark... It is the same with dyed, sprinkled, illuminated, colored, floral, wavy, marbled, and so-called Turkish paper. The same for gold, silver and brocade paper."[14]

In the second half of the 18th century owing to new fashions, colored paper, wallpaper, cardboard, cardboard lids and papier-maché were manufactured.[15]

Artists required special paper for copperplate engraving. The leading producers of this finely grained paper of spotless, silken surface and light quality were to be found in France and Basle. In 1806 the Berlin Art Academy invited entries for a national competition on the production of copper engraving paper. All the paper samples that were entered, however, proved to be unusable and too expensive. The experts from the Academy missed the silken softness and the golden tone that the French copperplate paper had, which allowed the print to stand out so clearly. Goethe described in his biography on the artist Philipp Hackert how Philipp and his brother Georg vom König received a commission to set up a papermill capable of producing good copper engraving paper.[16]

In the late 19th century, printers were increasingly self-confident in their craftsmanship and anxious to put it to the test. For them it was a question of making clear technical distinctions between the rough woodcut, soft lithograph, clear etching. This is especially plain to see in Edgar Degas' lithographs, above all in his life studies. Sometimes

Biographie des Malers Philipp Hackert, wie Philipp und sein Bruder Georg vom König den Auftrag erhalten, eine Papiermühle einzurichten, in der gutes Kupferdruckpapier hergestellt werden kann.[16]

Im späten 19. Jahrhundert, mit zunehmendem Selbstbewußtsein des Druckerhandwerks, waren Drucker bestrebt, ihr Können zu zeigen. Es ging ihnen nun darum, auch die unterschiedlichen Techniken klar herauszustellen, als groben Holzschnitt, als weiche Lithographie, als klare Radierung. Deutlich wird dies beispielsweise bei Lithographien von Edgar Degas, vor allem in seinen Aktdarstellungen. Verschiedentlich ist – wahrscheinlich bewußt, um die Materialität zu zeigen – auf der „falschen" Seite des Papiers gedruckt worden, so daß man in der bildlichen Darstellung auch alle Linien des Papiers, einschließlich des Wasserzeichens, erkennen kann. Diejenige Seite des Papiers, die beim Schöpfvorgang auf dem Sieb liegt, ist die „falsche" und weniger weich. Diese Tendenz setzt sich fort bis zu den Löschpapieren, auf denen Expressionisten Holzschnitte druckten.[17]

Die Ansprüche an die Papiermacherei und – nach Einführung der Papiermaschinen ab 1830 – an die Papierfabrikation stiegen ständig in bezug auf Spezialisierung und Produktionsmenge. Jede Verwendungsart stellt bis heute spezifische Anforderungen und bedarf somit jeweils eines speziellen Papiers.

Bis ins schreib- und lesefreudige 18. Jahrhundert erfuhr Papier allgemein eine hohe Wertschätzung. „Ein Papier ist ein solch vornehmes Wesen", schreibt gegen Ende des 17. Jahrhunderts der berühmte Augustinermönch und Prediger in Wien, Abraham de Santa Clara, „daß es auch in der höchsten Monarchen Hand gehalten wird, ja darauf Päpstliche und Kaiserliche Namen und Ehren-Titel geschrieben werden."[18] An anderer Stelle beschreibt er den vielfältigen Einsatz von Papier: „Ein Papier ist ein Werkzeug des Gelehrten, ist ein Vorrat der Bücher. Ein Papier ist der Hausrat der Kanzlei, ist ein Schatz der Schüler, ein Erhalter der menschlichen Freundschaft. Mein Papier, du bist

they were – probably on purpose to show the texture – printed on the "wrong" side so that all the lines of the paper including the watermarks are visible. The side of the paper that lies face down on the mould during the dipping procedure is the "wrong" side because it is less soft. This tendency continues up to the Expressionists' use of blotting paper for printing their woodcuts.[17]

The demands on papermaking and – following the introduction of papermaking machinery in 1830 – on paper manufacture rose steadily as regards specialization and the quantity produced. Each type of usage makes specific demands, requiring a specific grade of paper.

Well into the writing and reading-crazed 18th century, paper was generally very highly esteemed. "Paper is such a distinguished creature," the famous Augustine monk and preacher, Abraham de Santa Clara, wrote in Vienna toward the end of the 17th century, "that it is held in the hand of the highest monarch and has papal and imperial names and honorary titles written on it."[18] Elsewhere he described the many uses of paper: "Paper is a tool of the scholar, a storehouse for books. Paper is the household goods of the chancellery, a treasure for students, a keeper of human friendship. Dear paper, you are a really magnificent thing!"[19] The product, paper, and its manufacture served as a parable of life and of Christian teaching. In 1664 Wolfgang Jacob Dümler described paper production in Nuremberg: "The spectator is reminded of the resurrection: in the same way as the old clothes and the fouled and beaten rags are lifted beautiful and pure out of the vat and become a new sheet, so the foulness of the grave rusts out the roots of our sin and a beautiful and transfigured body rises on the Day of Judgement."[20] In 1612 the poet and scholar of law, Conrad Rittershausen, thanked his patron Christoph Girsner, scribe for the council of Nuremberg, for "the welcome annual gift of paper: it is not only a precious bounty, but its purity corresponds to the purity of your friendship and is as welcome to him as silver and gold."[21] The

wirklich eine herrliche Sach!"[19] Das Produkt Papier und seine Produktion dienten sogar als Gleichnis des Lebens und der christlichen Lehre. Wolfgang Jacob Dümler beschreibt 1664 die Nürnberger Papierherstellung: „Es kan sich auch der Zuseher der Auferstehung erinnern: Gleichwie auf der Papyrmühle die alten Kleider und deroselben Hader-Lumpen gefäulet, erstämpffet und hernach wieder schön und rein aus der Bütten heraus geschöpfft und ein neuer Bogen wird: Also durch die Grabesfäule rostet an uns aus die Sünden-Wurtzel und stehet am Jüngsten Tag auf ein schöner und verklärter Leib."[20] 1612 bedankt sich der Poet und Rechtslehrer Conrad Rittershausen bei seinem Gönner Christoph Girsner, Ratsschreiber in Nürnberg, für das alljährliche willkommene Geschenk des Papieres: Es sei nicht nur eine kostbare Gabe, seine Reinheit entspreche der Reinheit ihrer Freundschaft und daher sei es ihm erwünschter als Silber und Gold.[21] Der Theologe Thomas Fuller schreibt in der 1662 erschienen ‚History of the Worthies of England' Papieren landesspezifische Eigenschaften zu: „Das Papier spiegelt in gewissem Sinne den Charakter des Landes wider, in dem es hergestellt wurde; die venezianischen sind sauber, dünn und gefällig, die französischen leicht und schmiegsam und die holländischen dick, behäbig und stark, in dem sie aus ihrer Schwammigkeit die Tinte auffangen."[22] Noch Benjamin Franklin vergleicht mehr als ein halbes Jahrhundert später die Erwachsenen ihren Charakteren gemäß mit den unterschiedlichen Papiersorten. Der Stutzer ist ein Schuldschein, der Verschwender ein „Pariser Assignat", der Habgierige ein Packpapier, der Dichter ist Makulatur, das unschuldige Mädchen weißes Papier, der große Geist Royalpapier, die handfesten Arbeiter Konzeptpapier.[23]

Eine erste etwa 1000 Blatt umfassende Sammlung von Papieren und Wasserzeichen, die sich heute im Britischen Museum in London befindet, hatte der englische Bibliothekar Humphrey Wanley angelegt. In einem Brief von 1699 berichtet er, daß er einheimische Papiere in den Farben Braun, Grau, Blau,

theologian Thomas Fuller in 'History of the Worthies of England' published in 1662 endows paper with features specific to the province. He wrote that paper reflects in a certain way the character of the countryside in which it is made. He thought Venetian paper was clean, thin and pleasing, the French light and pliant and the Dutch thick, portly and strong in that it trapped the ink in its sponginess.[22] Even Benjamin Franklin more than half a century later compares the character of adults with different grades of paper. The dandy is a promissory note, the spendthrift a Paris assignat, the miser a sheet of wrapping paper, the poet waste paper, the innocent girl white paper, the great thinker royal paper, the robust worker scratch paper.[23]

The first collection of paper and watermarks comprising about 1000 sheets can be found today in the British Museum in London and was begun by the English librarian, Humphrey Wanley. In a letter from 1699 he reports that he possesses native paper in brown, grey, blue, red and black and oriental paper from East India, Persia, Turkey and China, written and printed on.[24]

From the 18th century paper has become a product that is no longer scarce and precious, but is used without thinking. In 1789 the author of a Japanese textbook on papermaking: "Consumers who know nothing of papermaking and how laborious the production of paper is, use it so wastefully as though it were worthless dust. This regretful carelessness will bring on the punishment of the gods."[25] Likewise in 1789 a 'Bittschrift des Papiers an die Gelehrten besonders von teutscher Art und Kunst' was published which criticized the abuse of paper. Georg Christoph Lichtenberg bitingly exclaimed that each pure sheet of paper was worth more than the most beautifully printed page.[26]

Today paper is for most people an everyday product that is unheedingly used and thrown away. The beauty of the texture and the many color nuances of the respective papers go as unnoticed as their tactile, optic and acoustic qualities. Or who

Rot und Schwarz besitzt und morgenländische Papiere aus Ostindien, Persien, der Türkei und China, beschrieben und bedruckt.[24]

Vom 18. Jahrhundert an ist das Produkt Papier nicht mehr knapp und kostbar, sondern wird bedenkenlos verbraucht. 1789 mahnt der Autor eines japanischen Lehrbuches der Papiermacherei: „Die Verbraucher, des Papiermachens unkundig und nicht wissend, wie mühevoll die Herstellung des Papiers ist, gehen oft so verschwenderisch damit um, als ob es wertloser Staub wäre. Diese bedauernswerte Sorglosigkeit wird aber die Strafe der Götter nach sich ziehen."[25] Ebenfalls 1789 erschien eine ‚Bittschrift des Papiers an die Gelehrten besonders von teutscher Art und Kunst', in der der Mißbrauch des Papiers kritisiert wird. Georg Christoph Lichtenberg äußerte bissig, daß jeder reine Papierbogen wertvoller sei als das schönste bedruckte Papier.[26]

Heute ist Papier für die meisten Menschen ein alltägliches Produkt, das unbeachtet verbraucht und weggeworfen wird. Die Schönheiten der Strukturen im Papier und die vielfältigen farblichen Nuancen des jeweiligen Papiers bemerken wir nicht, ebensowenig die haptischen, die optischen und die akustischen Qualititäten von Papieren. Oder wer achtet schon auf das Aussehen der Milchtüte, der Brötchentüte, des Hygienepapiers, des Zeitungspapiers, des Kartons, achtet schon darauf, wie diese unterschiedlichen Papiersorten sich anfühlen, wie sie vielleicht riechen, welche Geräusche von ihnen ausgehen, wenn wir sie befühlen, knüllen, zerreißen, wegwerfen?

Aufmerksame Papierliebhaber waren und sind viele Dichter und bildenden Künstler. Rainer Maria Rilke schrieb 1899 zum Fragment aus Richard Beer-Hofmann in sein Tagebuch: „Seine Schrift spricht mit, das Papier, der Duft, der beim Umblättern wach wird."[27] Der Maler und Buchkünstler William Morris war einer der Wahrer des handgeschöpften Papiers. Welche Bedeutung er der Wahl des Papiers beimaß, geht aus den Zielen hervor, die er 1891 bei der Gründung seiner ‚Kelmscott

really takes note of how the milk carton, the bread bag, the toilet paper, the newspaper, the cardboard box looks, how these different grades of paper feel, how they smell, what noises they produce when we touch, crumple, tear and dispose of them?

Observant paper fanciers are often found among the company of poets and visual artists. In 1899 Rainer Maria Rilke wrote in his dairy about a fragment by Richard Beer-Hofmann: "His script speaks out, the paper, the fragrance comes to life when the pages are turned."[27] The painter and book designer William Morris was one of the preservers of the craft of handmade paper. The significance he accorded to his choice of paper is notable in the report he gave when he founded the 'Kelmscott Press' in 1891. He discussed how he thought about what paper to use and how he naturally had to take handmade paper into account because of its durability and its appearance. It would have been false economy to sacrifice paper quality to price. He need only make up his mind about which sort to choose. First the paper had to be made of pure linen ragstock and hard, i.e., with a good glazing. And secondly it had to be laid but not so much so that it looked rough. He found himself of one mind with the papermakers of the 15th century. So he used a sheet of paper from Bologna around 1473 as a sample.[28]

Press' niederlegte: „Natürlich mußte ich handgeschöpftes Papier in Betracht ziehen, der Dauerhaftigkeit und des Aussehens wegen. Ganz falsche Sparsamkeit wäre es, des Preises wegen die Qualität des Papiers zu vernachlässigen. So also brauchte ich bloß über die Sorte schlüssig zu werden. Erstens mußte das Papier aus reinem Leinenhadern bestehen und hart sein, das heißt fest geleimt. Und zweitens sollte es gerippt sein, aber nicht so stark, daß es ein rauhes Aussehen bewirkt. Ich fand, daß ich darin mit den Papiermachern des 15. Jahrhunderts einig war. So nahm ich mir ein Papier aus Bologna um 1473 als Muster.[28]

II. 2. Wertigkeit von Material

Von der Antike bis zum Ende des 18. Jahrhunderts wurde ein Kunstwerk primär über seine Inhalte rezipiert; das Material spielte eine untergeordnete Rolle. Man ging von der Vorstellung aus, daß die Idee aller Dinge in ihrem vollkommenen Zustand stofflos ist. Der Werkstoff hatte sich weitgehend der künstlerischen Form unterzuordnen. Die Materialien waren in eine Rangordnung gebracht, die davon bestimmt war, wie wenig sie die zugrundeliegende Idee in ihrer Reinheit zu trüben vermochten.[29]

Erst im 19. Jahrhundert griff die auf das Material bezogene ästhetische Theorie. Das Material wurde allmählich selbständiges Medium der Kunst; Materialgerechtigkeit war nun ein Kriterium für ein gutes Kunstwerk. Das hatte nach und nach den Abbau der Werkstoffhierarchie zur Folge. In jedem Material erkannte der Künstler schließlich den spezifischen unnachahmlichen Eigenwert. Konsequenzen daraus zogen nachdrücklich die Avantgardekünstler seit dem Kubismus. Vorläufer in der Hochschätzung auch „armer" Materialien war Edgar Degas (*1834 Paris – †1917 Paris). 1881

II.2. The legitimacy of the material

From antiquity to the end of the 18th century an artwork was primarily experienced by means of its content; the material played a secondary role. The thinking behind this was that the idea of each and every thing in its perfect state is incorporeal. The material was supposed to be subject to the art form. Materials were placed in an order of rank according to how little they disturbed the purity of the basic idea.[29]

Not till the 19th century did the aesthetic theory regarding material come in here at all. Material per se gradually became an independent medium for art; the legitimacy of the material was only one criterium for a good work of art. Consequently and little by little the hierarchy of materials came to an end. The artist then came to recognize in each material its own specific inimitable value. It was the artists of the avant-garde who drew the most forceful conclusions. A forefather for the esteem awarded to "poor" materials was Edgar Degas (*1834 Paris – † 1917 Paris). In 1881 in the Impressionist section of the Salon des Indépendants in Paris he exhibited 'The Little Fourteen-Year-Old

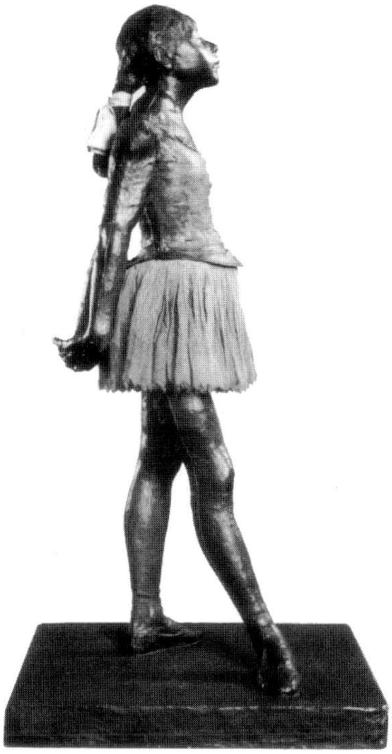

Edgar Degas: Die kleine vierzehnjährige Tänzerin, 1879/80. Wachs, Baumwollrock, Satin-Haarband, Haar heute mit Wachs überzogen. Höhe 95,2 cm / Edgar Degas: The Little Fourteen-Year-Old Dancer, 1879/80. Wax, cotton skirt, satin hair ribbon, hair now covered with wax. Height 95.2 cm. Paris, Musée d'Orsay

stellte er auf der Impressionistenausstellung des Salon des Indépendants in Paris ‚Die kleine vierzehnjährige Tänzerin' aus, die 1879/80 entstanden war. Die Wachsfigur, mit dem Pferdeschwanz aus echtem Roßhaar, fleischig koloriert, bekleidet mit echten Kleidern, Leinenmieder, weißem Gazerock und Ballettschuhen, löste in der Kunstwelt Entsetzen aus. Neben Kritikern, die das „junge Ungeheuer" an Jahrmarktschaustücke und Museumspräparate der Zoologie oder Physiologie erinnerte, verteidigte der Kritiker und Dichter Joris-Karl Huysmans Degas' Figur vehement. „Alle Ideen des Publikums über Bildhauerei, über die kalten, leblosen, weißen Erscheinungen, über diese denkwürdigen, seit Jahrhunderten wiederholten schablonenmäßigen Werke werden umgestürzt. Tatsache ist, daß Monsieur Degas die Tradition der Bildhauerkunst umgestoßen hat, genau wie er seit langem an den Konventionen der Malerei rüttelt. [...] Mit ihrem Fleisch, das lebt und von der Arbeit der Muskeln durchfurcht wird, ist diese Statuette der einzig wirklich moderne Versuch, den ich in der Bildhauerei kenne." Huysmans weist auf Werke hin,

Dancer', a work done in 1879/80. The wax figure with a ponytail made of real hair, flesh-toned, dressed in real clothes, a linen corset, white gauze skirt and ballet shoes, created a reaction of horror in the world of art. In the face of critics who were reminded by this "young monster" of show pieces at fairs and prepared samples at museums of zoology or physiology, the critic and poet, Joris-Karl Huysmans, hotly defended Degas' figure. "All the ideas the public has of sculpture, of the cold, lifeless, white apparitions, of those questionable, stereotyped works produced for centuries, have been overturned. The fact is that Monsieur Degas has overthrown the tradition of sculptural art, just like he has for years shaken the conventions of painting [...] With her flesh that is alive and furrowed by the working of the muscles, this statuette is the only really modern experiment that I know of in sculpture." Huysmans refers to other works that could have influenced Degas: "By taking up the methods used in old Spanish painting, Monsieur Degas with his original talent makes them directly into something quite special, quite

die Degas beeinflußt haben könnten: „Indem er die Methode der alten spanischen Malerei wieder aufnimmt, macht Monsieur Degas sie durch die Originalität seines Talents unmittelbar zu etwas ganz Besonderem, ganz Modernem. Gleich wie gewisse geschminkte und bekleidete Madonnen, gleich wie jener Christus der Kathedrale von Burgos, dessen Haare wirkliche Haare, dessen Dornen wirkliche Dornen und dessen Bekleidung aus wirklichem Stoff besteht.“[30]

Vergleichbares findet sich wenig. Gustave Moreau und Medardo Rosso bezogen kunstfremde Materialien in ihre Figuren ein. Doch dies blieben isolierte, nur wenig bekannte Experimente, die ein neues Denken, weitab von reglementierter Kunst, signalisierten. Ein ähnliches Signal ist einem Brief von Vincent van Gogh Ende Februar/Anfang März 1883 an seinen Freund van Rappard zu entnehmen: „Morgen bekomme ich einige interessante Gegenstände von diesem Müllablageplatz.“ Von der Sammlung ausgedienter Eimer, Körbe, Kessel, Ölkannen, Draht werde er träumen und diesen Winter ordentlich daran arbeiten.[31]

Die Reflexion über Materialität und Stofflichkeit von Fläche, Farbe, Technik findet sich um 1890 bei Maurice Denis: „Ein Bild ist wesentlich eine plane, von Farben in einer bestimmten Anordnung bedeckte Oberfläche.“[32] Exemplarisch hierfür sei Felix Vallotton genannt mit einem von mehreren Beispielen aus dem Jahr 1897, ‚Les passants (scène de rue)‘.

Bildträger ist ein rötlichbrauner Karton mit feinen Fasereinschlüssen. Seine Farbigkeit und grafische Struktur stehen an mehren entscheidenden Stellen im Bild großflächig unbemalt und unbehandelt. Die Schönheit des Materials ist zum Sprechen gebracht worden.

Im Spätwerk von Paul Cézanne bleiben ebenfalls weite Teile der Leinwand unberührt. Die Sensibilität für stoffliche Qualität des Bildträgers spricht aus dieser Handhabung. Pablo Picasso verselbständigt die Farben in der Blauen und Rosa Periode. Die Papiers collés entstehen aus logischer Folge.

modern. Just like certain Madonnas, dressed in clothes and with their faces made up, just like the Christ in the Burgos Cathedral whose hair is real hair, whose thorns are real thorns and whose clothing is made of real fabric.”[30]

It is difficult to find anything comparable. Gustave Moreau and Medardo Rosso incorporated art-alien material into their figures. But these were isolated and little known experiments that signalled a new way of thinking far beyond regimented art. A similar signal can be inferred in a letter from Vincent van Gogh written to his friend van Rappard at the end of February/beginning of March 1883: “Tomorrow I am getting some interesting objects from the dump.” He will dream of this collection of worn buckets, baskets, kettles, oil pitchers, wire and this winter do a lot of work on them.[31]

A reflection on the materiality and texture of surface, paint, and technique can be found around 1890 by Maurice Denis: “A picture is essentially a flat surface covered with colors assembled in a particular order.”[32] Felix Vallotton is a good instance of this, here with one of many examples from the year 1897, ‘Les passants (scène de rue)’. The picture is painted on red-brown carton with inclusions of fine fiber. Its color and graphic texture are left unpainted and untreated at several crucial places in the picture. The beauty of the material is given expression.

In Cézanne’s late works, as well, large parts of the canvas remain untouched. A sensitivity to the physical quality of the picture support is expressed here. Pablo Picasso allows the colors to take on a life of their own in his blue and pink periods. Papiers collés are the next logical consequence.

In arts and crafts and in folk art, paper was very early on a favorite work material. The oldest form of fabricating with paper is surely Origami, the Japanese art of folding, that began in the Heian Period (794–1185). It did not at first serve as entertainment but was reserved for religious purposes. The collage probably also had its origin

Im Kunsthandwerk und in der Volkskunst ist Papier schon sehr früh beliebtes Werkmaterial gewesen. Die älteste Form der Gestaltung mit Papier ist wohl die japanische Faltkunst Origami, die während der Heian-Periode (794 – 1185) entstand. Zunächst diente sie nicht der Unterhaltung, sondern war religiösen Zwecken vorbehalten. In Japan hat wahrscheinlich auch die Collage ihren Ursprung; hier ist sie erstmals im 12. Jahrhundert nachweisbar. Der Papierschnitt, d. h. das Schneiden oder Ritzen mit einem spitzen Gegenstand, ist eine „natürliche" Form der kunsthandwerklichen Behandlung von Papier, ebenso wie das Falten und das Zusammensetzen oder Kleben. Es ist anzunehmen, daß diese Techniken zu allen Zeiten und in all jenen Kulturen entwickelt wurden, die papierähnliche Produkte herstellten. So wurde der Papierschnitt bereits im 1. Jahrtausend v. Chr. in Mexiko beim Beschreibstoff Tapa eingesetzt. Im frühen 16. Jahrhundert in Persien nachweisbar, gelangte er von dort in die Türkei und um 1600 nach Westeuropa. Materialbilder in Klebetechnik finden im 16. Jahrhundert in Europa Verbreitung. Die Raritätenkammern des 17. Jahrhunderts waren mit Gegenständen und Materialien aus fremden Ländern gefüllt. Dement-

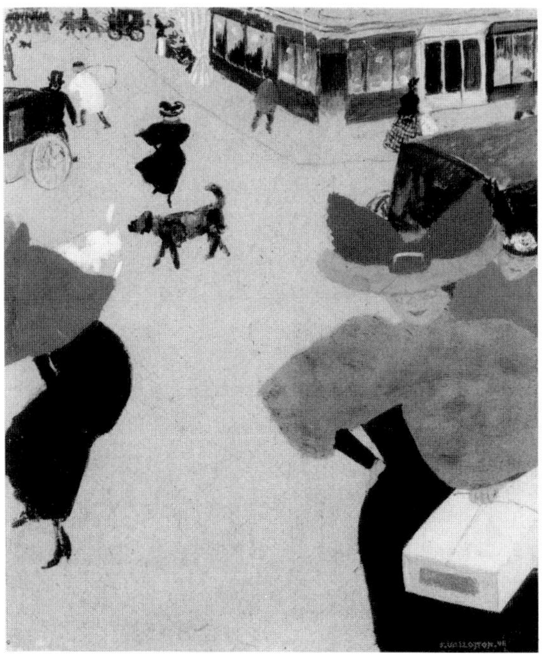

in Japan; it can be traced back to the 12th century. Papercutting, i. e., cutting or scratching with a sharp instrument, is a "natural" form of treating paper in arts and crafts, just as is folding, assembling or pasting. It can be assumed that similar techniques were developed at all times and in all those cultures that made paper-like products. For instance, in 1000 B. C. in Mexico, papercutting was used on the inscribable material of tapa. In the early 16th century it was found in Persia and went from there to Turkey and then to western Europe around 1600. Pictures made of pasted material are found in the 16th century in all of Europe. The 17th century cabinets of curiosities were filled with objects and materials from foreign lands. Consequently articles like glass eyes and glass tears, genuine hair, beetles, straw or seed were incorporated into paintings and sculpture. The devotional paintings of the 17th and 18th centuries could be true artworks of collaged or also movable parts of paper. Baroque artists used paper and papier-maché for their models, decorations and show pieces. Sculptures and reliefs made of papier-maché, some as far back as around 1570, can be found preserved in some private collections and

Felix Vallotton: Une rue (coin de rue), 1895. Gouache auf Karton. 35,9 x 29,9 cm / Felix Vallotton: Une rue (coin de rue), 1895. Gouache on cardboard. 35.9 x 29.9 cm

sprechend inkorporierte man Gemälden und Skulpturen Materialien wie z. B. Augen und Tränen aus Glas, echtes Menschenhaar, Käfer, Stroh oder Samenkörner. Die Andachtsbilder des 17. und 18. Jahrhunderts konnten wahre Kunstwerke aus collagierten oder auch beweglichen Papieren sein. Künstler des Barock verwandten für ihre Modelle, Dekorationen und Schaustücke Papier und Papiermaché. Skulpturen aus Papiermaché und Reliefs, einige sogar aus der Zeit um 1570, sind in manchen Privatsammlungen und Museen erhalten. Papiermachémanufakturen wurden im 18. Jahrhundert in Deutschland, Italien und England gegründet. Das wohl schönste und aufwendigste Imitat in Papiermaché ist Schloß Ludwigslust in Mecklenburg, das zur Zeit restauriert wird. Aus Geldmangel wurden hier nach 1765 Stuckornamentik, Büsten, Reliefs, Skulpturen, Möbel und viele Gegenstände aus Papiermaché geformt und aufwendig bemalt. 1793 entstand in Norwegen das Imitat des Pantheons in Rom aus Papiermaché. Die Kirche überdauerte immerhin 37 Jahre.

Ausschneidebögen und Guckkastendioramen mit perforierten Kupferstichen erfreuten sich steigender Beliebtheit. Die unter der Bezeichnung „Kulissenbilder" in Augsburg entstandenen Bildszenen sind in mehrere Teilflächen zerlegt und in einen Leporellofalz eingeklebt. Beim Auseinanderziehen entsteht eine räumliche Bildarchitektur. Aus der Zeit um 1757 ist bei Mitteilungen und Geschäftswerbeblättern eine bestimmte Falttechnik erhalten. Flexibilität und Leichtigkeit des Materials Papier werden auch beim zusammenlegbaren Reiseglobus aus Stuttgart um 1815 genutzt. Eine Spielzeugarmee aus der Zeit um 1810 entstand nur aus Papierfaltungen und anschließender Bemalung. Um die Mitte des vorigen Jahrhunderts erfand man Bilderbücher – heute bezeichnet man diese als Pop-up-books –, in denen durch Klappen und Ziehen bestimmter Teile neue Bildelemente sichtbar oder Funktionen ausgelöst werden.

Der Erfindungsreichtum in bezug auf Papier kannte keine Grenzen.

museums. Papier-maché manufactures were founded in the 18th century in Germany, Italy and England. What is probably the most beautiful and costliest imitation created out of papier-maché is Ludwigslust Castle in Mecklenburg, which is now in restoration. Because of a lack of funds after 1765, the ornamental plasterwork, busts, reliefs, sculptures, furniture and many objects were made out of papier-maché and painted with great care. In 1793 in Norway, an imitation of the Roman Pantheon was built in papier-maché, and the church lasted a full 37 years.

Cut-out sheets and peep-show dioramas with perforated copperplate engravings became more and more popular. The scenery that was painted in Augsburg and called "stage scenes" were cut down into several sections and pasted together into accordion folds. When pulled open again, the painted architecture formed its own space. From the time around 1757 a certain technique for folding notifications and shop advertisements was devised. The flexibility and lightness of paper were put to use in a foldable world globe made in Stuttgart around 1815. In approximately 1810 an entire toy army was made solely from folded paper that was then painted. Around the middle of the last century picture books were invented – today called pop-up books – in which by raising or pulling certain parts, new images became visible or new functions came into play.

Invention referring to paper knew no bounds.

After 1860 with the help of new techniques such as chromolithography, blanking and stamping, the production of luxury paper began. Paper experienced its high point as a substitute for expensive materials, so that it was now possible for the broad population to buy the "signs of supremacy" of the aristocracy, the wealthy and the powerful, if only as surrogate articles. Almost everything could be found in paper form: for children there were paper theaters, dress-up dolls, games, masks, Easter eggs; for adults lingerie and jewelry; for interior decoration lampshades,

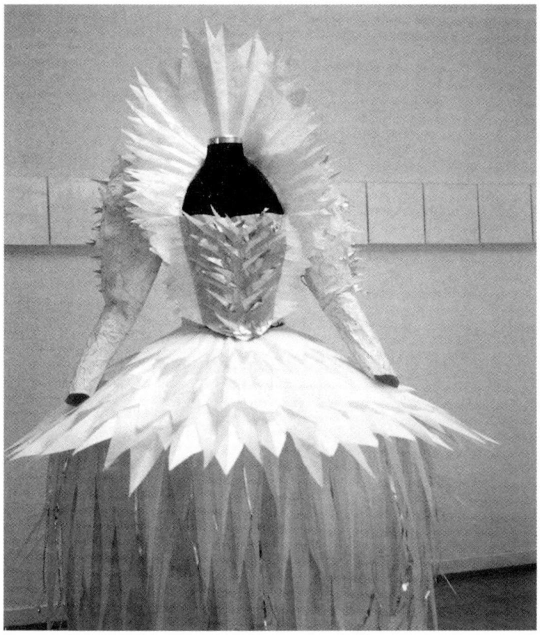

Hanjo Nagel: Surel, 1990. Geformtes Altpapier. 82 x 75 x 60 cm / Hanjo Nagel: Surel, 1990. Waste paper, moulded. 82 x 75 x 60 cm

Papierkostüm für die Performance zur Papierausstellung 1981 in Düren / Paper costume for the performance at the Paper Art exhibition 1981 in Düren

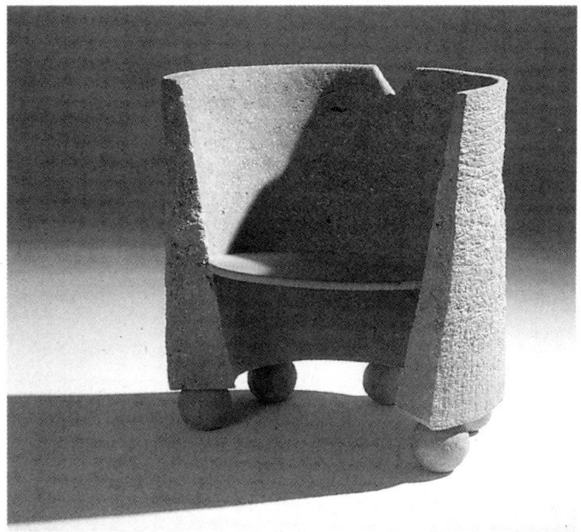

Nach 1860 begann mit Hilfe der neuen Techniken wie Chromodruck, Stanzung und Prägung die Luxuspapierherstellung. Papier erlebte seine Hochblüte als Ersatzstoff für teure Materialien, so daß jetzt auch die breite Bevölkerung die Möglichkeit hatte, die „Herrschaftszeichen" von Adel, Reichtum und Macht zu erwerben, allerdings als Surrogatartikel. Aus Papier gab es nun fast alles: Für Kinder Papiertheater, Anziehpuppen, Spiele, Masken, Ostereier; für Erwachsene Wäsche und Schmuck; für die Inneneinrichtung Lampenschirme, Gardinen, Tafeldekorationen, Blumen, Bilderrahmen und Stuck, zu jeder Gelegnheit, für den Karneval, für Feste, Bälle und Beerdigungen. Die Erzeugerfirmen publizierten Kataloge und Musterbücher. Es erschienen praktische Anleitungen zur Erstellung von Ersatzgegenständen aus Papier und Pappe. In diesen Büchern liest man von Papierimitationen jeglicher Art, wie man Elfenbein-, Horn- und Lederimitationen fertigen kann, feuersichere, wasserfeste und leuchtende Papiere fabriziert, wie man Flaschen aus Papier, unzerbrechliche Tintenschreibtafeln, Hufbeschläge, Gasleitungen, Eisenbahnräder oder Knöpfe aus Papier herstellt. 1880 nutzte man Papier als Baumaterial für einen Fa-

curtains, table decorations, flowers, picture frames and stucco, for every occasion, for carnival, for parties, balls and burials. The manufacturing companies published catalogues and books of samples. There were publications that gave practical instructions for creating surrogate articles made of paper and cardboard. These give directions for paper imitations of every kind: to make ivory, horn and leather imitations, paper that is fire- or waterproof or luminescent, bottles, unbreakable ink writing tablets, horseshoes, gas line pipes, train wheels or buttons – all out of paper. In 1880 paper was used to build a factory chimney in Breslau. Around 1850 in Dresden a clock was fabricated, including all its precision mechanics, out of paper. Shortly after 1900 a house was built in Pigeon Cove, Rockport/Massachusetts that still can be seen today, in which all the furnishings, even the piano, was made of rolled newspaper that was coated with a waterproof varnish.

Up to and including the present, paper, cardboard or papier-maché have been used for many different reasons. Above all in the mid-sixties, industrial companies developed fashion innovations out of paper and cardboard that met the needs of a waste-

brikschornstein in Breslau. In Dresden schuf man um 1850 eine Uhr einschließlich aller Feinmechanik aus Papier. Kurz nach 1900 baute man in Pigeon Cove, Rockport, Massachusetts, ein heute noch zu besichtigendes Haus mit allem Inventar – auch einem Klavier – aus gerolltem Zeitungspapier, das anschließend mit einer imprägnierenden Flüssigkeit überzogen wurde.
Bis in unsere Zeit werden Papier, Karton oder Papiermaché aus unterschiedlichsten Gründen verwendet. Vor allem Mitte der 1960er Jahre entwickelten Industriebetriebe Modeneuheiten aus Papier und Pappe, die den Bedürfnissen der neuen Wegwerfgesellschaft entsprachen. Kleider und Unterwäsche aus Papier kamen in den Handel. Für Bühne und Perfomances sind sie heute ebensowenig eine Seltenheit wie Schmuck aus Papier.[33] Die Pappfaltmöbel von Ellen Raake aus Hanau stellten 1967 eine Konzeption für faltbare Möbel aus Wellpappe vor. Es wurden Herzberger Möbel aus Vollpappe mit kunststoffbeschichteter Oberfläche angeboten. Hübner + Schuster aus Stuttgart baute Großspielzeuge aus starkem Wellkarton, kunststoffbeschichtet und abwaschbar. Die Volkshaus-Pala-Bau GmbH Fulda bot ein Volkshaus aus Pappe an. Hübner + Schuster ging 1972 mit einem Raumzellenhaus aus Wellkarton auf den Markt. Die Außenhaut bestand aus einer fugenlos aufgebrachten Deckschicht glasfaserverstärkten Polyesters. Auf dem Olympiagelände in München wurden Gruppen dieser Papp-Eder als Aufenthaltsräume, Teeküchen, Sanitärräume und Erste-Hilfe-Stationen genutzt. 1982 schuf der Architekt Bernard Lagneau in Bourges/Frankreich einen 20 Meter hohen und an der Basis 15 Meter im Durchmesser messenden Turm aus 240 Kuben aus Karton.[34] Für die Weltausstellung 1992 in Sevilla konstruierte der Schweizer Architekt Vincent Mangeat einen Turm ganz aus Papier. Er hatte eine Höhe von 38 Metern und einen Durchmesser von 12 Metern.[35]

producing society. Paper clothing and lingerie came onto the market. For the stage and for performances these are just as usual as is paper jewelry.[33] In 1967 Ellen Raake from Hanau, Germany designed foldable cardboard furniture that introduced a concept for making portable furniture from corrugated paperboard.
Herzberger furniture made of massive cardboard glazed with a plastic coating was put on the market. Hübner & Schuster in Stuttgart built large toys of strong corrugated paperboard that was plastic coated and washable. In 1972 Hübner & Schuster came onto the market with a house made up of individual rooms of corrugated paperboard. An outer layer of fiberglass-reinforced polyester was applied seamlessly to the outside surface. On the terrain of the 1972 Olympics in Munich, groups of these paper-eders were erected as lobby areas, tea kitchens, infirmaries, and first-aid stations. In 1982 the architect Bernard Lagneau designed in Bourges, France, a tower 20 meters high with a base diameter of 15 meters made up of 240 cubes of cardboard.[34] For the 1992 World's Fair in Sevilla, the Swiss architect, Vincent Mangeat, built a tower completely out of paper. It was 38 meters high and 12 meters in diameter.[35]

II. 3. Papiers collés und Kartonplastiken – Georges Braque und Pablo Picasso

Techniken und Themen der Volkskunde haben die Entwicklung der Moderne beeinflußt. Das hier angesprochene Beispiel Degas weist darauf ebenso hin wie Äußerungen und Werke von Wassily Kandinsky, Marc Chagall und vielen mehr. Die Kunst seit Aufbruch der Moderne hat systematisch neue Inspirationsquellen erschlossen. Die kategoriale Trennung zwischen Kunst, Volkskunst und Antikunst war bereits bei den Pionieren der Moderne aufgehoben. Theodor Adorno warnte eindrücklich, theoretische Erkenntnisse der Moderne auf Ähnlichkeiten mit älterer Kunst zu reduzieren. Nur durch den bewußten künstlerischen Umgang mit Material und Technik wird aus dem Werk mehr als eine Bastelei. Erst das eingeklebte Stück Papier der „papiers collés“ bei Braque und Picasso hat jene geistige Zündkraft, die den Effekt und die Fingerfertigkeit der Vorformen übersteigt. Georges Braque (* 1882 Argenteuil – † 1963 Paris) und Pablo Picasso (* 1881 Màlaga – † 1973 Mougins) schufen einen neuen Typus von Malerei: Die alltägliche Welt in Form von realen Materialien – wie Tapetenreste, Zeitungsfetzen, Wachstuch, Stoffe – wird Gegenstand hoher Kunst.[36]

Picassos Vorliebe für Alltagsobjekte zeigte bereits erste Ansätze in einer Zeichnung von 1899, ‚Mann mit Zeitungssausschnitt‘, in die er am rechten Rand den Zeitungsausschnitt mit dem Porträt einer Dame integrierte. Die Tuschzeichnung auf braunem Papier von 1908, ‚Badende‘, enthält eine eingeklebte zentrale Darstellung: eine leicht übermalte Eintrittskarte für den Louvre. 1911 klebte er in das ovale Gemälde ‚Der Brief‘ eine echte Briefmarke. Mit der Erfindung der Papiers collés realisierten die Kubisten ihr Ziel, Elemente in die Kunst einzuschließen, die – wie der Dichter Guillaume Apollinaire 1913 feststellt – „bereits durchtränkt sind mit menschlichem Leben.“[37] Picassos Interesse an Taktilem und am Material fand bildlich den

II.3. Papiers collés and cardboard sculptures – Georges Braque and Pablo Picasso

Techniques and themes from folk art had a great effect on the development of modernism. The example of Degas as previously cited is an indication of this, as are the comments and works by Vassily Kandinsky, Marc Chagall and many others. Since the outset of modernism, art has systematically been opened up to new sources of inspiration. The separation into the categories of art, ethnic art and anti-art had already been swept aside by the pioneers of modernism. Theodor Adorno warned emphatically, however, that the theoretical perceptions of modernism should not be reduced to mere similarities to older art forms. Only by a conscious aesthetic approach to material and technique can the work become more than just a figment of handicraft tinkering. It was that first piece of paper pasted into Braque's and Picasso's papiers collés which provided the mental spark that surpassed the effect and the artistic dexterity of the originals. Georges Braque (*1882 Argenteuil – † 1963 Paris) and Pablo Picasso (*1881 Màlaga – † 1973 Mougins) created a new type of painting: the everyday world in the form of actual materials – scraps of wallpaper, newspaper, wax cloth, fabric, etc. – became an object of high art.[36]

Picasso's preference for everyday objects could already be seen in a drawing he did in 1899, 'Man with Newspaper Clipping', when he integrated a portrait of a woman cut out from a newspaper into the righthand side of the picture. The ink drawing on brown paper from 1908, 'Bathers', has at its center an insertion of an entrance ticket to the Louvre over which he then partly painted. In 1911 he pasted a real stamp onto the oval painting 'The Letter'. With the invention of papiers collés, the cubists realized their goal of inserting elements into art that – as noted by the poet Guillaume Apollinaire in 1913 – "are already saturated with human life."[37] Picasso's interest in the tactile and in

ersten Höhepunkt im ‚Stilleben mit Rohrstuhlgeflecht' vom Mai 1912. Picasso verwandte hier verschiedene Materialien in unorthodoxer Manier. Das aufgedruckte Muster des Wachstuchs liefert die Illusion des Rohrgeflechts; es handelt sich nicht um reales Geflecht. Das aufgeklebte Papier gibt vor, etwas anderes zu sein, als es ist. Das umrahmende Seil ist konkretes Objekt.[38]

Im Sommer 1912 fiel Braque eine Rolle Tapete in Eichendekor ins Auge, die ihn faszinierte. Er schnitt Stücke aus und integrierte sie als Hauptbestandteile in eine Zeichnung. Anfang September 1912 entstand so das Papier collé ‚Obstschale und Glas'. Beeindruckt von Braques neuem Werk komponierte Picasso im Oktober/November sein Papier collé ‚Gitarre und Notenblatt'. Die eingeklebten Papiere stehen gleichwertig neben gemalten Bildpartien. In Braques ‚Obstschale mit Glas' übernimmt die holzmasrige Tapete die Rolle des Tisches und die der Wand im Hintergrund. Außer einigen Schriftzügen und einer Traubendolde erkennt man schwer konkrete Objekte. Wichtig erscheint das Zusammenwirken der wenigen Formen. Die Texturen der Holzmasertapete wirken den gezeichneten Flächenstrukturen entgegen. Diese wiederum variieren zwischen kräftiger Strichstruktur und einer leichten Schraffur, bei der die Rippung des Papieruntergrundes eine weitere Textur im Blatt benennt.

Das Bestreben, reine Flächentexturen einander entgegenzusetzen und daraus das Bildganze zu bestimmen, vollendete Picasso in seinem Papier collé vom November 1912, ‚Glas und Suze-Flasche'. Fast ausschließlich aus geschnittenen Papieren entwickelte er eine Dramatik strukturierter und farbiger Flächen, die einen ständigen Kampf von Raum und Fläche bestreiten. Wie in einem Vexierbild kippt die Raumtiefe sogleich wieder um in eine verkürzte Perspektive nach vorn aus dem Bild heraus; dann wieder wirken nur Flächen in einer Ebene gegeneinander. Graues Velinpapier, braunes Packpapier, ebenmäßig glattes Papier in Tiefschwarz, Weiß und Blau agieren neben Zeitungs-

the material reached its first highpoint in 'Still Life with Chair Caning' from May 1912. In it Picasso used several different materials in an unorthodox manner. The printed pattern of the wax cloth supplies the illusion of woven cane; it is not real cane. The pasted paper pretends to be something it is not. The rope that frames the picture is a concrete object.[38]

In the summer of 1912 Braque's notice was drawn to a roll of wallpaper with an oak pattern that fascinated him. He cut pieces out of it and integrated these as the main elements in a drawing. At the beginning of September 1912 the papier collé 'Fruit Bowl and Glass' came about in like manner. Impressed by Braque's new work, Picasso composed his papier collé 'Guitar and Sheet Music' in the following October/November. The inserted bits of paper stand on equal footing with the painted sections of the picture. In Braque's 'Fruit Bowl and Glass', the wood grained wallpaper takes over the role of the table and of the wall in the background. Except for some lettering and a bunch of grapes, it is difficult to discern any concrete objects. What seems important is the interaction between the few forms. The texture of the simulated-wood wallpaper works contra the drawing executed on the flat planes. The drawing, on the other hand, varies between powerful strokes and lightly applied hatching, whereby the ribbed paper base provides still another texture in the work.

The attempt to set off the pure surface textures one against the other and make of them a pictorial whole was brought by Picasso to perfection in his papier collé from November 1912, 'Glass and Bottle of Suze'. Using paper cutouts almost exclusively, he dramatized these as textured vs. colored planes in constant conflict between space and plane. Resembling a visual puzzle, space seems to tilt back into depth or to spring forward into a foreshortened perspective and out of the picture; then on the flat surface it is again only the planes that vie against each other. Gray vellum, brown wrapping paper, smooth glossy paper in dark black,

ausschnitten und geblümten Tapetenresten. Ein Etikett des Aperitifs ‚Suze' bildet suggestiv den Zentralpunkt. Die spezifische Materialität der einzelnen Papiere wird durch ihre strategisch kontrollierte Gegenüberstellung subtil herausgefiltert. Präzis und zielbewußt in Form geschnitten, unterscheidet die Dramatik des Vor und Zurück die unterschiedliche Materialität und die variierende Konsistenz der Papiere. Die Zeitungsausschnitte, strukturiert durch die grafisch flirrenden Elemente von Buchstaben und Zeilen, beseelt eine haptisch fragile Leichtigkeit. Kompositorisch bilden sie in der Gegenüberstellung zu den glatten Papieren das räumliche Element. Die bunten, glatten Papiere dagegen verweisen optisch und haptisch auf Dichte und Stabilität. Unmittelbar wird das taktile Bewußtsein, die Materialerfahrung des Betrachters mit Papier, in die Komposition einbezogen. Die Tapete, die Zeitung, das Packpapier als alltägliche Erfahrungen werden bewußt gemacht. Der Be-

white and blue are in interaction alongside of sheets of newspaper and floral wallpaper. The bottle label of the aperitif 'Suze' is suggestively placed at the center. The specific materiality of the single pieces of paper is subtly reinforced by a strategically controlled confrontation. Precisely and purposefully cut into forms, the different parts underline the drama of the backwards/forwards tilt and of the different materiality and varying consistency of the paper. Newspaper clippings, structured by the graphically whirling elements of lettering and printed lines, have an aura of tactile fragility and lightness. As to composition, they form the spatial element set against the glossy paper. On the other hand, the colored, glossy paper represents, optically and haptically, condensation and stability. Tactile awareness is directly included in the composition, i.e., the experience of different materials the viewer brings with him. The wallpaper, the newspaper, the wrapping paper, as part of everyday experience, are

Pablo Picasso: Glas und Suze-Flasche, 1912. Aufgeklebtes Papier, Gouache und Kohle. 65,4 x 50,2 cm / Pablo Picasso: Glass and Bottle of Suze, 1912. Pasted paper, gouache and charcoal. 65.4 x 50.2 cm

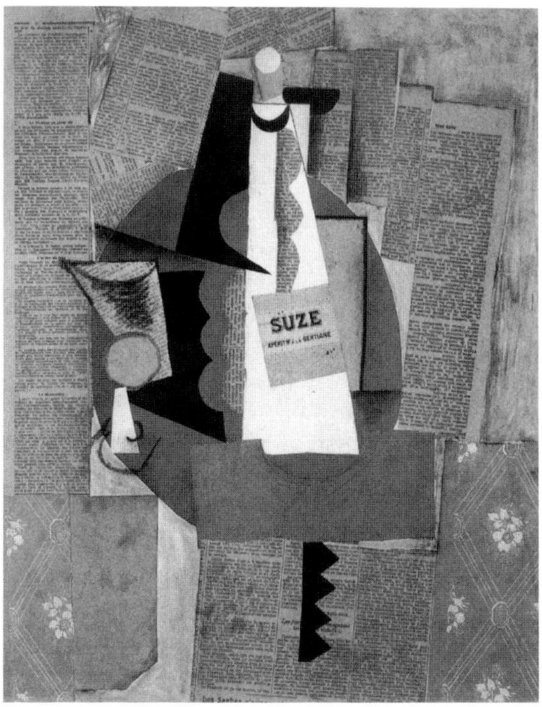

Pablo Picasso: Maquette für die ‚Guitarre', Paris, Oktober 1912. Konstruktion aus Karton, Schnur und Draht (restauriert). 65,1 x 33 x 19 cm / Pablo Picasso: Maquette for 'Guitar', Paris, October 1912. Construction of cardboard, string, and wire (restored). 65.1 x 33 x 19 cm

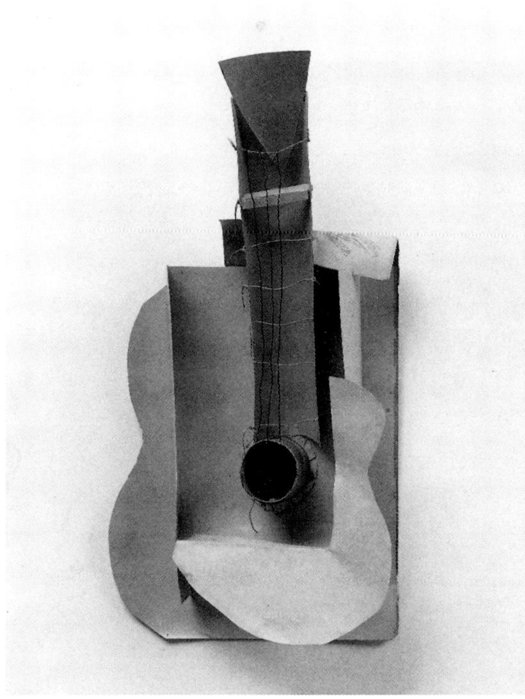

trachter wird unmittelbar über das Material angesprochen. Mit den Augen und über die Psyche wird er Teilnehmer des Bildes. Papiere, „bereits durchtränkt mit menschlichem Leben", werden zur populären Komposition.

Picasso und Braque verstanden ihr Atelier als Ort handwerklicher Arbeit. Sie untersuchten die Erweiterung der Kunst aufs Alltägliche mit neuen Materialien, 1912 und 1913 vor allem mit Papier. Sie nutzten Karton, Papiere in vielen Farben und Mustern, Sand, Sägemehl, Metallspäne, Ripolinlack, Blechschablonen, Rasiermesser, Kämme, Handwerksutensilien, um ihre Idee von einer „populären" Ikonographie zu verwirklichen. Apollinaire und André Salmon verglichen das Bemühen von Picasso und Braque um das volkstümlich Einfache mit dem Bemühen des Dichters François de Malherbe, der den Jargon der Hafenarbeiter studierte, um die eigene Sprache anzureichern.[39]

Den Papiers collés gingen Papierplastiken voraus, zunächst von Braque, später von Picasso. Braque schuf seine erste Papierplastik wahrscheinlich bereits 1911. Picasso hatte der Baugerüstcharakter dieser frühen Braqueschen Papierplastiken an die Doppeldeckerflugzeuge der Gebrüder Wright erinnert.[40]

Die einzige und auch nur in einem Foto vom Februar 1914 erhaltene Papierplastik von Braque ist malerisch aufgebaut und zeigt mehrere aus Papier geformte Objekte als Raumplastik. Unterhalb der Standfläche ist der untere Teil eines gebrauchten Kartons mit angeheftetem Boden angebracht, also ein Objet trouvé. Die Objekte oberhalb der Standfläche dagegen erhielten eine neu geformte Gestalt aus Papier und Pappe. Die ersten Papierplastiken von Braque müssen aber ebenso wie diejenigen von Picasso Einzelobjekte und nicht Arrangements mehrerer Objekte zum Dreidimensionalen gewesen sein. Außerdem liegt die Vermutung nahe, daß Braque bereits Mitte 1911 bemalte Papierreliefs schuf, die er durch die Bezeichnung „papiers peints" ganz deutlich von den Papierplastiken und Papiers collés unterschied. Auch Picasso formte

imparted to our consciousness. The viewer is directly addressed by the material. With his eyes and via his psyche he participates in the picture. These papiers collés, "directly saturated with human life", become popular compositions.

Picasso and Braque understood their atelier to be a place of handicraft. They investigated the expansion of art into the world of the everyday through the use of new materials, above all between 1912 and 1913, of paper. They utilized cardboard, paper (in

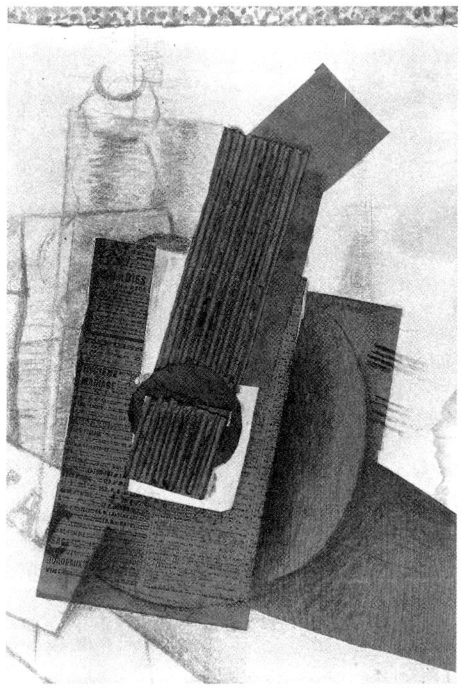

Georges Braque: Nature morte à la Guitare, 1912. Collage, Zeichnung, Aquarell, Gouache. 48,3 x 31,8 cm /
Georges Braque: Still Life with Guitar, 1912. Collage, drawing, water color, gouache. 48.3 x 31.8 cm

many colors and patterns), sand, sawdust, metal shavings, Ripolin enamel paint, tin stencils, razor blades, combs, tools, all in order to realize their idea of a "popular" iconography. Apollinaire and André Salmon compared Picasso's and Braque's pursuit of folk simplicity to a similar pursuit of the poet François de Malherbe, who studied the jargon of dockworkers to enrich his own vocabulary.[39]
Sculptures made of paper preceded papiers collés and were first produced by Braque and then

seine ersten Papierkonstruktionen, Gitarren, nicht aus gemischten Materialien. Mit Ausnahme der Saiten verwandte er nur Karton.[41] Seine Kartongitarre fotografierte Picasso mehrfach inmitten verschiedener Arrangements von Papiers collés aus Zeitungspapieren. Die ausgeschnittenen Formen der Gitarre und deren räumliches Zusammenwirken dienten ihm offenbar als Vorlage zur Übertragung ins Zweidimensionale. William Rubin vermutet hier einen deutlichen Hinweis darauf, daß diese Kartonplastiken der eigentliche Ideenstifter der Papiers collés waren. In den Papiers collés aus Zeitungspapieren übernehmen die ausgeschnittenen Flächen aus Zeitungspapier mit ihren vielen Grautönen aus dem Zusammenspiel von Buchstaben und Zeilen eine Art pointillistische Schattierung. Die Halbtöne bei der Papierplastik resultieren aus dem Wechselspiel von Licht und Schatten. Die Struktur des Papiers wird auch hier ganz bewußt in seiner Materialität und Oberflächenwirkung zum Kompositionsmittel.[42]

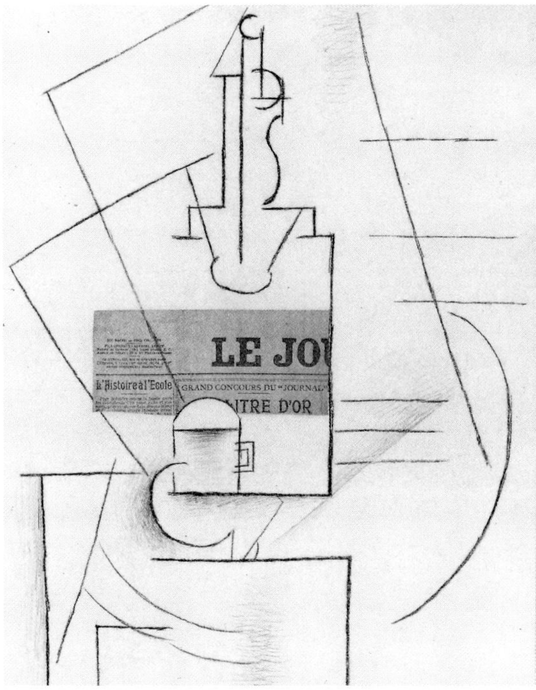

Pablo Picasso: Flasche, Tasse, Zeitung, 1912. Zeichnung und Collage mit Zeitungspapier. 63 x 48 cm / Pablo Picasso: Bottle, Cup and Newspaper. Drawing and collage with newspaper, 1912. 63 x 48 cm

Picasso. Braque created his first paper sculpture probably in 1911. Picasso was reminded by the scaffold-like character of Braque's early paper sculpture of the Wright brothers' double-decker airplanes.[40]

The only paper sculpture of Braque that exists in a photograph (a single one from February 1914) is built up in a painterly way, showing several paper objects formed into a spatial sculpture. Under the base on which it stands, the lower part of a used carton with pasted bottom has been attached, i. e., an objet trouvé. The objects above the base, in contrast, were given a newly wrought form of paper and cardboard. Braque's first paper sculptures, like Picasso's, must have been single objects and not several objects three-dimensionally arranged. There is also a strong suspicion that Braque had in mid-1911 already done some painted paper reliefs that he called "papiers peints" that were clearly distinguishable from his sculpture and his papiers collés. Neither did Picasso mix different materials to make his first paper constructions: guitars. With the exception of the strings, they consisted of nothing but cardboard.[41] Picasso photographed his cardboard guitar several times set in the center of different arrangements of papiers collés from newspapers. The cut-out forms of the guitar and their spatial interaction were to serve him apparently as a model for a later date should he transfer them to two-dimensionality. William Rubin sees here a clear indication that these cardboard sculptures were the actual inspiration for the papiers collés. In the papiers collés, the areas cut from newspapers with their many gray tones and their interplay of letters and lines of text take on a kind of pointillist shading. The half-tones of the paper sculpture are a result of the interaction of light and shade. The texture of the paper, its materiality and surface effect, is also consciously used here as a means of composition.[42]

II. 4. Collage

Das zweidimensionale Papier übernimmt in den Papiers collés die Rolle des plastischen Ausdrucksmittels. Die tradierte Guckkastenperspektive wird in Flächen aufgelöst. Je nach Materialität, Farbe oder Muster tritt die Papierfläche in den Vordergrund oder Hintergrund. Das Bild entwickelt sich zum räumlichen Flachrelief. Picasso hatte dies zunächst mit Papierschnitten, die er zu Gitarrenkartonplastiken konstruierte, erprobt. Die oben erwähnten Atelierfotos verdeutlichen das Vor und Zurück des Flächenreliefs im Raum.

Der Futurismus inkorporiert 1911/12 dem Flächenraum der Papiers collés die rhythmischen Wiederholungen und damit die dynamische Raumstruktur im Zustand der Simultaneität. Der Futurismus schafft ein dynamisches Relief der Welt im Zustand der Unruhe. Prozesse entwickeln sich nicht nacheinander, sondern in der Gleichzeitigkeit von Vergangenheit, Gegenwart und Zukunft.

II.4. Collage

The two-dimensional paper in the papiers collés takes over the role of plastic expression. The conventional peep-show box perspective is broken down into planes. According to texture, color or pattern, the paper plane steps forward into the foreground or retreats into the background. The picture develops to a low relief. Picasso tried this out at first with paper cut-outs that he constructed into guitar sculptures. The photos he took in his atelier (see above) show clearly how his low reliefs move forward and back in space.

In 1911/12 Futurism took the flat planes of the papiers collés, the rhythmic repetitions and the resulting dynamic spatial structure and incorporated them into a state of simultaneity. Futurism presented a dynamic relief of the world in a state of unrest. Processes do not develop one after the other, but develop within the simultaneity of past, present and future.

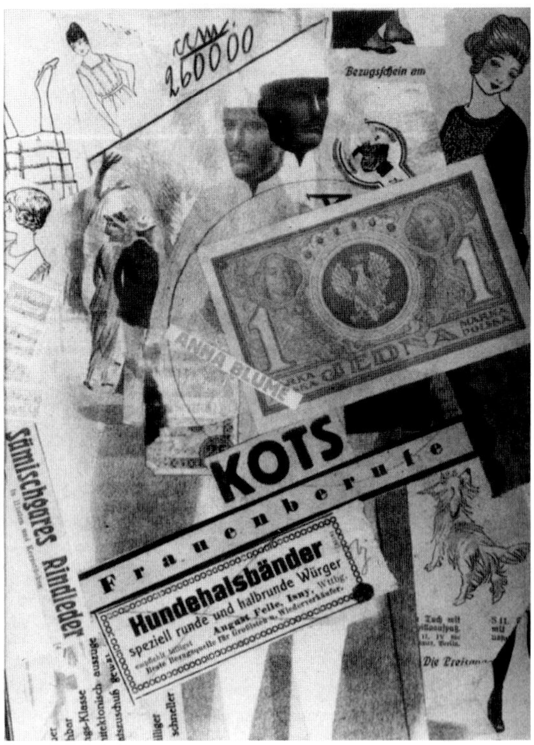

Kurt Schwitters: Das Kotsbild, 1920. Collage. 27 x 19,4 cm /
The Kots Picture, 1920. Collage. 27 x 19.4 cm

Den Prototyp einer zweidimensionalen futuristischen Collage mit Papier klebte Carlo Carrá aus Papieren und Zeitungsausschnitten. ‚Manifestazione interventista' erschien am 1. August 1914, kurz vor Ausbruch des Ersten Weltkrieges, in der Zeitung ‚Lacerba' in Paris. Aus dem Zentralpunkt rotieren mit ungeheurer Dynamik bedruckte Papierstreifen explosionsartig in alle Richtungen aus dem Bild heraus. Bei den Futuristen wird die Collage erstmals zum Zeitdokument aus Fetzen von Nachrichten, aus Reklame, Musikskizzen. Befreiten Worten gleich rollen Buchstaben zu Lauten und Geräuschen aus, jonglieren und purzeln eine Überfülle simultaner Informationen ins Bild.[43] Die Collage des Futurismus arbeitet hauptsächlich mit der Typographie des bedruckten Papiers.

Weiterentwickelt wird das futuristische Text- und Geräuschbild kurze Zeit später im Dadaismus. Bedruckte Papierfragmente werden nun in neue Sinnzusammenhänge gestellt. Separat betrachtet können die Bilder und Zeichen grundverschiedene Aspekte beleuchten. Im gegenseitigen Wechselspiel erhalten sogar nicht zusammengehörige Realitätsebenen eine verblüffende, tiefsinnige Bedeutung.

Im Werk von Kurt Schwitters (* 1817 Hannover – † 1948 Ambleside/Großbritannien) wird die Collage zum tragenden Prinzip. Er strebt nicht das Gesamtkunstwerk im Sinne von Kandinsky an, sondern will, konsequenter als Futuristen und Dadaisten, alles in ein zeitliches Zusammenspiel setzen und die Grenzen verwischen. Kunst bedeutet für ihn Integration aller Bereiche, auch der Technik. Aus dieser Lebenshaltung heraus ist die Collage, das Zusammenführen aller Künste, aller Erscheinungsformen, die logische Konsequenz. In seinen ‚Merz'-Bildern und ‚Merz'-Objekten verwandte Schwitters neben anderen Materialien Papiere jeglicher Herkunft und Art.

Für das Werk von Max Ernst (* 1891 Brühl/Köln – † 1976 Paris) spielt die Collage eine wesentliche Rolle. Ausgehend von bereits bestehendem visuellem Material eröffnet er Möglichkeiten, die den

The prototype of a two-dimensional futuristic collage with paper was the one that Carlo Carrá pasted out of paper and newspaper clippings. Called 'Manifestazione interventista', it was printed on 1 August 1914 just before the outbreak of World War I in the newspaper 'Lacerba' in Paris. From the center, printed strips of paper rotate with enormous dynamism like an explosion in all directions out of the picture. In the hands of the Futurists for the first time, the collage becomes a document of the times made up of scraps of news, advertising, sheets of music. Words that are liberated roll letters to notes and sounds, juggle and toss an overflow of simultaneous information onto the picture.[43] The Futurist collage chiefly works by means of the typography of the printed page.

A short time later, the Futuristic text and sound picture was to be further developed by Dada. Printed paper fragments were now set into a new context of meaning. Viewed separately, the pictures and signs explain basically different aspects, while in reciprocal interplay, levels of reality that do not even belong together assume an astonishing degree of profundity.

In the work of Kurt Schwitters (*1887 Hannover – †1948 Ambleside/Great Britain) the collage became the dominant principal. He did not pursue the Gesamtkunstwerk [all-encompassing work of art] in Kandinsky's sense, but, more consistently than the Futurists and the Dadaists, wanted to establish all arts within a timed interplay and efface the boundaries between them. To him art meant an integration of all the arts, also technology. For such an attitude to life, the collage, which brings all arts and all physical manifestations together, is the logical consequence. In his 'Merz' pictures and 'Merz' objects Schwitters used, along with other materials, paper of every type and origin.

For the work of Max Ernst (†1891 Brühl/Cologne – †1976 Paris) the collage played an essential role. Starting from already existing visual material, he activated possibilities that completely changed the original sense of the picture elements. As early as

ursprünglichen Sinn der Bildelemente völlig verändern. Bereits 1919 beginnt Max Ernst den ästhetischen Hintergrund der Papiers collés um neue Spielarten zu erweitern. Bis in die späte Schaffensphase hat er diesem Bildmedium immer neue, ganz persönliche Techniken abverlangt. Collage ist für ihn auch „Verneinung, als Möglichkeit des Widerstands gegen die Überflutung von Bildern und deren grenzenlose Mischung“[44].

Die Collage als Denkprinzip eröffnete für die Kunst des 20. Jahrhunderts bis dahin unbeachtete Wege mit unerwarteten Möglichkeiten. In bezug auf Papier erschloß sie die Sensibilität für dieses facettenreiche Material.[45]

1919 Max Ernst began to expand the aesthetic background of papiers collés to include new varieties. Up into his late period he demanded of this pictorial medium ever new and very personal techniques. To him collage is also "negation, a possibility of resisting the deluge of pictures and their endless combination."[44]

For the art of the 20th century, the collage as a conceptual principle initiated strategies with unexpected potentialities that till then had gone unnoticed. In relation to paper, it developed a sensibility to this many-facetted material.[45]

II. 5. Endlospapier – Material und Funktion

Der rasche technische und wirtschaftliche Aufschwung hatte um 1900 in verschiedenen Ländern Werkbünde entstehen lassen[46], die in Architektur und Kunstgewerbe Material- und Werkgerechtigkeit anstrebten. In den schönen Künsten waren es die Futuristen, die Maschinen und Technik verherrlichten. Als Folge der Orientierung an Technischem und an „reiner“ Malerei des Kubismus und Futurismus zeichnete sich um 1913 eine erste konstruktivistische Bewegung ab. Die Suche nach der reinen Form beschäftigte von nun an eine Reihe von Malern und Malergruppierungen in Europa, einschließlich Rußland, vor allem nach dem „künstlerischen Zusammenbruch“ durch den Ersten Weltkrieg. Der technisch erschlossene Raum an sich wird zum „Material“.

Das Bauhaus, 1919 in Weimar gegründet, erneuerte die mittelalterliche Vorstellung vom Gesamtkunstwerk. Elementarbegriffe von Form, Farbe, Material und deren Zusammenwirken wurden handwerklich unter Anleitung von bedeutenden Künstlern, „Meister“ genannt, erprobt. Nach dem Umzug des Bauhauses von Weimar nach Dessau fand 1926 eine

II.5. Continuous paper – Material and function

The rapid technical and economic upswing that occurred around 1900 resulted in the establishment of workmen associations ('Werkbund') in different countries,[46] which pursued the legitimacy of material and of workmanship in architecture and the handicrafts. In the fine arts it was the Futurists who glorified machinery and technology. As a result of Cubism's and Futurism's orientation toward the technical and toward "pure" painting, the first Constructivist movement emerged around 1913. The search for pure form became an occupation of a series of painters and art groups in Europe including Russia, especially after the "artistic breakdown" of World War I. Space per se is technically exploited and becomes itself the "material".

The Bauhaus, founded in 1919 in Weimar, revived the medieval idea of the Gesamtkunstwerk [the all-encompassing work of art]. Elemental definitions of form, color, material and their combination were probed under the direction of well-known artists called "masters". After the move from Weimar to Dessau in 1926, a restructuring took place. It was no longer Johannes Itten's basic theory, stressing

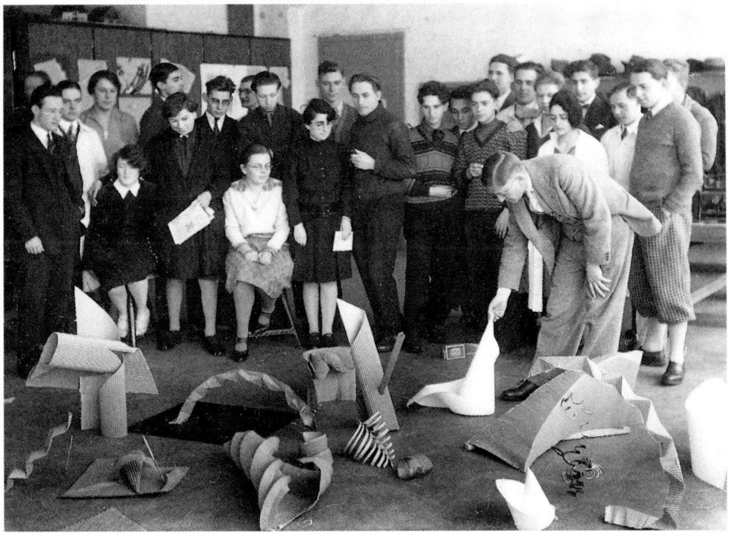

Josef Albers mit seinem Vorkurs am Bauhaus, um 1928 / Josef Albers with his class at the Bauhaus, about 1928

Umstrukturierung statt. Nicht mehr die Grundlehre von Johannes Itten mit Betonung des sinnlich Wahrnehmbaren von Farbe und Qualität der Materialien stand im Vordergrund, sondern das „basic design". Dynamische Kräfte und Funktionen von Materialien wurden abgefragt.
Der Purist Josef Albers (* 1888 Bottrop – † 1976 New Haven/Connecticut) fand im biegsamen, leichten Material Papier das Mittel für die reine Form. Er schätzte die speziellen Eigenschaften des planen, maschinell hergestellten, bahnenförmigen und endlosen Materials und vor allem die sich daraus ergebenden reinen Raumformen. Im Vorkurs ließ Albers die Bauhaus-Schüler Funktion und Form von Endlospapier frei und spielerisch erarbeiten. Das Produkt Endlospapier war für ihn Ausdruck der technisch-industriellen Zeit. Auf der Grundlage der Erfahrungen mit dem Material Papier entwickelte Albers seine zweckfreie Gestaltungslehre. 1928 veröffentlichte er in der Bauhaus-Zeitschrift den grundlegenden Aufsatz über ‚Papierarbeiten aus neuer Sicht'.
Wegen der Bedeutung in bezug auf das Endlospapier in seiner technischen Schönheit und reinen Form sei er hier zusammenfassend wiedergegeben: In einer wirtschaftlich orientierten Zeit geht es um die ökonomische Formgebung, die von den Faktoren Funktion und Material bestimmt wird. Vor

the sensual perception of color and the quality of the material, which became the leading doctrine, but "basic design". Now in demand were the material's dynamic forces and functions.
The purist Josef Albers (*1888 Bottrop – †1976 New Haven/Connecticut) found the means to pure form in the pliant and light material of paper. He treasured the special qualities of the flat, continuous material mechanically produced in rolls and, above all, the pure forms in space that could be made from it. In his introductory course, Albers had the Bauhaus students work with and experience, freely and playfully, the form and function of a roll of paper. The product of continuous paper was for him an expression of the technological and industrial times. On the basis of his experience with paper, Albers developed his own purpose-free art theory. In 1928 he published in the Bauhaus Magazine the fundamental essay, 'Paperworks from a New Point of View'. Because of the significance his formulation has for continuous paper as regards its technical beauty and purity of form, it is here reviewed in brief: In times of economic orientation, it becomes necessary to render form economically, something that is determined by the factors of function and material. Before you can recognize function, you must first study the working material. Inventive construction and a fresh responsiveness to discovery

der Erkenntnis der Funktion steht das Studium des Werkstoffs. Erfindendes Bauen und entdeckendes Aufmerken werden erst durch vorurteilsfreies Probieren und spielerisches Basteln im Material entfaltet. Ausgangspunkt ist das Material, das möglichst ohne Werkzeug bearbeitet werden soll, damit engster Materialkontakt mit den Fingerspitzen besteht. Papier wird in der Industrie und im Handwerk häufig liegend und flach verklebt gebraucht. Eine Seite des Papiers verliert dabei meist seinen Ausdruck, die Kante wird fast nie genutzt. Die Bauhaus-Schüler verwenden Papier stehend, uneben, plastisch bewegt, beiderseitig und kantenbetont. Anstatt zu kleben, binden, stecken, nähen, nieten sie, befestigen es also anders und untersuchen es auf seine Leistung bei Zug- und Druckbeanspruchung hin. Selbständiges, konstruktives Denken wird verlangt, darüber hinaus das Erproben weiterer unüblicher Materialien wie Wellpappe, Drahtgewebe, Cellophan, Etiketten, Zeitungen, Tapeten, Stroh, Konfetti, Zündholzschachteln, Papierschlangen, Grammophonnadeln, Rasierklingen. Planerisches Denken in bezug auf Stoffauswahl und Arbeitsvorgänge soll geschult werden. „Überlegung ist der billigste Verschleiß“[47], schreibt Albers. Jedes Material wird möglichst ohne Verschnitt verbraucht. Die Aktivierung der Negativa, die gleiche Bewertung von Positiva und Negativa läßt keinen Materialrest übrig. Jedes Element muß gleichwertig sein. So verschwinden Sockel und Rahmen. Auch die Leistungssteigerung des Papiers durch Knicken oder andere Arrangements erprobte Albers.[48] Räumliches Denken, genaues Beobachten, neues Sehen, feinstes Materialgefühl für Struktur, für Werkstoff, für Oberfläche sind Neuerungen des Bauhaus-Gedankens, der auch nach dem Zweiten Weltkrieg in vielen Kunstrichtungen weiterlebt.[49]

Die Reinheit des Papiers und seine Flexibilität nutzten einige Bildhauer. Nachzutragen ist, daß Naum Gabo und Antoine Pevsner einige der frühen Skulpturen in den Jahren 1920 bis 1925 aus Papier konstruierten, bei denen der technisch erschlossene Raum als „Material“ der Kunst nur mit einem

can first be developed by prejudice-free experimentation and playful tinkering with the material. The starting point is the material, which should be fashioned without tools if at all possible, so that the closest contact between the material and the tips of the fingers can take place. Paper is often utilized in industry and in handicrafts while prone and pasted while flat. One side of the paper loses most of its expression as a result, the edge is hardly ever used. Students of the Bauhaus work with paper when it is standing, uneven, in three-dimensional movement, in a two-sided and edge-oriented way. Instead of pasting, tieing, inserting, sewing, riveting it, they fasten it differently and examine how it stands up to pull and pressure. Individual and constructive ways of working are what is required, and beyond that the testing of other unusual materials like corrugated paper, wire mesh, cellophane, labels, newspaper, wallpaper, straw, confetti, match boxes, paper streamers, gramophone needles, razor blades. Strategic thinking is to be schooled as to choice of material and work procedure. “Planning ahead is the cheapest wear and tear,”[47] Albers writes. Each material is to be used if possible in full, i. e., without wastage. By activating negatives and assessing positives and negatives as equals, you see to it that no material is left over. Each element must be held in equal esteem. In this way, pedestal and frame disappear. The increased performance of paper by folding or other manipulation is something Albers also tried out.[48] Spatial thinking, exact observation, new ways of seeing, the finest feel for material, for texture, for working matter, for surfaces, all are innovations of Bauhaus thinking, which after World War II still lives on in many art movements.[49]

The purity of the medium of paper and its flexibility were implemented by several sculptors. A footnote that needs adding here is the fact that Naum Gabo and Antoine Pevsner constructed some of their earliest sculptures in the years 1920 to 1925 in paper, whereby the technically exploited space as “material” for art was exclusively defined by an

„offenen“ oder transparenten Werkstoff definiert werden durfte.
Manche Plastik mit „natürlichem, reinen“ Fluß erweckt den Eindruck, aus dem „reinen“ Fluß der Papierbahn hervorgegangen zu sein. Beispiel sind die gedrehten Räume in Max Bills endlosen Bändern. So wurde Papier zum formbildenden Medium.

"open" or transparent material. Thus, many a sculpture with "natural, pure" flow gives the impression of having originated from the "pure" flow of the paper roll. An example of this is the spiralled spaces of Max Bill's continuous bands. In this way paper became a form-creating medium.

III. Demontage des traditionellen Kunstbegriffs – Material wird autonom
III. Dismantling the traditional definition of art – Material becomes autonomous

III. 1. Materialität – das Tafelbild stirbt

Das erste Jahrzehnt nach dem Zweiten Weltkrieg ist in der bildenden Kunst geprägt von einem abstrakten Expressionismus in unterschiedlichen Spielarten wie Action-painting, Informel, Tachismus, lyrischer Expressionismus. Die stark strukturierte Oberfläche, der Materialreiz bewegt viele Künstler. Einer der Begründer des Informel, Jean Fautrier (* 1898 Paris – † 1964 Chatenay-Malabry/ Paris) entwickelte nach 1940 einen markanten haptischen Stil: Den Bildgrund stellte er selbst her und zwar aus Papier, Klebstoff und Farbpaste, die er, vermischt mit farbigen Pudern, in mehreren Schichten mit einem Palettenmesser auftrug. In den noch feuchten, rissigen, spröden Grund ritzte er hieroglyphenartige Figurationen.[50]
Jean Dubuffet (* 1901 Le Havre – † 1985 Paris) mischte 1945/46 ähnliche Malpasten aus Asphalt, Teer und Bleiweiß, die u. a. mit Sand, Stroh, Kohlenstaub und vielem mehr angereichert waren. Graffitiartige Linien zog er mit einem Löffel oder Messer in die Paste ein. Seine Ausstellung im Mai 1946 in der Galerie Drouin in Paris wurde zum Skandal. Das Publikum war empört über den Gebrauch von Schlamm und dem Abfall aus dem Mülleimer. Ohne unterscheidende Wertung arbeitete Dubuffet mit Materialien wie Holz, Dreck, Schmet-

III.1. Materiality – End of easel painting

The visual arts in the first decade after World War II were marked by a many-facetted Abstract Expressionism: Action Painting, Art Informel, Tachisme, Lyric Expressionism. Many artists were affected by highly textured surfaces, i. e., by the appeal of the material. One of the founders of Art Informel, Jean Fautrier (*1898 Paris – †1964 Chatenay-Malabry/ Paris), developed after 1940 a bold haptic style: he fabricated himself the picture base out of paper, glue and paint that he mixed with colored powders and applied in several layers with a palette knife. Into this still damp, cracked and brittle ground, he scratched hieroglyphic-like figurations.[50]
In 1945/46 Jean Dubuffet (*1901 Le Havre – †1985 Paris) mixed similar paint pastes from asphalt, pitch and white lead that he enriched, with sand, straw, coal dust, etc. He drew graffiti-like lines with a spoon or knife into the paste. His exhibition in May 1946 in the Galerie Drouin in Paris became a scandal. The public was incensed by his use of mud and waste products from the trash. Without making any distinction in value, Dubuffet worked with materials like wood, dirt, butterflies, plants, tin foil. In 1954 he made small figures of tin foil, papier maché, sponges, volcanic rock, and wood. In 1959 he created additional heads of crumpled tin foil and

terlingen, Pflanzen, Silberpapier. 1954 entstanden kleine Standbilder aus Silberpapier, Pappmaché, Schwämmen, Vulkangestein und Holz. 1959 schuf er Köpfe aus zerknülltem Silberpapier und Pappmaché, beides „ärmliche" Materialien, denen zuvor in der Kunst kein Wert beigemessen wurde. Die krustige Oberflächenstruktur des Pappmaché und die metallene Qualität des Silberpapiers ermöglicht neue plastische Qualitäten. Es ist die Schönheit des Häßlichen, die Wege des Erkennens eröffnet. Ende 1959 entstand die Bildfolge ‚Matériologies', reliefartige Bilder aus zerknüllten Silberpapierteilen oder aus Pappmaché, Kunststoffpasten, Sand, Glimmer. Die autonome Sprache der Materialien ist auch hier zum äußerten getrieben. Das Material in seinem Verhalten, seiner Textur, seiner Farbe bestimmt die Komposition, es wird selbst zur Form.[51]

Fautrier und Dubuffet hatten Bereiche erobert, die der jüngere Antonio Tàpies (* 1923 Barcelona) konsequent weiterentwickelte. Materie selbst wird auch bei ihm zum Thema. 1946 erprobte er die Stofflichkeit krustiger Farbschichten mit Einkerbungen primitivistischer Figurationen. Die Bild-

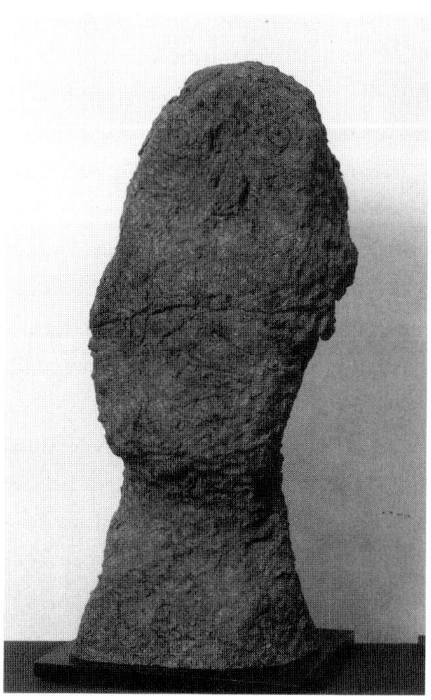

Jean Dubuffet: Pince bec, 1960. Pappmaché. Höhe 95 cm / Jean Dubuffet: Pince bec, 1960. Papier-maché. Height 95 cm

papier maché, both "poor" materials which up to then had not been artistically esteemed. The crusty surface structure of papier maché and the metallic property of the tin foil made new plastic qualities possible. It is the beauty of the ugly that initiates new ways of perception. At the end of 1959 came the first series of paintings called 'Matériologies', relief-like pictures of crumpled scraps of tin foil or of papier maché, synthetic pastes, sand, mica. The autonomous expressiveness of the materials is again carried to its extreme. The way material behaves, its texture, its color, determines the composition; it itself becomes the form.[51]

Fautrier and Dubuffet had probed those areas that the younger Antonio Tàpies (*1923 Barcelona) then consistently continued to develop. The material per se also became his theme. In 1946 he tested the physicality of crusted paint layers by gouging out primitivist figurations. The picture surface was broken down into relief-like layers made of a type of mortar. He applied the paint very thickly with a palette knife and scraped it off again in such a way that the texture of the canvas was laid bare. In 1946/47, inspired by the collage techniques of Max Ernst and Kurt Schwitters, he integrated found objects into the picture plane such as newspaper, tin foil and string. Utensils with traces of secondhand use, also paperboard, paper, newspaper, manage to lend his works up to his late creative years the flair of starkness, mystical silence and contemplative supra-sensuality.

The works of Tàpies, Alberto Burri (*1915 Città di Castello) and Dubuffet herald a new relationship to reality which is manifested in literal ways by the younger generation of artists. The spokesman of the New Realists in France, the art critic Pierre Restany, announced on 16 April 1960 in the manifesto 'Nouveaux Réalistes' that the time of the easel painting was at an end and traditional mediums were completely exhausted; hail the beginning of a "new realism of pure sensitivity".[52] With this break away from the subjective isolation of Tachisme and Abstract Expressionism,

oberfläche unterteilte er in reliefartige Schichten aus mörtelartiger Masse. Die Farbe trug er mit dem Spachtel dick auf und schabte sie wieder ab, so daß Gewebestrukturen der Leinwand freiliegen. Inspiriert von der Collagetechnik bei Max Ernst und Kurt Schwitters integrierte er 1946/47 Fundstücke in die Bildfläche wie Zeitungspapier, Silberpapier, Schnüre. Utensilien mit Alltagsspuren, auch Karton, Papier, Zeitungen geben seinen Werken bis in die späten Schaffensjahre das Flair von Schlichtheit, mystischem Schweigen und meditativ Übersinnlichem.

Die Werke von Tàpies, Alberto Burri (* 1915 Città di Castello) und Dubuffet künden vom neuen Realitätsbezug, der sich in einer jüngeren Künstlergeneration buchstäblich manifestiert. Der Wortführer der Neuen Realisten in Frankreich, der Kunstkritiker Pierre Restany, verkündet am 16. April 1960 im Manifest ‚Nouveaux Réalistes' den Beginn eines „neuen Realismus der reinen Sensibilität", da die Zeit der Tafelmalerei vorüber sei und man die traditionellen Mittel vollkommen ausgeschöpft habe.[52] Mit diesem Ausbruch aus der subjektiven Isolation des Tachismus und des abstrakten Expressionismus wird alles möglich: Alle Materialien, aller Abfall, alles Materielle und Nichtmaterielle werden von nun an für die Kunst erschlossen.

Bereits Umberto Boccioni (* 1882 Reggio Calabria – † 1916 Verona) forderte im ‚Manifest der Futuristischen Skulptur' von 1912 die Erweiterung des Materialienkanons um Karton, Glas, Eisen, Zement, Haare, Leder, Stoff und elektrisches Licht, weil es nur so gelingen könne, die Wesenselemente der bildnerischen Sensibilität zurückzugewinnen.

Auch Wladimir Tatlin (* 1885 Moskau – † 1953 Moskau) formte Materialreliefs aus Papier, Eisen, Teer, Glas, Parkett und Baumwolle.

Naum Gabo (* 1890 Brjansk – † 1977 Waterbury/Connecticut) und Antoine Pevsner (* 1886 Orel/Rußland – † 1962 Paris) proklamierten im ‚Realistischen Manifest' von 1920: „Wir wissen, daß jedes Ding sein eigenes Wissensbild hat; Stuhl, Tisch, Telefon, Buch, Haus, Mensch... das alles sind voll-

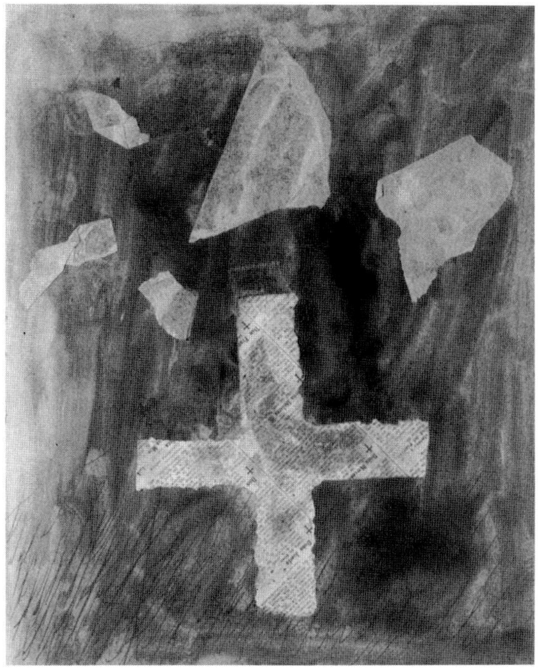

Antoni Tàpies: Creu de paper de diari, 1946/47.
Aquarell und Collage auf Papier. 40 x 31 cm /
Antoni Tàpies: Creu de paper de diari, 1946/47.
Water color and collage on paper. 40 x 31 cm

everything becomes imaginable. All materials, all waste products, everything material and non-material are from now on exploitable by art.

In the 'Manifesto of Futurist Sculpture' Umberto Boccioni (*1882 Reggio Calabria – †1916 Verona) had already in 1912 called for the expansion of the canon of art to include paperboard, glass, iron, cement, hair, leather, cloth, and electric light, because only in this way could the essence of pictorial sensitivity be regained. Vladimir Tatlin (*1885 Moscow – †1953 Moscow), too, created material reliefs out of paper, iron, pitch, glass, parquet and cotton. Naum Gabo (Naum Pevsner *1850 Bryansk – †1977 Waterbury/Connecticut) and Antoine Pevsner (*1886 Orel/Russia – † 1962 Paris) proclaimed in the 1920 'Realistic Manifesto': "We are aware that each thing has its own cognitive image; chair, table, telephone, book, house, man... all are complete worlds with their own rhythms and their own planetary orbits."[53]

ständige Welten mit eigenem Rhythmus und eigenen Planetbahnen."[53]

Marcel Duchamp (* 1887 Blainville – † 1968 Paris) hatte 1913 mit seinem ersten Ready-made, dem Rad eines Fahrrads, das Dogma zerstört, ein Kunstwerk müsse von Künstlerhand erschaffen sein: Er zeigte die ästhetischen Qualitäten eines industriellen Serienartikels. Die neue moralische Aufgabe der Nouveaux Réalistes ist jetzt das Erkennen von Ästhetik, Schönheit und damit Kunst, ein wesentlicher Teil des Schaffensprozesses besteht nun im Finden.[54]

Arman (* 1928 Nizza) häuft abgenutzte Gegenstände, Abfälle, Schutt, Unrat in durchsichtige Behälter. 1962 füllte er die Briefe von Pierre Restany in einen Objektkasten und erklärt die ‚L'Affaire du courrier' zum Kunstwerk. Christo (* 1935 Gabrovo/Bulgarien) verschnürt 1958 erste Gegenstände – Pappkartons. Gemalte Porträts verhüllt er in Papier und Stoff.[55] Plakatabrisse als Manifestationen von Alltagskultur werden durch die ord-

Marcel Duchamp (*1887 Blainville – †1968 Paris) with his first ready-made, a bicycle wheel, had destroyed the dogma that an artwork must be created by the hand of the artist: he showed the aesthetic quality of the mass-produced article. The new moral mission of the Nouveaux Réalistes now is to perceive the aesthetical, the beautiful and, therefore, art; an essential part of the creative process becomes the act of finding.[54] Arman (*1928 Nice) piles up used articles, waste products, rubble, or refuse into transparent containers. In 1962 he filled a glass case with letters written by Pierre Restany and declared 'L'Affaire du courrier' to be an artwork. Christo (*1935 Gabrovo/Bulgaria) tied up his first objects in 1958: cardboard cartons. He wrapped painted portraits in paper and cloth.[55] Posters, partially ripped from billboards, as manifestations of everyday culture and put into a new order by the hand of the artist became the theme of François Dufrêne (*1930 Paris – † 1982 Paris), Raymond Hains (*1926 Saint-Brieuc),

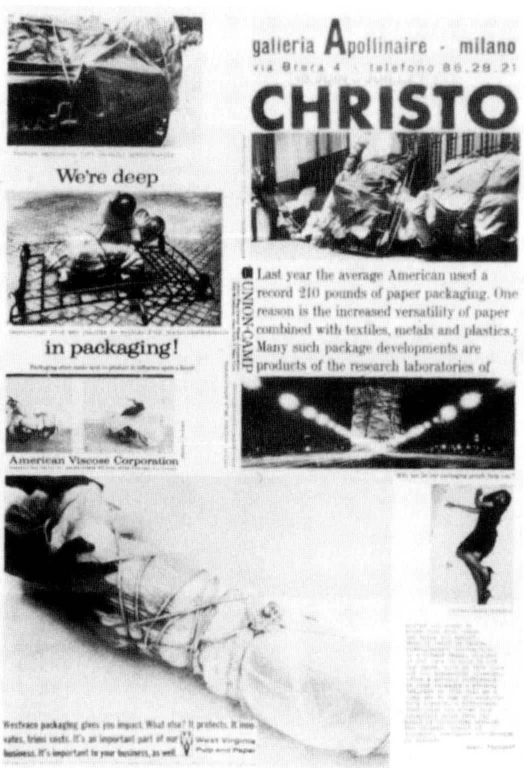

Christo: Faltblatt zur Ausstellung Christo, Galerie Apollinaire, Mailand, Juni 1963 / Christo: Folder of the Christo exhibition, Gallery Apollinaire, Milan, June 1963

nende Hand des Künstlers zum Bildthema bei François Dufrêne (* 1930 Paris – † 1982 Paris), Raymond Hains (* 1926 Saint-Brieuc), Mimmo Rotella (* 1918 Cantanzaro/Kalabrien) und Jacques Mahé de la Villeglé (* 1926 Quimper).
Yves Klein (* 1928 Nizza – † 1962 Paris) wandelt die Befreiung des Geistes von der Materie, die unendliche Ausdehnung des Raumes und die immaterielle Sensibilität, die in den Kosmogonien der Rosenkreuzer angesprochen sind, zum künstlerischen Konzept. 1948 „signierte" er sein erstes Kunstwerk, den Himmel über Nizza. 1950, während der Arbeit bei einem Einrahmer in London, trug er Farbpulver auf Pappvierecke auf. Es sind dies seine ersten Monochromien. Um dieselbe Zeit konzipierte er die ‚Symphonie Monotone', bestehend aus einem einzigen Ton, der 20 Minuten anhält. 1957 inszenierte er sein erstes ‚Immatériel', den völlig leeren Raum einer Galerie, als Ausdruck äußerster Sensibilisierung und Entgrenzung. 1958 startete er die „Lebenden Pinsel": Mit blauer Farbe bemalte Modelle hinterlassen Abdrücke auf Leinwand oder Papier.[56]
Niki de Saint Phalle (* 1930 Paris) schoß 1960 Farbkapseln auf die Leinwand, die beim Aufprall zerplatzten. Schwung- und Schwerkraft, Verlauf und Verteilung der Farbe sind dem Zufall unterworfen. Daneben entstehen Assemblagen aus Alltagsmüll, darunter beschriebene Papiere, Verpackungspapiere und glitzernde Papiere. Die ersten ‚Nanas', in ihrer Form bezug nehmend auf frühe Kulturen, bildete sie 1963/64 aus Pappmaché und bemalte sie zunächst gedeckt und später farbenfreudig.[57] Die Malmaschinen von Jean Tinguely (* 1925 Fribourg/Schweiz – † 1993 Paris), zunächst als Karikaturen gestischer Malerei gedeutet, negieren die persönliche Handschrift des Künstlers und stellen damit das Kunstwerk von Künstlerhand in Frage.

Mimmo Rotella (*1918 Cantanzaro/Calabria) and Jacques Mahé de la Villeglé (*1926 Quimper).
Yves Klein (*1928 Nice – †1962 Paris) proclaimed the liberation of the spirit from matter, the infinite expansion of space, and the immaterial sensitivity that are spoken of in the cosmogony of the Rosicrucians and transformed these into an artistic conception. In 1948 he "signed" his first artwork, the sky over Nice. In 1950, while working at a picture framer's in London, he applied powdered color onto cardboard squares. These were his first monochromes. Around the same time he conceived the 'Symphonie monotone', which consisted of a single tone that lasted 20 minutes. In 1957 he staged his first 'Immatériel', the completely empty room of a gallery as an expression of utmost sensitivity and of boundaries overcome. In 1958 he began the series 'Living Brush': nude models covered in blue paint left their imprint on canvas or paper.[56]
In 1960 Niki de Saint Phalle (*1930 Paris) shot color capsules at canvases; they exploded on contact. Momentum and gravity, the course and the distribution of the paint are subject to chance. Along with this, assemblages of everyday waste, including paper covered in writing, wrapping paper and glitter paper. She made the first 'Nanas', their form a reference to earlier cultures, from papier maché and painted them, at first in subdued, later in bright colors.[57] The painting machines of Jean Tinguely (*1925 Fribourg/Switzerland – † 1993 Paris), at first interpreted as caricatures of intellectual art, negate the personal signature of the artist and thereby question the artwork as something necessarily formed by an artist's hand.

III. 2. Freiheit im Urzustand

Die Nouveaux Réalistes in Paris sind keine solitäre Erscheinung. Kunst als Ausdruck einer Gesellschaft, deren Weltbild durch grundlegende Veränderungen in Wissenschaft und Technologie entscheidend erweitert ist, bedarf adäquater Ausdrucksmöglichkeiten. Fast gleichzeitig in Frankreich, Italien, Deutschland, der Schweiz, Österreich, Jugoslawien, den Niederlanden, Belgien, Großbritannien und Schweden sind Künstler vom leidenschaftlichen Impuls erfaßt, das neueröffnete Potential von Wirklichkeit künstlerisch zu erforschen. Es bewegt sie die gemeinsame Suche nach unbegrenzten immateriellen Räumen, die Eroberung neuer Dimensionen.

Neben Objekten und Rauminszenierungen werden Happening, Décollage-Happening und Fluxus Äußerungen einer sensibilisierten Haltung allem Materiellen und Immateriellen gegenüber, die die Künstler über Europa hinaus auch in den USA und Japan verbindet. Auf der Grundlage dadaistischen und futuristischen Gedankenguts entsteht das totale, vom Zufall bestimmte Gesamtkunstwerk.

Etwa ein Jahrzehnt später thematisierten die Arte-Povera-Künstler erneut arme Materialien und etablierten sie in vergeistigte Dimensionen der Kunstphilosophie.

Die zweite Aufbruchphase der bildenden Kunst kündet sich gegen Ende der 50er Jahre mit Macht an, beeinflußt und vorangetrieben von der Neuen Musik, die bereits zu Beginn der 50er Jahre neue, bislang ungehörte Klangwelten erobert hatte. Das Weltzentrum der neuen Klangdimensionen stellte bis 1965 Köln dar, wo 1951 am NWDR unter Leitung von Herbert Eimert das erste ‚Studio für Elektronische Musik' gegründet worden war. In der Sendereihe ‚Musikalisches Nachtprogramm' kamen aktuelle Fragestellungen zu Wort.

Hier trafen sich u. a. auch Komponisten, die für die bildende Kunst wichtig wurden, wie Mauricio Kagel, Nam June Paik und Charlotte Moorman sowie John Cage.

III.2. Freedom in the primal state

The Noveaux Réalistes in Paris were not a solitary phenomenon. Art as an expression of a society whose cosmic view has been decisively expanded by basic changes in science and technology was in need of an adequate means of expression. Almost simultaneously in France, Italy, Germany, Switzerland, Austria, Yugoslavia, the Netherlands, Belgium, Great Britain and Sweden, artists were caught up in a passionate impulse to investigate aesthetically the newly available potential of reality. What moved them was the common search for unlimited immaterial space, the conquest of new dimensions.

Along with objects and installations there were Happenings, Décollage Happenings, and Fluxus, which were utterances of a sensitized attitude vis-à-vis matter and anti-matter, linking artists beyond Europe to those in the US and Japan. Based on mental concepts from Dadaism and Futurism, the all-encompassing artwork comes into being determined by chance.

Approximately one decade later, Arte Povera took up "poor" materials again as a theme and established them within a spiritualized dimension of aesthetic philosophy.

The second eruptive phase of the visual arts arrived forcefully on the scene towards the end of the 50s, influenced and propelled by New Music, which already at the beginning of the 50s had probed an innovative and literally unheard universe of sound. Up to 1965 the world center for the new dimensions of sound was the city of Cologne, where in 1951 at NWDR under the direction of Herbert Eimert, the first 'Studio for Electronic Music' was founded. In the broadcast series 'Musikalisches Nachtprogramm' [Musical Night Program], the latest developments were debated. Here many young talents converged, including composers, who became important for art, such as Mauricio Kagel, Nam June Paik and Charlotte Moorman, as well as John Cage.

In Paris hatte sich um Pierre Schaeffer und Pierre Boulez ebenfalls eine Gruppe junger Komponisten geschart, deren Bestreben es war, das bereits von Natur aus vorhandene Klang- und Geräuschpotential zu neuen Ordnungen zu führen. John Cage hatte Ende der 40er Jahre in den USA begonnen, Klänge und Geräusche des Alltags zu erschließen.
Die elektronische Musik eröffnete zudem Zugang zu Klangerscheinungen der Elektronik, die in der bisherigen Musik nicht bekannt waren. Diese große Erweiterung des Klangspektrums, diese ungeheure unstrukturierte Freiheit, erforderte Gestaltungsideen, die nicht durch Musizieren auf Spielinstrumenten, sondern nur aus dem Klang selbst, dem „Material", gewonnen werden konnten.[58] Otto Piene (* 1928 Laasphe/Westfalen), einer der Hauptvertreter von ZERO, erinnert sich: „Wir verfolgten ähnliche Gedanken, wie sie bereits zuvor in der elektronischen Musik in Köln eröffnet waren. Mit neuen technischen Mitteln Räume zu erschließen und zu formulieren war auch unser Ziel."[59]
Der Gruppe ZERO, der neben Otto Piene Heinz Mack (* 1931 Lollar/Hessen) und später Günther Uecker (* 1930 Wendorf/Mecklenburg) als fester Kern angehörten, brach radikal mit den traditionellen Bildvorstellungen. Ähnlich der elektronischen Musik verfolgten diese Künstler auf der Grundlage neuer Technik die Erweiterung der Wahrnehmungskapazität. Licht und Bewegung erschienen ihnen die Mittel, um in den unbegrenzten immateriellen Raum vorzustoßen. Licht wird zum bestimmenden Element des gesamten visuellen Spektrums und Bewegung zum Ausdruck der Unendlichkeit von Zeit. Ähnliche Tendenzen wie ZERO in Düsseldorf verfolgen in Mailand die Gruppe T, in Amsterdam die Gruppe Null, in Paris die Groupe de Recherche d'Art Visuel GRAV. Manzoni reiste zwischen Paris, Düsseldorf, Mailand, Amsterdam umher als unermüdlicher Ideenfinder.
Bevorzugte Farbe zur Darstellung von Licht, von Weite und Freiheit ist Weiß als Bündelung der Gesamtheit aller Farbspektren, der der damals vieldiskutierte Begriff des „weißen Rauschens" aus

In Paris a group of young composers had also banded together around Pierre Schaeffer and Pierre Boulez, whose goal it was to direct the potentiality found in the tones and sounds available in nature toward a new systematization. John Cage had begun in the 40s in the USA to study tones and sounds in the everyday world.
In addition electronic music opened the way to sound phenomena of electronics till then unknown in music. This expansion in the spectrum of tonality, this enormous unstructured freedom required creative ideas capable of arising (not from playing music on instruments) solely from the tone itself, the "material".[58] Otto Piene (*1928 Laasphe/Westphalia), one of the chief representatives of the art group ZERO, remembers: "We pursued similar ideas to those already opened up by the electronic music in Cologne. It was our goal to exploit and formulate space by new technical means."[59]
ZERO, whose hard-core members were – with Otto Piene – Heinz Mack (*1931 Lollar/Hessen) and later Günther Uecker (*1930 Wendorf/Mecklenburg), broke radically with the traditional idea of a painting. Similar to the path taken by electronic music, these artists strove to expand man's perceptive capacity by the introduction of new techniques. Light and motion seemed to them the means to advance into unlimited, immaterial space: light becomes the determining element of the total visual spectrum and motion the expression of the infinity of time. Similar tendencies to ZERO in Düsseldorf were pursued by the groups T in Milan, Null in Amsterdam, and the Groupe de Recherche d'Art Visuel GRAV in Paris. Manzoni traveled between Paris, Düsseldorf, Milan and Amsterdam as a tireless instigator of ideas.
The preferred color for representing light, distance and freedom was white, the focus of the total color spectrum, which corresponded to the much debated concept of the "white noise" of electronic music. For paper art new ways were opened up by ZERO and its related art movements. Paper in its whiteness, its pliancy, its lightness and variability corresponds

der elektronischen Musik gleichgesetzt werden kann. Für die Papierkunst eröffnen sich mit ZERO und den verwandten Kunstbestrebungen neue Wege. Das Papier in seiner Weiße, seiner Geschmeidigkeit, seiner Leichtigkeit und Variabilität entspricht den künstlerischen Zielen dieser Zeit. Papier kann leicht sein wie Luft, weit wie das All und löst sich durch Verbrennen auf in Nichts; es kommt der Vorstellung des Immateriellen sehr nahe.

Die weite, unerschöpfliche Bandbreite des Optischen, Haptischen und Akustischen steht den Künstlern nun zur Verfügung. Im Literarischen eröffneten Futuristen und Dadaisten mit ihren vielgestaltigen Lautgedichten neue Wege wie beispielsweise Kurt Schwitters mit der ‚Ursonate'. Hieraus entwickeln sich in logisch-philosophischer Fortführung vielfach Varianten bis hin zu Hans G Helms Werk ‚Fa:m' Ahniesgwow' von 1959, das im Umfeld des Kölner elektronischen Studios entstand und hier Bedeutung für die elektronische Analyse der Sprache als Klangmaterial hatte. Die reine Linie und nichts als die Linie auf Papier wird zum Inbegriff allen Wissens, vergleichbar mit Weiß, mit Licht, mit „weißem Rauschen". Sie taucht in der Literatur bei Claude Pascal als Vorwort zu einem Katalog von Yves Klein und in der Kunst bei Manzoni auf. Auf die Rolle eines Endlospapiers zeichnete er seine Linie der Unendlichkeit, die alle Probleme von Komposition und Größe in der Weite des Weltalls hinter sich läßt.[60] Verwandt ist die unendliche Linie dem 20minütigen Ton der Sonate von Yves Klein, die ihre Wurzeln auch im ‚Gesang der Fische' von Morgenstern wiederfindet. Klein nennt die Erweiterung solchen Daseinsbewußtseins das „Erschaffen der Freiheit im Urzustand".[61]

Papier entpuppt sich in bezug auf dieses Gedankengut als geeignetes Medium, Raumordnungen und Erlebniswelten neuer Dimensionen zu erschließen.

to the aesthetic goals of the times. Paper can be light as air, as extensive as outer space and, when lit, dissolve in flames to nothingness; it comes very close to the concept of the immaterial.

The broad, inexhaustible range of the optical, the tactile and the acoustic were now available to artists. In literature the Futurist and Dadaist sound poetry in its many forms had thrown open new aspects, as had Kurt Schwitters' 'Ursonate' [Primal Sonnet]. Many variants developed out of these in logic and philosophic continuation up to Hans G Helms' work 'Fa:m'Ahniesgwow' from 1959, that had its origin in proximity to the Cologne electronic studio and was significant for its electronic analysis of speech as sound material. The pure line and nothing but the line on paper becomes the symbol of all knowledge, similar to white, to light, to the "white noise", and appears in literature in a foreword written by Claude Pascal to a catalogue on Yves Klein and in art with Manzoni. On a roll of continuous paper he draws his line of infinity that cedes all problems of composition and size to the vastness of outer space.[60] The infinite line of the 20-minute long tone in the sonnet by Yves Klein is related to this, which in turn has is roots in 'Gesang der Fische' (Song of the Fishes) by Morgenstern. Yves Klein called the expansion of such existential consciousness the "creation of freedom in a primal state".[61]

In reference to such ideas, paper turns out to be the suitable medium for the investigation of spatial systems and event-related worlds of new dimensions.

IV. Papier wird autonom – ZERO, Umfeld und danach

IV. Paper becomes autonomous – ZERO, associated groups and the aftermath

ZERO lehnt das expressiv gemalte Tafelbild ab. Der emotionalen Gestik des Informel, dem psychischen Automatismus, der subjektiven Spontaneität und den „archaischen", amorphen Texturen, die häufig wie Vulkanlandschaften wirken, setzt ZERO strenge Strukturen entgegen. Neue Methoden der Herstellung und neue Materialien wie Kunstharz, Polymerfarben, Kaolin, Gips, Rauch und Licht, Nägel, Aluminiumfolie, Glas, Spiegel, Lichtraster kommen zum Einsatz. Oskar Holweck und Jan Schoonhoven wählen Papier und Papiermaché. Die neuen Materialien erfordern neue Methoden der Bildherstellung. In Reaktion auf den subjektiven Gestus der älteren Malergeneration wird alles Handschriftliche zurückgedrängt. Man wendet halbmechanische Techniken an und nimmt damit Arbeitsmethoden von Dada und Max Ernst auf. Uecker nutzt Kämme, Stäbe oder Nagelbürsten, um Strukturen in die Farbmaterie zu ritzen, Fontana durchlöchert seine Papiere und Bilder mit Locheisen und Messer, Graubner setzt mit Farbe getränkte Kissen ein, um Abdrücke zu machen, Mack nimmt Scheibenwischer, Gummischaber, Mavignier Nagelköpfe und Piene Rastergitter aus Karton oder Metall.[62]

ZERO rejects the painted easel picture. ZERO sets against the emotional gestures of Art Informel, of psychic automatism, of subjective spontaneity and against the "archaic" and amorphic textures that often look like volcanic landscape, its own stark structures. New methods of production and new materials like synthetic resins, polymer paints, kaolin, plaster, smoke and light, nails, aluminum foil, glass, mirrors, light templates come into use. Oskar Holweck and Jan Schoonhoven choose paper and papier-maché. The new materials require new methods of art production. In reaction to the subjective gestural style of the older generation of artists, everything that smacks of a personal signature is rejected. Semi-mechanical techniques are used, thereby taking over work methods used by Dada and Max Ernst. Uecker uses combs, rods or nailbrushes to scratch structures into the paint material, Fontana perforates his paper and pictures with punch and knife, Graubner uses cushions drenched in color to make imprints, Mack takes windshield wipers, rubber scrapers, Mavignier the heads of nails and Piene templates made of cardboard or metal.[62]

IV. 1. Licht und Feuer

„Und das Licht ist da und dringt überall hin, und nicht ich male, sondern das Licht“, sagte Otto Piene 1961.[63] Bereits 1959 schrieb er in der ZERO-Zeitschrift: „Ich bemühe mich um die Reinheit der Farbe und Klarheit des Bildes. Das Licht ist die erste Bedingung aller Sichtbarkeit. Das Licht ist die Sphäre der Farbe. Das Licht ist das Lebenselement des Menschen und des Bildes [...] Die Mittel sind gefunden, der Malerei unter Beibehaltung ihrer Disziplin kraft des Lichtes so viel übersetzte Sinnlichkeit zu geben, daß sie aus der rationalen Deutbarkeit des Zeichenhaften in den Bereich der malerischen Schönheit tritt, in der der Weg des Geistes über die Sinne führt. Sie wird strahlende Fülle gewinnen, ihr Leuchten wird den Menschen treffen. Die Reinheit des Lichts wird sie befähigen, reine Empfindungen zu wecken.“[64] Das Licht soll nicht mehr nur Beleuchtung für ein Bild sein, sondern wird selbst aktiver Teil des Kunstwerks. Erst durch die Brechungen an Hindernissen kann sich Licht artikulieren. Je nach Lichteinfall ist die Wirkung verschieden. Es entstehen Lichtschwingungen, die beim Betrachter wie Vibrationen erscheinen.

In diesem Prozeß ist die aktive Bewegung, das „Wandern“, des Betrachters gefragt.

Otto Piene begann 1955, das Licht „als Sphäre der Farbe“ zu erobern.[65] Selbstfabrizierte Lochraster aus Karton setzte er dem Licht entgegen. 1957 entstanden die ersten Rasterbilder, Vorläufer der ‚Lichtballette‘. Die geometrischen Rastersiebe formte er aus Plakatkarton. Jeder Bogen in der Größe 70 mal 100 Zentimeter wird von Hand mit verschieden großen Locheisen mit 7000 bis 10 000 Löchern pro Bogen durchstoßen. Installationen von „Lichtmodellen“ wenden bis zu 40 Rastersiebe. Die Löcher stehen in wechselnder Ordnung in unterschiedlicher Dichte zueinander. Leichte Unregelmäßigkeiten sind beabsichtigte Ausdrucksmittel. Durch Übereinanderlegen und Verschieben der Rasterplatten entwickeln sich Interferenzen.

IV.1. Light and fire

“And the light is there and penetrates everywhere, and it is not I who paints but the light,” Otto Piene said in 1961.[63] Already in 1959 he wrote in the ZERO magazine: “I work hard to achieve the purity of the color and the clarity of the picture. Light is the first condition of visibility. Light is the sphere of color. Light is the life element of man and of the picture [...] The means have been found to give painting (with its discipline maintained by the power of light) so much transformed sensuality that it is able to leave the realm of the rational interpretation of the signs and step into that of graphic beauty, which leads toward the path of the spirit over the senses. It will gain radiant fullness, its glow will strike mankind. The purity of light will enable it to awaken pure sensation.”[64] Light should no longer only be the lighting for the picture, but itself become an active part of the artwork. Not till it is refracted from obstacles can light be articulated. The angle of light decides its varied effect. There are light oscillations that appear to the viewer as vibrations. In this process the viewer's active movement (“wandering”) is called for.

Otto Piene began in 1955 to conquer light “as a sphere of color”.[65] He set self-fabricated, pierced paperboard templates against the light. In 1957 the first template pictures were made, prototypes of the ‘Light Ballets’. The geometric template screens he made of heavy poster paper. Each sheet, 70 times 100 centimeters, was punctured with holes made by hand-held punches of different sizes, 7000 to 10 000 holes per sheet. Installations of light models require ut to 40 template screens. The holes are set in alternating order and in varying density to each other. Slight irregularities are intentional means of expression. By overlapping and shifting the screens, you create interferences.

“That I use paper is based on the procedure,” Otto Piene explains. “Paper/paperboard is light, flexible and can be easily perforated. Metal is heavy, is

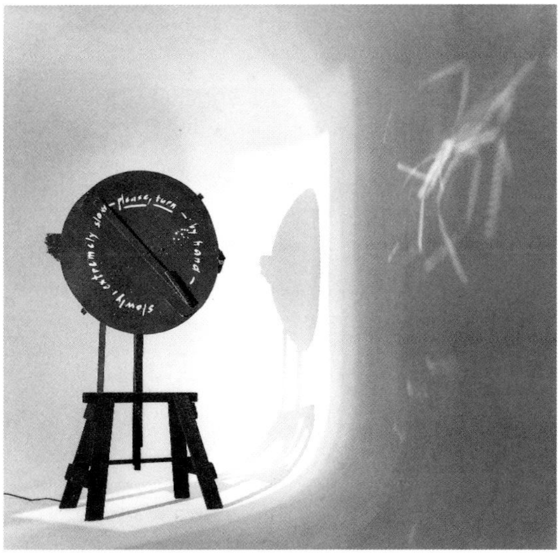

Otto Piene: Lichtballett ‚Please turn', 1961. Scheibenprojektor aus Karton und Holz. 210 cm hoch, 110 cm Durchmesser / Otto Piene: Light Ballet 'Please turn', 1961. Disk projector made out of cardboard and wood. Height 210 cm, diameter 110 cm

Otto Piene: Lichtraster-Montage, 1958. Perforierter Karton und Lichtprojektor / Otto Piene: Light template assemblage, 1958. Perforated pasteboard with light projector

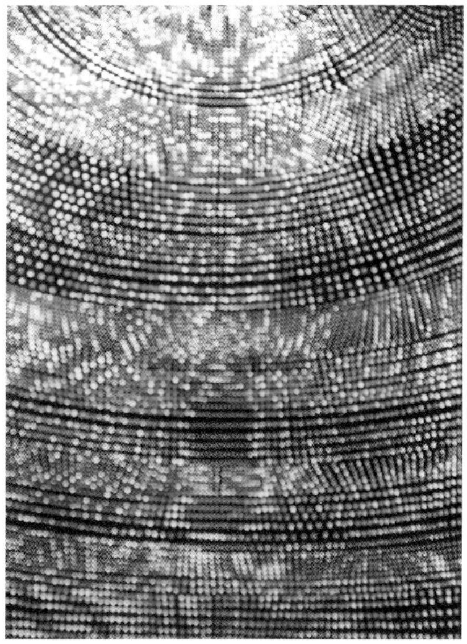

Otto Piene: Erstes mechanisches Lichtballett, 1960. Atelier Piene, Düsseldorf. 9. Abendausstellung ‚ein fest für das Licht' / Otto Piene: First Mechanical Light Ballet, 1960. Studio Piene, Düsseldorf. 9th evening exhibition 'a celebration for the light'

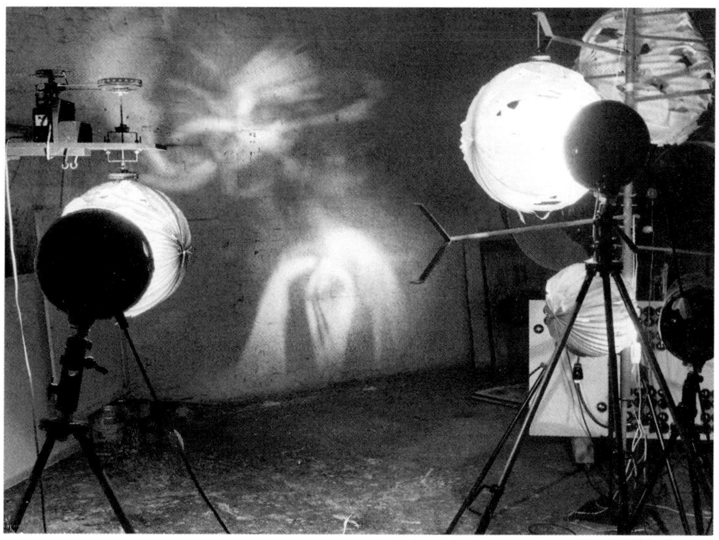

„Daß ich Papier nahm, ist im Vorgang begründet", erklärt Otto Piene. „Papier/Karton ist leicht, flexibel und läßt sich ohne Mühe perforieren. Metall ist zu schwer, ist schwerfällig. Die Arbeit wird dadurch langwierig."[66] Seine ersten Lichtmaschinen formte er aus Lampions, Bauholz, Pappe und Eisenstativen.[67] Wieder mit Hilfe der Rastersiebe entwarf Piene 1959 einen neuen Bildtypus: die Rauchzeichnungen und Rauchbilder auf Papier oder Leinwand als Manifestation des Elementes Feuer. Der durch die Löcher der Raster dringende Rauch einer Kerze oder einer Petroleumlampe bildet auf dem darüberliegenden Papier ein Punktraster. Je nach Steuerung erscheinen helle bis schwarze flächige Punkte, die sich in ihrer Dichte und Helligkeit unterscheiden. Sie suggerieren Raum und Vibration. Durch Firnisüberzug entstehen Reflexe und „Lichtnuancen im Dunkeln".[68] Rauch gestaltet das autonome Blatt Papier. Das Blatt wird zum Instrument, das Nuancen einer optischen Energie auffängt.

„Ich würde gerne meine Individualität als Autor noch weniger spürbar werden lassen, eine Kraft wie das Licht noch souveräner wirken lassen, damit die Materialität noch weiter aufgehoben und noch größere Freiheit gewonnen wird." In Pienes Lichtballetten erhält die Kraft des Lichtes beeindruckende Selbständigkeit. Das Licht „tanzt" nach einer gewissen „choreographischen" Abfolge, die mit Tönen als Leitstrahlen „orchestriert" wird. Die Lichtballette sind „Raumerfüllungen". Das Licht erreicht die meisten Orte im Raum. Der Erlebende hat so den Eindruck, Mitelpunkt des Geschehens zu sein. „Den Betrachter mitten ins Bild"[69] zu setzen, war bereits unerfülltes Bestreben der Futuristen. In Pienes Lichtballetten geht das Bild durch den Betrachter hindurch. Er fühlt sich als Teil des Lichtes, empfindet es als Selbstverständlichkeit wie das Ein- und Ausatmen.[70] Das erste Lichtballett in der Düsseldorfer Galerie Schmela inszenierte Piene noch mit Papprastersieben, hinter denen er Handlampen hin- und herbewegte. Auch die Scheiben der ersten Lichtmaschinen sind aus techni-

cumbersome. The work becomes tedious."[66] He also formed his first light machines out of structural wood, lanterns and paperboard.[67]

Again with the help of template screens, Piene designed a new type of picture in 1959: the smoke drawings and smoke pictures on paper or canvas are manifestations of the element of fire. The smoke of a candle or petroleum lamp that penetrates the holes in the template forms a pattern of dots on the paper above it. According to the manipulation, the two-dimensional dots are light to black and differ in density and lightness. They suggest space and vibration. With a coat of varnish, reflections are added and, "light nuances in the dark".[68] Smoke designs the autonomous sheet of paper. The sheet becomes an instrument that catches the nuances of optical energy.

"I would like my individuality as author to be even less noticeable, to allow a force like the light to be even more sovereign so that materiality is further suspended and greater freedom is won." In Piene's light ballets, the energy of the light attains impressive independence. The light "dances" according to a certain "choreographic" succession that is "orchestrated" with tones as lightray direction. The light ballets are "space fulfillments". The light reaches most corners of the room. The spectator thus has the impression of being in the middle of the event. To set "the viewer in the center of the picture"[69] was an unrealized goal of the Futurists. In Piene's light ballets the picture goes right through the spectator. He feels himself a part of the light and finds it as natural as breathing.[70] The first light ballet was staged by Piene for the Düsseldorf Galerie Schmela still using paperboard template screens, behind which he moved handheld lights back and forth. The disks of the first light machines were, for technical reasons, also perforated cardboard. Not till later did Piene use metal and felt.[71]

Today Otto Piene is acknowledged as the pioneer of Sky Art. He has come quite a way towards fulfilling the ZERO dream of invading cosmic dimensions

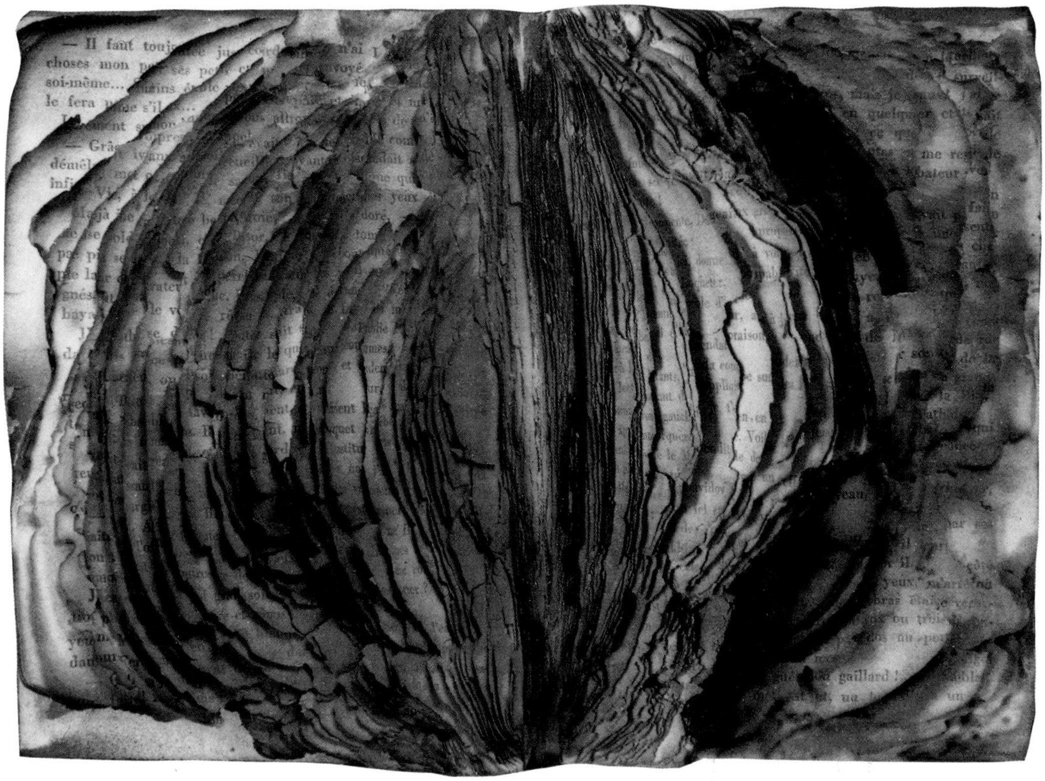

Bernard Aubertin: Livre brulé, 1962. 27 x 30 cm / Bernard Aubertin: Livre brulé, 1962. 27 x 30 cm

schen Gründen perforierte Pappen. Erst später verwendet Piene Metall und Filz.[71]

Heute gilt Otto Piene als der Pionier der Sky art. Dem ZERO-Traum, in kosmische Dimensionen mit Hilfe des Lichtes vorzudringen, ist er ein gutes Stück nähergerückt. Mit gigantischen Luftschleifen und Regenbögen belebt er in den USA die Weite des Himmels.

Feuerbilder, rotierende Feuerscheiben, Feuerschachteln im Taschenformat, raumgreifende Feuerwege – „Bernard le rouge" hat im Feuer sein Medium gefunden. Mit der Gruppe ZERO stellte Bernard Aubertin (*1934 Fontenay-aux-Roses/Seine) seit 1961 vielfach aus. Seine Suche nach Universellem, nach Absolutem jenseits von Form und Farbe verbindet ihn mit ZERO. Rot – nicht ein Farbton, sondern viele Varianten – steht für das Universum, für Feuer, Blut, Wärme, Energie, Dynamik. Feuer bedeutet Aubertin Farbe und Licht; es ist für ihn untrennbar mit dem Material Papier ver-

with the help of light. Using gigantic loops of air and rainbows, he enlivens the vast heavens above the United States of America.

Fire pictures, rotating fire disks, pocket-size fire boxes, paths of fire that invade space – "Bernard le rouge" has found his medium in fire. Bernard Aubertin (*1934 Fontenay-aux Roses/Seine) has since 1961 often participated in ZERO exhibitions. His search, beyond form and color, for the universal, the absolute is what links him to this group. Red – not one color but many varieties – stands for the unvierse, for fire, blood, warmth, energy, dynamics. For Aubertin, fire means color and light and is inseparably bound up with the material of paper. Brands are marked by fire in many grades of red and black. Fire paints images in and with paper. These fire signs resemble icons. The subjective signature disappears behind the anonymity of the burnt paper image. Paper burns, flames rise from the paper, heat is generated, colors

bunden. Feuer hinterläßt Brandmale in vielen Rot- und Schwarzstufungen; Feuer malt Bilder in und mit Papier. Diese Feuerzeichen gleichen Ikonen. Die subjektive Handschrift verschwindet in der Anonymität des gebrannten Papierbildes. Papier verbrennt, dem Papier entsteigen Flammen, Hitze wird erzeugt, Farben leuchten auf, das verkohlte Papier erzeugt Geruch, und das verbrennende Papier knistert und knackt. Die glimmenden Reste hinterlassen Reste von Papier: graue Asche und verkohltes Schwarz.
Aubertin verbrennt auch Bücher. Das Erzeugen von Ohnmacht beim Anblick des verzehrenden Feuers ist hier beabsichtigt, ebenso wie die Vermittlung des Gefühls der Verlorenheit angesichts der Unendlichkeit von Zeit und Raum.[72] Aubertin will das Gefühl sensibilisieren, den Blick schärfen, den Verstand aus seiner Lethargie befreien und den Menschen auf seine Möglichkeiten von Freiheit stoßen.

are illuminated, the charred paper gives off a smell, and the burning paper crackles and snaps. The glimmering remains leave paper remains behind: gray ash and charred black.
Aubertin also burns books. The feeling of powerlessness when watching the consuming fire is intentionally generated, just as is the feeling of being lost when faced with the infinity of time and space.[72] Aubertin wants to school our feelings, to sharpen our eyes, to free our mental powers from lethargy and to prod man to an awareness of his possibilities for freedom.

IV. 2. Weiß – Struktur

„Zero ist Weiß", heißt es im ZERO-Manifest. „Die Fleckenlosigkeit des Weiss zog uns an. Wir sahen darin Reinheit und Licht."[73] Weiß ist manchem ZERO-Künstler Innbegriff der Seinserfahrung. Weiß ist befreit von Erinnerungs- und Ausdruckswerten. Weiß ist reine Energie und zugleich Stille. Weiß summiert alle Farben in sich. „Die Stille ist tönend genug. Die Schwingung erscheint uns bewegter als die Niederschrift der Bewegung", schreibt Otto Piene, „die Nuancen erregen unseren Atem und steigern die Kraft unserer Farben. Das eine Leuchten strahlt uns mehr, als die vielen Farben können."[74] Die feinen Abstufungen der Monochromie, die Vibrationen der Farbe entstehen durch Unebenheiten, durch Strukturen, durch Reflexionen des Lichtes. ZERO-Künstler wählten neben Weiß auch Silber und Gold. Für Yves Klein war Blau die Farbe der Immaterialität.

IV.2. White – Structure

"Zero is white," it says in the ZERO manifesto. "The spotlessness of white attracted us. We saw it as purity and light."[73] White is for some ZERO artists the essence of an experience of being. White is free of memory and expressive values. White is pure energy and stillness at the same time. White is the sum of all colors. "Silence is sound enough. Vibration seems to us more moving than the recording of all movement," writes Otto Piene, "the nuances agitate our breathing and increase the power of our color. To us the one illumination shines brighter than many colors could."[74] The fine gradations of monochromism, the vibrations of the color are arrived at by means of irregularities, by texture, by reflections of the light. ZERO artists, besides white, chose silver and gold. For Yves Klein it was blue that was the color of immateriality.

„Ich habe mich für eine weiße Zone entschieden als äußerste Farbigkeit, als Höhepunkt des Lichtes, als Triumph über das Dunkel“, schreibt Günther Uecker. „Der Zustand Weiß kann als Gebet verstanden werden, in seiner Artikulation ein spirituelles Erlebnis sein.“[75] In verschiedenen Kulturen gilt Weiß als absolute Seinserfahrung. Auf den Symbolwert Weiß bezog sich seit jeher die katholische Liturgie, für die Weiß Reinheit und Heiligkeit, Entmaterialisierung bedeutet. Malewitsch demonstrierte mit seinem ‚Weißen Quadrat auf Weiß‘ die reine Gegenstandslosigkeit. Fontana schrieb 1946 das ‚Weiße Manifest‘.

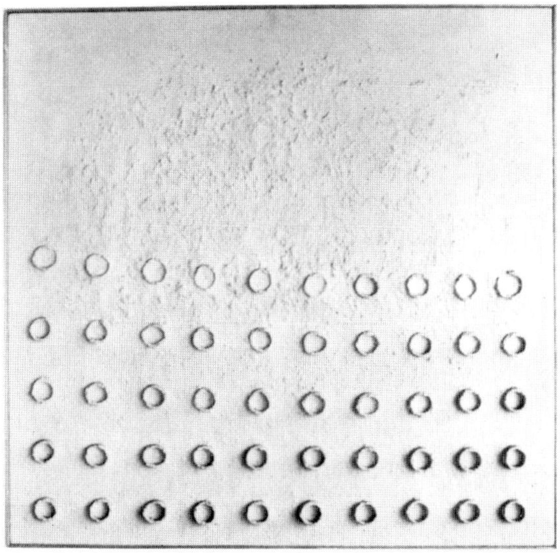

Günther Uecker: Formationsauflösung, 1958. Papprohre und Kunstharz auf Leinwand, monochrom weiß. 100 x 100 cm / Günther Uecker: Decomposed Formation, 1958. Cardboard tubes and synthetic resin on canvas, monochrome white. 100 x 100 cm

In seiner frühen Schaffensphase hat Uecker nicht nur Nägel durch weiße Übermalungen entmaterialisiert. Er verarbeitete auch Pappröhrchen und Korken. Der neue Bildraum entsteht mit Hilfe der Struktur von abgesägten Röhrchenstümpfen. Diese kleinen unregelmäßigen Kreise bilden ihrerseits eine sich hinziehende Bahn fortschreitend undeutlicher werdender größerer Kreise, die immer tiefer in den weißen Bildgrund sinken oder, auf gleiche Höhe geschnitten, ein Linienquadrat formen, wobei die Linien nicht exakt gezogen sind. Unebenheiten irritie-

“I decided on a white zone as the extremist color quality, as the highpoint of light, as triumph over darkness,” writes Günther Uecker. “The state of whiteness can also be understood as a prayer, in its articulation as a spiritual experience.”[75] In different cultures white is considered an absolute existential experience. Catholic liturgy has always been drawn to the symbolic value of white, which it sees as pure, saintly and immaterial. Malevich demonstrated pure abstraction with his ‘White on White’. In 1946 Fontana wrote the ‘White Manifesto’.

It was not only nails that Uecker in his early phase painted over in white. He also used cardboard tubes and bottle corks. The new pictorial space was created with the help of a structure of sawed-off tube stumps. The small, irregular circles generate in turn a lengthening row of ever vaguer and larger circles that sink ever deeper into the white ground or, cut to the same height, form a square of lines imprecisely drawn. Irregularities irritate the serial uniformity. The light plays over the white elevations and openings. The result is a vibration of many shades of gray.

In the years 1957 to 1959, Uecker studied the relationship of line and of dot to the flat plane. Of special interest for paper art are the drawings he made in 1959, in which he examined the structure of a line of squares. The square makes its appearance as an additive row. Serial regularity is something Uecker also achieved by folding the paper. The paper is folded in such a way that ridges are formed, raised above the picture plane. These linear elevations he then dyed with graphite.[76]

Jan Schoonhoven (*1914 Delft/Netherlands) created his first white reliefs out of papier-maché. The serial principle that Uecker in his drawings arrived at by folding, Schoonhoven achieved by forming elevations out of papier-maché. He too painted his structures white. Squares or rectangles are lined up into serial structures. Irregularities in the raised ridges are consciously included. The angle of light and the reflections on the white of the flat plane

ren das serielle Gleichmaß. Das Licht spielt mit den weißen Erhöhungen und Öffnungen. Vibration in vielen Grauschattierungen ist das Ergebnis.
In den Jahren 1957 bis 1959 untersuchte Uecker in Zeichnungen das Verhältnis von Linie und Punkt zur Fläche. Im Hinblick auf Papierkunst sind die Zeichnungen von 1959 von Interesse, in denen er Strukturen von Quadratreihen untersucht. Das Quadrat tritt als additive Reihe auf. Das Gleichmaß des Seriellen hat Uecker durch Faltungen der Papiere erreicht. Durch das Falten entstehen Stege, die sich über der Fläche erheben. Die linearen Erhebungen färbte er mit Graphit ein.[76]
Jan Schoonhoven (* 1914 Delft/Niederlande) schuf 1960 seine ersten weißen Reliefs aus Papiermaché. Das serielle Prinzip, das Uecker in seinen Zeichnungen durch Faltung erreichte, komponiert Schoonhoven mit Stegen aus Papiermaché. Auch er übermalt seine Strukturen weiß. Quadrate oder Rechtecke reihen sich zu seriellen Bildstrukturen. Unregelmäßigkeiten der Stege sind bewußt eingeplant. Der Lichteinfall und die Lichtreflexe im Weiß der Flächen und Stege bewirken ein vibrierendes Rasterspiel. Die Konstruktionen, Stege oder quadratische und rechteckige Fächer, sind immer aus Karton aufgebaut, mit Papierstücken beklebt und weiß gestrichen.[77]
Leo Erb (* 1923 St. Ingbert/Saar) ist bis heute einer der konsequentesten Vertreter von ZERO, obwohl er nie mit dieser Gruppe ausgestellt hat. Die Reduzierung der künstlerischen Mittel allein auf die Linie und das Weiß eröffnet im Immerwiederkehrenden die Kraft und Weite seiner Kompositionen. Bereits Ende der 40er Jahre ritzte er Linienformationen in weißen Karton. Unabhängig von den ersten Versuchen von Yves Klein oder ZERO suchte er nach einer neuen Bildform ohne Gestik, ohne informelle Handschrift, ohne Farbe und Pinsel. Werkzeug ist das Messer, mit dem er den Karton oder das Papier mit Linien stigmatisiert, an denen das Licht sich in vielstufigen Schatten bricht. Die Schnittlinien, in den Jahren 1947 bis 1951 noch als strukturale Gegenüberstellungen richtungsvari-

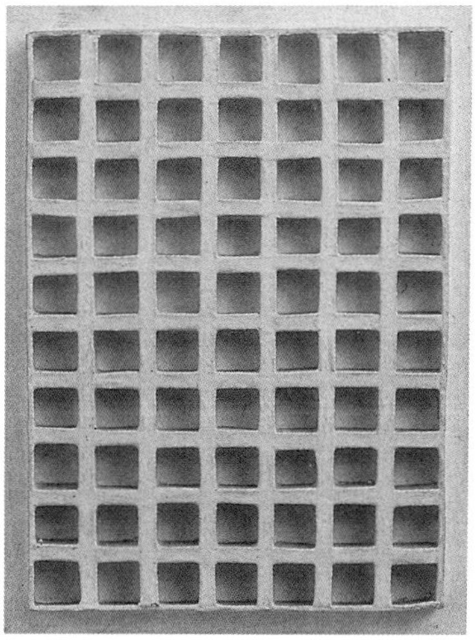

Jan Schoonhoven: R 70-30, 1970. Pappmaché-Relief. 33 x 24 cm / Jan Schoonhoven: R 70-30, 1970. Pappmaché-relief. 33 x 24 cm

and of the ridge make for a game of serial vibration. The constructions, ridges, or square and rectangular cubbyholes are always composed of paperboard, pasted with pieces of paper and painted white.[77]
Leo Erb (*1923 St. Ingbert/Saar), to the present day, is one of the most consistent representatives of ZERO, although he never took part in their exhibitions. His reduction of all mediums of artistic expression to the line and to the color white in constant repetition shows the force and the breadth of his compositions. As early as the 40s he scratched line formations into white cardboard. Independently of the first attempts made by Yves Klein or ZERO he began a search for a new picture form without gesture, without an Art Informel style, without color or brush. His tool was the knife with which he stigmatized lines into the paper and over which the light breaks in graded shades. The lines set in different directions from 1947 to 1951 he gradually in 1957 began to line up geometrically parallel. Today he rips the paper and places the torn edges mostly in horizontal parallel arrangement one below the other. Irregularities in the traces of the rip or in the edges cast from paper pulp enliven the texture. Torn edges placed closer

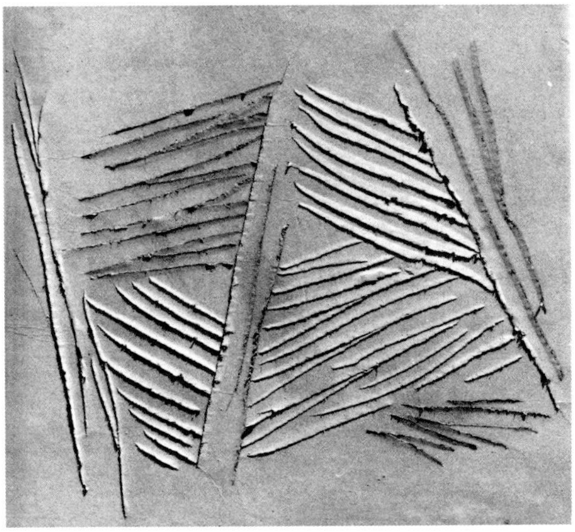

Leo Erb: Ohne Titel, 1949. Papierschnitt. 26 x 26,5 cm / Leo Erb: Untitled, 1949. Paper cut. 26 x 26.5 cm

ierend gesetzt, führt Erb erst allmählich 1957 zu geometrischem Parallelverlauf. Heute reißt er Papier und setzt die Reißkanten als meist waagerechtes Parallelgefüge untereinander. Unebenheiten der Reißspuren oder Gußkanten beleben das Strukturgefüge. Enger gestellte Reißkanten, Störungen im Gleichmaß, rhythmisieren das Bild. Der Lichteinfall auf die gerissenen oder gegossenen Erhebungen erzeugt den Eindruck von Linie.[78]
Oskar Holweck (* 1924 St. Ingbert/Saar) stellte seit 1958 vielfach mit ZERO aus. Für ihn ist das weiße Papier ausschließliches Material. Dem Papier gewinnt er Formen der eigenen Beschaffenheit ab. Die Brechungen des Lichtes an der Oberfläche und in den Hohlräumen sind Bestandteil der Komposition. „Das Papier hat seine eigene Struktur und Textur. Es trägt somit die Gestalt, die ich ihm gebe, bereits in sich." In den ersten Jahren „malte" Holweck Bilder in Papier, indem er das Papier durch Einkerbungen oder Ritzungen verletzt. Es entstehen serielle Strukturen. In den 70er Jahren formte er Objekte aus mechanisch oder thermisch behandeltem Papier. In Fortführung des Bauhaus-Gedankens erarbeitet er seine Bilder und Objekte allein aus dem Material heraus. Er biegt, knickt, knüllt, faltet, drückt, preßt, staucht, klopft, reißt das Pa-

together, disruptions in the regularity, give the picture a certain rhythm. The way the light falls onto the torn or poured raised areas creates the impression of lines.[78]
Oskar Holweck (*1924 St. Ingbert/Saar) often took part in ZERO exhibitions. His material is exclusively white paper. He coaxes shapes out of the paper's inner constitution. The fracturing of light on the surface and in the hollows are a part of the composition. "The paper has its own structure and texture. It already carries within itself the construction that I give it." In the first years Holweck "painted" pictures in paper by an assault on the paper with notches or scratches. Serial structures were the result. In the 70s he began forming objects out of paper that had been mechanically or thermically treated. In continuation of the idea of the Bauhaus, he elaborates his pictures and objects solely from the material itself. He bends, pleats, crumples, folds, exerts pressure on, compresses, hammers or tears the paper. "The incursion on the paper material occurs mostly under the strict maintenance of metric sequences of motion in the form of lines, rows and latticed patterns. It reacts to my cautious, often faint discourse with what is for me an ever surprising and hardly predictable, rich expression of forms and colors. While working I live in constant conflict between my action and the re-action of the work material."[79]
"The white sheet of paper is like a field of snow. The sensitivity of the white surface immediately absorbs every trace,"[80] Maria Reuter writes (*1929 Flensburg). She takes a sheet of paper and gives it a small pleat or makes a tear. The surface turns into a vivid relief. François Morellet (*1931 Cholet) also limits himself to a minimal infringement on the paper. By folding transparent paper and then overlapping and grading it by tones, he arrives at optically spatial constructions. His geometrical abstractions impress you by their reduction and logic. In 1963 Morellet participated in a ZERO exhibition. Hermann de Vries (*1931 Alkmaar/

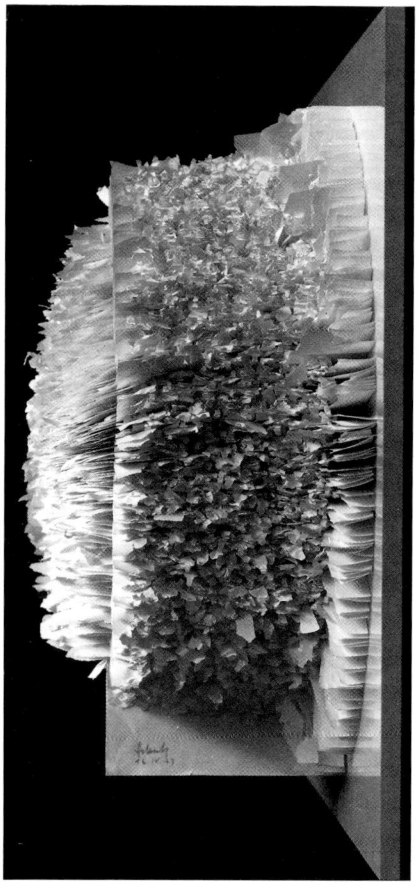

Oskar Holweck: 16 IX 74, 1974. Unbedrucktes Buch. 70 x 70 x 30,5 cm / Oskar Holweck: 16 IX 74, 1974. Unprinted book. 70 x 70 x 30.5 cm

pier. „Der Eingriff in das Papiermaterial geschieht meist unter strenger Beibehaltung metrischer Bewegungsabläufe in Form von Zeilen, Reihen und Rastern. Auf meine behutsame, oft karge Ansprache reagiert es mit einer für mich immer wieder überraschenden und kaum vorhersehbaren reichen Formen- und Farbensprache. Ich lebe während meiner Arbeit ständig in Konflikt zwischen meiner Aktion und der Reaktion des Werkstoffs."[79]

„Der weiße Bogen Papier gleicht einem Schneefeld. Die Empfindlichkeit der weißen Fläche nimmt sofort jede Spur auf"[80], schreibt Maria Reuter (* 1929 Flensburg). Sie fügt einem Blatt Papier eine kleine Kniffalte bei oder reißt es ein. Die Fläche wird zum belebten Relief. Auch bei François Morellet (* 1926 Cholet) ist der Eingriff ins Blatt auf ein

Netherlands) was a member of the Dutch group 'Null' close to Schoonhoven and was publisher of their magazine; he participated in the larger ZERO exhibitions from 1962 on. He started in 1960 to develop objects in pure white. Simple, geometric elements were set in rows of 20 to 30, expressing an aesthetic program with many hallmarks of minimalist and concrete art. In 1962 he began to incorporate chance and relativity into his works. Turi Simeti (*1929 Alcano/Italy), in proximity to ZERO and Fontana, worked on white structures of differing materiality. For instance, he sets white canvas against white-painted corrugated cardboard.[81] For Tom Mosley (*1927 Stoke-on-Trent/Great Britain) white paperboard is an adequate means of expression. Paperboard cut-outs are arranged into geometric reliefs and spatial structures, allowing the angle of light to design the picture. Alan Reynolds (*1926 Newmarket/Suffolk) works in a related way. In 1969 he produced his first relief designs, in 1978 his first constructions with modular cubes. Characteristic for the Constructivist, Henryk Stazevski (*1894 Warsaw – †1988 Warsaw), were his paperboard cutouts. He rhythmized flat white surfaces by allowing geometric areas to protrude. Bruno Erdmann (*1915 Darmstadt) worked in the 60s and 70s with structures of paper, whose geometry and transparency resulted from restrained, almost monochrome paper painting.[82]

Herbert Zangs (*1924 Krefeld) occupies a unique position. Since 1953 he has developed new fields of material structure in paper, paperboard and cardboard. A found object triggers a concept of design. It determines the formal and constructive principles. He makes banal things, mostly painted over in white, into something alien, disturbing. What interests him is the tactile, the brittle. Here he follows the tradition of Fautrier and Tapiès. The way he composes his designs, however, corresponds to the ideas of ZERO in as far as he declares white to be his own special color and implies the principle of the series and the rhythmic. Painting the work

Minimum beschränkt. Indem er transparentes Papier einknickt, erhält er durch die Überlagerung und Abtönung optische Raumkonstruktionen. Seine geometrischen Abstraktionen beeindrucken durch ihre Reduktion und Folgerichtigkeit. Morellet stellt 1963 mit ZERO aus. Hermann de Vries (* 1931 Alkmaar/Niederlande) war Mitglied der holländischen ‚Null'-Gruppe um Schoonhoven, Herausgeber ihrer Zeitschrift und beteiligte sich ab 1962 an den großen ZERO-Ausstellungen. Von 1960 an entwickelte er Objekte in reinem Weiß. Einfache, geometrische Elemente reiht er 20- bis 30fach zu ästhetischen Bildprogrammen minimal-konkreter Prägung. 1962 beginnt er, Zufall und Relativität in seine Werke einzubeziehen.

Turi Simeti (* 1929 Alcano/Italien) erarbeitet im Umfeld von ZERO und Fontana weiße Strukturen unterschiedlicher Materialität. Beispielsweise setzt er weiße Leinwand gegen weißgestrichene Wellpappe.[81] Für Tom Mosley (* 1927 Stoke-on-Trent/Großbritannien) ist weißer Karton adäquates Ausdrucksmittel. Kartonschnitte ordnet er zu geometrischen Reliefs und Raumstrukturen, bei denen das einfallende Licht zum bildnerischen Gestalter wird. In verwandter Weise verfährt Alan Reynolds (* 1926 Newmarket/Suffolk). 1969 entstehen erste Reliefgestaltungen, 1978 erste Konstruktionen mit modulen Kuben. Charakteristisch für den Konstruktivisten Henryk Stazewski (* 1894 Warschau – † 1988 Warschau) sind seine Papierkartonschnitte. Plane weiße Flächen rhythmisiert er durch geometrische Felder, die herausgestellt sind. Bruno Erdmann (* 1915 Darmstadt) untersuchte in den 60er und 70er Jahren Strukturen von Papieren, deren Geometrie zueinander und deren Transparenz, aus der verhaltenen fast monochromen Malerei mit Papier resultiert.[82]

Eine eigenwillige Position nimmt Herbert Zangs (* 1924 Krefeld) ein. Seit 1953 entwickelt er neue Positionen von Materialstrukturen in Papier, Karton und

François Morellet: Dreieck, auf ein Viertel gefaltet, 1977. Tusche auf Transparentpapier. 60 x 60 cm / François Morellet: Triangle Folded to a Square, 1977. Ink on transparent paper. 60 x 60 cm

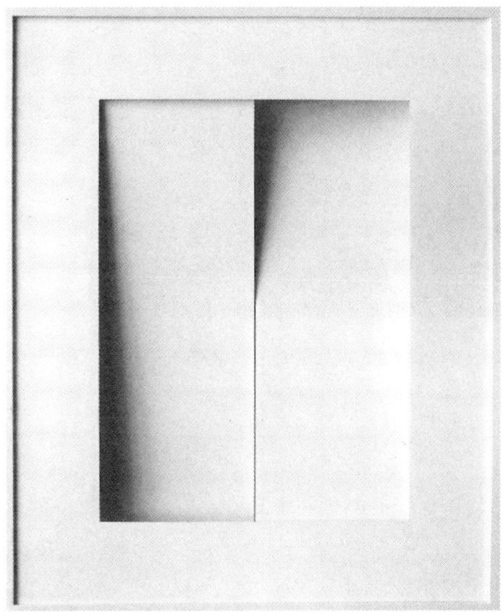

Tom Mosley: Shadow Box, 1980. Karton-Glas-Holzkasten. 87 x 67 x 10 cm / Tom Mosley: Shadow Box, 1980. Box of cardboard, glass, wood. 87 x 67 x 10 cm

Maria Reuter: Faltung, vor 1981. Papier. 58 x 78 cm / Maria Reuter: Folding, prior to 1981. Paper. 58 x 78 cm

Pappe. Das Fundstück wird Auslöser einer bildnerischen Idee. Es bestimmt die formalen und gestalterischen Prinzipien. Banale, zumeist weiß übermalte Dinge verfremdet er, stört sie. Das Spröde, das Haptische am Material interessiert ihn. Damit steht er in der Tradition von Fautrier und Tapiès. Seine kompositorische Gestaltungsweise aber entspricht den Gedanken von ZERO insofern, als er Weiß zu einer seiner speziellen Farben erklärt und das serielle, rhythmische Prinzip impliziert. Das Zumalen mit weißer Farbe verdeckt nicht und erhebt das Werk auch nicht in die Immaterialität, sondern verdeutlicht extrem die Strukturen des Bildes und seine haptischen Qualitäten, zumal er den weiß zugemalten Karton oft erst im Nachhinein formt und knickt, wodurch die Farbe wieder aufbricht. So macht das Kunstwerk einen „gebrauchten" Eindruck. Zangs' Vorgehensweise, bereits benutzte Pappe und verformten Karton mit einfachsten Mitteln zu gestalten bzw. unverändert zu belassen, erinnert an die Nouveaux Réalistes und Fluxus. Joseph Beuys äußerte 1975 über Zangs: „Er war immer auf der Suche nach dem Billigsten in Makulatur, Packpapier... Er lieferte eine ganze Reihe von Gegenbildern, an denen man sehr viel Orientierung finden konnte."[83]

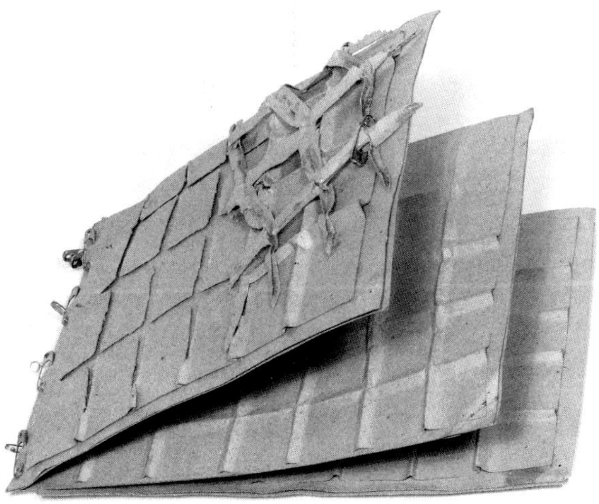

Herbert Zangs: Anti-Buch, 1963. Verschiedene Papiere, Pappe. 32 x 42 cm / Herbert Zangs: Anti-Book, 1963. Different papers, cardboard. 32 x 42 cm

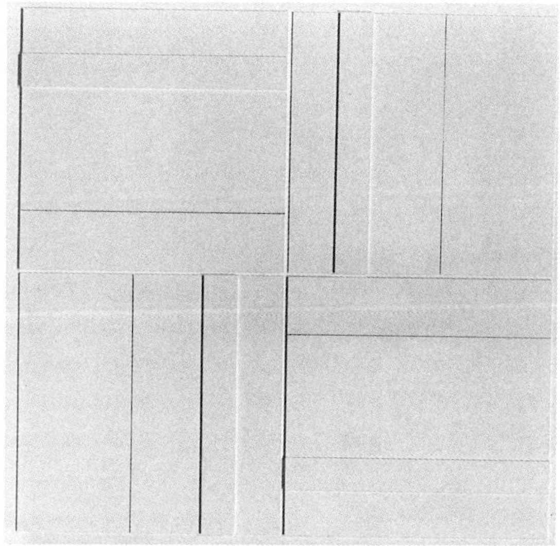

Alan Reynolds: Structures – Group II (Z) 2 (second smaller variation), 1983. Behandelte Pappe auf Holzgrund. 59 x 59 x 4 cm / Alan Reynolds: Structures – Group II (Z) 2 (second smaller variation), 1983. Treated cardboard on a wood base. 59 x 59 x 4 cm

white does not cut-off and does not raise the work into immateriality, but rather extremely clarifies the structure of the picture and its tactile qualities, especially since he often first paints the cardboard in white before he forms and bends it, whereby the color often flakes off again. In this way the artwork looks "used". Zangs' way of proceeding by re-arranging secondhand paperboard and deformed cardboard using the simplest means, or simply leaving it as found recalls the Nouveaux Réalistes and Fluxus. Joseph Beuys said of Zangs: "He was always on the lookout for the cheapest waste product, wrapping paper... He provided a whole range of counter-pictures that give you a great deal of orientation."[83]

IV. 3. Schneiden, Falten, Konstruieren

ZERO, Konkrete Kunst und Bauhaus bilden die Grundlagen für eine Papierkunst, die sich seit den 50er Jahren hauptsächlich in Europa entwickelt. Das Material ist das maschinell hergestellte Papier, in Format geschnitten oder endlos, in jeder Dicke, auch als Karton. Wichtig ist den meisten Künstlern die gleichmäßige, glatte Oberfläche ohne sichtbare Strukturierung. Struktur und Räumlichkeit werden erreicht durch das Behandeln des Papiers wie Schlitzen, Schneiden, Knicken, Falten, dann Übereinanderlegen oder -setzen und Kleben oder Zusammenbauen. Farbe wird entweder erzielt durch die Eigenfarbigkeit der Papiere oder durch Bemalen und Bezeichnen.[84]
Für Jiři Hilmar (* 1937 Hradec Králove/CFSR) ist Papier neben Holz das wichtigste Arbeitsmittel. Aufgespanntes Papier ritzt er geometrisch auf, wodurch dünne Auffaltungen entstehen. Er arbeitet gern mit serieller Reihung neben- und untereinander. Seine so entstandenen Werke erwecken zunächst den Eindruck von Perfektion. Doch leichte Unregelmäßigkeiten der aufragenden zarten Papierecken suggerieren behutsame Wellenbewegungen, die über die hauchdünnen Papierchen wehen. Milan Mölzer (* 1937 Prag – † 1976 Düsseldorf) bezeichnete sich selbst als einen Ästheten mit schneidendem Messer. Seine Messerschnittob-

IV. 3. Cutting, folding, engineering

ZERO, Concrete Art and the Bauhaus established the basis for a paper art that since the 50s has chiefly been a European development. The material is that of mechanically produced paper, cut into sheets or left continuous, in every thickness, also as paperboard. What is important for most of the artists is an even, smooth surface without visible texture. Structure and three-dimensionality are arrived at by the treatment of the paper such as slitting, cutting, pleating, folding, then layering and

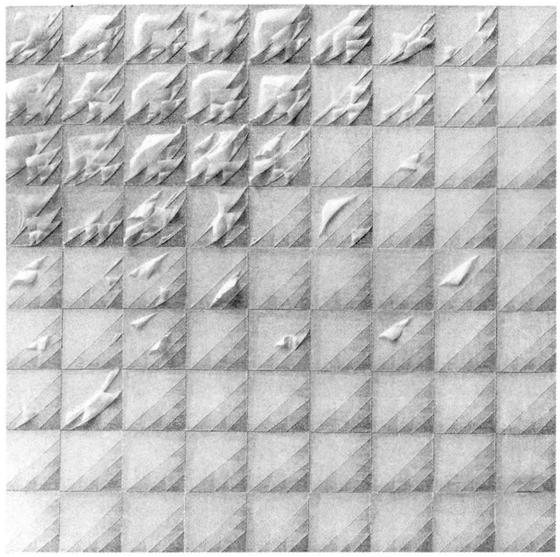

Jiři Hilmar: Ohne Titel, 1974. Transparentpapier. 80 x 80 cm / Jiři Hilmar: Untitled, 1974. Transparent paper. 80 x 80 cm

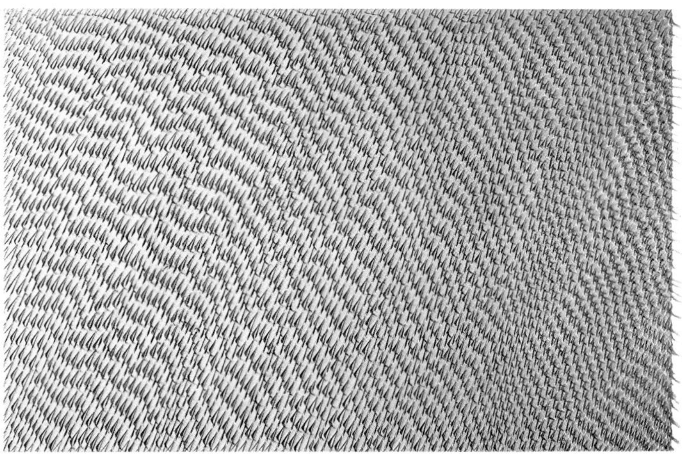

Milan Mölzer: Ohne Titel, 1980. Papier auf Papier, Messerschnitte. 100 x 100 cm / Milan Mölzer: Untitled, 1980. Paper on paper, knifeslits. 100 x 100 cm

jekte bestehen aus mehreren Lagen weißen Papiers, das auf der Unterseite farbig bemalt ist. Die übereinander geklebten Papierflächen spaltet Mölzer vielfach auf. Feine Papierhaare wölben sich. Die verschiedenen Farben der einzelnen Schichten leuchten auf. Dem gleichmäßigen Rhythmus der gebogenen „Fäden" entströmen zarte Farbwellen. In mehreren Werkgruppen untersuchte Hartmut Böhm (* 1938 Kassel) die Relation von übereinanderliegenden „konkreten" Zeichnungen in bezug auf sichtbare und unsichtbare Segmente, auf Anwesenheit und Abwesenheit von Bestimmungsgrößen. Klaus Staudt (* 1932 Ottendorf) erarbeitet aufgrund weißer Kartonschnitte neue Beziehungen zwischen Lichteinfall, Konstruktion und serieller Reihung. Tibor Gayor (* 1929 Rákospalota/Ungarn) entwickelte 1967 räumliche Faltobjekte und 1972 Faltungen von Blättern, die in serieller Reihung ein Raum-Flächen-Spiel entwickeln. Eberhard Fiebig (* 1930 Bad Harzburg) hat sich in seinen Papierarbeiten und in seiner Plastik konsequent dem Prinzip der Eroberung von Raum durch Faltung verschrieben.[85] Für Axel Heibel (* 1943 Lahnstein) ist Faltung und Schneiden das Gestaltungsprinzip. Papier wird in einfachen geometrischen Formen eingeschnitten und dann aufgeklappt. Die Veränderung der Flächen erreicht er nicht durch

Axel Heibel: Buchobjekt – D,1, 1978. 64 Seiten, Faltung, schwarze Tuschelinien. 35,2 x 25,2 x 1,2 cm / Axel Heibel: Book Object - D,1, 1978. 64 pages, folded paper, black ink lines. 35.2 x 25.2 x 1.2 cm

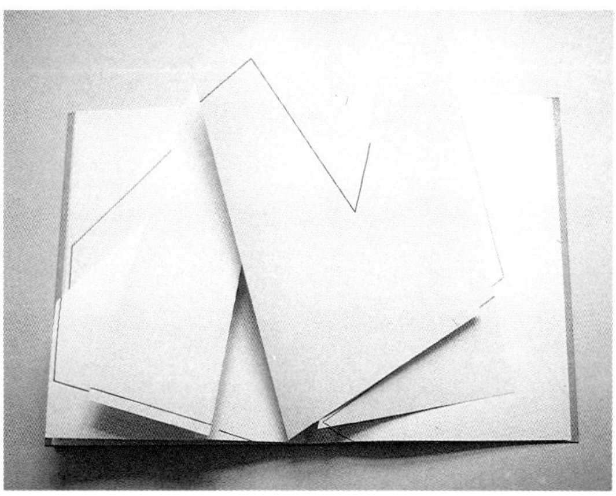

pasting or assembling. Color is either that provided by the tone of the paper itself or by painting and drawing.[84]

For Jiři Hilmar (*1937 Hradec Králove/ Czechoslovakia) paper along with wood is the most important work medium. He slits stretched paper into geometrical patterns, letting the narrow slashes gape. He likes working with serial sequences of one-alongside and one-below another. Arrived at in this way, his works give a first impression of perfection. But slight irregularities in the delicate, upright paper corners suggest discreet wavy movements that flutter over the extremely thin paper. Milan Mölzer (*1937 Prague – †1976 Düsseldorf) called himself an aesthete with a sharp knife. His knife-slit objects consist of white paper painted in color on the underside and then layered. He then cut the overlapped and pasted paper in many places into slivers with his knife; fine paper hairs arch upwards. The different colors of the single layers flash. Delicate waves of color in even rhythm stream from under the arched "threads". In several groups of work Hartmut Böhm (*1938 Kassel) probed the relationship of overlapped "concrete" drawings as regards their visible and invisible segments, the presence and absence of determined formats. Klaus Staudt (*1932 Ottendorf), on the basis of white paperboard cutouts, elaborated new relationships between light angle, construction and serial sequences. Tibor Gayor (*1929 Rákospalota/Hungary) developed spatial folding objects in 1967 and in 1972 folded sheets that in serial rows play a game of depth vs. plane. Eberhard Fiebig (*1930 Bad Harzburg) has consistently dedicated himself to the principle of the conquest of space through folding.[85] For Axel Heibel (*1943 Lahnstein) folding and cutting is his principle means of design. Paper is cut into simple geometric forms and then clapped open. An alternating surface is arrived at not by adding alien forms, but simply by pleating some of the planes that are part of the whole. The progressional opening and closing of folds changes the

Hinzufügen fremder Formen, sondern lediglich durch Falten von Teilflächen, die Teil des Ganzen sind. Das prozessuale Öffnen und Schließen durch Falten verändert Beziehungen und den Zusammenhang von Linien. Von 1967 an entstehen ein- und mehrflächige Faltobjekte aus monochromem Karton. Seit 1970 entwickelt er die Kartonfaltungen zu vielschichtigen Objekten, deren plastische und farbliche Zuordnungen veränderbar sind.

Reinhard Klessinger (* 1947 St. Blasien) arbeitet mit Überlagerungen von Transparentpapieren, denen er durch Ausschneiden oder Ausreißen bildliche Gestalt gibt. Die Einblicke und Durchblicke in den einzelnen Papierschichten überlappen sich oder auch nicht. Die verschiedenen Helligkeitswerte, die dadurch entstehen, suggerieren Raum und Bewegung. Heiko Tappenbeck (* 1936 Braunschweig) erforscht die spezifischen Reaktionen von Papierqualitäten wie Packpapieren oder Pappen. Er bricht bzw. reißt die Papiere über einer Kante und schichtet die Reißspuren aufeinander. Es entstehen Reliefs mit klarer Schichtungsstruktur. Reißunebenheiten und -fehler definieren serielle Strukturelemente. Die Bildobjekte von Jo Enzweiler (* 1934 Büdingen/Saarland) sind Ergebnisse eines materialgerechten Umgangs mit Karton. Durch Risse oder sonstige Eingriffe formen sich Strukturlinien in zarten Weiß-, Grau- und Brauntönen. Als Segmente gereiht, ergeben sich bildnerische Prozeßabläufe. Wolf Ebener (* 1936 Bonn) reißt, schneidet und ritzt Karton und erhält so materialspezifische, divergierende Strukturen. Der Schnitt ist klar und plastisch, die geritzte Linie zartes grafisches Element, und die Reißspur ergibt diffuse Halbtonschatten.

Erwin Heerich (* 1922 Kassel) baut seit 1959 Kartonobjekte, die streng nach den Regeln der Geometrie und Stereometrie konstruiert sind. Gerade das Material ist es, das die Gedanken des Betrachters auf den künstlerischen Kern der Plastiken lenkt: Die Plastik ist definiert durch den Mantel, der einen Raum umschließt; der leichte, verletzliche Karton entspricht der Idee der Körperlosigkeit.

relationship and the context of the lines. Beginning in 1967 he folded objects composed of one and more layers of planes out of light monochrome paperboard. From 1970 on he developed a way of folding paperboard into many-layered objects, whose three-dimensional and color classifications are changeable.

Reinhard Klessinger (*1947 St. Blasien) works by overlapping transparent paper, which he shapes aesthetically by cutting out or tearing. The "insights" into and through the individual paper

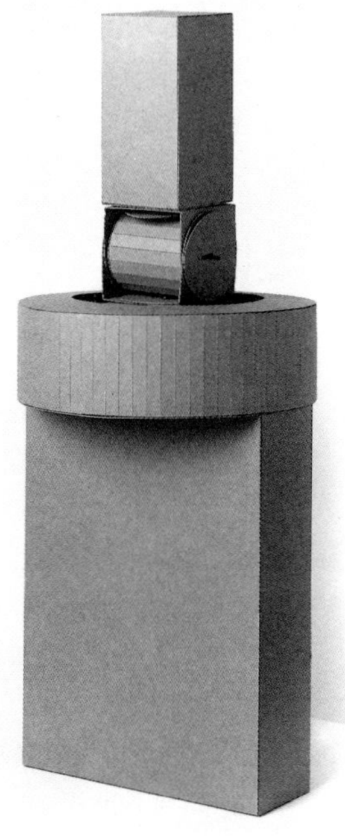

Erwin Heerich: Kartonplastik, 1969. 65 x 22 x 22 cm /
Erwin Heerich: Cardboard Sculpture, 1969.
65 x 22 x 22 cm

layers may overlap or not, as the case may be. The different gradations of light that result suggest space and motion. Heiko Tappenbeck (*1936 Brunswick) does research into the specific reactions of certain types of paper such as wrapping paper or cardboard. He breaks or tears the paper along an edge and layers the traces left by these rips above one another. Reliefs of a clear, layered structure are

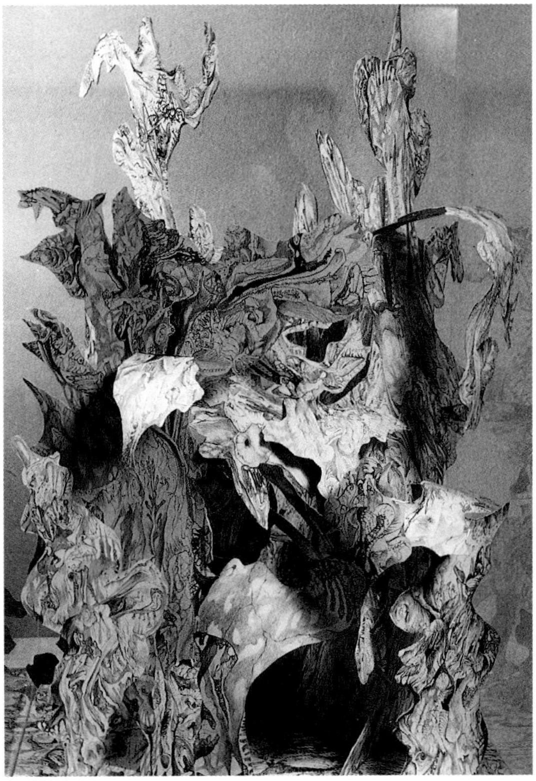

Bernard Schultze: Höhlen-Papier-Migof, 1972.
Papierplastik, Bleistift auf weißem Karton, Plexi-Cover.
67,5 x 41 x 41 cm / Bernard Schultze: Cave-Paper-Migof, 1972. Paper sculpture, pencil on white cardboard, plexi cover. 67.5 x 41 x 41 cm

Heerichs Konzept orientiert sich hier am mittelalterlichen Denken, wonach dem Werkstoff eine rein dienende Funktion zugeschrieben wird, um allein die Idee zur Anschauung zu bringen. Zur Ausführung gelangten Heerichs Vorstellungen von Raum und Plastik in den Bauten der Museumsinsel Hombroich bei Neuss.[86]
Der Maler und Objektkünstler Bernard Schultze (* 1915 Schneidemühl/Westpreußen) geht einen ganz anderen Weg. Um im Sinne des Informel eine materialhafte, haptische Oberflächenstruktur seiner Reliefs zu erreichen, verwendete er 1954 Papier und nutzte dessen Manipulationsmöglichkeiten für seine zerklüfteten Mallandschaften. Bevor er zu arbeiten begann, bereitete er die Leinwand oder Hartfaserplatte reliefartig vor, indem er gerolltes, gedrehtes oder zerdrücktes Seidenpapier aufklebte. Anfang der 60er Jahre begann Schultze

the result. Irregularities and errors made in tearing the paper are what define the serially composed textural elements. The objects of Jo Enzweiler (*1934 Büdingen/Saarland) are the result of an approach that calls for the legitimacy of the material, in this case, paperboard. By tearing or other manipulation, he creates structural lines in pale white, gray or brown tones. The final picture reflects the progressional course of these lined-up segments. Wolf Ebener (*1936 Bonn) tears, cuts and carves out cardboard and thus obtains materially specific and diverging structures. The cut is clear and plastic, the carved line a delicate graphic element, its trace provides diffuse half-shadows.
Since 1959, Erwin Heerich (*1922 Kassel) has been making his cardboard objects that are constructed strictly according to the rules of geometry and stereometry. It is the material itself that draws the viewer's attention to the aesthetic kernel of the sculpture: the sculpture is defined by the mantle enclosing a space; the light, vulnerable paperboard corresponds to the notion of disembodiment. Heerich is orientated towards a medieval concept of thinking whereby the material is seen to serve a purely functional capacity, so that the idea alone is made visible. Heerich's conceptions of space and sculpture were realized in the design of the museum buildings on the Island of Hombroich near Neuss.[86]
The painter and object artist, Bernard Schultze (*1915 Schneidemühl/West Prussia), took a completely different approach. In order to obtain an Art Informel material-like and haptic texture for his reliefs, he took up paper as a work material in 1954 and used the possibilities for manipulation that it offered to create his craggy paint-landscapes. Before he began to work, he prepared the canvas or hardboard by pasting on rolled, twisted and compressed tissue paper, forming it into a relief. In the early 60s, Schultze began his series of figurative, fabled creatures. He also made some paper reliefs and three-dimensional 'Paper-Migofs', open cutouts in space, whereby 'informel' drawing

die Reihe seiner figurativen Fabelwesen. Es entstanden auch einige Papierreliefs und dreidimensionale ‚Papier-Migofs', offene Papierschnitte im Raum, deren Flächen ihre vibrierende Kraft durch informelle Zeichnungen erhalten. Naturhaftes und Phantastisches formt sich züngelnd zur Einheit. Ein Gegenbild von Welt wird aufgestellt.[87]

IV. 4. Prägen

Der Blindprägedruck spielt z. B. im Werk von Günther Uecker eine gewichtige Rolle. Mit diesem Verfahren ist es ihm möglich, seine Intentionen von Licht und Struktur zu vervielfältigen. Er schuf seit 1960 mehrere Bücher mit Prägedrucken, Mappenwerke und viele Einzelblätter. Der schöpferische Akt beginnt bei der Herstellung des Druckstocks. Auf Holzplatten schlägt Uecker Nägel in entsprechende Formformation und Richtung. Als Papier verwendet er dickes, griffiges Büttenpapier. Er verletzt es nicht, um eine Verräumlichung der Papierfläche zu erzielen, wie dies Fontana durch Schnitte oder Stiche bewerkstelligt. Uecker verformt, aber zerstört das Papier nicht. Er schafft sensible Grafiken mit zarten Valeurs immateriellen Licht-Schatten-Spiels.

Das Prägen hat seine Geschichte im Münzprägedruck, im Pressen von Ornamenten in den Goldgrund mittelalterlicher Gemälde, im Prägen in Ton und anderen Materialien. Doch erst gegen Ende des 17. Jahrhunderts entwickelte man Methoden zum Prägen von Papier, zunächst zur Herstellung von Brokatpapieren. Gegen Ende des 18. Jahrhunderts kam der reine Blindprägedruck auf. Porträts und Wappen druckte man auf Karton oder Pappe, die weiße Oberfläche überzog man mit Lack, so daß sie wie Porzellan wirkte. Im Biedermeier gab es u. a. geprägte Briefpapiere oder Bilderbögen. Um 1850 kam in Wien der Naturselbstdruck auf, der auch in Verbindung mit Stanzung, beispielsweise zur Herstellung von Spitzenpapieren, genutzt

over the surface provided them with a vibrating force. The natural and the fantastic are formed into a flickering entity. A counter-world comes to life.[87]

IV. 4. Embossing

The blind-stamped or embossed print plays an important role, for instance, in the work of Günther Uecker. With this technique he found it possible to make his intentions of light and texture into multiples. Since 1960 he has created several books with blind prints, folder collections and many single sheets. The creative act begins with the manufacture of the wooden block for printing. He pounds nails into hardboard in certain formal patterns and directions. The handmade paper he uses is thick and granular. He does not, as did Fontana by slashing or piercing, damage it so that its surface can achieve the desired spatiality. Uecker deforms but does not destroy the paper. He creates sensitive graphic works with subtle nuances of immaterial light and shade.

The historical background of embossing goes back to the striking of coins, the impressing of ornamental designs into the gold ground of medieval paintings and into clay and other materials. But it was not till the end of the 17th century that methods were developed to make imprints on paper, at first for the production of brocade papers. Towards the end of the 18th century the pure embossed print came into production. Portraits and coats of arms were imprinted onto paperboard or cardboard, the white surface was covered in lacquer so that it looked like porcelain. During Biedermeier, embossed letter paper or broadsheets were made. Around 1850 in Vienna the printing on natural materials like leaves

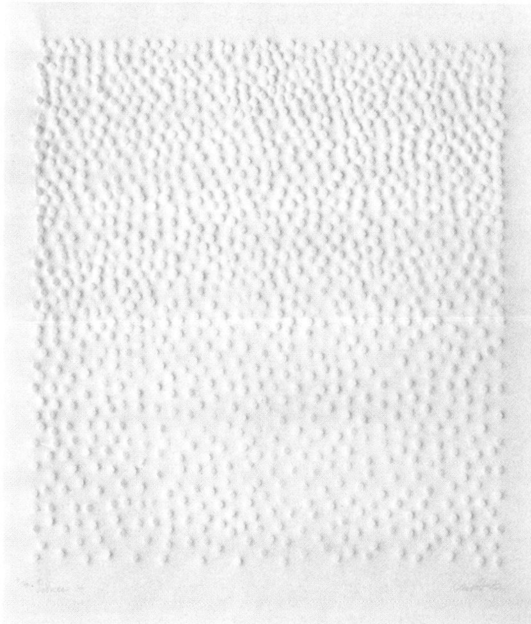

Günther Uecker: Schnee, 1972. Prägedruck auf Bütten. 60 x 49,5 cm / Günther Uecker: Snow, 1972. Embossed print on handmade paper. 60 x 49.5 cm

Günther Uecker: Regen, 1972. Prägedruck auf Bütten. 60 x 49,5 cm / Günther Uecker: Rain, 1972. Embossed print on handmade paper. 60 x 49,5 cm

wurde. Das Prägeverfahren wurde bis in die Moderne nur für Gebrauchsgrafik verwandt.

Rolf Nesch (* 1893 Obereßlingen – † 1975 Oslo) entwickelte um 1925 eine Art von Prägedruck, indem er Löcher in Metallplatten ätzte, die beim Abdruck im Papier wie erhabene Blasen aussahen. In späteren Jahren lötete er Drähte und andere Materialien auf Druckplatten und erhielt so Druckgrafik mit Reliefierungen. Der Brite Stanley William Hayter (* 1901 London – † 1988 Paris) vom Pariser Atelier 17 erweiterte in den 30er Jahren, beeinflußt von japanischen Drucken, die Palette der Prägeverfahren.[88] Max Ernst nutzte seit den 50er Jahren Blindprägedrucke, um sie mit Radierung und Aquatinta weiterzugestalten. Antonio Tapiès prägte seine Farbradierungen und -lithographien wegen des haptischen Eindrucks plastisch. Ben Nicholson (* 1894 Eight Bells/Dänemark – † 1982 London) überarbeitete Blindprägungen mit Aquarellfarben, um den Eindruck eines Originals zu erzielen. Hans Arp (* 1886 Strasbourg – † 1966 Basel) nutzte seine Holzreliefs auch als Druckstöcke für Prägungen.

originated, which combined with embossing, was used for the manufacture of quality paper. This type of impressing was used up to modern times only for the applied graphic arts.

Rolf Nesch (*1893 Obereßlingen – †1975 Oslo) developed around 1925 a kind of blind-stamped print by etching holes into metal plates that when printed onto paper look like ennobled bubbles. In later years he soldered wire or other materials onto printing plates and in this way was able to print relief-like graphic designs. Stanley William Hayter (* 1901 London – † 1988 Paris) of Atelier 17 in Paris, influenced by Japanese prints, expanded the range of embossing methods in the 30s.[88] From the 50s on, Max Ernst used blind-stamped prints so as to combine them with etchings and aquatints. Antonio Tapiès embossed his color etchings and lithographs because he liked the tactile, plastic impression they gave. Ben Nicholson (* 1894 Eight Bells/Denmark – † 1982 London) worked blind-stamped prints over with water color to give the impression of an original. Hans Arp (* 1886 Strasbourg – † 1966

Georges Braque stellte 1959 Pappgravierungen her.[89] Er schnitt dünne Pappe in Form; wegen der Flexibilität des Materials variieren die verschiedenen Drucke. Enrico Baj (* 1924 Mailand) und Werner Schreib (* 1925 Berlin – † 1969 Berlin) entwickelten den Materialdruck.

Für die neue Konkrete Kunst wird der Blindprägedruck seit den 50er Jahren geeignetes Ausdrucksmittel. Das Wechselspiel von Licht und Schatten kann auf der plastisch geformten Oberfläche visualisiert werden. Blindprägungen gibt es bei Etienne Hajdu (* 1907 Turda/Rumänien) und Birgit Skiöld (* 1923 Schweden – † 1982 Großbritannien), bei Josef und Anni Albers, Jan Schoonhoven, Piero Manzoni, Günther Uecker, Heinz Mack, Herman de Vries, Jasper Johns (* 1930 Allendale/ South Carolina) Raimund Girke (* 1930 Heinzendorf/Schlesien), Enrico Castellani (* 1930 Castelmassa/ Italien), Harry van Kuyk (* 1929 Nijmwegen/Niederlande), Horst Antes (* 1936 Heppenheim), Leo Erb, Klaus Staudt und Jean le Noble (* 1940 Haarlem/Niederlande).[90]

Basle) used his wood reliefs also as block impresses. Georges Braque produced cardboard engravings in 1959.[89] He cut light paperboard into form; because of the flexibility of the material, the different prints vary. Both Enrico Baj (* 1924 Milan) and Werner Schreib (* 1925 Berlin – † 1969 Berlin) developed the material print.

For the new Concrete Art, the blind-stamped print has since the 50s become a suitable medium of expression. The interplay between light and shade is made visible on the three-dimensional surface. Embossed prints were created by Etienne Hajdu (* 1907 Turda/Rumania) and Birgit Skiöld (* 1923 Sweden – † 1982 Great Britain), by Josef and Anni Albers, Jan Schoonhoven, Piero Manzoni, Günther Uecker, Heinz Mack, Herman de Vries, Jasper Johns (* 1930 Allendale/South Carolina), Raimund Girke (* 1930 Heinzendorf/Silesia), Enrico Castellani (* 1930 Castelmassa/Italy), Harry van Kuyk (* 1929 Nijmwegen/Netherlands), Horst Antes (* 1936 Heppenheim), Leo Erb, Klaus Staudt and Jean le Noble (* 1940 Haarlem, Netherlands).[90]

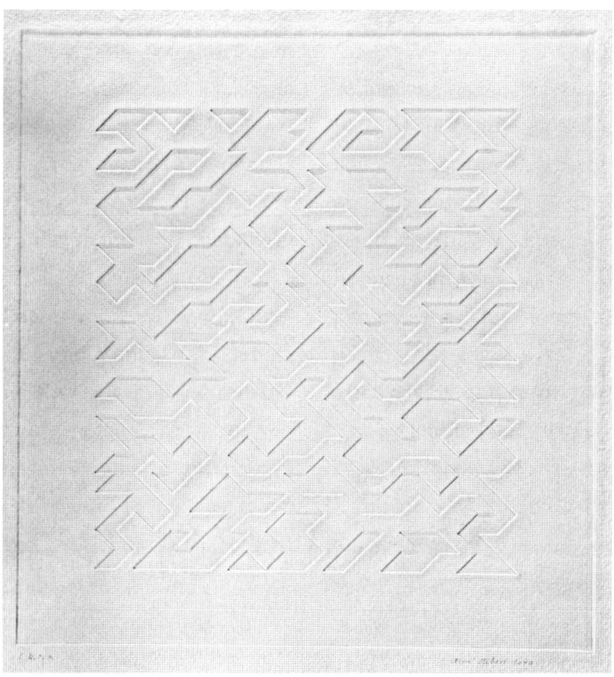

Anni Albers: Mountainous IV, 1978. Papierprägedruck von Radierplatte. 56,2 x 52,7 cm / Anni Albers: Mountainous IV, 1978. Relief print from etched plate. 56.2 x 52.7 cm

IV. 5. Natürliche Prozesse

Das Material spielt in der bildenden Kunst eine entscheidende, ja existenzbestimmende Rolle. Der Künstler ist abhängig von der stofflichen Substanz, aus der er ein Bildhauerwerk, eine Malerei, eine Grafik, ein Objekt herstellen will; er muß also das „Eigenleben" der Stoffe, die Beschaffenheit, die Reaktionen auf andere Materialien, auf Umwelteinflüsse, auf Naturgegebenheiten wie Hitze, Kälte, Feuchtigkeit und vieles mehr kennen und berücksichtigen. In der Geschichte der Kunst gibt es zahlreiche Erwähnungen von Fehlleistungen, wie das häufig zitierte Beispiel von Leonardo da Vinci zeigt. Er hatte 1503 den Auftrag, den Palazzo Vecchio in Florenz mit einem Wandgemälde auszuschmücken. Aufgrund einer neuen Behandlung des Malgrundes trockneten die Farben nicht, sondern flossen ineinander.[91]

Viele Kunstwerke haben heute nicht mehr das ursprüngliche Aussehen, sondern chemische und physikalische Prozesse haben im Laufe der Zeit Patina, Krakelee, Wölbungen, Holzwurmspuren – bei Papier Verfärbungen, Zersetzungen, Pilzzerfraß und Schimmel – entstehen lassen. Heere von Restauratoren versuchen, diese Veränderungen aufzuhalten oder rückgängig zu machen. Bereits Goethe bemerkte in seinen ‚Wahlverwandtschaften': „Wie über die Menschen, so über die Denkmäler läßt sich Zeit ihr Recht nicht nehmen."[92]

Prozeßhafte Vorgänge, orientiert am natürlichen Zerfall und am Eigenleben von Material und Natur, sind seit den ausgehenden 50er Jahren Ausdrucksmittel der bildenden Kunst – auch in bezug auf Papierkunst.

Im Frühwerk von Franz Erhard Walther (* 1939 Fulda) ist Papier und Karton entscheidendes Werkzeug, um in Materialprozessen zum künstlerischen Ziel vorzustoßen. Die für Walther typische Form der Rahmenzeichnung taucht 1962 bei den Blättern mit Ölrändern auf. Alle vier Ränder der Blätter werden in Öl getaucht. Grad des Eintauchens und Dauer des Vorgangs bestimmen die Intensität der Prozeß- und Materialspuren. „Ich war mit den illusionistischen Mit-

IV. 5. Natural processes

The material plays a crucial, even an existentially determinant role in the visual arts. The artist is dependent on the material substance from which he must produce a sculpture, a painting, a graphic work or an object; which means, he must be aware of and respect the "identity" of the material, its property, its reaction to other materials, to environment, to natural givens like heat, cold, dampness, etc. The history of art makes mention of many instances of spurious innovations, notably the often cited example of Leonardo da Vinci. In 1503 he was given a commission to adorn the Palazzo Vecchio in Florence with a fresco. Because of a new treatment of the ground, the colors did not dry but flowed into one another.[91]

Many artworks no longer look like they did originally, but chemical and physical processes have in the course of time allowed patina, craquelé, warp, woodworm traces and – in the case of paper – discoloration, corrosion, fungus, molds to develop. Armies of restorers attempt to arrest or reverse these changes. Goethe had already noted in his 'Wahlverwandschaften': "As it does over man so over monuments, Time refuses to relinquish her right."[92]

Process-like procedures, oriented towards natural corrosion, the individual identity of the material and of nature, have since the 50s been a means of expression in the visual arts, also in relation to paper.

In the early work of Franz Erhard Walther (*1939 Fulda) paper and paperboard were crucial tools in advancing his aesthetic goals by material processes. What for Walther is a typical form of framed drawing emerged in 1962: single sheets with oil edging. All four edges of the page were dipped in oil. The degree and duration of the dip determine the intensity of the traces left by this process on the material. "I had finished with the illusionistic mediums of painting. I was looking for new mediums. One of them was to have a substance that penetrates the paper and not, like the normal run of paint, sits on the surface. I took vegetable oil,

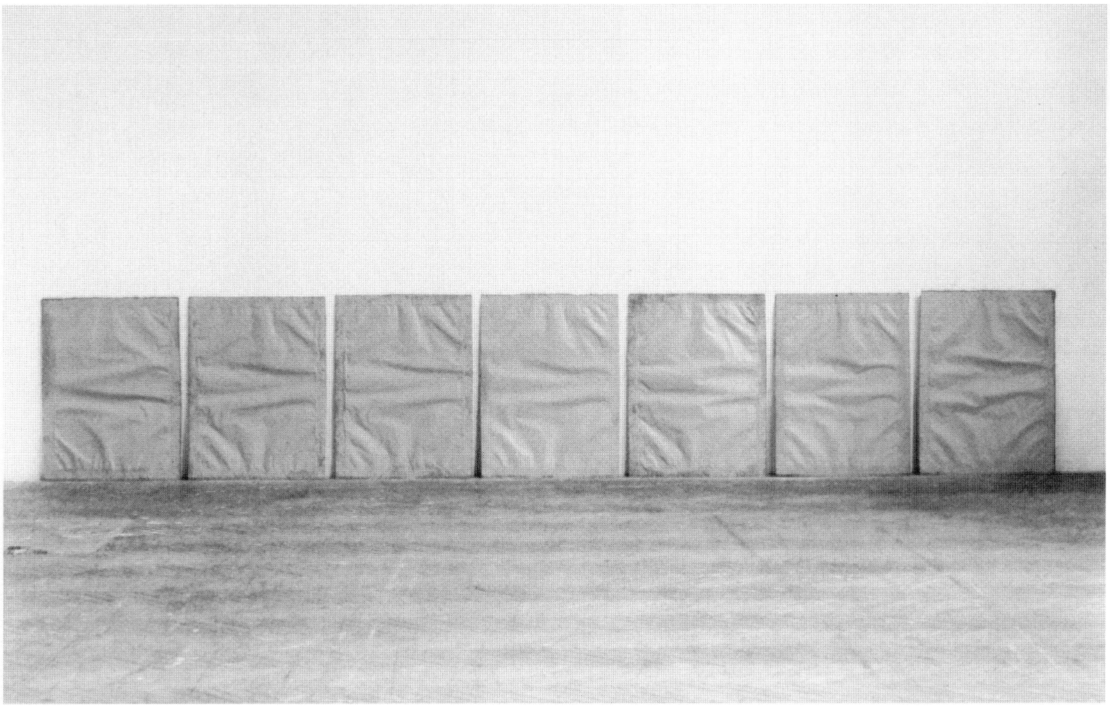

Franz Erhard Walther: Sieben Packpapierpackungen II (mit breitem Rand, unterschiedliche Stärken), 1963. Gelbliches Packpapier, Kleister, Pflanzenöl. Je 100,5 x 74 cm / Franz Erhard Walther: Seven Wrapping Paper Packages II (with broad margins, of different thickness), 1963. Yellowish wrapping paper, paste, vegetable oil. Each 100.5 x 74 cm

teln der Malerei fertig. Ich suchte nach neuen Mitteln. Eines davon war: Substanzen zu haben, die in Papier eindringen und nicht, wie die gängigen Farben, auf der Oberfläche sitzen. Ich nahm Pflanzenöl, Kaffee, Sojasoße und Erde, die Papierbögen betrachtete ich als flache Körper, und als Formpunkt war der Rahmen noch immer brauchbar. Von damals rührt mein bis heute sehr starkes Interesse an der Wirkung von Zusammenfassungen gleicher oder sich ähnelnder Formen."[93] Im selben Jahr nahm Walther Klebungen mit Papier vor. Strukturen bildeten sich je nach Klebespur und Menge des Klebers und schufen so die ersten Kissenformen. Vorausgegangen waren Beobachtungen an Rückseiten von Zeichnungen. Sie hatten Ausbeulungen und Faltungen. Dieses Phänomen forcierte er, indem er die Ränder mit braunen Papierklebestreifen besetzte, die sich nach dem Trocknen, der Papierlaufrichtung entsprechend, zusammenzogen und weitere Beulen und Knitterungen bewirkten. Die Blätter präsen-

coffee, soya sauce and soil; the sheets of paper I viewed as flat bodies and, as always, the frame was usable as a formation point. It's from that time that my (still today) very strong interest in the effect of collections of the same or very similar forms dates back."[93] In the same year Walther began to paste paper. Texture was created according to the traces and amount of paste, and so the first cushion forms came about. What preceded these were observations he made on the backs of drawings that had bulges and creases. This phenomenon he provoked by pasting the edges with brown paper strips that, after drying and respective of the bias of the strips, shrank and created further bumps and pleats. The sheets of paper were then exhibited from the back. The first air-filled pads were made. Mostly in the years 1962 and 1963 Walther probed the aesthetic effect of paper per se, based on its material property and reaction to handling, pasting, and to substances. "For me it was a question of the

tierte er von den Rückseiten. Die ersten luftgefüllten Wulste entstanden. Walther erprobt hauptsächlich in den Jahren 1962 und 1963 die malerischen Wirkungen von Papieren aus sich selbst heraus, begründet durch die Materialeigenschaften und Reaktionen auf Berührung, Verklebung und auf Substanzen. „Mir kam es auf die Materialprozesse an. Mich interessierten dabei weniger die Bilder selbst als die Idee der Formlosigkeit als Anfangspunkt."[94] Materialprozesse an Papieren unterschiedlicher Art löst er aus und beobachtet sie bei Klebungen, Schichtungen, Überdeckungen, beim Zusammenfügen, bei Teilungen, Abrissen, Faltungen, Füllungen, bearbeiteten Fundstücken und beidseitiger Bearbeitung. Im Sommer 1962 war durch Zufall Wasser auf einen Stapel von Papieren gesickert. „Ich erkannte den Materialprozeß als bedeutsam für mich. Vorher hatte ich die Prozesse immer zu steuern gesucht. Jetzt hatte ich plötzlich das überzeugende Resultat eines weitgehend selbständigen Materialprozesses vor Augen."[95] Die radikale Ablehnung traditioneller Bildvorstellungen bei der jungen Künstlergeneration löste die Suche nach neuen Aktionsfeldern und unkonventionellen Herstellungsmethoden aus. Natürliche Prozesse wie Zersetzen, Verschimmeln, Wachsen rücken ins Blickfeld. In der Zeit um 1960 geht es primär noch nicht um die Darstellung des Prozeßverlaufs, sondern um das Ergebnis, um das Endprodukt Kunstwerk. Aber die Grenzen des Bildes werden immer weiter gesprengt. Auch Atelier, Straße und Landschaft ersetzen den Bildraum. Die klassischen Malutensilien erweitern sich immer mehr und werden schließlich nicht nur durch Licht

material processes. What interested me was less the pictures themselves than the idea of formlessness as a starting point."[94] He instigates different kinds of material processes on paper and observes what happens after pasting, layering, covering, assembling, dividing, tearing, folding, filling, using found objects and working on both sides.
In the summer of 1962 by pure chance, water leaked onto a pile of paper. "I recognized this process as being very important to me. Formerly I had always tried to direct the processes. Suddenly the convincing result of an almost completely independent material process was staring me in the face."[95]
The radical rejection by the younger generation of artists of traditional concepts of painting triggered the search for new fields of action and unconventional methods of production. Natural processes like corrosion, mold, growth came into their own. At that time, around 1960, it was not yet primarily a matter of representing the course the process took, but the resulting end product, the artwork. However the boundaries of the picture did get ruptured more and more. The studio, the street and the countryside began to replace the picture plane. The classical painting tools in the end expanded more and more to include not only light and fire but also fat, soil, plants, yoghurt, air, fog or water. In 1970 the process took on a life of its own. The procedure itself is foregrounded. Natural, everyday processes become art: wandering shadows, growing grass, mildewing paper. Time plays a central role. Artists intervene in the natural, physical, chemical, biological process.[96]

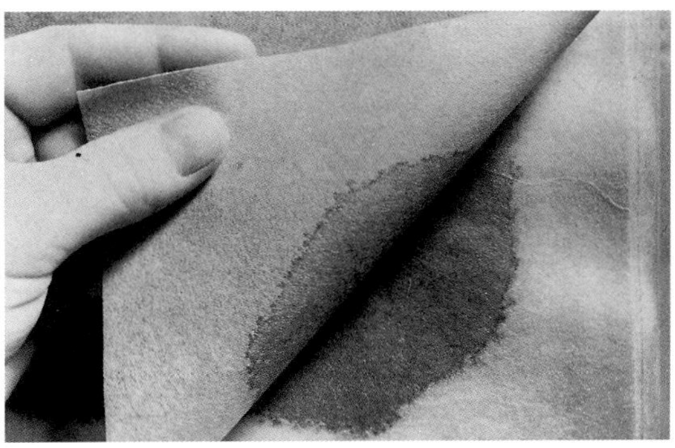

Gotthard Graubner: Sickerbuch, 1954. Auflage 6. Ölfarbe auf Synthetik-Vliespapier. 32 x 28,1 cm / Gotthard Graubner: Seeping Book, 1954. Edition of 6. Oil paint on synthetic fleece paper. 32 x 28.1 cm

und Feuer, sondern auch durch Fett, Erde, Pflanzen, Yoghurt, Luft, Nebel oder Wasser ersetzt. Um 1970 verselbständigt sich der Prozeß. Der Vorgang rückt ins Blickfeld. Natürliche, alltägliche Prozesse werden Kunst: wandernder Schatten, wachsendes Gras, schimmelndes Papier. Zeit spielt dabei eine zentrale Rolle. Künstler schalten sich in den natürlichen, physikalischen, chemischen, biologischen Prozeß ein.[96]

Gotthard Graubner (* 1930 Erlbach) arbeitet mit der Saugfähigkeit von Papier. Ins ‚Sickerbuch' von 1964 läßt er Farben sich einsaugen, eine von der Vorderseite, die andere von der Rückseite.[97]

Im Œuvre von Joseph Beuys (* 1921 Kleve – † 1986 Düsseldorf) finden sich mehrfach Papiere, in die Fett oder Ölfarbe eingezogen sind oder andere Substanzen Papier verändert haben. Auch Schimmelbefall akzeptiert er als kompositorisches Mittel.[98] Die Fluxus-Künstlerin Takako Saito (* 1929 Sabae-Shi/Japan) läßt seit den 70er Jahren ‚Wasserzeichnungen' in Wasser aus Düsseldorf und Reggio Emilia entstehen. Papierblätter taucht sie in Wasser, in dem Stempelfarbe aufgelöst ist und auf dessen Oberfläche eine Ölschicht schwimmt. Die Papiere saugen nach dem Prinzip des Zufalls Öl und Stempelfarbe auf. Die so entstandenen ‚Wasserzeichnungen' werden anschließend mit assoziationsreichen Wortverbindungen bedruckt wie ‚Fire Glass' oder ‚Emotion Chair'.[99] Daniel Hees (* Düsseldorf) läßt Tee in Karton oder Tusche in Papier weiterarbeiten.[100] In den Jahren 1988/90 schuf Wolf Kahlen (* 1940 Aachen) einen Zyklus mit über 120 Blättern, die ‚Naga'-Altölzeichnungen. „Ich setze nach meditativer Konzentration ein willentlich/unwillentliches Zeichen mit einem dicken Pinsel, in Autoaltöl getaucht, aufs saugfähige Papier und ziehe mich dann zurück. In acht bis zehn Tagen saugt sich das Öl ins Papier, und es entfaltet sich die organisch-chemische Welt der Strukturen des Chaos. Ich weiß nach Jahren jetzt, wohin, wie weit und wo das Öl stehen bleibt."[101]

Hans Peter Alvermann (* 1931 Düsseldorf) läßt 1960/61 ein Schimmelbuch entstehen, nachdem

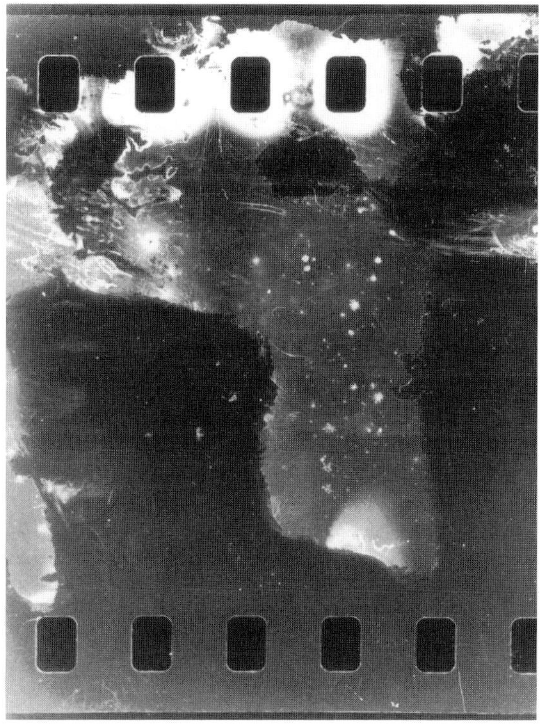

Wolf Kahlen: Gerettete Bilder, 1980. Rolle, Foto auf Papier. 80 x 300 cm (Detail) / Wolf Kahlen: Rescued Pictures, 1980. Roll, photograph on paper. 80 x 300 cm (detail)

Gotthard Graubner (*1930 Erlbach) works with the absorbency of paper. In his 'Sickerbuch' (Seeping Book) from 1964 he allows paint to seep in, one color from the front and another from the back end.[97]

There are numerous examples in the œuvre of Joseph Beuys (*1921 Kleve – †1986 Düsseldorf) that consist of paper saturated with fat or oil paint or with other substances that have changed it. He, too, accepted mildew as a compositional medium.[98] Since 1960 the Fluxus artist Takako Saito (*1929 Sabae-Shi/Japan) has made 'Wasserzeichnungen' (Water Drawings) in water from Düsseldorf and from Reggio Emilia. She dips sheets of paper into water, in which stamp ink has been dissolved and on which surface a layer of oil floats. The paper absorbs oil and stamp ink according to the principle of chance. The 'Wasserzeichnungen' that thus originate are then printed with word compounds rich in association like 'Fire Glass' or 'Emotion Chair'.[99] Daniel Hees (* Düsseldorf) lets tea go to work on cardboard or drawing ink on paper.[100]

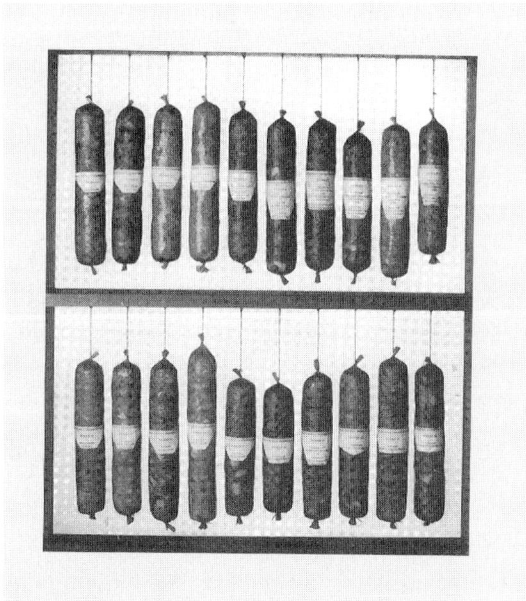

Dieter Roth: Georg Wilhelm Friedrich Hegel: Werke in 20 Bänden, 1974. Suhrkamp-Taschenausgabe zerkleinert, mit Gewürzen und Schweineschmalz in Wurstdärmen. Durchmesser 6 cm, Höhe ca. 30 cm, an Holzgestell, 100 x 85 x 14 cm / Dieter Roth: Georg Wilhelm Friedrich Hegel: Works in 20 volumes, 1974. Suhrkamp pocket edition minced, with spices, pork lard, in sausage skins. Diameter 6 cm, height ca. 30 cm, on wooden rack, 100 x 85 x 14 cm

durch Zufall angefeuchtetes Büttenpapier von Schimmel befallen war.[102] Marcel Duchamp hatte bereits 1918 ein Prozeßbild zum Kunstwerk erhoben. 1918 züchtete er über eineinhalb Jahre auf einer Glasplatte eine Staubschicht, die er zum Bild ‚Elevage de Poussière' fixierte.[103] Dieter Roth (* 1930 Hannover) arbeitet oft mit Schimmel. 1969 entsteht ein Schimmelblatt aus Sauermilch auf weißem Bütten.[104] Ab 1961 entwickelt er Literaturwürste. Zerschnittene Ausgaben des ‚Daily Mirror' werden mit heißem Wasser und Gelatine vermischt und in einen Wurstdarm gefüllt. Weitere Exemplare von Literaturwürsten entstehen nach althergebrachten Wurstrezepten; die fleischliche Substanz wird jeweils durch zerkleinertes Papier verschiedener Zeitschriften ersetzt.[105]

Yves Klein setzte bewußt Naturkräfte wie Wind und Regen zur Vollendung seiner ‚Kosmologien' ein.[106] Unerwartete Spuren von Regen und Schneeflocken berücksichtigte Emil Nolde (* 1867 Nolde/Südtondern – † 1956 Seebüll/Nordfriesland) in einigen sei-

In the years 1988 to 1990 Wolf Kahlen (*1940 Aix-la-Chapelle) did a cycle of over 120 sheets, the 'Naga' used-oil drawings. "After meditative concentration and with a thick brush dipped into used car oil I set down a voluntary/involuntary sign onto absorbent paper and then withdraw. In eight to ten days the paper soaks up the oil and the organic, chemical world of the structures of chaos unfold. I now, after years, know where and how far the oil is heading and where it will halt."[101]

In 1960/61 Hans Peter Alvermann (*1931 Düsseldorf) allowed a book to mildew after handmade paper had by chance become damp and then moldy.[102] Marcel Duchamp had already in 1918 promoted a processed image to an artwork. For over one and a half years he raised dust on a pane of glass that he then had photographed: 'Élevage de poussière'.[103] Dieter Roth (*1930 Hannover) often works with mold. In 1969 a sour milk fungus was allowed to form on handmade white paper.[104] From 1961 on, he developed literature sausages. Cut up issues of the 'Daily Mirror' were mixed with hot water and gelatine and filled into sausage gut. Many literature sausages were made according to old minced meat recipes; the meaty substance was replaced with chopped-up paper from newspapers.[105]

Yves Klein consciously deployed natural forces like wind and rain for the completion of his 'Cosmologies'.[106] Unintentioned traces of snowflakes were used by Emil Nolde (*1867 Nolde/Südtondern – † Seebüll/North Friesland) in some of his water paintings.[107] Jochen Gerz (*1940 Berlin) did not himself write on paper but in 1971 exposed it to the weather. Wind, rain, dirt, birds managed to inscribe it. He exhibited these sheets of paper with a description of the procedure.[108] The dedication that Wolfgang Mally (*1952 Magdeburg) has shown to the observation of processes is probably responsible for the most detailed and systematic documentations. These are each composed of 365 days of daily checks. In 1977/78 he exposed 365 sheets of paper each to the three elements of water, air and earth. He documented the corrosive process by

ner Aquarelle.[107] Jochen Gerz (* 1940 Berlin) beschreibt Papier nicht selbst, sondern setzt es 1971 der Witterung aus, Wind, Regen, Schmutz, Vögel sorgen für die Beschreibung. Ausgestellt hat er diese Papiere mit einem Beschreibungsvorgang.[108] Die Prozeßbeobachtungen von Wolfgang Mally (* 1952 Magdeburg) sind wohl die detailliertesten und systematischsten Dokumentationen. Sie umfassen jeweils 365 Tage mit täglichen Kontrollen. 1977/78 setzte er 365 Papiere den drei Elementen Wasser, Luft, Erde aus. Den Zersetzungsprozeß dokumentiert er, indem er jeden Tag „konserviert". Das jeweilige Papier eines Tages wird auf Leinwand aufgeklebt. 365 Papiere hängt er in den Fluß, 365 Papiere legt er auf das Dach seines Ateliers, 365 Papiere vergräbt er in der Erde. Täglich entnimmt er ein Blatt dem Wasser, der Luft, der Erde, solange, bis die Blätter zerfallen und unauffindbar sind. Im Wasser vollzieht sich der Zersetzungsprozeß am schnellsten, nämlich innerhalb von 58 Tagen – in der Erde innerhalb von 69 Tagen und in der Luft in 89 Tagen.[109] Papier ist für die 1945 geborene Japanerin Yaeko Osono lebendiges Naturwesen. Sie arbeitet mit Pa-

"conserving" every day. The paper relevant for that day was pasted on canvas. 365 sheets of paper were hung into the river, 365 were placed on the roof of his atelier, 365 were buried in the earth. Every day he removed one sheet each from the water, from the air and from the earth until the remaining paper had decayed completely and could no longer be found. The corrosive process was fastest in water, namely within 58 days; in the earth within 69 days and in the air within 89.[109]
Paper is for the Japanese Yaeko Osono, born in 1945, a natural living creature. She works with paper in nature and lets sunshine, rain, dew, frost and wind participate in the composition. The 'Four Seasons Cupola' from 1992 is made of rolls of Shoji, a thin but sturdy paper that is used in Japan instead of glass panes. Some of this paper contained seeds and earth, grass remnants, disintegrating leaves. Other paper was corroded by salty sea water in which it had lain for days. Some rolls of paper bore traces of weathering from frost and snow that had "worked" on them for weeks. Other paper was branded with fire.[110] In 1987 Gunther Keusen had

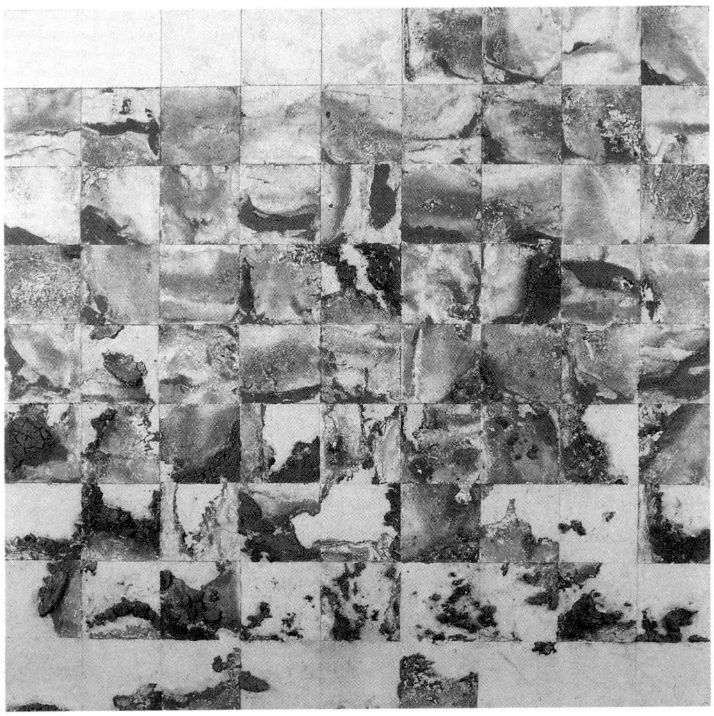

Wolfgang Mally: Papier im Wasser 0–58 Tage, 1981. 90 x 90 x 4 cm / Wolfgang Mally: Paper in Water 0–58 Days, 1981. 90 x 90 x 4 cm

pier in der Natur und läßt Sonnenschein, Regen, Tau, Frost und Wind an der Gestaltung mitwirken. Die ‚Jahreszeiten-Kuppel' von 1992 besteht aus Bahnen von Shoji, einem dünnen, dennoch festen Papier, das in Japan anstelle von Glasscheiben verwendet wird. Einige Papiere enthalten Samen und Erde, Spuren von Gräsern, zerfallenes Laub. Andere Papiere hat das salzige Meerwasser zersetzt, in dem es Tage lag. Manche Papierbahn trägt Verwitterungsspuren von Frost und Schnee, die es über Wochen „bearbeiteten". Weitere Papiere hat Feuer mit Brandmalen bezeichnet.[110] Gunther Keu-

nature itself paint on paper with elderberries.[111] One of Spoerri's students, Martin Weimar (*1959 Ulm), lets grass and flowers grow on handmade paper. In 1986 he sowed diverse grass seeds on the handmade paper pages of a book that were lined with watermarks. Different kinds were sown, creating the impression of writing. In paper, kept warm, damp and well-lit, the script began to grow.[112] In 1988 he planted tulip bulbs in shoes of handmade paper; they bloomed and faded during the course of the exhibition.[113] In 1990 Terese Murak (*1949 Kielce/Poland) sowed garden cress on handmade

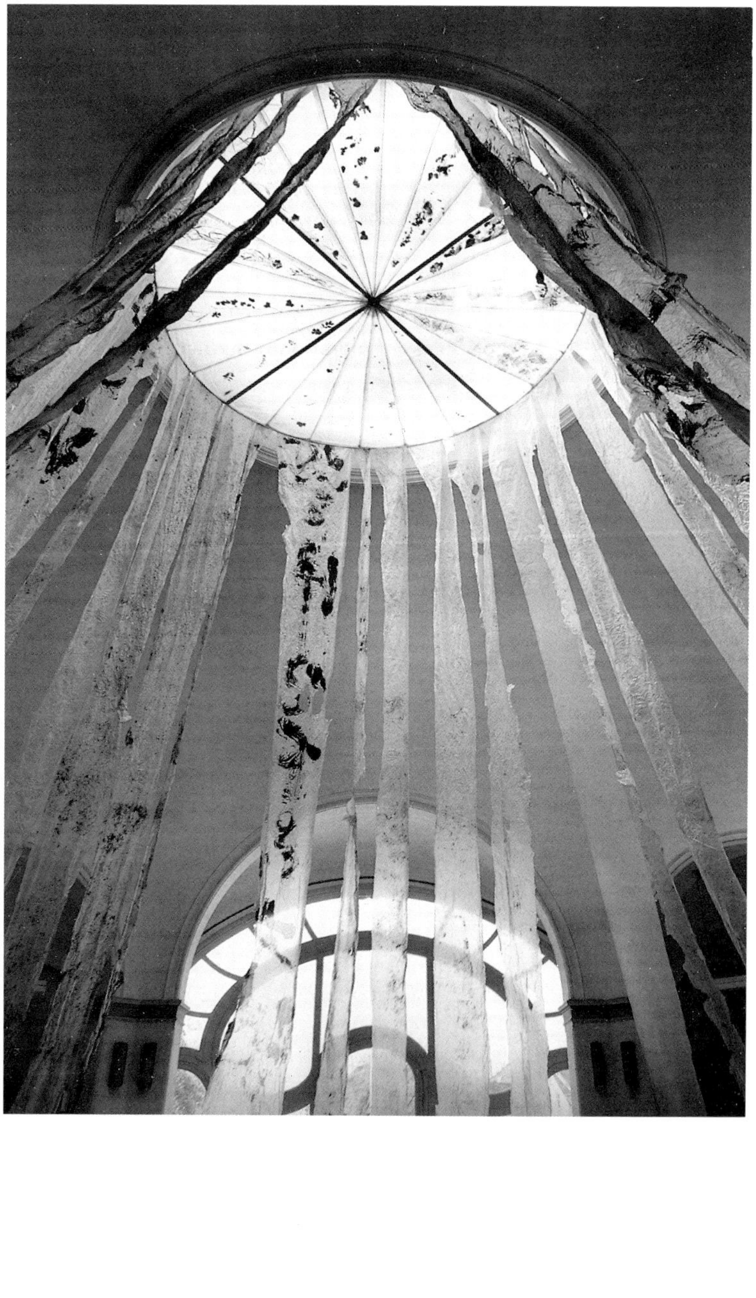

Yaeko Osono: Wasser, Feuer, Luft, Erde in den vier Jahrszeiten, 1992. Reispapier, Steine, Holz, Erde. Höhe 12 m / Yaeko Osono: Water, Fire, Air, Earth through the Seasons, 1992. Ricepaper, stones, wood, earth. Height 12 m

sen läßt 1987 die Natur mit Holunder selbst malen.[111] Bei dem Spoerri-Schüler Martin Weimar (* 1959 Ulm) wachsen Gräser und Blumen in handgeschöpftem Papier. 1986 sät er diverse Grassamen in handgeschöpfte Buchseiten, die durch Wasserzeichen liniert sind. In diese sind Samen verschiedener Sorten gesät, wodurch der Eindruck eines Schriftbildes entsteht. Im Papier, warm, feucht und hell gehalten, beginnt die Schrift zu wachsen.[112] In Schuhe aus handgeschöpftem Papier pflanzt er 1988 Tulpenknollen; sie erblühten und verwelkten während der Ausstellung.[113] Terese Murak (* 1949 Kielczewice/Polen) sät 1990 Kressesamen in handgeschöpftes Papier, ließ es wachsen und vergehen. „Die Geschichte der Welt ist für mich Wachstum, sinnvoll und zielstrebig gelenkt durch den immanenten Geist."[114]

Regen, Schnee, Feuer und Hitze, Licht, Schmutz, Öl, Samen sind aktive Gestalter. Ihre Kräfte und Zufälligkeiten übernehmen das Handschriftliche des Künstlers. Papier reagiert besonders empfindlich auf jedwede Veränderung. Brandfärbungen, Löcher aus Verwesung oder Zersetzung, Verschmutzungen, aber auch Gräser, Blumen und Schimmel werden Komposition. Papier wird nicht mehr beschrieben oder bemalt, sondern die Substanz des Papiers wird angegriffen, verändert und löst im Extremfall seine Materialität auf. Der Zufall ist bewußt eingeplant.

Fotochemische Prozesse und deren „Fehlleistungen" sind seit Erfindung der Fotografie bekannt. Das Aufbelichten von Gegenständen hat Man Ray mit den ‚Rayogrammen' bekannt gemacht. Robert Rauschenberg (* 1925 Port Arthur/Texas) variierte das Verfahren 1950. Verschiedene Gegenstände legte er auf Blaupauspapier und setzte diese dem Sonnenlicht aus. Es entstanden die ‚Blue Prints'. Shoichi Ida (* 1941 Kyoto/Japan) bezeichnet als sein frühestes Kunstwerk ein Blatt Papier, das er als Junge unter einen Stein legte und viele Jahre später wieder vergilbt und von der Natur bearbeitet hervorholte.[115] Timm Ulrichs (* 1940 Berlin) schreibt 1968 ‚Fotogramme' auf Tapeten, indem er die Bil-

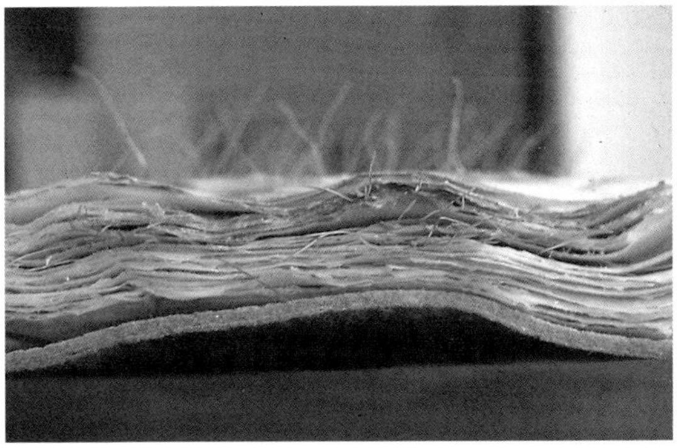

Martin Weimar: Taumel-Lolch, 1986. Gebundene Bücher, bestehend aus handgeschöpftem weißem Papier mit Einschlüssen von Grasarten (Samen). 75 x 120 x 40 cm / Martin Weimar: Taumel-Lolch, 1986. Bounded books, consisting of handmade white paper with insertions of grass (seeds). 75 x 120 x 40 cm

paper and allowed it to wax and then wither. "The history of the world for me is growth that the immanent spirit meaningfully steers towards an end."[114] Rain, snow, fire and heat, light, dirt, oil, seed are active designers. Their force and chance occurrence replace the personal touch of the artist. Paper especially reacts very sensitively to every kind of change. Coloration from burns, holes from decay and corrosion, grime, but also grasses, flowers, and mildew become means of composition. Paper is no long written or painted on, but the substance of the paper is attacked, changed and, when pushed to the extreme, its materiality dissolved. Chance is consciously built in.

Photo-chemical processes and their "mis-takes" have been around since the invention of photography. The flashed lighting up of objects became known through Man Ray's 'Rayogrammes'. Robert Rauschenberg (*1925 Port Arthur/Texas) brought new variation to this technique in 1950. He placed several articles onto blueprint paper and exposed them to sunlight. These became his so-called 'Blue Prints'. Shoichi Ida (*1941 Kyoto/Japan) says that his first artwork was a sheet of paper that as a boy he placed under a stone and many years later brought to light again, yellowed and marked by nature.[115] In 1968 Timm Ulrichs (*1940 Berlin) wrote 'Photogrammes' onto wallpaper by removing

der von der Wand abnimmt. Ihre „Abdeckung" haben Verfärbungen auf der Tapete bewirkt. Der Totalkünstler Ulrichs fordert vom Publikum eine neue Sensibilität, ein emanzipiertes Mitdenken. Er eröffnet eine neue Einstellung zu den Vorgängen und Dingen des Alltags, indem er Wörter wörtlich nimmt, geläufige Sachverhalte und Abläufe stört und dadurch verblüffende Erkenntnisse erzielt.[116]
Das Wort Blatt als Homonym für zwei ganz unterschiedliche Bedeutungen ist 1969 Thema für den Künstler. Das Laubblatt gleicht er dem Papierblatt an, indem er es rechteckig auf DIN A 7 beschneidet: Natur als Vorstellungs-, Sprach- und Begriffswelt.[117]
Ein Blatt Papier, geschöpft im Basler Papiermuseum aus reinen Hadern der Sorte Richard de Bas, ist das Urblatt für eine malerische Philosophie auf 150 Blättern, die Rémy Zaugg (* 1943 Courgenay/Schweiz) in den Jahren 1970 bis 1988 schuf. Die ‚Reflexionen auf und über ein Blatt Papier' umfassen 1800 bis 2000 Bögen, die im Siebdruck in mindestens drei und höchstens 14 Druckvorgängen mit dem Urblatt bedruckt werden. Das reproduzierte Urblatt ist also Abbild und somit Malerei: Sehen ist so schwierig wie denken.[118]
„Der Traum ist ein Papier", schreibt Heinar Kipphardt, und Michael Lentz sagt: „Meine einzige Hoffnung ist leeres Papier."[119]

the pictures from the wall. Their "cover-up" had discolored the wallpaper. Ulrichs, the comprehensive artist, demands a new sensibility from the public, an emancipated way of cooperative thinking. He offers a new approach to the processes and things of everyday life by taking words literally, by disturbing the current circumstance and the normal course, thereby producing striking insights.[116] The German word "Blatt" as a homonym for two different meanings [Blatt as page/sheet or Blatt as leaf] is in 1969 subject for the artist. He makes the leaf analogous to the sheet of paper by cutting it to a postcard-sized rectangle. Nature as a world of concept, of language and of definition.[117]
A sheet of paper of Richard de Bas quality, handmade in the Basle Paper Museum from pure rags, is the original design for a philosophy of painting on 150 pages that Rémy Zaugg (*1943 Courgenay/Switzerland) created in the years from 1970 to 1988. Reflections on and about a sheet of paper are composed of 1800 to 2000 pages each silkscreened with the original design in at least 3 and at most 14 work processes. The reproduced original is thus a copy and also a painting; seeing is just as difficult as thinking.[118]
"The dream is a paper," writes Heinar Kipphardt, and Michael Lentz says, "My only hope is blank paper."[119]

Timm Ulrichs: Das Wort ‚Blatt' als Homonym, 1966. Baum-Blatt, als Kunst-Blatt gerahmt; Baum-Blätter mit Seitenzahlen numeriert, 1969; Baum-Blätter, rechteckig auf DIN A 7 beschnitten, 1969 / Timm Ulrichs: The German Word 'Blatt' as Homonym, 1966. Tree leaf framed as art leaf/sheet; tree leaves with numbered pages, 1969; tree leaves, cut rectangular to DIN A 7, 1969

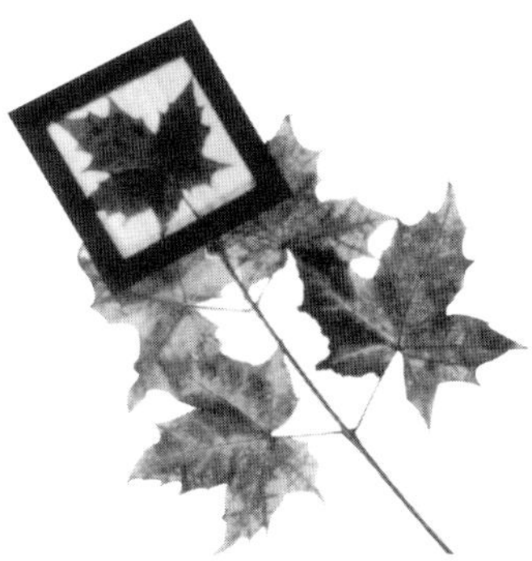

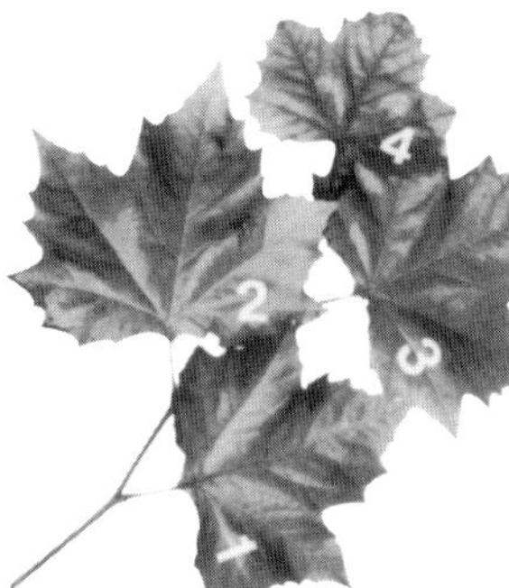

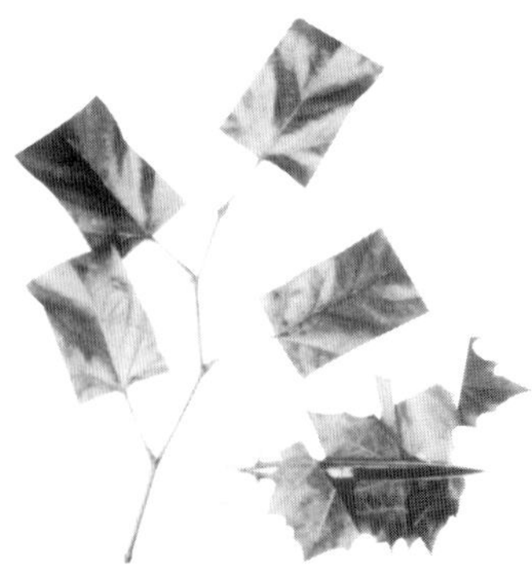

V. Papier und Pulp – Medium der Kunst

V. Paper and pulp – Mediums for art

V. 1. Wiederentdeckung des handgeschöpften Papiers

Die Anfänge der Papierkunst in Europa fallen in die späten 50er und beginnenden 60er Jahre. Basismaterial ist das maschinell vorgefertigte, glatte weiße Papier oder der weiße Karton. Künstler wie Joseph Beuys, Herbert Zangs oder die Nouveaux Réalistes nützten bereits gebrauchtes, mit Verletzungsspuren behaftetes Papier, Packpapier, Karton und Pappe, in einigen Fällen auch Papiermaché. Papier erweist sich als ideales Mittel, die neuen künstlerischen Ziele – die äußerste Reduktion der Sprachmittel und der individuellen Handschrift – zu verwirklichen. Papier, setzt man es natürlichen Prozessen aus, wird schließlich „von selbst", aus sich selbst, zum Kunstwerk.

In den USA verläuft die Kunstentwicklung dieser Zeit unter anderen Vorzeichen, wenn auch die junge Generation den ausdrucksstarken abstrakten Expressionismus sowie alles Mythische und Symbolische ebenfalls ablehnte. Bestimmte Merkmale des Action-painting erfuhren neue Varianten, so wurde die Wirkung der taktilen Oberfläche entdeckt; auch der Bezug zur Großstadt sowie zur Umwelt spielte nun eine wichtige Rolle. Robert Rauschenberg, beeinflußt von John Cages Forderung, die Grenzen zwischen Kunst und Leben nie-

V. 1. Handmade paper is rediscovered

The beginnings of paper art in Europe take place in the late 50s and early 60s. The basic material is that of prefabricated, glossy, evenly white paper or white paperboard. Artists like Joseph Beuys, Herbert Zangs or the Nouveaux Réalistes utilized second-hand paper, i. e., paper, paperboard and cardboard in damaged condition, in some cases also papier-maché. Paper proved to be an ideal medium for realizing the new goals of art: the utmost reduction of expressiveness and of the individual signature. Too, paper, when once exposed to natural processes, becomes an artwork "on its own" and from within.

In the US, the art of the times developed under other signs. The young generation rejected abstract expressionism and its emotionality, as well as everything mythical and symbolic. However, certain characteristics of Action Painting were given new twists; in this way the affect of tactile surfaces were discovered, and the relationship to the big city as well as to the environment played an important role. In 1950/51 Robert Rauschenberg, influenced by John Cage's call to tear down the boundaries between art and life and impressed by his opinion that the banal and the common have aesthetic potentiality, made completely white paintings on

derzureißen, und von dessen Ansicht beeindruckt, daß auch das Banale und Gewöhnliche ästhetische Möglichkeiten enthalte, schuf 1950/51 vollständig weiße Gemälde, auf denen nur der Schatten der Besucher sichtbar war. Als Malgrund der ganz schwarzen Bilder nahm er zerknittertes und zerrissenes Zeitungspapier, um eine unregelmäßige Oberfläche zu erhalten. Rauschenberg, der seine ersten „combine paintings" aus Tauenden, Lumpen, Zeitungen, Postkarten konstruierte, verfolgte ähnliche Tendenzen wie die Nouveaux Réalistes.[120]

Um dieselbe Zeit entdeckten Künstler wie Jackson Pollock (* 1912 Cody/Wyoming – † 1956 East Hampton/New York), Willem de Kooning (* 1904 Rotterdam) und Robert Motherwell (* 1915 Aberdeen/Washington – † 1991 Provincetown/Massachusetts) die Materialreize des handgeschöpften Papiers. Sie verwendeten es wie Leinwand für Gemälde. Häufig benutzten sie „mißlungene", unebene, an den Rändern „zernagte" Papiere des Papiermachers Douglass Morse Howell.

Gleichzeitig erlebte die Druckgrafik eine neue Blüte. Nicht mehr die absolute Uniformität eines jeden Blattes einer Auflage interessierte, sondern die Variation und Individualität. Die Eigenqualität des handgeschöpften Papiers erregte Aufmerk-

Garner Tullis: Renaissance Man, 1968–1974. Geformtes handgeschöpftes Papier aus einem recycelten Gemälde. 28 x 32 cm / Garner Tullis: Renaissance Man, 1968-1974. Moulded handmade paper from recycled painting. 28 x 32 cm

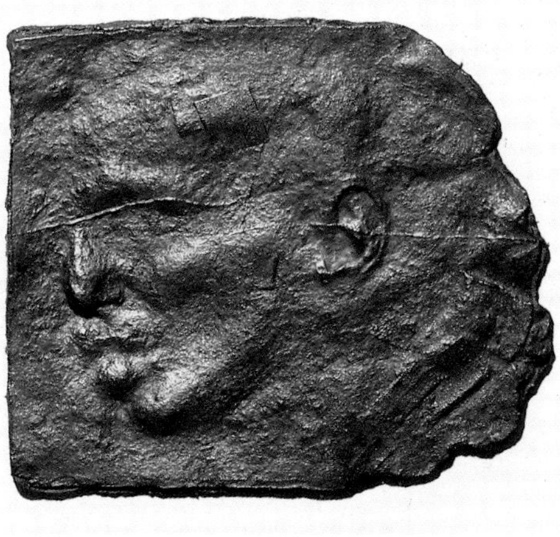

which only the shadow of the viewer was visible. As grounding for his completely black paintings he used crumpled and torn newspaper to obtain an irregular surface. Rauschenberg's first "Combines" were paintings constructed from rope ends, rags, newspaper, postcards, pursued goals similar to the Nouveaux Réalistes.[120]

Around the same time, artists like Jackson Pollock (* 1912 Cody/Wyoming – † 1956 East Hampton/New York), Willem de Kooning (* 1904 Rotterdam) and Robert Motherwell (* 1915 Aberdeen/Washington – † 1991 Provincetown/Massachusetts) discovered the special material appeal of handmade paper. They treated it as equal to canvas as a surface for paint. They often utilized the "miscarried", uneven, ragged-edged productions of the papermaker Douglass Morse Howell.

At the same time the graphic arts were undergoing a renaissance. No longer was it the absolute uniformity of each sheet of an edition that was interesting, but the variation and the individuality. What excited attention was the singular quality of handmade paper. The pioneers in this field were those artists who were themselves also printers, in the US, e. g., Garner Tullis, William Weege and Alan Shields. William Stanley Hayter expanded the art of engraving by the use of surrealist, automatist techniques and by experiments with color and structure. In Norway Rolf Nesch imprinted relief effects into his engravings with the aid of found objects. From the middle of the 60s many artists used handmade paper for limited editions. Jim Dine (*1935 Cincinnati/Ohio) printed his work on paper from the mills of Fabriano (Italy) and Richard de Bas (France). Ronald B. Kitaj (* 1932 Chagrin Falls/Ohio) used Japan paper; Henry Moore (* 1898 Castleford/Yorkshire – † 1986 Hadham/London) used that of Barcham Green, Great Britain, ordering special paper with his own watermarks. Victor Pasmore (1908 Chelsam/Great Britain) did his printing on approximately four meter long, specially made-to-order Arches paper (France).[121] The papermill of Carta Lafranca founded in Switzerland

samkeit. Pioniere auf diesem Gebiet waren Künstler, die auch selbst Drucker waren, in den USA z. B. Garner Tullis, William Weege und Alan Shields. William Stanley Hayter erweiterte die Druckgrafik durch Verwendung surrealistischer automatischer Techniken und durch Experimente mit Farben und Strukturen. In Norwegen preßte Rolf Nesch seinen Druckgrafiken mit Hilfe von Fundobjekten Reliefeffekte ein. Seit Mitte der 60er Jahre verwendeten viele Künstler handgeschöpftes Papier für limitierte Auflagen. Jim Dine (* 1935 Cincinnati/Ohio) druckte auf Papier des Mühlen Fabriano (Italien) und Richard de Bas (Frankreich). Ronald B. Kitaj (* 1932 Chagrin Falls/Ohio) verwendete Japanpapier, Henry Moore (* 1898 Castleford/Yorkshire – † 1986 Hadham/London) benutzte Papier von Barcham Green (Großbritannien). Er bestellte dort Papier mit eigenem Wasserzeichen. Victor Pasmore (* 1908 Chelsam/Großbritannien) druckte auf etwa vier Meter langem, eigens hergestelltem Arches-Papier (Frankreich).[121] Die 1968 in der Schweiz gegründete Papiermühle Carta Lafranca druckt auch heute noch für bekannte Künstler wie André Evrard, Jean-Edouard Augsburger, François Morellet oder Enrico Castellani und publiziert Editionen auf Papieren mit einem Gewicht zwischen 200 Gramm/Quadratmeter bis zu über 1000 Gramm/Quadratmeter, die eigens für die Handdrucktechniken entwickelt wurden.

In Großbritannien ist John Mason (*1927 Nebraska), der Sohn des Grafikers J. H. Mason, für die Wiederentdeckung des handgemachten Papiers von Bedeutung. Im Jahr 1954 begann er mit ersten Experimenten für den Bereich der Buchbinderei. Am Leicester College of Art gründete er ein Papierstudio, in dem er mit seinen Studenten experimentierte. Von 1960 an veröffentlichte er in seiner ‚Twelve by Eight Press' Bücher und lud Publizisten ein, auf handgeschöpftem Papier zu drucken. Als Wiederentdecker des handgeschöpften Papiers gilt in den USA der Papiermacher, Drucker und Sammler Dard Hunter (1883–1966). Sein grundlegendes Buch ‚Papermaking – The History and Tech-

in 1968 still today does printing for well-known artists like André Evrard, Jean-Edouard Augsburger, François Morellet and Enrico Castellani and publishes editions on paper specially developed for handprinting techniques and weighing between 200 to over 1000 grams per square meter.

John Mason (* 1927 Nebraska) is the son of the graphic designer, J. H. Mason, and of great importance for the rediscovery of handmade paper in Great Britain. In 1954 he began his first experiments in the field of bookbinding. At the Leicester College of Art he founded a paper studio, where he experimented with his students. From 1960 on he published his 'Twelve by Eight Press' books and invited publicists to do their printing on his handmade paper.

The papermaker, printer and collector, Dard Hunter (1883–1966), is acknowledged as the man who rediscovered handmade paper in the States. His

Douglass Morse Howell in seinem Atelier in Riverhead/New York, 1984 / Douglass Morse Howell in his studio in Riverhead/New York, 1984

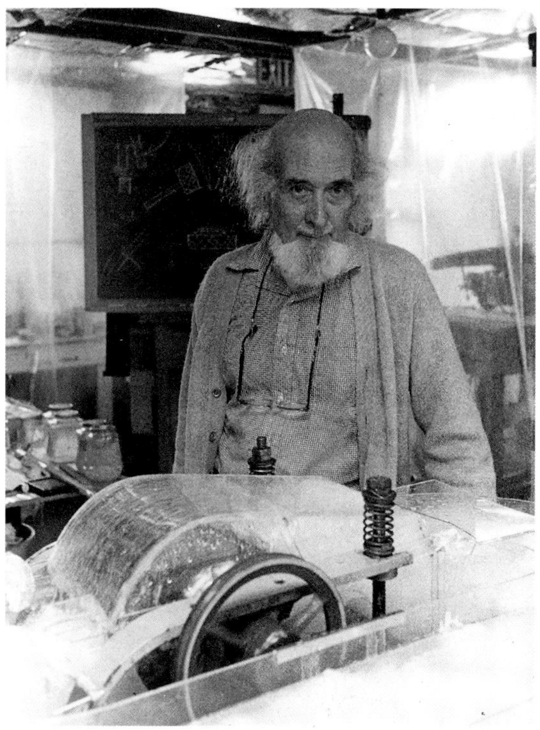

nique of an Ancient Craft', erstmals veröffentlicht in New York 1943, hatte große Breitenwirkung.[122] Wegweisend für die Papierkunst in den USA ist der Papiermacher und Drucker Douglass Morse Howell (* 1906 New York). In den 40er Jahren stellte er seine ersten Papiere ohne chemische Zusätze aus Leinen und später aus Flachs her. 1946 schöpfte er die ersten bunten Papiere aus verschieden gefärbten Leinen und veröffentlichte das erste Buch auf handgeschöpftem Papier. William Stanley Hayter testete 1946 Howells Produkte im New Yorker Atelier 17. Joan Miró (* 1893 Montroig/Barcelona – † 1983 Palma de Mallorca) sah diese und nahm sie mit. Jackson Pollock und seine Frau Lee Krasner besuchten Howell 1951. Beide arbeiteten von nun an mit dessen Papieren. Eine ganze Reihe amerikanischer Künstler verwendeten in den folgenden Jahren Howells Papiere, unter ihnen Jasper Johns (* 1930 Allendale/South Carolina) und Larry Rivers (* 1923 New York). 1951 erhielt Howell vom Metropolitan Museum of Art in New York den Auftrag, für den Museumsshop Druckgrafiken Albrecht Dürers von Originalplatten zu drucken. Howell unternahm viele Versuche, um das texturreiche Papier der Dürer-Originale herzustellen.[123] 1950 begann er, Papier plastisch zu formen. Die Figuren aus gefärbtem Pulp, in der Bütte eingefangen, wurden 1955 in der Betty Parsons Gallery in New York ausgestellt. 1959 fertigte Howell erstmals Papier aus Blue jeans. Sein Studiolabor auf Long Island entwickelte sich zu einem Zentrum für die Kunst der Papierherstellung. Künstler, Wissenschaftler und interessierte Laien studierten und diskutierten mit ihm.

standard book 'Papermaking – The History and Technique of an Ancient Craft' was first published in New York in 1943 and had wide-ranging influence.[122] The papermaker and printer, Douglass Morse Howell (* 1906 New York), was the trailblazer for paper art in America. In the 40s he introduced his first paper with no chemical additives made of linen and later of flax. In 1946 he made the first colored paper out of different tones of linen and published the first book on handmade paper. In 1946 William Stanley Hayer tested Howell's products at his New York Atelier 17, which Joan Miró (* 1893 Montroig/Barcelona – † 1983 Palma de Mallorca) saw there and took away with him. Jackson Pollock and his wife, Lee Krasner, visited Howell in 1951. Both of them worked from then on with his paper. A large number of American artists used Howell's paper in the following years, among them Jasper Johns (* 1930 Allendale/South Carolina) and Larry Rivers (* 1923 New York). In 1951 Howell was given a commission by the Metropolitan Musuem of Art in New York to print an edition of Albrecht Dürer's graphic art from the original plates. Howell undertook many attempts to manufacture the highly textured paper of the Dürer originals.[123] In 1950 he began to form paper three-dimensionally. His figures of colored pulp lifted from the vat were shown in 1955 in the Betty Parsons Gallery in New York. In 1959 Howell made paper for the first time from blue denim jeans. His studio and laboratory on Long Island developed into a center for the craft of paper production. Artists, scientists and interested laymen came to study and discourse with him.

V. 2. Anfänge der Papierkunst mit Pulp

1962 lehrte Howell den Leiter des Druckerzentrums an der Cranbrook Academy of Art in Michigan, Laurence Barker (* 1930 Houston/Texas), das Papiermachen und gründete dort im folgenden Jahr das erste Lehrinstitut für Handpapiermacherei in den USA. Während seiner siebenjährigen Lehrtätigkeit bildete er neue Generationen von Papiermachern heran wie Walter Hamady, John Koller, Aris Koutroulis, Winifred Lutz und Roland Poska, die Papiermühlen oder kleinere Verlage eröffneten und ihrerseits wieder anderen beibrachten, wie man handgeschöpftes Papier herstellen und für die Kunst nutzen kann. Seit 1970 betreibt Barker ein eigenes Papiermacherstudio in Barcelona. Er arbeitete zusammen mit Robert Rauschenberg, Joan Miró, David Hockney und Roy Lichtenstein. Seine Lehrtätigkeit war grundlegend für die heutige Papierkunst aus Papierpulp.

Laurence Barker: Ohne Titel, 1963. Malerei mit Papierstoff. 55 x 95 cm / Laurence Barker: Untitled, 1963. Paper pulp painting. 55 x 95 cm

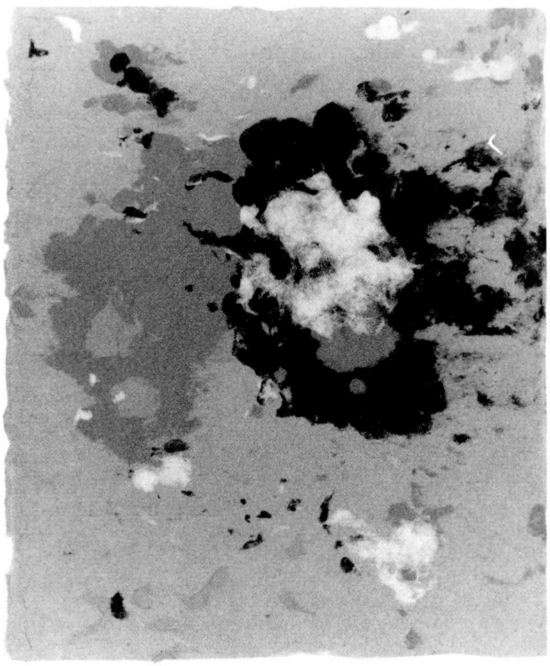

V.2. The beginnings of paper art from pulp

In 1962 Howell taught the director of the Printing Center at the Cranbrook Academy of Art in Michigan, Laurence Barker (* 1930 Houston/ Texas), the craft of papermaking and the following year founded there the first teaching institute for handmaking paper in the US. During his seven years of teaching he trained new generations of papermakers like Walter Hamady, John Koller, Aris Koutroulis, Winifred Lutz and Roland Poska, who later opened papermills or small publishing companies and in their turn trained others to handmake paper and use it for art. Since 1970 Barker has run his own papermaking studio in Barcelona. He has worked with Robert Rauschenberg, Joan Miró, David Hockney and Roy Lichtenstein. His teaching has been fundamental for today's paper art made from paper pulp.
The Institute for Experimental Printmaking is recognized as an important stimulus to the expansion of paper art to the west coast of the US, founded by Garner Tullis (* 1939 Cincinnati/Ohio) in Santa Cruz, California in 1973 and to which a handmade paper studio was attached. He worked with Louise Nevelson (* 1930 Kiev), Jean Dubuffet, Jim Dine, Sam Francis (1923 San Mateo/California) and Alan Shields. In 1974 he taught Jules Heller the craft of papermaking, who in turn taught it to generations of artists at the Arizona State University in Tempe.[124] New techniques generated new forms of paper art: in the Tullis studio Charles Hilger and Harold Paris developed the vacuum table that allowed water to be rapidly siphoned off, making unusual printing techniques and three-dimensional works possible.
In the early 70s artists, printers and papermakers founded workshops where other artists could become instructed in their techniques and skills. Alongside of many private studios, special mention is owed the Twinrocker Handmade Paper Mill opened in 1971 by Kathryn and Howard Clark in

Wichtig für die Verbreitung der Papierkunst an der Westküste der USA wurde das 1973 gegründete Institute for Experimental Printmaking von Garner Tullis (* 1939 Cincinnati/Ohio) in Santa Cruz/Kalifornien, dem ein Handpapiermacherstudio angegliedert ist. Er arbeitete zusammen mit Louise Nevelson (* 1930 Kiew), Jean Dubuffet, Jim Dine, Sam Francis (* 1923 San Mateo/Kalifornien) und Alan Shields. 1974 lehrte er Jules Heller die Papiermacherei, der an der Arizona State University in Tempe wiederum Generationen von Künstlern die Handpapiermacherei und den künstlerischen Umgang mit Papier beibringt.[124] Neue Techniken generierten neue Formen der Papierkunst. Im Tullis-Studio entwickelten Charles Hilger und Harold Paris den Vakuumtisch, der durch schnelles Absaugen des Wassers ungewöhnliche Drucktechniken und dreidimensionale Werke ermöglicht.

In den frühen 70er Jahren gründeten Künstler, Drucker und Papiermacher Werkstätten, in denen sie Künstlern ihre Technik und Kunstfertigkeit nahebrachten. Neben vielen privaten Studios ist vor allem die Twinrocker Handmade Paper Mill zu nennen, die 1971 von Kathryn und Howard Clark in Brookston/Indiana, eröffnet wurde. Twinrocker trug viel dazu bei, die Technik des Papierschöpfens in westlicher und östlicher Manier nach modernen Gesichtspunkten zu entwickeln. Ausrüstungen wurden entworfen und produziert, Workshops angeboten. Magnolia Editions in Oakland/Kalifornien ist eine weitere wichtige Werkstatt, ebenso Carriage House Handmade Paperworks, gegründet 1975 in Brookline/Massachusetts von Elaine und Donna Koretsky. Elaine Koretsky betreibt Grundforschungsarbeit in bezug auf Faserqualitäten und Färbung.[125]

In ihrem vergleichsweise kurzen Leben hat die Papierkunst relativ großen Einfluß auf die amerikanische Kunstszene genommen. Seit Mitte der 70er Jahre wurden Papiermühlen und -werkstätten von einer immer größer werdenden Zahl von Papierkünstlern nur für eigene Zwecke oder auch als Workshop eingerichtet. Einige wichtige Museen in

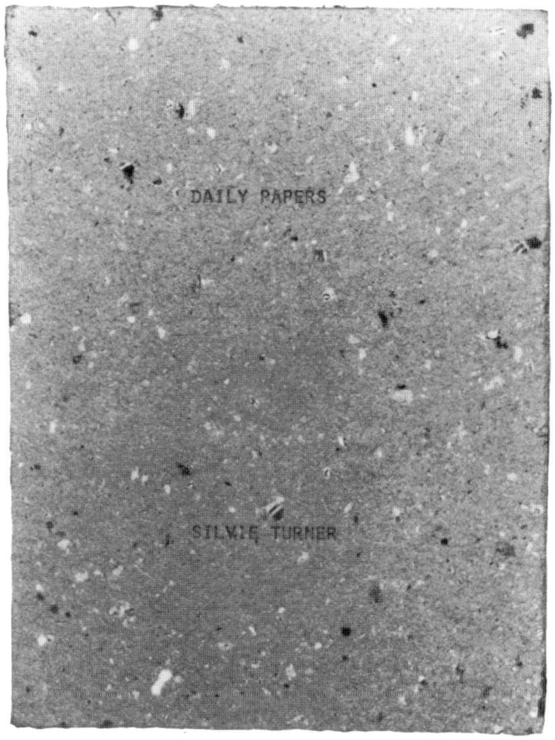

Silvie Turner: Daily Papers, 1980. Handgeschöpftes Papier aus Zeitungen. Buchobjekt. 16,5 x 12,3 cm / Silvie Turner: Daily Papers, 1980. Paper handmade from newspapers. Book object. 16.5 x 12.3 cm

Brookston/Indiana. Twinrocker contributed a great deal to the development of modern aspects of papermaking technique in the manner of the west and the east. There they designed and fabricated equipment and gave training workshops. Magnolia Editions in Oakland, California is a further important production shop, as well as the Carriage House Handmade Paperworks founded in 1975 in Brookline/Massachusetts by Elaine and Donna Koretsky. There Elaine Koretsky works on basic reasearch related to fiber quality and dye.[125]

Despite its comparitively short life, paper art has managed to have a relatively large impact on the American art scene. Since the middle of the 70s, papermills and production shops have been established by an ever larger number of paper artists either for their own purposes or as workshops. Some important US museums have brought paper as an artform to public attention.[126]

den USA haben auf Papier als Kunstform aufmerksam gemacht.[126] Konferenzen brachten Künstler mit Kuratoren, Kritikern und Papierherstellern zusammen.[127] Immer mehr Schulen und Universitäten bieten das Fach Papierherstellung an.

Die Verbreitung der Papierkunst aus Pulp ging in Europa zunächst nur schleppend voran. Nur wenige Künstler versuchten sich in den 70er Jahren im Medium Papier. Der Schweizer Ingenieur und Künstler Fred Siegenthaler (* 1935 Obergerlafingen/Schweiz) arbeitete um 1970 für Künstler wie Joan Miró, Marc Chagall, Jasper Johns, Horst Antes und Meret Oppenheim.[128] In London gründete Silvie Turner (* 1946 Yorkshire/Großbritannien) 1976 eine Handpapiermacherei.[129] Maureen Richardson (* 1930 Großbritannien) kam 1970 zur Handpapiermacherei und etablierte 1976 die Plant Papers Mill in Herefordshire/Großbritannien. Sie züchtet die Pflanzen, aus denen sie die Papiere herstellt, meist selbst. Jacky Perry (* 1941 Wonthaggi/Australien) lehrt seit 1976 das Handwerk des Papiermachens an der Glasgow School of Art. Heinz-Dieter Pietsch (* 1944 Glogau/Schlesien) erarbeitete 1976 seine ersten Experimente in Papier am Royal College of Art in London. Ian Tyson (* 1933 Wallasey/Großbritannien) begann mit der Papierkunst 1979 am City Literary Institute in London und in der Papiermühle Barcham Green in Kent. Im italienischen Reggio Emilia hatten sich wie in Fabriano zu Beginn der 80er Jahre Zentren für Papierkunst entwickelt. Dora Maurer (* 1937 Budapest) erhielt 1979, Géza Mészáros (* 1943 Budapest) 1980 die Möglichkeit, in einer Papierfabrik in Budapest mit Rohmaterial zu experimentieren. In den Niederlanden arbeiten seit der Zeit um 1970 Peter (* 1946 Rijswijk/Niederlande) und Pat Gentenaar (* 1949 San Francisco) mit verschiedenen Fasern. Sie entwickelten auch neues Arbeitsmaterial. In Deutschland gibt es vier Ausbildungsstätten für Papierkunst. 1982 richtete Eduardo Paolozzi (* 1924 Edinburgh) an der Akademie der Bildenden Künste in München eine Papierwerkstatt ein und unterrichtete das Fach an der Sommerakademie Salzburg. Andreas von Weiz-

Conferences have been staged where artists can meet curators, critics and paper manufacturers.[127] More and more schools and universities are offering papermaking as part of their curriculum.

Paper art made of pulp spread at first very slowly in Europe. By the 70s only very few artists had tried their hand at the medium of paper. The Swiss engineer and artist, Fred Siegenthaler (* 1935 Obergerlafingen/Switzerland), around 1970 worked for artists such as Joan Miró, Marc Chagall, Jasper Johns, Horst Antes and Meret Oppenheim.[128] In London Silvie Turner (* 1946 Yorkshire/Great Britain) founded a handmade paper works in 1976.[129] Maureen Richardson (* 1930 Great Britain) started handmade papermaking in 1970 and in 1976 set up the Plant Papers Mill in Herefordshire/Great Britain. She herself grows most of the plants from which she makes the paper. Jacky Perry (* 1941 Wonthaggi/Australia) has taught the craft of making paper in the Glasgow School of Art. In 1976 Heinz-Dieter Pietsch (* 1944 Glogau/Silesia) did his first experiments in paper at the Royal College of Art in London. Ian Tyson (* 1933 Wallasey/Great Britain) in 1979 began paper art at the City Literary Institute in London and at the Barcham Green Papermill in Kent. At the beginning of the 80s an Italian center for paper art had developed in Reggio Emilia in addition to the one that already traditionally existed in Fabriano. Dora Maurer (* 1937 Budapest) in 1979 and Géza Mészáros (* 1943 Budapest) in 1980 were given the opportunity to experiment with raw material at a paper factory in Hungary. In the Netherlands around 1970 Peter (* 1946 Rijswijk/Netherlands) and Pat Gentenaar (* 1949 San Francisco) worked with different fibers. They also developed new working material. In Germany there are four training centers for paper art. In 1982 Eduardo Paolozzi (* 1924 Edinburgh) fitted out a paper workshop at the Academy of the Visual Arts in Munich and gave courses in the craft at the Salzburg Summer Academy. Andreas von Weizsäcker (* 1956 Essen) became his successor.

säcker (* 1956 Essen) hat seine Nachfolge angetreten. An der Universität Paderborn lehrt seit 1983 Dorothea Reese-Heim (* 1943 Sindelfingen). Eine Papierwerkstatt unterhalten die Universitäten Osnabrück und Mainz.

Erst seit der ersten Hälfte der 80er Jahre ist in Europa ein reges und stetig sich erweiterndes Interesse an der Papierkunst aus Pulp festzustellen. Die Welle der Studiogründungen und der Experimente, die in den 60er und 70er Jahren in den USA zu beobachten war, hat nun auch Europa erfaßt. Seit 1980 werden Ausstellungen zum Thema Papierkunst in Europa immer häufiger gezeigt, so die seit 1986 im Zweijahresrhythmus durchgeführte ‚Internationale Biennale der Papierkunst' durch das Leopold-Hoesch-Museum und das Papiermuseum Düren. 1986 wurde in Düren die International Association of Hand Papermakers and Paper Artists (IAPMA) gegründet. Sie zählt heute etwa 450 Mitglieder in 33 Ländern. 1987 fand in Maastricht das Symposium ‚PaperArt' mit Ausstellungen, Vorführungen und Vorträgen statt.

In fast allen Ländern der Welt arbeiten seit den 70er Jahren immer mehr Künstler im Medium Papier. Ausstellungen, Konferenzen und Vereinigungen brachten Papierkünstler aus aller Welt zusammen.[130] Die ‚Internationale Handpapier-Konferenz' fand erstmals 1975 in Appelton/Wisconsin statt, die zweite 1976 in Santa Barbara/Kalifornien, die dritte 1978 in San Francisco; 1980 waren Honolulu, 1983 Kyoto und 1993 Toronto Tagungsorte. Die Konferenz wird stets begleitet von Papierkunstausstellungen. Die Ausstellung 1983 in Kyoto zeigte Papierskulpturen von 50 japanischen und koreanischen Künstlern. Die Ausstellung ‚New American Paperworks', arrangiert vom World Print Council, San Francisco, wanderte in den Jahren 1982 bis 1985 durch die USA und Asien mit den Ausstellungsorten Houston/Texas, Birmingham/Alabama, Kyoto/Japan, Fukuoka/Japan, Seoul/Korea, Taegu/Korea, Hongkong, Manila/Philippinen und Singapur. 1984 organisierte Language Plus an der Universität Québec ein internationales Symposium.

Dorothea Reese-Heim (* 1943 Sindelfingen) has been teaching at the University of Paderborn since 1983. Both the Universities of Osnabrück and Mainz also maintain paper workshops.

Not till the first half of the 80s has any strong and steadily expanding interest in paper art made of pulp been at all notable in Europe. It was then that the wave of studio foundings and experiments observable in the 60s and 70s in the US spread to Europe. Since 1980 exhibitions on the theme of paper art have been mounted more and more often in Europe, including the 'International Biennale of Paper Art' that since 1986 has been put on every two years conjointly by the Leopold Hoesch Museum and the Paper Museum in Düren. Also in 1986 an International Association of Hand Papermakers and Paper Artists (IAPMA) was founded in Düren. Today it has approximately 450 members from 33 countries. In 1987 the 'PaperArt' Symposium took place in Maastricht with exhibits, shows and lectures.

In almost all the countries of the world since the 70s, there are more and more artists working in the medium of paper. Exhibitions, conferences and associations have brought paper artists together from around the world.[130] The 'International Handpaper Conference' first took place in 1975 in Appelton/Wisconsin, the second in 1976 in Santa Barbara/California, the third in 1978 in San Francisco, in 1980 in Honolulu, in 1983 in Kyoto and in 1993 in Toronto. Each time it was accompanied by paper art exhibitions. The exhibit in 1983 in Kyoto showed the paper sculpture of 50 Japanese and Korean artists. The exhibit 'New American Paperworks' arranged by the World Print Council in San Franciso went on tour in the years from 1982 to 1985 throughout the US and Asia in the following places: Houston/Texas; Birmingham/Alabama; Kyoto/Japan; Fukuoka/Japan; Seoul/Korea; Taegu/Korea; Hong Kong; Manila, the Philippines; and Singapore. In 1984 Language Plus organized an international symposium at the University of Quebec. Australia set up the first

Australien richtete die erste nationale Papierkonferenz 1987 in Hobart/Tasmanien aus. Die erste südafrikanische Handpapiermacherkonferenz war 1987 in Johannesburg. 1988 wurde in Kyoto die Paper Academy gegründet, in der Papier in historischer, konservatorischer, wirtschaftlicher und künstlerischer Hinsicht Thema ist. Die zweite ‚Internationale Biennale der Papierkunst' 1988 ging als Wanderausstellung von Düren nach Aalborg/Dänemark und in drei japanische Museen, in das Museum of Kyoto, The Hall of Awa Japanese Handmade Paper, Tokushima, und in das Azabu Museum of Arts and Crafts, Tokyo. Die Kongresse der IAPMA fanden seit 1987 in Barcelona, Reno/Nevada, Basel, Budapest, Toronto und Noordwijkerhout/Niederlande, statt.
Die Verbreitung der Papierkunst ging zunächst von den USA aus, auch durch Künstler, die in andere Länder oder Erdteile übersiedelten. Umgekehrt zog es Künstler aus Kanada, Brasilien und Europa in die USA. Japan, Korea, Nepal, Burma, Thailand, die Philippinen und Mexiko sind für Papierkünstler Studienländer, um andere Techniken der Papierherstellung und Rohstoffgewinnung zu erlernen. Die sehr andersartige Materialität dieser Papiere erweitert entscheidend die Möglichkeiten künstlerischer Gestaltung.[131]
Seit etwa 1970 ist Pulp und handgeschöpftes Papier beliebtes Material in den USA und seit Mitte der 80er Jahre in Europa. Das Revolutionäre am Pulp ist, daß es den Künstlern nun möglich ist, bereits ihr Material im Entstehungsprozeß zu beeinflussen und zu bestimmen. Die Siebform bestimmt Größe und Struktur. Der Pulp hat seine unterschiedliche Konsistenz je nach Fasermaterial; seine unterschiedliche Farbigkeit resultiert entweder aus der Färbung durch die Faser oder durch Hinzufügen von Farbpigmenten. Pulpbilder können aus vielen Schichten Papier bestehen, die in nassem Zustand aufeinandergepreßt werden. Strukturen entstehen, indem zwischen die Schichten Objekte eingeschlossen werden oder Stoffe, Papiere und ähnliches auf die Schichten gepreßt werden.

national paper conference in 1987 in Hobart/Tasmania, Australia. The first South African Handpaper Makers Conference was held in 1987 in Johannesburg. In 1988 the Paper Academy was founded in Kyoto, where paper in its historical, conservatorial, economic and artistic aspects is the theme. In 1988 'The Second International Biennale of Paper Art' went on tour from Düren to Aalborg/Denmark and to three Japanese Museums: the Museum of Kyoto, the Hall of Awa Japanese Handmade Paper in Tokushima and the Azabu Museum of Arts and Crafts in Tokyo. Since 1987 the congresses of the IAPMA have taken place in Barcelona, Reno/Nevada, Basle, Budapest, Toronto and Noordwijkerhout/Netherlands.
Paper art spread at first from the United States, also through US artists who settled in other counties and on other continents. While, vice versa, there were artists from Canada, Brazil and Europe who were drawn to the US. To paper artists the countries of Japan, Korea, Nepal, Burma, Thailand, the Philippines and Mexico are where one can learn other techniques of papermaking and of raw material extraction. The quite unfamiliar materiality of this paper expands the possibilities of artistic design enormously.[131]
Since approximately 1970, pulp and handmade paper has been a popular material in the US and since the middle of the 80s also in Europe. The revolutionary aspect of pulp is that it allows the artists to influence and determine their material during its production. The screen form determines the size and the texture. The pulp acquires its different consistency according to the fiber, its different coloring from the dye of the fiber or from the addition of pigments. Pulp pictures can consist of many layers of paper that are pressed together when wet. Structures arise when objects are enclosed between the layers or when cloth, paper, etc. are pressed onto the layers. Sometimes a paper layer runs into the next one, is transparent or frayed, and acquires by means of an alien fiber or color a rich variety of structure. Relief-like

Manche Papierschicht verläuft in die nächste, ist durchsichtig oder zerfasert, gibt durch die andersartige Faserigkeit oder Farbigkeit variationsreiche Struktur. Reliefierungen, Eindrücke sind möglich. In trockenem Zustand können auch Teile aufgenäht oder geklebt werden. Neben den zweidimensionalen Farbbildern gibt es Reliefs, entweder gegossen und naß auf dem Sieb getrocknet oder im Schnellverfahren auf dem Vakuumtisch getrocknet, was ausladendere plastische Formen erlaubt.

Künstler, die mit Papier arbeiten, kommen aus vielen Bereichen der Kunst, aus dem der Grafik, der Bildhauerei, der Malerei, der Textilkunst und Töpferei. Jeder Künstler bringt in das neue Medium Papier seine Erfahrungen, seine Sensibilität und Begabung, sein Bedürfnis nach Entwicklung von Techniken ein. So kommt es zu den unterschiedlichsten Gestaltungen.

impressions are possible. Once in a dry state, the layers can have other parts applied to them by sewing or pasting. Along with two-dimensional pictures, there are also reliefs, either dried on the mould after being poured while wet or dried by the faster method of the vacuum table, which allows larger plastic forms.

Artists who work with paper come from many areas of art, from the graphic arts, sculpture, paintings, textile design and pottery. Each artist brings his experience, his sensitivity and talent, his need to evolve techniques with him into the new medium of paper. The result is the most differentiated of creations.

V. 3. Bekanntmachen durch Arrivierte

Eines der bedeutendsten experimentellen druckgrafischen Zentren unserer Zeit und das berühmteste Studio für die Herstellung von Papierkunst ist Tyler Graphics Ltd. in Mount Kisco/New York, das von Kenneth Tyler geleitet wird. Wichtige Künstler schufen hier, wo die technischen Voraussetzungen vorhanden sind, wo umfassendes Wissen und Können sowie die Freude an Innovativem das Arbeitsklima prägen, bedeutende Kunstwerke. Tyler arbeitete z. B. mit Josef Albers, Anthony Caro, Ron Davis, Richard Hamilton, David Hockney, Paul Jenkins, Ellsworth Kelly, Roy Lichtenstein, Robert Motherwell, Kenneth Noland, Claes Oldenburg, James Rosenquist, Alan Shields und Frank Stella zusammen.

Diese Künstler sind es auch gewesen, die die neue revolutionäre Art der Papierkunst bekannt und populär machten und ihr einen Stellenwert innerhalb der Kunst gaben.

V. 3. Paper becomes known by the company it keeps

One the most significant, experimental graphic arts centers of our time and the most famous studio for the production of paper art is Tyler Graphics Ltd. in Mount Kisco, New York, which is run by Kenneth Tyler. Important artists have created notable works there, where the technical prerequisites are available, where comprehensive knowledge and skill, as well as the joy of innovation, have been responsible for a favorable working climate. Tyler has worked e. g. with Josef Albers, Anthony Caro, Ron Davis, Richard Hamilton, David Hockney, Paul Jenkins, Ellsworth Kelly, Roy Lichtenstein, Robert Motherwell, Kenneth Noland, Claes Oldenburg, James Rosenquist, Alan Shields and Frank Stella. It were these artists who made the new revolutionary paper art known and popular and gave this new field its status within the arts.

1965 betrieb der damals 21jährige Kenneth Tyler seinen ersten Drucker-Workshop, die berühmt gewordene Gemini G.E.L. in Los Angeles. 1974 übersiedelte er an die Ostküste und gründete Tyler Graphics Ltd. in Bedford Village/New York.
Nachdem Tyler 1972 in Kyoto Papiermühlen und Papierarbeiten aus handgeschöpftem Papier gesehen hatte, suchte er nach Möglichkeiten der direkten Zusammenarbeit mit Künstlern in einer historischen Papiermühle.
Robert Rauschenberg (* 1925 Port Arthur/Texas), bekannt für seine ungewöhnlichen Experimente in der Kunst, schien der geeignete Partner. Er hatte sich bereits 1970 mit „Papierkunst" auseinandergesetzt. Für den Titel seiner Kartoncollagen aus diesem Jahr nutzte er das Wortspiel „cardbirds" – „cardboards". Tyler, der für Rauschenberg 1967 verschiedene Techniken untersucht hatte, Fotografien und Material aus Zeitungen in Grafiken zu integrieren, gelang es, den Künstler für seine Ideen zu begeistern.

Already in 1965 as a young man of 21, Kenneth Tyler ran his first lithography workshop, the now famous Gemini G.E.L. in Los Angeles. In 1974 he settled on the east coast and founded Tyler Graphics Ltd. in Bedford Village/New York.
After Tyler had seen the papermills and the works made of handmade paper in Kyoto – this was in 1972 – he began to seek out artists with whom he could work directly in the ambience of an historic papermill.
Robert Rauschenberg (* 1925 Port Arthur/Texas), famous for his unusual experiments in art, seemed the ideal partner. He had already in 1970 experienced his first encounter with "paper art". For the title of his paperboard collages from that year he coined the pun "cardbirds", i. e., cardboards. In August of 1973 both men journeyed together to Ambert in the south of France to the historic papermill, Richard de Bas, in order to carry out their first paper project. Prior to this Rauschenberg had developed methods by which colored pulp could

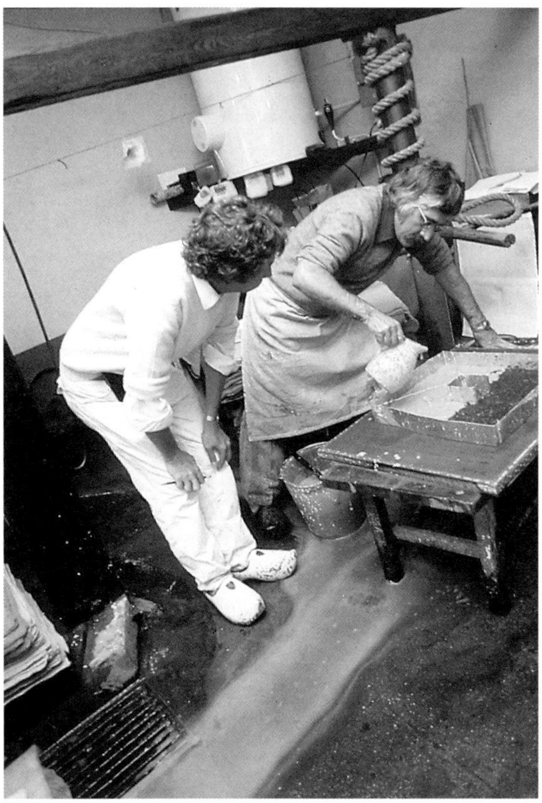

Robert Rauschenberg beobachtet Kenneth Tyler bei der Herstellung der Serie ‚Pages and Fuses' in der Papiermühle Richard de Bas, Frankreich, 1973 / Robert Rauschenberg watches as Kenneth Tyler pours paper pulp for the 'Pages and Fuses' project at Richard de Bas paper mill, France, 1973

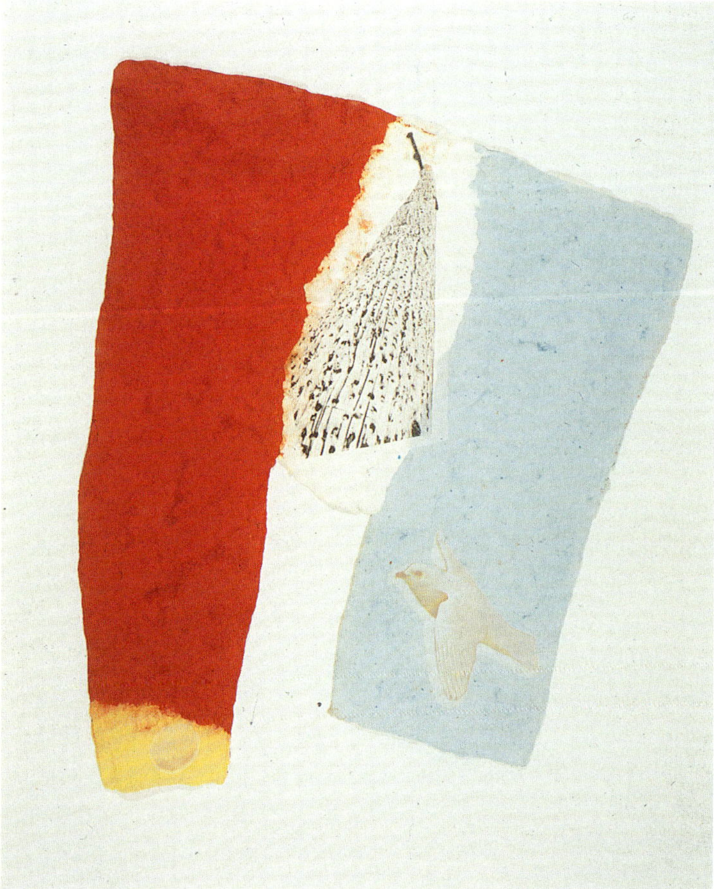

Robert Rauschenberg: Link (aus ‚Pages and Fuses'), 1973/74. Gefärbter und gepreßter Papierpulp. Siebdruck, Collage. Auflage 29. 65 x 51 cm /
Robert Rauschenberg: Link (from 'Pages and Fuses'), 1973/74. Colored and pressed paper pulp. Screenprint, collage. Edition of 29. 65 x 51 cm

Im August 1973 fuhren beide nach Ambert in Südfrankreich, um dort in der historischen Papiermühle Richard de Bas ihr erstes Papierprojekt durchzuführen. Rauschenberg entwickelte Arbeitsmethoden, nach denen farbiger Pulp in Objekten genutzt werden kann. „Er schlug vor, daß ich mit dem Prägen von bedrucktem Seidenpapier auf oder in handgeschöpftem Papier experimentieren sollte", berichtet Kenneth Tyler. „Wir entwickelten Siebe für Vierfarbdruck aus Collagematerial, das der Künstler bereitstellte. Wir druckten die Bilder mit auf Wasser basierender Tinte auf speziell maschinell hergestelltem Seidenpapier, mit dem uns Bernard Guerlain von Special Papers versorgte."[132] Diese in den USA bedruckten Papiere wurden in Ambert Teil der Kompositionen.
Rauschenberg schuf in vier Tagen zwölf verschiedene Bildvorlagen für Editionen: die Serie der fünf

be used to make objects. "[He] suggested I experiment with incorporating printed tissue paper onto or in handmade papers," Kenneth Tyler reported. "We developed four-color process screens from collage material the artist supplied and we printed the images with water base inks onto special, machine-made tissue paper that Bernard Guerlain of Special Papers obtained for us."[132] This paper printed in the US now became in Ambert a part of the compositions.
In four days Rauschenberg created twelve different images for editioning, the series of five paper paintings 'Pages' and the seven-part series 'Fuses'. 'Pages' were done on off-white duplex sheets handmade with a mould; cord, twine, and old remnants of printed cloth were imbedded. The 'Fuses' series with the titles 'Roan', 'Hind', 'Scow', 'Bit', 'Vale', 'Vale State I', 'Link' is more colorful and

Papiergemälde ‚Pages' und die siebenteilige Serie ‚Fuses'. Die ‚Pages' sind mit dem Sieb geschöpfte gebrochenweiße Doppelblätter; Schnüre, Zwirn und bedruckte Stoffreste wurden eingebettet. Die Serie ‚Fuses' mit den Titeln ‚Roan', ‚Hind', ‚Scow', ‚Bit', ‚Vale', ‚Vale State I', ‚Link' ist farbenfreudiger und erinnert an Rauschenbergs Verfahren der Combine paintings. Auf die geschöpften Doppelseiten wurde mit Hilfe von Schablonen farbiger Papierstoff aufgegossen. Zudem wurden die bereits bedruckten Seidenpapiere auf den nassen, gefärbten Papierstoff gelegt und dann zwischen Filzen zusammengepreßt. Nach dem Pressen verbanden sich die aufgelagerten dünnen Seidenpapiere vollständig mit dem Grundblatt. Die wasserlösliche Tinte blutete leicht aus, so daß auch kompositorisch eine Einheit generiert wurde.

In diesen vier Tagen in Ambert entstanden etwa ein Drittel der insgesamt 300 Blätter. Marius Peraudeau und seine Mitarbeiter vollendeten die Edition anhand der vorhandenen Blätter. Jedes Blatt hatte Modellcharakter. Variationen waren vom Künstler gewünscht und technisch bewußt nicht ausgeschlossen.

Zwar hatten in den späten 60er Jahren bereits Künstler wie Alan Shields, William Weege, Joel Fisher und Garner Tullis mit Papier gearbeitet, doch erst das Projekt in der Richard-de-Bas-Mühle erregte weltweit die Aufmerksamkeit der Kunstwelt und lenkte den Blick auf das neue Medium. Diese große Resonanz hing sicherlich auch mit der Person Rauschenbergs und seiner Bedeutung für künstlerische Innovationen zusammen.

Im Jahr 1975 wurde Robert Rauschenberg von einer reichen, an zeitgenössischer Kunst interessierten Familie nach Ahmedabad/Indien, eingeladen; dort erarbeitete er ein weiteres Papierprojekt.

Die Arbeit begann im Mai 1975 und dauerte einen Monat. Hier in der Textilhauptstadt Indiens entschied sich Rauschenberg für ein Projekt aus Baumwolldrucken, Papierstoff und Bambusstreifen, die in großem Überfluß vorhanden waren. Die Rauschenberg-Werke entstanden in einer Papier-

recalls Rauschenberg's experience with his combines. Colored paperpulp was poured into tin moulds on top of the handmade duplex papers. Then the already printed tissue paper was laid onto the wet, dyed paperpulp and couched between felt layers. After pressing, the layer of thin tissue paper was completely fixed to the base paper. The water base inks bled slightly so that a compositional unity resulted.

In these four days in Ambert approximately one-third of the 300 papers were created. Marius Peraudeau and his colleagues completed the edition on the basis of those at hand. Each sheet of paper was in the nature of a prototype. Variations were devoutly to be wished for by the artist and technically not consciously ruled out.

Although in the late 60s artists like Alan Shields, William Weege, Joel Fischer and Garner Tullis had already worked with paper, it was the project in the Richard de Bas Mill that attracted worldwide attention to the new medium. This considerable repercussion was certainly dependent on the person of Rauschenberg and his significance for artistic innovation.

In the year 1975 Robert Rauschenberg was invited by a rich family interested in contemporary art to Ahmedabad, India where he worked on another paper project.

The project began in May 1975 and lasted one month. In this textile capital of India, Rauschenberg decided to do a project using cotton prints, paper pulp and bamboo strips, all available in excess. Onto a layer of pulp poured on a mould, a sheaf of bamboo strips and scraps of cloth were arranged. A second layer of pulp was then poured over this; the work was laid between felt layers, couched and later hung up to dry on racks. This is the way the first series of five paper works called 'Bones' came about. These rather relief-like prototypes were followed by a three-dimensional six-part series called 'Unions'. The work material, besides paperpulp, was rags, brick mud, twine, bamboo, and brilliantly colored silk. Inspired by the traditional material of Indian

mühle. Auf ein Sieb goß man eine Lage Pulp und ordnete verschnürte Bambusstreifen sowie Stoffreste darauf an. Eine zweite Lage Pulp wurde darübergegossen, dann legte man die Arbeiten zwischen Filze und gautschte sie. Zum Trocknen wurden sie auf Gestelle gehängt. So entstand die erste Serie von fünf Papierarbeiten, ‚Bones'.
Diesen eher reliefartigen Prototypen folgte die dreidimensionale sechsteilige Serie ‚Unions'. Arbeitsmaterialien waren neben Papierstoff Lumpen, Ziegelschlamm, Zwirn, Bambus und hochglänzende Seide. Inspiriert vom traditionellen Material für den indischen Hausbau, luftgetrocknete Ziegel, begann Rauschenberg mit dem Ziegelschlamm in Verbindung mit Papierpulp zu experimentieren. Sein Bestreben war es, Papierpulp in irgendeiner Weise körperhaft zu gestalten. Aufgrund von Ratschlägen eines indischen Handwerkers entwickelte er eine Möglichkeit, Ziegelschlamm und Papierpulp zu kombinieren. „Traditionell werden dem Luftziegelschlamm gewisse Ingredienzen als Insektenschutz beigemengt. Diese aromatischen Gewürze, Griechenmoor-Pulver und gemahlene Tamarindensaat, wurden mit Kreide, Pflanzenharzpulver und Kupfersulfat vermischt. Dieses wurde zu einer Paste verarbeitet und in den Schlamm untergerührt. Rauschenberg bezeichnete die Masse als ‚Lumpen-Schlamm'."[133] Diesen „Lumpenschlamm" formte er mit seinen Händen und fügte Schnur, Zwirn, Bambus und hochglänzende Seide zu dreidimensionalen Objekten, den ‚Unions'.
Materialbilder sind für Robert Rauschenberg Ausdruck seiner Lebensphilosophie. Elemente der Alltagswelt führt er über eine poetische Bildsprache zur künstlerischen Komposition. Er zeigt das Ästhetische der Dinge, die im konsumgesteuerten Alltag ihrer Beachtung beraubt wurden. „Malerei hat sowohl mit der Kunst als auch mit dem Leben zu tun. Keines von beiden läßt sich künstlich herstellen... Ich meine, ein Bild ist wirklich, wenn es aus Teilen der wirklichen Welt gemacht ist."[134] Rauschenberg entwickelte 1953 seine ersten Combine paintings, denen eine Collagetechnik aus vorgefer-

housing, namely open-air dried adobe, Rauschenberg began to experiment with "adobe mud" in combination with paper. His goal was to give paperpulp in some way or other a bodily form. Based on the advice of an Indian artisan, he developed a means of combining adobe and paper. "The tradition in using this material was to add certain ingredients to the adobe to protect it from insects. These aromatic spices, fenugreek powder and ground tamarind seed were mixed with chalk powder, gum powder and copper sulphate. Gum powder and tamarind seed were mixed to a paste with water and then added to the mud. Rauschenberg called this substance 'rag mud'."[133] This "rag mud" Rauschenberg further shaped by hand and introduced rope, twine, bamboo and brilliantly colored silk into the three-dimensional objects, the 'Unions'.
Material paintings are for Robert Rauschenberg an expression of his philosophy of life. Via poetic images he brings elements of the everyday to an artful composition. He shows the aestheticism of objects that have been robbed of any value in a world of daily consumerism. "For Rauschenberg, painting has to do with art but also with life, neither of which can be produced artificially. A painting is real when it is made from parts of the real world."[134] In 1953 Rauschenberg had developed his first "combines", paintings based on a collage technique of pre-fabricated consumer articles and abstract easel paintings. The paper works can be considered as being in the distinct line of these combines. Materials typical of the place of artistic creation, with which and from which the inhabitants live, filtered by selection and recombination, are formulated into art.
Kenneth Noland (* 1924 Ashville/North Carolina) was one of the first well-known artists to deal intensively with paperpulp painting. With intelligence, originality, skill and fantasy he raised the craft of papermaking to the dimension of art. Noland recognized that working with colored paperpulp was faster and more direct than painting.

tigten Konsumartikeln und abstrakt gemaltem Tafelbild zu Grunde liegt. Die Papierarbeiten kann man als Sondergruppe der Combine paintings auffassen. Typische Materialien des Entstehungsortes, mit denen und von denen die Bewohner leben, werden durch Herausfiltern und Wiedervereinen zur Kunst formuliert.

Zu den ersten namhaften Künstlern, die sich intensiv mit Papierpulpmalerei auseinandersetzten, gehört Kenneth Noland (* 1924 in Ashville/North Carolina). Mit Intelligenz und Originalität, mit Geschick und Phantasie hat er das Handwerk des Papiermachens in die Dimension Kunst erhoben.

Noland erkannte, daß das Arbeiten mit farbigem Papierstoff schneller und direkter ist als Malen. Ein Pinsel ist nicht nötig, man arbeitet mit den Händen. An die Stelle einer leeren Leinwand kann ein bereits farbig gestalteter Papiergrund treten. Form- und Farbstrukturen entstehen aus übereinandergeschichteten farbigen Pulps, auch können ausgeschnittene Papiere und alle möglichen Materialien in die Papierschichten eingebettet werden. Es ist

A brush is unnecessary; you work with your hands. An empty canvas is replaced by an already color-worked ground of paper. Structures of form and color arise from the overlayering of dyed pulp; cutout paper and every possible material can also be imbedded into these paper layers. It is possible to emboss structures or have them determined by the kind of mould used. Paper was at times his favorite medium because it fulfilled his specific understanding of a direct treatment of color and texture. Noland's first paper works were done in 1976 when he participated in a paper workshop given by the sculptor, Garner Tullis, at Bennington College. Making paper by hand so inspired Noland that, on his return to Vermont, he set up a paper studio in North Hoosick/New York.

For Noland, papermaking became just as familiar a procedure as applying color to canvas, for him it was a transfer process. He need not wait for the color to dry or the acids to bite; and, above all, he was not dependent on anyone else to do the printing.

Kenneth Noland und Kenneth Tyler arbeiten an ‚Horizontal Stripes', 1978 /
Kenneth Noland and Kenneth Tyler working on 'Horizontal Stripes', 1978

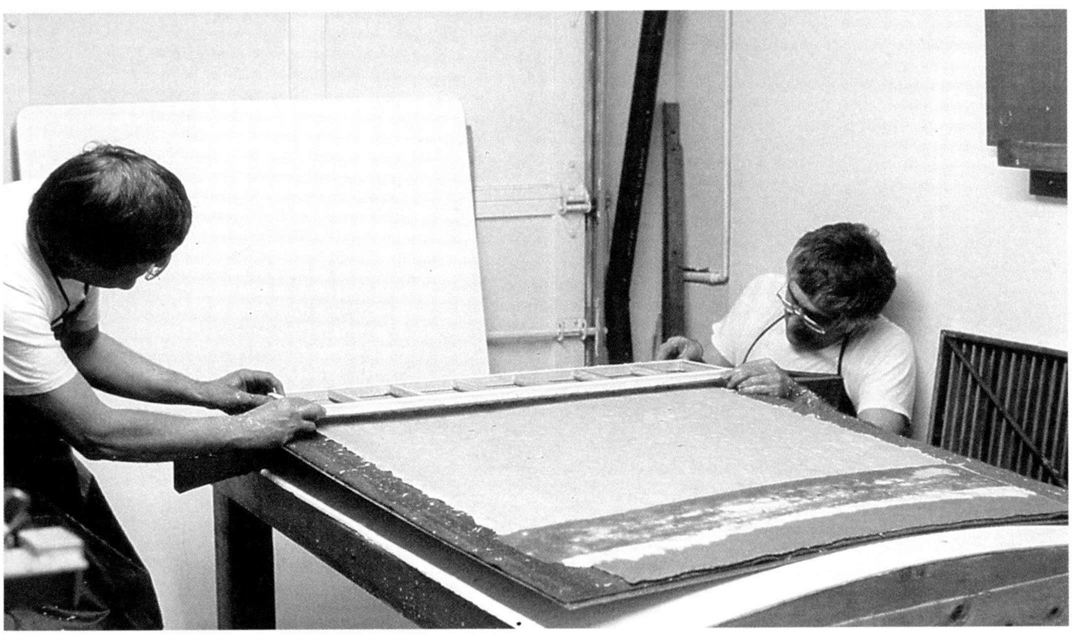

Kenneth Noland: Circle I, II – 42
(aus dem ‚Handmade Paper Project'),
1978. Gefärbter und gepreßter Papierpulp. Monoprint. 50,8 x 40,6 cm /
Kenneth Noland: Circle I, II – 42
(from the 'Handmade Paper Project'),
1978. Colored and pressed paper
pulp. Monoprint. 50.8 x 40.6 cm.

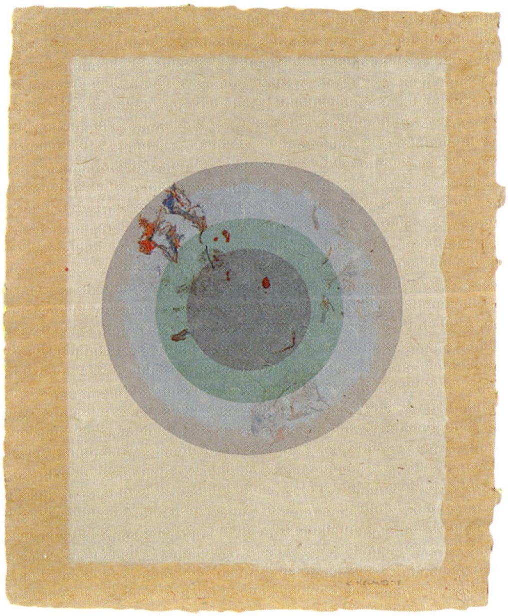

möglich, Strukturen einzuprägen oder gleich von der Siebbeschaffenheit bestimmen zu lassen. Papier wurde für Noland zeitweise bevorzugtes Medium, weil hier sein spezifisches Verständnis vom direkten Umgang mit Farbe und mit Textur möglich ist.

Seine ersten Papierarbeiten schuf Noland 1976, als er an einem Papier-Workshop teilnahm, den der Bildhauer Garner Tullis am Bennington-College gab. Das Papierschöpfen begeisterte Noland so, daß er nach seiner Rückkehr aus Vermont ein Papierstudio in North Hoosick/New York, einrichtete. Für ihn war die Papierherstellung ein genauso vertrauter Vorgang wie das Auftragen von Farbe auf die Leinwand, sie erschien ihm wie ein Umwandlungsprozeß. Er mußte nicht darauf warten, daß Farbe trocknete oder Säuren ihre Wirkung taten, und er war vor allem von niemandem abhängig wie beim Drucken.

Für die Werkstatt von Tyler Graphics war die Zusammenarbeit mit Kenneth Noland eines der ersten Großprojekte. 1978 entstanden mehr als 200 Werke aus Papierpulp, und zwar Nolands Serien ‚Circles', ‚Horizontal Stripes' und ‚Diagonal Stripes'. Das Wesentliche dieser Blätter ist die Be-

One of the first large projects done in the workshop of Tyler Graphics was the collaboration with Kenneth Noland. In 1978 more than 200 images out of paperpulp were produced, Noland's series 'Circles', 'Horizontal Stripes' and 'Diagonal Stripes'. The essential feature of these works is the treatment of paperpulp as color applied in the elemental geometric forms of rectangle and circle. At first glance the different images produced seem similar, but not one is the same as the next. The colors vary in many tones, from nebulous blues and bright yellows to delicate purples or murky greys. Sometimes the image dominates, sometimes the structure. The surface can be fragile and wafer-thin or thick like incrusted cardboard. Noland used oriental and western fibers as well as particles of colored paper. Before beginning each series, sometimes before each image, he decided on the color, the texture and the thickness of the base sheet. He chose the rags to be cut up into pulp and later dyed and, by his choice of mould, determined the format of the sheet. The kind of mould also determined the texture, the thickness, and the translucency of the paper. Then began the painting process with colored pulp. This is kept in buckets or containers and classified by color. Noland

Kenneth Noland: Horizontal Stripes I–5 (aus dem ‚Handmade Paper Project'), 1978. Gefärbter und gepreßter Papierpulp. 130 x 85 cm / Kenneth Noland: Horizontal Stripes I–5 (from the 'Handmade Paper Project'), 1978. Colored and pressed paper pulp. 130 x 85 cm. © Tyler Graphics Ltd.

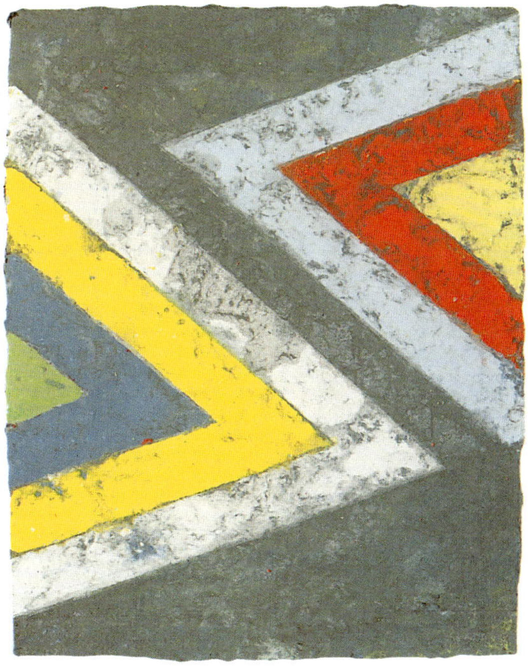

Kenneth Noland: Diagonal Stripes TP VI–3 (aus dem ‚Handmade Paper Project'), 1978. Gefärbter und gepreßter Papierpulp. 110 x 85 cm / Kenneth Noland: Diagonal Stripes TP VI–3 (from the 'Handmade Paper Project'), 1978. Colored and pressed paper pulp. 110 x 85 cm. © Tyler Graphics Ltd.

handlung des Papierstoffs als Farbe in den reduzierten geometrischen Formen von Rechteck und Kreis. Auf den ersten Blick ähneln sich viele Arbeiten, doch kein Blatt gleicht dem anderen. Die Farben variieren in vielfach schillernden Tönen, von trübem Blau und kräftigem Gelb bis hin zu zartem Purpur oder verwaschenem Grau. Manchmal dominiert die Farbe, manchmal die Struktur. Die Oberfläche kann zart und hauchdünn sein oder dick wie verkrusteter Karton. Noland verwandte orientalische und westliche Fasern sowie Farbpapierpartikel. Vor jeder Serie, manchmal vor jedem Blatt, bestimmte er zunächst die Materialität, die Farbe, Textur und Dicke des Basisblattes. Er suchte die Fasern aus, die, zu Stoff zerkleinert, später gefärbt werden und mit Hilfe eines Siebes die Blattform erhalten. Die Art des Siebes bestimmt die Griffigkeit, die Dicke, die Struktur und Lichtdurchlässigkeit des Papiers. Dann beginnt die Malerei mit farbigem Papierstoff.

Er befindet sich in Eimern oder Behältern, geordnet nach Farben. Verschiedenste Blau- und Grüntöne, alle möglichen Töne in Gelb, Grau, Fuchsia, Pfirsich wählte Noland. Er mischte und kreierte an die hundert Farbtöne. Auf das Basispapier legte er einen Plastikrahmen, dessen Stege die Flächenformen der Darstellung bestimmen. In die Felder drückte und klopfte er farbigen Pulp, manchmal verschmierte er ihn mit den Händen, um unregelmäßige Kanten zu erzielen, oder schüttete Wasser über den Pulp, damit die Farbe ins Basisblatt versickerte und ausblutete. Nach Beendigung der Farbaufschichtungen wurde der Plastikrahmen entfernt und die nasse Malerei zwischen Filzen gepreßt. Die verschiedenen, noch feuchten Papierflieslagen verbinden sich nun zu einer durchgehenden Oberfläche untrennbar miteinander.

Das Pressen verändert das Aussehen des Bildes. In nassem Zustand ist das Gemälde dick und farbig brillant. Der Trocknungsprozeß läßt die Farbe eigenartig gesättigt und matt werden. Auch dringen die aufeinandergeschichteten farbigen Pulps ineinander und vermischen sich zu neuen Farbtönen.

chose different tones of blue and of green, all imaginable tones in yellow, gray, fuchsia, peach. He mixed and created up to one hundred hues. Onto the base sheet he laid a plexiglass frame divided into bands that determined the shape of the surface presentation. He pressed and patted the colored pulp into these bands, sometimes smearing it on with his hands so as to obtain irregular edges, or poured water over the pulp so that the color of the base paper oozed and bled. After the stratification of color was completed, the plastic frame was removed and the wet painting pressed between felt layers. The levels of still damp paper now became fused into an unbroken and inseparable surface.

Hydraulic compression changes the appearance of a picture. In a wet condition the painting is thick and glossy-colored. The drying procedure gives it a strangely matte look. The stratified layers of colored pulp permeate each other and become contiguous, creating new hues.

Once dried, the paintings were then very sparingly reworked; Noland stained the work with new color, did additional screenprinting or, in the case of 'Circles' for instance, added lithographic circles. The base paper of 'Circle I' he chose in peach or beige made from a laid mould. Onto this he couched a ragged-edge, colored circle from a wove mould and onto this another smaller transparent, rectangular sheet. He made the second rectangle with a flexible mould from one of three oriental fibers – Kozo, Gampi and Mitsumata. Bright bits of cutup rag paper, wool and silk threads were added. All the layers meld together and produce a new color scheme. The final circle (printed by lithographic process) overlaps the paper and the pulp and creates additional colors.

For 'Circle II' Noland couched onto the rectangular sheet a smaller one from the same color pulp so that the two forms subtly echo each other. Then he couched three concentric, differently-colored circles onto the sheet and into the center a ring of Gampi fiber. The finely articulated gampi fibers accentuate the circlular shape.

Die trockenen Gemälde bearbeitete Noland anschließend sparsam weiter, indem er Farbe in das Blatt einbeizte, im Siebdruckverfahren behandelte oder bei den ‚Circles' beispielsweise mit Hilfe der Lithographie Kreise aufdruckte.

Das Basisblatt in ‚Circle I' wählte er pfirsich- bzw. beigefarben, geschöpft auf einem gerippten Sieb. Darauf gautschte er einen gekanteten farbigen Kreis, geschöpft mit einem gewebten Sieb, und darüber ein kleines, transparentes, rechteckiges Blatt. Ein zweites Rechteck stellte er aus den drei orientalischen Fasern Kozo, Gampi und Mitsumata mit Hilfe eines beweglichen Bambussiebs her. Helle Stücke zerschnittenes Papier, Wolle und Seidenfäden fügte er ein. Alle Schichten durchdringen sich, erzeugen neue Farbigkeiten. Der im lithographischen Verfahren aufgedruckte Kreis, der Papiere und Pulp überlappt, läßt weitere Farben entstehen.

In ‚Circles II' gautschte Noland auf das rechteckige Rundblatt ein quadratisches in gleicher Struktur und gleicher Farbe, so daß die beiden Rechtecke

With each series Noland developed his process further. He discovered new ways to use paperpulp like paint.[135]

In the following months of the year 1978, from August to October, another sensational painting project was initiated. The English painter and graphic artist, David Hockney (* 1937 Bradford/Great Britain), created 29 pictures of colored paperpulp. Hockney turned enthusiastically to this new medium that fuses painting with paper production. Tyler had shown him the paperpulp work that Kenneth Noland and Ellsworth Kelly had done. "They were stunningly beautiful," Hockney found with surprise. "This was a thing I had never seen or used before. I think mediums can turn you on... So I said I'll have a go [...] Ken explained that you can add dyes to the pulp and the color would be more vivid and stronger than applying paint on the surface... Using this process, you are forced to be very bold, and you cannot be finicky with it, you can't use lines at all. At first I said, I love using lines... But gradually I realized that you

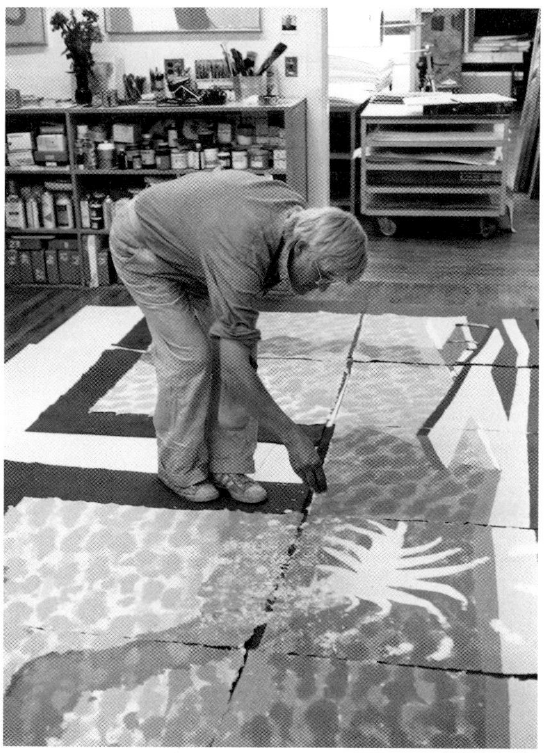

David Hockney streut gefärbten Pulp auf einen Teil des zwölfteiligen ‚Paper Pool' (‚A Large Diver'), 1978 / David Hockney sprinkling bits of colored pulp onto a section of the 12 panel 'Paper Pool' entitled 'A Large Diver', 1978.
© Tyler Graphics Ltd.

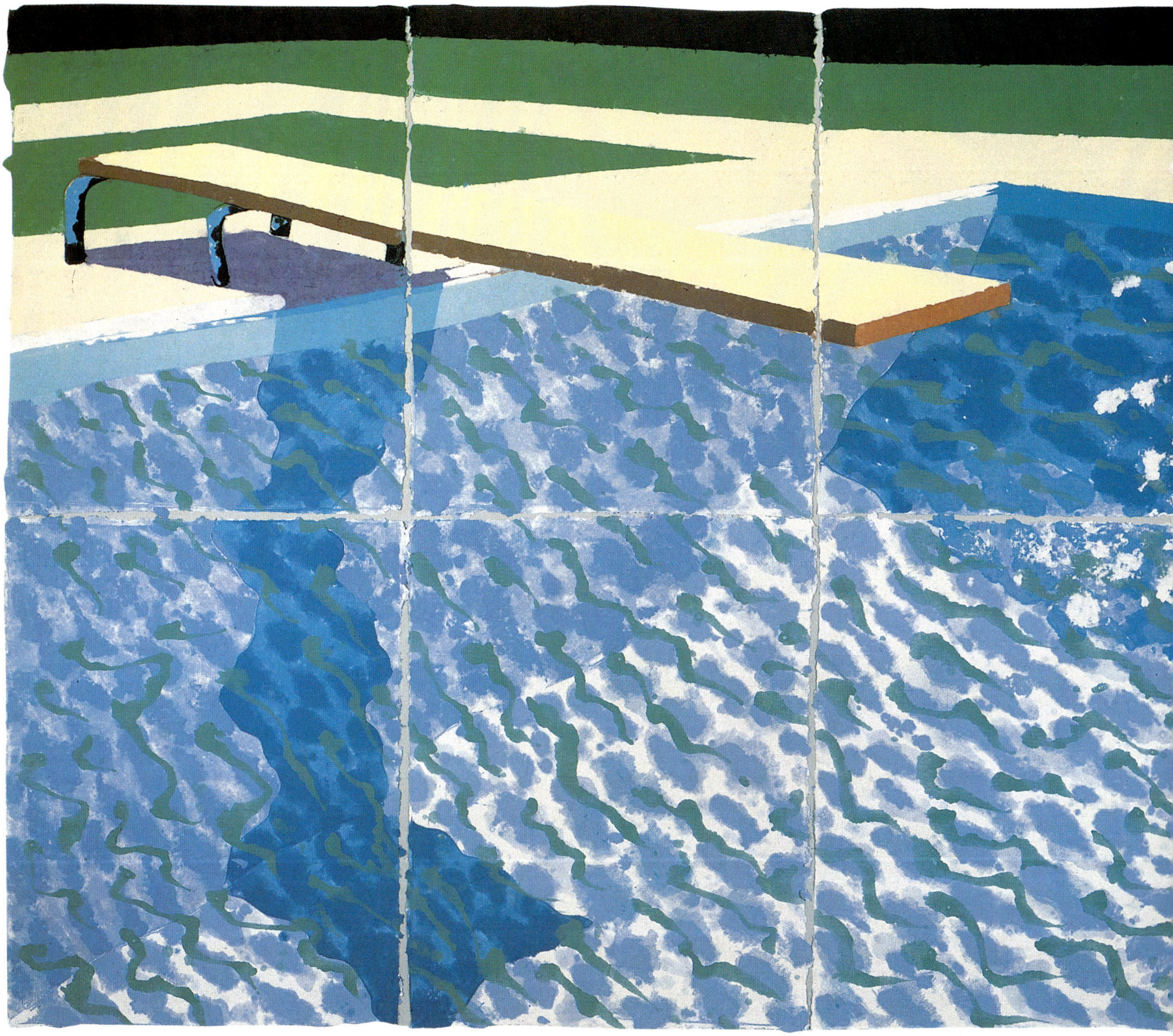

David Hockney: A Large Diver (Paper Pool 27), 1978. Gefärbter und gepreßter Papierpulp. 12 Blätter. 183 x 434 cm / David Hockney: A Large Diver (Paper Pool 27), 1978. Colored and pressed paper pulp. 12 sheets. 183 x 434 cm. © Tyler Graphics Ltd.

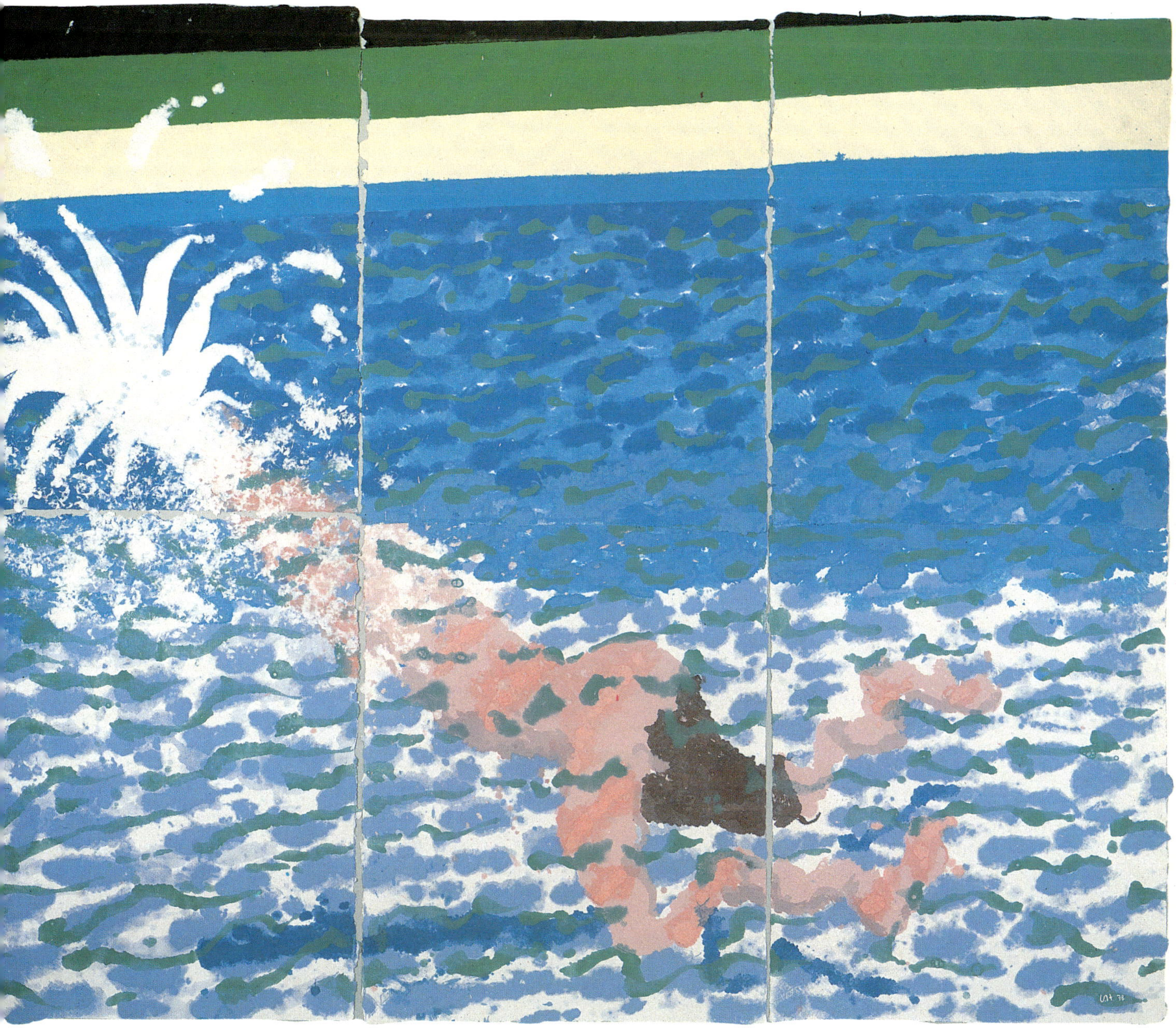

zartfarben korrespondieren. Dann gautschte er drei konzentrische, verschiedenfarbene Kreise in die Mitte des Blattes und ins Zentrum einen Klumpen Gampifasern. Die feinzeichnende Gampifaser verstärkt die Kreisform.

In jeder Serie entwickelte Noland das Verfahren weiter. Er fand neue Wege, Papierpulp wie Farbe zu verwenden.[135]

In den anschließenden Monaten des Jahres 1978, von August bis Oktober, entstand bei Tyler Graphics ein weiteres Aufsehen erregendes Malereiprojekt. Der englische Maler und Zeichner David Hockney (* 1937 in Bradford/Großbritannien) schuf zusammen mit Kenneth Tyler 29 farbige Papierpulpbilder. Mit Enthusiasmus wandte Hockney sich der neuen Technik zu, in der Malerei und Papiergewinnung ineinander verschmelzen. Tyler hatte ihm Papierpulpmalereien von Kenneth Noland und Ellsworth Kelly gezeigt. „Sie sind atemberaubend schön", äußerte Hockney staunend. „Nie zuvor hatte ich so etwas gesehen oder angewandt. Ich entschloß mich, das neue Medium zu erproben, neue Medien faszinieren mich [...] Ken erklärte mir, daß man dem Papierpulp Farben beimischen kann, daß die Farbe lebendiger und stärker als beim Auftragen auf die Oberfläche wirkt [...] Man muß sehr großflächig arbeiten, nicht kleinteilig oder genau, man kann keine Linien verwenden [...] Dies störte mich zunächst, da die Linie in meiner Arbeit wichtig ist. Aber nach und nach erkannte ich, daß man mit Sieben und Schablonen so arbeiten kann, als ob man die Umrisse ‚zeichnete'. Alle Farben goß man einfach in die Schablonen nebeneinander; der Metallsteg trennte sie. Diese imaginäre Linie blieb auch nach dem Pressen und Trocknen."[136]

Hockney entschied sich, nicht wie Noland oder Kelly abstrakt mit Papierpulp zu malen. Als erster Künstler erprobte er im neuen Medium die gegenständliche Malerei mit schlichten, eindeutigen Farbformen. Als Thema wählte er Tylers Swimmingpool. Tagelang studierte er den Pool, zeichnete und fotografierte ihn zu verschiedensten Tages- und Nachtzeiten, beobachtete die Licht- und Farbverän-

could work with moulds, as if 'drawing' the form with little metal moulds, and pour all the colours next to one another."[136]

Hockney decided not to paint abstractions with paperpulp as Noland and Kelly had done. He was the first artist who tried out the new medium using the stark, simple color forms of representational painting. As his theme he chose Tyler's swimming-pool. For days he studied the pool, drew and photgraphed it at all times of the day and night, observed the light and colors changes, the distortions in form caused by a diver. Finally Hockney had established his color scale and completed his standardized color drawings. Moulds of tin metal were constructed to conform with the shapes on the drawings. These stencils of bold and simple forms were laid onto the freshly made base sheets. Hockney then poured colored paperpulp into the empty moulds and afterwards carefully removed the moulds. He completed the work with direct, freehand application of colored pulp and paint. Pulp in liquid form was spooned on, poured, painted on, dripped. Sometimes he toned down the hard edges by smearing or beating them with his hands or fingers. Utensils such as brushes, combs, a garden hose or also rain served to attain certain textures or effects.

Water is a subject on which Hockney has created variations ever since 1964. It fascinated him to fix a moving element like water into a motionless picture. The swimming-pool interested him as an artifcial container for nature that was set up in nature: the reflection of light on and below its surface, the transparency of the water, the effects of shade on the pool floor, the distortion of forms under water, the disembodied shadows of a diver, and the idea of painting water in a medium that had been produced with untold quantities of water. "The point about water is you can look at it in so many different ways; it's always different; you can choose what you want to look at... I was using my hands in the pulp, trying to blend colour into colour. These have the most mysteries; they looked,

derungen und die Formverzerrungen eines Tauchers. Schließlich legte Hockney seine Farbskala fest und fertigte die maßstabgerechten Farbzeichnungen. Auf der Grundlage dieser Zeichnungen wurden die Schablonen aus galvanisierten Metallstreifen konstruiert. Die Schablonen mit den einfachen, kühnen Formen legte man auf die frischgeschöpften Basisblätter. Die leeren Schablonenformen goß Hockney voll mit farbigem Pulp. Am Ende wurden die Schablonen vorsichtig entfernt. Er beendete die Arbeit durch freihändiges, direktes Auftragen von farbigem Pulp und flüssiger Farbe. Flüssiger Pulp wurde aufgelöffelt, gegossen, gemalt, getropft. Manchmal milderte Hockney die Kanten durch Verstreichen oder Einklopfen mit den Händen oder Fingern. Hilfsmittel wie Bürsten, Kämme, ein Gartenschlauch oder auch der Regen dienten der Erzielung bestimmter Texturen und Effekte.

Wasser ist ein Thema, das Hockney seit 1964 immer wieder variierte. Ihn fasziniert die Vorstellung, das niemals stillstehende Wasser in ein bewegungsloses Bild zu bannen; ihn interessiert das Schwimmbad als künstlich geschaffener Behälter für Natur, aufgestellt in der Natur, die Spiegelung des Lichtes auf der Oberfläche und darunter, die Durchsichtigkeit des Wassers, die Schattenwirkungen auf dem Grund, die Verzerrung der Formen unter Wasser, der entmaterialisierte Schatten eines Tauchers und die Vorstellung, Wasser zu malen mit einem Medium, das mit unendlich viel Wasser hergestellt wird.

Wasser kann man auf sehr unterschiedliche Weise betrachten. Man kann sich aussuchen, was man sehen will. Nachts bei eingeschaltetem Unterwasserlicht blickt man direkt unter die Oberfläche, weil das Licht im Schwimmbad an der Oberfläche des Wassers aufhört. Alles darüber ist Schwarz, ebenso das Sprungbrett, unter dem das Licht angebracht ist. „Mit Wasser ist es so – es sieht immer anders aus, je nachdem, wie man schaut; man kann sich aussuchen, was man anschauen möchte [...]“, stellte Hockney fest. „Ich faßte den Pulp mit

they even began to make the swimming-pool begin to look mysterious...as if it's all from 'The Magic Flute'," Hockney related.[137]

In the first works of his series 'Paper Pools', Hockney was satisfied with the largest paper format that Tyler could create (127 cm x 81 cm). But this did not satisfy him for long. At first Hockney took six of these base papers, later he took twelve, and put them down side by side and worked on them as on one large painting. The four and a half meter long picture that ensued was created freehand, without moulds. He simply used a piece of metal to fix the borders between color fields while pouring the pulp onto the base sheet.

At the end of his work David Hockney declared: "Finally I realized, because I had these buckets full of blue and buckets full of green, if this was paint and I was doing a painting I wouldn't have the nerve to just throw it around like this and pour it on. [...] [These pictures] probably look better in real life than they do in reproduction because the paper is very beautiful, the surface, there is no such thing as a flat colour, and they are very subtle at times. They are like painting... And they also helped me in another way: painting in England before I kept saying I thought the paintings were getting too gray, too tight and I kept getting finicky and I wanted to be bolder; I figured it was harder to be bolder and these works now allowed me to be bolder."[138]

'Colored Paper Images' is what Ellsworth Kelly (* 1923 Newburgh/New York), the main exponent of the "hard-edge" school, called his paper paintings that he made exclusively out of colored paper pulp. They came about during an eight-month stay at Tyler Graphics in 1976 with the assistance of Tyler and John Koller. Kelly laid colored pulp he had designed and shaped by moulds onto still wet, white, handmade paper. In order to test the special tones and shades, Kelly mixed about 50 different colors. During compression the colors bled a little. A series of 20 prints in an edition of 9 to 23 variations resulted.

den Händen an, versuchte, die Farben miteinander zu mischen. Die Farben hatten etwas Geheimnisvolles, eine geheimnisvolle Ausstrahlung; durch sie wirkte selbst der Swimming-pool geheimnisvoll ... wie aus einem Märchen."[137]

In den ersten Arbeiten seiner Serie ‚Paper Pools' begnügte Hockney sich mit dem größten Format eines Basisblattes (127 x 81 cm), das Tyler schöpfen konnte. Doch dies genügte Hockney für seine Kompositionen bald nicht mehr. Also legte er zunächst sechs Basisblätter, später zwölf Basisblätter nebeneinander, an denen er gleichzeitig übergreifend wie an einem großen Gemälde arbeitete. Die viereinhalb Meter langen Bilder entstanden sogar freihändig, ohne Schablonen. Für die geraden Abgrenzungen zwischen den Farbflächen benutzte er einfach ein Stück Metall, während er den Farbpulp auf das Basisblatt goß.

Am Ende seiner Arbeit stellte David Hockney fest: „Schließlich erkannte ich angesichts dieser Eimer mit blauer und grüner Farbe, der Farbe, mit der ich malen würde, daß ich sie nicht einfach umstoßen und über das Bild gießen konnte. [...] [Diese Bilder] sehen vielleicht besser im Original aus als in einer Reproduktion, weil das Papier, seine Oberfläche wunderschön ist, da gibt es keine verwaschene Farbe, gleichzeitig sind die Farben aber sehr nuanciert. Sie sind wie ein Gemälde... Und sie besaßen einen weiteren Vorteil: Als ich in England malte, sagte ich immer, ich hätte den Eindruck, die Bilder würden zu grau, zu wenig großzügig, ich empfand mich als zu pedantisch, und ich wollte großzügiger arbeiten; ich kam zu dem Schluß, daß es schwierig sei, großzügiger zu arbeiten, und in diesen Arbeiten hatte ich die Chance, es zu werden."[138]

‚Colored Paper Images' nennt der Hauptvertreter des „hard edge" Ellsworth Kelly (* 1923 Newburgh/ New York) seine Papiermalereien, die er ausschließlich mit farbigem Papierpulp gestaltete. Sie entstanden während eines achtmonatigen Aufenthaltes bei Tyler Graphics im Jahr 1976 unter der Mithilfe von Tyler und John Koller. Auf noch nasses,

The intention of these 20 paper paintings was to give the color its own "concrete" reality. In prints I to XII Kelly formed the mostly bright colored planes organically soft and geometrically sharp. In prints XIII to XX he set clear color planes in the form of broad stripes, triangles and rectangles to vie with each other. These cannot claim to be truely monochrome, since the color planes shimmer like moiré.[139]

Frank Stella (*1936 Malden/Massachusetts) has since 1966 carried out several graphic projects with Tyler. In 1975 he made a series of reliefs that he shaped solely from paperpulp. Onto a traditional dipping screen the moulds for the different segments of the relief were sewn. After many trials the paper quality was found that gave the best and most stable form. For technical reasons it was necessary to dry the wet composition on the mould for 72 hours; not till then did the paper attain the correct firmness. Each of the almost 200 reliefs, consisting of six basic forms, was individually

Ellsworth Kelly arbeitet an ‚Colored Paper Images', 1976 /
Ellsworth Kelly working on 'Colored Paper Images', 1976.

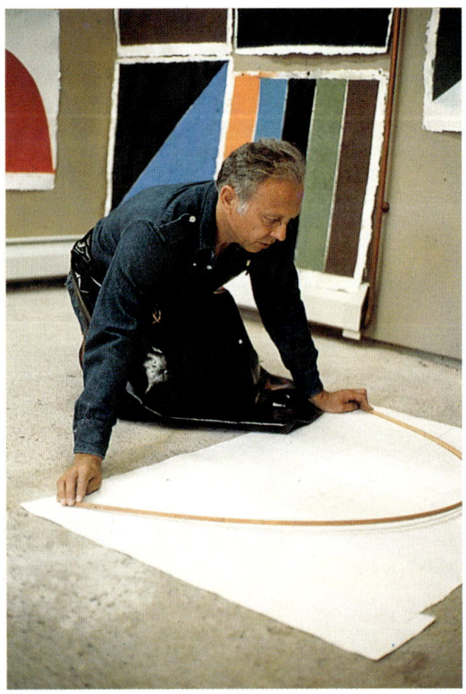

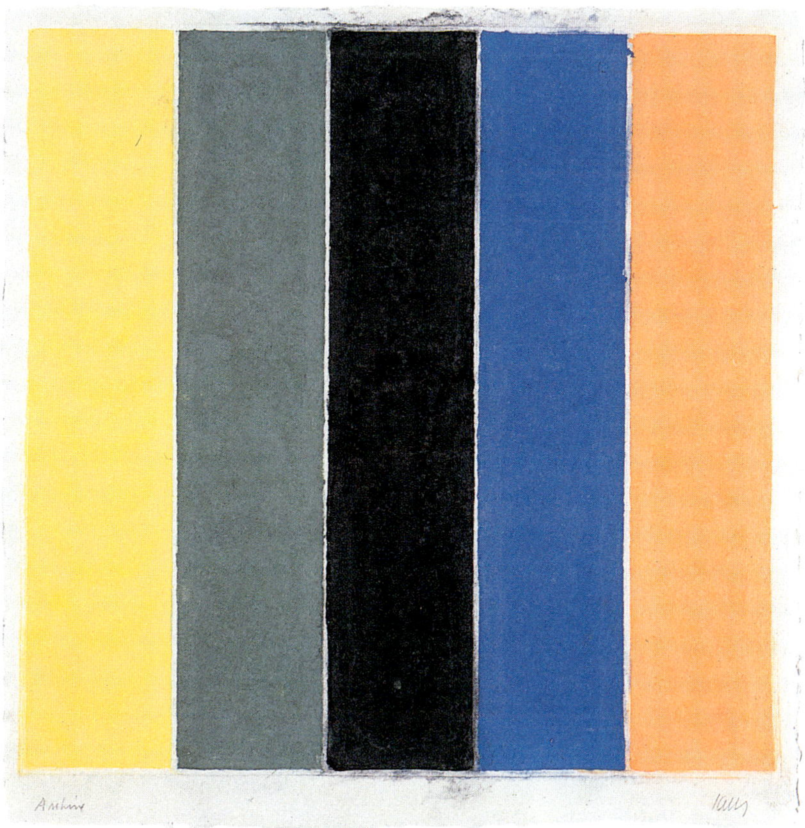

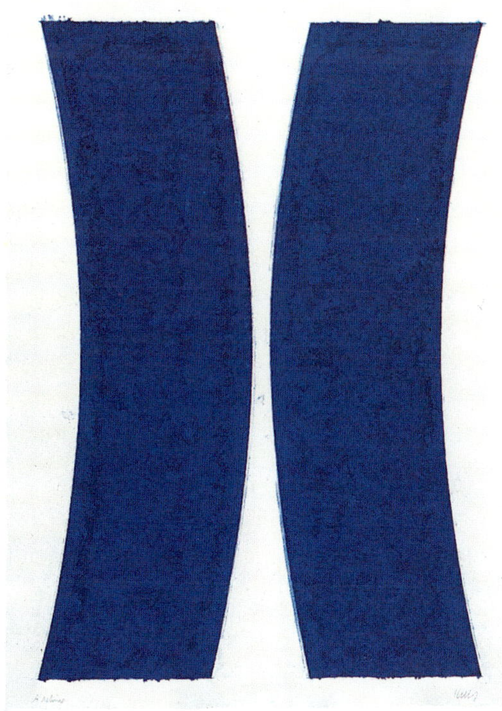

Ellsworth Kelly: Colored Paper Image XIII, 1976. Gefärbter und gepreßter Papierpulp. 81,9 x 79,4 cm / Ellsworth Kelly: Colored Paper Image XIII, 1976. Colored and pressed paper pulp. 81.9 x 79.4 cm. © Tyler Graphics Ltd.

Ellsworth Kelly: Colored Paper Image V, 1976. Gefärbter und gepreßter Papierpulp. 118,1 x 82,6 cm / Ellsworth Kelly: Colored Paper Image V, 1976. Colored and pressed paper pulp. 118.1 x 82.6 cm © Tyler Graphics Ltd.

weißes geschöpftes Papier brachte Kelly Lagen von gefärbtem Pulp, geformt durch Schablonen, die er entworfen hatte. Um die speziellen Farbtöne und Farbschattierungen zu erproben, mischte er an die 50 Farben. Während des Preßvorgangs bluteten die Farben ein wenig aus. Es entstand eine Serie von 20 Blättern in einer Edition von jeweils 9 bis 23 Variationen.

Die Intention dieser 20 Papiermalereien ist es, der Farbe eine eigene ‚konkrete' Realität zu geben. In den Blättern I bis XII formte Kelly die meist starkfarbene Farbfläche organisch weich und geometrisch klar. In den Blättern XIII bis XX setzte er klare Farbflächen in Form von breiten Streifen, Dreiecken und Vierecken gegeneinander. Eine exakte tatsächliche Monochromie liegt nicht vor. Die Farbflächen changieren in sich in vielfachen Werten.[139]

Frank Stella (* 1936 Malden/Massachusetts) hatte seit 1966 grafische Projekte zusammen mit Tyler durchgeführt. 1975 entstand eine Reihe von Reliefs, die er allein aus Papierpulp formte. Auf ein traditionelles Schöpfsieb wurden die Schablonen für die Reliefsegmente aufgenäht. Nach langen Versuchen fand man diejenige Papierqualität, die am besten eine stabile Form ergab. Aus technischen Gründen wurde es notwendig, daß die nasse Papierreliefkomposition auf der Schöpfform 72 Stunden trocknete; erst dann hatte das in Form geschöpfte Papier seine Festigkeit erlangt. Jedes der nahezu 200 Reliefs, bestehend aus sechs Grundformen, collagierte oder bemalte Stella individuell. Die Relieffierungen unterliegen sowohl in den Farben wie auch in den Formen rhythmisch variierenden Prinzipien. Ein spannungsreiches Spiel von Farben und Formen erzeugt Schwingungen im visuellen Raum.[140]

Ein Hauptwerkzeug ist für Alan Shields (* 1944 Harrington/Kansas) die Nähmaschine. Bereits während seiner Studienzeit kam er, sicherlich beeinflußt von den genähten und ausgestopften Stoffobjekten von Claes Oldenburg, auf den Gedanken, Leinwände mit einer Nähmaschine zusammenzusetzen. Das Studio des Künstlers wirkt ungewöhn-

collaged or painted by Stella. The relief effects, in color as well as in form, are subject to rhythmically varied principles. A highly wrought play of color and form generates visual vibrations in space.[140]

For Alan Shields (* 1944 Harrington/Kansas) a prime tool has proved to be the sewing machine. Already during his student days, certainly influenced by the sewn and stuffed cloth objects of Claes Oldenburg, he got the idea to stich canvases together on a sewing machine. The studio of the artist looks unusual: next to stacked bolts of silk and cotton material, as well as twine, sewing machines can be seen, also the kind that work automatically and simultaneously with thick and thin thread.

Alan Shields has since 1971 often worked in the medium of paper and done so using very different techniques. Together with William Weege and Joe Wilfer, who ran the Jones Road Print Shop and the Upper U.S. Paper Mill in Wisconsin, respectively, he designed about 30 editions. His first project with Kenneth Tyler he carried out in 1978, followed by others in 1980 and 1984/85. Shields was enthusiastic about the new possibilities that Tyler had discovered for working with paperpulp and handmade paper, especially the new dimensions that the vacuum table with separate pump now made feasible. Shields said: "Ken expanded the papermaking far beyond my wildest dreams."[141]

In the late 80s Alan Shields worked together with the paper sculptress, Karen Stahlecker, in Achorage/Alaska, where she was teaching at the Visual Art Center and at the university. Alan Shields used a great range of techniques which gave his paper works their very tactile effect, their rich scale of color and their sculptural impact with many angles of light and shade. The works mostly consist of several layers of handmade sheets of paper of different thickness and fiber texture. The base sheet is either left white or is worked up graphically into color. Over this, for instance, voluminous sheets of latticed paper are laid, one on top of the other. The latticework looks like relicts of a picture that has

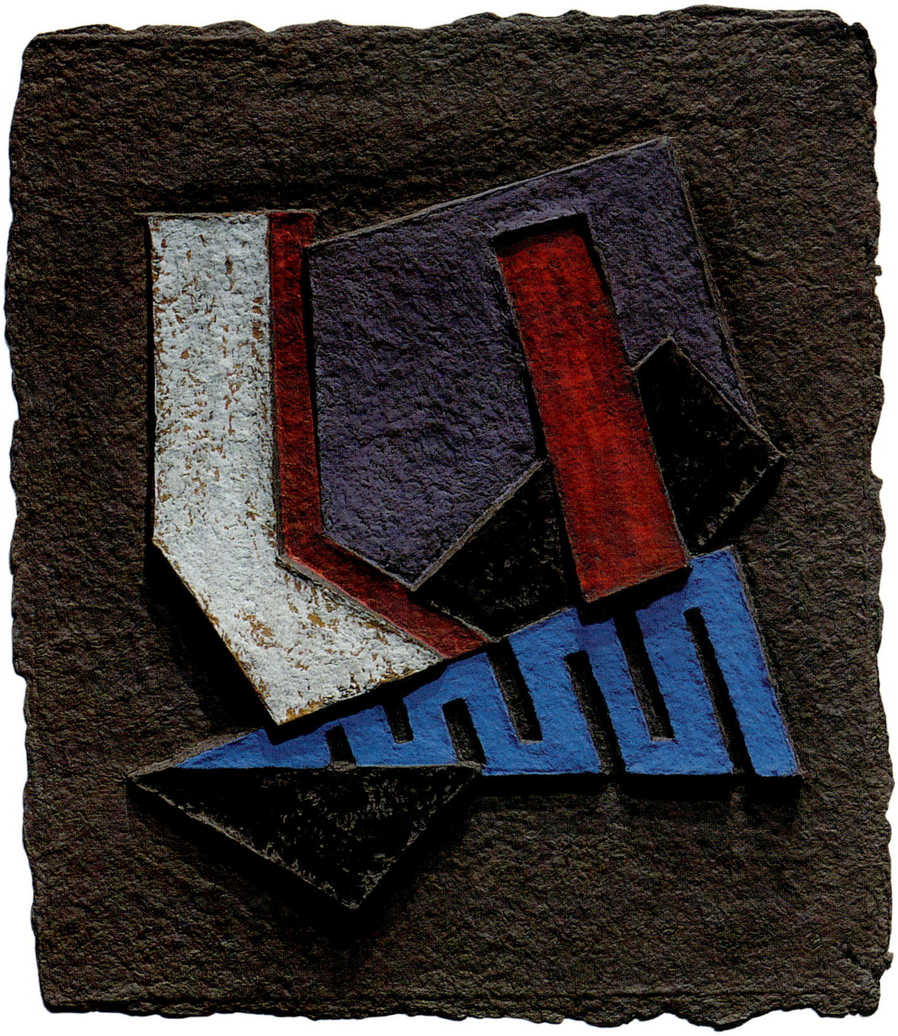

Frank Stella: Kozangródek (II), T. P. 9 (aus dem ‚Paper Relief Project'), 1975. Gefärbter und gepreßter Papierpulp; handkoloriert. 66 x 54,6 x 4,4 cm / Frank Stella: Kozangródek (II), T. P. 9 (from the 'Paper Relief Project'), 1975. Colored and pressed paper pulp, hand colored. 66 x 54.6 x 4.4 cm. © Tyler Graphics Ltd.

lich: Neben gestapelten Seiden- und Baumwollstoffballen sowie Garnen sieht man Nähmaschinen, auch solche, die automatisch und simultan sowohl mit dicken als auch dünnen Garnen produzieren.
Im Medium Papier arbeitet Alan Shields seit 1971 immer wieder und in Verbindung mit unterschiedlichsten Techniken. An die 30 Editionen gestaltete er zunächst zusammen mit William Weege und Joe Wilfer, die in Wisconsin den Jones Road Print Shop und die Upper U.S. Paper Mill betreiben. Sein erstes Projekt mit Kenneth Tyler führte Shields 1978 durch; es folgten weitere in den Jahren 1980 und 1984/85. Shields war begeistert von den neuen Möglichkeiten, die Tyler für das Arbeiten mit Papierpulp und handgeschöpftem Papier gefunden hatte. Vor allem der Vakuumtisch mit einer separaten Absaugpumpe eröffnete neue Dimensionen. Shields äußerte: „Ken Tyler expandierte die Papiermacherei in Regionen, die ich mir in meinen wildesten Träumen nicht vorgestellt hatte.“[141] In den späten 80er Jahren arbeitete Alan Shields mit der Papierbildhauerin Karen Stahlecker in Anchorage/Alaska, zusammen, die dort am Visual Art Center und an der Universität lehrt. Für seine Papierarbeiten nutzt er eine große Bandbreite an Techniken, um die überaus haptische Wirkung, die palettenreiche Farbigkeit und die plastische Wirkung, Licht- und Schatteneinfälle eingeschlossen, zu erzielen. Die Werke bestehen meist aus mehreren Lagen von geschöpften Blättern unterschiedlicher Dicke und Faserkonsistenz. Das Basisblatt bleibt entweder weiß oder wird grafisch farbenreich gestaltet. Darüber erheben sich beispielsweise voluminöse, geschöpfte Papiere in Gittermuster, auch mehrere übereinander. Die Gitterstäbe wirken wie Relikte eines weggeschnittenen Bildes. Der Blick auf das Bild des Basisblattes wird zwar ermöglicht, doch die Gitterformationen der darüberliegenden Papierschichten verdecken weite Bereiche. Gleichzeitig eröffnen sie jedoch neue Dimensionen von Farbe und Raum. Andere Werke zeigen ein Deckblatt mit Ritz- oder Lochmuster, so daß das Basisblatt lediglich durchschimmert. Die verschiedenen Papierlagen sind zusammengenäht.

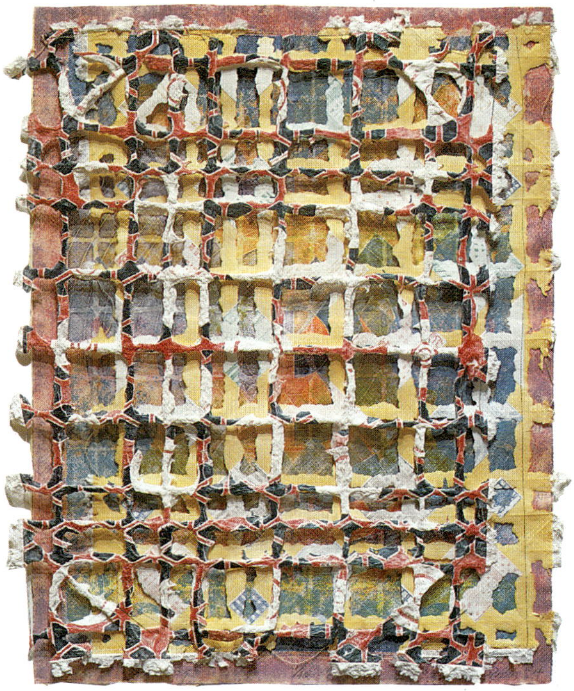

Alan Shields: Milan Fog, 1984. Holzschnitt, Radierung, Aquatinta, genäht, collagiert, handgeschöpftes Papier. 101 x 81,3 cm / Alan Shields: Milan Fog, 1984. Woodcut, etching, aquatint, stitching, collage, handmade paper. 101 x 81.3 cm. © Tyler Graphics Ltd.

been cut away. Though the view onto the base sheet is possible, the lattice design of the paper layer above it covers large areas. At the same time it creates new dimensions of color and space. Other works have a cover sheet with patterns of slits or holes, so that the base sheet only shimmers

Alan Shields (links) und Steve Reeves ziehen einen Druck von ‚Uncle Ferdinand's Route‘, Juli 1985 / Alan Shields (left) and Steven Reeves pulling an impression of 'Uncle Ferdinand's Route', July 1985. © Tyler Graphics Ltd.

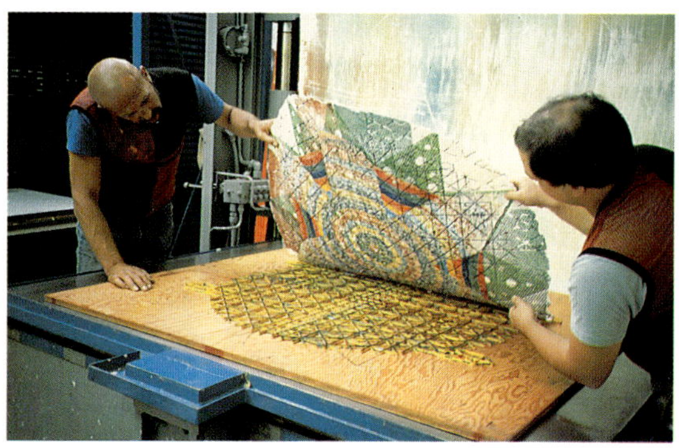

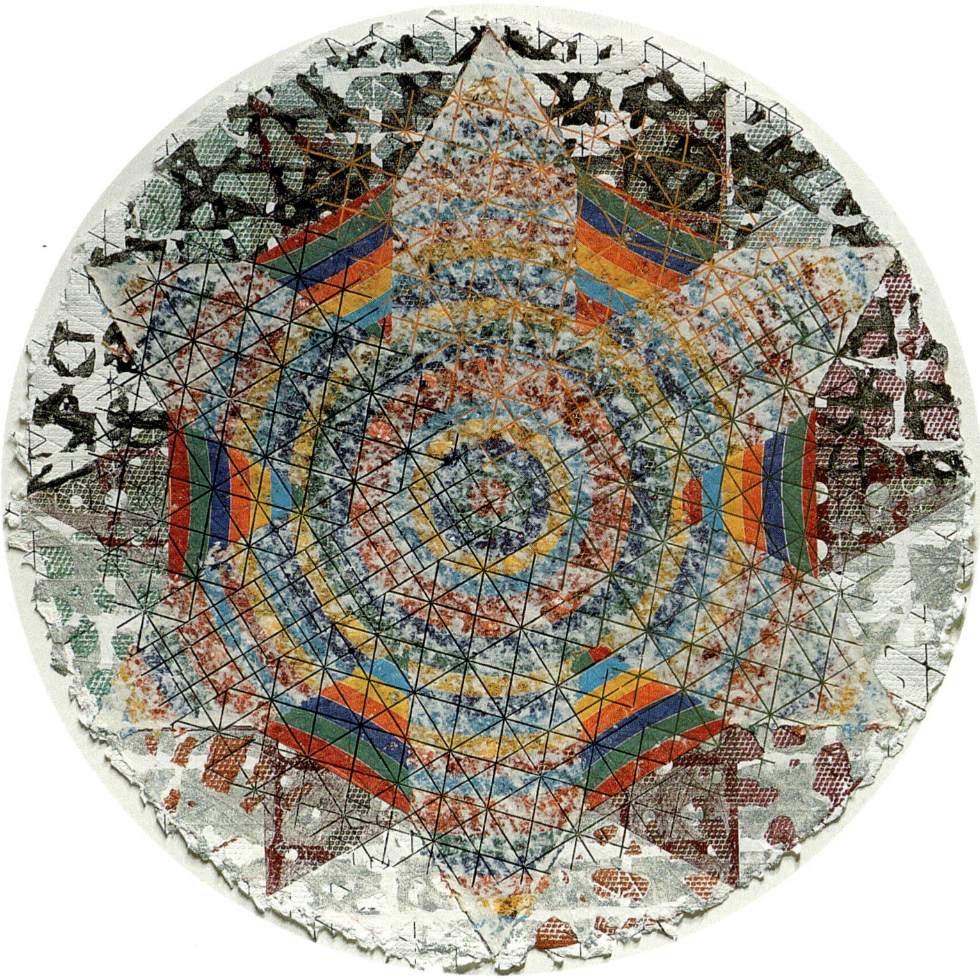

Alan Shields: Uncle Ferdinand's Route. Aus: The Raggedy Circumnavigation Series, 1985. Durchmesser 119,4 cm. Geprägt, Siebdruck, Holzschnitt, Collage, handgeschöpftes Papier / Alan Shields: Uncle Ferdinand's Route. From: The Raggedy Circumnavigation Series, 1985. Diameter 119.4 cm. Relief, screenprint, woodcut, collage, handmade paper.

Auch die Nähtespur wird zum grafischen Gestaltungselement. Die Gittermuster der Bildschichten entstehen oft nicht durch Stanzung oder Wegschneiden; zu ihrer Herstellung entwickelte Tyler Graphics eigens Schöpfsiebkonstruktionen, damit das Blatt bereits als Gitterform geschöpft wird.
1984/85 entstand in achtmonatiger Zusammenarbeit mit Tyler Graphics eine Serie kreisförmiger Papierpulparbeiten mit bis zu sieben Papierschichtüberlagerungen in vielen grafischen Techniken. Ein Werk dieser Serie mit dem Titel ‚The Raggedy Circumnavigation' widmet Alan Shields ‚Uncle Ferdinand', Fernando Magellan, dem ersten Überquerer des Pazifischen Ozeans. Das runde Basisblatt ist weiß belassen. Die Arbeit hat die künstlerische Wirkung und Kraft eines Denkmals für den großen Seefahrer. Die runde Form steht als Zeichen für die Weltkugel. Vom Zentrum der Welt, der Mitte des Kreises, expandieren kreisähnliche Farbstreifensegmente wellenförmig auf die Peripherie zu. Allerdings wird die klare Farbstreifengestaltung in weiten Teilen nebelartig überlagert. Der Funktion eines Steuerrades nicht unähnlich, hat diese oberste Papierschicht die Form eines breiten Pfeilsystems. Es kragt in seinen Spitzen bis an den Rand, führt damit den Blick des Betrachters über die Dimensionen des Blattes hinaus. Diese flauschig dünne Schicht aus weißem Papierpulp überdeckt die klaren Farben wie Wolkenschleier. Die breite Randzone des Werkes gibt aufgrund der vielfältigen Musterstrukturschichtungen und ihrer reich gestalteten Farbdifferenzierungen dem Werk intensive Plastizität und Tiefenwirkung. Die Phantasie des Betrachters wird in die Unendlichkeit von Raum und Zeit geleitet.
Es liegt in der Intention des Künstlers, seine Philosophie von Welt nicht nur im Kunstwerk zu dokumentieren, sondern auch durch Bildtitel den Betrachter zu lenken. Die Bild- und Serientitel nehmen Bezug auf Lebenssituationen und Ereignisse. Alle zusammen, so äußerte Alan Shields, stellen ein Epitaph des eigenen Lebens dar.

through. The different layers of paper are sewn together. The seams are also a part of the overall graphic design. The lattice pattern of the picture layers are not always a result of punching or cutting out; Tyler Graphics developed new mould constructions so that the sheet could be dipped directly with this pattern.
In 1984/85 during an eight-month collaboration with Tyler Graphics, Alan Shields did a series of round paperpulp works with up to seven paper layers in many graphic techniques. One work in this series with the title 'The Raggedy Circumnavigation' was dedicated to 'Uncle Ferdinand' (Fernando Magellan) the first man to cross the Pacific Ocean. The round base sheet has been left white. The work has the artistic function and effect of a monument to the great explorer. The round form stands for the globe. From the center of the world, the middle of the circle, wavy stripes of color extend outwards to the periphery. However, the clear colors of the stripes are overlaid and made nebulous in many places. Not unlike a steering wheel, this upper layer of paper is in the form of a broad system of arrows. Its tips reach to the edge, directing the eyes of the observer to the dimensions beyond the paper. This thin fluffy layer of white paperpulp covers the clear base colors like a veil of cloud. The broad zone at the border of the painting gives the work intense plasticity and depth through the many layered patterns and rich assortment of differentiated color. The fantasy of the viewer is directed at the infinity of time and space.
It is part of the intention of the artist to document his philosphy of the world not only in the artworks, but also to orient the viewer by the titles. The titles of the pictures and the series are related to situations and events. Taken together, says Alan Shields, they represent an epitaph to one's own life.

V. 4. Malerei mit Pulp und Papier

Die professionellste Werkstatt für Papiermalerei und Handpapiermacherei in Europa ist diejenige des Künstlers John Gerard (* 1955 Michigan). Sein profundes papier- und kunsthistorisches Wissen – er war in den Jahren 1979 bis 1984 Kurator der Sammlungen an der Cranbrook Academy of Art in Michigan – prädestiniert ihn zum idealen Mitarbeiter für Künstler. Er siedelte 1992 von Berlin, wo er im Künstlerhaus Bethanien seit 1985 eine Papierwerkstatt betrieb, nach Rheinbach bei Bonn über. Mit ihm arbeiten so bekannte Künstler wie A. R. Penck (* 1939 Dresden), Frank Badur (* 1944 Oranienburg/Berlin), Kuno Gonschior (* 1935 Wanne-Eickel), Shinkichi Tajiri (* 1923 Los Angeles), Ian Tyson (* 1933 Wallasey/Großbritannien) und Felix Droese (* 1950 Singen/Hohentwiel).

Der japanische Bildhauer Tajiri gestaltete zusammen mit John Gerard kleine quadratische Pulpmalereien von geballter Kraft. Der Abdruck einer Kordel schlängelt sich – eingeengt durch die Begrenzungen des Formats – in Linien über das Blatt. Es bilden sich Schlingen, die im Begriff sind, sich zu Knoten zusammenzuziehen. Manche Kordel entfranst zu Greifern. Die Werke sprechen von Gewalt und Erotik. Der aggressive Charakter potenziert sich durch die schreiende Farbigkeit, mit der das Relief der Kordel

V.4. Painting with pulp and paper

The most professional workshop in Europe for paperpainting and handpaper making is that of the artist John Gerard (* 1955 Michigan). His profound knowledge of paper and art history – from 1979 to 1984 he was curator of the collections at the Cranbrook Academy of Art in Michigan – predestines him as the ideal partner for artists. In 1992 he moved from Berlin, where since 1985 he had run a paper workshop in the Künstlerhaus Bethanien, to Rheinbach outside of Bonn. Famous artists have collaborated with him, such as A. R. Penck (*1939 Dresden), Frank Badur (* 1944 Oranienburg/Berlin), Kuno Goschior (* 1935 Wanne-Eickel), Shinkichi Tajiri (* 1923 Los Angeles), Ian Tyson (* 1933 Wallasey/Great Britain) and Felix Droese (*1950 Singen/Hohentwiel).

The Japanese sculptor Tajiri together with John Gerard designed small square pulp paintings of dense energy. Held to the designated boundaries, the imprint of a cord winds its way in lines across the paper. Loops are formed that seem about to pull together into knots. Some of the cord is frayed into claws. The works express violence and eroticism. The aggressive character is multiplied by the shrill colors which accentuate the cord relief. "I am

Skinkichi Tajiri arbeitet in der Papierwerkstatt von John Gerard, 1987 / Skinkichi Tajiri working in the paper studio of John Gerard, 1987

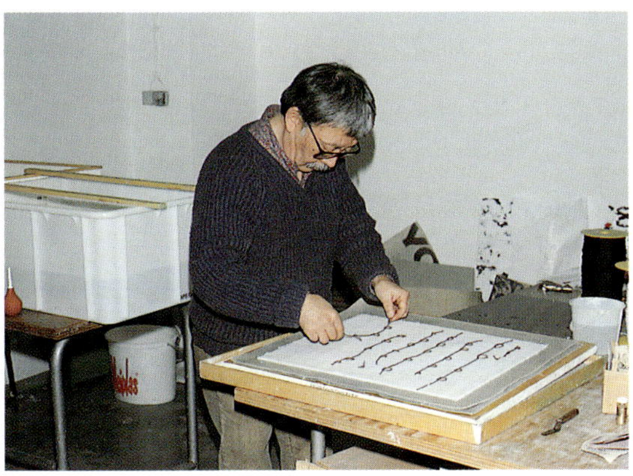

A. R. Penck und John Gerard arbeiten am Buch ‚Wallenstein', 1991 / A. R. Penck and John Gerard working on 'Wallenstein' book, 1991

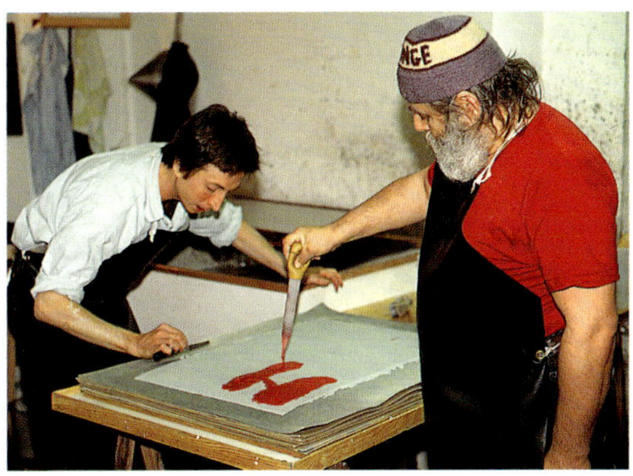

hervorgehoben ist. „Mich interessiert die Arbeit mit Papier, um zu erfahren, was man alles damit machen kann und wo es mich künstlerisch hinführt.“[142]
John Gerard malt zartfarbene Gemälde aus Faserstoff und farbigen Papierfragmenten. Sotirakis Charalambou (* 1947 London) arbeitete in den 80er Jahren mit farbigem Fasermaterial, das auf eine Grundfläche verbracht wird und sich während des Sprühvorgangs zur flockigen Oberfläche verknotet. Es entstanden Farblandschaften mit zerklüfteter, changierender Oberfläche. Auch für K. Reith Blake (* 1951 Huntingdon/Kanada) ist Papier zugleich sowohl Farbe als auch Leinwand. Die Künstlerin kam 1977 von der Druckgrafik zur Papiermalerei. „Die frustrierende Begrenztheit der Möglichkeiten mit den handelsüblichen Papieren und die allgemeine große Unkenntnis über den Charakter von Papier haben viele von uns Studenten dazu gebracht, mit jeder nur denkbaren Unterlage für Drucke zu experimentieren und auch mit Pulp.“[143] John Babcock gießt farbige Pulps zu Gemälden mit Farbfeldern, -streifen und Zeichen. Die unterschiedlichen Fasern und Farben, aus denen die Pulps bestehen, weisen differierende Eigenschaften der Lichtabsorption

John Babcock: Bid for Heaven, 1986. Frei gegossener Papierstoff aus pigmentierter Baumwoll- und Abakafaser. 101,6 x 104,1 cm / John Babcock: Bid for Heaven, 1986. Free cast paper, pigmented cotton and abaca fiber. 101.6 x 104.1 cm

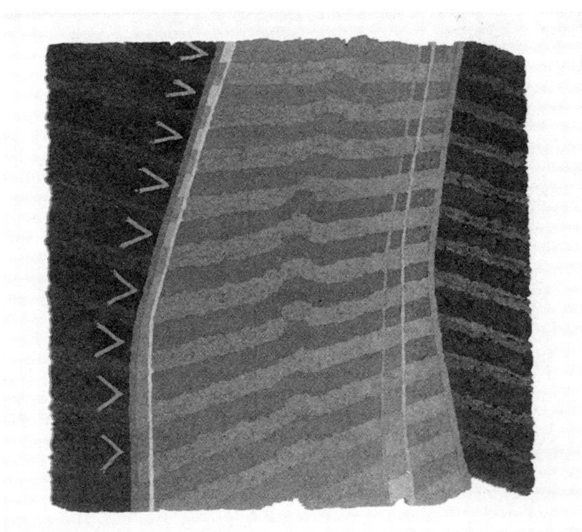

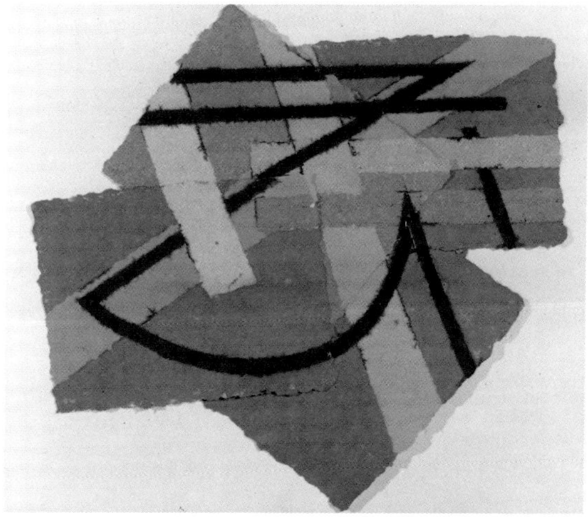

Clinton Hill: Bold Maneuver, 1984. In Form gegossenes handgeschöpftes Papier. 117 x 119,5 cm / Clinton Hill: Bold Maneuver, 1984. Mould formed handmade paper. 117 x 119.5 cm

interested in working with paper in order to learn what all can be done with it and where it leads me artistically.“[142]
John Gerard paints delicately colored paintings out of pulp and colored paper fragments. Sotirakis Charalambou (*1947 London) worked in the 80s with colored rag paper that was applied to a base by a spraying process, knotting into floculated forms on the surface. These became color landscapes, craggy, shimmery. For K. Reith Blake (* 1951 Huntingdon/Canada) paper is simultaneously color and canvas. The artist switched in 1977 from lithographic printing to paper painting. “I had just completed printmaking studies where the frustrating limitations of commercial rag papers and a great ignorance about paper character generally had driven several of us to printing onto just about every experimental substrate possible.”[143] John Babcock pours colored pulp into paintings of color fields, stripes and figures. The different rags and colors out of which the pulp is made have differing properties of light absorption. Any shift in the light or in the angle from which it is viewed changes the color of the picture. Clinton Hill (* 1922 Payette/Idaho) began in 1973 to collaborate with John and Kathy Koller

auf. Je nach Lichteinfall oder Blickwinkel ändert sich die Farbigkeit des Bildes. Clinton Hill (* 1922 Payette/Idaho) begann 1973 in Zusammenarbeit mit John und Kathy Koller von HMP Papers in Woodstock Valley/Connecticut, mit Pulp zu arbeiten. Es entstanden großflächige Gemälde, die aus einzelnen Papieren zusammengesetzt eine Gesamtkomposition ergeben. Joan M. Hall (* 1952 Mansfield/Ohio) verbindet Pulpmalerei mit grafischen Techniken. Ihre Bildinstallationen bestehen aus sehr harten, gefärbten Papieren aus Baumwolle, Abaka und Flachs. Sie sind in unregelmäßige Form gebracht, mit vielen Zeichen bedruckt und zu einem farbenfreudigen Formkonglomerat zusammengefügt. Fast monochrome Papierbilder fertigt Wolfgang Finck (* 1945 Neukloster/Mecklenburg). In den späten 70er Jahren prägte er dem Papier während des Trocknens geometrische Strukturen ein, in den frühen 80er Jahren arbeitete er mit farbigen Papieren, deren Umrißformen von Raute, Sechseck, Kreis er zu Sequenzen fügte. In den späten 80er Jahren

of HMP Papers in Woodstock Valley/Connecticut on works in pulp. This resulted in paintings of large planes that when brought together made up one comprehensive composition. Joan M. Hall (* 1952 Mansfield/Ohio) combines pulp painting with graphic techiniques. Her installations are made up of very tough colored pulp made of cotton, abaca (Manila hemp) and flax. She shapes the pulp to irregular forms, prints it with many figures and brings them together in a colorful conglomerate. Wolfgang Finck (* 1945 Neukloster/Mecklenburg) creates paperpulp pictures that are almost monochrome. In the late 70s he embossed paper during its drying process with geometric structures; in the early 80s he shaped colored paperpulp into diamond, hexagon, and circle contours and then joined them into sequences. In the late 80s he placed ciphers on the picture that covered the picture plane. Hans-Dieter Pietsch (* 1944 Glogau/Schlesien) for the first time experimented with paper in 1977 while studying at the Royal

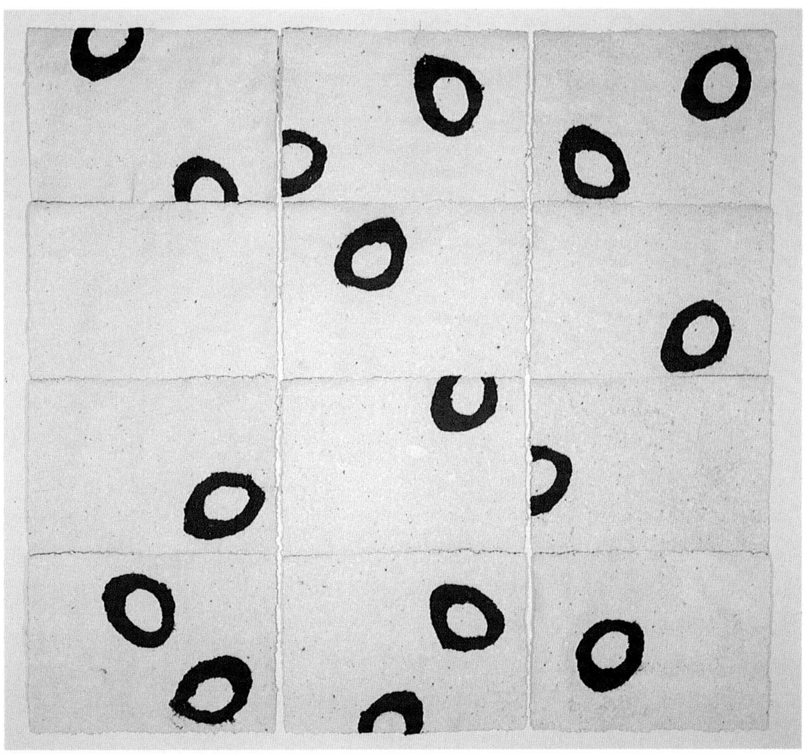

Wolfgang Finck: Ohne Titel, 1989. 12teilig, geschöpfte und gegossene Papiere. 230 x 245 cm / Wolfgang Finck: Untitled, 1989. 12 panels, handmade cast papers. 230 x 245 cm

setzte er zudem Chiffren ins Bild, die seriell den Bildgrund überziehen. Heinz-Dieter Pietsch (* 1944 Glogau/Schlesien) experimentierte erstmals 1977 am Royal College of Art in London mit Papier. Ihn interessiert die Umsetzung von Motiven der Stadtarchäologie in bröcklige, zerfaserte Papierstruktur.
Eine Pionierin der Papierkunst ist Golda Lewis (* New York). 1960 begann die Bildhauerin, in Papierstoff archaische Figurationen zu ritzen und Gemälde mit Pulp zu malen. In den folgenden Jahren komponierte sie Materialien wie Holzsplitter und Lederreste als grafische Elemente in die Papiermasse ein. 1970 wurde die Straße ihr Aktionsfeld. Die Rißstrukturen auf Asphalt und Zement fungierten als Ausgangspunkt künstlerischer Reflexion in Gemälden und schließlich in Stelen aus grobrissigem, sprödem Papierpulp.
Papier kann aus allen Pflanzenfasern gewonnen werden. Die haptische Qualität und die optische Wirkung differieren dabei sehr. Künstler, die vor allem mit der Materialität und der Naturfarbe von Papieren arbeiten, bauen oft ihre Pflanzen selbst an oder sammeln sie, um daraus ihren speziellen Faserstoff zu schaffen. Maureen Richardson (* 1930 Großbritannien), Helmut Becker (* 1931 Castor/Kanada), Helmut Frerick (* 1952 Neustadt/Schwarzwald), Randi B. Studsgarth (* 1938 Kopenhagen), Virginia Sigwald (* 1954 Buenos Aires), Chava Pressburger (* Prag) oder Claudine Péters-Ropsy (1940 Brüssel), Pat Gentenaar (* 1949 San Francisco), Ingrid Evans (* Berlin), Lore Burger (* 1933 Schleswig), Aurelia Muñoz (* 1926 Barcelona) beispielsweise schaffen Papierkunstwerke von äußerst haptischer, teils fragiler, teils massiver Qualität. Versuche, Papier aus Pflanzenfasern herzustellen, unternahmen bereits Wissenschaftler im 18. Jahrhundert. Neben René-Antoine Réaumur, Albert Seba und J. E. Guerttard ist Jacob Christian Schaeffers sechsbändige Veröffentlichung ‚Versuche und Muster ohne alle Lumpen [...] Papier herzustellen' (1765–1771) die berühmteste.
Mancher Künstler erweitert auch die Möglichkeiten, den Papieren durch Tinkturen eine andere Materialität zu geben. Helmut Löhr (* 1955 Lünen) legt Pa-

College of Art in London. What interested him was the transformation of motifs from city archaeology into crumbly, raveled paper structures.
Golda Lewis (* New York) is a pioneer paper artist. In 1960 the sculptress began to scratch archaic figurations into rag paper and to paint with pulp. In the following years she worked material like wood chips and leather remnants into the paper mass as graphic elements. In 1970 the street became her field of action. The fissured structure of asphalt and cement was the starting point for her artistic reflection in paintings and finally in pillars of coarsely-cracked and brittle paper pulp.
Paper can be made from any kind of plant fiber. Its tactile quality and optical effect differ accordingly. Artists who work, above all, with the materiality and the natural color of paper often grow their own plants or collect them, in order to make special pulp. Maureen Richardson (* 1930 Great Britain), Helmut Becker (* 1931 Castor/Canada), Helmut Frerick (* 1952 Neustadt/Black Forest), Randi B. Studsgarth (* 1938 Copenhagen), Virginia Sigwald (* 1954 Buenos Aires), Chava Pressburger (* Prague) or Claudine Péters-Ropsy (1940 Brussels), Pat Gentenaar (* 1949 San Francisco), Ingrid Evans (* Berlin), Lore Burger (* 1933 Schleswig), Aurelia Muñoz (* 1926 Barcelona), for example, create paper art that is extremely haptic, whether fragile or massive. Attempts to produce paper from plant fiber had already been made in the 18th century by scientists. Along with René-Antoine Réaumur, Albert Seba and J. E. Guerttard it was Jacob Christian Schaeffer's six-volume publication 'Versuche und Muster ohne alle Lumpen [...] Papier herzustellen' (1765–1771) that was the most famous report.
By using tinctures, some artists expanded the possibility to give paper another materiality. Helmut Löhr (* 1955 Lünen) lays papers of different color and structure one above the over and stains them so that textures and colors shine through and the total effect of the picture comes from all the layers together. Stephan Runge (* 1947 Barghausen)

piere unterschiedlicher Farbe und Struktur übereinander, tränkt sie, so daß Strukturen und Farben durchscheinen und die überlagernden Papiere gemeinsam das Bild ergeben. Stephan Runge (* 1947 Barghausen) bearbeitet einfarbige Papiere mit Enzymen und Lösungen. Der chemische Prozeß, der vom Künstler beeinflußt und gestoppt wird, verursacht die Vielfaltigkeit und die Farbgestalt im Papier.

allows enzymes and solutions to do their work on uni-colored paper. The chemical process – initiated, influenced and brought to an end by the artist – causes the variety and the pattern of the colors in the paper.

V. 5. Der neue Begriff von Landschaftsmalerei

Eine neue Form von Landschaftsmalerei übermittelt Helmut Dirnaichner (* 1942 Kolbermoor/Oberbayern). Er malt mit Asche aus Hölzern, zermahlenen Steinen, Mineralien und Erden und bindet diese körnigen oder staubähnlichen Farben mit

V. 5. Landscape painting defined in a new way

A new form of landscape painting is mediated by Helmut Dirnaichner (* 1942 Kolbermoor/Upper Bavaria). He paints with wood ash, ground stones, minerals, and soil and binds their granular or dustlike colors with cellulose. The choice of

Helmut Dirnaichner: Lapislazuli, Vulkan, Auripigment, 1989. Lapislazuli, Auripigment, Vulkan Paricutín, Jonotefaser. 207 x 315 cm /
Helmut Dirnaichner: Lapis lazuli, Volcano, Auripigmentum, 1989. Lapis lazuli, auripigmentum, volcano paricutín, jonote fiber. 207 x 315 cm

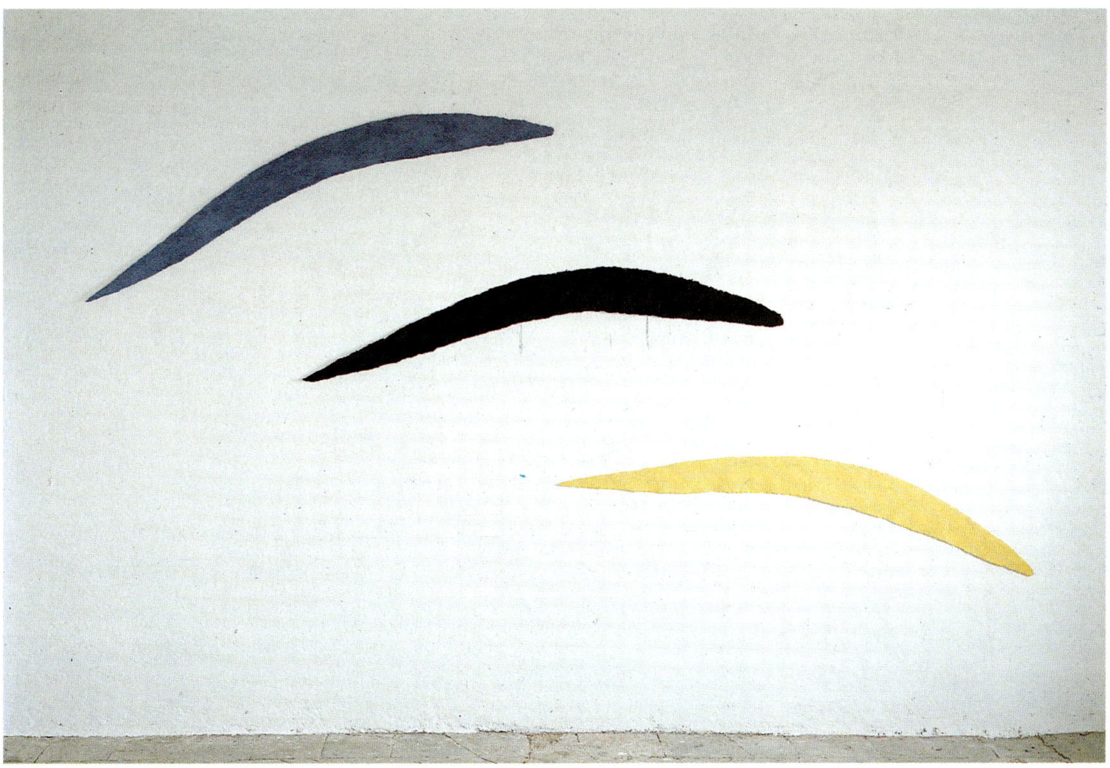

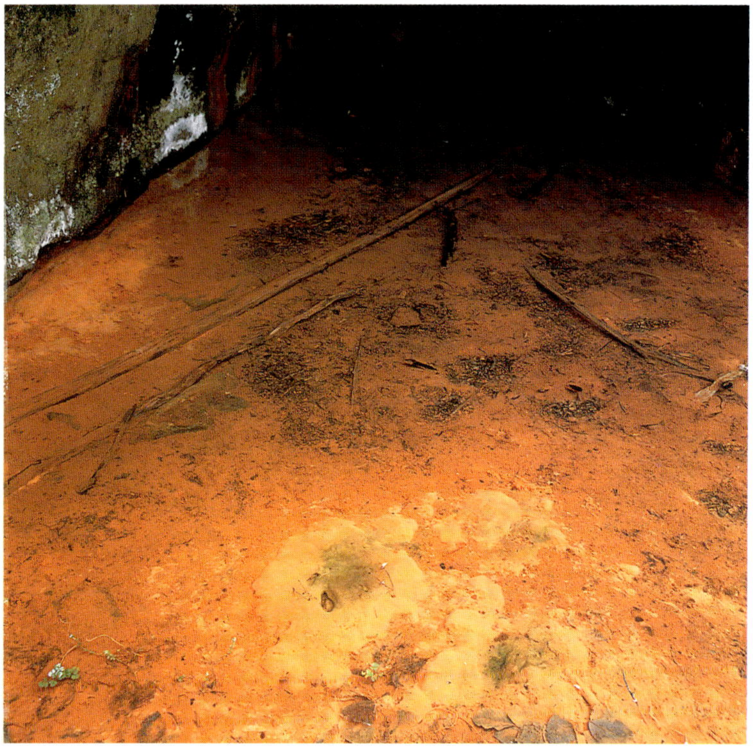

Miloš Šejn: Spuren des Eisens, 1987. Erd- und Pflanzenpigmente in Papierstoff, Installation, 9 Teile (Ausschnitt). 190 x 285 x 95 cm / Miloš Šejn: Traces of Iron, 1987. Paper dyed with soil and plant pigments (detail). Installation, 9 parts. 190 x 285 x 95 cm

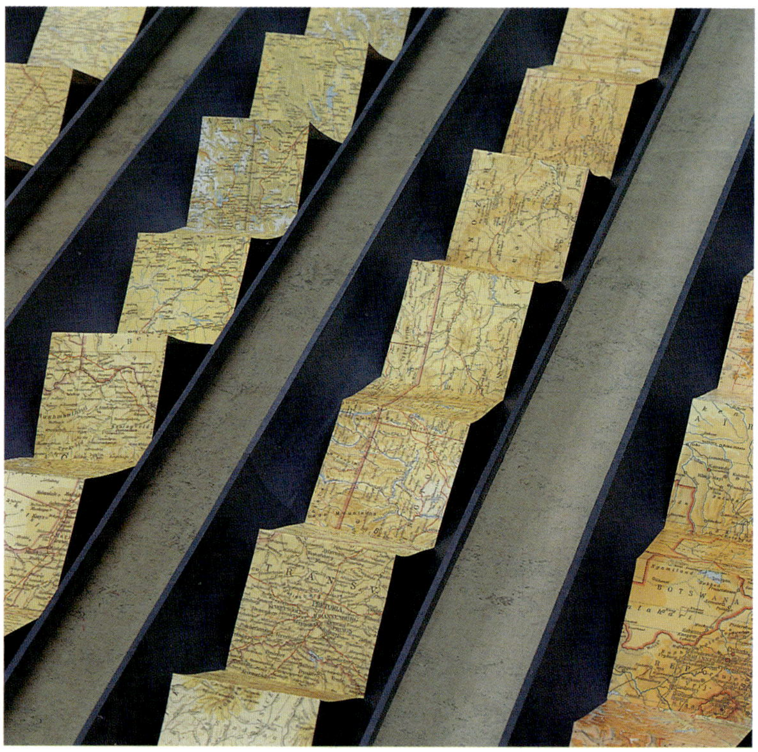

Urbain Mulkers: WØCXS – Armada, 1987. Collage mit Atlasfragmenten, 49 Stücke. 300 x 7 cm / Urbain Mulkers: WØCXS – Armada, 1987. Collage with fragments of an atlas, 49 pieces. 300 x 7 cm

Zellulose. Die Wahl des Materials und die jeweilige Farbigkeit charakterisieren die Natur einer Region. Dirnaichners Arbeiten sind Berichte von Landschaften. Für ihn stellen Naturmaterialien Speicher von Geschichte dar. Man muß diese nur erfragen, ertasten, erforschen. Dirnaichners Werke verstehen sich als Naturbilder auf überhöhter geistiger Ebene. In der Reduktion allein auf die Wertigkeit von Material liegt die transzendentale Kraft. Die empfindlichen, fragilen Werke aus Grundwerten der Natur verweisen zudem auf Vergänglichkeit. „Ich beschäftige mich in meiner künstlerischen Arbeit ausschließlich mit Naturmaterialien, die in Beziehung zur Kultur, zu einer Landschaft und den Menschen stehen", schreibt der Künstler. Auslösendes Erlebnis war ein Arbeitsaufenthalt in Mexiko im Frühjahr 1985 bei den Otomi, dem einzigen Indianerstamm, der heute noch Papier aus der Faser des Jonotebaumes schlägt. „Die Jonotefaser, aus der seit präkolumbianischer Zeit die heiligen Papiere und Codices entstehen, habe ich in Verbindung gebracht mit den Erden der Sierra Norte de Puebla."[144]

Miloš Šejn (* 1947 Jablonec nad Nisou/Böhmen) dokumentiert Landschaften in Papier. Erde, Moos, Farnkraut, Holz, Blätter schließt er durch Einreiben in die Landschaftsaufnahmen ein.[145]

Kathryn Lipke (* 1939 Cooperstown/North Dakota) mischt ihre Papiere mit Ton, um den Eindruck einer krustigen Erdoberfläche zu erzeugen. Ihre ‚Earthworks' fungieren als Aufzeichnungen menschlicher Existenz.[146]

Am Beispiel der Thematik Landschaft wird deutlich, daß in den 80er Jahren nicht nur Pulp und handgeschöpftes Papier als adäquate Materialien genutzt werden. Auch maschinell hergestelltes und bereits bedrucktes oder beschriebenes Papier bleibt beliebtes Arbeitsmaterial. Die weitgespannte Ausdrucksbreite des Papiers und des Pulps in jeglicher Form, Art und Qualität wird von Künstlern als Medium differenziert eingesetzt.

Urbain Mulkers (* 1945 Schulen/Belgien) arbeitet mit bereits bedrucktem und beschriebenem Papier.

material and the respective colors characterize the nature of a region. Dirnaichner's works are reports on the countryside. For him the natural materials represent an historical storehouse. One only need question, touch, explore them. Dirchaichner's works can be understood as pictures of nature at an enhanced spiritual level. Their reduction to the value of the material gives them their transcendental force. At the same time the sensitive, fragile works made from the basic ingredients of nature point to their own transience. "In my artwork I am engaged exclusively with natural materials that in relation to culture stand for a landscape and for man," the artist wrote. The initial event for him was a stay in Mexico in the spring of 1985 with the Otomi, the only Indian tribe that still today makes paper from the fibers of the jonote tree. "I have brought together the jonote fiber, which has served since pre-Columbian times for sacred papers and codes, with the soil of the Sierra Norte de Puebla."[144]

Miloš Šejn (* 1947 Jablonec nad Nisou/Bohemia) documents countrysides in paper. Earth, moss, ferns, wood, leaves he uses to rub into the reproductions of landscapes.[145]

Kathryn Lipke (*1939 Cooperstown/North Dakota) mixes her papers with clay to create the impression of an encrusted earth surface. Her 'Earthworks'-pieces function as reports on human existence.[146]

The example of the theme of landscape painting makes clear that in the 80s it was not only pulp and handmade paper that were used as adequate materials. Mechanically produced paper and second-hand paper already printed or written on were also popular working materials. The broad-ranging expressive quality of paper and pulp of every type, quality and format is deployed by artists as a medium in quite distinctive ways.

Urbain Mulkers (* 1945 Schulen/Belgium) works with paper that has already been printed or inscribed. He creates landscapes in new dimensions from maps and atlases. Transformed in shape and context they stand for a world-embracing universal language.

Er schafft mit Landkarten und Atlanten Landschaften neuer Dimensionen. Transformiert in Form und in Zusammenhang stehen sie für eine weltverbindende Universalsprache.
‚Mappamondo' von Michelangelo Pistoletto (* 1933 Biella/Italien) besteht aus einer Kugel aus gepreßtem Zeitungspapier. 1966 wurde sie durch die Straßen gerollt und 1968 mit einem Drahtgehäuse, das die Breiten- und Längengrade der Erde darstellt, umgeben. Die Kugel aus Zeitungen gehört zur Gruppe der ‚Oggetti di Meno', der ‚Minus-Objekte', mit denen der Künstler Wahrnehmungserfahrungen endgültig in die Außenwelt drängen will, um sich selbst zu befreien. „Eine einzelne Arbeit ist ein Wort eines Gesprächs, das die Dauer eines Lebens haben könnte, und gleichzeitig ist es eine in sich abgeschlossene Sprache [...] Nur die Wahrnehmung entscheidet, welches Material von Fall zu Fall ausgewählt wird – alle Materialien sind für mich geeignet."[147]
Andreas von Weizsäcker (* 1956 Essen) arbeitete im Jahr 1992/93 intensiv mit Kartenmaterial, das durch die politischen Neugliederungen plötzlich zum Altmaterial geworden war. Sein riesiges Werk ‚Atlas' nimmt Bezug auf Caspar David Friedrichs ‚Eismeer' von 1821. Der formale Bildaufbau Friedrichs ist in ein polykubisches, asymmetrisches

'Mappamondo' by Michelangelo Pistoletto (* 1933 Biella/Italy) consists of a globe make of compressed newspaper. In 1966 it was rolled through the streets and in 1968 it was provided with a wire casing that represents the latitudes and longitudes. The globe of newspaper belongs to the 'Oggetti di Meno' series, the minus objects, which the artist, once and for all, wants to banish to the outside world so that he can be free of them. "A single work is a word in a conversation that can last a lifetime and at the same time is an enclosed language... It is only the perception that decides which material is chosen for one occasion or another; to me all materials are suitable."[147]
Andreas von Weizsäcker (* 1956 Essen) worked in 1992/93 intensively with maps that had with one blow become out of date due to geographic restructuring. His gigantic work 'Atlas' relates to Caspar David Friedrich's 'Eismeer' from 1821. Friedrich's formal composition is translated into a polycubic, asymmetrical conglomeration of archaic blocks. Their visible surfaces are covered in maps of continents and oceans: a collaged world, unorthodox and utopian in the way it has come together. The original title of Friedrich's picture 'The Failure of Hope' makes the enigma clear: 'Hope' was the name of the ship that sank in the sea

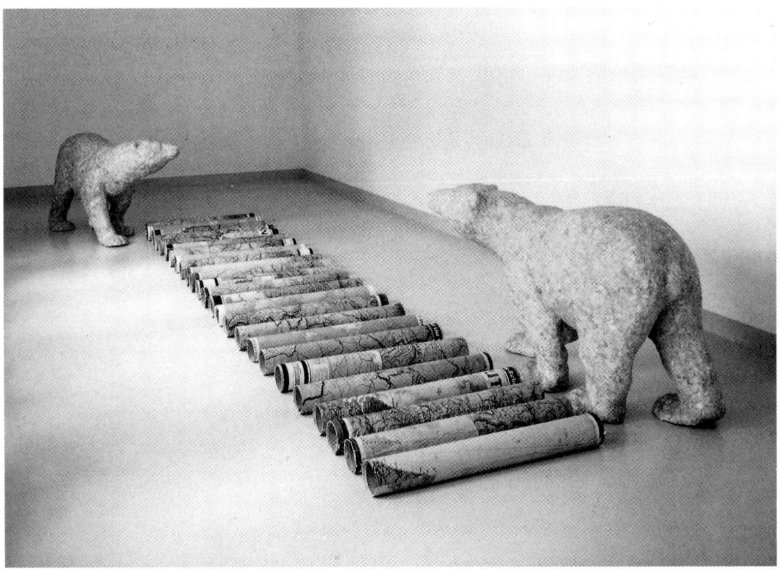

Andreas von Weizsäcker: Weißt du noch, 1992. Recycelte Landkarten von Ost- und Westdeutschland. 700 x 132 x 80 cm /
Andreas von Weizsäcker: Remember When, 1992. Recycled maps of East and West Germany. 700 x 132 x 80 cm

Formkonglomerat archaischer Blöcke übersetzt. Ihre sichtbaren Außenflächen überziehen Landkarten und Meere. Eine collagierte Welt, die sich unorthodox und utopisch zueinanderschiebt, ist entstanden. Der ursprüngliche Titel von Friedrichs Bild, ‚Die gescheiterte Hoffnung', verdeutlicht die Hintergründigkeit des Werkes – ‚Hoffnung' hieß das dargestellte untergegangene Schiff, Friedrich spielt jedoch auf das aktuelle politische Geschehen an. ‚Die gescheiterte Hoffnung', ‚Eismeer', ‚Atlas' – die drei Begriffe verbindet Gemeinsames auf dem Hintergrund der gescheiterten Hoffnung auf Weltfrieden. ‚Atlas' trägt schwer an der Welt. Die erste Arbeit mit Kartenmaterial schuf Andreas von Weizsäcker 1992 aus recycleten Berlin-Stadtplänen aus der Zeit vor der Wiedervereinigung Deutschlands. Das Berliner Bärenpaar, getrennt durch eine lange Reihe von Kartenrollen, fragt: „Weißt du noch?" und verweist damit auf die neue politische und schwierige menschliche Situation.

of ice; Friedrich was, however, referring to the political situation at the time. 'Atlas' strains to carry the weight of the world. Andreas von Weizsäcker's first work with maps was made from recycled city maps of Berlin before re-unification. The two Berlin bears, separated by a long row of rolled up maps, ask nostagically: "Remember When?" and refer to the difficulties in the new political and human situation.

V.6. Zeichnung im Papier

Papier kann Zeichen in sich verbergen und zwar als Wasserzeichen. Diese alte Technik machten sich manche Künstler zunutze. Horst Antes schuf 1969 in Zusammenarbeit mit Fred Siegenthaler die Mappe ‚Agamemnon 3' mit 16 Blättern, in denen verschiedene Zeichnungen als Wasserzeichen eingelassen sind.[148] Ian Tyson zeichnete 1985 seine ersten geometrischen Bilder in Papier in der Mühle Barcham Greene/Kent mit dem Titel ‚Wasserzeichen'.[149] Die Papiermacherei hatte er 1979 am City Literary Institute in London erlernt.

Meret Oppenheim schuf 1971 in Zusammenarbeit mit Fred Siegenthaler eine ‚Wolken-Serie' mit elf unterschiedlichen Wasserzeichenmotiven. Das Verbergen, die Unzugänglichkeit des Objekts, ist Grundtenor vieler ihrer Arbeiten. Unter einem Pelzkleid z. B. verbirgt sie 1936 Porzellan, ihre Bilder an der Wand verdeckt sie 1969 mit Kaninchendraht.

V. 6. Signs drawn in paper

Paper can conceal signs in the form of watermarks. This very old technique has been put to use by some artists. In 1969 Horst Antes in collaboration with Fred Siegenthaler created the portfolio 'Agemennon 3' with 16 single sheets, into which different signs had been inserted in the form of watermarks.[148] Ian Tyson in 1985 drew his first geometric pictures on paper in the Barcham Green Papermill in Kent and called them 'Watermarks'.[149] He had learned papermaking at the City Literary Institute in London in 1979.

Meret Oppenheim in collaboration with Fred Siegenthaler in 1971 created 'Cloud Series' with eleven different watermark motifs. Concealment, the inacessibility of the object, is the basic tenor of her work. In 1936, for instance, she hid porcelain under a coating of fur; in 1969 she covered her pictures on the wall with rabbit wire. She did not entrust

Meret Oppenheim: Meine Fahne, 1974. Wasserzeichen. 28,5 x 23 cm / Meret Oppenheim: My Flag, 1974. Watermark paper. 28.5 x 29 cm

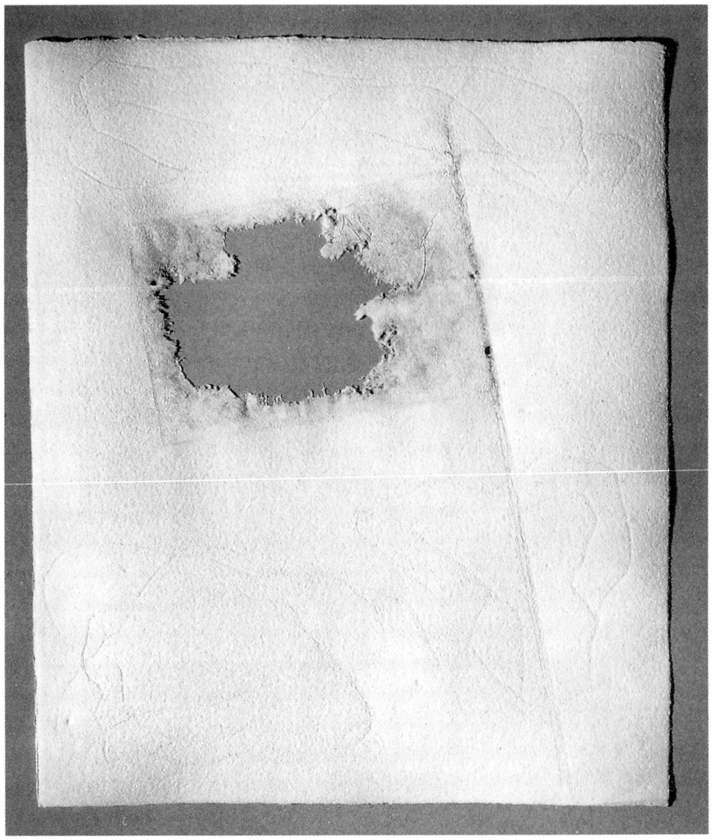

Horst Antes: Kopffüßler. Aus: Agamemnon 3, 1969. Wasserzeichen. 30,5 x 21,5 cm / Horst Antes: Kopffüßler. From: Agamemnon 3, 1969. Watermark paper. 30.5 x 21.5 cm

A. R. Penck: Schöpfsieb mit Wasserzeichen für das Buch ‚Zachor', 1990 hergestellt in der Werkstatt von John Gerard. 46 x 36 cm / A. R. Penck: Mould with watermark for the book 'Zachor', made 1990 in the paper studio of John Gerard. 46 x 36 cm

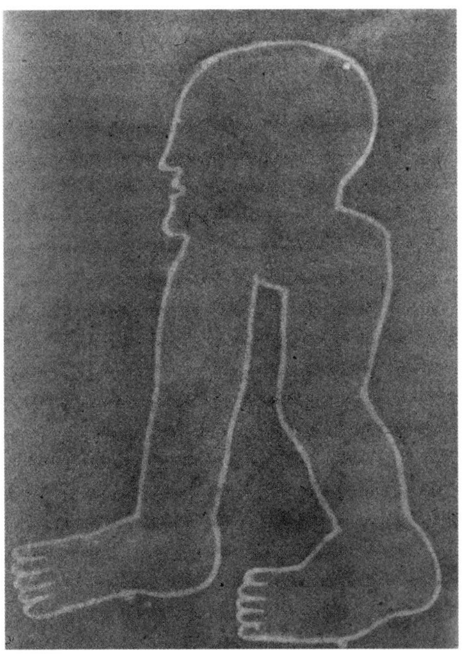

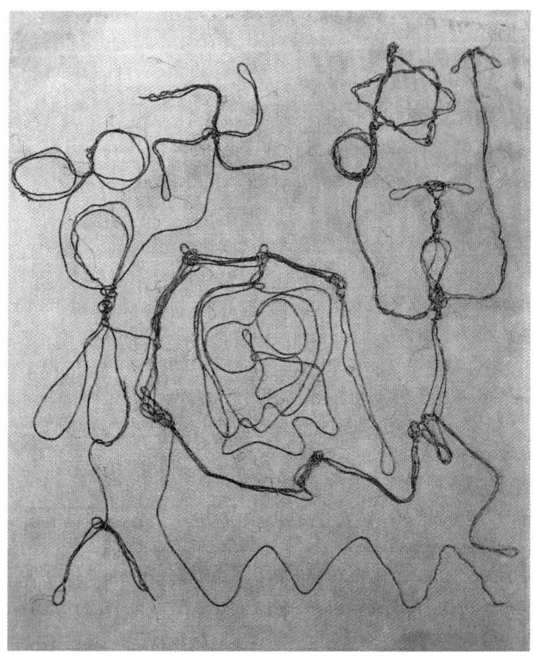

Auch Papier benutzt sie, um zu verbergen. Ihre Zeichen vertraut sie nicht der Oberfläche an, vielmehr ruhen sie als Wasserzeichen im Papier. Die Unzugänglichkeit der Botschaft verleiht das Flair des Besonderen. Erst das durchflutende Licht eröffnet das Geheimnis.
A. R. Penck kreierte 1990 in der Werkstatt von John Gerard eine Blattfolge ‚Zachor' mit inkorporierten Liniendiagrammen. Die Linien graben sich in den dicken, dichten schwarzen Papiergrund ein. Ausschließlich ein Streiflicht macht die Zeichnung sichtbar, die durch Drahtstege auf dem Schöpfsieb verursacht ist. Nur das „abgeschöpfte" Bild ersteht als Kunstwerk.
Andreas von Weizsäcker kultivierte beim Schöpfvorgang Fehler und Unregelmäßigkeiten, um ein gestaltendes Vokabular aus dichten und durchscheinenden Bereichen im Papier zu erzielen. Zudem unterstützte er durch Auftropfen von Wasser die Formbildung. Die so entstandenen großformatigen Wasserzeichnungen in Indigoblau erwecken Assoziationen an Kosmisches, an Weltraumatmosphäre.

her signs to the surface; they are lodged as watermarks in the paper. The inacessibility of the message lends it the flair of the extraordinary. Not till it is lit from behind does it reveal its secret.
A. R. Penck in 1990 created in John Gerard's workshop the series 'Zachor' with incorporated linear diagrams. The lines were recessed in the thick and dense black paper base. Only a raking light makes the image visible that was caused by a wire mark on the mould. It is solely the handmade sheet that emerges as the work of art.
Andreas von Weizsäcker intentionally cultivated errors and irregularities during the moulding process, so as to attain a creative vocabulary of thick and translucent areas in the paper. And, by dripping water onto the paper, he abetted the creation of formations. The large-scaled watermarks in indigo blue that are the result awaken associations of the cosmos and outer space.

V. 7. Das „Dazwischen"

Das Recycling war in den 1970er Jahren in den USA eine gängige Methode, Materie zu vergeistigen. Papierstoff wird u. a. aus getragener Kleidung hergestellt. Im Kunstwerk ersteht das recycelte Kleidungsstück in gleichem Aussehen, jedoch in anderer Materialität und Konsistenz.
Für Joel Fisher (* 1947 Salem/Ohio) ist Recyceln ein philosophischer Akt, der auf ostasiatischer Geisteshaltung beruht. Die bestehende materielle Existenz löst sich zugunsten einer neuen auf, ein Vorgang des Loslösens und gleichzeitig neuer Bindung. Fisher verschrieb sich 1969 dem Papier aus einer bestimmten philosophischen Lebenshaltung heraus. Seine letzten Acrylbilder nannte er „grundlose Bilder"[150], weil sie keine Trägerfläche

V.7. The "between"

In the 70s in the US recycling was a normal procedure for spiritualizing matter. Paper stock is made from worn clothing, among others. In the work of art, the recycled article of clothing is resurrected to look the same, but in another materiality and consistency.
For Joel Fisher (* 1947 Salem/Ohio) recycling is a philosophic act based on an Asiatic mentality. The present material existence is dissolved so that a new one can take its place, a simultaneous process of dissolution and a new fusion. In 1969 Fisher devoted himself to paper as a medium out of a certain philosophy of life. His previous acrylic paintings he had called "groundless" [150] because they had no picture support, but consisted of many

haben, sondern lediglich aus mehreren Acrylschichten bestehen, die auf einer Glasplatte aufgetragen und nach dem Trocknen abgenommen worden waren. „Plötzlich, eines Tages, sah ich ein Stück Papier, das ich gerade gemacht hatte. Ich konnte Papier als ein effizientes ordnendes System verstehen. Hier war eine Substanz, die sich selbst zusammenhielt, ohne Bindemittel; es war reiner als Farbe, die Pigmente enthält und eines Mediums bedarf [...] Reines Papier ist ausdrücklich auf die Probleme der Malerei ausgerichtet [...] Ich nannte das Papier einfach ‚Grund' und betrachtete es als eine Position, auf die ich mich verlassen konnte. Es wurde zu einem Punkt Null der reduktionistischen Tendenz, die ich verfolge." Im Jahr 1971 sammelte Joel Fisher erstmals seine Kleider. „Ich dachte mir, daß Kleidung auf ähnliche Weise eine Art Pufferzone darstellt wie die Schicht unter dem Papier [...] Manchmal erschien es mir, als ob Kleidung eine Farbschicht wäre, lose auf den Körper aufgetragen. Ich wollte all dies Material in meine Arbeit einbringen [...] Ich wollte meine Kleider in Papierblätter verwandeln." Fisher zerschnitt die Kleider, entfernte die Reißverschlüsse und Knöpfe und fütterte die Holländermühle. „Am Ende der Woche hatten wir 88 Stücke Papier und einen Beutel mit Reißverschlüssen. Es war das schönste Papier, das ich je gesehen hatte."[151] Die Arbeit wurde auf der ‚documenta 5' 1972 ausgestellt. Für die Ausstellung im Victoria and Albert Museum in London erstellte der Künstler 1971 eine Arbeit aus recycelten Toilettenpapierrollen des Museums mit der Aufschrift „Eigentum der Regierung".[152] Im selben Jahr sammelte er in Paris die kleinen gelben Metrobil-

layers of acrylic paint applied to a plate of glass and peeled off when dry. "Suddenly one day I was confronting a piece of paper I had just made. I could understand paper as an efficient ordering system. Here was a substance that held itself together without binder; it was purer than paint which required pigment and medium... Pure paper addresses itself articulately to the problems of painting... I simply called the paper 'ground' and considered it a position upon which I could build. It became a zero point for the reductionist tendency I was involved in." In 1971 Joel Fisher collected his first pieces of clothing. "I was thinking how clothing, like the layer under the paper ... is a buffer ... Sometimes it was as if clothing were a layer of paint loosely applied to the body. I wanted to put all this material into my work. I wanted to turn my clothing into sheets of paper." Fisher cut up the clothes, with zippers and buttons removed, and put them through a Hollander beater. "By the end of the weekend we had 88 pieces of paper and a bag of zippers. I thought it was the most beautiful paper I had ever seen."[151] The work was shown in 1972 at 'documenta 5'. For an exhibition in the Victoria and Albert Museum in London in 1971 the artist created a work out of rolls of the museum's toilet paper stamped "Government Property".[152] In the same year in Paris he started collecting the discarded yellow Metro tickets that could be found lying everywhere and made them into artworks.
In 1972 Fisher created a series made from Rauschenberg's discarded trash. In 1975 there was a legendary recycling event that took place in the museum in Mönchengladbach. Fisher collected all

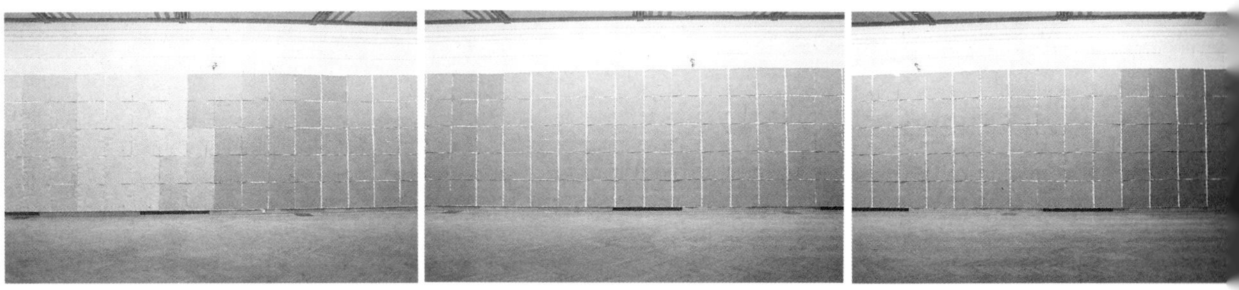

lets, die überall weggeworfen herumlagen, und formte sie neu zu Kunstwerken. Aus Rauschenbergs weggeworfenem Müll gestaltete Fisher 1972 eine Blattfolge. Ein legendäres Recyclingereignis vollzog sich 1975 für seine Ausstellung im Museum in Mönchengladbach. Fisher sammelte alle seine Werke aus sieben Jahren, denen er habhaft werden konnte, zermahlte sie zu Papierstoff und schuf damit neue Bilder. „Die alten Stücke, die den Brei bildeten, hatten allerdings ihre eigene und ausgeprägte Individualität. „Sie unterschieden sich deutlich nach Format und Farbe, nach Struktur und Gewicht der Papiermasse, nach Zahl und Art der Zusammenfügung von einzelnen Blättern und nach ihrer Geschichte, das heißt nach ihrem Entstehungsjahr und nach den Umständen und Motivationen ihrer Entstehung", erläuterte Museumsdirektor Johannes Cladders in seiner Eröffnungsrede zur Ausstellung.[153] Die alten Stücke blieben in den neuen zwar materiell und ideell enthalten, waren jedoch nicht in alter Form lesbar. „Man könnte die Ausstellung eine Retrospektive nennen", sagte Cladders weiter. „Alle alten Papierarbeiten sind in ihr anwesend – und sie sind es zugleich auch wiederum nicht. Geschichte ist hier nicht eliminiert, sie präsentiert sich nicht als zeitliches Nacheinander. Sie ist abgesunken auf den Grund, auf dem sich Anfang und Ende aufheben. Sie ist aufgegangen in eine Ordnung ohne individuelle Begrenzungen." Der Welt der ostasiatischen Gedankengänge sei Fisher „ein erhebliches Stück nähergekommen als das Werk eines Yves Klein". Die geistige und

his works from the last seven years that he could get a hold of, ground them into paper stock and made new pictures from them. "The old pieces that made up the paper mass had their own strong individuality. They were quite distinctive as to format and color, the structure and weight of the paper stock, number and type of new configuration from the single pieces and to history, i. e., the year created and the circumstances and motivation for their creation," the museum director, Johannes Cladders, explained in his speech at the opening.[153] The old pieces were in matter and spirit contained in the new but without being legible in their old form. "You could call the exhibition a retrospective," Cladders continued. "All the old paper works are present in it – and then again they are not. History has not been eliminated here; it is not presented in temporal linearity. It has sunk to the bottom where beginning and end are in suspension. It has unfolded into an order without individual boundaries." The world of oriental mentality "is quite a bit closer [to Fisher] than the work of someone like Yves Klein." The mental and creative force of the early works and their history was integrated into the new works. The constant re-working of his own works and of secondhand clothing is typical for Fisher's art at certain periods. With the concept of recycling he associates biographic, aesthetic and philosophic concepts. According to him the artist is only a storehouse and guardian of the traces left behind. The use of his own clothing is, in the sense of individual

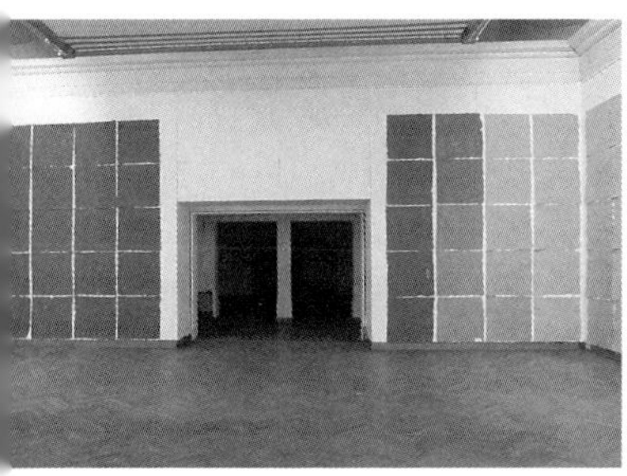
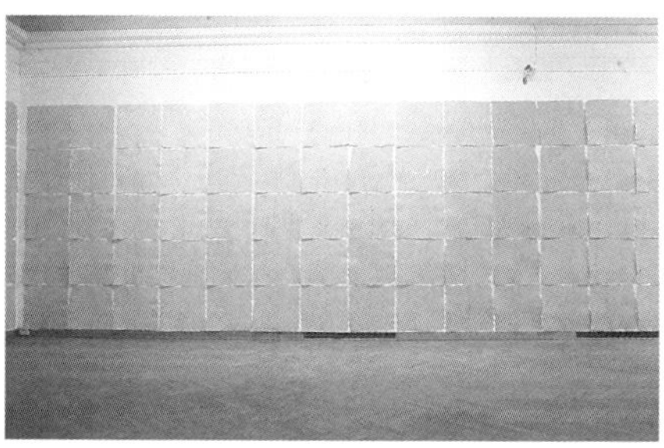

Joel Fisher: Ein unwiderruflicher Schritt. Städtisches Museum Abteiberg, Mönchengladbach 1975. 1977 im Palais des Beaux-Arts, Brüssel. 420 Blätter recycelte Papierkunstwerke, jedes 70 x 70 cm / Joel Fisher: It is an irrevocable action. Städtisches Museum Abteiberg Mönchengladbach 1975. Installed 1977. Palais des Beaux-Arts, Brussels. 420 sheets recycled paper art works, each 70 x 70 cm

schöpferische Kraft der früheren Werke und ihre Geschichte wurde in die neuen Kunstwerke integriert. Das ständige Umarbeiten eigener Kunstwerke und getragener Kleidung ist typisch für Fishers Kunst in manchen Perioden. Mit dem Konzept des Recycling verbindet er biographische, ästhetische und philosophische Vorstellungen. Seiner Meinung nach ist der Künstler nur Bewahrer und Hüter von Spuren. Das Verwenden der eigenen Kleidung ist im Sinne von individueller Mythologie der letzte Versuch, Herrscher der Spur zu werden. Das Papier ist nicht selbst Idee, sondern enthält eine Art Idee. „Innerhalb des Papierblattes besteht strukturelle Homogenität", sagt Fisher, „Rückseite und Vorderseite, Inneres und Äußeres, alles ist gleich."[154] Die Idee bleibt verborgen.

Mystik und eine innige Verbundenheit mit der Natur kennzeichnen viele Papierkunstwerke. Ein Beispiel hierfür gibt der Japaner Yoichi Takada (* 1956 Osaka). Seine Werke atmen Lyrik und Eleganz und erfordern meditative Sammlung. Takada, der an die vollständige systematische Verbundenheit aller Elemente der Umwelt miteinander glaubt, ist demütiger Betrachter der Natur. Seine Werke ver-

mythology, the last attempt to become master over these spoors. The paper is not itself the idea, but contains a kind of idea. "Within the sheet of paper there is a great structural homogenity," Fisher says, "back, front, inside, and outside are all equal."[154] The idea remains latent.

Mysticism and an inner alliance with nature is characteristic of many works of paper art. An example for this is the Japanese Yoichi Takada (* 1956 Osaka). His works respire lyricism and elegance and call for meditative composure. Takada, who believes in a complete and systematic bond between all the elements in our world, is a humble observer of nature. His works attempt to bring together this unity and this interplay – namely the principle of time that transforms through motion, angle of light and changes in humidity – into one object. During the process of events, space and atmosphere are ever re-defined.

The Japanese Shoichi Ida (* 1941 Kyoto) refers in his art concepts to nature and its apparitions. His works, which he often cryptically calls "surface is the between", contain all the phenomena of life such as feelings, sense, judgments, changes, memories,

Yoichi Takada: Tamatsubasa, 1985. Japanpapier, Bambus, Stein, Messing, Blei. Höhe 24 cm, Länge 70 cm / Yoichi Takada: Tamatsubasa, 1985. Japanese Paper, bamboo, stone, brass, lead. Height 24 cm, length 70 cm

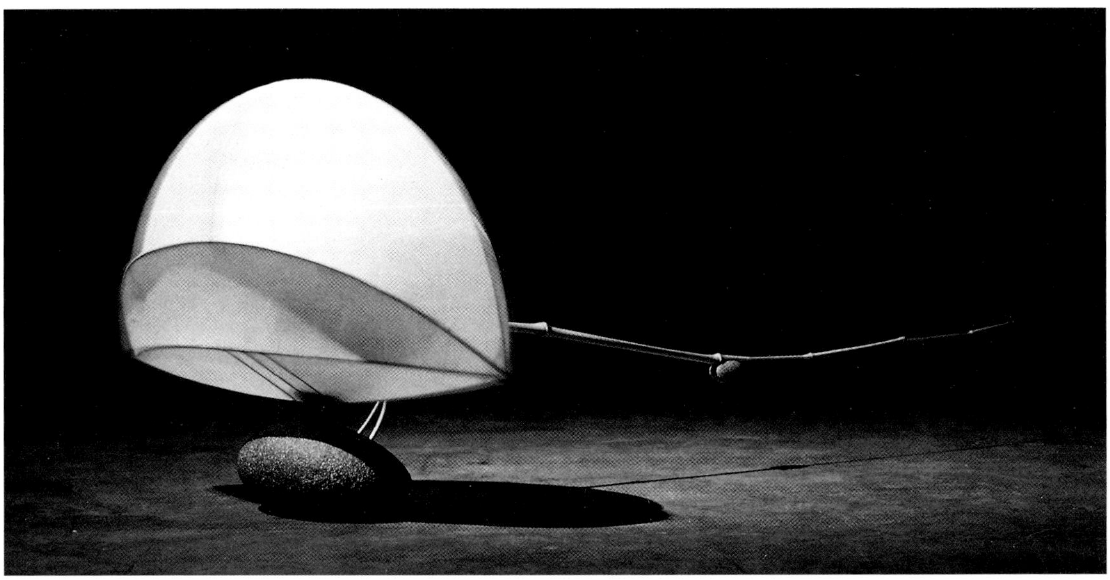

suchen diese Einheit und dieses Zusammenspiel – nämlich das Prinzip der Veränderung in der Zeit durch Bewegung, Lichteinfall und Feuchtigkeitswechsel – in einem Objekt zusammenzufassen. Raum und Atmosphäre definieren sich im zeitlichen Ablauf immer wieder neu.
Auch der Japaner Shoichi Ida (* 1941 Kyoto) bezieht sich in seinen Werkkonzepten auf Natur und ihre Erscheinungsformen. Seine Arbeiten, die er oft als verdeckende „Oberfläche Dazwischen" bezeichnet, beinhalten alle Phänomene des Lebens wie Gefühle, Sinne, Urteile, Veränderungen, Erinnerungen, kulturelle Unterschiede. Wichtig ist für ihn der Schaffensprozeß, weil er hier die natürlichen und physikalischen Prozesse physisch und psychisch beobachten und begreifen kann.
Das Bild sei das „Dazwischen", philosophiert Eng Tow (* 1947 Singapur). Schöpfsieb und Papierpulp bilden bei der Entstehung des Werkes eine Einheit und bedingen sich gegenseitig. Doch nach dem Abgautschen des Blattes verbleibt das Urbild unentrinnbar im Sieb gefangen. Was als Papierkunstwerk sichtbar ist, ist lediglich das Abbild des Urbildes. Hintereinandergehängt erzeugen die hauchdünnen Papiere Raumbilder: Der Raum zwischen den Blättern wird Teil des Kunstwerkes.
Auch für Christa Feuerberg (* 1955 Essen) liegt das Bild „dazwischen", jedoch in weniger philosophisch-mystischer Betrachtungsweise als bei Ida. Sie schneidet unregelmäßige Konturen aus Papier und schafft so eine komplexe Form. Papier ist zwar Zeichen, aber nicht das eigentliche Werk. Dieses ist vielmehr ausgeliefert an den Raum dazwischen, an den Zwischenraum. Es ist zwar ein sinnlich erfahrbares Bild, aber kein greifbar existentes.

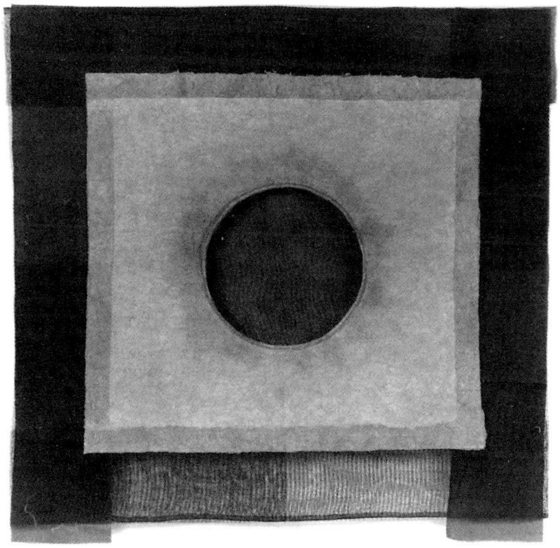

Shoichi Ida: Die Oberfläche liegt Dazwischen – Zwischen Vertikal und Horizont, 1987/88. Gartenprojekt. Verschiedene Materialien. 113 x 108 x 29 cm / Shoichi Ida: The Surface is the Between – Between Vertical and Horizon, 1987/88. Garden Project. Mixed Media. 113 x 108 x 29 cm

cultural differences. What is important to him is the process of creation, because it is here that he can physically and psychically observe and understand the natural and physical processes.
The picture is the "between", Eng Tow (* 1947 Singapore) philosophizes. The mould and the paper pulp become a unity during the creative process and mutually condition each other. Yet after the couching of the paper, the original picture remains inescapably behind in the mould. What is visible as a work of paper art is not the master picture but the copy. Hung one behind the other, the wafer-thin papers create spatial pictures. The space between the sheets becomes part of the artwork.
Also for Christa Feuerberg (*1955 Essen) the picture is "in-between", if less philosophically and mystically than for Ida. She cuts irregular contours out of paper and makes them into a complex form. Though paper is the sign, it is not the actual work. This is supplied more by the space in-between, the interval. It can be sensually experienced as an image, but is not palpably existent.

V.8. Papierschnitt

Im letzten Lebensjahrzehnt schuf Henri Matisse (* 1869 Cateaue – † 1954 Nizza) die ‚Papiers découpés', Meisterwerke konzentrierter Vereinfachung in Farbe und Arabeske. Er „zeichnete" mit der Schere: Zunächst bemalte er große Bogen mit Wasserfarben und schnitt dann mit der Schere Formen, die er solange ordnete und kombinierte, bis ein ausgewogenes Nebeneinander reiner Farben entstand. „In Farbe direkt hineinzuschneiden, erinnert mich an die unmittelbare Arbeit der Bildhauer in Stein", schrieb Matisse.[155] Nach der ‚Jazz'-Serie, 1947 veröffentlicht, entstanden noch zahlreiche Scherenschnitte, weibliche Akte, Akrobaten, Figurengruppen im Schwimmbad. Bereits in den 30er Jahren hatte Matisse Papierschnitte für Vorstudien zu Wandgemälden und für Kostüme genutzt.

1988 stellte der Bildhauer Eduardo Chillida (* 1924 San Sebastián/Spanien) eine neue Werkgruppe, die ‚Gravitaciónes', vor. Es handelt sich um 47 Papierarbeiten in meist zwei oder drei Lagen von Papieren, die in Form geschnitten, übereinandergelegt, an wenigen Stellen mit dünner brauner Kordel angenäht und frei schwebend aufgehängt sind, eine Mischung aus Collage und Relief. Die verwendeten Papiere zeugen von der Freude an der haptischen und optischen Qualität von Handgeschöpftem. Chillida wählte auffällige Materialitäten, handgeschöpfte Papiere mit unregelmäßigem Rand, oft ein wenig gewellt, uneben tonig angebräunt oder cremig in der Farbstruktur, dick ge-

V. 8. Paper cut-outs

In the last decade of his life Henri Matisse (* 1869 Cateaue – † 1954 Nice) created his 'papiers découpés', masterworks of concentrated simplicity in color and arabesques. He "drew" with scissors: first he painted large sheets with waterpaint and from them cut forms that he combined and arranged until a counterpoised row of pure color emerged. "Cutting into color reminds me of a sculptor's direct carving," Matisse wrote.[155] After the 'Jazz' series printed in 1947, he did many other silhouettes: female nudes, acrobats, figures in a swimming-pool. Matise had used cut-outs as early as the 30s as preliminary studies for murals and for costumes.

In 1988 the sculptor Eduardo Chillida (* 1924 San Sebastián/Spain) introduced a new work group, 'Gravitaciónes'. These are 47 paperworks of mostly two or three layers of paper, cut to form, stacked, sewn together at a few places with thin brown twine and hung so as to swing free, a mixture of collage and relief. The use of this medium is proof of the joy he finds in the tactile and optical quality of handmade paper. Chillida chose striking materials: handmade papers with irregular edges, often slightly warped, bronzed unevenly or with a creamy color structure, thickly moulded or wafer-thin and fibrous. Irregularities in the tone and uneveness in the surface are welcome means of composition. In 1992 a lightly marbled, cork-like paper can be seen, in 1993 a thick handmade and a firm brown paper that looks like leather are notable. The large-scaled series of

Henri Matisse: Frauen und Affen, 1952. Gouache auf Papier, geschnitten und geklebt und Kohle auf weißem Papier. 77 x 286 cm /
Henri Matisse: Women and Monkeys, 1952. Gouache on paper, cut and pasted, and charcoal on white paper. 77 x 286 cm

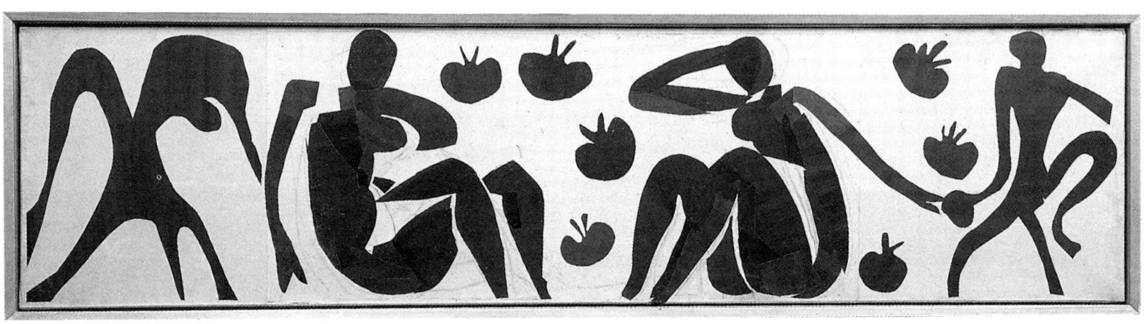

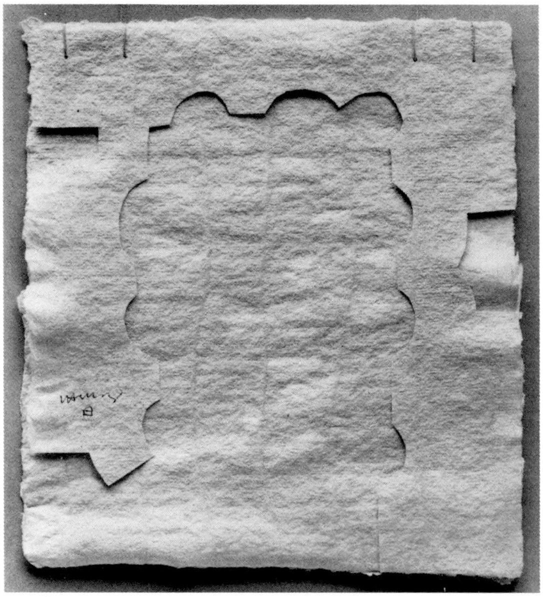

Eduardo Chillida: Gravitation L 15, 1990. Papier. 22 x 20 cm /
Eduardo Chillida: Gravitation L 15, 1990. Paper.
22 x 20 cm

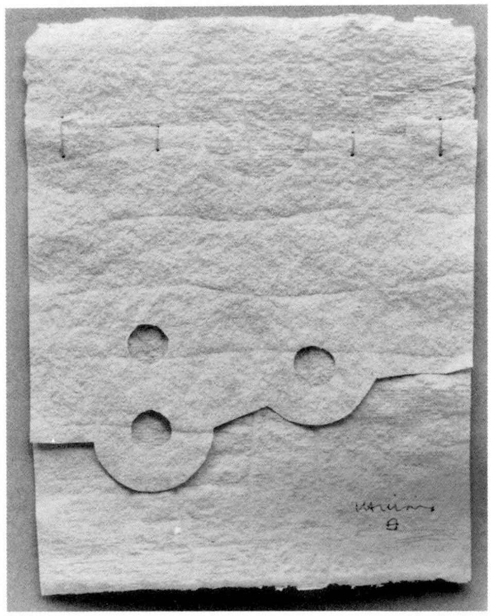

Eduardo Chillida: Gravitation L 17, 1990. Papier. 23 x 18 cm /
Eduardo Chillida: Gravitation L 17, 1990. Paper.
23 x 18 cm

schöpft oder auch hauchzart und fasrig. Differenzen in der Tonigkeit und Unebenheiten in der Papierfläche sind willkommene Kompositionsmittel. 1992 fällt ein leicht marmoriertes, im Aussehen korkähnliches Papier besonders auf, 1993 ein dickes handgeschöpftes und ein griffiges bräunliches, das wie Leder wirkt. Die gleichzeitig entstandenen großformatigen ‚Gravitaciónes' aus Filz unterstützen die Betonung auf die haptische Qualität von Material. Meist sind die Deckblätter in archaische Form geschnitten und mit einem Blatt ähnlicher Farbqualität und Struktur an den beiden Hängepunkten zusammengenäht. Beide Papiere schweben voreinander, die Schwerkraft bestimmt ihre Anordnung. So erweist sich der Raum zwischen den Papieren als Teil des Kunstwerks. Wie bei den Skulpturen wird auch bei den Papierschnitten der „innere" Raum Kompositionsmittel, hier aber auf zweifache Weise. Die ausgeschnittene Papierfläche des Deckblattes bildet das negative Raumvolumen, die stehengebliebene Papierform das positive Material. Positiv- und Negativform befinden sich in einem Spannungsverhältnis zuein-

'Gravitaciónes' made of felt are done during the same time and underline the emphasis on the haptic quality of the material. The upper sheets are mostly cut in archaic form and sewn to a sheet of paper of similar color and structure at the two points of suspension. The two papers float one before the other; gravity determines their order. In this way the space between the sheets of paper becomes part of the artwork. As with the sculpture, the "inner" space between the cut-outs is a medium of composition, in this case in two ways. The top cut-out sheet of paper forms the negative volume of space, the immobile paper sheet forms the positive material. Positive and negative forms find themselves in a state of mutual tension. The concept of spatiality is underlined by the irregular color and texture of the papers. Flat black pieces or linear forms reinforce once again the three-dimensionality and point up the contrast between the natural materiality of handmade paper and the smooth, solid, saturated black plane.
The paper cut-out was for Felix Droese (* 1950 Singen/Hohentwiel), especially characteristic for the years 1978 to 1981, when dark, heavy, stock

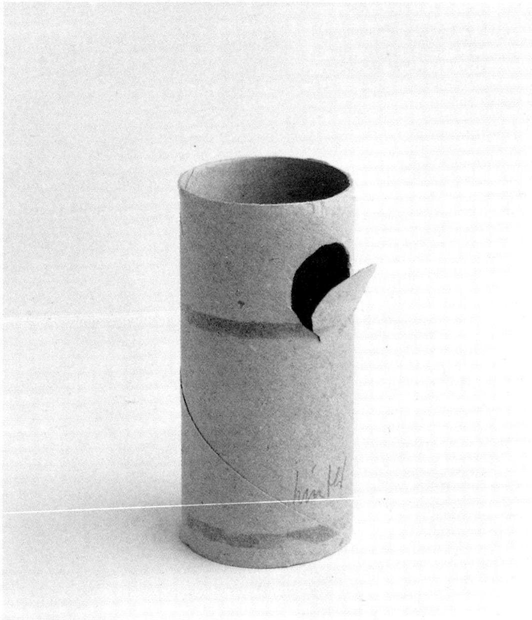

Felix Droese: Regenwald, 1987. Scherenschnitt in Klopapierrolle. Je 9,5 x 4,5 cm / Felix Droese: Rain Forest, 1987. Cut-out in toilet paper roll. Each 9.5 x 4.5 cm

ander. Unterstützt wird die Vorstellung von Räumlichkeit durch die unregelmäßige Farb- und Materialstruktur der Papiere. Schwarze Flächenstücke oder Linienformen unterstreichen einmal mehr die dreidimensionalen Effekte und verdeutlichen den Gegensatz von der natürlichen Materialität des handgeschöpften Papiers und der glatt gesetzten, satt-schwarzen Farbfläche.

Der Papierschnitt ist für Felix Droese (* 1950 Singen/Hohentwiel) vor allem in den Jahren 1978 bis 1981 charakteristisch, als er dunklen, schweren Fotokarton bevorzugt als Material verwendete. Die Werkgruppe der Papierschnitte arbeitet mit Positiv-Negativ-Formen. Die Leerstellen beziehen die Wand als hellen Grund in die Komposition ein. Sie bilden den Kontrapunkt zur Silhouette des schwarzen Schnitts, dessen Papier sich wölbt und dadurch im Licht Plastizität erhält. Bewegung, Dynamik vermitteln sich allein aus den schwarzen Formen vor weißem Grund. Droeses Themen beziehen sich auf Alltägliches, befassen sich mit den lautlosen kleinen Kriegen im Alltag, die zerstörend

cardboard was a favorite material. The cut-out series uses postive-negative forms. The intervals between them bring the wall as light grounding into relation to the composition. They are counterpoints to the silhouettes of the black cut-outs, the paper of which is arched and attains therefore a certain plasticity in the light. The movement and dynamics come solely from the fact that the black forms are foregrounded to the white. Droese's themes are based on the everyday; they take up the small and muted battles of daily life that can be so destructive. His presentations and his titles leave room for thought. Expansion of the canon of material to include stock cardboard and simultaneous use of tissue paper with newspaper, cardboard, gauze, string, wood, metal and glass were, above all, to be seen in the work for 'documenta 7' in 1982, 'I Killed Anne Frank'. The materials he uses are crushed, torn, printed on and painted over. What is thrown away, used, worthless is turned into a worthy means of composition. Droese regards all materials with equal favor; he respects each of their histories, their life traces, their wounds. Material remains very much alive.[156]

Felix Droese: Hafenbild, 1987. Scherenschnitt aus verschiedenfarbigen Kartons, Pappen und Papieren. 21 x 22,5 cm / Felix Droese: Arbor Picture, 1987. Cut-out from differently colored cardboards and papers. 21 x 22,5 cm

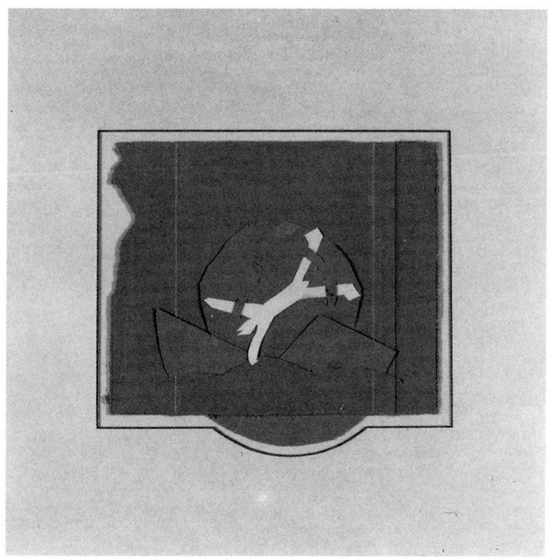

sein können. Seine Darstellungen und die Bildtitel lassen Platz zum Nachdenken. Die Erweiterung des Materialkanons von Fotokarton auf die gleichzeitige Nutzung von Seidenpapier mit Zeitungspapier, Karton, Gaze, Schnur, Holz, Metall und Glas ist vor allem in der Arbeit für die ‚documenta' 1982, ‚Ich habe Anne Frank umgebracht', angewandt. Die Materialien nutzt er zerdrückt, zerrissen, bedruckt und zugestrichen. Das Weggeworfene, Gebrauchte, Wertlose wird zum wertvollen Kompositionsmittel. Alle Materialien bedenkt Droese mit gleicher Gunst; er hat Achtung vor deren eigener Geschichte, ihren Lebensspuren, ihren Wunden. Material bleibt lebendig.[156]

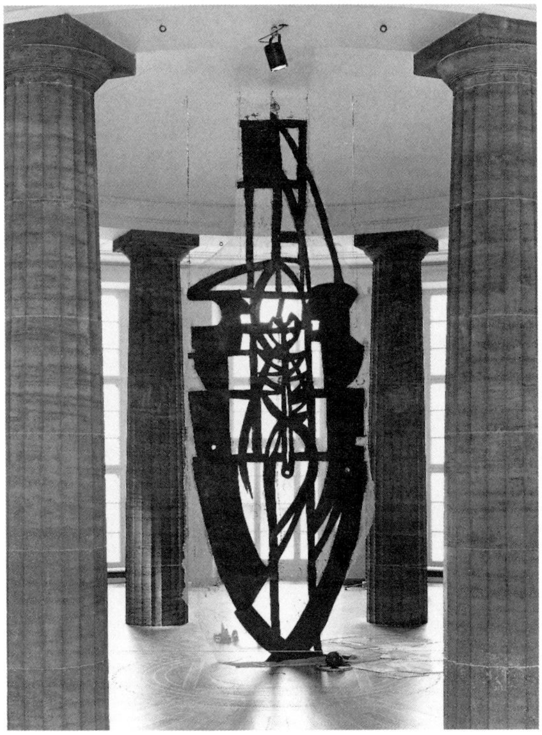

Felix Droese: Ich habe Anne Frank umgebracht, 1981. Hauptteil: Papierschnitt. 735 x 230 cm / Felix Droese: I Killed Anne Frank, 1981. Main part: paper cut-out. 735 x 230 cm

V. 9. Papier und Kommunikation

Papier ist über die Jahrhunderte Trägermaterial von Informationen gewesen. Nun aber ist es untrennbar mit der Information verbunden und wird selbst Medium. Silvie Turner (* 1946 Yorkshire/Großbritannien) schuf 1980 ein Dokument ihres täglichen Umgangs mit Tageszeitungen und Zeitschriften. Sie zermahlte während der Dauer einer Woche die jeweils gelesenen Zeitungen und schöpfte daraus ihr „Tagesblatt", Montag: ‚Guardian', Dienstag: ‚Arts Review' usw. Ein Tagebuchblatt faßt die Mitteilungen einer Schrift komprimiert zusammen. Das Wissen bleibt von nun an verborgen und ist nicht mehr entzifferbar.

Michael Petry (* 1960 El Paso/Texas) konservierte 1986 drei Wochen „Wahrheit" des ‚Daily Mirror'. Auf witzige Weise prangert er die Wichtigkeit und den Wahrheitsgehalt vom Inhalt der Zeitungen an. ‚Three Weeks of the Truth' sind 21 Buchstaben, die 21 Ta-

V. 9. Paper and communication

Over the centuries paper has been a conveyor of information. Now it has become inseparable from the information and is itself a medium. Silvie Turner (* 1946 Yorkshire/Great Britain) created in 1980 a document of each day's occupation with newspapers and journals. One week long she ground up the newspapers she had read and from this composed her own "Daily". Monday: 'Guardian', Tuesday: 'Arts Review', etc. One diary page summarized the information from one condensed text. From now on the facts remain concealed and no longer decipherable.

Michael Petry (* 1960 El Paso/Texas) in 1986 conserved three weeks of "truth" from the 'Daily Mirror'. In a witty way he denounces the importance and the accuracy of newspaper contents. 'Three Weeks of the Truth' are 21 letters of the alphabet that correspond to 21 daily newspapers

geszeitungen und drei Wochen „Wahrheit“ entsprechen. Der jeweilige Gehalt der Tageszeitungen unterscheidet sich lediglich durch höhere oder geringere Grauwerte, durch mehr oder weniger Druckerschwärze, durch den Gehalt an Geschriebenem.

Norbert Stockheim (* 1947 Düren) thematisiert die Schnellebigkeit und die Nachrichtenvielfalt. 1982 weist er mit der Aktion ‚Ich bin eine Zeitung‘ auf gleichgeschaltete Charakteristika von Zeitung und eigener Person, auf die im Wesen begründete strukturelle Vielfalt, auf die Veränderbarkeit und die Vergänglichkeit hin.

Die Arbeit des russischen Neo-Avantgardisten Dmitri Prigov (* 1940 Moskau) beruht auf der intellektuellen und spirituellen Kommunikation. Einen wichtigen Platz nehmen die Werke mit Zeitungspapier, dem Medium der Alltagssprache ein. Ein Text der ‚Prawda‘ wird schon durch den Namen der Zeitung – „Prawda“ gleich „Wahrheit“ – in einen größeren philosophischen, metaphysischen Zusammenhang gestellt. Überschriften und Namen politischer Persönlichkeiten tauchen hinter Codewörtern wie Glasnost, Menetekel, Koschmar (Alptraum) auf. Symbole und Zeichen stellen einen Bezug zu übergeordneten kulturellen Werten her. Ein Auge, das Auge Gottes, wird z. B. zum Symbol für den Ursprung allen Bewußtseins und schafft eine magische Aura.[157]

Verbrauchte Zeitungen und Altpapier bergen für den Macher HA Schult (* 1939 Parchim) „Botschaf-

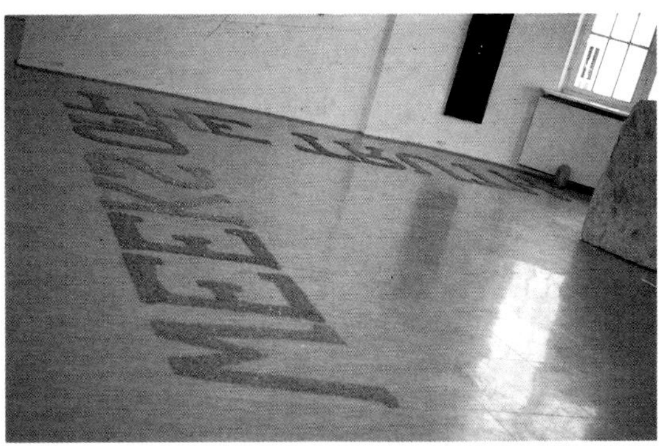

Michael Petry: Drei Wochen der Wahrheit, 1986. Breite 90 cm, Länge 19,20 m / Michael Petry: Three Weeks of the Truth, 1986. 90 cm wide, 19.20 m long

and their “truth”. The respective contents of the daily newspapers differ only in a higher or lower degree of gray, in more or less printing ink, in the volume of print.

Norbert Stockheim (* 1947 Düren) takes the short shelf-life and the multiplicity of the news as his theme. In 1982 with his action ‘I Am a Newspaper’ he points out how a newspaper and his own person are equally geared, their respective structural variety grounded in nature, as well as their changeability and transience.

The work of the Russian neo-avantgardist, Dmitri Prigov (* 1940 Moscow), is based on intellectual and spiritual communication. His works with paper, with the medium of everyday language, are accorded an important place. A text from the ‘Pravda’, already by the clarification of its name Pravda = Truth, is established in a larger philosophic and metaphysical context. Headlines and names of political personalities appear behind code words like glasnost, menetekel (writing on the wall), koschmar (nightmare). Symbols and signs are set in relation to overriding cultural values. An eye, the eye of God, becomes, for instance, a symbol for the origin of all consciousness and radiates a magical aura.[157]

To the “maker” HA Schult (* 1939 Parchim), used newspaper and wastepaper harbor are “messages of our time”. Since 1968 he has been performing actions with wastepaper, pointing to the consumerism of an over-technologized society that creates its own trash present. In 1969 HA Schult filled the Schack Street in Munich with five tons of wastepaper in order to start a public discussion on art and the environment. In 1976 he covered St. Mark’s Square in Venice kneehigh in old newspapers and consumer literature, “messages of the times” repeated ad infinitum. The total environment of St. Mark’s Square showed “time brought to a standstill”. In 1980 Schult built a giant wall of wastepaper in front of the Cologne cathedral for the exhibition ‘Now! Time…’. For the gigantic reality-collage ‘New York Now!’ in 1983 Schult poured a river of newspapers

ten unserer Zeit". Seit 1968 veranstaltet er Aktionen mit Altpapier. Er weist damit auf den Konsumrausch einer übertechnisierten Gesellschaft hin, die eine Abfallgegenwart schafft. 1969 füllte HA Schult die Schackstraße in München mit fünf Tonnen Altpapier, um eine öffentliche Diskussion über Kunst und Umwelt in Gang zu setzen.
1976 bedeckte er den Markusplatz in Venedig kniehoch mit verbrauchtem Zeitungspapier, mit Konsumliteratur, mit sich vieltausendfach wiederholenden „Botschaften der Zeit". Das totale Environment des Markusplatzes zeigte eine zum „Stillstand gebrachte Zeit". 1980 baute Schult für die Ausstellung ‚Jetzt! Zeit...' vor den Kölner Dom eine riesige Papierwand aus Altpapier. Für die gigantische Realitätscollage ‚New York Now!' 1983 goß Schult in die Washington Street in New York einen Fluß in Form von Tageszeitungen.
Papier ist jedem vertraut. Deshalb ist dieses alltägliche Material für den in Barcelona lebenden Amerikaner Thomas Pupkiewicz (* 1950 Cleveland/ Ohio) geeignet, ein neues Publikum für Kunst zu erschließen. Seine Papierobjekte erstehen in vertrauter Erscheinungsform als Faltkarten, Schachteln, Bücher. Nur so kann seiner Ansicht nach aus Kunst Kommunikation entstehen. Dieses Prinzip realisierte er in provokanter Weise 1984 in der denkmalgeschützten Gasse vor dem Picasso-Museum in Barcelona. Den Bewohnern war es nach der Restaurierung nicht mehr erlaubt, ihre Wäsche in der Gasse aufzuhängen und zu trocknen. Pupkiewicz ersetzte die Wäsche durch Bögen seines langlebigen, wasserbeständigen Papiers in Form von Wäschestücken.
Der englische Bildhauer David Mach (* 1956 Methil Fife/Großbritannien) baut Assemblagen aus Gebrauchsgut. Er stapelt Papier, Bücher oder Zeitschriften in Form eines Rolls-Royce, eines U-Bootes oder abstrakter Skulpturen. Ordnungen ähnlicher Tendenz finden sich bei Richard Long, der Fundstücke, beispielsweise Steine und Treibholz, zu geometrischen Formen arrangiert, oder bei Tony Cragg, der Abfallmaterialien wie Spielzeugautos und Stücke von Plastikobjekten in Flächenformen ordnet und nach Far-

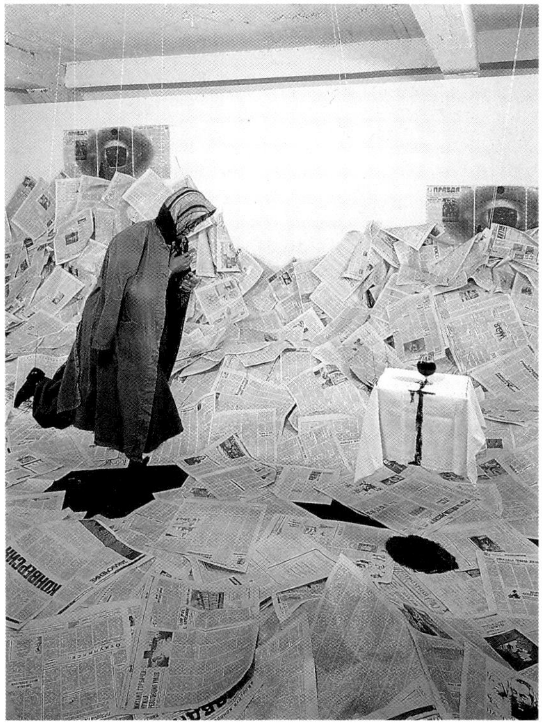

Dmitri Prigov: Schneemann, 1991. Zeitungen. Installation (Ausschnitt) / Dmitri Prigov: Snowman, 1991. Newspapers. Installation (detail)

onto Washington Street in New York. Paper is familiar to everybody. That is why this everyday material is so suitable for the American Thomas Pupkiewicz (* 1950 Cleveland/Ohio) living in Barcelona in his attempts to create a new public for art. His paper objects emerge in the familiar shapes of folding cards, boxes, books. Only in this way can, according to him, communication become art. In 1984 this is the principle that he provocatively realized in the narrow street in front of the Picasso Museum in Barcelona, an area under historical protection. After the restoration, the inhabitants were no longer allowed to hang out their wash to dry in the street. Pupkiewicz replaced their laundry with sheets of his own longlasting, waterproof paper shaped in the form of pieces of laundry.
The English sculptor David Mach (* 1956 Methil Fife/Great Britain) makes assemblages out of consumer goods. He stacks paper, books or newspapers into the shapes of a Rolls-Royce, a

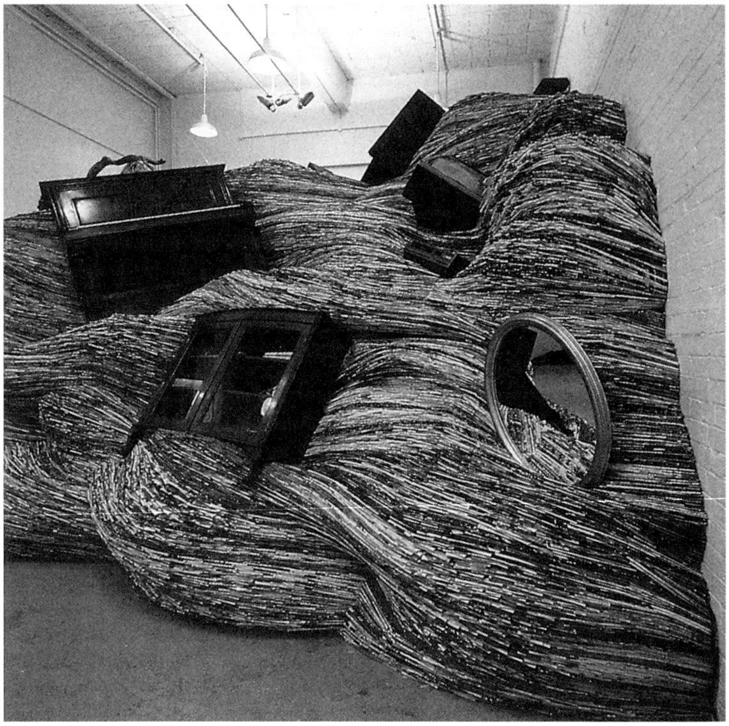

David Mach: Fuel for the Fire, 1986. Zeitschriften, Möbel. Installation /
David Mach: Fuel for the Fire, 1986. Journals, furniture. Installation

ben zerstreut. Die Assemblagen von Mach sind gestapelte Großobjekte. Sie werden aus Zeitschriften oder Büchern vor Ort gebaut, sind an den Platz gebunden. Bei einem Standortwechsel wird die Ordnung zerstört. Die Zeitschriften und Bücher können ihre Reise erst fortsetzen, wenn das Kunstwerk aufgehoben ist. Das Baumaterial landet nach Auflösung des Kunstwerkes unbeschädigt in den Antiquariaten. Mach verbraucht kein Material. Von Zeitschriften und Büchern bleiben keine Spuren der Benutzung: Kunst muß keine Spuren hinterlassen. David Machs Werke wenden sich gegen die Reiselust von Kunst.

Der Belgier Denmark (* 1950 Antwerpen) nimmt die Beendigung der Reiselust und ihren Neubeginn in verwandelter Form zum Thema. Der Ort, an dem die Reise des Papiers ein Ende findet, ist das Archiv, das der Welt das Papier entzieht. Hier ist es zu lebenslänglicher Unbeweglichkeit verurteilt, vor dem Verfall bewahrt, erhält einen Grad von Ewigkeit. Denmark baut Archive aus zerschnittenen, zusammengepreßten Buch- oder Zeitungsstapeln. Er gibt diesen eine eigene Form des „Aufbewahrens“,

submarine or an abstract sculpture. Arrangements with a similar tendency can be found in the work of Richard Long who groups foundling stones and driftwood into geometric forms. Or Tony Cragg who takes waste material like toy cars and pieces of plastic objects, arranges them into planar forms and according to color. Mach's assemblages, on the other hand, are large, stacked objects. They are built out of newspaper or books directly on the site and are bound to the location. When the site is changed, the arrangement is destroyed. The newspapers and books can take up their journey through life when the artwork is suspended. The building material, undamaged, then goes straight to the antique shops. Mach does not use any material. There remain no traces of use on the magazines and books: art must not leave any traces. David Mach's works protest against art's mania for travel.
The Belgian, Denmark (* 1950 Antwerp), takes as theme the end of all travel lust and a new beginning in transformed shapes. The paper journey comes to an end in an archive, a place

eine Form, in der die Vergangenheit nicht mehr lesbar, sondern verborgen ist, also keine Rolle mehr spielt. Parallel zur Aktion des Schreibens hat er die Aktion des Schneidens entwickelt: horizontal von links nach rechts, von oben nach unten. „Frei von Bedeutung und Bezug zum Text wird das Wort nur als Spur an die Oberfläche gebracht“, meint Denmark[158], der deshalb seine Objekte „Tote Archive“ nennt. Für ihn ist Papier, das nicht mehr reisen kann, totes Papier. So bringt er Bücher, Magazine, Zeitschriften als Kunstwerke wieder in den Kreislauf. Sie gehen auf eine neue Reise in die Museen, Galerien und Sammlungen.

„Das einzige, was von der Geschichte übriggelassen worden ist“, sagt der Chinese Huang Yong Ping (* 1954 Quanzhou/Fujian), „ist eine große Menge an Worten und Schriften. Weil die Geschichte selbst nicht sprechen kann, befinden wir uns inmitten eines großen Müllhaufens. Dazu gehört auch die Kultur, die die Menschen manipuliert.“[159] Um neue Wege zu finden, muß man Tradiertes zer-

Denmark: Drei Archivblöcke, 1991. Schulhefte, Schulbankholz. 136 x 33 x 29 cm / Denmark: Three Archive Blocs, 1991. School exercise books, wood from school desks, metal ribbon. 136 x 33 x 29 cm

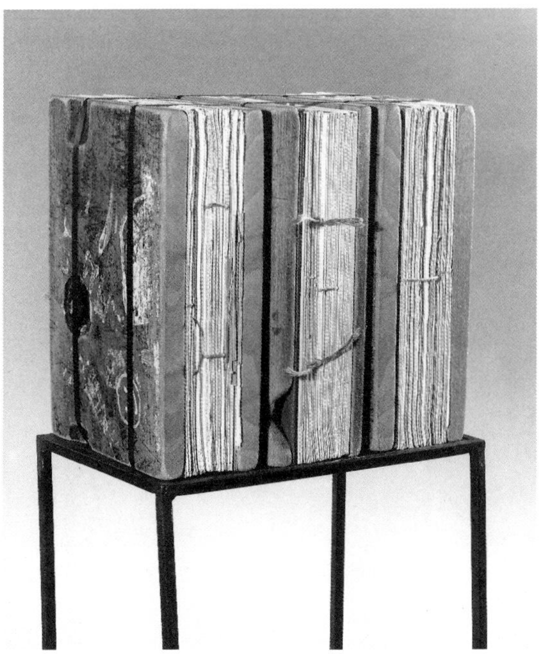

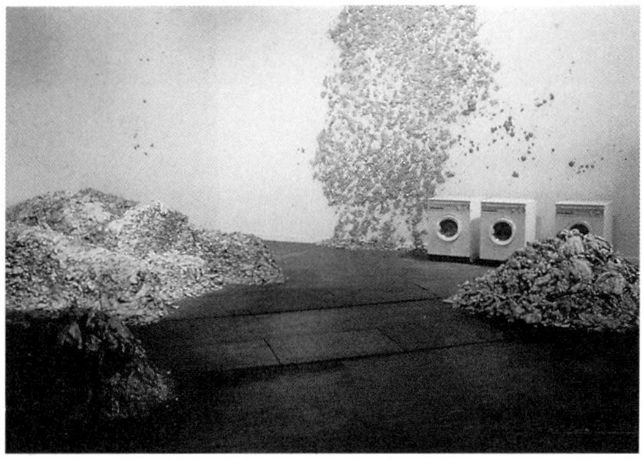

Huang Yong Ping: Magiciens de la Terre, 1989. Installation Centre de Culture de d'Art moderne Georges Pompidou, Paris / Huang Yong Ping: Magiciens de la Terre, 1989. Installation Centre de Culture de d'Art moderne Georges Pompidou, Paris

where paper is withdrawn from the world. Here it is sentenced to lifelong immobility, is preserved from decay, attains a degree of eternity. Denmark builds archives out of cut-up, compressed stacks of books or newspapers. He gives these their own form of "conservation", a form in which the past is no longer legible, but hidden, i. e., no longer plays a role. Parallel to the action of writing he has developed the action of cutting: horizontal from left to right, from top to bottom. "Liberated from any meaning and reference to the text, the word is only brought to the surface as a trace," Denmark believes,[158] who names the works accordingly "Dead Letters". Paper that can no longer travel is for him dead paper. So he brings books, magazines, newspapers into circulation again as artworks. They go on new tours to museums, galleries and collections.

"All that has been left over from history," the Chinese Huang Yong Ping (* 1954 Quanzhou/Fujian) says, "is a great many words and scripts. Because history itself cannot speak, we find ourselves in the midst of a huge trash heap. Culture is also a part of this, manipulated by man."[159] In order to go new ways, man must destroy the existing traditions. At the end of 1987 Huang placed the book 'History of Chinese Painting' together with a Chinese translation of a history of

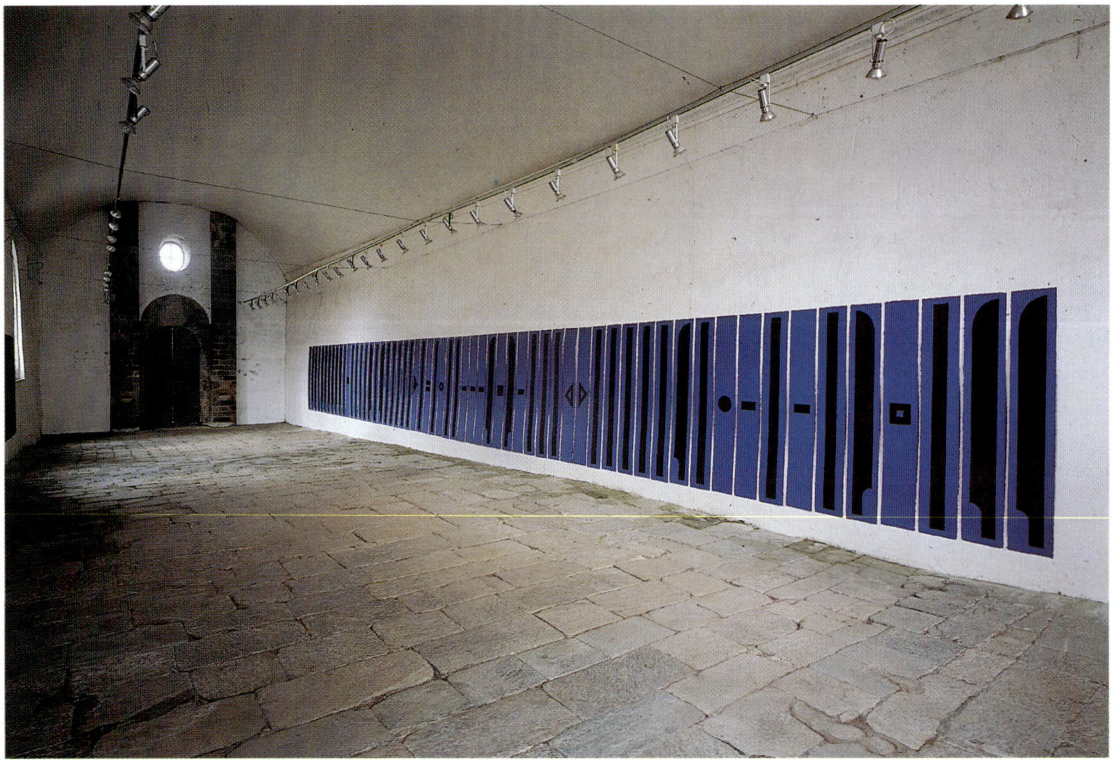

Ulrich Wagner: Umkehr, 1993. Büttenpapiere mit aufgegossenen Zeichen aus pigmentiertem Papierbrei. 24,5 x 6,5 m, je 190 x 27 cm. Installation Chapelle St. Fiacre Giudel, Frankreich / Ulrich Wagner: Return, 1993. Rag paper with cast symbols from pigmented paper pulp. 24,5 x 6,5 m, each 190 x 27 cm. Installation Chapelle St. Fiacre Giudel, France

stören. Ende 1987 wusch Huang in einer Waschmaschine die ‚Geschichte der chinesischen Malerei' zusammen mit einer chinesischen Übersetzung einer Geschichte der modernen westlichen Malerei. Es entstand ein Papierbrei, eine ironisch gemeinte Verbindung zwischen westlicher und östlicher Kunst. 1989 wusch er im Centre Pompidou in Paris in mehreren Waschmaschinen Druckerzeugnisse. Das Papier wurde in ein südchinesisches Grabmal aus Papierbrei in Form einer Schildkröte umgewandelt, das Zeichen für ewiges Leben.[160]

Im Extremfall ist ein Buch nicht mehr lesbar. Die ersten Künstler, die das Buch als Kunstobjekt erarbeiteten, waren in den 60er Jahren Dieter Roth, Gerhard Rühm, Franz Erhard Walther und Timm Ulrichs. Eine differenzierte Skala von Ansatzpunkten hat sich seitdem entwickelt.

Dieter Roth ließ alle Materialien, die als Seiten zusammengebunden sind, als Buch gelten; die Sach-

modern western art, into a washing machine and started the wash cycle. A porridge of paper was the result, an ironic link between western and eastern art. In 1989 in several washing machines located at the Centre Pompidou in Paris, he laundered printed matter. The paper mash was then transformed into a southern Chinese grave stone in the form of a turtle, the sign for eternal life.[160]

In the most drastic cases the book is made illegible. The first artists that made the book into an art object were Dieter Roth, Gerhard Rühm, Franz Erhard Walther and Timm Ulrichs in the 60s. Different ways of going about this have since evolved.

Dieter Roth left all the materials as was, bound into page form; the information was then painted over, destroyed, burned. But it can just as well be that special paper made from eastern or western plant fibers are simply assembled into pages of a beautiful

aussage wird zugemalt, vernichtet, verbrannt. Es können aber auch besondere Papiere aus östlichen oder westlichen pflanzlichen Fasern einfach nur schöne Papierseiten ergeben. Bei Hubertus Gojowczyk (* 1943 Oels/Schlesien) verbleibt vom ursprünglichen Buch lediglich eine verfremdete Teilaussage. Der Italiener Vito Capone (* 1935 Rom) „schreibt“ Bücher durch Graben und Skulptieren von handgeschöpftem dickem Papier. Die punktartigen Erhöhungen und Mulden formen miteinander geometrische Zeichen, Spuren von verschlüsselten Botschaften.
Botschaften transportiert auch Ulrich Wagner (* 1959 Köln). Er arbeitet mit Zeichen, die zwar erkennbar und deutbar, also Informationen in sich bergen, nicht aber eindeutig lesbar sind. Wenige konstruktive Elemente reihen sich zur Niederschrift. Kreise, Quadrate, Dreiecke und Balken fügen sich in immer neuen Konstellationen zum Ganzen, entziehen sich dem deutbaren Zugriff und lassen Spannungsverhältnisse entstehen. Seine gegossenen Papierzeichen in den gegossenen Papiergrund wirken wie Rückgriffe auf archaische Schriftformen, wie codierte Texte. Karg wie seine Formensprache ist sein Farbvokabular. Klares Blau auf Weiß, manchmal ein Schwarz oder Gelb geben dem klaren Formenrhythmus die Klangfarbe.

book. In the case of Hubertus Gojowczyk (* 1943 Oels/Silesia) only a partial and alienated statement remains from the original book. The Italian Vito Capone (* 1935 Rome) “writes” books by digging and sculpting into thick, handmade paper. The elevations and depressions in combination form geometric signs, traces of codified messages.
Ulrich Wagner (* 1959 Cologne), too, transports messages. He works with signs that, though recognizable and interpretable, that is, informational, are not unambiguously readable.
A few constructive elements form rows of script: circles, squares, triangles, bars come together in ever new constellations to form a whole that denies any explicable appropriation. The paper signs poured onto the paper base look like regressions to archaic script, like coded texts. His vocabulary of color is as spare as his repertoire of forms. Clear blue on white, sometimes a black or yellow, provides a tonal color for the clear, formal rhythm.

V. 10. Papierskulptur

Die Verbindung von Papier und Skulptur eröffnet ein reiches Spektrum künstlerischer Möglichkeiten. Vorläufer finden sich in den Konstruktionsplastiken von Braque und Picasso und in den materialspezifischen Formbildungen vom Bauhaus.
Den ersten Höhepunkt erlebt die dreidimensionale Papiergestalt im Umfeld von ZERO. Sie charakterisiert sich als eine in sich geschlossene Form. Licht- und Schattenspiel in Papierreliefs und intensiver noch die Lichtballette von Otto Piene setzen die Papierskulptur in Bezug zum Raum. Der Betrachter erlebt das Kunstwerk im Raum.[161] Um dieselbe Zeit erweitern Künstler in den USA und Europa ihr Vo-

V. 10. Paper sculpture

Paper and sculpture in combination open a rich spectrum of artistic possibilities. The prototypes here are the constructive objects made by Braque and Picasso and the materially specific creations of the Bauhaus.
The first highpoint is the three-dimensional paper constructions in and around ZERO. They are characterized by a closed-off form. A play of light and shadow in paper reliefs and more intensely in Otto Piene's light ballets sets the sculpture in relation to space. The viewer experiences the artwork within its spatial surroundings.[161] At the same time the artists in the US and Europe were

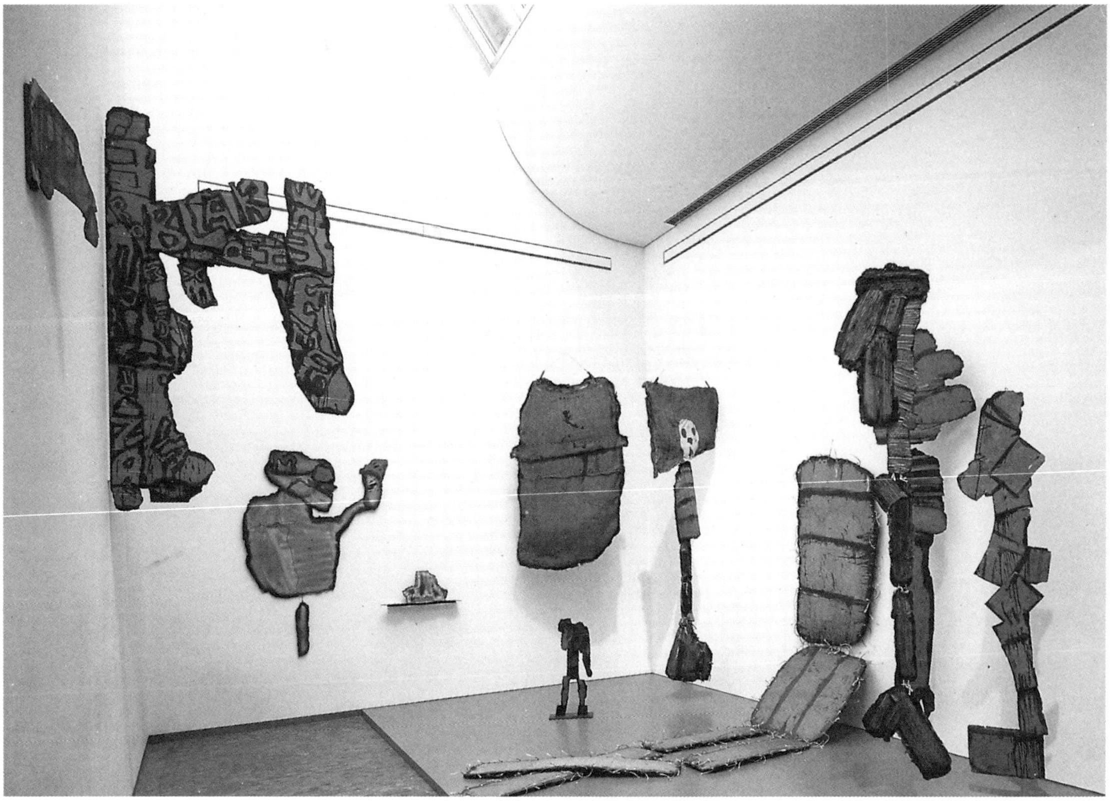

Claes Oldenbourg: Die Straße, 1960. Installation. Pappe, Stoff, Schnur / Claes Oldenbourg: The Street, 1960. Installation. Cardboard, textiles, string

kabular um Environment und Happening. Kunstwerke entstehen, die das Publikum einbeziehen und außer dem Sehvermögen auch das Hören, Riechen und Tasten beanspruchen. Nicht nur die französischen Nouveaux Réalistes hatten „Abfallprodukte" für die Kunst entdeckt und bezogen sich damit auf die Ready-mades von Marcel Duchamp. Intensiver noch ergriffen die Amerikaner Allan Kaprow (* 1927 Atlantic City/New Jersey), Jim Dine (* 1935 Cincinnati/Ohio) und Claes Oldenburg (* 1929 Stockholm) in ihren Environments Besitz von Situationen im Alltag und vom Abfall der Großstadt.

Oldenburg inszenierte seine Ausstellungen als totale Environments. Seine ersten Räume aus Zeitungspapier und Holz stellte er 1959 in der Cooper Union Library in New York aus. 1960 war in der Judson Gallery New York das Environment ‚The Street' zu sehen, Figuren, Zeichen und Gegenstände aus

expanding their vocabulary to include environments and happenings. Artworks emerge that incorporate the public and demand the use of hearing, smell and touch besides that of sight. It is not only the French Nouveaux Réalistes who discover "waste products" for art in reference to the readymades of Marcel Duchamp. It is the Americans, Allan Kaprow (* 1927 Atlantic City/ New Jersey), Jim Dine (* 1935 Cincinnati/Ohio) and Claes Oldenburg (* 1929 Stockholm), who even more intensively take over everyday situations and the debris of the city.

Oldenburg staged his exhibitions as total environments. His first rooms of newspaper and wood he installed in 1959 in the Cooper Union Library in New York and in 1960 in the New York Judson Gallery the environment 'The Street'. Figures, signs and objects are made of cardboard, corrugated paper, newspaper and sacking that he

Pappe, Wellpappe, Zeitungspapier sowie Sackleinen, die er aus dem Abfall der Lower East Side geholt hatte. Wohl mit Recht wurde vermutet, daß die Figuren aus gebrauchtem und teilweise vom Künstler schwarz bemaltem Karton in Beziehung zu den Einwohnern und deren ärmlicher Einrichtung in den Slums stehen.[162] Er führte in diesem Environment sein erstes Happening ‚Snapshots from the City', auf. Das Triviale, das Banale thematisiert Oldenburg in einer Bilderwelt ohne hierarchische Ordnung. Dem entspricht die Nutzung von einfachstem und billigstem Material, aus dem er seine frühen Straßen-Environments inszeniert. Pappe und Zeitungspapier, seinen Hauptmaterialien, beläßt er die spezifische Ausdruckssprache, die gewellte, rauhe Struktur, die haptische Qualität. Sich selbst sieht der Künstler lediglich als ausführendes Medium.
Den Nachbildungen wirklicher Gegenstände in Karton, Gips oder Kunststoff folgen überdimensionierte Nachbildungen von Eßwaren und schließlich von Gebrauchsgegenständen wie Badewanne, Waschbecken in „harter" Ausgabe (Pappe) und in „weicher" Ausgabe (Stoff oder Vinyl, manchmal gefüllt mit Pappe). Schafft Oldenburg in seinem frühen Werk ein neues Bewußtsein von Wirklichkeit durch den Gebrauch von einfachem und gebrauchtem Material, wird dies im späteren Werk durch ge-

picked from the rubbish of the Lower East Side. It was assumed, probably rightly, that the figures made of used cardboard and partly painted black stood in relation to the inhabitants and their poor accomodation in the slums.[162] He performed his first happening 'Snapshots from the City' in this neighborhood. Oldenburg thematizes the trivial, the banal in a world of imagery lacking any hierarchical order. This corresponds to the use of the simplest and cheapest material with which to stage his early street environments. He leaves cardboard and newspaper, his main materials, to their own specific expressiveness: their warped, raw texture and haptic quality. The artist sees himself as a mere medium for their implementation.
The duplication of real objects in cardboard, plaster or plastic are followed by over-sized re-creations of food and finally of everyday, functional articles like bathtubs and sinks made of cardboard in a "hard" version (cardboard) and of cloth or vinyl (sometimes filled with cardboard) in a "soft" one. If Oldenburg created a new awareness of reality in his early work by the use of simple and secondhand material, in his later work he achieved the same by the over-sized reproduction of everyday objects. Their haptic quality helps rid them of a sense of isolation in face of reality; their huge scale disturbs the normal visual expectation of the viewer.

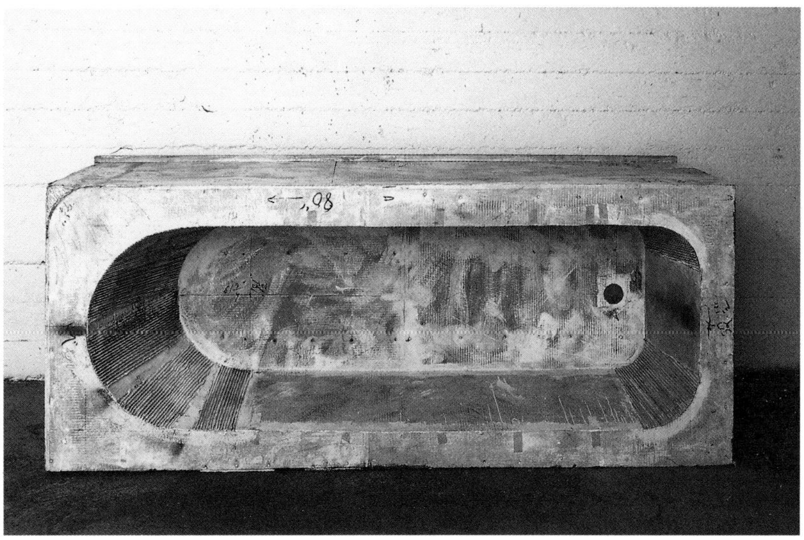

Claes Oldenburg: Badewanne, 1966. Harte Fassung. Pappkarton, Holz, Bleistift, Ölfarbe. 79,5 x 204 x 69,5 cm / Claes Oldenburg: Bath Tub, 1966. Hard model. Cardboard, wood, pencil, oils. 79.5 x 204 x 69.5 cm

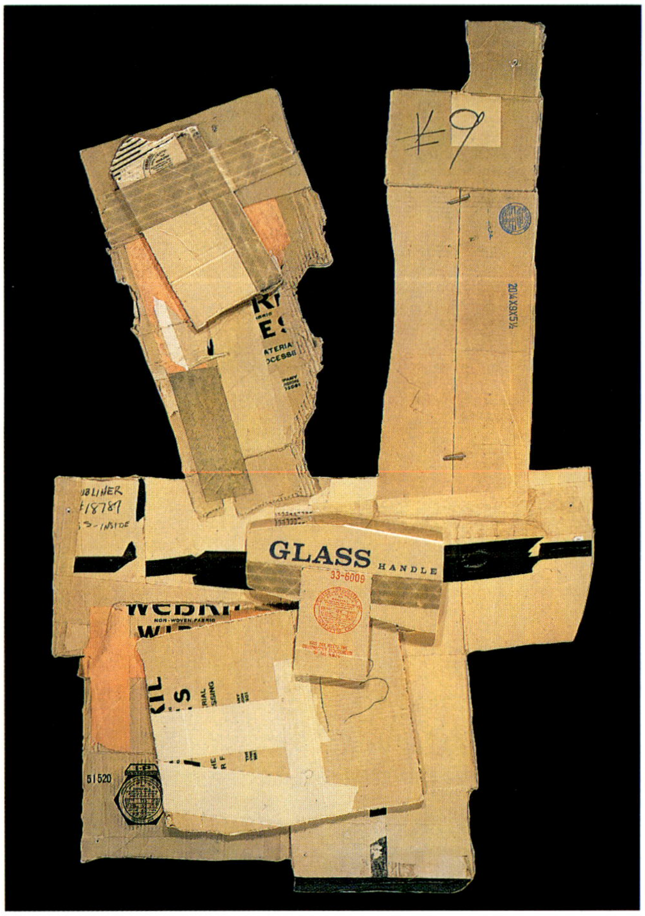

Robert Rauschenberg: Cardbird II. Aus: ‚Cardbird Series', 1971. Lithographie, Siebdruck, Collage. 137,2 x 85,1 cm / Robert Rauschenberg: Cardbird II. From: 'Cardboard Series', 1971. Lithograph, screen print, collage. 137.2 x 85.1 cm. © Tyler Graphics Ltd.

treue, aber überdimensionale Abbildungen von Alltagsobjekten erreicht. In ihrer haptischen Qualität verlieren sie an Isolation der Realität gegenüber, durch ihre Größe stören sie die Sehgewohnheiten des Betrachters. Oldenburg, für den Pappe so vergänglich ist wie Leinwand[163], nutzt Pappe und Wellpappe nicht nur in den „hard"-Versionen. Sie dienen ihm bis heute auch, um Modelle von Großskulpturen zu erstellen. Das Material in seiner Struktur kommt zum Tragen. Die haptischen und optischen Qualitäten der Pappe, wie die Wellenkonstruktion an den Schnitträndern oder die leichte Rippung der Oberfläche, geben den Modellen einen spezifischen Charakter. Die Modelle behaupten ihre eigenständige Existenz.[164]

Oldenburg, for whom cardboard is just as impermanent as canvas,[163] does not only use cardboard and corrugated paper in hard versions. They serve him still today for making preliminary models of his large sculptures. The material is brought into play in all its structural property. The haptic and optic qualities of cardboard and the corrugated construction of the cut edges or the slight ribbing on the surface give these models their specific character; they are able to claim an independent existence.[164]
Robert Rauschenberg, who had already in 1952 done a series of cardboard collages, in which (usually) untreated paperboard was the picture support and the picture surface in one, and who was fascinated by the

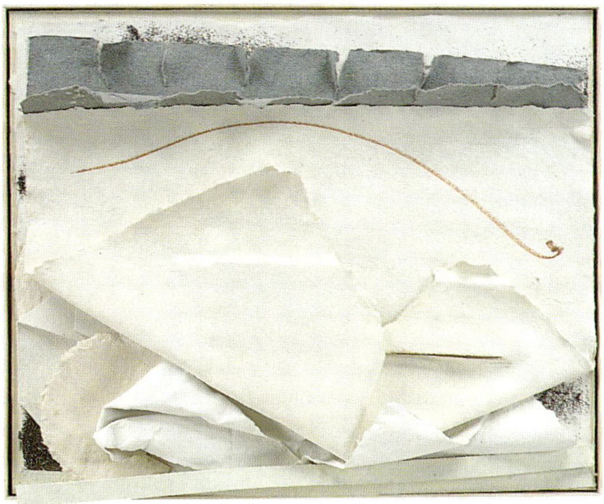

Anthony Caro: No. 53. Untitled. Aus: ‚Paper Relief Sculptures', 1982. Handkolorierte Skulptur. 66,7 x 80 x 11,4 cm / Anthony Caro: No. 53. Untitled. From: 'Paper Relief Sculptures', 1982. Hand colored sculpture. 66.7 x 80 x 11.4 cm. © Tyler Graphics Ltd.

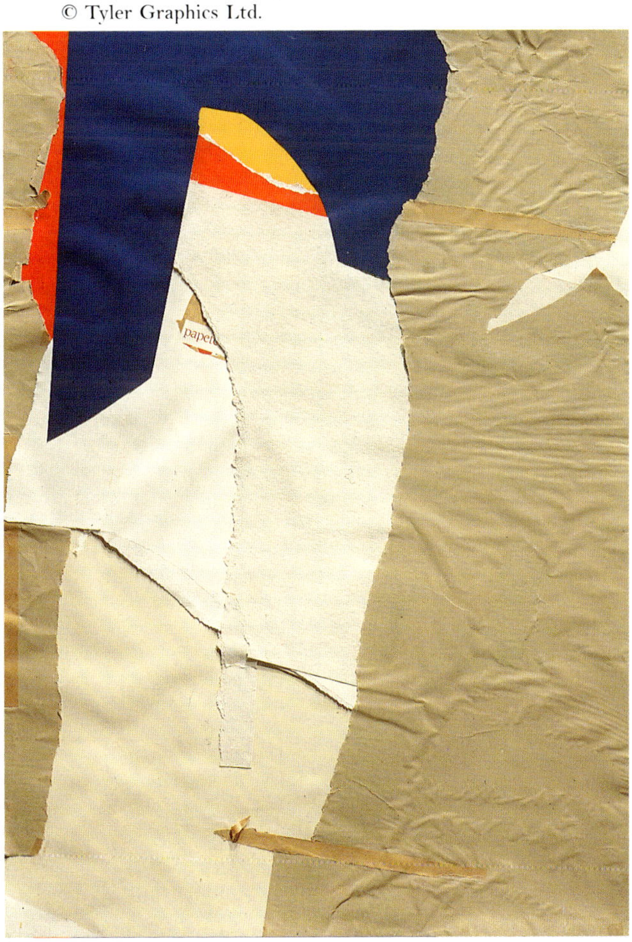

Robert Motherwell: America – La France Variations II, 1984. Lithographie, Collage. 115,6 x 73,7 cm / Robert Motherwell: America – La France Variations II, 1984. Lithograph, collage. 115.6 x 73.7 cm. © Tyler Graphics Ltd.

Robert Rauschenberg, der bereits 1952 eine Reihe von Kartoncollagen fertigte, in denen meist unbehandelter Karton Bildträger und Bildoberfläche zugleich ist, und den die „Geschichte" der gefundenen Kartons faszinierte, schuf Anfang der 70er Jahre Kartonreliefs mit Fundspuren, denen er weitere Verletzungen beibrachte. „Nach einiger Zeit und einem gewissen Widerstand kam ein Verlangen in mir auf, mit Material des Überflusses und der Weichheit zu arbeiten. Etwas, das mittels seiner eigenen Sprache eine Sammlung von Verbindungslinien liefert."[165]

Robert Motherwell (* 1915 Aberdeen/Washington – † 1991 Provincetown/Massachusetts) schuf 1984 eine Serie von Papiercollagen, in denen die Materialität der verschiedenen Papiersorten Struktur und Farbe bestimmte und das Papier selbst zur Flächenskulptur wird.

Anthony Caro (* 1924 London) erarbeitete 1981 eine Serie von Papierskulpturen bei Tyler Graphics. Ihn interessierte die besondere Materialität des handgeschöpften Papiers. Griffige Papiere mit betont unregelmäßigem Rand brachte er gebogen, gefaltet oder geknüllt zur Form. Es entstanden Reliefs und vollplastische Formen. Die Farbigkeit resultiert meist aus den Papieren selbst. Die unterschiedlichen Weißtöne, das lebendige Licht-Schatten-Spiel und die variierenden Strukturen der geschöpften

"history" of this found material, created in the 70s cardboard reliefs with traces of their past to which he added further mutilation. He reports how, after a time and a certain amount of resistance, he had felt a need to work with surplus material that was soft. That is, with something that has its own language, supplying it with a network of connective lines.[165]

Robert Motherwell (* 1915 Aberdeen/Washington – † 1991 Provincetown/Massachusetts) created in 1984 a series of paper collages in which the materiality of different kinds of paper determined the structure and color, and the paper itself became a planar sculpture.

In 1981 Anthony Caro (* 1924 London) worked on a series of paper sculptures at Tyler's. He was interested in the materiality of handmade paper. Taking sturdy paper with a markedly irregular edge, he bent, folded, crumpled it into form, creating reliefs and three-dimensional forms. Color was usually the extension of the paper itself. The different white tones, the vivid play of light and shadow and the varying textures of the handmade paper are part of the composition. Caro, won over to paper as a medium, composed a second series of paper sculptures in Ohama, Japan in 1990, this time out of Japanese Washi paper.

Andy Warhol (* 1930 Pittsburgh/Pennsylvania – † 1987 New York) created in 1964 a series of simple

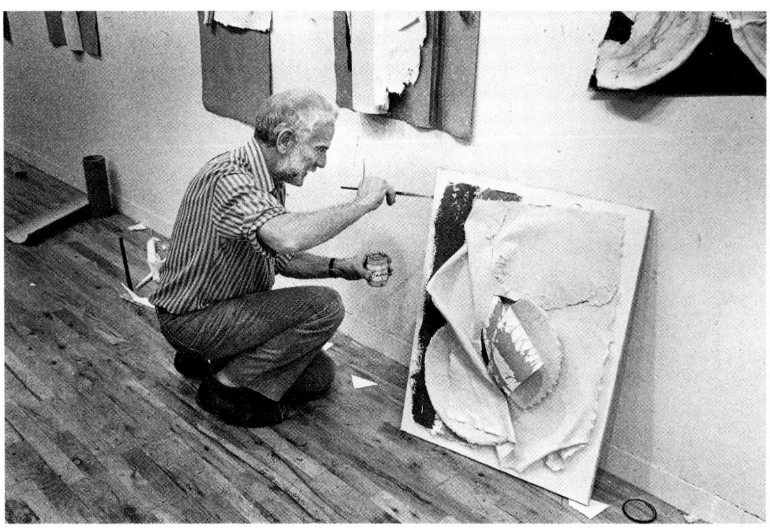

Anthony Caro malt an ‚No. 114. Untitled' aus der ‚Paper Relief Sculptures Series', Tyler Graphics Artist's Studio, 1981 / Anthony Caro painting 'No. 114. Untitled' from the 'Paper Relief Sculptures Series', Tyler Graphics Artist's Studio, 1981. © Tyler Graphics Ltd.

Papiere sind Kompositionsbestandteil. Caro, überzeugt vom Medium Papier, komponierte 1990 in Ohama/Japan eine zweite Serie von Papierskulpturen, diesmal mit dem japanischen Papier Washi.
Andy Warhol (* 1930 Pittsburgh/Pennsylvania – † 1987 New York) schuf 1964 Serien einfacher Kartons, die sich jeder im Supermarkt hätte besorgen können: die ‚White Brillo Boxes' und ‚Yellow Brillo Boxes'. Doch aus Pappe sind die Warhol-Objekte nicht. Es sind vielmehr Nachbildungen aus Sperrholz mit entsprechendem Signet. Nur wegen Schwierigkeiten mit dem Zoll stellte Warhol 1968 in Stockholm originale Brillo-Kartons aus.
Zum Teil mehrräumige Installationen aus Wellpappe und Karton, in denen der Betrachter zwischen die Figuren treten kann, baute der junge Maler und Bildhauer Bertram Jesdinsky (* 1960 Bonn – † 1992 Wuppertal) seit 1984 und griff damit das Thema des Environments mit Pappe in buchstäblich real-phantastischer Weise auf. In Möbeln und Gegenständen aus Pappe agieren tierähnliche Figuren, die sich durch menschliche Verhaltensweisen auszeichnen. Mit Bemalung sparte der Künstler nicht. In der Kölner Galerie Krings-Ernst war 1985 eine Badezimmersituation zu sehen: In einer Badewanne sitzen zwei Figuren, die sich mit einer kleinen Waschmaschine und einem Sägefisch beschäftigen. Die Figur vor der Wanne zeigt aufgespießt auf einem langen Stab eine Koffernähmaschine. Ein großer Vogel sitzt auf einem Haus und hält einen Diaprojektor auf seinem Oberschenkel. Zwei Vogelmenschen tragen eine Straße mit Häusern und Laternen. Dahinter öffnet sich ein höhlenartiger Gang, der in einem kapellenartigen Raum mit zwei Fenstern aus Transparentpapier endet. Die Inszenierungen aus Fiktion und Realität, kombiniert mit der haptischen Materialität Pappe mit realitätsnahen, skizzenhaften Bemalungen machen die Faszination von Jesdinskys begehbaren Räumen aus. Um seine Wellpappenplastiken zu stabilisieren, überzog er von 1989 an die Oberflächen mit farbigem Epoxydharz. Die Plastiken wirken nun kostbar wie Keramiken.[166]

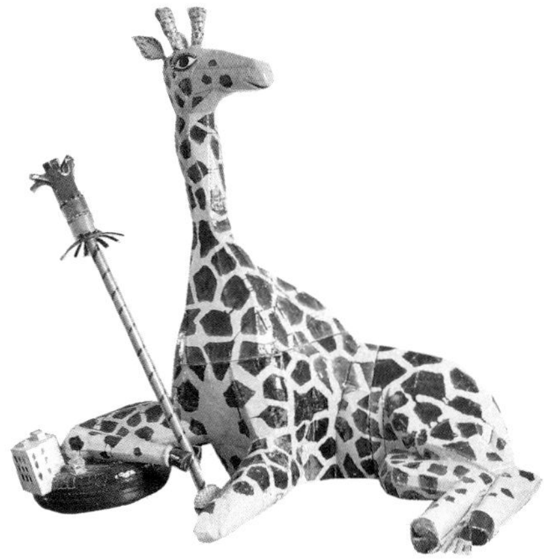

Bertram Jesdinsky: Giraffe, 1988. Pappmaché und Epoxydharz. 2 x 2 x 2 m / Bertram Jesdinsky: Giraffe, 1988. Papier maché and epoxyd resin. 2 x 2 x 2 m

cartons that anyone could have taken home from the supermarket: 'White Brillo Boxes' and 'Yellow Brillo Boxes'. But these Warhol objects are not made of cardboard. They are, in fact, imitations made of plywood with the respective labels. It was only because of difficulties with Swedish customs that in 1968 in Stockholm Warhol used genuine Brillo cartons.
The young painter and sculptor Bertram Jesdinsky (* 1960 Bonn – † 1992 Wuppertal) had since 1984 built corrugated paper and cardboard installations consisting sometimes of several compartments into which the viewer could step between the figures, hereby taking up the theme of paperboard environments in a literal, realist-fantasist manner. In interaction with furniture and objects made of cardboard are animal-like figures characterized by human behavior. The artist does not spare the paint. In 1985 in the Galerie Krings-Ernst a bathroom situation was depicted: in a bathtub two figures were seated who are occupied with a small washing machine and a swordfish. The figure in front displayed a portable sewing machine impaled on a long pole. A large bird was seated on a house holding a slide projector on its thigh. Two bird-

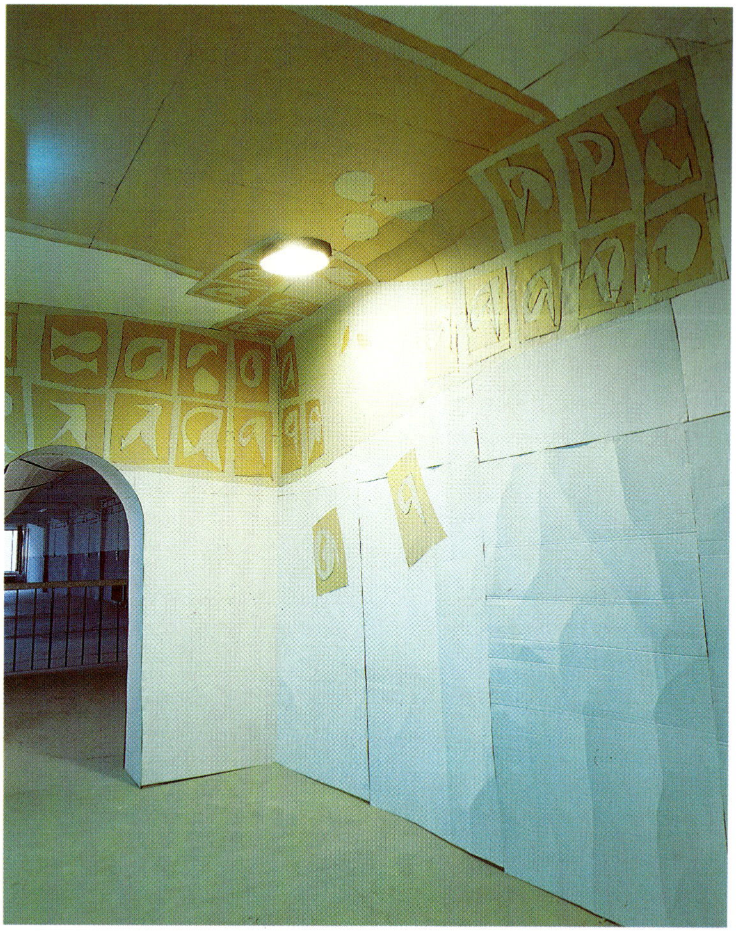

Bertram Jesdinsky: ‚Cicero', Installation, Düsseldorf 1990 / Bertram Jesdinsky: 'Cicero'. Installation, Düsseldorf 1990

Michael Kortländer (* 1953) arbeitet seit 1981 mit Wellpappe. Die frühen Werke bestehen aus planimetrischen Elementen, die geordnet und rhythmisiert eine Raumskulptur ergeben. In den späten 80er Jahren baut er große Skulpturen in spröder und monumentaler Blockform. Ein meist einfarbiger Anstrich intensiviert die Strukturen der Pappe und deren Schnittstellen, verfremdet zugleich aber das materialspezifische Aussehen.
Scott Fine (* 1949 Moscow/Idaho) baut aus Wellpappe Alltagsobjekte in täuschend ähnlicher Nachbildung. Irritation ist Bestandteil der Formulierung. Das einfache Objekt ist in ein anderes Medium transponiert. Qualität und Ästhetik des Werkstoffes werden durch einen dünnen, lasierenden Farb-

men were carrying a street with houses and lanterns. In the background a cave-like passage opened out and ended in a kind of chapel with two windows of transparent paper. The stage-setting – part fiction, part reality – combined with the haptic materiality of cardboard, painted sketchily but realistically, is what makes up the fascination of Jesdinsky's walk-in world. In order to stabilize his corrugated paper structures, he had begun in 1989 to coat the surfaces with epoxy resins. The sculpture now looks as precious as ceramic.[166]
Michael Kortländer (* 1935) has worked since 1981 with corrugated paper. The early works are composed of planimetric elements that, provided with order and rhythm, make up a sculptural

auftrag betont oder durch eine dick aufgetragene Bemalung ignoriert.[167]
Ohne Rücksicht auf Wertigkeit sammelt Thomas Virnich (* 1957 Eschweiler) alles, was sich bearbeiten läßt, bevorzugt jedoch solche Materialien, die bereits den Charakter des Abgenutzten und Morbiden haben. Gestaltungsprinzip ist das Zerschneiden, Aufbrechen, Zerlegen und das anschließende Verpacken, Umhüllen, Ergänzen. Er nutzt nicht selten Pappe und Pappmaché. Die Papierobjekte bestehen meist aus mehreren miteinander verleimten Schichten von Wellpappe, Pappe und aufkaschierten Illustrierten, die als Basis der Zergliederung dienen. Wie Puzzleteile wirken die Einzelelemente, die oft mit Draht untereinander verbunden sind.[168]
Gerd O. Stegner (* 1951 Höheinöd/Pfalz) arbeitet vorwiegend mit Pappe und Papier. Neben Buchobjekten, deren „Seiten" und „Umschläge" oft verschnürt und zugemalt sind, entstehen Skulpturen aus gefundenen Kartons, Pappen und Packpapier, die, teils verschnürt, stets die rohe Materialkonsi-

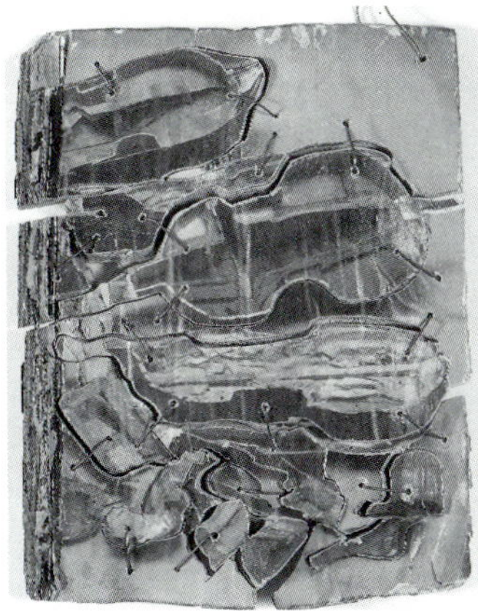

Thomas Virnich: Baßfutteral, 1990. Karton gesägt, Farbe, Draht. 30 x 23 x 2 cm /
Thomas Virnich: Bass-Fiddle Case, 1990. Cardboard sawed, paint, wire. 30 x 23 x 2 cm

installation. In the late 80s he built large sculptures in a reserved and monumental block form. A usually uni-colored coat of paint intensifies the textures of the cardboard and its cut edges and, at the same time, gives the material a look that distances it from its origin.
Scott Fine (* 1949 Moscow/Idaho) builds everyday objects of corrugated paper that are deceptively real. Irritation is part of the formulation. The

Ruth Handschin: Leuchtraum. Kunstverein Heilbronn 1992. 300 g fluoreszierendes Papier, Schwarzlicht /
Ruth Handschin: Glowroom. Kunstverein Heilbronn, 1992. 300 g fluorescent paper, black light

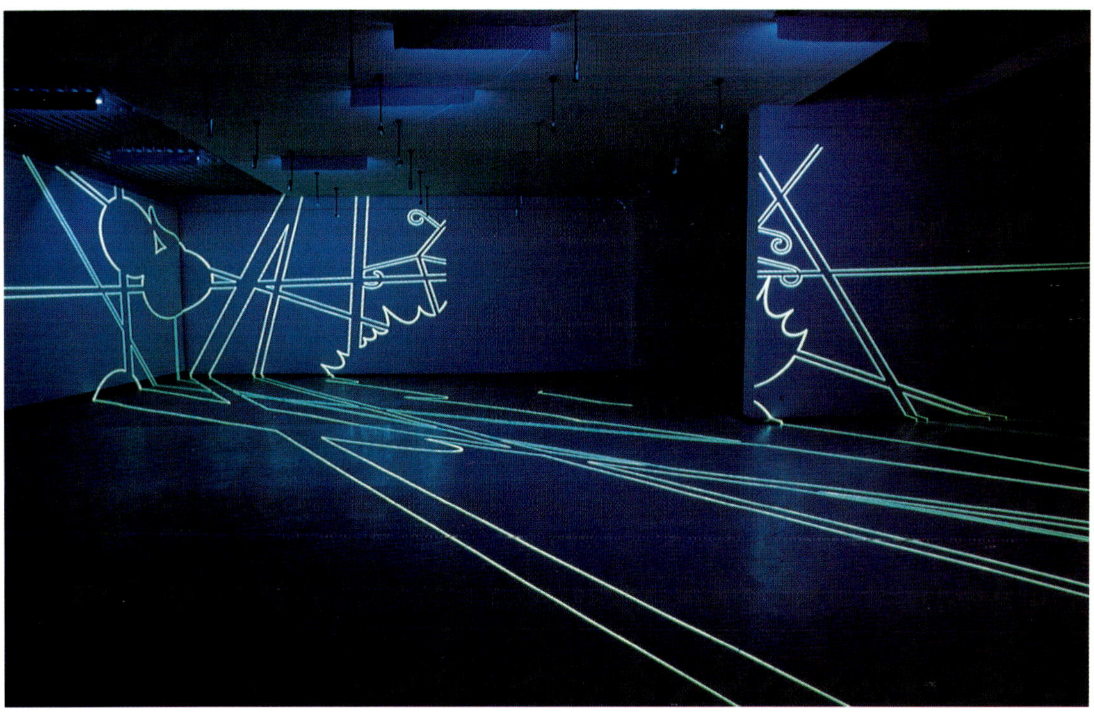

stenz und den Gegensatz der Papiermaterialien als Kompositionsmerkmale inkorporieren.
Farbige Lichtskulpturen im Raum mit fluoreszierendem Papier inszeniert Yvonne Goulbier (* 1953 Kaiserslautern). Papier schneidet sie in kleine Formen oder drückt und knickt es in Form und ordnet die Teile zum Raumarrangement.
Ausladende Lichtzeichnungen im Raum konstruiert Ruth Handschin (* 1949 Basel) mit fluoreszierenden Papierstreifen und Schwarzlicht. Überfordert vom extremen Hell-Dunkel-Gegensatz, beginnt das Auge von Linie zu Linie zu springen, so daß das Netz sich von Boden und Wänden abhebt und zur Raumskulptur wird.
Räume mit Objekten aus Papier, die in beredter Zwiesprache von Form und Materialität stehen, gruppierte Uwe Meier-Weitmar (* 1952 Bochum). Seit 1979 arbeitet er mit Papieren jeglicher Art. Er

simple object is transposed into another medium. The quality and aesthetics of the working material are emphasized when given a thin, color glazing or ignored when covered in thick paint.[167]
With no thought for its value, Thomas Virnich (* 1957 Eschweiler) collects anything that can be worked on, but prefers such materials that already have a used and morbid character. The principle of further design is based on cutting, breaking, segmenting followed by encasing, wrapping, completion. From time to time he uses cardboard and papier-maché. The paper objects are mostly made up of several layers pasted together of corrugated paper and cardboard and laminated magazine illustrations that serve as the foundation for the fragmentation. The single elements function like pieces of a puzzle that are often wired together.[168]

Uwe Meier-Weitmar: Ohne Titel, 1985. Papier, Band, Lack, Folie, Dispersion. 340 x 700 cm /
Uwe Meier-Weitmar: Untitled, 1985. Paper, cord, varnish, foil, dispersion paint. 340 x 700 cm

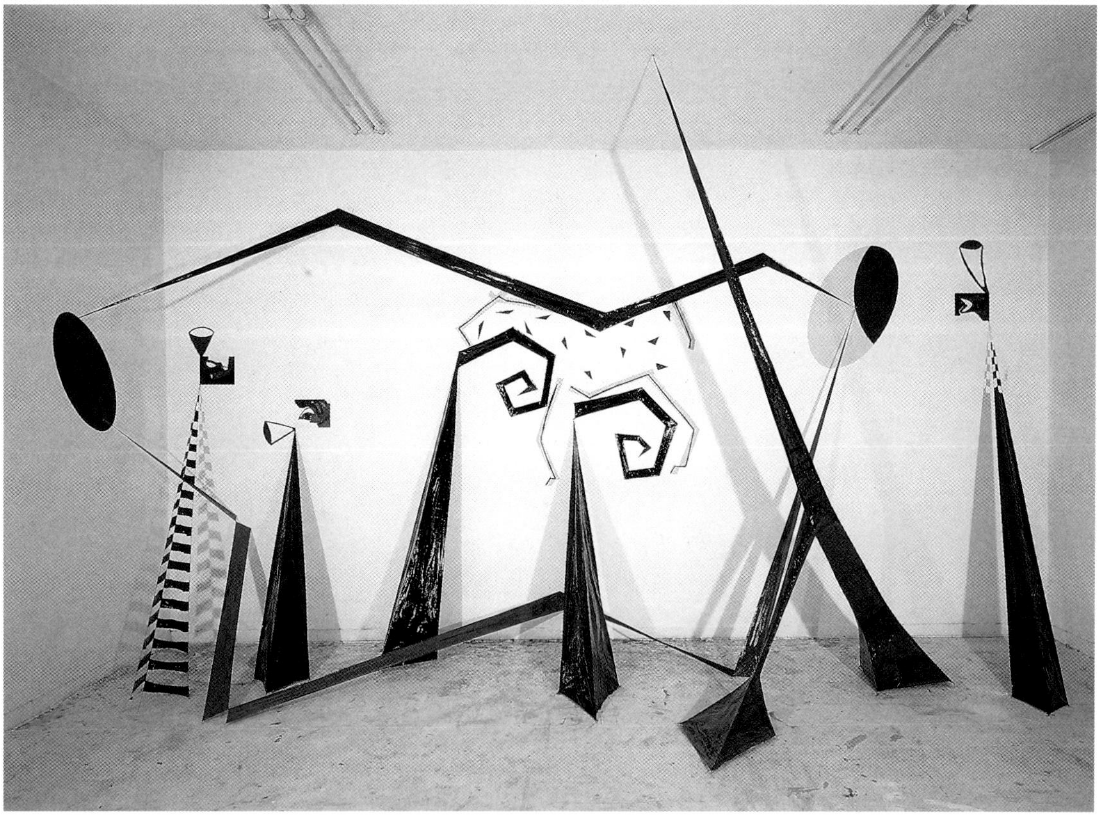

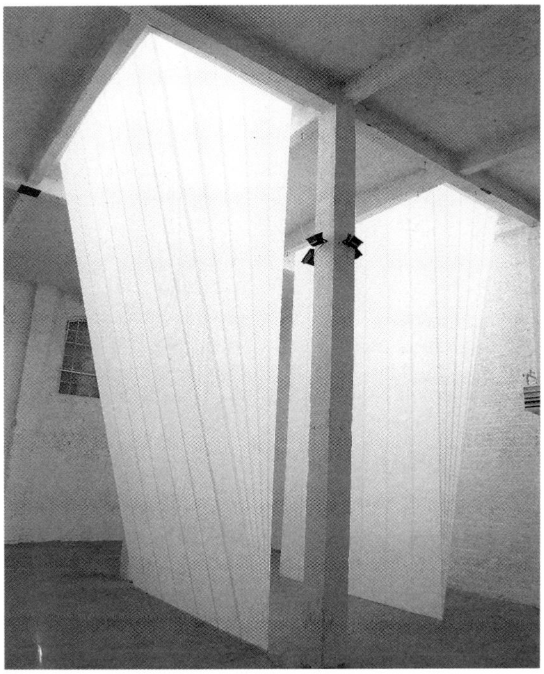

Annette Sauermann: Zwei Lichtkeile, 1992. Installation Wachsfabrik Köln. Stahlseil, Seidenpapier, Tageslicht. Höhe 805 cm, Breite 205 cm, Tiefe 400 cm / Annette Sauermann: Two Light Wedges, 1992. Installation Wachsfabrik Cologne. Steel rope, satin paper, daylight. 805 cm high, 205 cm wide, 400 cm long

realisiert in diesem Medium Installationen, plastische Stilleben und Scherenschnitte. Farbigkeit erhalten sie durch die Kombination vorgefundener Papiere oder durch Pigmentierung von Pulp.

Skulpturen, die das Tageslicht einfangen und formen, baut Annette Sauermann (* 1957 Essen). Sie arbeitet mit dünnem, durchscheinendem Seidenpapier, das gestrafft wird durch senkrechte, mit Hilfe eines Gewichtes zum Boden gezogene Stahlseile. Die Schwerkraft gibt der Papierskulptur die Form. Der Wind, der durch das Oberlicht dringt oder durch das Begehen des Raumes entsteht, erzeugt Bewegung und Geräusche. Das Licht, das durch das Oberlicht fällt, nimmt innerhalb der Papierskulptur körperhafte Gestalt an und verändert sich und damit die Skulptur im Tagesverlauf stetig.

Mit Transparenz von Papier komponiert auch Jane Balsgaard (* 1939 Kopenhagen). Ihre lichtbeeinflußten Skulpturen von nahezu schwereloser Substanz bestehen oft aus hauchdünnem Papier, das

Gerd O. Stegner (* 1951 Höheinöd/Palatinate) works chiefly with cardboard and paper. Along with book objects whose "pages" and "covers" are often lashed together and covered in paint, he makes sculptures out of found cardboard, paperboard and wrapping paper that, partially tied, incorporate the consistency of the different raw materials and their contrast as compositional elements.

Yvonne Goulbier (* 1953 Kaiserslautern) creates stage-settings of fluorescent light sculptures. She cuts paper into small shapes or compresses and bends it into form and arranges the parts into an installation.

Ruth Handschin (* 1949 Basle) constructs sweeping light drawings out of fluorescent strips of paper and black light. The eye, overtaxed by the extreme light/dark contrast, begins to leap from line to line so that the whole complex lifts off from the walls and floor and becomes a spatial sculpture.

Uwe Meier-Weitmar (* 1952 Bochum) groups objects of paper, which stand in eloquent dialogue of form and materiality with each other, into rooms. Since 1979 he has worked with paper of every kind. In this medium he has realized installations, three-dimensional still-lives and cut-out silhouettes. Their color comes from the combination of that inherent in the paper he finds or the pigmentation in the pulp.

Sculptures that catch and shape the daylight are built by Annette Sauermann (* 1957 Essen). She works with thin, translucent tissue paper that is, with the help of weights, stretched to the floor by vertical steel wires. Gravity gives the paper sculpture its form. The wind, which enters through the skylight or results from the movement through the room, assumes a bodily presence in the paper sculpture, changes over the course of the day and transforms the sculpture.

Jane Balsgaard (* 1939 Copenhagen) also uses the transparency of paper to compose. Her light-influenced sculptures of almost weightless substance often consist of wafer-thin paper that the artist has produced from vegetable substances. The paper

die Künstlerin aus Substanzen der Vegetation fertigte. Die Papiere inkorporieren de facto Natur, die die Materialität, die Struktur und die Farbigkeit des jeweiligen Papiers bestimmt. Jane Balsgaards Werk ist deutlich von Elementen naturorientierter Philosophie beeinflußt, wie auch an ihren Außenskulpturen aus dem leicht vergänglichen Material Papier zu erkennen ist. Naturprozesse finden hier die substantielle Verdeutlichung durch Veränderung, Schwingung und Verwesung, verursacht durch Luft, Wind und Regen. Ähnliche Ziele verfolgt Helmut Frerick (* 1952 Neustadt/Schwarzwald) in manchen seiner Skulpturen.
Die Japanerin Kyoko Ibe (* 1941 Nagoya) baut mit tapisserieähnlichen Gehängen aus geformtem Washi Raumkonstruktionen, die durch Licht und Spiegelungen in imaginäre Dimensionen weisen.
Lore Bert (* 1936 Gießen) schuf 1982 erste Collagen mit fernöstlichen Papieren und 1985 ihre er-

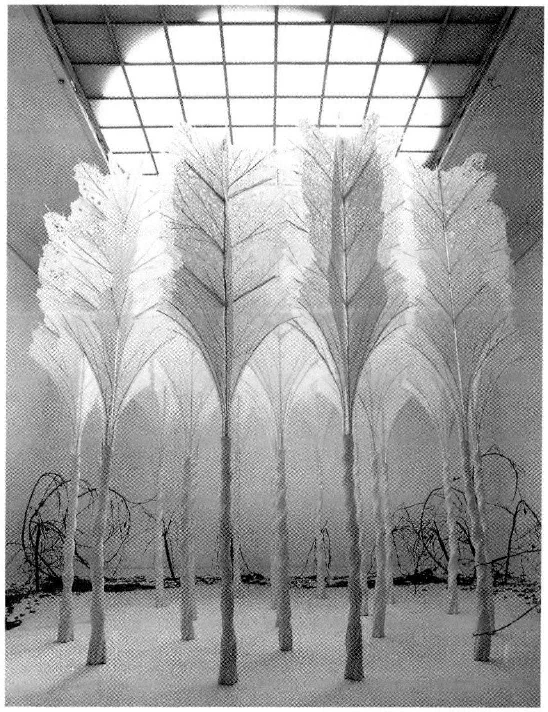

Karen Stahlecker: Letzter Bestand, 1991/92. Handgeschöpftes Papier aus Kozo und Gampi mit Wasserzeichen, Papiere aus Baumwolle, Sisal und Fasermischungen für Stamm-/Säulen-Formen, versteifte Fasern in natürlichem Zustand oder auch mit Pigment gefärbt. Höhe 435 cm, Durchmesser 450 cm / Karen Stahlecker: The Last Stand, 1991. Handmade papers of kozo and gampi with watermarks. Paper of cotton, sisal and mixed fibers for cast trunk/column forms. Stiffened fibers both natural and with pigment. Height 435 cm, diameter 450 cm

Jane Balsgaard: Kuben mit Schatten, 1991. Weideruten und handgeschöpftes Papier. Je ca. 220 x 170 x 190 cm / Jane Balsgaard: Cubes with Shadow, 1991. Willow switches, and handmade paper. Each about 220 x 170 x 190 cm

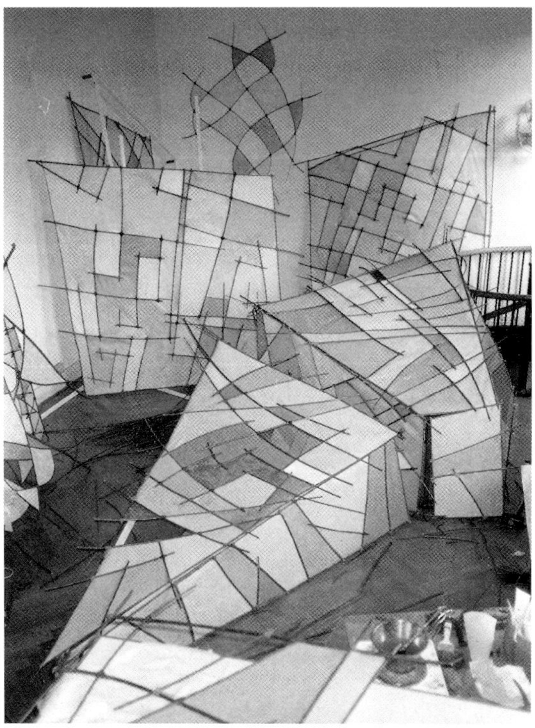

incorporates de facto nature, which determines the materiality, the structure and the color of the respective paper. Jane Balsgaard's work has been clearly influenced by elements of a nature-oriented philosophy, as is easily recognizable in her outdoor sculptures out of the light, transient material of paper. Natural processes are here given substantial manifestation by the change, oscillation and decay caused by air, wind and rain. Helmut Frerick (* 1952 Neustadt/Black Forest) pursues similar goals in his sculptures.
The Japanese Kyoko Ibe (* 1941 Nagoya) creates tapestry-like hangings out of spatial constructions formed from Washi that by means of light and reflections call up imaginary vistas.

sten Raumobjekte. Zarte, nicht behandelte und nicht bemalte Papiere aus Korea und Japan formt sie zu Objekten und Raumordnungen, die die Leichtigkeit der Papiere transformieren und einen Zustand des Schwebens und der Schwerelosigkeit suggerieren.
Karen Stahlecker (* 1954 Chicago) nimmt in ihren großformatigen Skulpturen aus selbst hergestelltem Papier unterschiedlichster Fasern wie Kozo, Gampi, Sisal und Baumwolle Bezug auf die Natur und ihre Zerstörung. Papierschöpfen ist für Stahlecker ein anderer Aspekt von Natur im Sinne traditioneller japanischer Papiermacher, die glauben, daß die Natur das Papier schöpft und wir nur Assistenten sind.
Winifred Lutz (* 1942 Brooklyn/New York) gehört zu den amerikanischen Bildhauerinnen, die seit den

Lore Bert (* 1936 Giessen) in 1982 created her first collages with oriental paper and in 1985 her first space objects. Delicate, untreated and unpainted papers from Korea and Japan she forms into objects and spatial arrangements that are transformed by the lightness of the paper to a state of floating weightlessness.
Karen Stahlecker (* 1954 Chicago) in her large-scale sculptures (made of paper she makes herself from very different types of fibers like Kozo, Gampi, sisal, and cotton) refers to nature and its destruction. Papermaking is for Stahlecker another aspect of nature in the sense of the traditional Japanese papermakers who believe that nature makes the paper and we are only here to assist.
Winifred Lutz (* 1942 Brooklyn/New York) is one of the American sculptors that since the late 60s

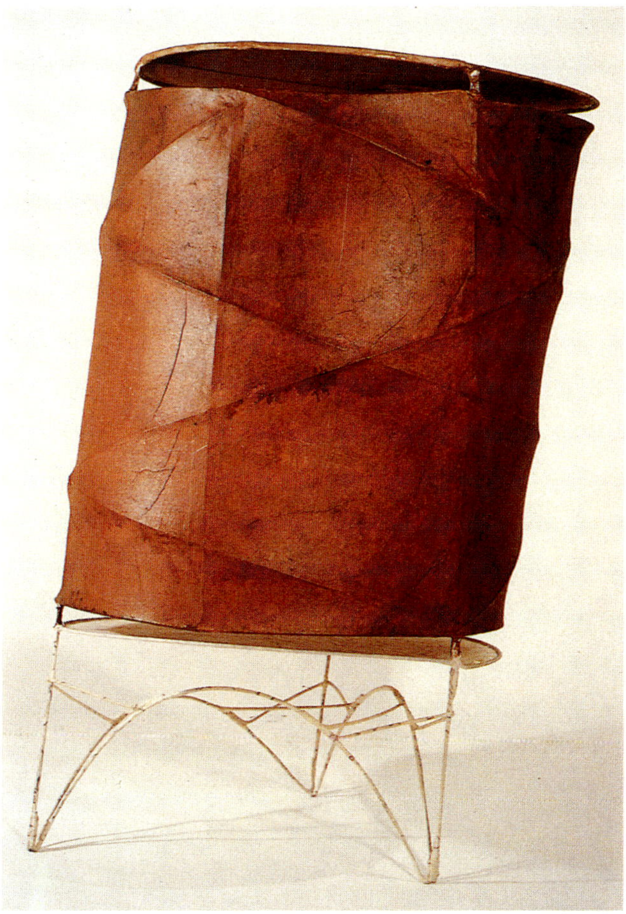

Masaji Kashio: Papiertrommel, 1988. Kozo-Papier, Gerbstoff, Eisendraht. 92 x 58 x 52 cm / Masaji Kashio: Paper Drum, 1988. Kozo paper, persimmon tannin, iron wire. 92 x 58 x 52 cm

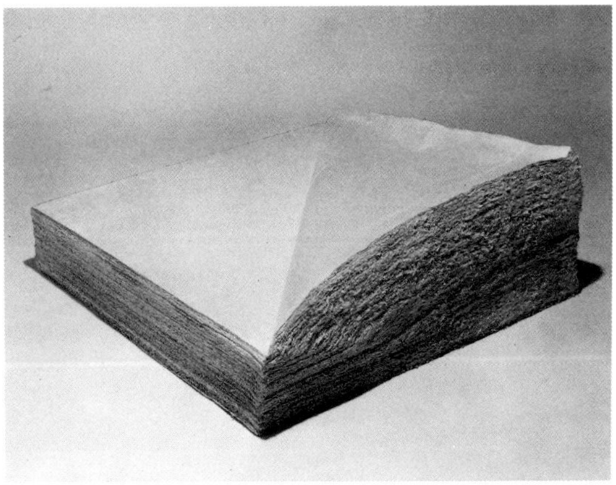

Kazuo Kadonaga: Paper No. 1 U, 1983. Japanpapier, handgemacht. 88 x 87 x 34 cm / Kazuo Kadonaga: Paper No. 1 U, 1983. Japan paper, handmade. 88 x 87 x 34 cm

späten 60er Jahren ausschließlich im Medium Papier arbeiten. Ihre oft metallen harten oder transluzenten Papiere stellt sie selbst her. Sie entwickelte neue Techiken, um Pulp in dreidimensionale Form zu bringen. Jede noch so unterschiedliche Materialität von Pulps transformiert sie in eine dem Papier wesenhaft eigen erscheinende Form. Materie und Formgestaltung bedingen sich gegenseitig. Das Licht spielt in allen ihren Skulpturen eine wichtige Rolle, Licht läßt Papier gläsern leuchten oder lederartig glatt glänzen.

Masaji Kashio (* 1933 Fukui Prefecture/Japan) kreiert Skulpturen von amorpher Formgebung mit eigentümlich glatter und glänzender Oberfläche. Über einen Drahtrahmen legt er in mehreren Schichten eine Art von Washi, das nach dem Trocknen sehr fest und stramm gespannt ist wie der Bezug einer Trommel. Die Farbigkeit entsteht durch Tränken mit Gerbsäure.

Kazuo Kadonaga (* 1946 Ishikwa-ken/Japan) arbeitet mit den vorgegebenen Papierformaten von Rechteck, Quadrat oder Dreieck. Er legt sie zu Stapeln zusammen, wobei die handgeschöpften Papiere an einem Rand kleiner und dichter sind und am anderen durch Abschälen erweitert und geöffnet wurden. Die Skulpturen reagieren auf die Umgebung, schrumpfen bei trockenem Wetter und quellen bei Feuchtigkeit.

Eva-Maria Andresen (* 1942 Wuppertal) arbeitet ebenfalls mit dem Blattformat. Bei ihr jedoch bleibt

have worked exclusively in the medium of paper. She makes her often hard, metallic or translucent papers herself. She has developed new techniques to bring pulp into three-dimensional form. Each type of materiality, no matter how divergent, she transforms to a formal manifestation that is inherent to that paperpulp. Material and form are mutually conditioned. Light plays an important role in all her sculptures; it allows paper to glow like glass or shine like leather.

Masaji Kashio (* 1933 Fukui Prefecture/Japan) creates sculptures of amorphous shape with a strange and smooth surface. He places over a wire frame several layers of a kind of Washi that, after drying, is stretched very firmly like the skin of a drum. The color results from a tincture of tannic acid.

Kazuo Kadonaga (* 1946 Ishikwa-ken/Japan) works with paper's given formats: rectangle, square or triangle. He heaps them into stacks, whereby the handmade paper is at one edge smaller and denser and at the other has been peeled away so as to widen and open. The sculptures react to the environment; they shrink when the weather is dry and swell when it is wet.

Eva-Maria Andresen (* 1942 Wuppertal) also works with the normal sheet of paper. This, however, is treated singly and becomes a sculpture in its specific materiality. Josephine Tabbert (* Jägersthal/Rominten) provides the hard and

das Papier Einzelstück und wird in seiner spezifischen Materialität zur Skulptur. Josephine Tabbert (*Jägersthal/Rominten) gibt der Materialität ihrer harten, widerstandsfähigen Papiere formentsprechende Gestalt. Materie wird in gewissermaßen alchemistischer Absicht sensibilisiert.

Bei Lena Liv (*1952 Leningrad) wird Fotografie zum Objekt. Fotos der Jahrhundertwende vergrößert sie, so daß die Dargestellten in Lebensgröße, aber in einem breiten Metallrahmen eingefangen, dem Betrachter als vergangene Wirklichkeit entgegentreten. Einzelelemente der Fotografie wie z. B. der Ball oder der Kreisel eines Kindes oder Schuhpaare einer Kindergruppe sind als Objekte in Papierpulp rekonstruiert und vor die Porträtierten plaziert. So erscheint eine Person aus der Vergangenheit in die Wirklichkeit versetzt beziehungsweise die Schuhe wirken wie ein Stück „liegengebliebener" Vergangenheit. Ein Zeitcluster wird verbildlicht.[169]

resistant paper she uses with its corresponding shape. Matter is sensitized by a kind of alchemical intention.

Lena Liv (* 1952 Leningrad) makes photography into an object. She enlarges photographs from the turn of the century so that those depicted are life size but, enclosed in a wide metal frame, confront the viewer as past reality. Single elements like a child's ball or top or pairs of shoes from a group of children are reconstructed in paperpulp and these objects placed before those in the portraits. Thus a person from the past appears to be transported to reality or the shoes seem a "left-over" remnant from the past. A time cluster is given an image.[169]

Lena Liv: Tre Bambini, 1991. Eisen, Foto, handgeschöpftes Papier, farbiges Pigment. Je 100 x 55 x 50 cm / Lena Liv: Tre Bambini, 1991. Iron, photograph, handmade paper, pigment. Each 100 x 55 x 50 cm

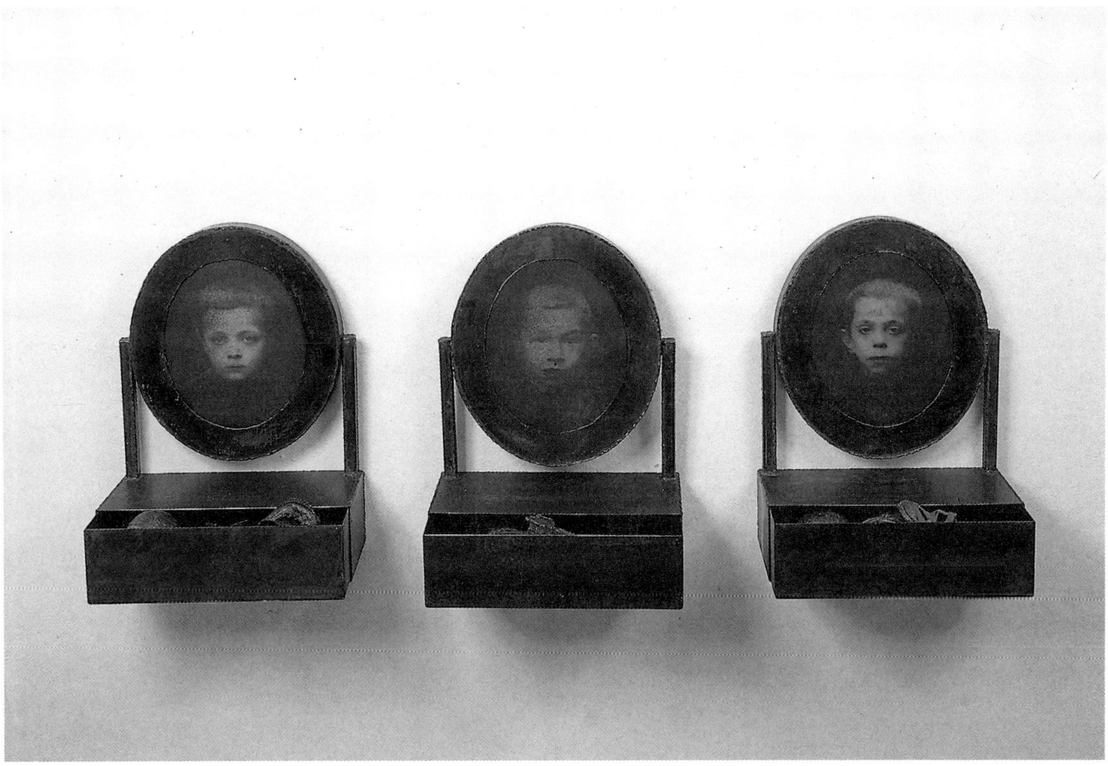

V. 11. Papier und Musik

Papier kann auch Instrument, kann Ton- und Klangerzeuger sein, denn jede Papierqualität hat ihre eigene charakteristische Klangfarbe. So klingt ein Tranzparentpapier klar und hart, eine Pappe dumpf. Die Größe des Papiers, die Form einer Pappe beeinflussen zudem das Klangspektrum. Aus dem Bespielen von Papier ergeben sich neue, spezifische Klang- und Geräuschmöglichkeiten. Früheste Beispiele, Papier als Musikinstrument zu nutzen, sind von den Futuristen und Dadaisten bekannt. In der Musik der 20er und beginnenden 30er Jahre, als Experimente mit Geräuschen und Geräuschinstrumenten nachhaltig betrieben wurden, nutzte man auch Papier und Pappe zur Klangerzeugung, so etwa bei Erik Satie, Jeff Golyscheff, Herbert Eimert oder Darius Milhaud. Seit den 1950er Jahren, als durch die elektronische Musik und die Musique concrète das gesamte Klangspektrum verfügbar wurde, setzte man Papiergeräusche in

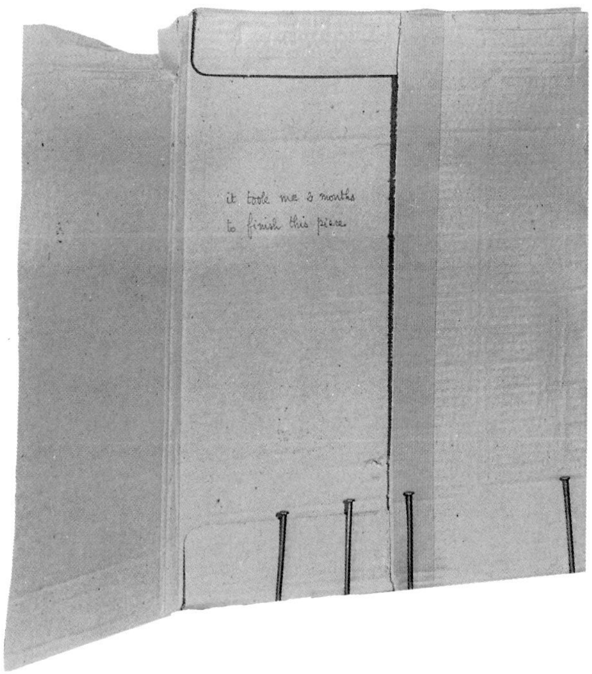

Robert Filliou: It took me 2 month to finish this piece, 1971. Holzplatte mit Nägeln und einem Kartonabriß. 41 x 44 x 13 cm / Robert Filliou: It took me 2 month to finish this piece, 1971. Wood panel with nails and a cardboard tear-off. 41 x 44 x 13 cm

V. 11. Paper and music

Paper can also be an instrument, can generate tones and sounds, since every quality of paper gives off its own characteristic resonance. A transparent paper, for instance, sounds clear and distinct, cardboard muffled. In addition, the size of the paper or the form of a cardboard influences the spectrum of sound. Playing on paper produces new, specific tones and sounds. The earliest known examples for the use of paper as a musical instrument were those created by the Futurists and Dadaists. In the music of the 20s and the early 30s when experiments with sounds and sound instruments were persistently carried out, paper and cardboard were used to create tones, e.g., Erik Satie, Jeff Golyscheff, Herbert Eimert or Darius Milhaud. Since the 50s and through Electronic Music and Musique concrète, when the whole spectrum of sound was made available, the tonality of paper was used in some compositions so that the transition from the visual arts to Happenings and Fluxus became fluent. A new emotional and mental liberation makes feasible the use of everyday sources of noise. The sound of reality and the poetry of the unheeded object are awarded a certain dignity. Not only natural sounds but above all also articles with definite everyday functions are given unexpected dimensions of ideas, feelings and sound. John Cage (* 1912 Los Angeles – † 1992 New York), one of the composers who initiated a completely transformed attitude toward material and influenced many composers and artists, noted down 'Music for Piano' (1952–1956) in relation to the thicker places in the paper. Benjamin Patterson (* 1939 Pittsburgh/Pennsylvania) composed a 'Paper Piece for 5 Players', a sensitive, at times vehement action on materials of differentiated tonality. The piece was performed at the beginning of the 60s in the studio of Mary Bauermeister in Cologne. The score comprises two handwritten letter-sized sheets. On the first page Patterson pasted five trading stamps.[170] Mauricio Kagel (* 1931 Buenos Aires)

manchen Kompositionen ein, der Übergang zur bildenden Kunst bei Happening und Fluxus ist nun fließend. Eine neue Empfindungs- und Denkfreiheit ermöglicht die Verwendung von alltäglichen Schallquellen aller Art. Der Klang der Realität und die Poesie der unbeachteten Dinge erhalten ihre Würde. Nicht nur Naturgeräusche, sondern vor allem auch Objekte mit festgelegter Alltagsfunktion erhalten unerwartete Vorstellungs-, Empfindungs- und Klangdimensionen. John Cage (* 1912 Los Angeles – † 1992 New York), einer der Komponisten, die eine völlig veränderte Einstellung zum Material initiierten und viele Komponisten und bildende Künstler beeinflußte, fixierte 1952 bis 1956 die ‚Music for Piano' nach Verdickungen im Papier. Benjamin Patterson (* 1934 Pittsburgh/Pennsylvania) komponierte ein ‚Papier-Stück für 5 Spieler', eine sensible, stellenweise heftige Materialaktion differenzierter Klanglichkeit. Das Stück wurde Anfang der 60er Jahre im Atelier von Mary Bauermeister in Köln aufgeführt. Die Partitur umfaßt zwei handgeschriebene DIN-4-Blätter. Auf die erste Seite klebte Patterson fünf Rabattmarken.[170] Mauricio Kagel (* 1931 Buenos Aires) bezog mehrfach Papier in seine Kompositionen ein. Nam June Paik (* 1932 Seoul/Korea) beeindruckte in den 60er Jahren in Köln durch ein Konzert mit einem Stück Papier, das er mit den Händen um ein sehr empfindliches Mikrophon preßte. Dann nahm er die Hände fort, und das Konzert begann: Das Papier öffnete sich langsam und sank in die Ausgangsposition zurück. Klangbild und visueller Eindruck steigerten sich gegenseitig. Takako Saito arbeitet seit 1964 mit Duft- und Klangwürfeln, gefüllt mit Reis, Sand oder Steinen. 1977 entsteht die ‚Music Bottle No. 1'. Beim Schütteln der Flasche erzeugen die eingeschlossenen Papierwürfel Geräusche wie von Brandung und Meeresrauschen.[171] Mit Würfeln aus Papier und Pappe zur Erzeugung von Klängen agiert Saito mehrfach bei Fluxus-Aktionen. 1977 führte sie in der Galleria Pellegrino in Bologna eine ‚Paper Music' auf. Papierwürfel verschiedener Größe hingen an Nylonfäden von der Decke. Die

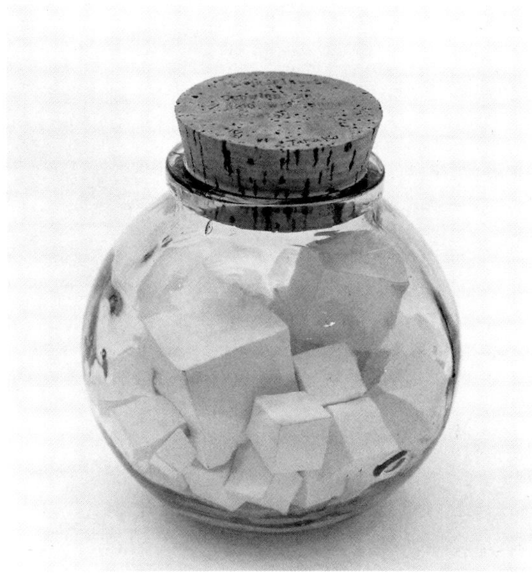

Takako Saito: Musikflasche, 1984. Handgefertigte Papierwürfel in verkorkter Flasche. Auflage 24 / Takako Saito: Music Bottle, 1984. Handmade papercubes in corked up bottle. Edition of 24

incorporated paper in his compositions several times. Nam June Paik (* 1932 Seoul/Korea) made an enormous impression in the 60s with a concert he gave by pressing a piece of paper with his hands around a very sensitive microphone. He then removed his hands and the concert began: the paper opened slowly and sank back to the initial position. Tonal and visual impressions went hand in hand. Takako Saito has worked since 1964 with scent and sound cubes filled with rice, sand or stones. In 1977 she did 'Music Bottle No. 1'. When the bottle is shaken, the enclosed paper cubes generate the roar of waves and the sea.[171] Saito has several times taken part in Fluxus actions by creating sounds with cubes of paper and cardboard. In 1977 she performed 'Paper Music' in the Galleria Pellegrino in Bologna. Paper cubes of different sizes hung on nylon threads from the ceiling. The threads were cut off with a scissors or a burning cigarette. The falling cubes engendered sounds. Further sounds were produced by players who scattered and stepped on the cubes. On a large piece of cloth hung at a height of five meters an additional amount of cubes had been placed that, once the

Fäden wurden mit einer Schere und einer brennenden Zigarette durchtrennt. Die fallenden Würfel erzeugten Geräusche. Weitere Klänge generierten Spieler durch das Verteilen und Treten der Würfel. Auf einem großen Stoffstück in fünf Meter Höhe lagen weitere Mengen von Papierwürfeln, die nach Durchschneiden der Halterungen auf den Boden fielen und wiederum Musik machten.[172] Auch Franz Erhard Walther (* 1939 Fulda) arbeitete zu Beginn der 60er Jahre mit Duftobjekten und Papiergeräuschen. Das ‚Papierkonzert' führte er 1963 erstmals in der Galerie Junge Kunst in Fulda auf. Bis 1981 folgten neun Aufführungsorte, u. a. 1972 die ‚documenta 5'.[173] Rolf Julius (* 1939 Wilhelmshaven) komponierte 1988 für Düren ‚Papierstücke'. Kleine zerknitterte Pergamentfetzen hingen an den Fenstern. Aus den versteckt angebrachten kleinen Lautsprechern erklangen minimale knisternde Papiergeräusche, als ob sich das Papier entspanne oder sich leicht im Windzug bewege. Der Raum schien durchtränkt von weit entfernten, leisen Klängen. Der Komponist Josef Anton Riedl (* München) nutzt seit 1961 Papier. „Papier ist ein dankbares Material, um Dinge auszudrücken, die ich mit traditionellen Instrumenten nicht ausdrücken kann", sagte Riedl anläßlich der Aufführung seiner ‚Paper Music' zur Papierbiennale 1988 in Düren.[174] Aus über 80 Sorten Papier hat Riedl eine etwa 20minütige Komposition geschaffen. 1990 entwarf er eine neue Komposition mit Papiergeräuschen und Stimme, die ‚Paper Music II – Lautgedichtfolge f'.

strings were cut, fell to the floor and produced music.[172] Franz Erhard Walther (* 1939 Fulda) worked at the beginning of the 60s with scent objects and paper sounds. 'Paper Concert' was performed in 1963 for the first time in the Galerie Junge Kunst in Fulda. Up to and including 1981 there followed nine other performance in different places, including 'documenta 5' in 1972.[173] Rolf Julius (* 1939 Wilhelmshaven) composed 'Paper Pieces' for Düren in 1988. Small, crumpled scraps of parchment were hung at the windows. From tiny hidden loudspeakers the sound of a fine rustling could be heard, as if the paper were breathing or moving lightly in a breeze. The room seemed saturated with soft, distant tones. The composer Josef Anton Riedl (* Munich) has used paper since 1961. "Paper is a rewarding material to express things that I cannot express with traditional instruments," Riedl said on the occasion of the performance of his 'Paper Music' at the paper biennale 1988 in Düren.[174] From over 80 kinds of paper Riedl composed his approximately 20 minute long piece. In 1990 he composed a new composition with paper sounds and voice called the 'Paper Music II – Sound Poem Sequence f'.

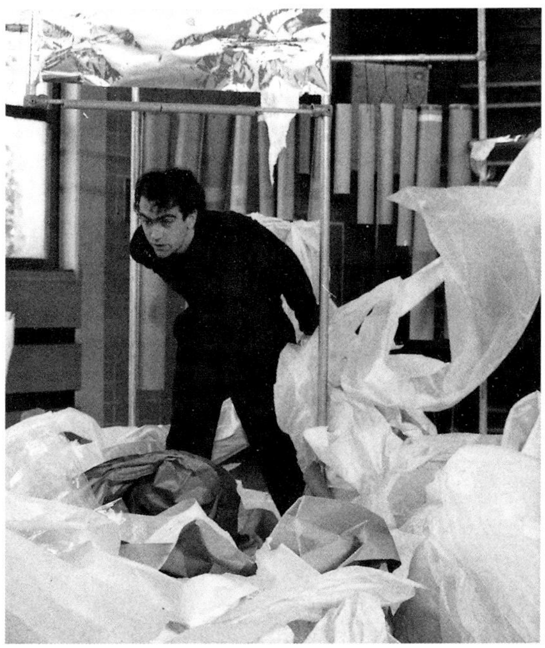

Josef Anton Riedl: Paper Music. Konzert 28. August 1988, Düren / Josef Anton Riedl: Paper Music. Concert August, 28, 1988, Düren

V.12. Papier und Sprache

Papier zeichnet sich durch ungeheure Anpassungsfähigkeit aus. In jedweder Form ist es in der bildenden Kunst des 20. Jahrhunderts zum selbständigen Medium geworden. Mit großem Selbstverständnis wird es von Künstlern geachtet und genutzt. Selbst Komponisten bezogen es in ihre Ausdruckssprache mit ein.

Auch die Sprache hat sich des Papiers bemächtigt, um Wertschätzung, Geringschätzung oder gar Ironie zum Ausdruck zu bringen. Wird ein Forschungs- oder Beratungsergebnis vorgetragen, sagt man „er las ein Papier“, man spricht von einem „Medienpapier“, oder „Staatspapier“, „Grundsatzpapier“ oder „Kirchenpapier“. Eine hohe Wertschätzung genießt das Papier im Bereich der Presse; hier wird die Bezeichnung für die Maschine sogar als Pars pro toto eingesetzt. Im Amerikanischen steht die Kurzform „paper“ für „newspaper“. Im Deutschen spricht man von der Zeitung als seinem „Blatt“, wobei das Blatt Papier das besondere ist: So heißt es denn auch „Flug-Blatt“ im Gegensatz zu „Fahr-Schein“. Hohen Wert erhält ein Papier, wenn Effekten und Aktien als „Wertpapiere“ bezeichnet werden oder die Rede von „Börsenpapieren“ und „Bankpapieren“ ist. Unsere Sprache befaßt sich mit Papier nicht nur im postiven Sinne: Gesetze stehen womöglich „nur auf dem Papier“, die Sache „bleibt Papier“ oder ist „nichts als Papier“, es „bleibt vor allem nur das Papier“. Das Papier tritt gelegentlich auch als Sinnbild der Ohnmacht, gekoppelt mit einer Prise Ironie in Erscheinung, wenn man sagt: „Papier ist geduldig“ oder jemanden als „Papiertiger“ bezeichnet. Papier kann besser und feiner sein als der Gedanke, wenn man äußert, jener Text sei „das Papier nicht wert“. Verächtlich spricht man bei einem Autor von einem „papierenen Stil“ oder äußert, der Redner bemächtigt sich einer „papierenen Sprache“. Heinrich Heine charakterisierte bisweilen mit Papiersorten Schreibstile. Kants Stil in der ‚Kritik der reinen Vernunft‘ nennt er einen „grauen, trockenen Packpapierstil“. In der Schrift

V.12. Paper and language

Paper is characterized by its enormous adaptability. In one form or another it has become an independent medium in the visual arts of the 20th century. It is regarded and used with the greatest matter-of-fact conviction. Even composers have made it a means of expression.

The word has also taken over paper to express high or low esteem or even irony. If a research or counselling result is publically announced, this is called “reading a paper“; there are “media papers” or “state papers”, “consitutional papers” or “church papers”. Paper is given a high evaluation in the press. The American word “paper” is the short form for “newspaper“; in German the newspaper is addressed as a “Blatt” [sheet], whereby the sheet of paper is something special as in “Flugblatt” [flyer] in contrast to “Fahr-Schein” [(travel) ticket]. Paper is given a very high value when securities are called “Wertpapiere” [literally, valuable papers] or when bank shares are said to be “Bankpapiere” and listed securities or stock “Börsenpapiere”. Our language does not only use paper in a positive sense: a law is possibly “only on paper” or facts are “just paper”. Paper stands occasionally for a symbol of powerlessness as in “paper is patient” or someone is called a “paper tiger”. Paper can be better or more refined than the thought expressed, as in a text that “isn’t worth the paper it’s printed on”. An author can be contemptuously accused of a having a “paper style” or a speaker a “paper language”. Heinrich Heine characterized certain writing styles according to kinds of paper. He called Kant’s writing in ‘The Criticism of Pure Reason’ “a dry, gray wrapping-paper style”. In his essay on Ludwig Börne Heine speaks of “sour stockpaper German” or of “vellum-lovely English”. He also wrote once that his head was free and cheery, his body so lame, so “wastepapery”.[175]

Above and beyond this, paper has meaning as a product, for instance when you speak of “paper money” in contrast to plastic money or credit cards.

über Ludwig Börne spricht Heine vom „sauren fließpapierenen Deutsch" und vom „velinschönen Englisch". Auch schreibt er einmal, daß sein Kopf frei und heiter sei, sein Leib aber gelähmt, so „makulaturig".[175]

Darüber hinaus hat Papier Produktbedeutung, wenn man vom „Papiergeld" im Gegensatz zum Plastikgeld der Scheckkarte spricht. Einen Spielzeugdrachen bezeichnet man auch als „Papiervogel". Die Pappe hält für beschreibende Spracherläuterungen her, wenn man von „pappig" gleich dickflüssig spricht, von „aneinanderpappen" als ein Aneinanderkleben und man in der Umgangssprache Brei als „Papp" bezeichnet. Ein „Pappenstil" ist eine Bagatelle, ein „Papierkrieg" jedoch nicht.[176]

A toy dragon is a "paper bird". Cardboard [Pappe] also serves for certain descriptive explanations as in "pappig" for thick fluids, as in something being "gepappt" or stuck together and in the colloquial expression of "Papp" for a porridge-like consistency. "Pappenstil" is a bagatelle but a "paper war" is anything but.[176]

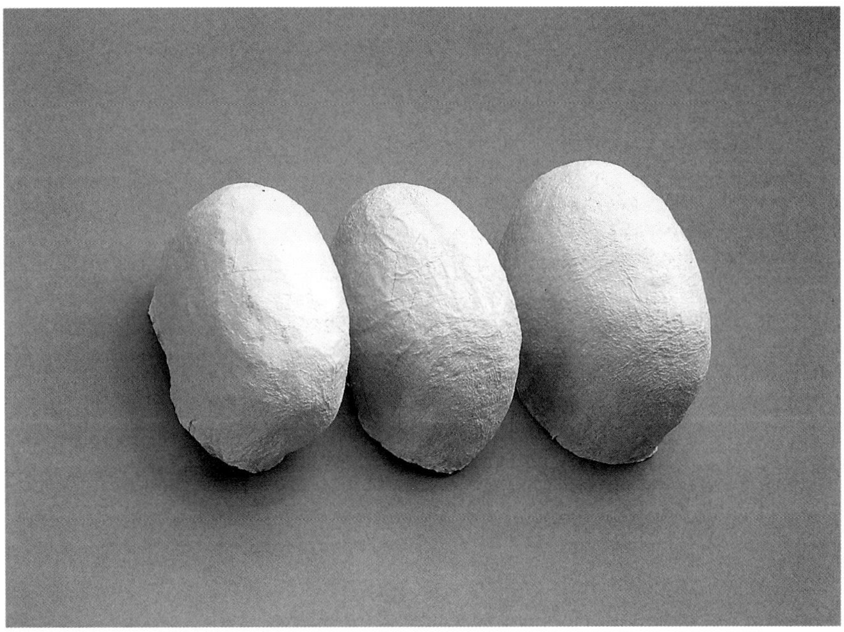

Irmel Droese: Drei Köpfe, 1987. Pappmaché, weiße Farbe. 15 x 21 x 10 cm / Irmel Droese: Three Heads, 1987. Papier maché, white paint. 15 x 21 x 10 cm

Anmerkungen

1 Eine Kulturgeschichte unter dem Oberthema „Papier" zu erarbeiten ist hier nicht beabsichtigt, zumal ein solches interdisziplininäres Unternehmen nahezu lebensfüllend wäre. Die unterschiedlichen Gesichtspunkte können an dieser Stelle lediglich angedacht werden. 2 Armin Renker: Beseeltes Papier. In: Vom Feinpapier. Stuttgart 1973², S. 12. 3 Vgl. Peter Tschudin: Geschichte des Papiers. In: Lothar Göttsching (Hrsg.): Papier in unserer Welt. Ein Handbuch. Düsseldorf, Wien, New York 1990, S. 11–16, sowie Günter Bayerl: Die Papiermühle. Vorindustrielle Papiermacherei auf dem Gebiet des alten deutschen Reiches – Technologie, Arbeitsverhältnisse, Umwelt. = Europäische Hochschulschriften III/260. Frankfurt/M., Bern, New York, Paris, 1987, S. 45–46. 4 Fritz Winzer: Kulturgeschichte Europas. Von der Antike bis zur Gegenwart. Braunschweig o. J., S. 340. 5 Nach Walter Koschatzky: Die Kunst der Graphik. Technik, Geschichte, Meisterwerke. München 1976², S. 69. 6 Bayerl 1987, S. 77; vgl. hierzu auch Irmgard Gerhards: Papier und Wissen im ausgehenden Mittelalter. In: III. Internationale Biennale der Papierkunst. Ausst. Kat. Düren 1990, S. 34ff. 7 Walter Dohmen: Die Lithographie. Geschichte – Kunst – Technik. Köln 1982, S. 169. 8 Nach Armin Renker: Das Buch vom Papier. Wiesbaden 1950, S. 191. 9 Andrew Robinson: An Aesthetic History of Paper in Prints. In: Paper – Art & Technology. The History and Methods of Fine Papermaking with a Gallery of Contemporary Paper Art. San Francisco 1979, S. 62. 10 Renker 1950, S. 190. Die Einbeziehung von farbigen Papieren in die Komposition eines Blattes ist m. W. nicht nachhaltig erforscht und bedarf einer gesonderten Untersuchung. Ebenso verhält es sich mit dem Rückbezug der Papierqualität und -struktur auf die Darstellung. Farbige und getönte Papiere fabrizierte man aus farbigen Lumpen oder durch Zusatz von Farbstoffen. Bis ins 18. Jahrhundert wurde das Färben quasi als Geheimwissenschaft gehegt. Vgl. Bayerl 1987, S. 320ff. Entscheidend für die Qualität eines Blattes waren die Qualität von Wasser, die Rohstoffe und die Aufbereitung, aber auch der Prozeß des Handschöpfens, der über die Gleichmäßigkeit von Dicke, Oberfläche und Form entschied. Glätten, Leimen und eventuell Färben konnten das Blatt veredeln. Normalerweise trachteten Künstler bis gegen Ende des 19. Jahrhunderts überwiegend danach, in der „hohen Kunst" die Abhängigkeit vom Material optisch unwirksam zu machen. Die besondere Leistung Dürers bestand darin, „materialbedingte Stilelemente der älteren Grafik soweit zu eleminieren, daß Kupferstich und Holzschnitt einander ähnlich werden im Dienste des in der Vorzeichnung niedergelegten ‚Bildes'." (Vgl. Günther Bandmann: Der Wandel der Materialbewertung in der Kunsttheorie des 19. Jahrhunderts. In: Beiträge zur Theorie der Künste im 19. Jahrhundert Bd. 1. Frankfurt/M. 1971, S. 147.) Papier und Pappe als Hilfsmittel der Künstler werden zu allen Zeiten benutzt. Für großformatige Wandbilder beispielsweise fertigte man Kartons im Maßstab 1 zu 1. In der Renaissance wurden solche Entwurfskartons schließlich als selbständige künstlerische Leistung bewertet. 11 Robinson 1979, S. 63–64. 12 Bayerl 1987, S. 88. Dieser besondere Anspruch Schillers an das Papier seiner Bücher mag wie ein erstes Aufkeimen von Materialbewußtsein erscheinen. In bezug auf die Kunst ist Schiller jedoch – wie bis ins 19. Jahrhundert charakteristisch – der Auffassung, daß jede Spur von Werkprozessen verdeckt und das Material durch den Künstler überwunden werden muß. 1795 schreibt er in seiner Abhandlung über die ästhetische Erziehung des Menschen: „Darin also besteht das eigentliche Kunstgeheimnis des Meisters, daß er den Stoff durch die Form vertilgt." Nach Bandmann 1971, S. 131. 13 Nach Renker 1950, S. 194–195. 14 Nach Bayerl 1987, S. 94. 15 Ebd., S. 94–95. 16 Ebd., S. 88–89 und S. 128. 17 Robinson 1979, S. 65. 18 Nach Renker 1950, S. 192. 19 Nach ebd., S. 165. 20 Nach Bayerl 1987, S. 119. 21 Nach ebd., S. 111. 22 Nach Renker 1950, S. 189. 23 Ebd., S. 192.

Footnotes

1 It is not my intention here to write a definitive cultural history of paper, an interdisciplinary undertaking that would entail a lifelong commitment. The various aspects can only be touched on. 2 Armin Renker, "Beseeltes Papier", in: Vom Feinpapier, (Stuttgart, 1973²) 12. 3 See Peter Tschudin, "Geschichte des Papiers," in: Papier in unserer Welt. Ein Handbuch, ed. Lothar Göttsching, (Düsseldorf, Vienna, New York, 1990) 11–16, as well as Günter Bayerl, "Die Papiermühle. Vorindustrielle Papiermacherei auf dem Gebiet des alten deutschen Reiches – Technologie, Arbeitsverhältnisse, Umwelt," = Europäische Hochschulschriften III/260, (Frankfurt/M., Bern, New York, Paris, 1987) 45–46. 4 Fritz Winzer, Kulturgeschichte Europas. Von der Antike bis zur Gegenwart, (Braunschweig, no year given) 340. 5 From Walter Koschatzky, Die Kunst der Graphik. Technik, Geschichte, Meisterwerke, (Munich, 1976²) . 6 Bayerl, 1987, 77. See also Irmgard Gerhards, "Papier und Wissen im ausgehenden Mittelalter," in: 3rd International Biennale of Paper Art, exhibition catalogue, (Düren, 1990) 34 ff. 7 Walter Dohmen, Die Lithographie. Geschichte – Kunst – Technik, (Cologne, 1982) 169. 8 From Armin Renker, Das Buch vom Papier, (Wiesbaden, 1950) 191. 9 Andrew Robinson, "An Aesthetic History of Paper in Prints," in: Paper – Art & Technology. The History and Methods of Fine Papermaking with a Gallery of Contemporary Paper Art, (San Francisco, 1979) 62. 10 Renker 1950, 190. The inclusion of colored paper in the composition of a sheet has, as far as I know, not been adequately researched and needs additional study, as does the case of the effect of paper quality and texture on the depiction. Colored and toned paper is made directly from colored rags of by adding color dyes. The craft of color dying was a quasi secret science well into the 18th century. See Bayerl 1987, 320ff. Crucial for paper quality was the quality of the water, the raw material and the preparation but also the handmaking process itself, which affected the regularity of thickness, surface and form. Glazing, sizing and dying could enhance the paper. Normally artists, up to the end of the 19th century, aimed at making their material for "high art" optically neutral. It was Dürer's special achievement to eliminate the material-conditioned style elements of former graphics in such a way as to make copperplate engraving and woodcut resemble one another in service to the given preliminary "design". Paper and cardboard were used by artists of all times as aids. For largescale mural painting, for example, cartoons were produced on a scale of 1 to 1. In the Renaissance such preliminary designs were then esteemed as independent artistic achievements. 11 Robinson 1979, 63–64. 12 Bayerl 1987, 88. That Schiller demanded such a high standard of paper for his books appears to be one of the first signs of an awareness of materiality. In relation to art, however, Schiller is of the opinion – as is characteristic – that every trace of the working process should be concealed and that the material is something the artist must overcome. In 1795 he wrote in his treatise on the aesthetic education of man: "So that is the secret of the master craftsman, that he eradicates matter through form." From Bandmann 1971, 131. 13 From Renker 1950, 194–195. 14 From Bayerl 1987, 94. 15 Ibid., 94–95. 16 Ibid., 88–89 and 128. 17 Robinson 1979, 65. 18 From Renker 1950, 192. 19 From ibid., 165. 20 From Bayerl 1987, 119. 21 From ibid., 111. 22 From Renker 1950, 189. 23 Ibid., 192. 24 Ibid., 165–166. 25 Bayerl 1987, 125. 26 Ibid., 125 and 127. 27 From Renker 1950, 196. 28 From ibid., 196–197. 29 Natural material was painted to transform its surface and elevate it to a new existence. Any traces of workmanship were to be concealed since it affected the character of perfection and spotlessness. See Bandmann 1971, 130–133. 30 From Karl-Ludwig Hofmann and Christoph Präger, "Provokation des Schönen. Kunst und Karton," in: Materialisation, exhibition catalogue, (Mannheim, 1987) no page given. 31 From ibid., no page given. 32 From Bandmann 1971, 148. 33 See Das Papier. Geschichte. Herstellung, künstlerische Gestaltung, exhibition catalogue (Düren, 1981) 84–92; 1st International Biennale of Paper Art, Handgeschöpftes, exhibition catalogue, (Düren, 1986) 67–83; 2nd International Biennale of Paper Art, Kunst macht Raum, exhi-

24 Ebd., S. 165–166. 25 Bayerl 1987, S. 125. 26 Ebd., S. 125 und S. 127. 27 Nach Renker 1950, S. 196. 28 Nach ebd., S. 196–197. 29 Das natürliche Material wurde bemalt, um es durch Verwandlung der Oberfläche in eine neue Existenz zu erheben. Spuren der handwerklichen Arbeit verdeckte man, da sie den Charakter des Vollkommenen und Makellosen beeinträchtigten. Vgl. Bandmann 1971, S. 130–133. 30 Nach Karl-Ludwig Hofmann und Christoph Präger: Provokation des Schönen. Kunst und Karton. In: Materialisation. Ausst. Kat. Mannheim 1987, o. S. 31 Nach ebd., Hofmann, o. S. 32 Nach Bandmann 1971, S. 148. 33 Vgl. Das Papier. Geschichte, Herstellung, künstlerische Gestaltung. Ausst. Kat. Düren 1981, S. 84–92; I. Internationale Biennale der Papierkunst. Handgeschöpftes. Ausst. Kat. Düren 1986, S. 67–83; II. Internationale Biennale der Papierkunst. Papier macht Raum. Ausst. Kat. Düren 1988, S. 67–69; III: Internationale Biennale der Papierkunst. Papier als Wissen. Ausst. Kat. Düren 1990, S. 178–181, PaperArt – 4. Internationale Biennale der Papierkunst. Papier und Natur. Ausst. Kat. Düren 1992, S. 170–177. 34 Le Papier. Ausst. Kat. Paris 1983, S. 162–167. 35 PaperArt. Ausst. Kat. Düren 1992, S. 102–103. Zum Themenkomplex Volkskunst, Architektur usw. aus Papier und Pappmaché vgl. Kurt Londenberg: Papier und Form. Krefeld 1972; Eberhard und Renate Fiebig, Karl Pobantz und Erik Spiekermann: Zauber des Papiers. Frankfurt/M. 1973; Le Papier. Ausst. Kat. Paris 1983; Christa Pieske: Das ABC des Luxuspapiers. Herstellung, Verarbeitung und Gebrauch 1860 bis 1930. Berlin 1993. 36 Nach Werner Spies: Max Ernst. Collagen, Ausst. Kat. Tübingen, Bern, Düsseldorf 1988/89, Köln 1988, S. 12. Braque selbst unterstreicht in seinem Aufsatz Pensées et réflexions sur la peinture, erschienen im Dezember 1917 in Nord-Sud, Paris, die schöpferische Freiheit, die die Papiers collés eröffnen: „Sie sind ebenfalls simple Fakten, doch durch den Geist geschaffen, und stellen einer der Rechtfertigungen für eine neue Figuration im Raum dar.“ Nach Eduard Fry: Der Kubismus. Köln 1974², S. 157. 37 Nach Diane Waldman: Collage und Objektkunst vom Kubismus bis heute. Köln 1993, S. 22. 38 Vgl. ebd., S. 25, sowie William Rubin: Picasso und Braque. Die Geburt des Kubismus. München 1990, S. 30–31. 39 Guillaume Apollinaire: Die Maler des Kubismus (1913). Dt. Ausg. Zürich 1956, S. 40, und Rubin 1990, S. 14. 40 Rubin 1990, S. 27. 41 Ebd., S. 52. Anm. 63 und 69. 42 Ebd., S. 29. 43 Dorothea Eimert: Der Einfluß des Futurismus auf die deutsche Malerei. Köln 1973. 44 Spies 1990, S. 7ff. 45 Das Thema Collage ist seit der grundlegenden Veröffentlichung von Herta Wescher: Die Geschichte der Collage. Köln 1974, mehrfach, auch ausgerichtet auf andere Spielarten, erweitert dargestellt worden. Deshalb wird die Collage als Sondertypus von Papierkunst hier nur gelegentlich Gegenstand der Betrachtung. 46 William Morris war einer der ersten Künstler, die das Bewußtsein für die Qualitäten des handgeschöpften Papiers wieder in die Druckkunst einbrachten. Vgl. Anm. 28. 47 Josef Albers: Papierarbeiten aus neuer Sicht von 1928. In: Londenberg 1972, S. 52. 48 Ebd., S. 54. Albers erprobte die äußerste Ausnutzung von Papier. Zeichenpapier in Grätenmusterfaltung, etwa 25 x 30 cm, 1 cm hoch, trägt zwei Menschen; der innere Teil von Zündholzschachteln, in engstem Kreis ineinandergesteckt, trägt mehr als eine Person. 49 Jasia Reichardt: „In den frühen 40er Jahren stand ‚Papier-Skulptur‘ auf dem Lehrplan des Pratt Institute, der Cooper Union, der Parsons School of Design und der Cleveland School of Art. In einem Handbuch über Papierskulptur riet Tadeusz Lipski 1947: ‚Wenn man anfängt, eine Papierplastik zu formen, muß man daran denken, daß hier mehr als ein Künstler am Werk ist, man selbst und das Papier.‘ [...] Papier-Skulptur entwickelte sich zwischen den Weltkriegen zu einem Kunsthandwerk. Sie war in den Schaufenstern der Kaufhäuser und als Dekoration bei Fenstern zu sehen. Hieraus entwickelten sich verblüffende Effekte der Papierkonstruktion und einige der Techniken, die heutzutage bei von Künstlern geschaffenen Büchern und Werken von konkreten und visuellen Dichtern vorliegen“. Nach II. Internationale

bition catalogue, (Düren, 1988) 67–69, 3rd International Biennale of Paper Art, Papier als Wissen, exhibition catalogue, (Düren, 1990) 178–181; Paper Art – 4th International Biennale of Paper Art, Papier und Natur, exhibition catalogue, (Düren, 1992) 170–177. **34** Le Papier, exhibition catalogue, (Paris, 1983) 162–167. **35** Paper-Art 1992 102–103. On the theme of folkart, architecture etc. made of paper and papier-maché see Kurt Londenberg, Papier und Form, (Krefeld, 1972); Eberhard and Renate Fiebig, Karl Pobantz and Erik Spiekermann, Zauber des Papiers, (Frankfurt/M., 1973); Le Papier, exhibition catalogue (Paris, 1983); Christian Pieske, Das ABC des Luxuspapiers. Herstellung, Verarbeitung und Gebrauch 1860 bis 1930, (Berlin, 1993) **36** From Werner Spies, Max Ernst. Collagen, exhibition catalogue, (Tübingen, Bern, Düsseldorf, 1988–89; Cologne, 1988) 12. Braque himself in his article "Penseés and réflexions sur la peinture," published in December 1917 in Nord-Sud, Paris, emphasizes the creative freedom that papiers collés allows: "They are simple phenomena, yet created by the intellect, and represent the justification for a new figuration in space." From Eduard Fry, "Der Kubismus," Cologne, 1974², 157. **37** See Diane Waldman, Collage und Objektkunst vom Kubismus bis heute, (Cologne, 1993) 22. **38** See ibid., 27, and William Rubin, Picasso und Braque. Die Geburt des Kubismus, (Munich, 1990) 30–31. **39** Guillaume Apollinaire, Die Maler des Kubismus, (1913; German Edition Zurich, 1956) 40, and Rubin 1990, 14. **40** Rubin, 27. **41** Ibid., 52, notes 63 and 69. **42** Ibid., 29. **43** Dorothea Eimert, Der Einfluß des Futurismus auf die deutsche Malerei, (Cologne, 1973). **44** From Spies 1990, 7. **45** The subject of collage, since the definitive publication by Herta Wescher Die Geschichte der Collage, (Cologne, 1971) has increasingly been depicted under a wider aspect that includes other varieties. Which is why the collage as a special kind of paper art is here only from time to time an object of research. **46** William Morris was one of the first artists to call for a renewed interest in the qualities of handmade paper for book printing. See note 28. **47** Josef Albers, "Papierarbeiten aus neuer Sicht von 1928," in: Londenberg 1972, 52. **48** Ibid., 54. Albers put paper to extreme tests. E. g., he found that one sheet of drawing paper, 1 cm thick, folded in a herringbone pattern, 25 x 30 cm, can bear the weight of two people; matchboxes thightly adjoined in a circle bear the weight of more than one person standing in its center. **49** Jasia Reichardt: "In the early 40s 'paper sculpture' was included in the curriculum of the Pratt Institute, the Cooper Union, the Parsons School of Design and the Cleveland School of Art. In a 1947 manual on paper sculpture, Tadeusz Lipski advised: 'When you begin to form a sculpture, you should remember that there is more than one person at work, yourself and the paper.' [...] Between the wars paper sculpture developed to a craft. It could be seen in the show windows of the department stores and as decoration in windows. Astonishing effects of paper construction were developed from this, as well as some of the techniques that are present today in artist's book objects and works created by concrete and visual poets." From 2nd International Biennale of Paper Art, exhibition catalogue, (Düren, 1988) 54. **50** In 1929 Fautrier has used prepared paperpulp as a picture ground; the material becomes more textural. Jean Fautrier, Gemälde und Zeichnungen, exhibition catalogue, (Bremen, 1993). **51** Dubuffet said: "My pictures are closely linked to the material and its behaviour. I speak of behaviour as one speaks of the behaviour of an animal. I see no difference between my paste and a cat. My bond to the material is like that of a rider to his horse." From Jean Dubuffet, exhibition catalogue, (New York, 1952) no page given. Further literature: Dubuffet, exhibition catalogue, (Berlin, Vienna, Cologne, 1980–81; Dubuffet, exhibition catalogue, (Martingny, 1993). The tachistes also mixed sand, sawdust and other textural substances into paint. Emil Schumacher confessed in 1959 that he often left the material to its own will, because he learned that it was wiser than all calculations. In: blätter + bilder, No. 1 (Würzburg, Vinna, 1959) 34. Around 1957, Schumacher made touch objects out of a construction of chicken wire with papier-maché applied to it, so as to underline materiality. See Andreas Franzke, Skulpturen und Objekte von Malern im 20. Jahrhundert, (Cologne, 1982) 213. **52** From 1960 – Les Nouvaux Réalistes, exhibition catalogue, (Paris, Mannheim, Winterthur, 1986–87) 70. **53** On Boccioni see Christa Baumgart, Ge-

Biennale der Papierkunst. Ausst. Kat. Düren 1988, S. 54. 50 Fautrier hatte bereits 1929 einen Malgrund aus präpariertem Papier benutzt; die Malerei wird stofflicher. Jean Fautrier. Gemälde und Zeichnungen. Ausst. Kat. Bremen 1993. 51 Dubuffet äußerte: „Meine Bilder sind eng mit dem Material und seinem Verhalten verknüpft. Ich spreche von Verhalten, wie man vom Verhalten eines Tieres spricht. Ich sehe keinen Unterschied zwischen meiner Paste und einer Katze. Meine Verbindung mit dem Material gleicht der des Reiters mit dem Pferd." Nach Jean Dubuffet. Ausst. Kat. New York 1952, o.S. Weitere Literatur: Dubuffet. Retrospektive. Ausst. Kat. Berlin, Wien, Köln 1980/81; Dubuffet. Ausst. Kat. Martigny 1993. Auch die Tachisten mischten den Farben Sand, Sägemehl und ähnliche strukturbildende Stoffe bei. Emil Schumacher gesteht 1959, daß er dem Material oft den Willen lasse, denn er habe erfahren, daß es weiser ist als alle Berechnungen. In: blätter und bilder, Heft 1, Würzburg, Wien 1959, S. 34. Schumacher schuf um 1957 Tastobjekte aus einem Gerüst aus Maschendraht mit aufgetragenem Papiermaché, um Stofflichkeit zu betonen; vgl. Andreas Franzke: Skulpturen und Objekte von Malern im 20. Jahrhundert. Köln 1982, S. 213. 52 Nach 1960. Les Nouveaux Réalistes. Ausst. Kat. Paris, Mannheim, Winterthur 1986/87, S. 70. 53 Zu Boccioni vgl. Christa Baumgart: Geschichte des Futurismus. Reinbek b. Hamburg 1966, S. 249. Zitat Gabo und Pevsner nach Kunst in der Revolution. Ausst. Kat. Frankfurt/M., Stuttgart, Köln 1972, o. S. 54 Nach 1960. Les Nouveaux Réalistes. Ausst. Kat. Paris, Mannheim, Winterthur 1986/87, S. 103. 55 Henno Lohmeyer und Felix Schmidt: Eulenspiegel oder Revolutionär. Der Kampf um den Reichstag. Berlin 1993, S. 70 und S. 73, sowie 1960 Les Nouveaux Réalistes. Ausst. Kat. Paris, Mannheim, Winterthur 1986/87, S. 103, Abb. aus Zeitungsanzeige. 56 Ebd., S. 47ff. und S. 235. 57 Niki de Saint-Phalle. Ausst. Kat. Bonn 1993. 58 Vgl. zu diesem Themenkomplex Herbert Eimert: Elektronische Musik, und ders.: Zur musikalischen Situation. Beides in: Elektronische Musik. Sonderheft. Technische Mitteilungen des NWDR Köln 1954, S. 4–5 und S. 42–46; Die 60er Jahre. Kölns Weg zur Kunstmetropole. Vom Happening zum Kunstmarkt. Ausst. Kat. Köln 1986; Herbert Eimert und Hans Ulrich Humpert: Das Lexikon der elektronischen Musik. Regensburg 1973. 59 Otto Piene in einem Gespräch mit Verf. am 28.1.1994. Vgl. auch Manfred Schneckenburger: Zero oder der Aufbruch zur immateriellen Struktur. In: Gruppe ZERO. Ausst. Kat. Düsseldorf 1988, S. 9: „Das Tafelbild entmaterialisiert sich zum Transformator für die Vibrationen optischer Energie. Aus der Überwindung des Tafelbildes gehen Projekte für Himmelsschauspiel, klimatische Landschaftsräume, pneumatische Architekturen, Kunststationen in der Wüste hervor. Viele Künstler glauben geradezu euphorisch an die Verschmelzung von Kunst, Technik, Wissenschaft." 60 Claude Pascal, ein Dichter-Freund von Yves Klein, schrieb einen Text ohne Worte aus einer schwarzen Linie auf weißem Papier als Vorwort zum Ausstellungskatalog Galerie Fernando Franco de Sarabia, Madrid; vgl. Hannah Weitemeier-Steckel: Zero – Zur Entwicklungsgeschichte einer Bewegung. In: ZERO. Bildvorstellungen einer europäischen Avantgarde 1958–1964. Ausst. Kat. Zürich 1979, S. 10. Herman de Vries veröffentlichte 1960 ein Buch mit leeren Blättern, wit – wit is overdaad – weiss ist übermäßig, in einer Auflage von 120 Exemplaren, und 1962 wit, ein Buch mit leeren weißen Seiten in einer Auflage von fünf numerierten Exemplaren. Vgl. Thomas Kellein: Fröhliche Wissenschaft. Das Archiv Sohm. Stuttgart 1986, S. 65. Zu Manzoni vgl. Germano Celant: Piero Manzoni. Aust. Kat. Paris 1991, S. 27. 61 Nach Weitemeier-Steckel 1979, S. 9. 62 Günther Uecker. Bilder und Zeichnungen. Ausst. Kat. Braunschweig 1979, S. 11f., und Ursula Perucchi-Petri: Zu den Bildvorstellungen von Zero. In: ZERO. Ausst. Kat. Zürich 1979, S. 41f. 63 Otto Piene: Das Licht malt. In: Otto Piene. 10 Texte Galerie nota München und dato. Frankfurt/M. 1961, S. 37. 64 Ders.: Über die Reinheit des Lichts. In: Otto Piene 1961, S. 11. 65 Perucchi-Petri 1979, S. 45. 66 Otto Piene im Gespräch mit Verf. am 20.12.1993.

schichte des Futurismus, (Reinbek/Hamburg, 1966) 249. Quotation Gabo and Pevsner from Kunst in der Revolution, exhibition catalogue, (Frankfurt/M., Stuttgart, Cologne, 1972) no page given. **54** 1960 – Les Nouveaux Réalistes 1960, 103. **55** Henno Lohmeyer and Felix Schmidt, Eulenspiegel oder Revolutionär. Der Kampf um den Reichstag, (Berlin, 1993) 70 and 73; and 1960 – Les Nouveaux Réalistes 1960, 103, reproduction from newspaper advertising. **56** Ibid., 47ff. and 235. **57** Niki de Saint-Phalle, exhibition catalogue, (Bonn, 1993). **58** On this subject see Herbert Eimert, "Elektronische Musik," and "Zur musikalischen Situation," both in Elektronische Musik, special issue, Technische Mitteilungen des NWDR, (Cologne, 1954) 4–5, 42–46. Die sechziger Jahre. Kölns Weg zur Kunstmetropole. Vom Happening zum Kunstmarkt, exhibition catalogue, (Cologne, 1986); Herbert Eimert and Hans Ulrich Humpert, Das Lexikon der elektronischen Musik, (Regensburg, 1973). **59** Otto Piene in a conversation with the author on 28 Jan. 1994. See also Manfred Schneckenburger, "Zero oder der Aufbruch zur immateriellen Struktur," in: Gruppe Zero, exhibition catalogue, (Düsseldorf, 1988) 9: "The easel painting immaterializes into a transformer for vibrations of optical energy. Out of this overthrow of the easel painting, projects come into being for sky dramas, climatic landscape, pneumatic architecture, art stations in the desert. Many artists believed almost euphorically in the synthesis of art, technology and science." **60** Claude Pascal, a poet friend of Yves Klein, wrote a text without words (a black line on white paper) as the foreword to an exhibition catalogue of the Galerie Fernando Franco de Sarabia in Madrid. See Hannah Weitemeier-Steckel, "Zero – Zur Entwicklungsgeschichte einer Bewegung," in: ZERO. Bildvorstellungen einer europäischen Avantgarde 1958–1964, exhibition catalogue, (Zurich, 1979) 10. Herman de Vries published a book in 1960 with empty pages, wit – wit is overdaad – white is superfluous, an edition of 120 copies, and in 1962 wit, a book with empty white pages, an edition with five numbered copies. See Thomas Kellein, Fröhliche Wissenschaft. Das Archiv Sohm, (Stuttgart) 65. On Manzoni see Germano Celant, Piero Manzoni, exhibition catalogue, (Paris, 1991) 27. **61** From Weitemeier-Steckel 1979, 9. **62** Günther Uecker. Bilder und Zeichnungen, exhibition catalogue, (Braunschweig, 1979) 11f., and Ursula Perucchi-Petri, "Zu den Bildvorstellungen von Zero," In: ZERO, exhibition catalogue, (Zurich, 1979) 41f. **63** Otto Piene, "Das Licht malt," in: 10 Texte Galerie nota und dato, (Frankfurt/M., 1961) 37. **64** Otto Piene, "Über die Reinheit des Lichts," in: Otto Piene 1961, 11. **65** Perucchi-Petri 1979, 45. **66** Otto Piene in a conversation with the author on 20 Dec. 1993. **67** Otto Piene in a conversation with the author on 28 Jan. 1994. **68** Perucchi-Petri 1979, 50. **69** Eimert 1973, 39ff. **70** Otto Piene, "Lichtballett," in: Otto Piene 1961, 16. **71** Otto Piene in a conversation with the author on 20 Dec. 1993. **72** Dorothea Eimert, "Papier als Wissen," in: 3rd International Biennale of Paper Art, exhibition catalogue (Düren, 1990) 12–13. Yves Klein in 1957 presented his first fire painting 'Feux de Bengale' and lit 16 fires on a blue monochrome painting at the opening. Similarly to Piene he did not use fire, as Burri did, to paint or to gesticulate, but to indicate immateriality. Paper has been burnt in many actions, like Milan Knizak in 1964 on the street in Prague or Jerzy Berés in 1973 in Lublin. See Elisabeth Jappe, Performance, Ritual, Prozeß. Handbuch der Aktionskunst in Europa, (Munich, 1993) 185 and 162. **73** Otto Piene in his speech at the opening of the exhibition 'Mack – Piene – Uecker' in the Kaiser-Wilhelm-Museum Krefeld, Haus, Lange, January 1963. From Perucchi-Petri 1979, 75. **74** Otto Piene, "Fragen," in: Otto Piene 1961, 22–23. **75** Günther Uecker in exhibition catalogue (Hannover, 1964–65). From Perucchi-Petri 1979, 76. **76** Gudrund Inboden, "Zeichnungen 1957–1959," in: Günther Uecker. Bilder und Objekte. Das zeichnerische Frühwerk. Prägedrucke, Prägestöcke und Frottage. Figuren und Bühnenbildentwürfe zum 'Parsifal', exhibition catalogue, (Stuttgart, 1976) 40–41. **77** Before Schoonhoven joined the avant-garde in the 50s, he had been working for some years on reliefs out of painted cardboard and papier-maché. They recall vegetable life or bizarre architecture. See Antje von Graevenitz, "Jan J. Schoonhoven – Der Zeichner," in: J. J. Schoonhoven. Zeichnungen 1940–1975, exhibition catalogue, (Düsseldorf, Rotterdam, Ulm 1975–76) 5–7. See also Ad Dekkers, Jan J. Schoonhoven, Peter

67 Otto Piene im Gespräch mit Verf. am 28.1.1994. 68 Perucchi-Petri 1979, S. 50. 69 Dorothea Eimert 1973, S. 39ff. 70 Otto Piene: Lichtballett. In: Otto Piene 1961, S.16. 71 Otto Piene im Gespräch mit Verf. am 20.12.1993. 72 Dorothea Eimert: Papier als Wissen. In: III. Internationale Biennale der Papierkunst. Ausst. Kat. Düren 1990, S.12–13. Yves Klein montiert 1957 sein erstes Feuerbild ‚Feux de Bengale' und zündet die 16 Feuer auf einer blauen Monochromie zur Vernissage an. Ähnlich wie Piene nutzt er das Feuer nicht, um wie Burri damit zu malen oder zu gestalten, sondern um auf die Immaterialität hinzuweisen. Papier wird vielfach in Aktionen verbrannt wie z. B. bei Milan Knizak 1964 auf der Straße in Prag oder Jerzy Berés 1973 in Lublin; vgl. Elisabeth Jappe: Performance, Ritual, Prozeß. Handbuch der Aktionskunst in Europa. München 1993, S.185 und S.162. 73 In: Otto Piene: Ansprache zur Eröffnung der Ausstellung ‚Mack – Piene – Uecker' im Kaiser-Wilhelm-Museum Krefeld, Haus Lange, Januar 1963. Nach Perucchi-Petri 1979, S.75. 74 Otto Piene: Fragen. Otto Piene 1961, S. 22–23. 75 Günther Uecker. In: Ausst. Kat. Hannover 1964–65. Nach Perucchi-Petri 1979, S.76. 76 Gudrun Inboden: Zeichnungen 1957–1959. In: Günther Uecker. Bilder und Objekte. Das Zeichnerische Frühwerk. Prägedrucke, Prägestöcke und Frottage. Figuren und Bühnenbildentwürfe zum ‚Parsifal'. Ausst. Kat. Stuttgart 1976, S. 40–41. 77 Bevor Schoonhoven sich Ende der 50er Jahre der Avantgarde anschloß, arbeitete er seit einigen Jahren an Reliefs aus bemaltem Karton und Pappmaché. Sie erinnern an Vegetabiles oder an bizarre Architekturen. Vgl. Antje von Graevenitz: Jan J. Schoonhoven – Der Zeichner. In: J. J. Schoonhoven. Zeichnungen 1940–1975. Ausst. Kat. Düsseldorf, Rotterdam, Ulm 1975/76, S. 5–7. Vgl. auch Ad Dekkers, Jan J. Schoonhoven, Peter Struycken, Carl Visser. Bilder, Plastiken, Zeichnungen aus dem Stedelijk Museum Amsterdam. Ausst. Kat. Bottrop 1977, S. 9–10. 78 Leo Erb. Eine Retrospektive. Ausst. Kat. Bergisch Gladbach 1993/94. 79 Oskar Holweck. In: Das Papier. Ausst. Kat. Düren 1981, Artikel Holweck. 80 Ebd., Artikel Reuter. 81 Only Paper. Papier als künstlerisches Medium. Bestandskatalog der Sondersammlung. Bergisch Gladbach 1992, S. 318. 82 Das Papier. Ausst. Kat. Düren 1981, Artikel Erdmann. 83 Joseph Beuys über Herbert Zangs. In: Herbert Zangs – Arbeiten 1953–1981. Ausst. Kat. Kleve 1982, S.17. 84 Vgl. hierzu folgende Kataloge: Papier als künstlerisches Medium. Heidelberg, Wanderausstellung 1980/82; Das Papier. Düren 1981; Medium Papier. Bergisch Gladbach 1982; Papier zu Papier gebracht. Farbe, Linie, Raum. Düren 1984; Papier. Berlin 1987; Only Paper. Bergisch Gladbach 1992. 85 Fiebig befaßte sich auch historisch und theoretisch intensiv mit der Thematik Papier. Er organisierte 1973 die Ausstellung ‚Zauber des Papiers' im Kunstverein Frankfurt; vgl. Ausst. Kat. Anm. 35. 86 Erwin Heerich. Ausst. Kat. Düsseldorf 1979. 87 Das Papier. Ausst. Kat. Düren 1981, Artikel Schultze. 88 Hayter gab 1927 seinen Beruf als Chemiker auf, ging nach Paris und gründete dort eine Werkstatt für Druckgrafik, das spätere Atelier 17, eine Experimentierstätte für Künstler wie Yves Tanguy, Joan Miró und Jean Arp. 1939 übersiedelte er nach New York, wo sein Atelier 17 sich zum Treffpunkt von Emigranten und amerikanischen Grafikern entwickelte. Das 1949 erschienene Lehrbuch über moderne grafische Techniken, New Ways of Gravure, geriet zum Standardwerk. 1950 kehrte er nach Paris zurück; sein Atelier wurde 1955 der Académie Ranon angegliedert. Vgl. Das Große Lexikon der Graphik. Braunschweig 1984, S. 286–269. 89 Vgl. Dora Vallier: Braque. Das graphische Gesamtwerk. Stuttgart 1982, S. 212. 90 Vgl. zum Thema Prägen Ulrike Eichler: Prägedrucke. In: Günther Uecker. Ausst. Kat. Stuttgart 1976, S. 47–52; Paperwork. Ausst. Kat. Canberra 1982, S.7–12. 91 Margarethe Jochimsen: Prozesse. Ansätze zur Erschließung des Terrains. Ausst. Kat. Bonn 1978, o. S. 92 Johann Wolfgang von Goethe: Wahlverwandtschaften. 2. Teil, 2. Kapitel, letzter Satz. 93 Franz Erhard Walther. Arbeiten 1959–1963. Ausst. Kat. Bonn 1981, zu Kat. Nr. 7. 94 Ebd., zu

Struycken, Carl Visser. Bilder, Plastiken, Zeichnungen aus dem Stedelijk Museum Amsterdam, exhibition catalogue, (Bottrop) 9–10. **78** Leo Erb. Eine Retrospektive, exhibition catalogue (Bergisch Gladbach, 1993–94) **79** Oskar Holweck, in: Das Papier, exhibition catalogue, (Düren, 1981) article "Holweck". **80** Ibid., article "Reuter". **81** Only Paper. Papier als künstlerisches Medium. Bestandskatalog der Sondersammlung, (Bergisch Gladbach, 1992) 318. **82** Das Papier, exhibition catalogue, (Düren, 1981) article "Erdmann" **83** Joseph Beuys über Herbert Zangs, in: Herbert Zangs – Arbeiten 1953–1981, exhibition catalogue, (Kleve, 1982) 17. **84** See the following catalogues: Papier als künstlerisches Medium, (Heidelberg, travelling exhibition 1980–82); "Das Papier," (Düren, 1981); Medium Papier, (Bergisch Gladbach, 1982); Papier zu Papier gebracht. Farbe, Linie, Raum, (Düren, 1984); Papier, (Berlin, 1987); Only Paper, (Bergisch Gladbach, 1992). **85** Fiebig studied very thoroughly the subject of paper including its historical and theoretical aspects. In 1973 he organized the exhibition in the Kunstverein Frankfurt, 'Zauber des Papiers', see exhibition catalogue note 35. **86** Erwin Heerich, exhibition catalogue, (Düsseldorf, 1979). **87** Das Papier, exhibition catalogue, (Düren, 1981), article "Schultze". **88** Hayter gave up his profession of chemistry, went to Paris in 1927 to found a workshop for the graphic arts, later to become 'Atelier 17', an experimental studio for artists like Yves Tanguy, Joan Miró and Jean Arp. In 1939 he moved to New York where his 'Atelier 17' became a meeting place for emigrants and American graphic artists. His textbook on modern graphic techniques, New Ways of Gravure (1949), became a standard textbook. In 1950 he returned to Paris; his atelier was incorporated in the Académie Ranon in 1955. See Das Große Lexikon der Graphik, (Braunschweig, 1984) 268–269. **89** See Dora Vallier, Braque. Das graphische Gesamtwerk, (Stuttgart, 1976) 212. **90** See on the subject of embossing Ulrike Eichler, "Prägedrucke," in: Günther Uecker, exhibition catalogue, (Stuttgart, 1976) 47–52; Paper Work, exhibition catalogue, (Canberra, 1982) 7–12. **91** Margarethe Jochimsen, Prozesse. Ansätze zur Erschließung des Terrains, exhibition catalogue, (Bonn, 1979) no page given. **92** Johann Wolfgang Goethe, Wahlverwandtschaften, part two, chapter two, last line. **93** Franz Erhard Walther. Arbeiten 1959–1963, exhibition catalogue, (Bonn, 1981) see catalogue number 7. **94** Ibid., see catalogue number 10. **95** Ibid., see catalogue number 10. **96** See Jochimsen 1978; 4th International Biennale of PaperArt, exhibition catalogue, (Düren, 1992). **97** See Myriam Wierschowski, Book Art in Europe 1. Buchobjekte aus Papier, exhibition catalogue, (Düren, 1993–94) 16. **98** See S. D. Sauerbier, "Poesie der Natur," in: 4th International Biennale of Paper Art, exhibition catalogue, (Düren, 1992) 32–33f. **99** See Fluxus. Aspekte eines Phänomens, exhibition catalogue, (Wuppertal, 1982) 173. **100** See Sauerbier 1992, 30. **101** In: Zufall als Prinzip. Spielwelt, Methode und System in der Kunst des 20. Jahrhunderts, exhibition catalogue, (Heidelberg, 1992) 244. **102** See Sauerbier 1992, 24. **103** See Übrigens sterben immer die anderen. Marcel Duchamp und die Avantgarde seit 1950, exhibition catalogue, (Köln, 1988) 88. **104** Dieter Roth, Gesammelte Werke Band 20. Bücher und Grafik Teil I aus den Jahren 1949–1971, 112. **105** Kellein 1986, 70–71. **106** See 1960 – Les Nouveaux Réalistes, exhibition catalogue, (Paris, Mannheim, Wintherthur 1986/87) 68. **107** See Joachimsen 1978, no page given. Nolde wrote in one of his letters, "I want so much for my work to grow out of the material." From Bandmann 1971, 138. **108** See Sauerbier 1988, 31. **109** See Das Papier, exhibition catalogue, (Düren, 1981), article "Mally". Mario Reis left untreated linen to be worked by the water in the river and called the works "Naturaquarelle" (natural water colors). **110** Dorothea Eimert, "Papier und Natur", in: 4th International Biennale of Paper Art, exhibition catalogue, (Düren, 1992) 9–10. **111** Sauerbier 1992, 28. **112** 1st International Biennale of Paper Art, exhibition catalogue, (Düren, 1986) 352. **113** Exhibited at the 3rd International Biennale of Paper Art, Düren, 1990. **114** From 4th International Biennale of Paper Art, exhibition catalogue, (Düren, 1992) 104. **115** Dorothea Eimert, "Papier und Natur", in: Papierkunst der Gegenwart, Deutschland – Japan, exhibition catalogue, (Berlin, 1990) 10. **116** Timm Ulrichs. Retrospektive 1960–1975, exhibition catalogue (Braunschweig, 1975) 25. **117** Ibid., 83. **118** Rémy

Kat. Nr. 10. 95 Ebd. 96 Vgl. hierzu Jochimsen 1978; 4. Internationale Biennale der Papierkunst. Ausst. Kat. Düren 1992. 97 Vgl. Myriam Wierschowski: Book Art in Europe 1. Buchobjekte aus Papier. Ausst. Kat. Düren 1993/94, S.16. 98 Vgl. S. D. Sauerbier: Poesie der Natur. In: 4. Internationale Biennale der Papierkunst. Ausst. Kat. Düren 1992, S. 32–33. 99 Vgl. Fluxus. Aspekte eines Phänomens. Ausst. Kat. Wuppertal 1982, S.173f. 100 Vgl. Sauerbier 1992, S. 30. 101 Zufall als Prinzip. Spielwelt, Methode und System in der Kunst des 20. Jahrhunderts. Ausst. Kat. Heidelberg 1992, S. 244. 102 Vgl. Sauerbier 1992, S. 24. 103 Vgl. Übrigens sterben immer die anderen. Marcel Duchamp und die Avantgarde seit 1950. Ausst. Kat. Köln 1988. S. 88. 104 Dieter Roth: Gesammelte Werke Band 20. Bücher und Grafik Teil I aus den Jahren 1949–1971, S.112. 105 Kellein 1986, S. 70–71. 106 Vgl. 1960 Les Nouveaux Réalistes. Ausst. Kat. Paris, Mannheim, Winterthur 1986/87, S. 68. 107 Vgl. Jochimsen 1978, o. S.; Nolde äußerte in einem seiner Briefe: „Ich will so gern, daß mein Werk aus dem Material herauswachse." Nach Bandmann 1971, S.138. 108 Vgl. Sauerbier 1988, S. 31. 109 Vgl. Das Papier. Ausst. Kat. Düren 1981, Artikel Mally. Mario Reis ließ unbearbeitetes Leinen vom Wasser des Flusses bearbeiten und nannte die Arbeiten „Naturaquarelle". 110 Dorothea Eimert: Papier und Natur. In: 4. Internationale Biennale der Papierkunst. Ausst. Kat. Düren 1992, S. 9–10. 111 Sauerbier 1992, S. 28. 112 I. Internationale Biennale der Papierkunst. Ausst. Kat. Düren 1986, S. 352. 113 Ausgestellt in der III. Internationalen Biennale der Papierkunst, Düren 1990. 114 Nach 4. Internationale Biennale der Papierkunst. Ausst. Kat. Düren 1992, S.104. 115 Dorothea Eimert: Papier und Natur. In: Papierkunst der Gegenwart, Deutschland – Japan. Ausst. Kat. Berlin 1990, S.10. 116 Timm Ulrichs. Retrospektive 1960–1975. Ausst. Kat. Braunschweig 1975. S. 25. 117 Ebd., S. 83. 118 Rémy Zaugg: Reflexionen auf und über ein Blatt Papier. Ausst. Kat. Basel 1993. 119 Nach Michael Lentz: papierfressen: In: III. Internationale Biennale der Papierkunst. Ausst. Kat. Düren 1990, S. 44. 120 Vgl. Barbara Rose: Amerikas Weg zur modernen Kunst. Von der Mülltonnenschule zur Minimal Art. Köln 1969, S. 221–222. 121 Vgl. Silvie Turner und Birgit Skiöld: Handmade Paper Today. London 1983, S. 225. 122 Eine Biographie über Dard Hunter erstellen Patricia Scott und Cathleen A. Baker, Chillicothe/Ohio. 123 Brief von Douglass Morse Howell an Verf. v. 15.12.1986; vgl. Douglass Morse Howell. Retrospective. Ausst. Kat. New York 1982. 124 Jules Heller: Papermaking. The White Art. New York 1978. 125 Elaine Koretsky: Color for Hand Papermaking. Carriage House Press 1983; weitere Papiermühlen vgl. Turner und Skiöld 1983, S. 256–161; Dorothea Eimert (Hrsg.): IAPMA International Association of Hand Papermakers and Paper Artists. Düren 1992; die Kataloge der Biennalen der Papierkunst, Düren 1981, 1986, 1988, 1990, 1992. 126 Rauschenbergs Pages and Fuses, Los Angeles County Museum of Art 1975; Works on Handmade Paper, Museum of Modern Art, New York 1976; The Handmade Paper Object, Santa Barbara Museum of Art 1976; New ways With Paper, National Collection of Fine Arts, Washington D. C. 1977/78; Paper as Medium, Smithsonian Institution, Washington D. C., Wanderausstellung durch 17 Stationen 1978–1980; New American Paperworks, Wanderausstellung des World Print Council San Francisco durch die USA und Asien 1982–1985. 127 Internationale Vereinigungen: IPH International Paper Historians (Basel); IAPMA International Association of Hand Papermakers und Paper Artists (Basel); Friends of Dard Hunter (Montpellier/Vermont). Publikationsorgane: IPH Information; IAPMA Bulletin und Newsletter; Hand Papermaking (Washington D. C.); Works on Paper. Newsletter of Papermakers of Australia (Hobart/Tasmania). 128 Vgl. I. Internationale Biennale der Papierkunst. Ausst. Kat. Düren 1986, S. 320. 129 Vgl. Das Papier. Ausst. Düren 1981. Artikel Turner und Anm.121. 130 Vgl. Dorothea Eimert: Eine kleine Geschichte der Papierkunst. In: II. Internationale Biennale der Papierkunst. Ausst. Kat. Düren 1988, S. 41 f. 131 Weitere Angaben hierzu vgl.

Zaugg, Reflexionen auf und über ein Blatt Papier, exhibition catalogue, (Basle, 1993). 119 From Michael Lenz, "papierfressen," in: 3rd International Biennale of Paper Art, exhibition catalogue, (Düren, 1990) 44. 120 See Barbara Rose, Amerikas Weg zur modernen Kunst. Von der Mülltonnenschule zur Minimal Art, (Cologne, 1969) 221–222. 121 See Silvie Turner and Birgit Skiöld, Handmade Paper Today, (London, 1983) 225. 122 A biography on Dard Hunter will be edited by Patricia Scott and Cathleen A. Baker, Chillicothe/Ohio. 123 Letter from Douglass Morse Howell to author on 15 Dec. 1986. See Douglass Morse Howell. Retrospective, exhibition catalogue (New York, 1982). 124 Jules Heller, Papermaking. The White Art, (New York, 1978) 125 Elaine Koretsky, Color for Hand Papermaking, (Carriage House Press, 1983); for other papermills see Turner and Skiöld 1983, 256–161; Dorothea Eimert (ed.), IAPMA. International Association of Hand Papermakers and Paper Artists, (Düren, 1992); the catalogues of the Biennali of Paper Art, (Düren, 1981, 1986, 1988, 1990, 1992). 126 Rauschenbergs Pages and Fuses, Los Angeles County Museum of Art, 1975; Works on Handmade Paper, Museum of Modern Art, 1976; The Handmade Paper Object, Santa Barbara Museum of Modern Art, New York, 1976; New Ways with Paper, National Collection of Fine Arts, Washington D. C. 1977/78; Paper as Medium, Smithsonian Institution, Washington D. C., travelling exhibition with 17 stations 1978–1980; New American Paperworks; travelling exhibition of the World Print Council San Fransicso through the U.S. and Asia 1982–85. 127 International Associations: IPH International Paper Historians (Basle); IAPMA International Association of Hand Papermakers and Paper Artists (Basle); Friends of Dard Hunter (Montpellier/Nevada). Publications: IPH Information; IAPMA Bulletin and Newsletter; Hand Papermaking (Washington D. C.); Works on Paper. Newsletter of Papermakers of Australia (Hobart/Tasmania) 128 See 1st International Biennale of Paper Art 186, 320. 129 See Das Papier, exhibition catalogue, (Düren, 1981) article "Turner" and Note 121. 130 Dorothea Eimert, "Eine kleine Geschichte der Papierkunst," in: 2nd International Biennale of Paper Art, exhibition catalogue, (Düren, 1988) 41f. 131 For further details see Eimert 1988, 42; and Eimert IAPMA, 1992, 10ff. 132 Kenneth E. Tyler and Rosamund Felsen, "Two Rauschenberg Projects," in: Paper. The World Print Council, (San Francisco, 1979) 81–82. Kenneth Tyler (*1931 East Chicago/Indiana) was in 1964–65 director of the Tamarind Lithography Workshop and worked among others with Albers. In 1965 he founded Gemini Ltd. in Los Angeles and was director and lithography printer till 1974. He worked with Hockney, Albers, Rauschenberg, Stella, Johns, Oldenburg, Lichtenstein. In 1974 he founded Tyler Graphics Ltd. in Bedford Village/New York. He continued to work together with the artists already named and won some of them over to working in pulp. In 1981 the Gemini Archive was set up in the National Gallery of Art in Washington, D. C. and in 1982 the Tyler Graphics Archive in the Walker Art Center in Minneapolis/Minnesota. Tyler arranged many travelling exhibitions with the works that were done in his workshop, among others, one through Japan in 1992–93. 133 Tyler and Felsen 1979, 86. 134 From José Pierre, DuMonts kleines Lexikon der Pop Art, (Cologne, 1978) 114. 135 See Judith Goldman, Kenneth Noland, (Tyler Graphics, Bedford Village/New York, 1978). 136 From Nikos Stangos (ed.), David Hockney. Paper Pools, (New York, 1980) 10. 137 From ibid., 48. 138 From ibid., 100. 139 Ellsworth Kelly. Colored Paper Images, (Tyler Graphics, Bedford Village/New York, 1976); Innovation in Collaborative Printmaking: Kenneth Tyler 1963–1992, exhibition catalogue, (Yokohama, 1992) 80. 140 See ibid., 168. 141 Ibid., 156. 142 Comment made by the artist to the author while preparing the text to the catalogue Contemporary Paper Art in Germany at Saint Louis Gallery of Contemporary Art, Saint Louis/Missouri, and others, 1989. 143 From 1st International Biennale of Paper Art, exhibition catalogue, (Düren, 1986) 110; for the other artists mentioned in this chapter, further information can be found in the catalogues to the Paper Art Biennali (Düren, 1986, 1988, 1990, 1992); see the article by Golda Lewis in the 1986 catalogue, 59–66. 144 From Dorothea Eimert, "Papier und Wert," in: Wertpapier, exhibition catalogue, (Munich, 1989) 5–6. 145 4th International Biennale of

Eimert 1988, S. 42, und Eimert IAPMA 1992, S. 10ff. 132 Kenneth E. Tyler und Rosamund Felsen: Two Rauschenberg Projects. In: Paper. The World Print Council. San Francisco 1979. S. 81–82. Kenneth Tyler (* 1931 East Chicago/Indiana) war 1964/65 Direktor des Tamarind Lithography Workshop; dort arbeitete er u. a. mit Albers. 1965 gründete er Gemini Ltd. in Los Angeles, wo er Direktor und Drucker bis 1974 war; er arbeitete mit Hockney, Albers, Rauschenberg, Stella, Johns, Oldenburg, Lichtenstein. 1974 gründete er Tyler Graphics Ltd. in Bedford Village/New York; er setzte die Zusammenarbeit mit den genannten Künstlern fort und gewann einige von ihnen zur Gestaltung mit Pulp. 1981 wurde das Gemini Archiv in der National Gallery of Art, Washington D. C. eingerichtet und 1982 im Walker Art Center, Minneapolis/Minnesota das Tyler Graphics Archiv. Tyler arrangierte viele Wanderausstellungen mit den bei ihm entstandenen Werken, u. a. 1992/93 durch Japan. 133 Tyler und Felsen 1979, S. 86. 134 Nach José Pierre: DuMont's kleines Lexikon der Pop Art. Köln 1978, S. 114. 135 Vgl. Judith Goldmann: Kenneth Noland. Tyler Graphics, Bedford Village. New York 1978. 136 Nach Nikos Stangos (Hrsg.): David Hockney. Paper Pools. New York 1980, S. 10. 137 Nach ebd., S. 48. 138 Nach ebd., S. 100. 139 Ellsworth Kelly: Colored Paper Images. Tyler Graphics, Bedford Village. New York 1976; Innovation in Collaborative Printmaking: Kenneth Tyler 1963–1992. Ausst. Kat. Yokohama 1992, S. 80. 140 Vgl. ebd., S. 168. 141 Ebd., S. 156. 142 Mitteilung des Künstlers an Verf. für die Textvorbereitung zum Katalog der Ausstellung ‚Contemporary Paper Art in Germany' in der Saint Louis Gallery of Contemporary Art, Saint Louis/Missouri u. a. 1989. 143 I. Internationale Biennale der Papierkunst. Ausst. Kat. Düren 1986, S. 110; zu den übrigen in diesem Kapitel genannten Künstlern weitere Informationen in den Katalogen der Papierbiennalen Düren 1986, 1988, 1990, 1992; vgl. den Aufsatz von Golda Lewis in Ausst. Kat. Papierbiennale 1986, S. 59–66. 144 Nach Dorothea Eimert: Papier und Wert. In: Wertpapier. Ausst. Kat. München 1989, S. 5–6. 145 Nach 4. Internationale Biennale der Papierkunst. Ausst. Kat. Düren 1992, S. 128. 146 Ebd., S. 100. 147 Nach Pontus Hulten: Territorium Artis: Ausst. Kat. Bonn 1992, S. 264. Vgl. Michelangelo Pistoletto. Ausst. Kat. Baden-Baden 1988. 148 Vgl. I. Internationale Biennale der Papierkunst. Ausst. Kat. Düren 1986, S. 90. 149 Ebd., S. 338. 150 Ein unwiderruflicher Schritt. Ausst. Kat. Joel Fisher. Mönchengladbach 1975, S. ‚1969', Spalte 2. 151 Ebd. 152 Ebd., S. 1971, 5. Spalte. 153 Manuskript zur Ausstellungseröffnung am 23. 9. 1975. 154 In: I. Internationale Biennale der Papierkunst. Ausst. Kat. Düren 1986, S. 154. 155 Henri Matisse: Jazz. München, 1959. S. 40. 156 Michael Schwarz: Felix Droese. Ich habe Anne Frank umgebracht. Frankfurt/M. 1988; Lucius Grisebach: Felix Droese. Reine Gesinnung. Ausst. Kat. Nürnberg. 1991. 157 Christine Pfeifer: Dmitrij A. Prigov. Mitteilungen der Krings-Ernst Galerie Köln o. J. 158 In: Art Paper. Ausst. Kat. Maastricht 1987, S. 48. 159 In: China Avantgarde. Ausst. Kat. Berlin 1993, S. 134. 160 Ebd. 161 Vgl. Kapitel IV.1 ‚Licht und Feuer', S. 50–54. 162 Hofmann und Präger 1987, o. S. 163 Ebd. 164 Vgl. Germano Celant: Claes Oldenburg. Coosje van Bruggen: A Bottle of Notes and Some Voyages. Sunderland 1988. 165 Nach Hofmann und Präger 1987; vgl. Handbuch Museum Ludwig Köln 1979; S. 662. 166 Claus Bach: Under the Boardwalk. In: Bertram Jesdinsky. Ausst. Kat. Düren 1991, o. S. 167 Hofmann und Präger 1987, o. S. 168 Rolf Wedewer: Am Beispiel Plastik. Konzeption und Form. Ausst. Kat. Leverkusen u. a. 1993, S. 93–103. 169 Eimert 1990, S. 14–15. 170 Fluxus 1982, S. 153. 171 Ebd., S. 166. 172 Jappe 1993, S. 203. 173 Ebd., S. 212. 174 Eimert 1989, S. 10. 175 Nach Bayerl 1987, S. 129. 176 Vgl. Dolf Sternberger: Papiergedanken. In: Das Papier. Ausst. Kat. Düren 1981, S. 15–19.

Paper Art, exhibition catalogue, (Düren, 1992) 128. **146** Ibid., 100. **147** From Pontus Hulten, Territorium Artis, exhibition catalogue, (Bonn, 1992) 264. See Michelangelo Pistoletto, exhibition catalogue (Baden-Baden, 1988). **148** See 1st International Biennale of Paper Art, exhibition catalogue, (Düren, 1986) 90. **149** Ibid., 338. **150** Joel Fisher. Ein unwiderruflicher Schritt, exhibition catalogue (Mönchengladbach, 1975) page "1969", column two. **151** From ibid. **152** Ibid., page "1971", column 5. **153** Manuscript of the opening of the exhibition on 23 Sept. 1975. **154** In: 1st International Biennale of Paper Art, exhibition catalogue (Düren, 1986) 154. **155** Henri Matisse, Jazz, (Munich, 1959) 40. **156** Michael Schwarz, Felix Droese. Ich habe Anne Frank umgebracht, (Frankfurt/M., 1988); Lucius Grisebach, Felix Droese. Reine Gesinnung, exhibition catalogue, (Nuremberg, 1991). **157** Christine Pfeifer: Dmitri A. Prigov. Mitteilungen der Krings-Ernst Galerie, (Cologne, no year given). **158** In: Art Paper, exhibition catalogue, (Maastricht, 1987) 48. **159** In: China Avantgarde, exhibition catalogue, (Berlin, 1993) 134. **160** Ibid. **161** See chapter IV. 1 "Licht und Feuer", 50–54. **162** Hofmann and Präger 1987, no page given. **163** Ibid.. **164** See Germano Celant, Claes Oldenburg, Coosje van Bruggen, A Bottle of Notes and Some Voyages, (Sunderland, 1988). **165** Hofmann and Präger 1987; see "Handbuch Museum Ludwig Köln, (Cologne, 1979) 662. **166** Claus Bach, "Under the Boardwalk," in: Bertram Jesdinsky, exhibition catalogue, (Düren, 1991) no page given. **167** Hofmann and Präger 1987, no page given. **168** Rolf Wedewer, Am Beispiel Plastik. Konzeption und Form, exhibition catalogue, (Leverkusen and elsewhere, 1993) 93–103. **169** Eimert 1990, 14–15. **170** Fluxus 1982, 153. **171** Ibid., 166. **172** Jappe 1993, 203. **173** Ibid., 212. **174** Eimert 1989, 10. **175** From Bayerl 1987, 129. **176** See Dolf Sternberger, "Papiergedanken," in: Das Papier, exhibition catalogue, (Düren, 1981), 15–19.

Literaturverzeichnis zur Papierkunst nach 1950

Bücher: Es sind nur solche genannt, die wenigstens ein Kapitel der Papierkunst widmen, nicht solche, die nur Kunsthandwerk, Papierhistorie oder Techniken der Papierherstellung behandeln. Es wurden nur die wichtigsten Ausstellungskataloge aufgeführt. Kataloge von Künstler-Einzelausstellungen sind nicht aufgenommen.

Bücher

John Mason: Papermaking as an Artistic Craft. Leicester 1959
Kurt Londenberg: Papier und Form. Krefeld 1972
Eberhard und Renate Fiebig, Karl Pobantz und Erik Spiekermann: Zauber des Papiers. Frankfurt/M. 1973
Vance Studley: The Art & Craft of Handmade Paper. London, New York 1977
Judith Goldmann: Kenneth Noland. New York 1978
Jules Heller: Papermaking. The White Art. New York 1978
Paulette Long (Hrsg.): Paper – Art & Technology. San Francisco 1979
Nikos Stangos (Hrsg.): David Hockney. New York 1980
Silvie Turner und Birgit Skiöld: Contemporary Handmade Paper. London 1983
Anne Vilsbøll: Papier Mageri 2. kunst og technik. Gylling 1990
Dorothea Eimert (Hrsg.): III. Internationale Biennale der Papierkunst. Heidelberg 1990.
Dorothea Eimert (Hrsg.): PaperArt 4. Papier und Natur. Köln 1992
Dorothea Eimert (Hrsg.): IAPMA International Association of Hand Papermakers and Paper Artists. Düren 1992

Aufsätze und Manuskripte

John Loring: American Prints from Fuses to Fizzles. In: Art in America, 1977, 65, Nr. 1
Dorothea Eimert: Das Papier – Ein Grundelement künstlerischen Gestaltens. In: Das Papier. Ausst. Kat. Leopold-Hoesch-Museum der Stadt Düren 1981, S. 81–82
Dorothea Eimert: Papier – Medium moderner Kunst. In: Medium Papier. Ausst. Kat. Städtische Galerie, Villa Zanders, Bergisch Gladbach 1982, S. 5–6
Shelley Krapes: A Painter's Way with Paper. In: Fiberarts. The Magazine of Textiles. Ashville/North Carolina, Juli/August 1982, S. 20
Ann Gora: Books without Words. In: Fiberarts. The Magazine of Textiles. Ashville/North Carolina, Juli/August 1982, S. 21
Bernhard Toale: Papermaking in the U.S.A. In: Fiberarts. The Magazine of Textiles. Ashville/North Carolina, Juli/August 1982, S. 34–38
Silvie Turner: Papermaking. In: Artists Newsletter. London, Supplement November 1983
Michael Schulte-Wintrop: Papier als künstlerisches Medium. Osnabrück 1983 (Examensarbeit, Manusk.)
Jessica Scarborough: Sculptural Paper. In: Fiberarts. The Magazine of Textiles. Asheville/North Carolina, März/April 1984, S. 32–35
Dorothea Eimert: Papier. Eine neue Sprache der Kunst. In: Textilforum. Hannover 1985, H. 4, S. 32–33
Dorothea Eimert: Papierkunst. In: Kunst und Handwerk, Düsseldorf 1986, H. 4., S. 226–230
Dorothea Eimert: Papier – Medium der modernen Kunst. In: Papier. Ausst. Kat. Museum für Verkehr und Technik. Berlin 1987, S. 109–127
Birgit Kötters: Papier als künstlerisches Medium. Untersuchungen von Gestaltungsprozessen. Osnabrück 1985 (Examensarbeit, Mansk.)

Bibliography on post – 1950 paper art

Books: listed are those books that include at least one chapter on paper art, not those only on the craft, the history or the techniques of papermaking. Only the catalogues of the most important exhibitions are mentioned and those on artists' solo exhibitions have not been included.

Books

John Mason: Papermaking as an Artistic Craft. Leicester 1959
Kurt Londenberg: Papier und Form. Krefeld 1972
Eberhard and Renate Fiebig, Karl Pobantz and Erik Spiekermann: Zauber des Papiers. Frankfurt/M. 1973
Vance Studley: The Art & Craft of Handmade Paper. London, New York 1977
Judith Goldmann: Kenneth Noland. New York 1978
Jules Heller: Papermaking. The White Art. New York 1978
Paulette Long (ed.): Paper – Art & Technology. San Francisco 1979
Nikos Stangos (ed.): David Hockney. New York 1980
Silvie Turner and Birgit Skiöld: Contemporary Handmade Paper. London 1983
Anne Vilsbøll: Papier Mageri 2. kunst og technik. Gylling 1990
Dorothea Eimert (ed.): III. Internationale Biennale der Papierkunst. Heidelberg 1990.
Dorothea Eimert (ed.): PaperArt 4. Papier und Natur. Cologne 1992
Dorothea Eimert (ed.): IAPMA International Association of Hand Papermakers and Paper Artists. Düren 1992

Articles and manuscripts

John Loring: American Prints from Fuses to Fizzles. In: Art in America, 1977, 65, no. 1
Dorothea Eimert: Das Papier – Ein Grundelement künstlerischen Gestaltens. In: Das Papier. Exhibition catalogue Leopold Hoesch Museum der Stadt Düren 1981, p. 81–82
Dorothea Eimert: Papier – Medium moderner Kunst. In: Medium Papier. Exhibition catalogue Städtische Galerie, Villa Zanders, Bergisch Gladbach 1982, p. 5–6
Shelley Krapes: A Painter's Way with Paper. In: Fiberarts. The Magazine of Textiles. Ashville/North Carolina, July/August 1982, p. 20
Ann Gora: Books without Words. In: Fiberarts. The Magazine of Textiles. Ashville/North Carolina, July/August 1982, p. 21
Bernhard Toale: Papermaking in the U.S.A. In: Fiberarts. The Magazine of Textiles. Ashville/North Carolina, Juli/August 1982, p. 34–38
Silvie Turner: Papermaking. In: Artists Newsletter. London, Supplement November 1983
Michael Schulte-Wintrop: Papier als künstlerisches Medium. Osnabrück 1983 (thesis, manuscript)
Jessica Scarborough: Sculptural Paper. In: Fiberarts. The Magazine of Textiles. Ashville/North Carolina, March/April 1984, p. 32–35
Dorothea Eimert: Papier. Eine neue Sprache der Kunst. In: Textilforum. Hannover 1985, 4, p. 32–33
Dorothea Eimert: Papierkunst. In: Kunst und Handwerk, Düsseldorf 1986, 4, p. 226–230
Dorothea Eimert: Papier – Medium der modernen Kunst. In: Papier. Exhibition catalogue Museum für Verkehr und Technik. Berlin 1987, p. 109–127
Birgit Kötters: Papier als künstlerisches Medium. Untersuchungen von Gestaltungsprozessen. Osnabrück 1985 (thesis, manuscript)
Michel Thomas: Peintre avec le papier. In: Textile /Art. Paris, fall 1985, 16, p. 18–24
Dorothea Eimert: Kleine geschiedenis van de Papierkunst. In: Arte Grafika. Driemaandelijks Tijdschrift voor de grafische en aanverwandte Kunstvormen. Antwerp, 1988/89, 1, 2, 3, 4

Michel Thomas: Peintre avec le papier. In: Textile /Art. Paris, Herbst 1985, 16, S. 18–24
Dorothea Eimert: Kleine geschiedenis van de Papierkunst. In: Arte Grafika. Driemaandelijks Tijdschrift voor de grafische en aanverwandte Kunstvormen. Antwerpen, 1988/89, H. 1, 2, 3, 4
Dorothea Eimert: Papier als künstlerisches Ausdrucksmittel. PapierKunstStücke. In: die waage, Zeitschrift der Grünenthal GmbH. Stolberg 1989, H. 4, S. 143–152
Dorothea Eimert: Papier als Werkstoff. In: Schiffe aus Papier. Vierzehn Beiträge über das hundert Jahre alte Hobby Karton-Modellbau. Worpswede 1989, S. 6–9
Dorothea Eimert: Papier als Medium. In: Kultur & Technik, Zeitschrift des Deutschen Museums. München 1990, H. 1, S. 40–46
Dorothea Eimert: Papierkunst. In: Lothar Göttsching (Hrsg.): Papier in unserer Zeit. Ein Handbuch. Düsseldorf, Wien, New York 1990, S. 17–21
Julia Reuschling: Papier als Wissen. Analyse eines künstlerischen Prozesses. Osnabrück 1990 (Examensarbeit, Manusk.)
Dorothea Eimert: Faszination Papier. In: Kompendium zeitgenössischer Handpressendrucke. Hamburg, 1990, 2, S. 6–10
Therese Weber: Papier und Ästhetik in Japan. In: Schweizerische Arbeitslehrerinnen-Zeitung. Basel 1990, 3, S. 15–29

Kataloge

Magie des Papiers. Kunstgewerbemuseum Zürich 1969/70
Robert Rauschenbergs Pages and Fuses. Los Angeles County Museum of Art 1975
The Handmade Paper Object. Santa Barbara Museum of Art, Santa Barbara/Kalifornien 1976
Paper Art. Galleries of the Claremont Colleges, Claremont/Kalifornien 1977
Paper Forms. Handmade Paper Objects. Hayden Gallery, Cambridge, Massachusetts 1977
New Ways with Paper. Smithsonian Institution, National Collection of Fine Arts, Washington/D. C. 1977/78
Paper as Medium. Smithsonian Institution, Washington D. C. 1978–80
With Paper, about Paper. Albright Knox Art Gallery, Buffalo/New York 1980
Papier als künstlerisches Medium. Galerie St. Johann, Saarbrücken, Kunstverein Heidelberg, 1980/82
Das Papier. Geschichte, Herstellung, künstlerische Gestaltung. Leopold-Hoesch-Museum der Stadt Düren 1981
papier navdihuje – papir navdùsuje. Galerie Ljubljana 1981
Papiri. izlozbeni salon doma jna. Zagreb 1982
erschöpft. 5 Künstler arbeiten mit Papier. Hamburg 1982
New American Paper Works (Jane Farmer for the World Print Council). San Francisco 1982
Making Paper. American Craft Museum, New York 1982
Medium Papier. Städtische Galerie Villa Zanders, Bergisch Gladbach 1982
Le Papier. Centre National d'Art et Culture Georges Pompidou, Paris 1983
Paperworks Canada/USA. Alberta College of Art Gallery, Calgary/Kanada 1983
Papiers. Galerie du CAC Pablo Neruda, Corbeil-Essonnes 1983
Paper as Image (Julie Lawson for Council of Great Britain). London 1983
Paper – Papier. Goethe-Institut London 1983
Le Papier – Un nouveau langage artistique. Musée des Arts Décoratifs, Lausanne 1983
Paper Trails. Bluecoat Gallery, Liverpool 1984
Papier zu Papier gebracht. Farbe, Linie, Raum. Leopold-Hoesch-Museum der Stadt Düren 1984
Papier Matière. Musée du Saguenay-Lac-St.-Jean, Alma-Québec 1984
Papier – Un langage artistique II. Musée des Arts Décoratifs, Lausanne 1985

Dorothea Eimert: Papier als künstlerisches Ausdrucksmittel. PapierKunstStücke. In: die waage, Zeitschrift der Grünenthal GmbH. Stolberg 1989, 4, p. 143–152
Dorothea Eimert: Papier als Werkstoff. In: Schiffe aus Papier. Vierzehn Beiträge über das hundert Jahre alte Hobby Karton-Modellbau. Worpswede 1989, p. 6–9
Dorothea Eimert: Papier als Medium. In: Kultur & Technik, Zeitschrift des Deutschen Museums. Munich 1990, 1, S. 40–46
Dorothea Eimert: Papierkunst. In: Lothar Göttsching (ed.): Papier in unserer Zeit. Ein Handbuch. Düsseldorf, Vienna, New York 1990, p. 17–21
Julia Reuschling: Papier als Wissen. Analyse eines künstlerischen Prozesses. Osnabrück 1990 (thesis, manuscript)
Dorothea Eimert: Faszination Papier. In: Kompendium zeitgenössischer Handpressendrucke. Hamburg, 1990, 2, p. 6–10
Therese Weber: Papier und Ästhetik in Japan. In: Schweizerische Arbeitslehrerinnen-Zeitung. Basle 1990, 3, p. 15–29

Catalogues

Magie des Papiers. Kunstgewerbemuseum Zurich 1969/70
Robert Rauschenbergs Pages and Fuses. Los Angeles County Museum of Art 1975
The Handmade Paper Object. Santa Barbara Museum of Art, Santa Barbara/California 1976
Paper Art. Galleries of the Claremont Colleges, Claremont/California 1977
Paper Forms. Handmade Paper Objects. Hayden Gallery, Cambridge, Massachusetts 1977
New Ways with Paper. Smithsonian Institution, National Collection of Fine Arts, Washington/D. C. 1977/78
Paper as Medium. Smithsonian Institution, Washington/D. C. 1978–80
With Paper, about Paper. Albright Knox Art Gallery, Buffalo/New York 1980
Papier als künstlerisches Medium. Galerie St. Johann, Saarbrücken, Kunstverein Heidelberg, 1980/82
Das Papier. Geschichte, Herstellung, künstlerische Gestaltung. Leopold Hoesch Museum der Stadt Düren 1981
papier navdihuje – papir navdùsuje. Galerie Ljubljana 1981
Papiri. izlozbeni salon doma jna. Zagreb 1982
erschöpft. 5 Künstler arbeiten mit Papier. Hamburg 1982
New American Paper Works (Jane Farmer for the World Print Council). San Francisco 1982
Making Paper. American Craft Museum, New York 1982
Medium Papier. Städtische Galerie Villa Zanders, Bergisch Gladbach 1982
Le Papier. Centre National d'Art et Culture Georges Pompidou, Paris 1983
Paperworks Canada/USA. Alberta College of Art Gallery, Calgary/Canada 1983
Papiers. Galerie du CAC Pablo Neruda, Corbeil-Essonnes 1983
Paper as Image (Julie Lawson for Council of Great Britain). London 1983
Paper – Papier. Goethe Institute London 1983
Le Papier – Un nouveau langage artistique. Musée des Arts Décoratifs, Lausanne 1983
Paper Trails. Bluecoat Gallery, Liverpool 1984
Papier zu Papier gebracht. Farbe, Linie, Raum. Leopold Hoesch Museum der Stadt Düren 1984
Papier Matière. Musée du Saguenay-Lac-St.-Jean, Alma-Québec 1984
Papier – Un langage artistique II. Musée des Arts Décoratifs, Lausanne 1985
Sculpture Textile. 12ème Biennale Internationale de la Tapisserie, Musée Cantonal des Beaux-Arts, Lausanne 1985
Fabriano (c)arte 1985. La scultura in carta, Fabriano 1985
1st International Biennale of Paper Art. Handmade Paper. Leopold Hoesch Museum der Stadt Düren 1986

Sculpture Textile. 12ème Biennale Internationale de la Tapisserie, Musée Cantonal des Beaux-Arts, Lausanne 1985
Fabriano (c)arte 1985. La scultura in carta, Fabriano 1985
I. Internationale Biennale der Papierkunst. Handgeschöpftes. Leopold-Hoesch-Museum der Stadt Düren 1986
Papierkunst. de onbegrensde moglijkheden. Stedelijk Museum Het Prinsenhof, Delft 1986
Papier und Skulptur. Zwischen Fläche und Dreidimensionalität. Gesellschaft für Aktuelle Kunst, Weserburg, Bremen 1986
Materialisation. Mannheimer Kunstverein 1987
Art-Paper. Jan van Eyck Academie, Maastricht 1987
Papier. Museum für Verkehr und Technik, Berlin 1987
II. Internationale Biennale der Papierkunst. Papier macht Raum. Leopold-Hoesch-Museum der Stadt Düren 1988 (Wanderausstellung: Nordjyllands Kunstmuseum Aalborg/Dänemark; Museum of Kyoto; The Hall of Awa Japanese Handmade Paper, Tokushimo; Azaba Museum of Arts and Crafts, Tokyo)
Outdoor Papers International. Galerie Frerick, Nideggen 1988
Papierreflexion. Städtische Galerie Waldkirch/Br. 1988
Paper. Form & Substance. Center for Visual Arts, New Jersey 1988
Papierkunst. Contemporary Papermakers from Germany. Saint Louis Gallery of Contemporary Art, Saint Louis/Missouri 1989 (Wanderausstellung Goethe-Institut Chicago, Goethe-Institut Vancouver)
Papierkunst. Städtische Galerie, Paderborn 1989
Wertpapier. Künstlerwerkstatt Lothringerstraße, München 1989
Papier wird Kunst. Kornhaus, Bern 1989
Paper in Art. Association of Art Nysted/Dänemark 1989
La Planète Papier. Centre d'Action Culturelle, Saint-Avold, 1989
Innovation: Papier. Galerie im Körnerpark, Berlin 1990
Papierkunst der Gegenwart. Japan – Deutschland, Bezirksamt Tempelhof, Berlin 1990
Papierkunst. Kunstverein Neustadt 1990
Handgeschöpftes – Papier. Museum für Kunsthandwerk, Gera 1991
Papierkunst – Material und Medium. Neckarwerke Esslingen 1991
Paperitaide Saksassa. Suomen PaperiTaideGalleria Kuusankoski/Finnland 1991
Papier. Musée d'Art et d'Histoire, Neuchâtel 1991
Papier = Kunst. Neuer Kunstverein Aschaffenburg 1992
Only Paper. Städtische Galerie Villa Zanders, Bergisch Gladbach 1992
Papiers libres. Grand-Hornu/Belgien 1992
Medium: Paper. Museum für Bildende Künste, Budapest 1992
Innovation in Collaborative Printmaking: Kenneth Tyler 1963–1992. Yokohama Museum of Art 1992/93 (Wanderausstellung)
Papier hier. Flottmann-Hallen, Herne 1993
Papier und Figuration. Flottmann-Hallen, Herne 1993
Papier und Konkrete Kunst. Flottmann-Hallen, Herne 1993
Papier und Raum. Flottmann-Hallen, Herne 1993
Künstlerische Arbeiten mit und auf Papier. Deutsches Buch- und Schriftmuseum der Deutschen Bücherei, Leipzig 1993
Papier. Musée du pays, Charmey (Hrsg.), Schweiz 1993/94
papier pur. Arbeiten mit Papier, Galerie untern Turm, Stuttgart 1994

Zeitschriften

Hand Papermaking. Amanda Degener und Michael Durgin (Hrsg.). Minneapolis/Minnesota
IAPMA Bulletin. Puck Bramlage (Hrsg.). Amsterdam
IAPMA Newsletter. Puck Bramlage (Hrsg.). Amsterdam

Papierkunst. de onbegrensde moglijkheden. Stedelijk Museum Het Prinsenhof, Delft 1986
Papier und Skulptur. Zwischen Fläche und Dreidimensionalität. Gesellschaft für Aktuelle Kunst, Weserburg, Bremen 1986
Materialisation. Mannheimer Kunstverein 1987
Art-Paper. Jan van Eyck Academie, Maastricht 1987
Papier. Museum für Verkehr und Technik, Berlin 1987
2nd International Biennale of Paper Art. Paper makes Space. Leopold Hoesch Museum der Stadt Düren 1988 (travelling exhibition: Nordjyllands Kunstmuseum Aalborg/Denmark; Museum of Kyoto; The Hall of Awa Japanese Handmade Paper, Tokushimo; Azaba Museum of Arts and Crafts, Tokyo)
Outdoor Papers International. Galerie Frerick, Nideggen 1988
Papierreflexion. Städtische Galerie Waldkirch/Br. 1988
Paper. Form & Substance. Center for Visual Arts, New Jersey 1988
Papierkunst. Contemporary Papermakers from Germany. Saint Louis Gallery of Contemporary Art, Saint Louis/Missouri 1989 (travelling exhibition Goethe Institute Chicago, Goethe Institute Vancouver)
Papierkunst. Städtische Galerie, Paderborn 1989
Wertpapier. Künstlerwerkstatt Lothringerstraße, Munich 1989
Papier wird Kunst. Kornhaus, Bern 1989
Paper in Art. Association of Art Nysted/Denmark 1989
La Planète Papier. Centre d'Action Culturelle, Saint-Avold, 1989
Innovation: Papier. Galerie im Körnerpark, Berlin 1990
Papierkunst der Gegenwart. Japan – Deutschland, Bezirksamt Tempelhof, Berlin 1990
Papierkunst. Kunstverein Neustadt 1990
Handgeschöpftes – Papier. Museum für Kunsthandwerk, Gera 1991
Papierkunst – Material und Medium. Neckarwerke Esslingen 1991
Paperitaide Saksassa. Suomen PaperiTaideGalleria Kuusankoski/Finland 1991
Papier. Musée d'Art et d'Histoire, Neuchâtel 1991
Papier = Kunst. Neuer Kunstverein Aschaffenburg 1992
Only Paper. Städtische Galerie Villa Zanders, Bergisch Gladbach 1992
Papiers libres. Grand-Hornu/Belgium 1992
Medium: Paper. Museum of Art, Budapest 1992
Innovation in Collaborative Printmaking: Kenneth Tyler 1963–1992. Yokohama Museum of Art 1992/93 (travelling exhibition)
Papier hier. Flottmann-Hallen, Herne 1993
Papier und Figuration. Flottmann-Hallen, Herne 1993
Papier und Konkrete Kunst. Flottmann-Hallen, Herne 1993
Papier und Raum. Flottmann-Hallen, Herne 1993
Künstlerische Arbeiten mit und auf Papier. Deutsches Buch- und Schriftmuseum der Deutschen Bücherei, Leipzig 1993
Papier. Musée du pays, Charmey (ed.), Switzerland 1993/94
papier pur. Arbeiten mit Papier, Galerie untern Turm, Stuttgart 1994

Periodicals

Hand Papermaking. Amanda Degener and Michael Durgin (eds.). Minneapolis/Minnesota
IAPMA Bulletin. Puck Bramlage (ed.). Amsterdam
IAPMA Newsletter. Puck Bramlage (ed.). Amsterdam

VI. PaperArt 5

5. Internationale Biennale der Papierkunst

5th International Biennale of Paper Art

Die Künstler The artists

Frank Badur
A. Harold Barreiro
Anthony Caro
Tony Cragg
Felix Droese
Joel Fisher
Horst Gläsker
Kuno Gonschior
Huang Yong Ping
Maria Orzel-Hercka
Jean-Luc Parant
Milko Pavlov
A. R. Penck
Michael Petry
Otto Piene
Dmitri A. Prigov
Reviva Regev
Eun Nim Ro
James Rosenquist
Takako Saito
Timm Ulrichs
Andreas von Weizsäcker

Frank Badur

1944 geboren in Oranienburg, lebt in Berlin 1963–69 Studium der Malerei an der Hochschule der Künste Berlin seit 1973 ein ständiges Atelier in Finnland 1975 Mitbegründer der Gruppe Systhema 1985 Berufung als Professor an die Hochschule der Künste Berlin Arbeitsaufenthalte: 1971 London 1982 USA Preise und Stipendien (Auswahl): 1984 Kunstpreis TetraPack – Werkstipendium des Kunstfonds Bonn – Mülheimer Bürgerpreis für bildende Kunst Ausstellungen (Auswahl): 1979 Galerie Schoeller, Düsseldorf 1983 Kunsthalle Bremen 1985 Neuer Berliner Kunstverein 1986 Galerie Repères, Paris 1989 Galerie Eward Thordén, Göteborg

1944 born in Oranienburg, lives in Berlin **1963–69** studies painting at the Hochschule der Künste Berlin **since 1973** permanent studio in Finland **1975** Co-founder of the group Systhema 1985 appointed professor at the Hochschule der Künste Berlin **work projects: 1971** London **1982** US **prizes and awards (selection): 1984** Kunstpreis TetraPack – grant of the Kunstfonds Bonn – Mülheimer Bürgerpreis für Bildende Kunst **exhibitions (selection): 1979** Galerie Schoeller, Düsseldorf **1983** Kunsthalle Bremen **1985** Neuer Berliner Kunstverein **1986** Galerie Repères, Paris **1989** Galerie Eward Thordén, Göteborg

Eine strenge kompositorische Gliederung zeichnet die Papiermalerei von Frank Badur aus. Farbbahnen und -flächen, schichtweise aufgegautscht, stehen in anderer Tonlage und differierender Textur nebeneinander. Das Gleichmaß der Farbfelder wirkt in der satten Dichte raumbildend. Die Farbe als Lichtmaterie ist von griffiger, samtener Substanz. Ein verhaltenes, gedämpftes Leuchten charakterisiert die Farben der Pulpmalereien.
In den neuesten Papiermalereien unterbricht Frank Badur die Strenge seiner Bildarchitektur. Ihn faszinierte die von John Gerard gefundene Möglichkeit, mit verklumpten Farb-Pulp-Einsprengseln allein durch den Schöpfvorgang zu komponieren. Die leuchtenden vielfarbigen Pulpspritzer durchziehen das Blatt seriell nach dem Prinzip des gesteuerten Zufalls. Es ist nicht mehr die reduzierte Einfarbigkeit, die oszillierend Farbschimmer erahnen läßt. Nun erströmen sich im dicken Papierstoff – sattfarben und leuchtend – Farbflecken in reicher Farbenskala.

A strict compositional arrangement is typical for Frank Badur's pulp paintings. Stripes and planes of color, couched in layers, lie one next to the other in different tones and varying textures. Color here is luminous material, a rough, velvety substance. The symmetry of the color fields in their saturated density creates space. A restrained and subdued lustre are characteristic for the colors of paperpulp paintings.
In the newest of these paintings, Frank Badur breaks with the strictness of his pictorial architecture. It fascinated him to work with the possibility invented by John Gerard, which allowed him to compose ad hoc with flocullated pulp during the moulding process. The luminous many-colored pulp speckles run through the paper sheet serially, according to the principle of manipulated chance. No longer is the coloring reduced, its oscillating shimmer a color you must guess at. Now clear – saturated and bright – flecks of paint in rich color schemes flow through the thick paper stock.

Frank Badur: Nella Was Here, 1991. Papierarbeit. Multiple. 148 x 108 cm. Auflage 15 /
Frank Badur: Nella Was Here, 1991. Paperwork. Multiple. 148 x 108 cm. Edition of 15

A. Harold Barreiro

1958 geboren in New York, lebt in Köln 1977–80 Studium der Musikperformance und Kunst am Atlanta College/Georgia 1983 Pantomimeunterricht an der Mirage School of Corporal Mime, Boston/Massachusetts 1981 Kompositionsunterricht am Guitar Study Center, New York 1986 Umzug nach Deutschland 1988 Aufenthalt in Italien seit 1976 zahlreiche Klavierkonzerte, Performances und Klangaktionen, Fernseh- und Radioauftritte in Europa und den USA

1958 born in New York, lives in Cologne from 1977–80 studies music performance and art at Atlanta College/Georgia 1983 studies pantomime at the Mirage School of Corporal Mime, Boston/Massachusetts 1981 studies guitar at the Guitar Center, New York 1986 moves to Germany 1988 stay in Italy since 1976 numerous piano concerts, performances and sound events, TV and radio appearances in Europe and US

„Ein Körper ist immer ein KlangKörper und dessen Anwesenheit wird erst durch akustische und/oder visuelle Bewegung wahrgenommen. Ich wähle den Umgang mit Materialien nicht, um zu hören, WIE ein Körper klingt, sondern um darzustellen, daß er Klang ist."
Im Papier, einer bisher durch nichts zu ersetzenden Umformung des Holzes, bleiben die meisten der im Holz gespeicherten Informationen erhalten, und das Papier wird vom Menschen dazu benutzt, seinerseits seine Erinnerung darauf niederzuschreiben. Dabei überlagern sich natürliche und kulturelle Erinnerungen auf dem gleichen Material zu einem komplexen, voneinander unlösbaren Verbund. Mit seiner Musik strebt Barreiro an, eine ähnliche Komplexität aufzubauen. Er nutzt dabei aktiv einen Umstand, der jeder Musik zugrunde liegt, also keineswegs von ihm erst entdeckt werden mußte. In den Tonabständen eines Instruments sind Intervalle als universal gültige Proportionen virtuell gespeichert, werden erinnerungsfähig aufbewahrt. Beim Musizieren wird eine Erinnerung daran lebendig gemacht und in den Tonfolgen dem Zuhörer zur Anbindung an seine Erinnerungen und sein Wissen angeboten. In diesen individuellen Erinnerungen, die die Folgen von gelebter Zeit sind, werden Erinnerungen an die natürlichen, universellen Proportionsgesetze von den Erinnerungen

"A box is always a resonance box, and its presence is first noted when there is acoustic or visual movement. I do not choose my way of acting on materials in order to hear HOW a box sounds, but to show that it is sound."
Memory is the theme of the new composition. As a natural example of the storing of memories, Barreiro chose the tree and paper. In paper, which is a re-formation of the wood not replaceable by anything else, most of the information stored in the wood is retained and the resulting paper is used in turn by man to write down what he remembers. In the process, natural and cultural memories overlay each other on the same material to become a complex, inseparable consolidation. With his music, Barreiro strives to engineer a similar complexity. To do so, he actively uses a circumstance that is the basis for any music, that is, something that in no case needed to be discovered by him. In the distance between the notes of an instrument, intervals are virtually stored in universally valid proportions, that is, capable of memory. While music is played, a memory can come alive and its sequences of notes can be offered to the auditor as a link to his memories. In these individual memories that are the sequels of experienced time, memories of the natural, universal laws of proportion are overlaid by memories that are a

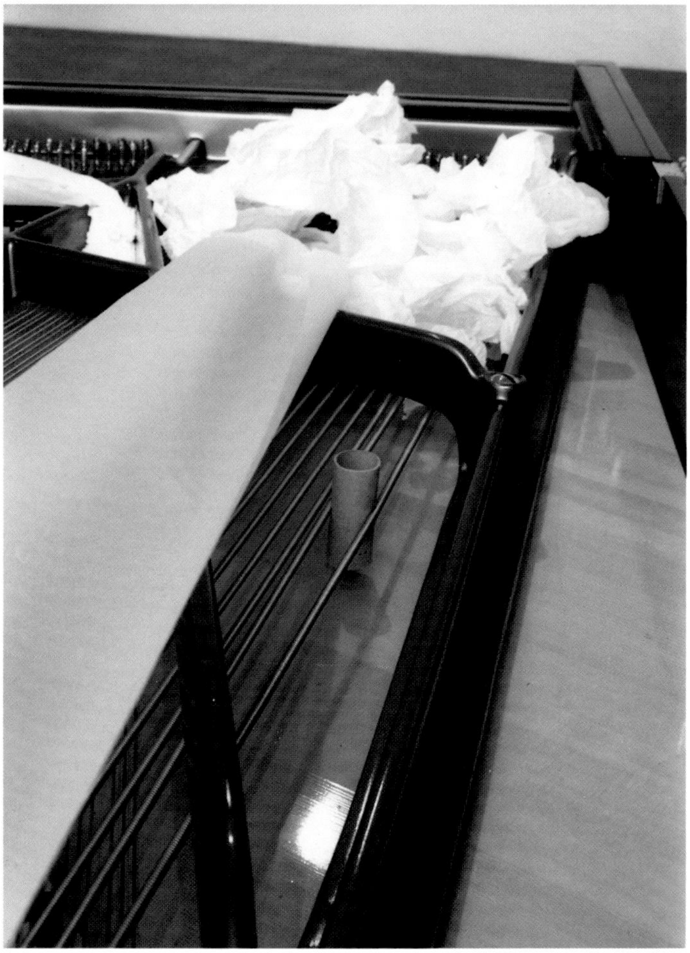

A. Harold Barreiro: Pianowerk mit Baum-Dokumenten, 1992.
Installation in der Galerie Sophia Ungers, Köln. Klavier und Papier /
A. Harold Barreiro: Piano Piece with Tree Documents, 1992.
Installation at the Gallery Sophia Ungers, Cologne. Piano and paper

überlagert, die sich aus kulturellem Wissen und kulturellen Erfahrungen zusammensetzen. Ohne die natürliche Basis hätte die kulturelle Erinnerung keine Chance, uns zu Gehör zu kommen. Ohne unsere invidiuelle Erinnerungsbereitschaft hätten die strukturierten Tonfolgen einer musikalischen Komposition kein Ziel. Nur durch diese Überlagerung zweier Erinnerungsformen kommt es zur Chance einer Kommunikation zwischen Musiker und Zuhörer, um die sich beide immer wieder erneut bemühen müssen. Das ist das Thema von Barreiros Komposition.

Peter Gerlach

blend of cultural knowledge and cultural experience. Without this natural base, the cultural memory would not have a chance to be heard. Without our individual fitness for memory, the structured sequence of notes in a musical composition would have no destination. Only as a result of this overlaying of two forms of memory is there any chance for a communication between musician and audience, which both must take constant pains to achieve. That is the theme of Barreiro's composition.

Peter Gerlach

Anthony Caro

1924 geboren in London bis 1944 Studium der Ingenieurwissenschaften am Christ College, Oxford anschließend Studium der Bildhauerei am Regent Street Polytechnic und den Royal Academy Schools, London, davon zwei Jahre lang Assistent von Henry Moore 1959 Reise in die USA, wo er David Smith begegnet 1963–65 Professor am Bennington College/Vermont 1953–67 Professor an der St. Martin's School of Art, London Ausstellungen (Auswahl): 1975 Große Wanderretrospektive mit Beginn im Museum of Modern Art, New York

1924 born in London **to 1944** studies engineering at Christ College, Oxford followed by study of sculpture at the Regent Street Polytechnic and the Royal Academy School London, including two years assistant to Henry Moore **1959** trip to US where he meets David Smith **1963–65** professor at Bennington College/Vermont **1953–67** professor at St. Martin's School of Art, London **exhibitions (selection): 1975** retrospective of his works in Museum of Modern Art, New York, which then went on tour

Anthony Caro vollendete 1993 in einem Zeitraum von einigen Wochen 35 freistehende Skulpturen bei Tyler Graphics. Es handelt sich um intime Arbeiten, die ganz anders als seine größeren Arbeiten in Stahl wirken (eine mit dem Titel ‚After Olympia' aus dem Jahr 1986/87 ist 230 Meter lang); die Papierskulpturen sind vergleichsweise klein. Dennoch beinhalten die Papierkonstruktionen intensive Hinweise auf die Architektur und zeigen eine Verwandtschaft mit den großen Metallarbeiten (einschließlich ‚After Olympia'). Tatsächlich sind diese neuen Papierskulpturen Ausdruck dessen, was Caro „Skulpitektur" nennt, eine Fusion von architektonischer Syntax mit abstrakter Bildhauerei. Sie weisen das Charisma von architektonischer Form und Raum auf und führen die Aufmerksamkeit des Betrachters in, über, durch und um die multidimensionalen Werke. Die Papierskulpturen sollen wie Gebäude von allen Seiten aus erfahren werden; sie sind optisch kinetische, sich wandelnde Konstruktionen.

Alle Arbeiten in dieser neuen Papierserie besitzen eine kastenartige oder säulenartige Zentralachse in Verbindung mit einem rechteckigen oder quadratischen Fuß. Einige haben architektonische Titel – wie zum Beispiel ‚Sailor's House' und ‚His

In his most recent paper project, Anthony Caro returned to Tyler Graphics Ltd. in Mount Kisco, New York, for a period of serveral weeks in 1993, completing 35 free-standing sculptures. These are intimate pieces, quite unlike some of his larger works in steel (one, entitled 'After Olympia', from 1986/87 measures 230 meters in length); the paper sculptures are very small in comparison. On the other hand, the paper constructions contain powerful references to architecture and are akin to the large metal works (including 'After Olympia'). Indeed, these new paper sculptures are expressions of what Caro calls "Sculpitecture", a fusion of architectural syntax with abstract sculpture. They carry the charisma of architectural form and space, bringing the viewer's attention into, over, through, and around the multi-dimensional creations. The paper sculptures, like buildings, ask to be experienced from all angles; they are visually kinetic, transmuting constructions.

All the works in this new paper series have a box-like or columnar central axis in addition to a rectangular or square footing. Some have architectural titles, 'Sailor's House' and 'His House' for example, but all are house-like abstractions with multiple entrances and exits. There is also a

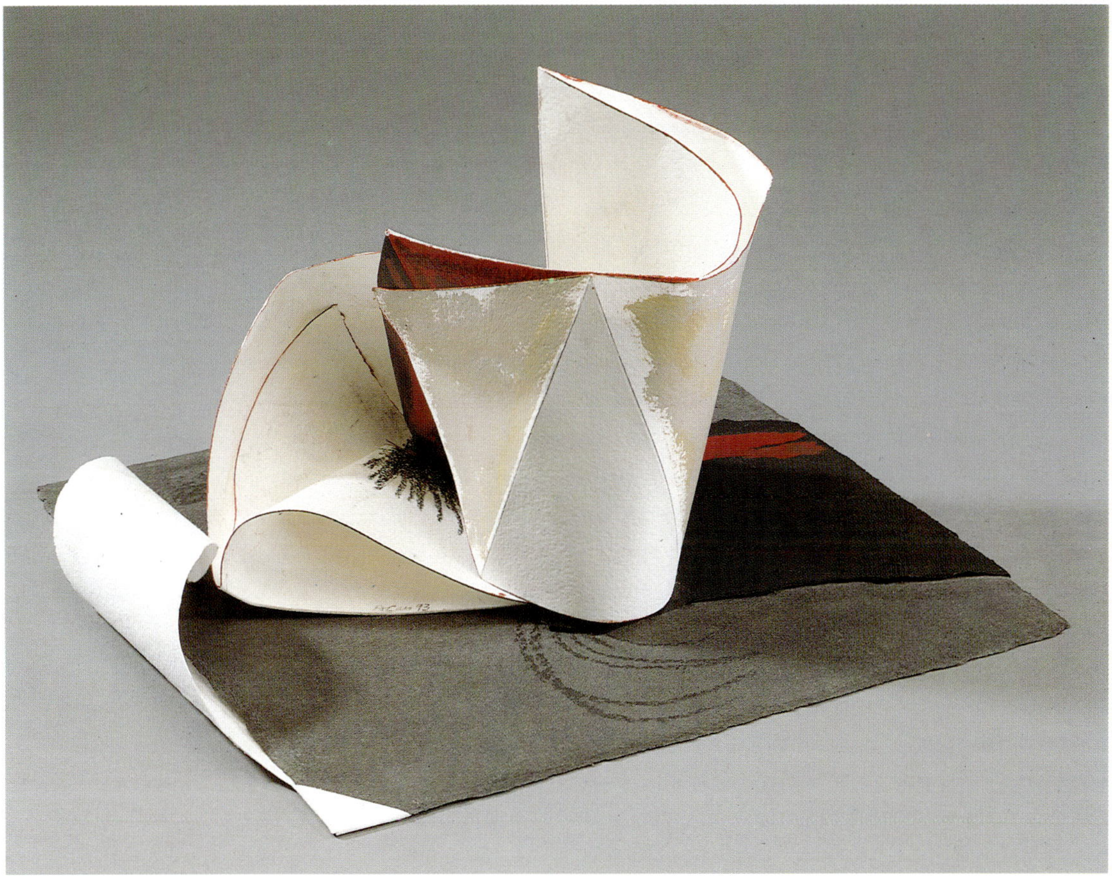

Anthony Caro: No. 5. Black Bird, 1993. Aus: Hand-Colored Paper Sculptures. Papierskulptur, handkoloriert. 27 x 42 x 40 cm / Anthony Caro: No. 5. Black Bird, 1993. From: Hand-Colored Paper Sculptures. Paper sculpture, hand colored. 27 x 42 x 40 cm. © Tyler Graphics Ltd.

House' – ,alle aber sind hausähnliche Abstraktionen mit vielen Ein- und Ausgängen. Es ist ein faszinierendes Schauspiel, wie Caro die Beweglichkeit des Papiers ausnutzt. Er windet ein neugeformtes Kozoblatt um einen Holzhammer oder eine Holzkugel, schichtet Baumwolle um Rohre oder einen Trichter, preßt neugeformte Bögen in Holzfasern oder auf gefärbte und geschnittene Holzblöcke. Während diese Papiere trocknen, nehmen sie die Formen dessen an, an das sie zeitweise gepreßt waren. Das von der Form gelöste Papier ist so gewichtslos wie ein Briefumschlag und wird zum „gefundenen" Element (so zum Beispiel der papierene Holzhammer in der Papierskulptur Nr. 6 ,Hat Box'). Abgesehen davon handelt es sich bei den in den Skulpturen eingebetteten Materialien um keine echten „Readymades". Caro enthüllt Bruchstücke aus gewöhnlichem Karton, Styropor, Malerpinsel, Schleifblätter oder Kisten für Weinflaschen, die in seine Kompositionen verwoben sind.

Es handelt sich um eine komplexe Ansammlung von handgefärbten Papieren und/oder handgeschöpftem Papier in verschiedenen Farben, unterschiedlichen Materialien, Pigmenten und Texturen. Jede kleine Skulptur, die zwangsläufig von allen Seiten erfahren wird, weist eine unwahrscheinliche Fülle und Bandbreite auf. Caro beabsichtigte, jeder eine gewisse visuelle „Überraschung" mitzugeben. Das ist ihm gelungen. Und auch das, was der Kritiker Michael Fried als die von Caro so gewandt ins Papier umgesetzte „erreichte Schwerelosigkeit" preist.

Marabeth Cohen-Tyler

fascinating play as Caro exploits the mercurial properties of paper. He wraps an newly-formed Kozo sheet over a wooden mallet or a sphere, wraps cotton pulp sheets around piping or a funnel, presses newly-formed sheets into wood grain or inked carved blocks, and as these papers dry they assume the shapes they once temporarily adhered to. Once removed from the forms, the shaped paper (for example, the paper mallet in paper sculpture number 6 'Hat Box') is as weightless as an envelope and becomes a "found" element. This is not to say that there are not genuine ready-made materials incorporated in these sculptures. Caro reveals a fragment of common cardboard, styrofoam, paint brush, sanding disks, or wine bottle casing, woven into the compositions.

These are complex assemblages of hand-colored papers and/or handmade papers of various colors, of diverse materials, pigments and textures. Each little sculpture, by necessity experienced in the round, has incredible breadth. Caro meant for each one to contain visual "surprise" and, yes, there is that and what critic Michael Fried praises as Caro's "achieved weightlessness", so aptly performed in paper.

Marabeth Cohen-Tyler

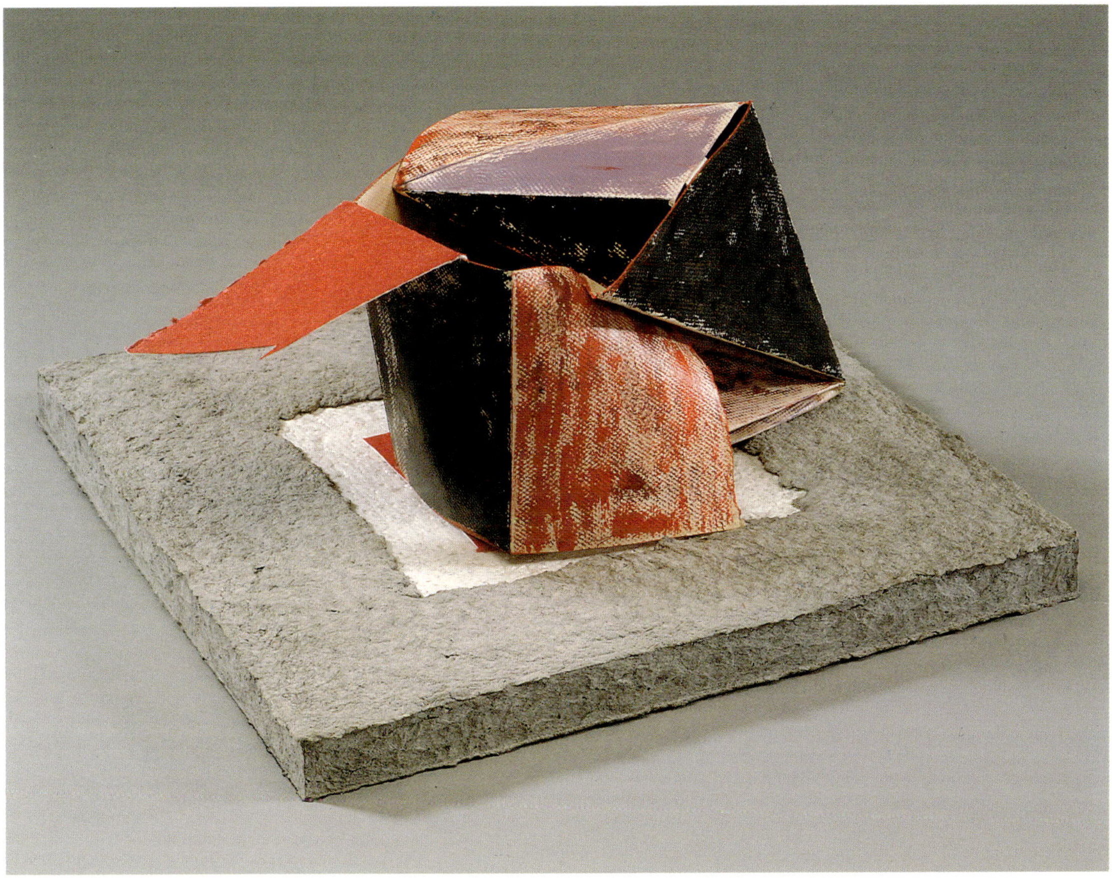

Anthony Caro: No. 14. Red Flap. Aus: Hand-Colored Paper Sculptures. Papierskulptur, handkoloriert. 17,8 x 35,6 x 35,6 cm /
Anthony Caro: No. 14. Red Flap. From: Hand-Colored Paper Sculptures. Paper sculpture, hand colored.
17.8 x 35.6 x 35.6 cm. © Tyler Graphics Ltd.

Tony Cragg

1949 **geboren in Liverpool, lebt und arbeitet in Wuppertal** 1969–70 **Studium am Gloucestershire College of Art, Cheltenham** 1970–73 **Studium an der Wimbledon School of Art** 1973–77 **Studium am Royal College of Art, London** 1988 **Professor an der Kunstakademie Düsseldorf** Preise (Auswahl): 1988 **Turner-Preis** Ausstellungen (Auswahl): 1979 **Lisson Gallery, London** 1980 **Galerie Konrad Fischer, Düsseldorf** 1981 **Whitechapel Gallery, London** 1982 **Nisshin Gallery, Tokyo** 1983 **Kunsthalle Bern** 1984 **Kölnischer Kunstverein** 1985 **Art & Project, Amsterdam** 1988 **Biennale Venedig** 1989 **Kunstsammlung Nordrhein-Westfalen, Düsseldorf** 1990 **Galerie Buchmann, Basel** 1991 **Wiener Sezession** 1993 **Knoll Galerie, Budapest**

1949 born in Liverpool, lives and works in Wuppertal **1969–70** studies at Gloucestershire College of Art, Cheltenham **1970–73** studies at Wimbledon School of Art **1973-77** studies at Royal College of Art, London **1988** professor at the Kunstakademie Düsseldorf **awards:** Turner-Preis **exhibitions (selection): 1979** Lisson Gallery, London **1980** Konrad Fischer Gallery, Düsseldorf **1981** Whitechapel Gallery, London **1982** Nisshin Gallery, Tokyo **1983** Kunsthalle Bern **1984** Kölnischer Kunstverein **1985** Art & Project, Amsterdam **1988** Biennale Venice **1989** Kunstsammlung Nordrhein-Westfalen, Düsseldorf **1990** Galerie Buchmann, Basle **1991** Wiener Sezession **1993** Knoll Galerie, Budapest

Aus der beeindruckenden Vielfalt von Pflanzen, die zelebrierend im Wind tanzen, werden einige zerstampft, zerschmettert, mit chemischem Speichel zermürbt, zu einer Art Faserbrei verdorben, um eine Substanz zu gewinnen, deren Moleküle mit geringfügig andersartiger Form bei gleicher Zusammensetzung als Panzer für Insekten gedient hätten.
Architektonische Baustoffe der Natur, die für ihre Zähigkeit bestraft und dazu verurteilt wird, sich für alles herzugeben: Eierkarton oder Gedicht, Parkzettel oder Zeichnung. Passepartout – die entsetzliche Carte blanche.

Tony Cragg

From the impressive multitude of plants that, revelling, dance in the wind, some will be trampled, crushed, corroded by chemical saliva, broken down into a kind of fiber mash, in order to produce a substance whose molecules with a slightly different form and identical composition could serve as an armored tank for insects.
An architectural building block of nature that for its very toughness has been punished and sentenced to passive transformation into anything and everything: egg carton or poem, parking ticket or drawing. A passe-partout – the carte blanche terrible.

Tony Cragg

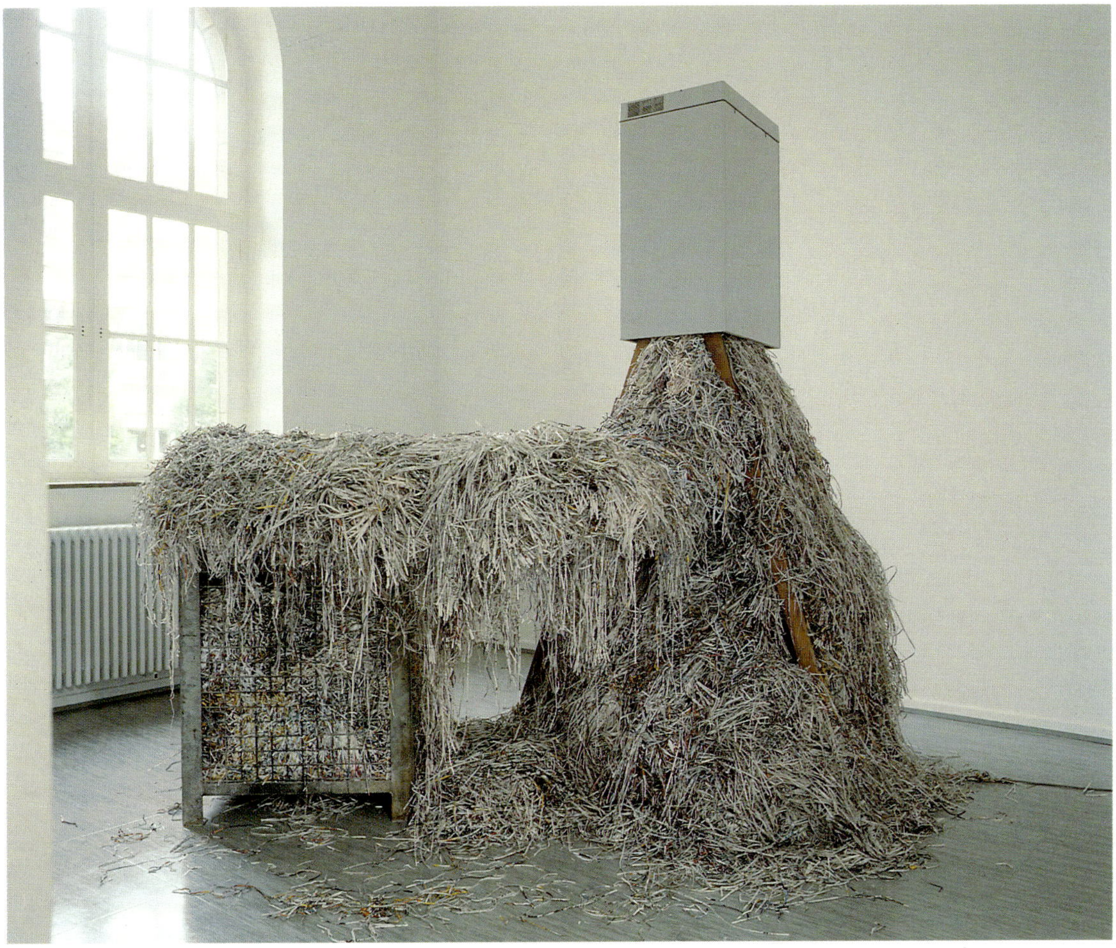

Tony Cragg: Tagelöhner, 1994. Papier und diverse Materialien. Rauminstallation. 240 x 265 cm, Höhe 250 cm /
Tony Cragg: Day-labourer, 1994. Paper and various materials. Installation. 240 x 265 cm, 250 cm high

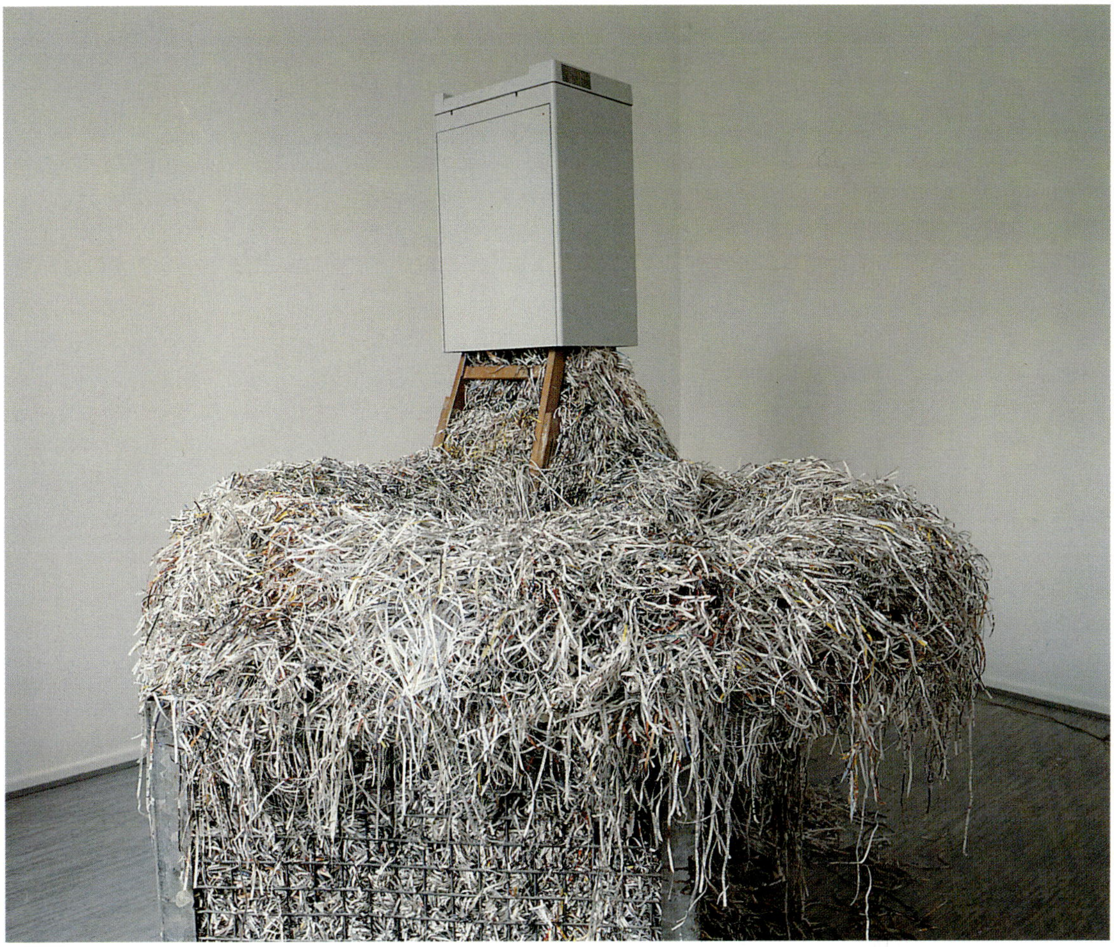

Tony Cragg: Tagelöhner, 1994. Papier und diverse Materialien. Rauminstallation. 240 x 265 cm, Höhe 250 cm /
Tony Cragg: Day-labourer, 1994. Paper and various materials. Installation. 240 x 265 cm, 250 cm high

Felix Droese

1950 geboren in Singen/Hohentwiel, lebt in Mettmann-Diepensiepen 1970–76 Studium an der Kunstakademie Düsseldorf bei Joseph Beuys 1983 Atelier in Paesens/Niederlande 1986–87 Professor für Malerei/Grafik an der Städelschule, Frankfurt/Main Kunstpreise: 1982 Förderpreis für junge Künstler des Landes Nordrhein-Westfalen 1987 Kunstpreis Glockengasse Köln Ausstellungen (Auswahl): 1980 Museum Bochum 1982 documenta 7, Kassel 1988 Biennale Venedig 1989 List Visual Arts Center am Massachusetts Institute of Technology, Cambridge/Massachusetts 1991 Kunsthaus Zürich 1991/92 Kunsthalle Nürnberg

1950 born in Singen/Hohentwiel, lives in Mettmann-Diepensiepen **1970–76** studies at Kunstakademie Düsseldorf under Joseph Beuys **1983** studio in Paesens/Netherlands **1986–87** professor for painting and graphic arts at the Städelschule, Frankfurt/M. **awards (selection): 1982** Förderpreis für junge Künstler des Landes Nordrhein-Westfalen **1987** Kunstpreis Glockengasse, Cologne **exhibitions (selection): 1980** Museum Bochum **1982** documenta 7, Kassel **1988** Biennale Venice **1989** List Visual Arts Center at Massachusetts Institute of Technology, Cambridge, Massachusetts **1991** Kunsthaus Zurich **1991/92** Kunsthalle Nuremberg

Pascals Kette
Sechs Wasserzeichen

Man stelle sich eine Anzahl Menschen vor, die alle in Ketten gelegt und zum Tode verurteilt sind. Täglich werden einige von ihnen vor den Augen der anderen erdrosselt. Die Überlebenden sehen ihr eigenes Los in dem ihrer Brüder und warten, Schmerz und Hoffnungslosigkeit in den Blicken, bis sie an die Reihe kommen. Dies ist das Bild vom Schicksale der Menschen.
Blaise Pascal

Herstellung: Die sechs Zeichnungen von Felix Droese wurden auf das Sieb übertragen von John Gerard, Rheinbach-Hilberath.
Papier: Hanf, handgeschöpft von John Gerard
Format: 43,5 x 31,5 cm
Auflage: 20 Exemplare, signiert, numeriert, datiert, 5 Exemplare, signiert, mit e. a. bezeichnet, datiert
1 Textheft: Auszug aus Blaise Pascals ‚Gedanken. Elend des Menschen'. Übersetzung von Bruno von Herber-Rohow. Leipzig und Jena, 1905
Herausgeber: Edition Odradek, Galerie Klaus Fischer, Berlin. Berlin 1994

Pascal's Chain
Six Watermarks

Imagine a number of people that have been put into chains and condemned to death. Every day some of them would be strangled before the eyes of the others. The survivors would see their own fate in that of their brothers and wait, their expressions full of pain and hopelessness, until it was their turn. That is the picture of man's fate.
Blaise Pascal

Production process: The six drawings by Felix Droese were transferred to the papermaking mould by John Gerard, Rheinbach-Hilberath.
Paper: Handmade of hemp by John Gerard
Format: 43.5 x 31.5 cm
Edition: 20 copies, signed, numbered, dated
5 copies, signed, first draft, dated
1 text: extract from Blaise Pascal's 'Pensées. La misère de l'homme'. Translated into German by Bruno von Herber-Rohow (Leipzig and Jena, 1905)
Publisher: Edition Odradek. Gallery Klaus Fischer, Berlin. Berlin 1994

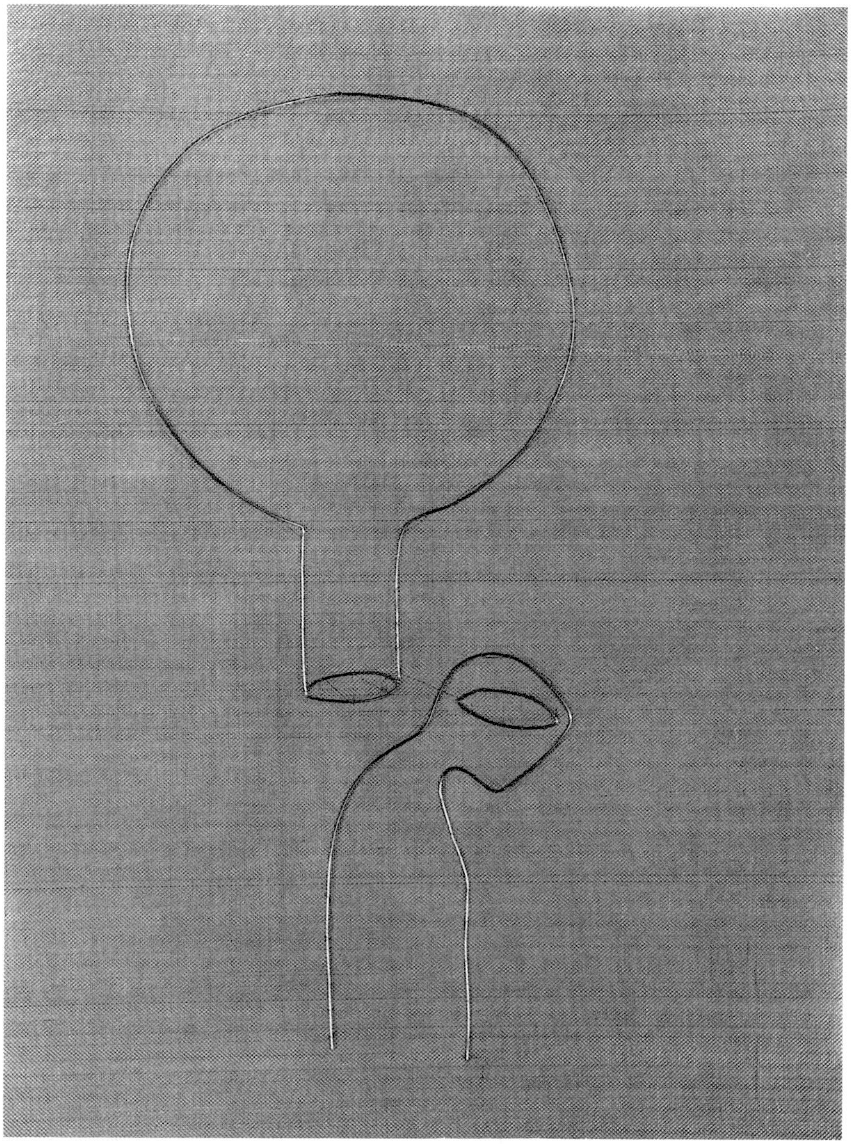

Eines von sechs Schöpfsieben für die sechs Wasserzeichen-Papiere von Felix Droese zu ‚Pascals Kette', 1994 / One of six moulds for the six watermark papers by Felix Droese's 'Pascal's Chain', 1994

Joel Fisher

1947 **geboren in Salem/Ohio, lebt in New York und North Troy/Vermont** 1965–69 **Studium am Kenyon College, Gambier/Ohio** 1969 **Übersiedlung nach New York** **seit** 1971 **regelmäßige Reisen nach Europa** 1980–82 **Professor an der Bath Academy of Art** seit 1989 **Professor an der School of Visual Arts, New York** Preise und Stipendien: 1974 **Stipendiat des DAAD in Berlin** 1993–94 **John Simon Guggenheim Fellowship** Ausstellungen (Auswahl): 1970 **Mansfield Fine Arts Centre, Mansfield/Ohio** 1972 **documenta 5, Kassel** 1975 **Städtisches Museum Abteiberg, Mönchengladbach** 1977 **Max Protech Gallery, New York** 1978 **Stedelijk Museum, Amsterdam** 1992 **International Bird Museum, South Hampton/New York** 1993 **Galerie Farideh Cadot, Paris**

1947 born in Salem/Ohio, lives in New York and North Troy/Vermont **1965-69** studies at Kenyon College, Gambier/Ohio **1969** moves to New York **since 1973** regular trips to Europe **1980–82** professor at the Bath Academy of Art **since 1989** professor at the School of Visual Arts, New York **prizes and grants: 1974** DAAD Grant in Berlin **1993–94** John Simon Guggenheim Fellowship **exhibitions (selection): 1970** Mansfield Fine Arts Centre, Mansfield/Ohio **1972** documenta 5, Kassel **1975** Städtisches Museum Abteiberg, Mönchengladbach **1977** Max Protech Gallery, New York **1978** Stedelijk Museum, Amsterdam **1992** International Bird Museum, South Hampton/New York **1993** Galerie Farideh Cadot, Paris

Hoch Droben auf der Pforten

Es geschieht in einem Augenblick: Das Schöpfsieb durchdringt die von der Wasseroberfläche gebildete Ebene und schöpft in diesem Augenblick eine neue Ebene, ein Blatt Papier. Dieses Blatt bildet eine frische Oberfläche; und es ist auch ein Abbild jener Grenze, die das Schöpfsieb durchdringen mußte, um es zu erschaffen. Es ist das Bild einer Grenze, eines Durchgangs, und es ist gleichzeitig ein Raum, in dem ein neues Universum (oder das Bild eines vergangenen) einen Grund finden kann.
Die Grenzfläche zwischen Wasser und Luft ist ein höchst bedeutsamer Übergang. Auch wenn Wasser in kleinen Mengen durchsichtig ist, manchmal die Dinge sogar vergrößert, so wirkt es in größeren Mengen oft verhüllend; es versteckt die Dinge unter seine Oberfläche. Wir kommen in den Bereich des Unsichtbaren, des zu Kleinen oder zu Dunklen oder zu Tiefen.
Die Herstellung von Papier ist ein einschneidender Akt der Trennung und der Auflösung. Bevor sich ein

Sitting on the Gate

It happens in an instant: the filter screen passes through the plane which is the surface of the water and at that instant creates a new plane which is a sheet of paper. This paper is a fresh new surface. It is also an image of the barrier that the filter screen passed through in order to create it. A barrier, a gate: an image of each and, simultaneously, a space in which a new universe (or an image of an old one) can find a base.
The interface between water and air is a most important threshold. Although water in small amounts is transparent and can even magnify, in larger quantities it often hides what is beneath its surface. This is the realm of the invisible, the too small or too dark or too deep.
Papermaking is a decisive act of seperation. Before a sheet of paper is formed, its pulp exists as a chaotic blend of microscopic cellulose fibers suspended in water. A filter screen is dipped into the water and slowly brought to the surface. The water falls back

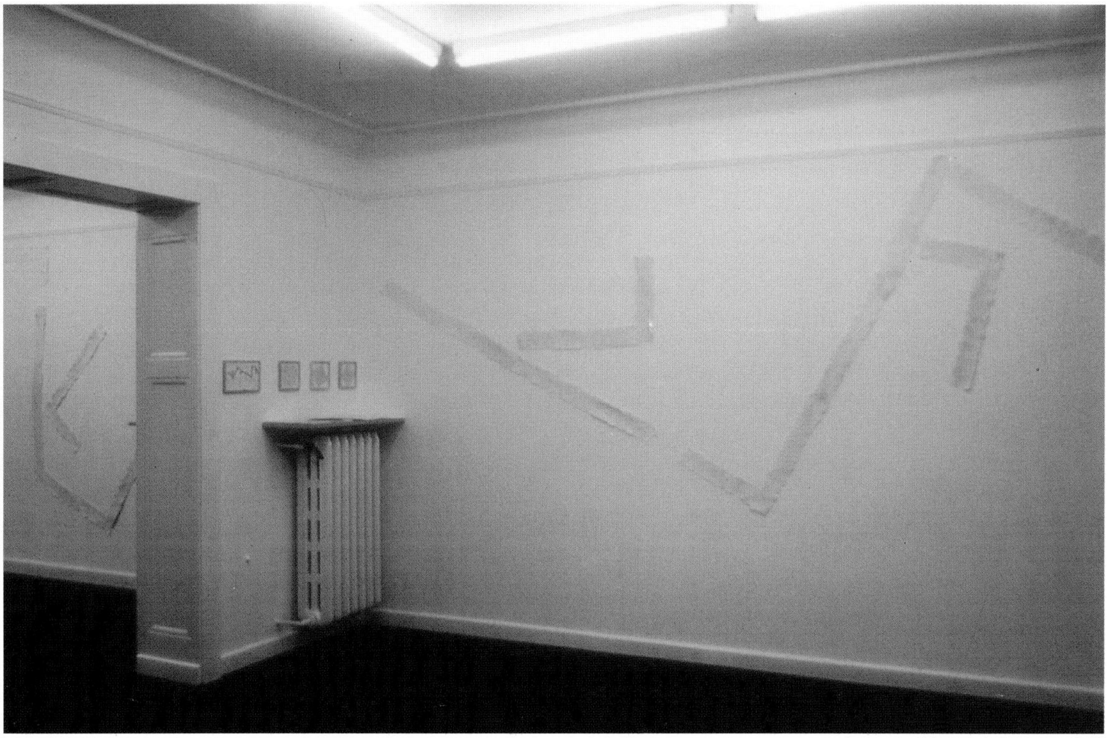

Joel Fisher: Installation in der New 57 Gallery, Edinburgh, 1980 /
Joel Fisher: Installation at New 57 Gallery, Edinburgh, 1980

Blatt Papier herausbilden kann, besteht die Papiermasse als eine chaotische Mischung mikroskopisch kleiner, in Wasser suspendierter Zellulosefasern. Man taucht ein Sieb in diesen Brei und hebt es langsam wieder zur Oberfläche empor. Das Wasser tropft ab, und im Sieb konstitutiert sich eine dünne Lage Papier. Dieses Blatt besteht aus einer Vielzahl kleiner Fasern, die sich zu einer Oberfläche mit eigener Struktur verfilzt haben. Einmal zu einem Blatt Papier geworden, sind diese Fasern stärker miteinander verbunden als je zuvor; sie brauchen keine äußeren Kräfte für ihren Zusammenhalt. Jede Faser hält sich an der nächsten und findet ihren festen Platz in einer nachbarschaftlichen Verkettung. Und so wie die Fasern im Prozeß der Auflösung von ihrer ursprünglichen Einheit getrennt werden, so verbinden sie sich selbst und ganz zwanglos zu einer neuen Einheit. Ein Blatt wie das andere ist das Ereignis von intensiven Beziehungen; und wenn zwei Blätter zusammengelegt werden, findet eine Vereinigung statt, in der sich die individuellen Papiere aufeinander beziehen. Diese Beziehung übersteigt die Verwandtschaft ihrer gleichartigen Herkunft. Die Beziehung erwächst aus ihrer Stellung zueinander, in der die ursprüngliche Trennung, zum Teil wenigstens, aufgehoben ist.

Joel Fisher

as the filter lifts a thin layer of paper into the air. This sheet consists of many small fibers interlocked in a self-structuring surface. After they have become a sheet of paper the small fibers have far stronger bonds with each other than they did before. They need no external force to keep them together. Each fiber holds and in turn is held in place by its neighboring fibers. Separated from their former unitiy, and without coercion, the fibers unifiy themselves anew. With the appearance of a second sheet of paper there is a second relational event. There is reunion as the two are placed together, and the individual papers interact. This is more than a contrast between where one sheet now is in relation to where it has been: all papers share that. Relation exists in position. The original separation is at least partially overcome.
Division controls the very heart of the process. Through division the individual instance appears, bringing a general sympathy for the total unity of its earlier fluid state. Paper is a medium of, as it were, a material reincarnation keeping, as it does, a memory of the vat. Its immediate past is one of paper's potentials. Caught between fragile memory and abundant potentials there is also something quite surprising to perceive: a blank sheet of paper is a very beautiful object.

Joel Fisher

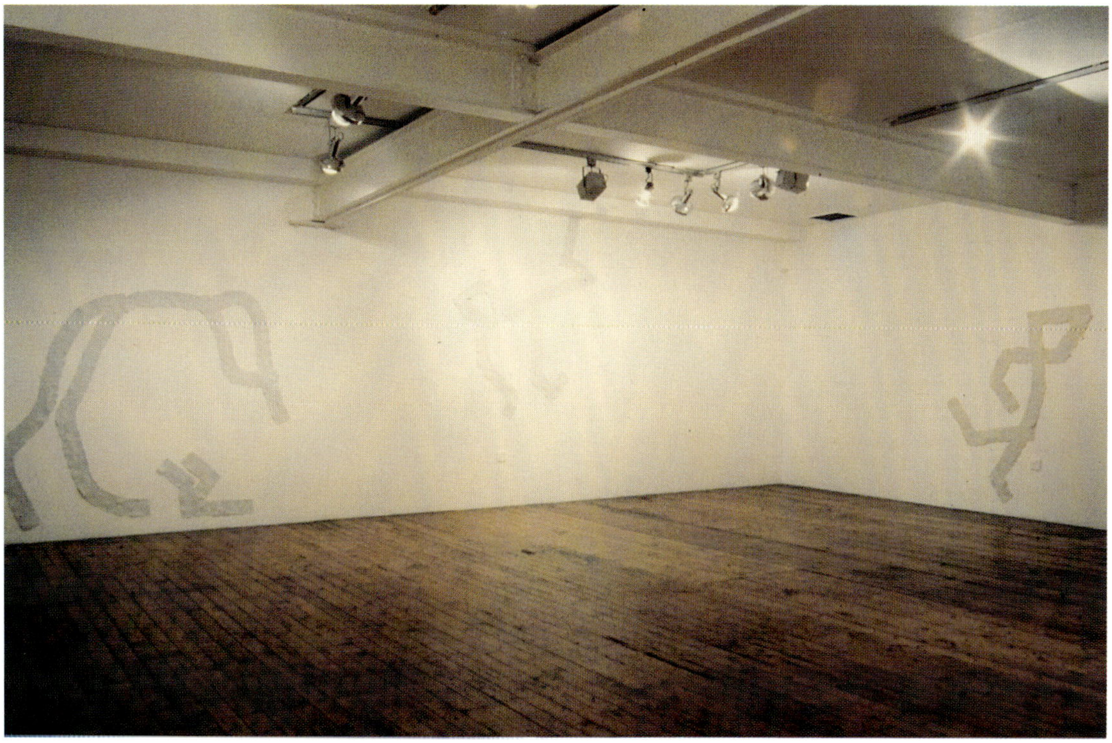

Joel Fisher: Installtion Riverside Studios, London 1982 /
Joel Fisher: Installation Riverside Studios, London 1982

Horst Gläsker

1949 **geboren in Herford** 1973–79 **Studium der Malerei an der Kunstakademie, Düsseldorf** 1975/76 **Aufenthalt in Italien** 1983, 1988–91 **Gastprofessur an der Kunstakademie Münster** Ausstellungen (Auswahl): 1980 **Musée d'Art Moderne de la Ville de Paris** 1980/81 **Kunst- und Museumsverein Wuppertal** 1981 **Neue Galerie Sammlung Ludwig, Aachen** 1983 **Groninger Museum** 1984 **Neuer Berliner Kunstverein** 1987 **Württembergischer Kunstverein, Stuttgart – Museum Abtei Liesborn** 1990 **Städtisches Gustav-Lübecke-Museum, Hamm** 1993 **Mediale, Hamburg**

1949 born in Herford **1973–79** studies painting at the Kunstakademie Düsseldorf **1975/76** stay in Italy **1983 and 1988–91** guest professor at the Kunstakademie Münster **exhibitions (selection): 1980** Musée d'Art Moderne de la Ville de Paris **1980/81** Kunst- und Museumsverein Wuppertal **1981** Neue Galerie Sammlung Ludwig, Aix-la-Chapelle **1983** Groninger Museum **1984** Neuer Berliner Kunstverein **1987** Württembergischer Kunstverein, Stuttgart – Museum Abtei Liesborn **1990** Städtisches Gustav-Lübecke-Museum, Hamm **1993** Mediale, Hamburg

Material spielte für Horst Gläsker immer wieder eine bedeutende Rolle. Aber nicht die Materialität war das Ausschlaggebende, sondern das Material als Welt- und Bild-Träger. In den 70er und 80er Jahren benutzte Gläsker industriell gefertigte Orientteppiche und Tapetenpapiere als Malgründe: Sie waren gleichermaßen Anstoß und Träger der Malerei. Immer wieder griff Gläsker in seinem Œuvre auf Materialien zurück, die Aura und eigene Welt mitbrachten.

Die Doppelbödigkeit dieser Situation fasziniert den Künstler. Was ihn zu neuem Gestalten reizt, ist das fertige Produkt, das einen definierten Platz in der Welt hat, ihm aber zugleich die Möglichkeit eröffnet, in vorzeitige Welten einzudringen. Horst Gläsker sieht das Immaterielle im Material – das trifft auf seine ornamentale Malerei ebenso zu wie auf sein figurativ-skulpturales Gestalten.

Gläskers Kunst definiert sich aus der Auseinandersetzung mit Vor-Bildern. Als Vor-Bilder gelten ihm „tief verlassene Kulturen". Ägyptische, etruskische, aber auch melanesische Figuren und Architekturen haben ihn angeregt und in seinen Formulierungen bestätigt. Bewußt hat er sich nie Anregungen in fremden Kulturen geholt. Sie begegneten ihm, und er konnte in sie hinabtauchen. Sicherheit gab ihm,

Material always played for Horst Gläsker a large role; but it was not materiality per se that counted, but the material as a conveyor of the world and the image. In the 70s and 80s Gläsker used industrially manufactured oriental carpets and wallpapers as paint ground: they were both impulse and support for the painting. Again and again Gläsker used materials in his œuvre that brought with them an aura and their own cosmos.

The equivocation of this situation fascinated the artist. What rouses him to new works is a finished product that has a defined place in the world, but at the same time offers the possibility to penetrate into former worlds. Horst Gläsker sees the immaterial in material; this applies to his ornamental painting just as much as it does his figurative/sculptural creations.

Gläsker's art is defined by its confrontation with pre-set images. For him such images mean those from "profoundly abandoned cultures". Egyptian, Etruscan, but also Melanesian figures and architecture have inspired him and confirmed his formulations. He has never consciously sought stimulus in foreign cultures. They crossed his path and he was able to submerge himself in them. What gave him assurance was the fact that he could

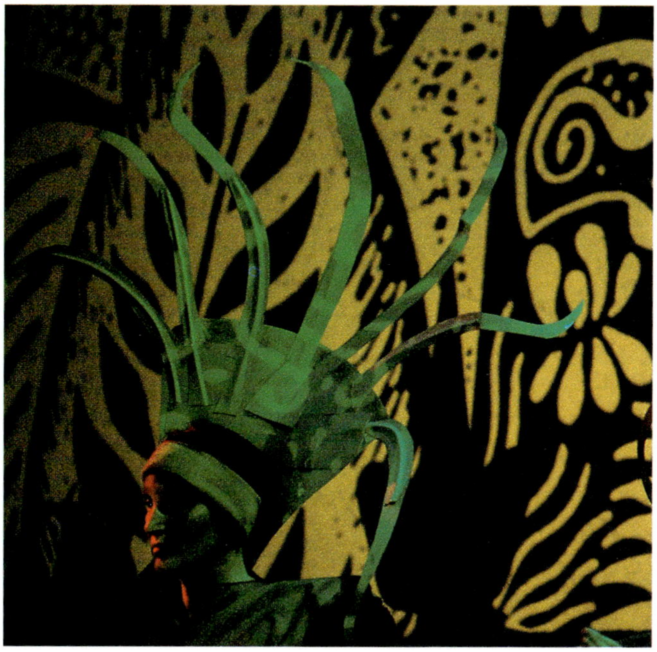

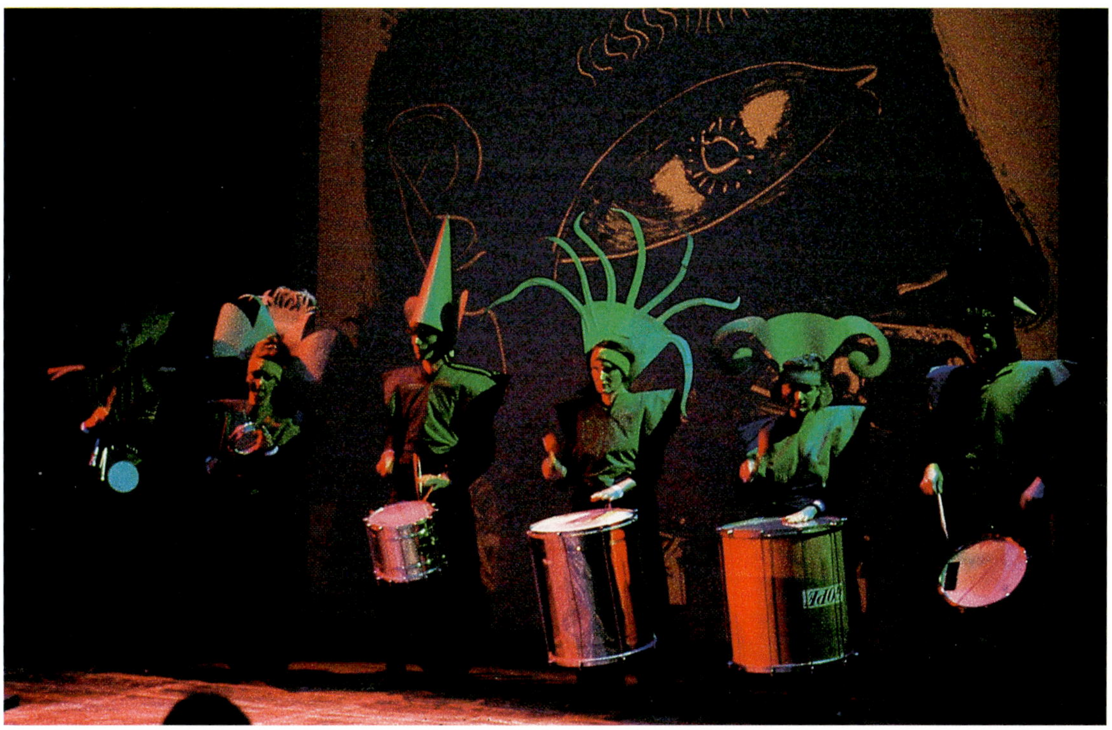

Horst Gläsker: Der Tanz des Schüttelgeistes und die Verführung des Tons. Lebende Bilder. Aufführung im Düsseldorfer Schauspielhaus und im Gasteig-Theater, München, 1991 / Horst Gläsker: The Dance of the Shivering Ghost and the Seduction of the Tone. Living pictures. Performance at the Schauspielhaus, Düsseldorf, and the Gasteig-Theater, Munich, 1991

daß er eine seinen Vorstellungen vergleichbare Welt-„Organisation“ ahnte: Seine Vor-Bild-Kulturen nahmen Formen gleichermaßen wichtig zum Geben wie zum Gestalten. „Sie wollten das Leben angenehm machen und auch das Überleben.“ Leben und Überleben angenehm zu machen, versteht Horst Gläsker nicht als materiellen Luxus, sondern als geistigen.

Seine Erzählungen wünscht Horst Gläsker sich „fabelhaft“, also mit witzig-satirischen, weniger mit moralisch-belehrenden Effekten. Gläsker wollte immer den Raum gestalten, denn nur er schließt den Künstler wie den Betrachter als selbstverständlichen Teil ein, integriert ihn in ein Weltbild. Malerei und Skulptur erscheinen deshalb in den Materialien, die der „Raum“ zur Verfügung stellt, das sind Lichtprojektionen oder Schattenbilder ebenso wie Kerzen-Zeichnungen und Erzählungen mit weißen Kieseln.

‚Weltliebesbilder‘ oder ‚Paradiesgarten‘ lauten die Titel für solche raumgreifenden Installationen, die mal den Erdboden bedecken, mal den Himmel beschreiben.

Teppiche und Tapeten gaben Gläsker bis in die 80er Jahre die Ornamente vor: Sie waren ein Ariadnefaden, der den Künstler aus dem Kompositionslabyrinth befreite. Malerei war die eine Befreiungsform aus dem strengen Schema, raumgreifende Installationen die andere. Horst Gläsker hebt gerne die eindeutige Bedeutung auf, ohne damit die Deutung unterbinden zu wollen. Die Möglichkeiten sind ihm wichtiger als die Realitäten. In seiner Kuppel im Treppenhaus des Museums ist deshalb auch der immaterielle Teil eigentlich der wirklichkeitsträchtigste: die Projektion.

Dünnes Papier bildet den Grund, aus dem die Figuren kommen, und Papiere bilden auch die (Licht)filter. Das Materialhafte ist die Bedingung für die sich luftig entfaltende Szenerie.

Heinz Thiel

divine in them one of his idea's comparative world-“organizations“: his archetypal cultures took on forms that were important both for giving and creating. “They want to make life and also survival pleasant.” To make living and surviving pleasant is something Horst Gläsker understands not to be a material, but a spiritual, luxury.

Horst Gläsker wants his narratives to be “fabulous”, that is with witty-satirical effects, rather than have a moral. Gläsker always wanted to arrange space, for he is the only one who naturally includes the artist as well as the observer, integrating him in the cosmic picture. Painting and sculpture appear for that reason in materials that “space” makes available: these are light projections or shadow pictures as well as candle drawings and narratives of white gravel.

'World-love Pictures' or 'Paradise Garden' are the titles for such space-invasive installations, that at times cover the ground, at times describe the heavens. Carpets and wallpaper were what supplied Gläsker with ornaments in the 80s: they were an Ariadne thread that led the artist out of the labyrinth of composition. Painting was one form of liberation from strict schema, space-inclusive installations the other. Horst Gläsker likes to suspend any one-to-one meaning, without wishing to undermine interpretation. The chances are more important for him than reality. In his cupola over the stairwell of the museum is therefore the immaterial part the most realistic: the projection. Thin paper makes up the ground out of which the figures rise. And paper also makes up the (light) filters. Material substantiality is the prerequisite for the airily unfolding scenery.

Heinz Thiel

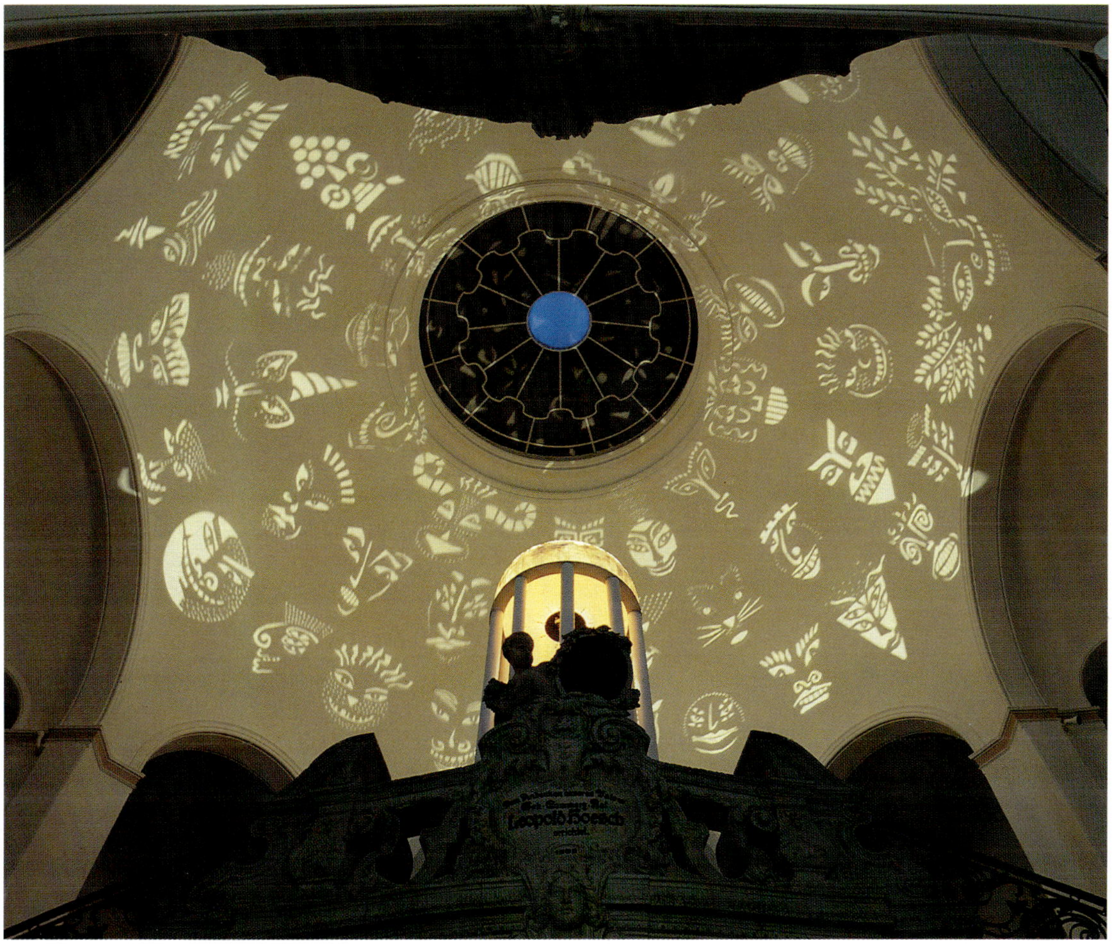

Horst Gläsker: Licht-Kuppel, 1994. Säulen: Pappe. Kuppel: Papier, mehrere Schichten geleimt, Figuren ausgeschnitten. Durchmesser 142 cm, Höhe 482 cm, Gesamthöhe 12 m / Horst Gläsker: Light-Cupola, 1994. Column: cardboard. Cupola: paper, various layers glued. Diameter 142 cm, height 482 cm, total height 12 m

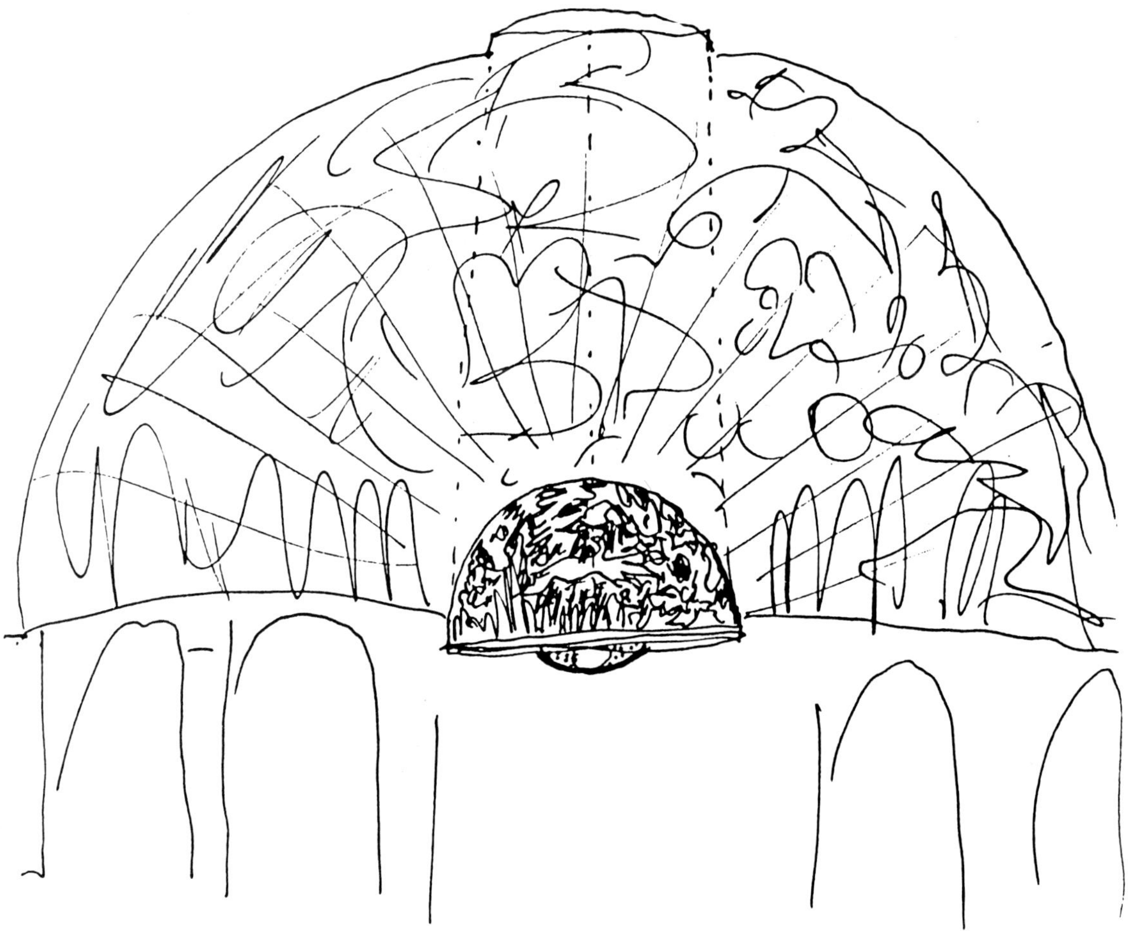

Horst Gläsker: Zeichnung für ‚Licht-Kuppel', 1994. Installation im Leopold-Hoesch-Museum, Düren /
Horst Gläsker: Sketch for 'Light-Cupola', 1994. Installation at the Leopold Hoesch Museum, Düren

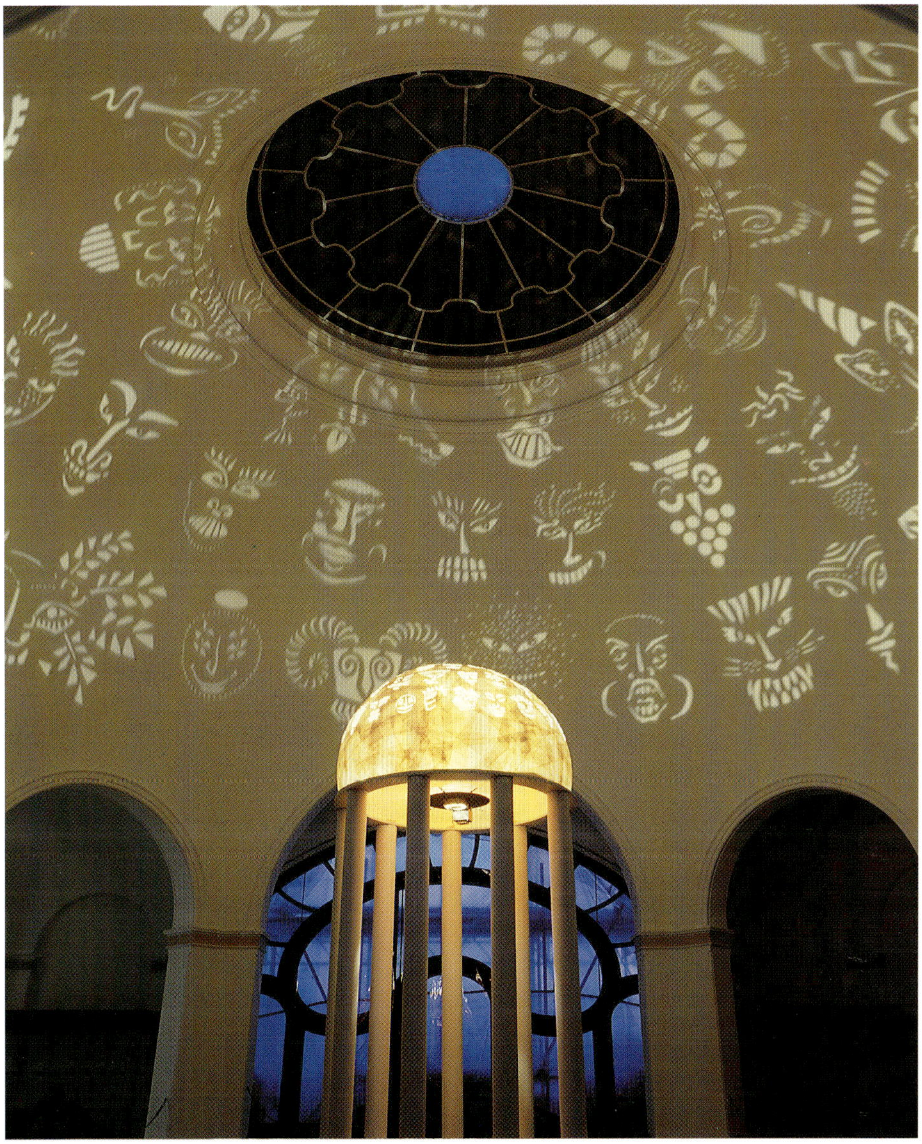

Horst Gläsker: Licht-Kuppel, 1994. Säulen: Pappe. Kuppel: Papier, mehrere Schichten geleimt, Figuren ausgeschnitten. Durchmesser 142 cm, Höhe 482 cm, Gesamthöhe 12 m /
Horst Gläsker: Light-Cupola, 1994. Column: cardboard. Cupola: paper, various layers glued. Diameter 142 cm, height 482 cm, total height 12 m

Kuno Gonschior

1935 **geboren in Wanne-Eickel, lebt in Bochum und Berlin** 1957–61 **Studium an der Kunstakakemie in Düsseldorf** bis 1963 **Studium an der Universität zu Köln** seit 1982 **Professur für freie Malerei an der Hochschule der Künste Berlin** Preise und Stipendien (Auswahl): **Kunstpreis Junger Westen, Recklinghausen – Wilhelm-Morgner-Preis, Soest** Ausstellungen (Auswahl): 1963 **Stedelijk Museum, Amsterdam – Staatliche Kunsthalle Baden-Baden** 1971 **Museum Schloß Morsbroich, Leverkusen – Wilhelm-Lehmbruck-Museum, Duisburg Museum Haus am Waldsee, Berlin** 1976 **Württembergischer Kunstverein, Stuttgart** 1977 **documenta 6, Kassel – Kunsthalle zu Kiel** 1979 **Karl-Ernst-Osthaus-Museum, Hagen** 1984 **und** 1990 **Galerie Schoeller, Düsseldorf** 1990 **Museum am Ostwall, Dortmund – Wilhelm-Hack-Museum, Ludwigshafen** 1991 **Galerie St. Johann, Saarbrücken**

1935 born in Wanne-Eickel, lives in Bochum and Berlin **1957–61** studies painting at the Kunstakademie Düsseldorf **to 1963** studies at University of Cologne **since 1982** professor for painting at the Hochschule der Künste Berlin **prizes and awards (selection):** Kunstpreis Junger Westen, Recklinghausen – Wilhelm-Morgner-Preis, Soest **exhibitions (selection): 1963** Stedelijk Museum, Amsterdam – Staatliche Kunsthalle Baden-Baden **1971** Museum Schloß Morsbroich – Wilhelm-Lehmbruck-Museum, Duisburg – Museum Haus am Waldsee, Berlin **1976** Württembergischer Kunstverein, Stuttgart **1977** documenta 6, Kassel **1977** Kunsthalle zu Kiel **1979** Karl-Ernst-Osthaus-Museum, Hagen **1984** and **1990** Galerie Schoeller, Düsseldorf **1990** Museum am Ostwall, Dortmund – Wilhelm-Hack-Museum, Ludwigshafen **1991** Galerie St. Johann, Saarbrücken

Farbe als dauernde Bewegung und als körperhaftes Volumen ist die malerische Vision von Kuno Gonschior. 1991 erweiterte er diese komplexe Auffassung von Farbe auf die Malerei mit Papierpulp. In der Papierwerkstatt von John Gerard entstanden zunächst vier Gemälde. Seinem Kompositionsprinzip der Farbflecken- und Farbpunktemalerei bleibt Gonschior auch hier treu.

Aus schwarz pigmentiertem Papiergrund leuchten Farbpunkte in gleichmäßiger Reihenformation. Eine ungeheure Farbkraft entströmt den großflächigen Punkten. Die Farbe wirkt fast fluoreszierend und überstrahlt ihre realen Begrenzungen. Die dicke Materialität des Papierstoffs gibt den Farben haptischen Charakter. Unterstützt wird die Wirkung durch den unregelmäßigen Rand, der aus dem Gieß- und Preßvorgang resultiert.

Color as constant motion and as tangible volume is Kuno Gonschior's vision of painting. In 1991 he widened his complex idea of color to include painting with paperpulp. In the paper workshop run by John Gerard, four paintings were at first completed. In them Gonschior remains true to his compositional principle of speckled dots of color. From a black pigmented paper ground, dots of paint light up in even rows. An enormous dynamism of color pulses through them. The dots seem almost fluorescent and their illumination extends beyond their actual boundaries. The thick materiality of the paperpulp gives the color its haptic character. This impression is bolstered by the uneven edge, whose effect is a result of the process of pouring and then moulding the paper stock.

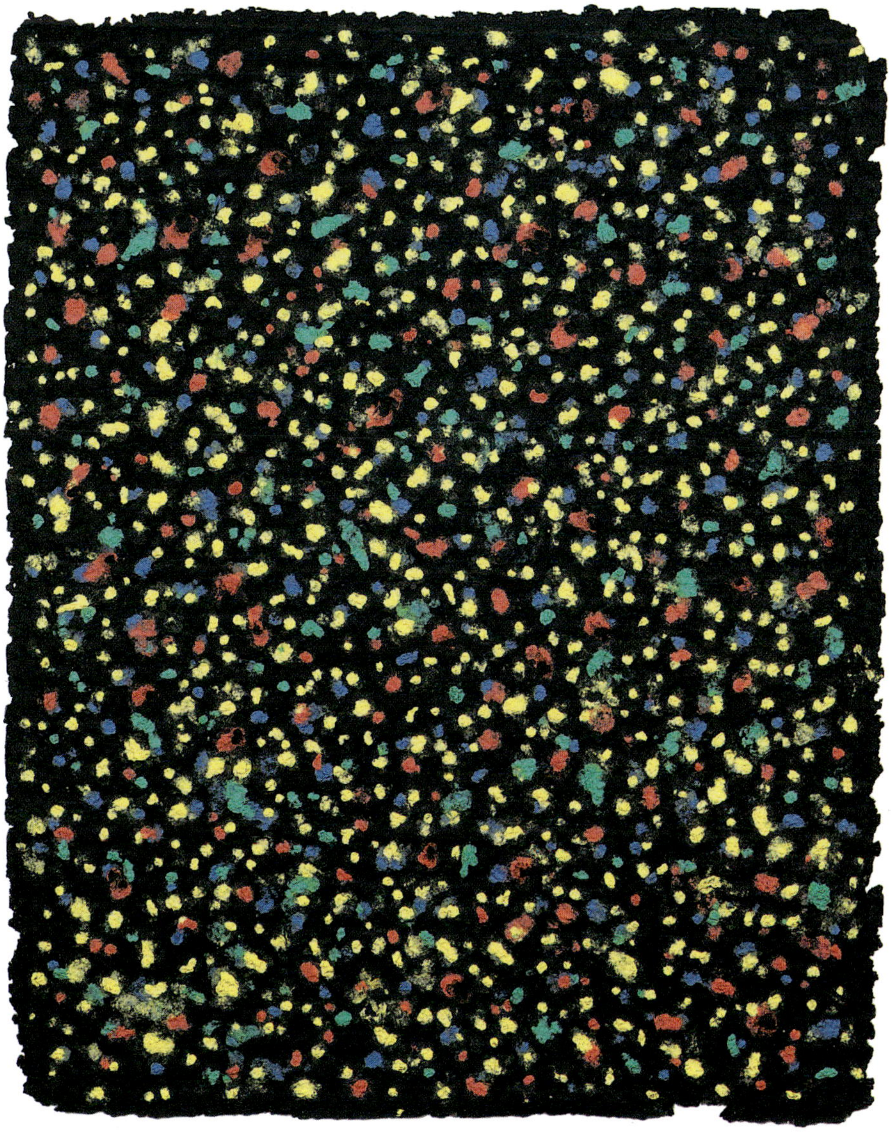

Kuno Gonschior: Blau-Grün-Gelb-Rot, Nr. 18. 9. 91, 1991. Pulpmalerei. 90 x 70 cm /
Kuno Gonschior: Blue-Green-Yellow-Red, No. 18 / 9 / 91, 1991. Pulp painting. 90 x 70 cm

Huang Yong Ping

1954 geboren in Quanzhou/Provinz Fujian, lebt seit 1989 in Paris Bis 1982 Studium der Malerei an der Akademie der Bildenden Künste Zhejiang/Hongzhou 1982–89 Lehrer an einer Mittelschule in Xiamen/Fuijan 1992 Stipendium, Schloß Solitude, Stuttgart Ausstellungen (Auswahl): 1983 Museum of Fine Arts, Xiamen 1986 Palace of Culture, Xiamen 1989 Centre National d'Art et de Culture Georges Pompidou, Paris 1990 Ecole des Beaux-Arts, Rouen und Avignon 1992 Galerie Froment & Putman, Paris 1993 Haus der Kulturen, Berlin 1994 New Museum of Contemporary Art, New York – Fondation Cartier pour l'art contemporain – Rijksmuseum Kröller-Müller, Otterlo/ Niederlande

1954 born in Quanzhou in the Fujian province of China, lives since 1989 in Paris **to 1982** studies painting at the Academy of Visual Arts Zhejiang/Hongzhou **1982–89** teacher at a school in Xiamen/Fuijan **1992** grant to study at Schloß Solitude, Stuttgart **exhibitions (selection): 1983** Museum of Fine Arts, Xiamen **1986** Palace of Culture, Xiamen **1989** Centre National d'Art et de Culture Georges Pompidou, Paris **1990** Ecole des Beaux-Arts, Rouen and Avignon **1992** Galerie Froment & Putman, Paris **1993** Haus der Kulturen, Berlin **1994** New Museum of Contemporary Art, New York – Fondation Cartier pour l'art contemporain – Rijksmuseum Kröller-Müller, Otterlo/Netherlands

Die Arbeiten Huang Yong Pings sind nicht leicht zu entschlüsseln; immer geben sie Rätsel auf. Bewußt spielen sie mit der Mehrdeutigkeit von Begriffen und deren Verständnis innerhalb der Kulturkreise (Fern) Ost-West.

1986 gründeten er und einige Künstlerkollegen die Gruppe ‚Xiamen-Dada', die mit verschiedenen spektakulären Ausstellungen und Aktionen in Kunstkreisen Diskussionen auslöste und ihre Besucher sowie die Offiziellen verwirrte: So endete eine Ausstellung mit der Verbrennung der Exponate; ebenfalls im Jahre 1986 zeigte die Gruppe in der Ausstellung ‚Ereignisse' nicht die erwarteten Bilder und Objekte, sondern präsentierte Fundstücke und Gerümpel aus der unmittelbaren Umgebung des Museums als Ausstellungsstücke. Da sie als Folge dieser Aktion nicht mehr öffentlich ausstellen konnte, hielt sie ihre Aktionen bis zu ihrer Selbstauflösung im Video fest.

Huang ging es in diesen Aktionen nicht um „Antikunst" im dadaistischen Sinne der 20er Jahre, sondern um das Nachdenken über eine „andere" Kunst und einen anderen Kunstbegriff.

The works of Huang Yong Ping are not easy to decipher; they are always puzzling. They consciously play with the double-meanings of concepts and their comprehension within the cultural climates of (far)east and west.

In 1986 in China he founded with some of his artist colleagues the group 'Xiamen-Dada' that with different spectacular exhibitions and actions sparked off discussions in art circles and confounded their visitors as well as the officials. One exhibition ended with the burning of the artworks. Again in 1986 in an exhibition 'Events', the group did not show the expected pictures and objects, but put articles and junk collected from the immediate vicinity of the museum on exhibition. When, as a consequence, the group was not allowed to exhibit again in public, they preserved all their actions on video tape until their disbandment.

These actions were for Huang not a question of "anti-art" in the sense of Dada from the 20s, but a way of contemplating "another" art and another concept of art. In his works he sought an "objective" work process in contrast to the

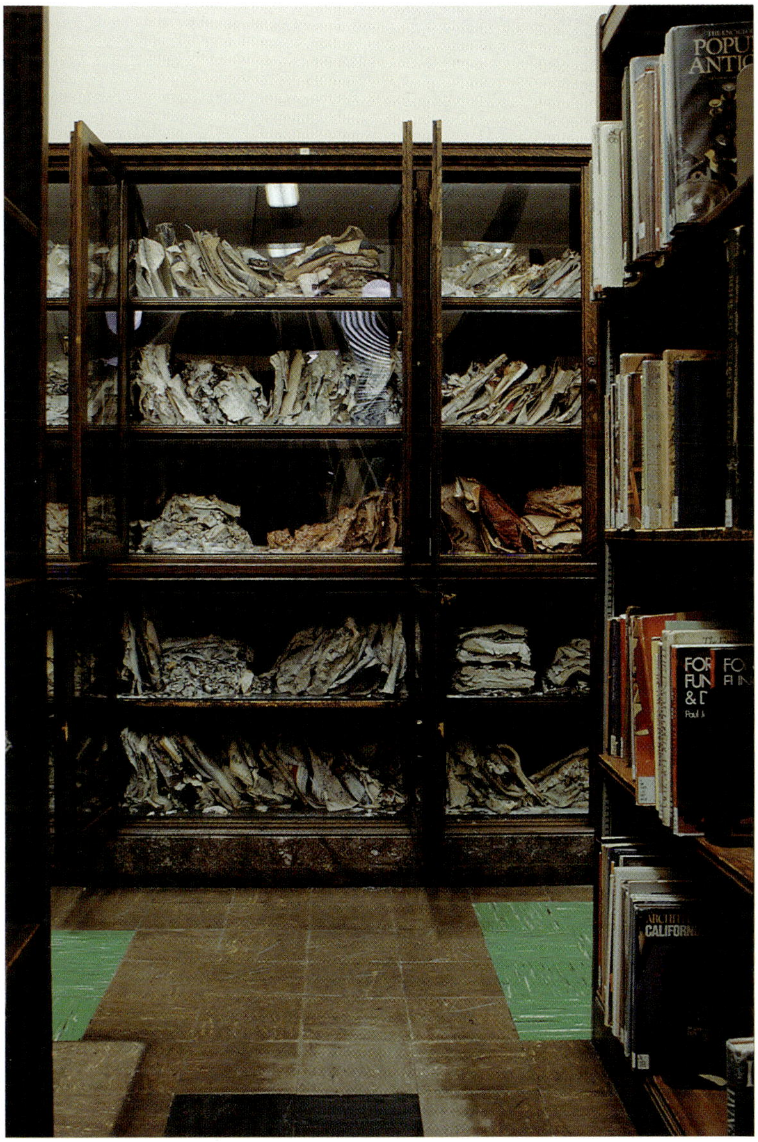

Huang Yong Ping: Unreadable Humidity, 1991. Carnegie-Bibliothek, Pittsburgh, Massachusetts / Huang Yong Ping: Unreadable Humidity, 1991. Carnegie Library, Pittsburgh/Massachusetts

In seinen eigenen Arbeiten suchte er den „objektiven" Herstellungsprozeß im Gegensatz zu einer subjektiv-gestischen Ausdrucksweise. Bestärkt und inspiriert wurde er hierin durch die damals gerade ins Chinesische übersetzten Schriften von Wittgenstein, Foucault und de Saussure ebenso wie durch die Arbeitsweise von Cage. Hinzu kam die kritische Aufarbeitung der Kulturrevolution und der Folgen in China sowie eine neue, intensive Auseinandersetzung mit der eigenen klassischen Tradition in Philosophie und Kunst, die während der Kulturrevolution verfemt war.

1987 entwickelte er Objekte (‚Scheibenläufer' oder ‚Roulette') mit übereinandermontierten drehbaren Scheiben, die dem Künstler Duktus, Farbe, Malstil, Zeit usw. vorgaben und damit eine „objektivere" Produktion ermöglichten. Als nächsten Schritt führte er die Waschmaschine in den Arbeitsprozeß ein. In Verbindung mit ihr wird das Papier zu einem seiner bevorzugten Materialien. Die Arbeit ‚Eine Geschichte der chinesischen Kunst und Kurze Geschichte der modernen Kunst nach zweiminütigem Waschen in der Waschmaschine' besteht aus einem Papierbreihaufen der beiden verarbeiteten Kunstgeschichtsbücher auf einer Glasplatte als Teil eines Objektes über einer Holzkiste. Auf humorvoll-ironische Weise werden hier die oft angestrengt-peinlichen Bemühungen um eine Verbindung von östlicher mit westlicher Kunst kommentiert. Daneben kommt Huangs generell skeptische Haltung gegenüber dem Absolutheitsanspruch von Niedergeschriebenem zum Ausdruck:

„Was uns die Geschichte übriggelassen hat, ist eine große Menge von Schriften und Texten ... Wir befinden uns mitten in einem großen Müllhaufen; darunter findet sich die Kultur – Philosophie, Religion und Kunst. Sie läßt sich beliebig manipulieren und aussortieren ... Wenn du dich nicht aus dem Müll des Textes (unserer Geschichte, unseres Denkes und unserer Kultur) erhebst, werden wir von verschiedenen Theorien, Wertvorstellungen und Predigten niedergedrückt werden."

subjective, gestural means of expression. He was supported and inspired by the writings of Wittgenstein, Foucault and de Saussure, who had just then been translated into Chinese, and by the working methods of Cage. Added to this was an emerging, critical reappraisal of the Cultural Revolution and its consequences for China as well as a new, intensive debate on China's own classical traditions in philosophy and art that had been banned during the revolution.

In 1987 he developed objects ('Scheibenläufer' or 'Roulette') with turntable disks, one above the other, that provided the artist with means of procedure, color, painting style, time, etc., making an "objective" production possible. His next step was to introduce a washing machine into the process, and in connection with this, paper became one of his preferred materials. The work 'A History of Chinese Art and A History of Modern Art after Two Minutes in the Washing Machine' consists of paper mash from the two art history books piled on a glass plate as part of an object mounted on a wooden case. Humorously, ironically, he thus comments on the often embarrassingly strained way an east-west connection in the field of art is sought. Also manifest here is Huang's skeptical view in general toward the claim of script to be absolute: "What history has left behind is a large amount of writings and texts ... We find ourselves in the midst of a heap of refuse, including culture, i. e. philosophy, religion and art. It can be manipulated and sorted at will ... If you do not lift yourself out of this debris of texts (our history, our thinking and our culture), you will be weighed down by different theories, cosmic concepts and sermons."

Through destruction, the opportunity simultaneously arises for something new. However, the cleansed must not necessarily mean the healed: "The act of 'bookwashing' is similar to Wittgenstein's idea when he said that certain expressions should be extracted from a language and sent to be cleaned, after which they could be re-instated as communication. I consider the

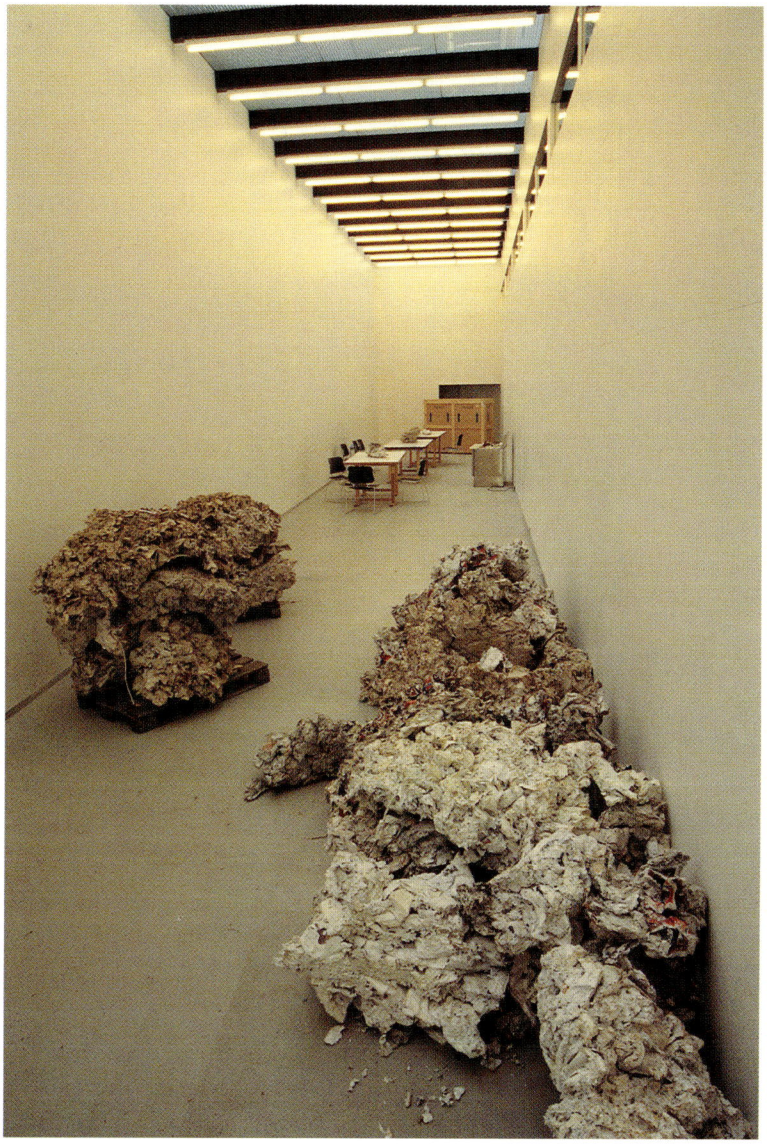

Huang Yong Ping: China Avantgarde, 1993. Kunsthalle Rotterdam /
Huang Yong Ping: China Avant-garde, 1993. Kunsthalle Rotterdam

Durch die Zerstörung ist gleichzeitig die Chance zu etwas Neuem gegeben. Allerdings muß das Gereinigte durchaus nicht das Geheilte bedeuten:
„Der Akt des ‚Buchwaschens' ähnelt im Grunde dem Gedanken Wittgensteins, als er sagte, daß bestimmte Ausdrücke aus einer Sprache herausgezogen und zum Reinigen gegeben werden müßten; danach könnten sie wieder in die Kommunikation zurückgeführt werden. Ich betrachte das Waschen von Büchern als Prozeß und zugleich als Ziel meiner Arbeit, da ich nicht glaube, daß eine ‚gewaschene' Sprache wieder in den Sprachgebrauch zurückkehren kann. Mit anderen Worten: Die Kommunikation selbst ist eine ‚schmutzige' Sache ..."
Das Neuentstandene bei Huang ist daher auch das nicht Erwartete, etwas, was nicht gleich wieder in eine Kategorie einordbar und beurteilbar ist. Erst in dieser Differenz wird der Betrachter als Individuum wirklich gefordert. Endgültige Interpretationsversuche lehnt Huang Yong Ping ab.
Seine Projekte, ob in den USA, Europa oder Asien, entstehen immer vor Ort, haben immer sowohl etwas mit seiner heimatlichen chinesischen Kultur als auch mit seinen Erfahrungen im westlichen Kulturkreis zu tun. Sein Interesse gilt den gegenseitigen Beeinflussungen verschiedener Kulturen. Er versteht die Begriffe „Ost" und „West" als fließende, nicht als statische Konzeptionen. Im Schaffensprozeß greift er auf das traditionelle chinesische Orakelbuch ‚Buch der Wandlungen' (Yi Jing) als Zufallsgenerator zurück.
In seiner Arbeit ‚Kiosk', Düren, arbeitet Huang Yong Ping mit durch den Betonmischer gedrehten Zeitschriften und Zeitungen. Sie sind Teil einer Form, die einerseits von einem französischen Zeitungskiosk herrührt, sich andererseits an der Form der chinesischen Pagode orientiert. Es ist eine „Ruine" vergangener Kulturen, ein Denkmal unsereres Zeitungs- und Zeitschriftenkonsums und unseres Überflusses.

Andreas Schmid

washing of books a process and at the same time the goal of my work, since I do not believe that a 'cleansed' language can be returned to verbal use. In other words: communication itself is 'something dirty'."
The newly created in Huang's work is therefore not what is expected, not something that is again immediately classifiable and judgeable. It is this difference that really challenges the individual as viewer. Huang Yong Ping rejects definitive interpretations. His projects, whether in the US, Europe or Asia, are always produced on the site itself and always have something to do with his native Chinese culture as well as with his experience in western cultural circles. His interest is centered on the mutual influences of different cultures. He understands the words "East" and "West" to be fluent, not static concepts. In the creative process he looks back to the traditional Chinese book of oracles, 'The Book of Changes' Yi Jing, as a generator of random chance.
In 'Kiosk' presented in Düren, Huang Yong Ping works with newspapers and magazines that have been rotated in a cement mixer. They partake, on one hand, of a form taken from a French newsstand kiosk and, on the other, are oriented to that of a Chinese pagoda. It is a "ruin" of past cultures, a monument to our newspaper and magazine consumption and to our affluence.

Andreas Schmid

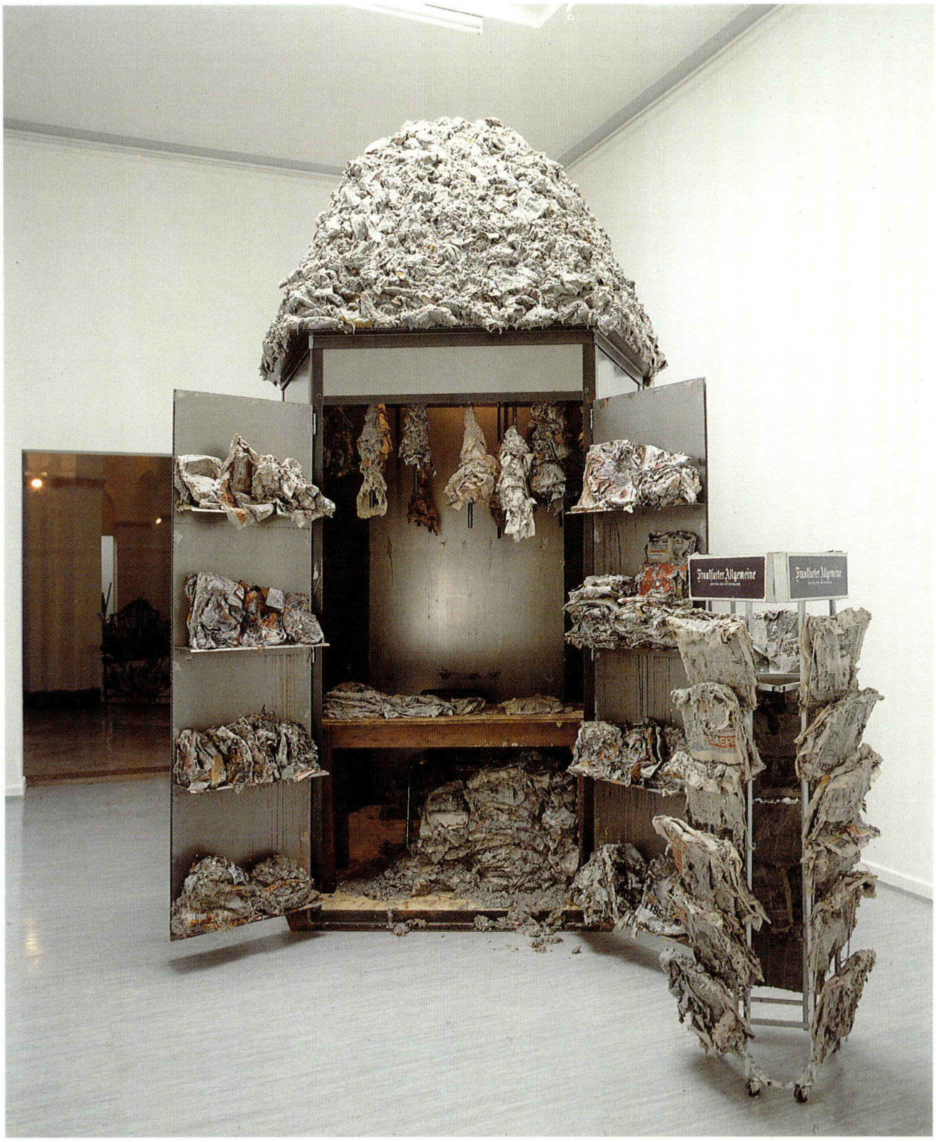

Huang Yong Ping: Kiosk, 1994. Metall, Zeitungen und Zeitschriften in der Betonmischmaschine behandelt. Grundfläche 240 x 265 cm, Höhe 370 cm / Huang Yong Ping: Kiosk, 1994. Metal, magazines, newspapers, rotated in a cement mixer. Ground 240 x 265 cm, height 370 cm

Maria Orzel-Hercka

1949 geboren in Katowice, lebt in Düren 1963–68 Studium an der Staatlichen Fachoberschule für bildende Künste in Katowice 1968–69 und 1971–72 Studium an der Kunstakademie in Krakau 1975–81 Kostümdesignerin bei Film, Fernsehen und Theater in Polen Kostümentwürfe und Performances (Auswahl): 1991 Kunstzug beim Kulturforum des Kreises Düren auf der Burg Nideggen 1992 4. Internationale Biennale der Papierkunst, Düren 1993 Galerie 68 elf, Köln

1949 born in Katowice, lives in Düren **1963-68** studies at the state school of Visual Arts in Katowice **1968–69 and 1971–72** studies at the Art Academy in Krakow **1975–81** costume designer for film, TV and theater productions in Poland **costume designs and performances (selection): 1991** art procession to the Burg Nideggen for the Kulturforum des Kreises Düren **1992** 4th International Biennale of PaperArt, Düren **1993** Galerie 68 elf, Cologne

Natur-Triptychon: Erde, Wasser, Luft – Bewegliche Bilder –

Zwischen Leopold-Hoesch-Museum und Papiermuseum entsteht eine Papierstraße mit beweglichen Bildern, Bühnenelementen und Kostümen. Es ist eine dreiteilige Inszenierung, die vor den Augen der Zuschauer bei offenem Vorhang entwickelt wird. Bewegliche Bilder, die Tanz, Geräusche und Musik beinhalten, vermitteln visuelle Erzählungen. Die natürlichen Formen des Papiers und des menschlichen Körpers werden ineinander zu neuen Proportionen verschmelzen, so wie die in Bewegung befindlichen Strukturen, Farben und Geräusche. Nur in Bewegung kann man die Bilder als Gesamtheit erfassen. Danach werden sie nur noch als Erinnerung zurückbleiben.
Ich bin in das Papier verliebt, habe keine Angst vor ihm. Ich kann die Bogen bemalen, zerschneiden, zerreißen, bekleben, sie formen. Ich respektiere ihre Individualität.
Ich bewundere die Natur und ihre ständige Bewegung. Sie ist der Ursprung für meine Arbeit. Wir Menschen leben zwar noch mit der Natur zusammen, aber die Umweltzerstörung wird fatale Folgen für uns mit sich bringen – nicht für die Natur, denn diese wird sich durchsetzen.

Maria Orzel-Hercka

Nature-triptych: Earth, Water, Air – Moving Pictures –

Between the Leopold Hoesch Museum and the Paper Museum a paper street has been established with moving pictures, stage elements and costumes. It is a three-part production that takes place and evolves before the audience without benefit of a curtain. Moving pictures, comprised of dance, sounds and music, present visual tales. The natural forms of the paper and of the human body are blended together to new proportions, as structures, colors and sounds in motion. Only in motion can the viewer take in the total sum of the pictures. Afterwards they remain only a memory.
I have fallen in love with paper, have no fear of it. The single sheets I can paint, cut, tear, paste, form. I respect their individuality.
I admire nature and the fact that she is in constant motion. She is the origin of my work. Though we humans live together with nature, the destruction of the environment will be fatal to us – though not for nature; she will pull through.

Maria Orzel-Hercka

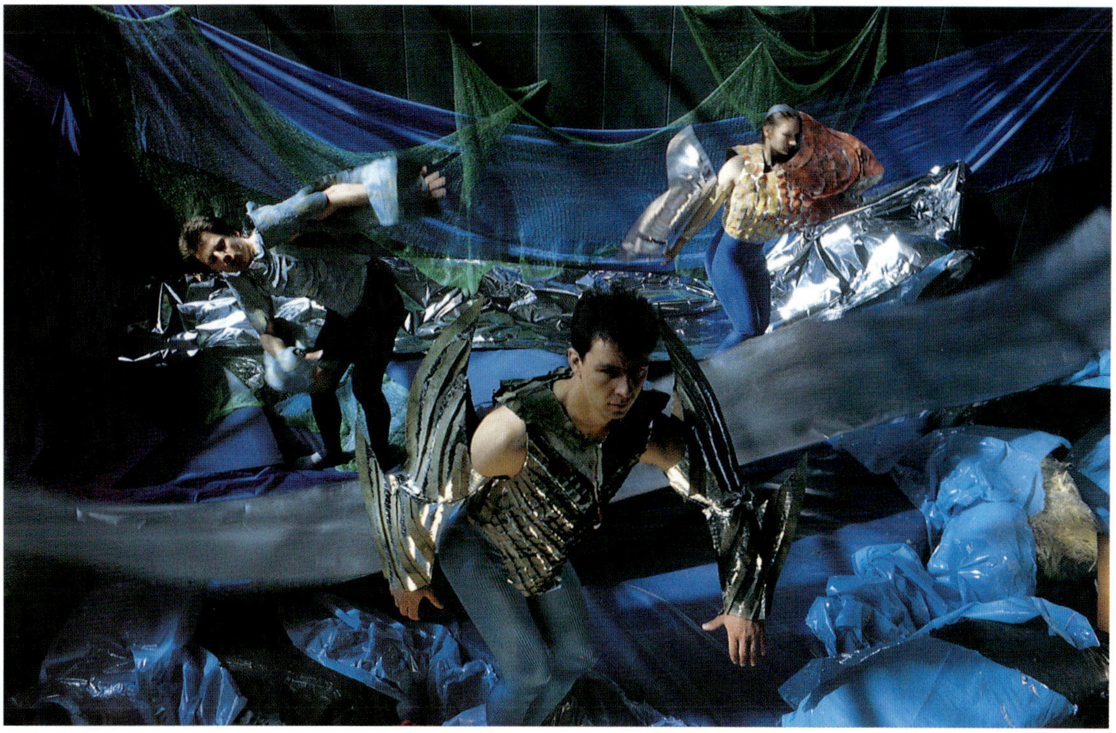

Maria Orzel-Hercka: Zweites Bild: Wasser, 1994. Bewegliches Bild mit Papier /
Maria Orzel-Hercka: Second Picture: Water, 1994. Moving picture with paper

Drei Bilder:

1. Erde: Spielort vor den Treppen des Leopold-Hoesch-Museums
   Atmosphäre: Geburt
   - rieselnder Sand, rollender Stein, Bäume und Wiesen
   - Kontakt mit Erdboden
   - rohes Papier, Zeitungspapier
2. Wasser: Spielort Weg im Grünen
   Atmosphäre: Hoffnung, Erfrischung
   - fließendes Wasser, schwimmende Fische
   - bemaltes Papier
   - klare, glänzende Silberpapiere
   - Meer – geheimnisvoll – Angst vor der Tiefe
   - blaue und kräftige Farben
   - Kontrast, Rhythmus
   - Bewegung – Wellen
3. Luft: Spielort von den Spitzen der Berge bis zum Tor des Papiermuseums
   Atmosphäre: Freiheit, Paradies
   - bewegliche Wolken, fliegende Vögel
   - gefärbtes Papier
   - Pastell, Aquarell, Ajour
   - schwebende, leichte Bewegung

Darsteller:
Erde: Karin Schüller, Kati Monchou, Silke Greiff, Helga Mönnich, Wilfried Baum
Wasser und Luft: Bewegungstheater Karambolage, Köln

Komposition und Live-Musik:
Last Affair (Gerald Doecke, Norbert Jorzik)

Three Pictures:

1. Earth: venue – before the steps of the Leopold Hoesch Museum
   Atmosphere: birth
   - trickling sand, rolling stones, trees, fields
   - contact with the ground
   - raw paper, newspaper
2. Water: venue – path into the green fields
   Atmosphere: hope, refreshment
   - running water, swimming fish
   - painted paper
   - clear, glossy silver paper
   - sea – mysterious – fear of the deep
   - blue and intense colors
   - contrast, rhythm
   - motion – waves
3. Air: venue – before the peaks of the hills up to the gate of the paper museum
   Atmosphere: freedom, paradise
   - moving clouds, flying birds
   - dyed paper
   - pastels, water color, à jour
   - floating, light movement

Characters:
Earth: Karin Schüller, Kati Monchou, Silke Greiff, Helga Mönnich, Wilfried Baum
Water and Air: Bewegungstheater Karambolage, Cologne

Composition and live music:
Last Affair (Gerald Doecke, Norbert Jorzik)

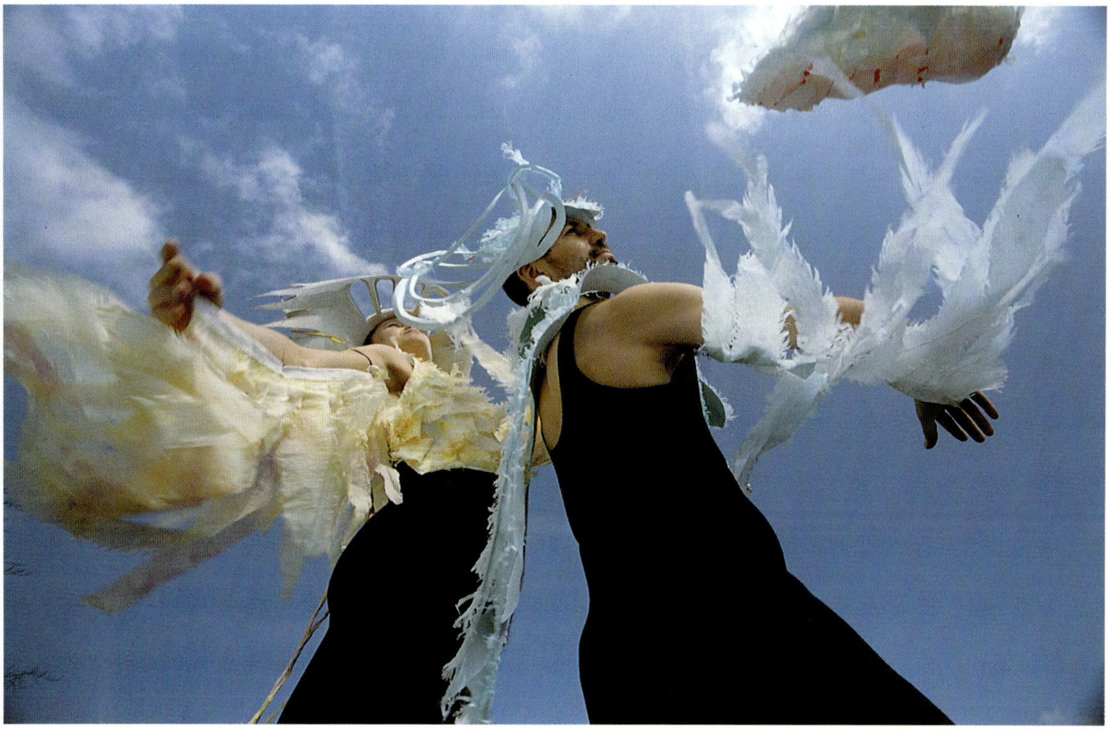

Maria Orzel-Hercka: Drittes Bild: Luft, 1994. Bewegliches Bild mit Papier /
Maria Orzel-Hercka: Third Picture: Air, 1994. Moving picture with paper

Jean-Luc Parant

1944 **geboren in Tunis, lebt in Bout des Bordes/Frankreich, bildender Künstler und Dichter** Ausstellungen (Auswahl): 1963 **Hôtel Colbert de Torcy** 1976 **Fondation Maeght** 1977 **Galerie Obliques, Paris** 1978 **Galerie Katia Pissaro** 1982 **Centre National d'Art et de Culture Georges Pompidou, Paris** 1985 **Musée de l'Art Moderne de la Ville de Paris** 1991 **Centre National d'Art et de Culture Georges Pompidou, Paris – Centre de création contemporaine, Tours** 1993 **Galerie Montaigne, Paris**

1944 born in Tunis, lives in Bout des Bordes/France, visual artist and writer **exhibitions (selection): 1963** Hôtel Colbert de Torcy **1976** Fondation Maeght **1977** Galerie Obliques, Paris **1978** Galerie Katia Pissaro **1982** Centre National d'Art et de Culture Georges Pompidou, Paris **1985** Musée de l'Art Moderne de la Ville de Paris **1991** Centre National d'Art et de Culture Georges Pompidou, Paris – Centre de création contemporaine, Tours **1993** Galerie Montaigne, Paris

Vom verschwindend Kleinen zum Unendlichen und zurück

Eine Kugel, um in der Dunkelheit zu kreisen, ein Text, um im Licht zu kreisen: mit seinen Augen die Sonne berühren und zurückkommen auf die nie versiegende und winzige Wiederholung derselben Gebärde. Nichts wiegen auf der Erde und in seinen Händen unablässig das Gewicht der Welt noch einmal schöpfen. Augen, Sexus, Tiere. Die Wörter noch einmal erfinden, die Zeit noch einmal erfinden, den Raum noch einmal erfinden. Die Sätze wuchern hervor wie lauter lebende Zellen, die Kugeln vermehren sich wie alle die Gedanken, die der Mensch hervorbringen könnte. Es gab keine erste Kugel, es sei denn ein anfängliches Staubkorn des Kosmos. Es wird kein letztes Wort geben, solange eine Stimme die Tage und die Nächte wird zählen können. Gleichviel, ob Dichter oder Bildhauer, König oder Künstler. Mit seinem Geschlecht die Sterne anschauen oder lieben auf Erden, daß einem darüber die Stimme versagt. Reglose Reise zwischen Leben und Tod, absoluter Taumel eines Gesangs, der die Ewigkeit umfaßt seit der gezählten Zeit einer irdischen Existenz. Titi und Jean-Luc, die Frau und der Mann, sind eins und sind alle Möglichkeiten. Die Bücher und die Kugeln, die Tinte

From the infinitesimal to infinity and back

A sphere for circulating in the darkness, a text for circulating in the light: to touch the sun with your eyes and return to the inexhaustible and minuscule repetition of the same gesture. To be weightless on the earth and never cease to recreate between your hands the weight of the world. Eyes, the sexual organs, animals. To reinvent words and time, reinvent space. Phrases proliferate like so many living cells; spheres multiply like all the thoughts producible by man. There was no primal sphere unless it was an initial speck of cosmic dust. There will not be a last word, as long as a voice exists to count the days and nights. Poet or sculptor, king or artist, it does not matter. To watch the stars with your sex or make such love on earth that it takes your voice away. An immobile voyage between life and death, the absolute vertigo of an interrupted chant that embraces eternity from the time ticked off by an earthly existence. Titi and Jean-Luc, the woman and the man, are one sole and every thing possible. Books and spheres, ink and earth, paper and sealing wax are one sole and every thing possible. To write and make spheres, the always different recommencement of the same chant. Time

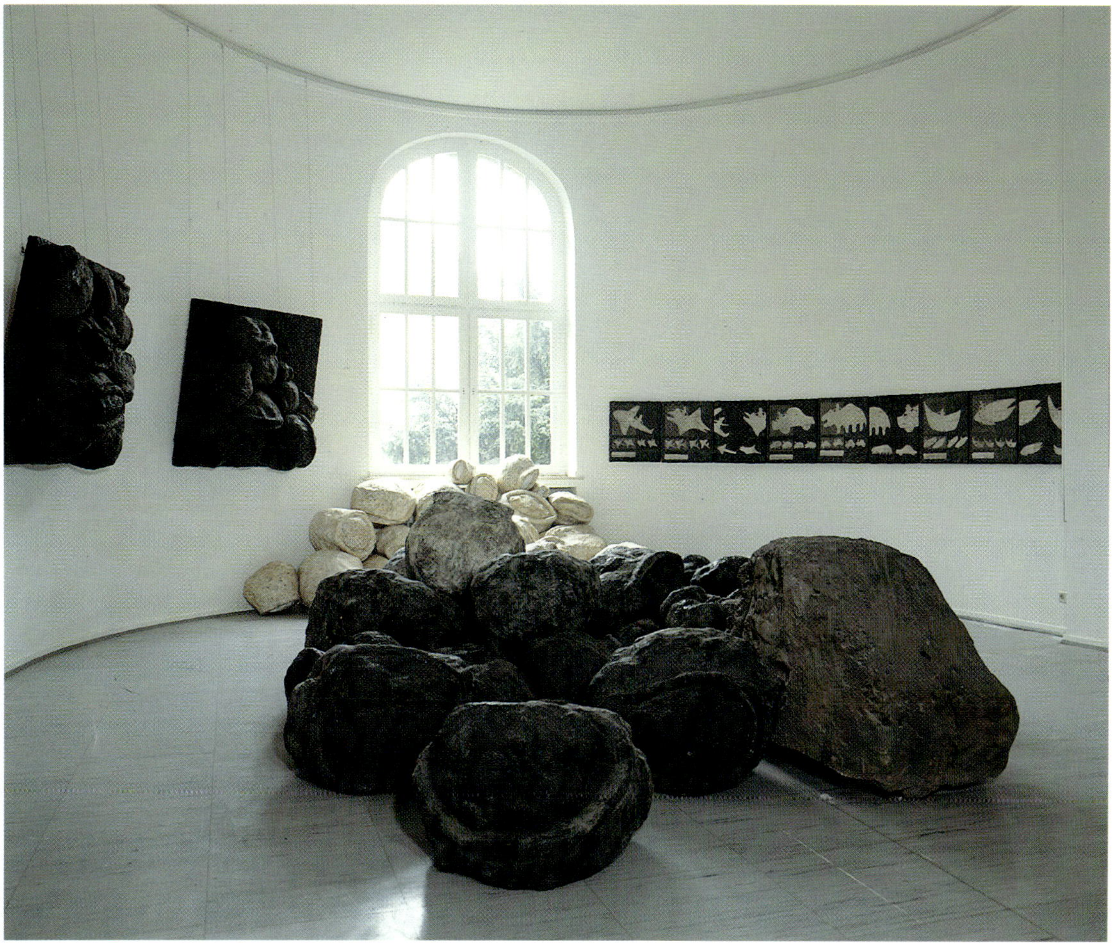

Jean-Luc Parant: Installation mit Kugeln, Tinte, Erde, 1994. Raumgröße 840 x 650 cm /
Jean-Luc Parant: Installation with spheres, ink, earth, 1994. Dimensions 850 x 650 cm

und die Erde, das Papier und der Siegellack sind eins und sind alle Möglichkeiten. Schreiben und Einkugeln, der immer andere Wiederbeginn der gleichen Psalmodie. In dieser grenzenlosen Wiederaufnahme der Gebärde und der Stimme existiert die Zeit nicht, gibt es keinen Unterschied mehr zwischen der Fruchtbarkeit in den Wörtern und der Vielzahl der Kugeln.

Jean-Michel Phéline

does not exist in this unceasing, unlimited rehearsal of gesture and voice; there is no longer a difference between the fecundity of words and the multitude of spheres.

Jean-Michel Phéline

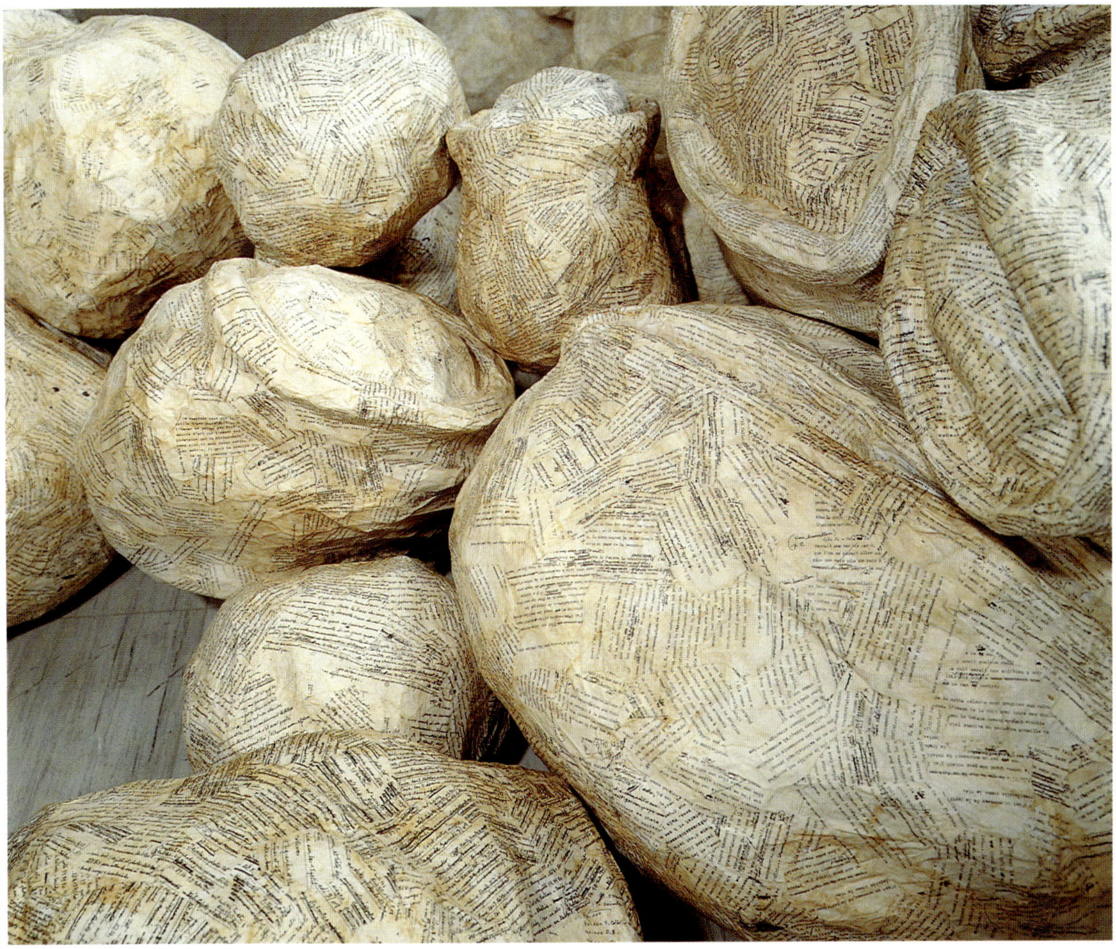

Jean-Luc Parant: Installation mit Kugeln, Tinte, Erde, 1994. Raumgröße 840 x 650 cm /
Jean-Luc Parant: Installation with spheres, ink, earth, 1994. Dimensions 850 x 650 cm

Milko Pavlov

1956 geboren in Aitos/Bulgarien, lebt in Sofia 1976–1979 Studium am Institut für Ökonomie und Wirtschaft, Sofia Ende der 80er Jahre mehrere Reisen in Europa Stipendien: 1993 Stipendium der Heinrich-Böll-Stiftung, Langenbroich Ausstellungen (Auswahl): 1991 Kulturzentrum, Zürich – Galerie Granero, Bern 1992 Galerie Hemus, Sofia 1993 Papiermuseum, Düren

1956 born in Aitos, Bulgaria, lives in Sofia **1976–1979** studies at the Institute for Economics and Business, Sofia **late 80s** takes several trips to Europe **grants: 1993** grant of the Heinrich-Böll-Stiftung, Langenbroich **exhibitions (selection): 1991** Kulturzentrum, Zurich – Galerie Granero, Bern **1992** Galerie Hemus, Sofia **1993** Papiermuseum, Düren

Milko Pavlov inszenierte für die Ausstellung ein Labyrinth. Das strukturreiche Material Wellpappenkarton erachtete er als geeignet, die philosophische Dimension dieses antiken Mythos zu verbildlichen. Der Künstler trat in einen Dialog mit dem Material. Der gesteuerte Zufall wurde dabei zum kompositorischen Prinzip.
Allein schon der Arbeitsprozeß mit Wellpappe verdeutlicht einen labyrinthischen Vorgang, äußerte der Künstler. Er verletzte die glatte Oberschicht des Wellpappenkartons, ritzte Spuren in sie ein, schnitt Elemente aus der Deckschicht aus und klebte die Pappefetzen wieder auf. Durch die Beschädigungen des deckenden pappefarbenen Basispapiers wird die gewellte, hellere Zwischenschicht zum bildkünstlerischen Element. Ritzungen erscheinen wie schluchtartige Einkerbungen. Fetzen des Pappebasispapiers formen sich zum reliefierten Formenkonglomerat.
Grafische Linienstrukturen, vielgestaltige Erhebungen und Eingrabungen überziehen die Weite der Bildfläche. Ruhige, unbehandelte Pappeflächen wechseln mit Kompositionsstrukturen von unentwirrbarer Dichte. Der Lichteinfall unterstreicht das Spannungsverhältnis der seriell gestreuten Strukturen und Flächen. Das Licht formt die Plastizität des Wandreliefs deutlich aus und läßt vielstufige Farbdifferenzierungen entstehen.

Milko Pavlov has staged a labyrinth for the exhibition. Corrugated paper is the highly textured material he found suitable to visualize the philosophic dimension of this ancient myth. The artist entered into a dialogue with the material, and manipulated chance advanced to a compositional priniciple.
The working process with corrugated paper alone implies a labyrinth approach, the artist said. He defaced the smooth outer surface of the corrugated paperboard, gashed traces into it, cut elements out of the top layer and pasted these cardboards shreds back again. Because of the damage to the upper cardboard-colored base paper, the corrugated and lighter-colored middle layer becomes a pictorial element. Gashes turn into canyon-like grooves. Shreds of the cardboard base paper come together to form almost three-dimensional conglomerations.
Graphic linear structures and many forms of elevations and hollows spread across the picture plane. Surfaces of tranquil, untreated cardboard alternate with compositional structures of inextricable density. The way light falls onto the serially scattered structures and planes underlines the tension between them. The light is what moulds and defines the plasticity of the wall reliefs and allows fine grades of color differentiation to become visible.

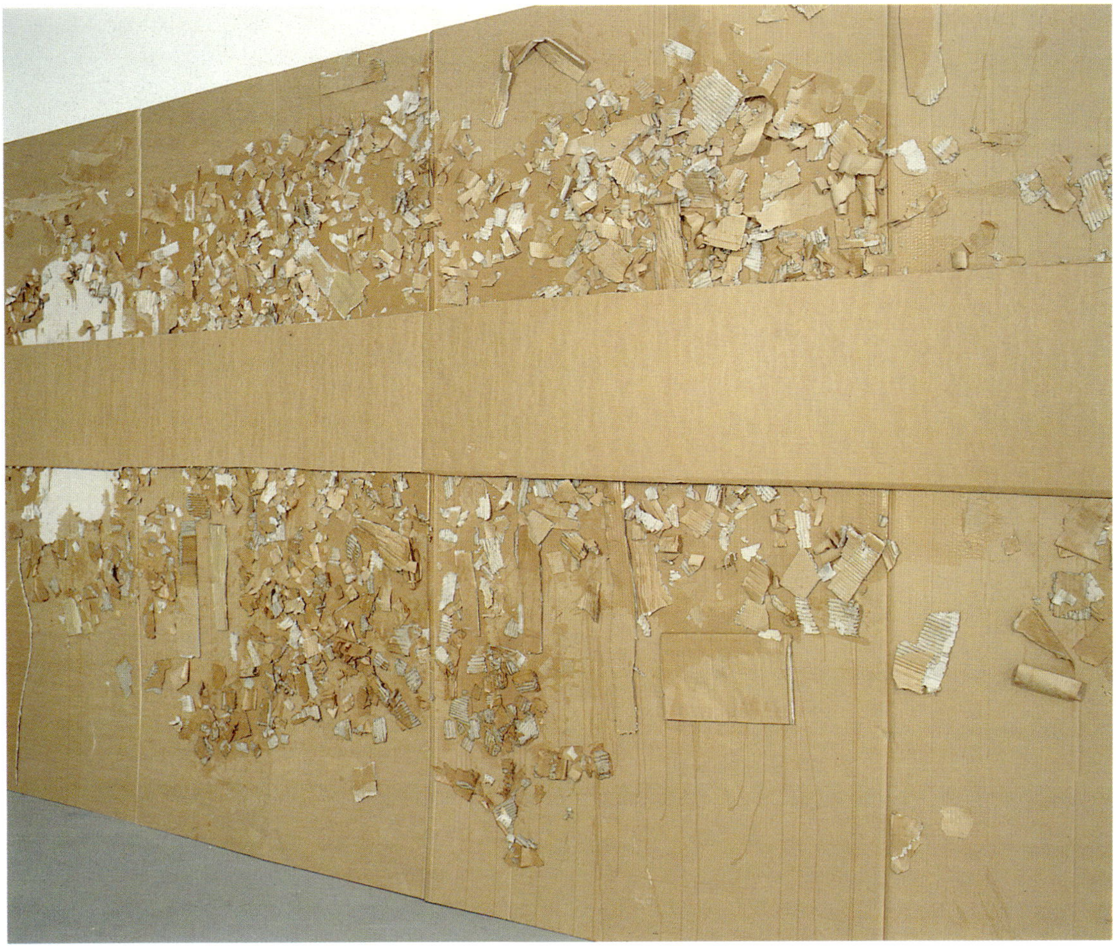

Milko Pavlov: Labyrinth, 1994. Wellpappenkarton. 200 x 900 x 100 cm (Ausschnitt) /
Milko Pavlov: Labyrinth, 1994. Corrugated paper. 200 x 900 x 100 cm (detail)

A. R. Penck

1939 in Dresden geboren, lebt in Dublin, Düsseldorf und New York 1956/57 nach Ablehnung zum Kunststudium an der Hochschule für Bildende Künste, Dresden, Studium an der dortigen Abendschule 1980 Ausreise in die Bundesrepublik Deutschland, läßt sich in Lörsfeld/Kerpen bei Köln nieder 1988 Berufung zum Professor an die Kunstakademie Düsseldorf Ausstellungen (Auswahl): 1968 Galerie Werner, Köln 1970 Museum Haus Lange, Krefeld 1975 Kunsthalle Bern 1981 Kunsthalle Köln 1988 Neue Nationalgalerie Berlin

1939 born in Dresden, lives in Dublin, Düsseldorf and New York **1956/57** after he is rejected at the Hochschule für Bildende Künste, Dresden, goes to night school there **1980** moves to the Federal Republic of Germany and settles in Kerpen near Cologne **1988** appointed professor at the Kunstakademie Düsseldorf **exhibitions (selection): 1968** Galerie Michael Werner, Cologne **1970** Museum Haus Lange, Krefeld **1975** Kunsthalle Bern **1981** Kunsthalle Cologne **1988** Neue Nationalgalerie Berlin

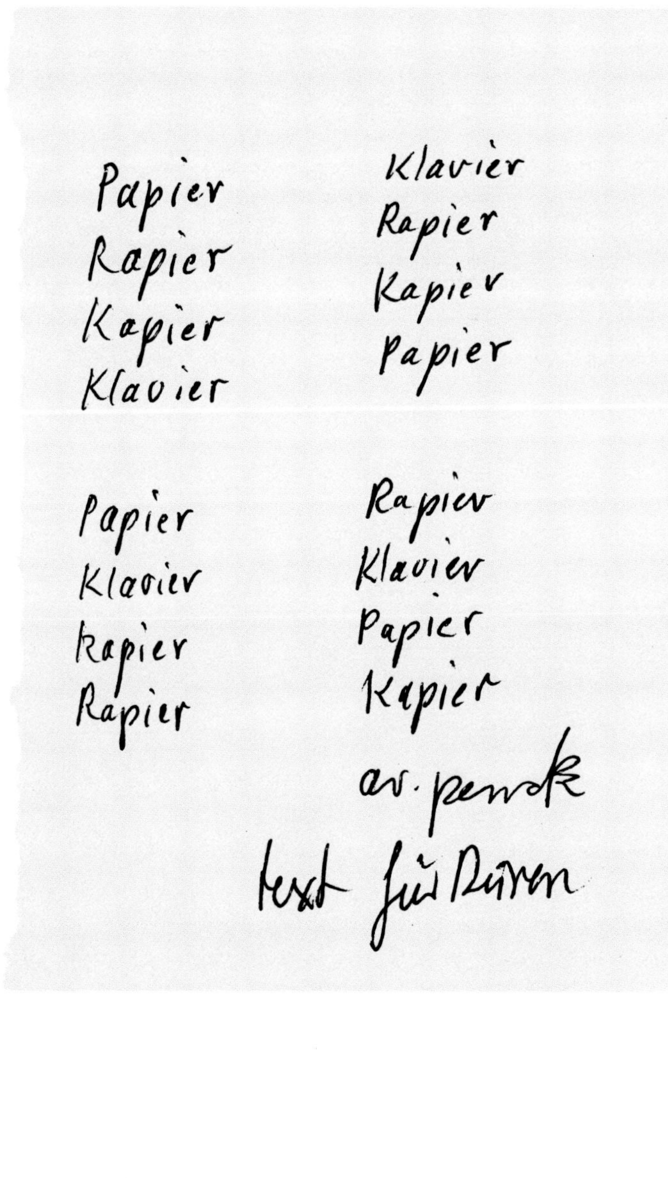

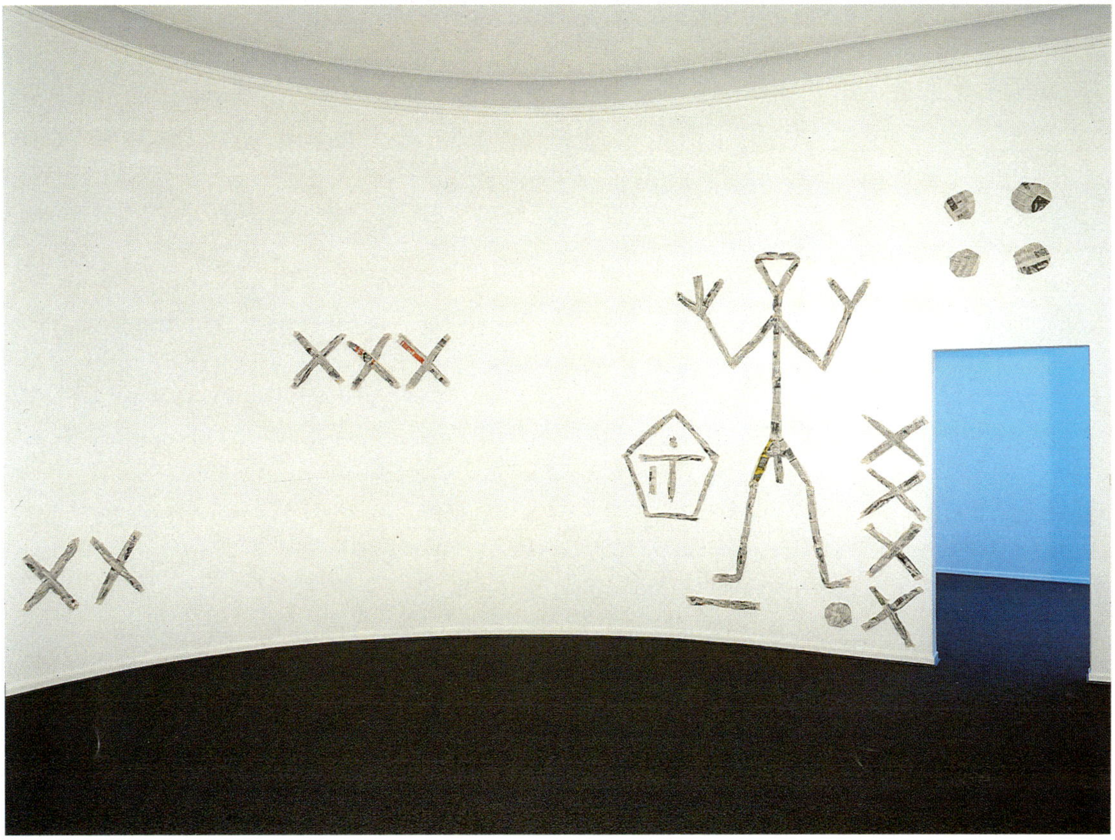

A. R. Penck: Neue Logik 17. 5. 94., 1994. Rauminstallation aus geknüllten Zeitungen. Raumgröße 680 x 680 cm /
A. R. Penck: New Logic 17 / 5 / 94., 1994. Installation with crumpled newspapers. Dimensions 680 x 680 cm

Michael Petry

1960 in El Paso, Texas, geboren, lebt seit 1981 in London bis 1981 Studium der Mathematik und bildenden Kunst an der Rice University, Houston/Texas 1982 Gründung der Media Arts Group 1990 gründet zusammen mit Nicolas de Oliveira und Nicola Oxley das Museum of Installation in London 1994 erscheint die gemeinsame Veröffentlichung ‚Installation Art' Installationen: 1982 Air Gallery, London 1983 Electrum Gallery, London 1983 Electrum and Aspects Gallery 1986 Coracle Gallery, London 1988 Slaughterhouse Gallery, London 1989 Ornamenta 1, Pforzheim 1990 Museum of Installation, London 1991 Galerie Mangisch, Zürich 1992 James Hockney Gallery, Farnham 1993 Biennale Venedig – Atlantis Gallery, London – Sydenham Hill Woods, London 1994 Kunst- und Ausstellungshalle der Bundesrepublik Deutschland, Bonn

1960 born in El Paso/Texas, lives in London since 1981 to 1981 studies mathematics and the visual arts at Rice University, Houston/Texas 1982 founds Media Arts Group 1990 founds together with Nicolas de Oliveira and Nicola Oxley the Museum of Installation in London 1994 joint publication 'Installation Art' is edited installations: 1982 Air Gallery, London 1983 Electrum Gallery, London 1983 Electrum and Aspects Gallery 1986 Coracle Gallery, London 1988 Slaughterhouse Gallery, London 1989 Ornamenta 1, Pforzheim 1990 Museum of Installation, London 1991 Galerie Mangisch, Zurich 1992 James Hockney Gallery, Farnham 1993 Biennale Venice – Atlantis Gallery, London – Sydenham Hill Woods, London 1994 Kunst- und Ausstellungshalle der Bundesrepublik Deutschland, Bonn

‚Der Schneesturm'

Ein Raum ist mit einem Schneesturm aus kleinen weißen und durchsichtigen beweglichen Papierstückchen gefüllt, die von der Decke herunterhängen und den Umriß eines großen, offenen Buches bilden. Ein Videogerät projiziert Bilder auf das Papier und die rückwärtige Wand. Jedes Papierstück wurde mit der Hand in ovale Stücke gerissen; die Form ähnelt der eines Fernsehpixels. Das durchsichtige Azetat wurde grob in die gleiche Form geschnitten. Beim Papier handelt es sich um Rives Druckpapier, das normalerweise für Radierungen oder Kunstbücher und -editionen in limitierten Auflagen verwendet wird.
Beim Eintreten sehen die Besucher zwei pyramidenartige Formen, die in den Raum hineinwachsen und als Bildteile „gelesen" werden können. Das Zentrum des Schneesturms liegt in der Dunkelheit, so wie es auch in der Natur wäre. Und wie bei

'The Blizzard'

A room is filled with a blizzard of small white and clear pieces of floating paper hung from the ceiling in the shape of a huge open book. A video is projected onto the paper and the back wall. Each piece of paper is handtorn to an oval shape similar to that of a television pixel. The clear acetate is roughly cut to a similar shape. The paper is Rives printing paper, commonly used for etchings and for fine art publications of limited edition books.
As viewers enter they see two pyramid shapes that grow larger in the room, it is possible to "read" part of the image. The centre of the blizzard is in darkness, as it would be in nature, and like a book, open it contains accessible information, while closed it is solely an object. The Blizzard itself has information (the video) projected onto it, and at the same time the internal paper pixels are in the shadow of the ones in front of them (as are those

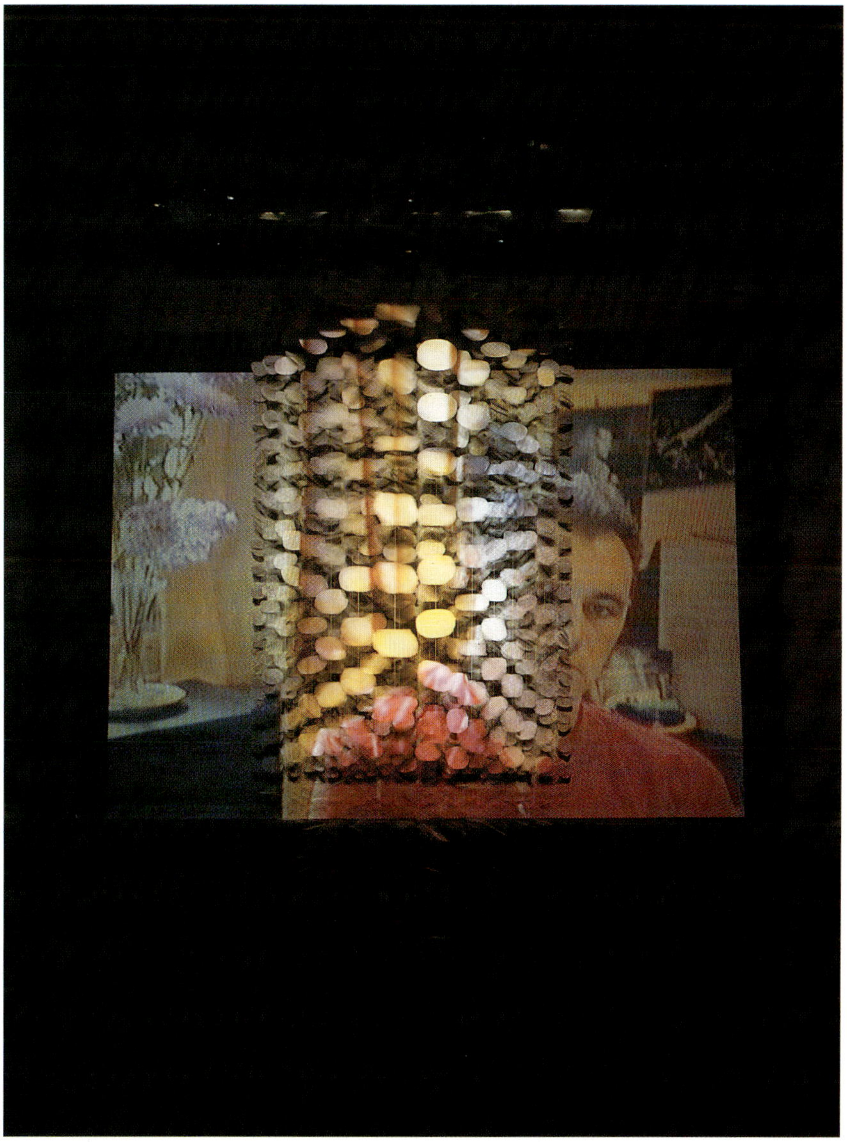

Michael Petry: Der Schneesturm, 1994. Rauminstallation. 680 x 980 cm /
Michael Petry: The Blizzard, 1994. Installation. 680 x 980 cm

einem Buch erhält man beim Öffnen Zugang zu Informationen, während es im geschlossenen Zustand ein Objekt ist. Der Schneesturm selbst projiziert Informationen (das Video), gleichzeitig befinden sich die hinteren Papierpixel im Schatten der vor ihnen liegenden (wie bei den Seiten eines Buches, die gerade nicht aufgeschlagen sind – sie existieren in dem Moment als Potential und Objekt). Der Betrachter kann die schwebenden Pixel als Objekt und Informationsträger sehen. Je weiter der Besucher in den Raum hineingeht, um so größer wirkt die jeweilige Videoprojektion auf das einzelne Pixel. So wird der Effekt erzielt, daß die Papierpixel wie Juwelen oder ein Sturm aus Licht aussehen.

Wenn man auf einen Fernsehschirm guckt, sind die Pixel hinter einer durchsichtigen Glasscheibe versteckt – ähnlich den Azetatpixeln. Das Licht dringt durch sie hindurch, wird aber auch in den Raum zurückgeworfen. Die Qualität vervielfältigt sich in Form und Inhalt. Klar bleibt nur, das Papier – ältestes Mittel des bequemen Informationsaustauschs – immer noch das haltbarste, ausdauerndste und möglicherweise sinnlichste Material ist. In Stein gemeißelte Information ist zwar widerstandsfähiger, kann jedoch für den heutigen Transfer von Informationen und Ideen nicht genutzt werden. Eine Computerdiskette ermöglicht den simplen Zugriff auf weltumfassende Daten, aber schon ein kurzes Zusammentreffen mit einem kleinen Magneten mag die mühevollen Anstrengungen von Jahren einfach ausradieren. Das Gefühl, schweres Papier in Händen zu halten, das Umdrehen einer Seite beim Lesen eines Buches, ein tränenbefleckter oder parfümierter Brief, der das ganze Sein der Geliebten in sich trägt, kann durch die elektronische Post oder das Flackern eines Computerbildschirms niemals ersetzt werden. Die Berührung, die Spur der letzten Berührung, der letzten Person, die das Papier angefaßt hat, diese Linie, die Zeugnis ablegt, ist nicht im Herzen einer Maschine zu finden. Für den Menschen ist Schreiben eine der größten Gaben der Zivilisation, grundlegend für

pages in a book that are not the ones opened to – they exist at that moment as potential, and as object). The viewer can see the suspended pixels and information carrier. The further the viewer is in the room, the bigger the actual video projection of individual pixels is. The efect of this is to make the paper pixels look like jewels, or a blizzard of light.

When one looks at a television screen the pixels are hidden behind a clear glass layer that is similar to the acetate pixels. The light passes through these, but also is reflected back into the room. The duality is duplicated in form and content. What remains clear is that paper, the oldest means of conveniently transporting information, remains the most durable, enduring, and possibly the most sensual. While information carved in stone is more durable, it cannot readly be used in the contemporary setting for the transfer of information and ideas. A computer disk may offer ease of global access, but only a brief encounter with a small magnetic field can wipe out years of effort. The feel of heavy paper in the hand, a page turned over while reading a book, a tear-stained or perfumed letter with the essence of a lover, can never be replaced by E-mail, or light on a computer screen. The touch, the trace of the last touch, the trace of the last person who touched that paper, that trill of molecular evidence can never be found inside the heart of a machine. It ist the human element that makes writing one of the greatest gifts of civilization, it is the cornerstone of all understanding. We "read" a picture, we even "read" a situation, is it no wonder that the written trace, the signature, the scratchings of culture hold the greatest allure for the homo mentis. The Electronic Age brings with it many gifts, as did the age of Enlightenment, but each are tempered by their faults. The book and the Power Book (this text was written on a Mac 165) both have a place, but time will tell which was more powerful.

There is a certain joy to be had standing lost in the center of a storm, to feel nature around one, to be a

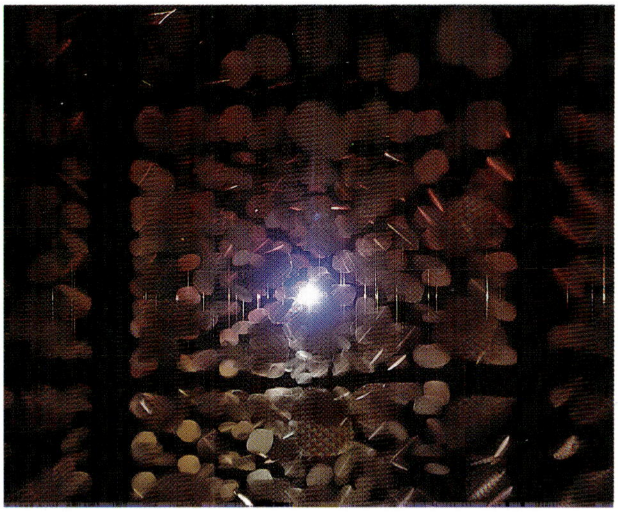

Michael Petry: Der Schneesturm, 1994. Rauminstallation. 680 x 980 cm /
Michael Petry: The Blizzard, 1994. Installation. 680 x 980 cm

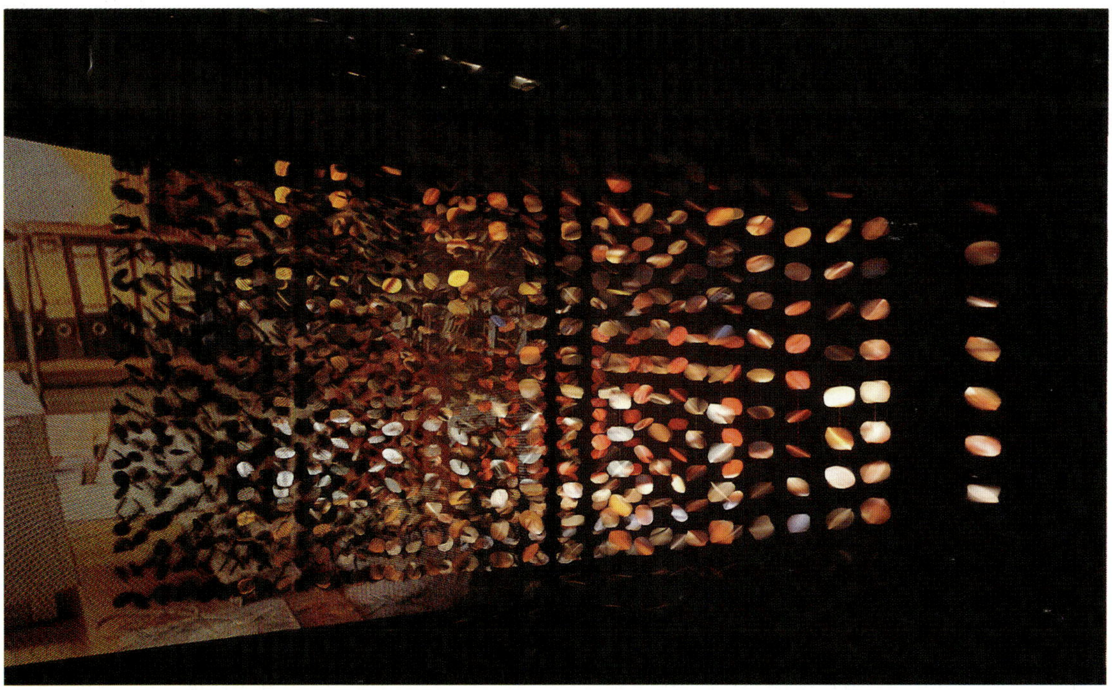

Michael Petry: Der Schneesturm, 1994. Rauminstallation. 680 x 980 cm (Ausschnitt) /
Michael Petry: The Blizzard, 1994. Installation. 680 x 980 cm (detail)

unser gesamtes Verstehen. Wir „lesen“ ein Bild, wir „lesen“ sogar eine Situation, daher ist es nicht verwunderlich, daß der Schriftzug, die Unterschrift, das Geschriebene einen sehr großen Reiz für den Homo mentis darstellen. So wie die Ära der Aufklärung bringt das elektronische Zeitalter viele Vorteile – beide besitzen aber auch ihre Fehler. Das Buch und das Power Book – dieser Text wurde auf einem Mac 166 geschrieben – haben beide ihren Platz; die Zeit wird zeigen, welches von beiden mehr Kraft hat.

Es kann schön sein, allein in der Mitte eines Sturms zu stehen, um sich herum die Natur zu fühlen, als Teil von ihr und dennoch getrennt – die Verlorenheit im Schneesturm gibt einem die wahre Gewißheit darüber, wie es ist, lebendig zu sein.

Michael Petry

part, and yet apart; to be lost in the blizzard is truly to know what it is to be alive.

Michael Petry

Video:
Eine Reihe von unglücklichen Zufällen lenkt einen jungen Mann von seinem Versuch ab, ein Gedicht von W. H. Auden abzuschreiben. Die Technik läßt ihn immer wieder im Stich, und am Ende taucht er den Computer gegen einen Füller, Tinte und altmodisches Schreibpapier aus. Videofilm von Raymond O'Daly
Soundtrack:
Die Partitur sieht die Stimme von Mark Rylance vor, der das Gedicht ‚Ode to Terminus‘ (Ode an den Endpunkt) liest; Musik von Gavin Greenaway und John Powell
Fotografie:
Edward Woodman
Unser spezieller Dank geht an: Berthold Bell, Peter Benedict, Nicolas de Oliveira, Leo Flynn, Juliane Jung, Scott Mason Morris und Robert Smith

Video:
A series of mishaps drives a young man to distraction as he attempts to copy a poem by W. H. Auden. Technology keeps breaking down and in the end he discards the computer for pen, ink and old fashioned writing paper. Video photography by Raymond O'Daly
Soundtrack:
The musical score will include the voice of Mark Rylance reading the poem 'Ode to Terminus'; music by Gavin Greenaway and John Powell
Still photography:
Edward Woodman
Special thanks to: Berthold Bell, Peter Benedict, Nicolas de Oliveira, Leo Flynn, Juliane Jung, Scott Mason Morris, and Robert Smith

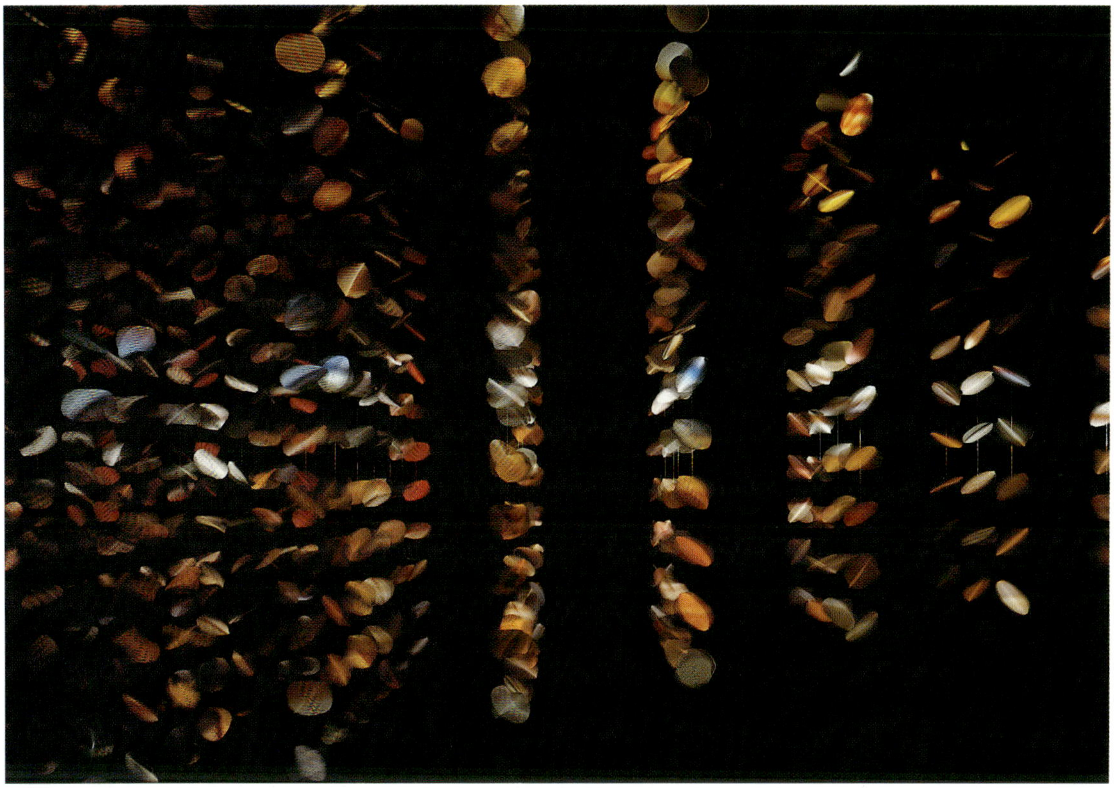

Michael Petry: Der Schneesturm, 1994. Rauminstallation. 680 x 980 cm /
Michael Petry: The Blizzard, 1994. Installation. 680 x 980 cm

Otto Piene

1928 geboren in Laasphe, Westfalen, lebt in Groton/Massachusetts, und Düsseldorf 1948–57 Studium der Kunst, Kunsterziehung und Philosophie in München, Düsseldorf und Köln 1957 zusammen mit Mack Gründer der Gruppe ZERO 1951–64 unterrichtet an der Modeschule Düsseldorf 1964 Gastprofessur für Malerei an der University of Pennsylvania, Philadelphia 1972–93 Professor für Umwelt-Kunst am Massachusetts Institute of Technology, Cambridge/Massachusetts 1993 Professor Emeritus seit 1974 Direktor des Center for Advanced Visual Studies am Massachusetts Institute of Technology, Cambridge/Massachusetts Ausstellungen und Events: 1959 Galerie Schmela, Düsseldorf 1965 Howard Wise Gallery, New York 1972 Olympia Regenbogen, XX. Olympische Spiele in München 1976 documenta 6 mit ‚Centerbeam' (CAVS/MIT) 1981 Direktor SKY ART Conference: 1981, Massachusetts Institute of Technology, Cambridge/Massachusetts 1982 Ars Electronica, Linz 1983 Stadt München 1986 Massachusetts Institute of Technology, Cambridge/Massachusetts 1990 Arttransition '90, Massachusetts Institute of Technology, Cambridge/Massachusetts

1928 born in Laasphe, Westphalia, lives in Groton/Massachusetts, and Düsseldorf **1948–57** studies art, art education and philosophy in Munich, Düsseldorf and Cologne **1957** founds the Group ZERO together with Mack **1951–64** lectures at the School of Fashion, Düsseldorf **1964** guest professor for painting at the University of Pennsylvania, Philadelphia **1972–93** professor for environment art at the Massachusetts Institute of Technology, Cambridge/Massachusetts **1993** professor emeritus **since 1974** director of the Center for Advanced Visual Studies at the Massachusetts Institute of Technology, Cambridge/Massachusetts **exhibitions and events: 1959** Galerie Schmela, Düsseldorf **1965** Howard Wise Gallery, New York **1972** Olympic Rainbow, XX. Olympic Games in Munich **1976** documenta 6, Kassel, with 'Centerbeam' (CAVS/MIT) **1981** director SKY ART Conference: 1981, Massachusetts Institute of Technology, Cambridge/Massachusetts **1982** Ars Electronica, Linz **1983** City of Munich **1986** Massachusetts Institute of Technology, Cambridge/Massachusetts **1990** Arttransition '90, Massachusetts Institute of Technology, Cambridge/Massachusetts

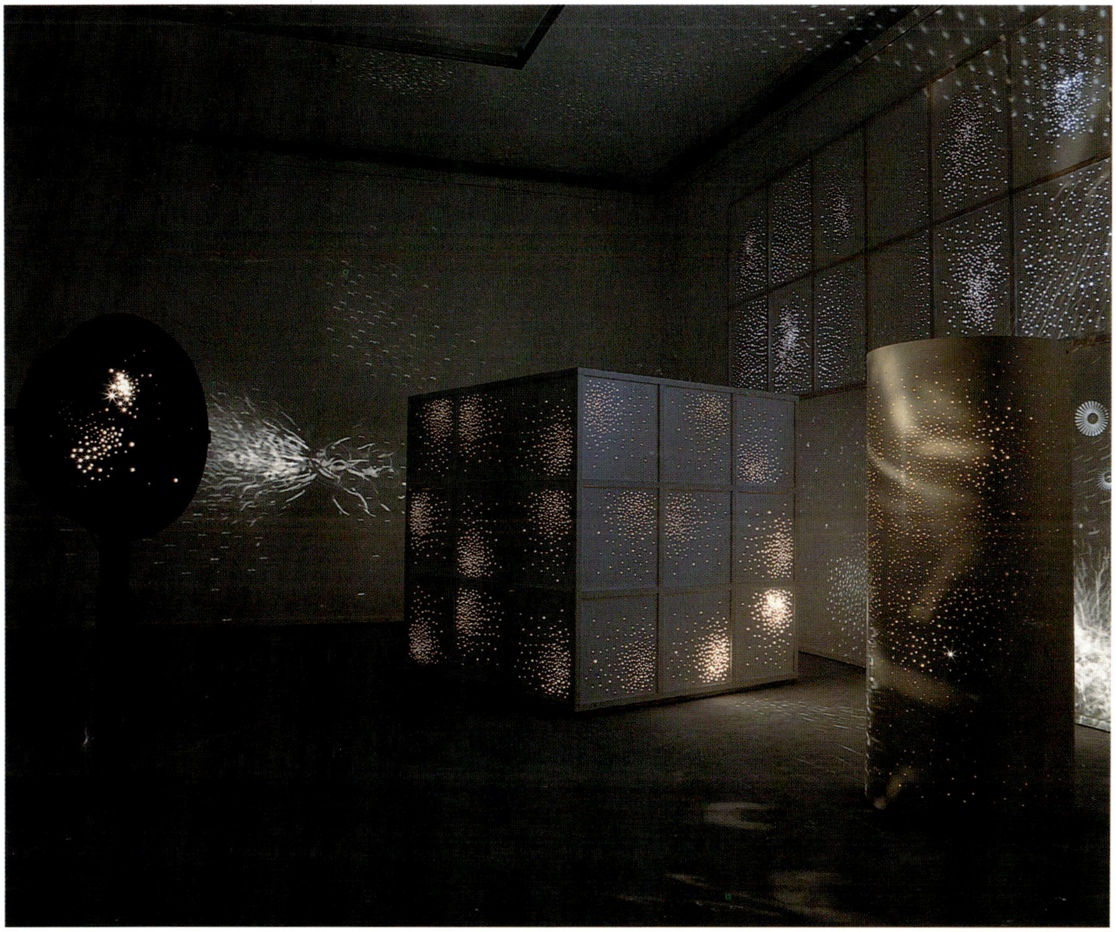

Otto Piene: Perforationen, 1979/94, 1961 und 1994. Rauminstallation. Perforierter Karton, Licht. Raumgröße 10,90 x 7,90 cm /
Otto Piene: Perforations, 1979/94, 1961 and 1994. Installation. Perforated cardboard, light. Dimensions 10.90 x 7.90 cm

Perforationen

Seit Beginn meiner Arbeit mit Licht als übergreifendem Medium haben Papiermateriale als Träger und Vermittler mitgespielt – seit den Mittfünfziger Jahren. Die Rastersiebe für die Rasterbilder waren auch Lichtsiebe fürs Lichtballett und Rauchsiebe für Rauchzeichnungen.
Bei den Rauchzeichnungen verkörpern die weißen Papierbögen Licht und Raum: Bei meinen Feuergouachen auf Karton findet ein „heißer Dialog“ statt zwischen brennender Farbe und der „Weißheit“ des Papiers. Von der Hitze angegriffen, wird Papier Brandfarbe und blättert ab zu organischer Form.
Mein Lichtraum ‚Perforationen‘ thematisiert „Licht und Papier“ (wie Lampions ‚Papier und Feuer‘ und Drachen ‚Papier und Wind‘ ausweisen). Zwei Arten von Licht sind im Spiel: Sonnenlicht/Tageslicht dringt durch die Fensterkästen mit Rastersieben und wandert mit der Erdbewegung zur Sonne „durch den Raum“. „Kunstlicht“ aus den Lichtkuben und -plastiken wandert entsprechend der internen Rotation. Es entsteht ein Lichtzelt mit sich überschneidenden und durchdringenden, langsamen Lichtschwärmen. Der Ton kommt von Bändern meiner alten Lichtballette von 1959 und 1961. Jedes der Zehntausende Rasterlöcher ist eine Linse für Lochkameraprojektionen. Die Papierkörper sind Schachteln, die Licht moderieren. Der Raum ‚Perforationen‘ ist ein Modelluniversum im Karton aus Karton.

Otto Piene

Perforations

Since the beginning of my work with light as a pervasive medium, paper as support and mediator has played a role – from the middle of the 50s. The template screens for making the stencil paintings were at the same time light screens for the light ballet and smoke screens for smoke drawings.
In the smoke drawings the white sheets of paper are incarnations of light and space. In my fire gouaches on cardboard, a “hot dialogue” takes place between burning color and the “white-wise” paper. Attacked by the heat, the paper becomes brand-marked and flakes away to an organic form.
My lightroom ‘Perforations’ thematizes “light and paper” (as lanterns do ‘paper and fire’ and kites ‘paper and wind‘). Two kinds of light are at work here: sunlight/daylight penetrates casement windows through template screens and wanders with the earth's movement around the sun “through the room”. “Artlight” from the light cubes and light sculpture wanders according to internal rotation. So a tent of light originates: of slow swarms of light that overlap and interpenetrate. The sound I use is that of tapes from my old light ballets from 1959 and 1961. Each of the ten thousand template holes is a lens for pinhole camera projections. The paper cubes moderate the light. The room ‘Perforations’ is a paper universe made of paper.

Otto Piene

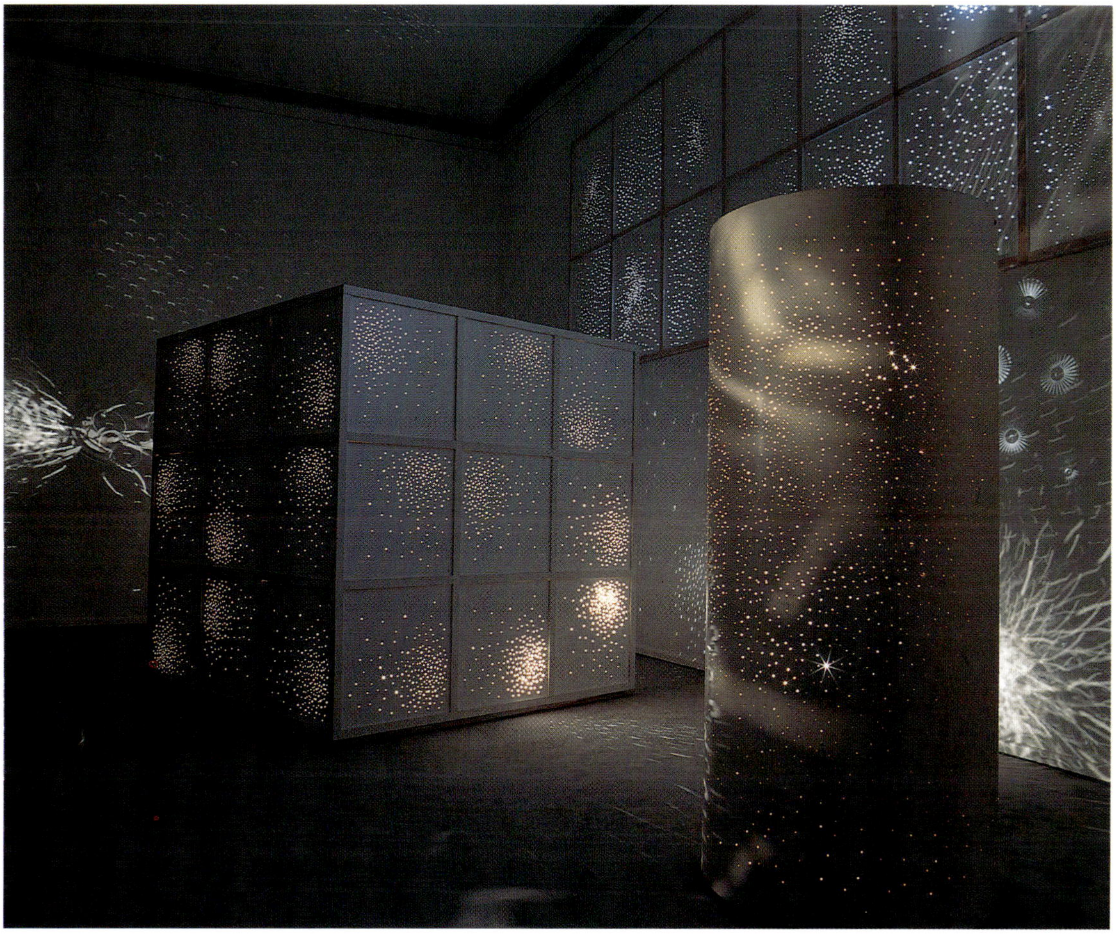

Otto Piene: Perforationen, 1979/94 und 1994. Rauminstallation. Perforierter Karton, Licht. Raumgröße 10,90 x 7,90 cm /
Otto Piene: Perforations, 1979/94 and 1994. Installation. Perforated cardboard, light. Dimensions: 10.90 x 7.90 cm

Dmitri A. Prigov

1940 **geboren in Moskau, lebt in Moskau** Einzel- und Gruppenausstellungen (Auswahl): 1987 **documenta** 8, **Kassel** 1988 **Kunstmuseum Bern – Krings-Ernst Galerie, Köln** 1989 **Struve Gallery, Chicago – Gallery of Contemporary Art, Saint Louis/Missouri – Institute of Contemporary Art, London** 1991 **Institute of Contemporary Art, Boston/Massachusetts** 1991 **Galerie Inter Art, Berlin – Krings-Ernst Galerie, Köln – Martin-Gropius-Bau, Berlin** 1992 **Groninger Museum**

1940 born in Moscow, lives in Moscow **solo and group exhibitions (selection): 1987** documenta 8, Kassel **1988** Kunstmuseum Bern – Krings-Ernst Galerie, Cologne **1989** Struve Gallery, Chicago – Gallery of Contemporary Art, Saint Louis/Missouri – Institute of Contemporary Art, London **1991** Institute of Contemporary Art, Boston/Massachusetts **1991** Galerie Inter Art, Berlin – Krings-Ernst Galerie, Cologne – Martin-Gropius-Bau, Berlin **1992** Groninger Museum

„Das Wichtige ist, den Namen von Dingen zu wissen. Die Kraft liegt in den Namen. Bezeichne eine Sache richtig, und sie wird dir dienen. Russische Kultur neigt zu einer solchen Magie – sie legt großen Wert auf Namen."

Dmitri Prigov, Interview mit Viktor Misiano in ‚Arts and Letters', in: Contemporanea, New York, Jan./Febr. 1989

"What's important is knowing the names of things. Power lies in names: call a thing by its true name and it will accomplish everything for you itself. Russian culture is, in general, inclined toward magic of this sort – it places great emphasis on names."

Dmitri Prigov, Interview with Viktor Misiano in 'Arts and Letters', in: Contemporanea, New York, Jan./Febr. 1989

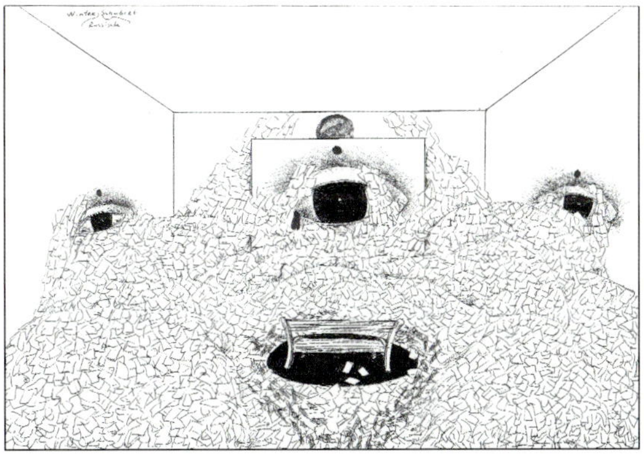

Dmitri A. Prigov: Winter Russische Reise, 1994. Skizze zur Rauminstallation mit Zeitungen. Zeichnungen. Gartenbank zu Schuberts ‚Winterreise'. Raumgröße: 10,90 x 7,90 cm /
Dmitri A. Prigov: Winter Russian Journey, 1994. Sketch for Installation with newspapers, drawings, garden bench on Schubert's 'Winterreise'. Dimensions 10.90 x 7.90 cm

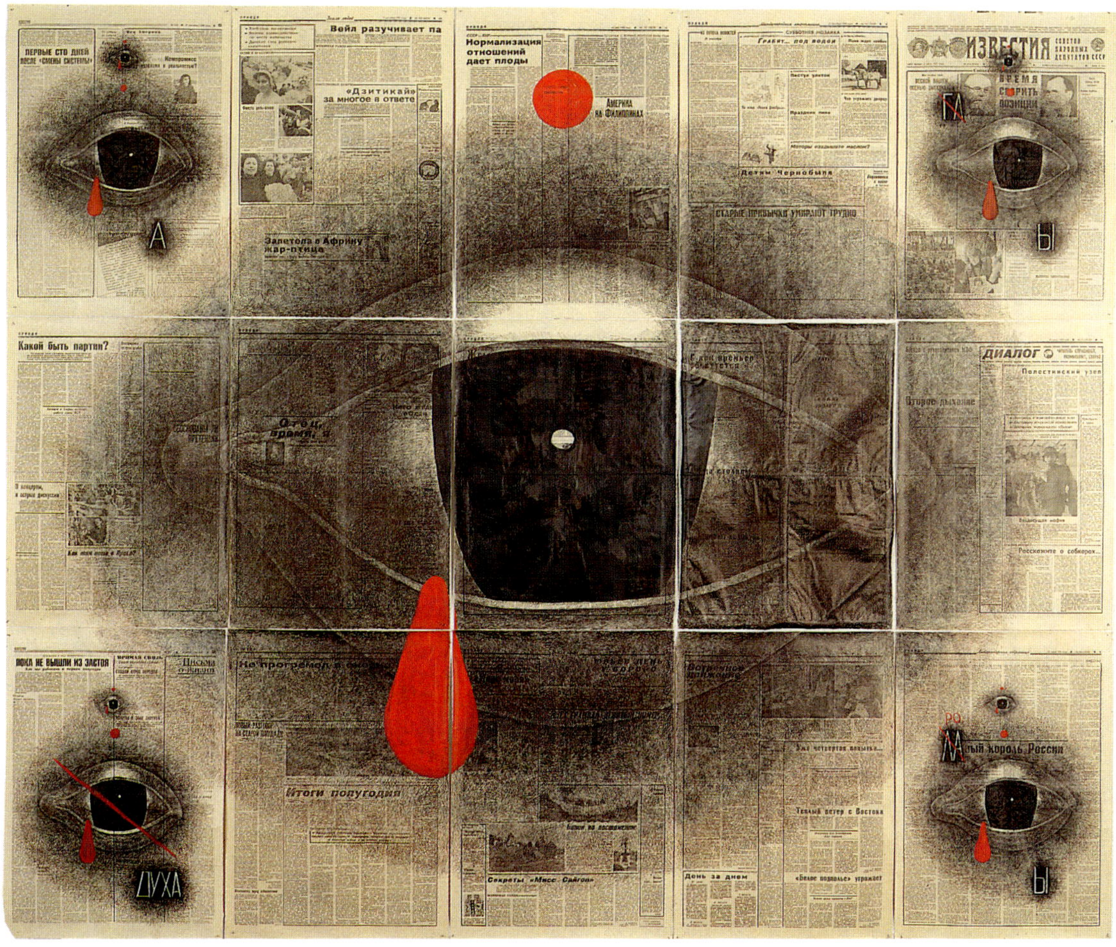

Dmitri A. Prigov: Glasa Asy, Ducha Grasy, 1991. Tusche, Acryl, Zeitungspapier. 178 x 210 cm /
Dmitri A. Prigov: Glasa Asy, Ducha Grasy, 1991. Ink, acrylic, newspaper. 178 x 210 cm

Reviva Regev

1936 geboren in Tel Aviv/Israel, lebt in Herzlya/Israel, unterrichtet am Art Teachers College, Tel Aviv 1993 Arbeitsaufenthalt in Japan Ausstellungen und Kurator-Tätigkeit (Auswahl): 1988 Brooklyn Museum, New York 1990 ‚Boundary of Peace' – Israeli-Palestinian Art Encounter 1991 Hara Museum of Contemporary Art, Tokyo The National Museum of Contemporary Art, Seoul/Korea

1936 born in Tel Aviv/Israel, lives in Herzlya/Israel, lectures at the Art Teachers College, Tel Aviv 1993 work project in Japan exhibitions and curatorship (selection): 1988 Brooklyn Museum, New York 1990 'Boundary of Peace' – Israeli-Palestinian Art Encounter 1991 Hara Museum of Contemporary Art, Tokyo – The National Museum of Contemporary Art, Seoul/Korea

In ihrer Installation für Düren 1994 mit dem Titel ‚Die opsimistische Urne' strömt Wasser aus einem „himmlischen" Krug in eine riesige „erderne" schwarze Urne aus Teerpappe. ‚Die opsimistische Urne' verbindet Trauer und Hoffnung.

Der Prozeß des Lebens, der Geburt, des Todes, verhält sich wie eine Urne, die sich davon abhält, für ihre Bestimmung zu symmetrisch, abgegrenzt und perfekt zu werden. Die „menschliche" Urne – die Unmöglichkeit, Reinheit ohne Veränderungen zu bewahren – wird in Reviva Regevs Arbeiten durch ihre Vorliebe für vergängliche Materialien transportiert. Die Zeitlichkeit impliziert Organisches, welches im Zeitpunkt seiner Blüte bereits den Verfall in sich dokumentiert – einen Verfall, der das gleiche Mitgefühl für Menschlichkeit einfordert: Das ist Reviva Regevs bildhauerische Plattform.

Einige Künstler konzentrieren sich auf eine spirituelle, kosmische, ideale Welt, während andere auf das Menschliche auf der Erde blicken. Reviva Regev gehört zu den letzteren. Sie leugnet nicht die Reinheit, die in dieser Installation durch das vom Himmel „fallende" Wasser verkörpert wird; klar und rein, mit einem Heiligenschein aus Licht. Aber sie unterstreicht die menschliche Identifikation mit dem leidenden Wesen der Urne.

Effie Carmel

In her installation for Düren 1994 – 'The Opsimistic Urn' – water pours from a "heavenly" jar into a giant "earthly" black urn made of tar paper. 'The Opsimistic Urn' combines sadness and hope.

The process of life, birth, death, is stored in an urn where it is kept from becoming too symmetrical, sharp, perfect for its own good. The impossibility of stabilizing purity in the human urn is conveyed in Reviva Regev's works through her preoccupation with perishable materials. Corroding temporality, everything organic whose very flowering is a manifestation of its descent into decay, a descent which appeals for the very same sympathy towards its humanness: this is Reviva Regev's sculptural platform.

Some artists concentrate on a spiritual, cosmic, ideal world, while others focus on what is human on earth. Reviva Regev is one of the latter. It is not that she denies purity, which is embodied in this installation in the water "falling" from heaven lucid and pure, haloed in light. But she underlines the human identification with the suffering nature of the jar.

Effie Carmel

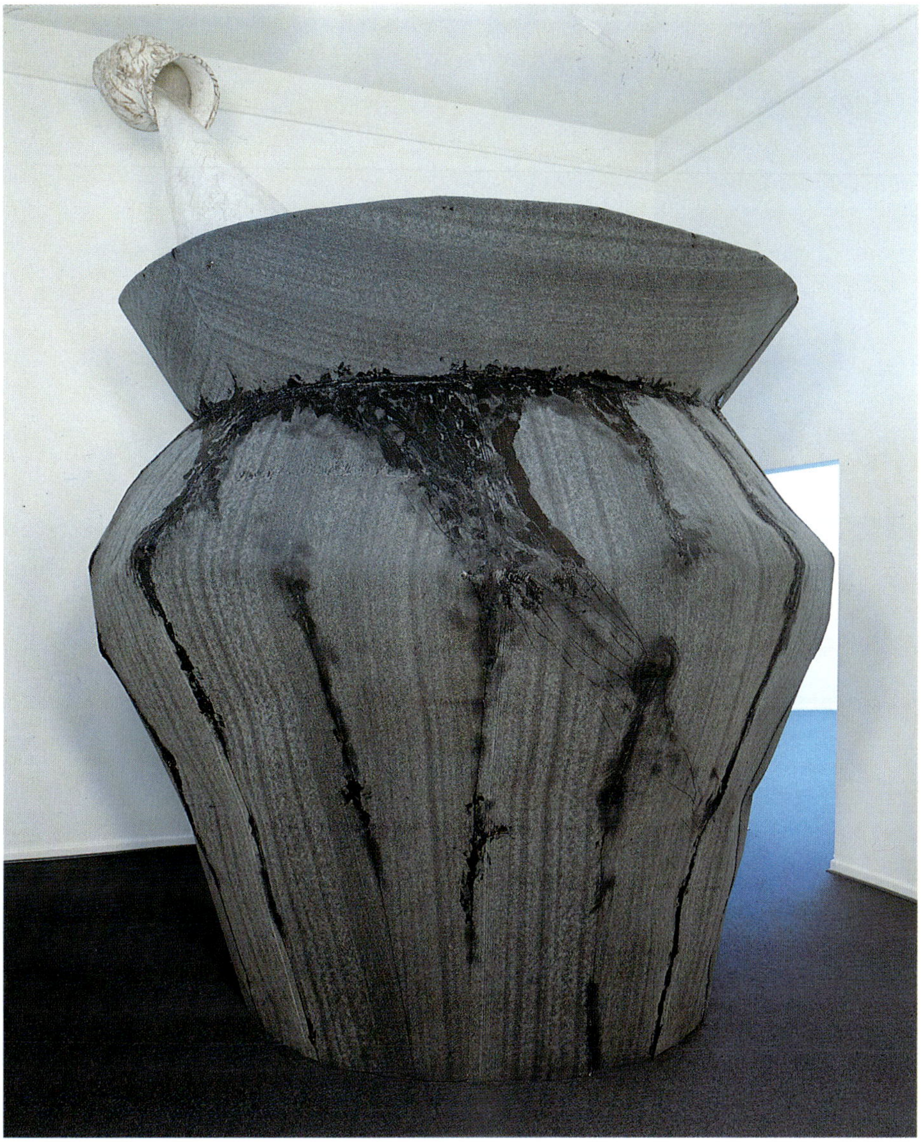

Reviva Regev: Die opsimistische Urne, 1994. Teerpappe und geformtes Japanpapier. 430 x 250 x 250 cm /
Reviva Regev: The Opsimistic Urn, 1994. Tar paper, moulded Japan paper. 430 x 250 x 250 cm

Eun Nim Ro

1946 **geboren in Chun-Zu/Korea** 1973–79 **Studium an der Hochschule für bildende Künste, Hamburg** 1990 **Professur an der Fachhochschule für Gestaltung, Hamburg** Stipendien: 1975–79 **DAAD Stipendium** 1982 **Freie und Hansestadt Hamburg Kunstfonds Bonn** 1984 **Barkenhoff-Stipendium, Worpswede** 1985 **BDI-Förderpreis** Einzelausstellungen (Auswahl): 1979 **Galerie vor Ort, Hamburg** 1986 **Het Apollohuis, Eindhoven** 1986 **Won Gallery, Seoul/Korea** 1987 **Davidson Gallery, Seattle/Washington** 1988 **Oldenburger Kunstverein** 1989 **Galerie Philippe Guimot, Brüssel** 1990 **Haus der Kulturen der Welt, Berlin** 1991 **Overbeck Gesellschaft, Lübeck** 1992 **Gallery Hyndai, Seoul/Korea** 1993 **Hordeland Kunstnersentrum, Bergen** 1993 **Gallery Lowe, New York**

1946 born in Chun-Zu/Korea **1973-79** studies at the Hochschule für bildende Künste, Hamburg **1990** professor at the Fachhochschule für Gestaltung, Hamburg **grants (selection): 1975–79** DAAD **1982** Freie und Hansestadt Hamburg – Kunstfonds Bonn **1984** Barkenhoff-Stipendium, Worpswede **1985** BDI-Förderpreis **solo exhibitions (selection): 1979** Galerie vor Ort, Hamburg **1986** Het Apollohuis, Eindhoven – Won Gallery, Seoul/Korea **1987** Davidson Gallery, Seattle/Washington **1988** Oldenburger Kunstverein **1989** Galerie Philippe Guimot, Brussels **1990** Haus der Kulturen der Welt, Berlin **1991** Overbeck Gesellschaft, Lübeck **1992** Gallery Hyndai, Seoul/Korea **1993** Hordeland Kunstnersentrum, Bergen **1993** Gallery Lowe, New York

Die Bewegung von Ruhe und Stille

Das Licht war der entscheidende Anstoß, daß Eun Nim Ro diesen Raum mit dem halbrunden Erker für sich wählte. Licht ist hier in einem fast metaphysischen Sinn gebraucht, denn es wird in der Installation weitgehend ausgesperrt; Papiere decken die Scheiben ab und lassen Helligkeit nur durch unregelmäßige Löcher zu.

Die Situation, die dadurch geschaffen ist, spiegelt zwei Momente aus der Erlebniswelt der Künstlerin wider: Kindheitserinnerungen und Erinnerungen an die erste Arbeitsphase nach Beendigung des Kunststudiums.

Papiere, wie sie Eun Nim Ro in ihrer künstlerischen Arbeit verwendet, sind in den 50er und 60er Jahren in Korea noch selbstverständlicher Teil des Alltags. Mit ihnen waren Türen und Fenster bespannt – sie ließen das Licht durch, gewährten aber weder Einblick noch Ausblick. Um „Einsicht" zu erlangen, mußte man mit dem nassen Finger ein kleines Loch

The movement of repose and stillness

It was the light that inspired Eun Nim Ro to choose this room with its semi-circular bay window. "Light" is here used in an almost metaphysical sense since it is restricted here to a minimum: paper covers the windows and allows in light through irregular holes.

The situation re-created here is a reflection on two moments in the life of the artist: memories from childhood and from her first phase of work after completing her art studies.

The type of paper that Eun Nim Ro uses in her art were still an unreflected part of everyday life in the Korea of the 50s and 60s. It curtained off doors and windows, allowing in light but no view out of or into the rooms. For "insight", you had to work a small hole into the paper with a wet finger. Rice paper is not only a tough, but also a pliable material. It is extremely tear-resistant and must therefore be "dissolved" in water. It was through such peepholes,

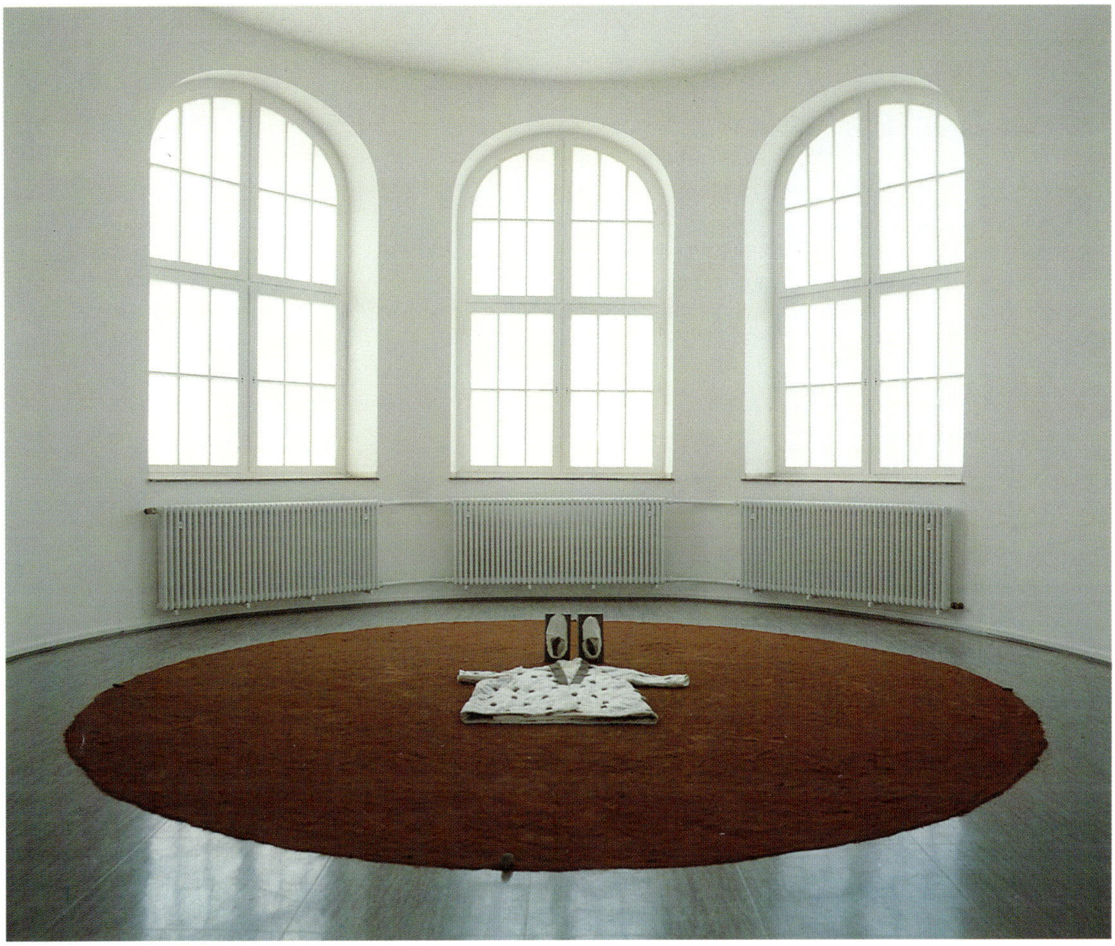

Eun Nim Ro: Meine Flügel sind meine Last, 1994. Rauminstallation. Ausschnitt. Reispapier, rote Tonerde. Durchmesser 470 cm /
Eun Nim Ro: My Wings Are My Burden, 1994. Installation. Detail. Rice paper, red alumina. Diameter 470 cm

in das Papier drehen. Das Reispapier ist ein sowohl zähes als auch weiches und biegsames Material. Es ist äußerst reißfest und muß deshalb mit Feuchtigkeit „aufgelöst“ werden. Durch diese „Gucklöcher“ wurde beispielsweise traditionell die Hochzeitsnacht beobachtet. Der Blick durch ein solches Loch verändert den Raumeindruck: Man nimmt den Raum gerundeter wahr, als er tatsächlicher ist; das Volumen wirkt dadurch besonders intensiv. Zugleich schwinden aber auch die Begrenzungen. Da sich in koreanischen Zimmern nur wenige Einrichtungsgegenstände befinden, hat man fast immer den Raum als „offenes“ Volumen vor sich, das weich und unbestimmt an Höhle und Weltkugel denken läßt.

Eun Nim Ro hat in ihrer Installation gewissermaßen den Innenraum akzentuiert. Die Löcher im Reispapier am Fenster sind nicht für das Herausschauen, sondern für das Hereinschauen gemacht – letzteres ist allerdings nicht real möglich, sondern nur als Projektion. Die Installation ist die Projektion eines Bildes nach innen, auf einen Innenraum. Der Realität wird dadurch die Wirklichkeit weitgehend abgesprochen.

Neben Malerei und Zeichnung hat sich die Künstlerin immer auch auf Installationen und performanceähnliche Aktionen eingelassen. Ihr Anteil, das Handeln, ist dabei wesentlich; es ist Zentrum und Verbindungsstück gleichermaßen. Das Ergebnis solchen Handelns ist wieder nicht mehr als ein „Spurenbild“, ein Erstarren der Bewegung. Das Handeln ist der Übergang innerhalb der Gegensätzlichkeit; es ist das, was Zufall und Ordnung verbindet.

Die Gegensätzlichkeit wird in dieser Rauminstallation sofort deutlich: In Opposition zum Licht der hellen, großen Erkerfenster hat die Künstlerin Erde und Steine gesetzt. Die konkrete, konzentrierte Materie steht zwar im Gegensatz zum Sphärischen des Lichts, aber durch ihre Position sind Erde und Steine wiederum auch das Zentrum, aus dem sich der Kreis entwickelt, dessen Ränder sich (als Fenster) dem Ungestalteten öffnen.

Erde, Fußstapfen, Kleid, Steine, Leben der Materie und Dasein des Menschen verbinden sich in diesen vier Teilen. Die Erde ist das Gedächtnis, das keinen

for example, that the wedding night was traditionally observed. A peep through such a hole changes the impression of space: a room appears rounder than it is, its volume especially intense. At the same time its boundaries disappear. Since there is little furniture in Korean rooms, you almost always find before you a space like an “open” volume, as soft and indeterminate as a cave or globe.

Eun Nim Ro has, so to speak, accentuated the interior of her installation. The holes in the rice paper over the windows have not been made for looking out, but for looking in, something not here possible in reality but only in the imagination. The installation is the projection of a picture turned inward onto an interior. What is actual has, for the most part, been denied reality.

Along with painting and drawing, however, the artist also mounts installations and performs actions. Her role, the action, in this is essential; it is both the center and the link. The result of her action is again no more than a “trace”, a fixing of movement. The action, itself the interface between the opposing forces, is what links chaos and order.

The opposition becomes immediately clear in this installation: as contrast to the light of the large, bright bay windows, the artist has placed earth and stones. Concrete, concentrated matter stands opposed to the sphere of light, but by their position the earth and stones are also the center out of which the circle develops, whose borders (as windows) open onto the unformed.

Earth, footprints, robe, stones – animated matter and the being of man are united in these four parts. The earth is the memory that never forgets a footstep, the robe is the re-possessed fetal membrane from within which man can still deny gravity. The material that Eun Nim Ro uses is a “symbol” of man’s origin: the paper from which the robe is made originates from the bark of the mulberry tree. He who dons the robe becomes a tree.

In this installation the robe is determined by the stones that hang from it; it is a “stone robe”. The

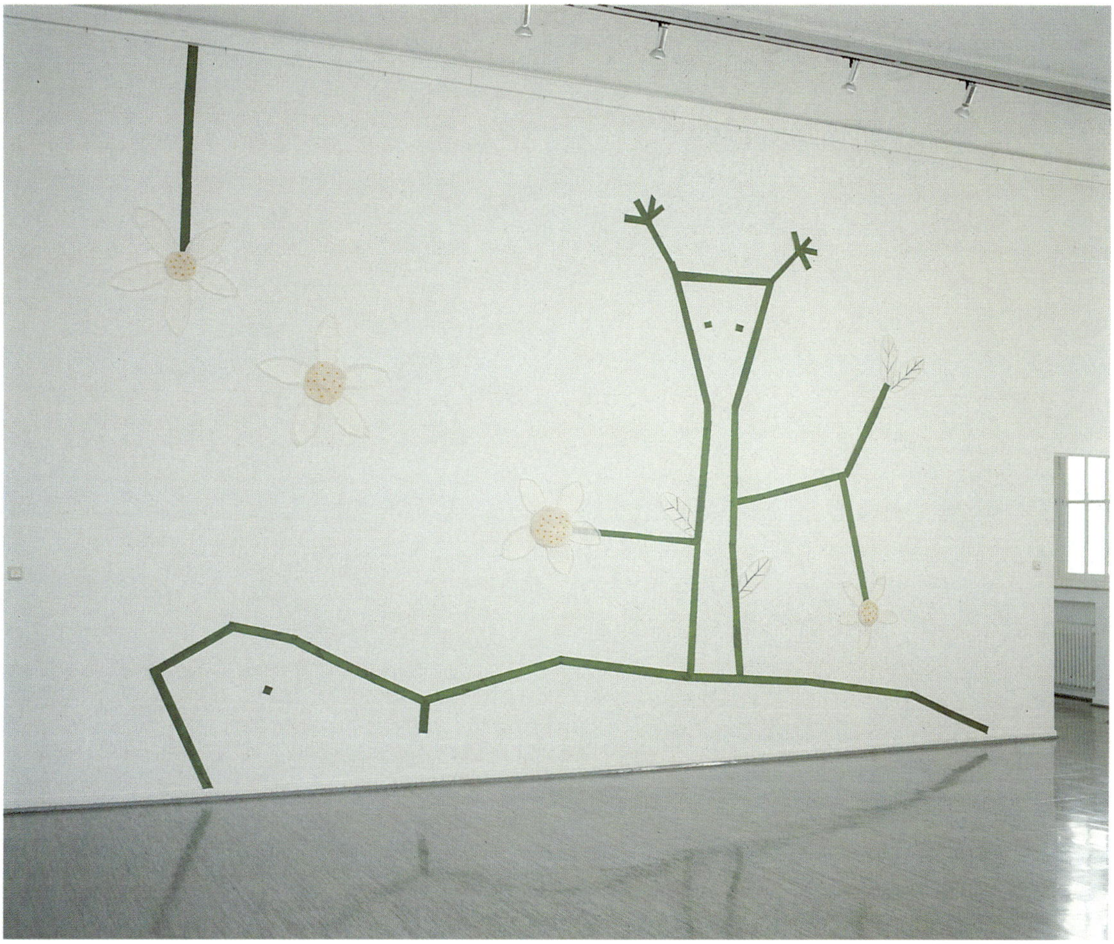

Eun Nim Ro: Meine Flügel sind meine Last, 1994. Rauminstallation. Ausschnitt. Reispapier. 460 x 750 cm /
Eun Nim Ro: My Wings Are My Burden, 1994. Installation. Detail. Rice paper. 460 x 750 cm

Schritt vergißt, das Kleid ist die zurückgewonnene Fruchtblase, in der der Mensch die Erdenschwere noch leugnen kann. Das Material, das Eun Nim Ro einsetzt, ist das „Bild" seines Ursprungs: Das Papier, aus dem das Kleid gemacht ist, hat ja seinen Ursprung in der Rinde des Maulbeerbaums. Der Mensch, der das Kleid trägt, wird zum Baum.

Das Kleid wird in dieser Installation bestimmt durch die an ihm hängenden Steine – es ist ein „Steinkleid". Die Steine machen das papierene Kleid zu einem Bild der Erdenschwere. Der Baum, der sich im Papier und zugleich auch im aufrechten Gang des Menschen offenbart, ist im Verständnis des Zen-Buddhismus die Verbindung zwischen Himmel und Erde und ein Bild von der nur abstrakt benennbaren „Kraft", die man nicht anders sichtbar machen kann.

Die Wände des Ausstellungsraumes „bilden" die Reflexion des Lichts: schwebende Blumen und versteckte, flüchtige Töne. Sie verweisen auf den sinnlichen, lebensalltäglichen Teil des Kosmos, auf Wachsen, Blühen, Reifen. In ihrer Künstlichkeit liegt ein Hinweis auf die Vergänglichkeit. Als „Bild", als Arrangement wird die Installation zum Stilleben, zur Metapher des Endes, und durch seine Beständigkeit, gewissermaßen durch seinen Kunstvorbehalt, auch zur Metapher des immer neuen Beginns. „Die Natur macht Kreise, auch wenn ich nicht da bin", schrieb Eun Nim Ro 1984 und spielte damit auf die Beständigkeit von Anfang und Ende an. Das Ich, das eigene Leben ist dabei der Prozeß der Erkenntnis in dieser zyklische Ewigkeit.

Künstlerisches Arbeiten bedeutet für Eun Nim Ro das Ausloten des kosmischen Raums, den sie, abgebildet in der Natur, durch „Liebe, Widerstand und Eifersucht" erkennt. Die Künstlerin durchläuft dabei wie die Natur immer wieder die gleiche Bahn. Deshalb ist es auch nicht verwunderlich, wenn sie für die Installation einen Titel gewählt hat, der bereits in ihrem Œuvre verankert ist: „Meine Flügel sind meine Last."

Heinz Thiel

stones make the paper robe an image of gravity. The tree, manifest in the paper and at the same time in man's upright stance, is according to Zen Buddhism the link between heaven and earth and symbol for what is defined abstractly as "energy", visible in no other way.

The walls of the exhibition room "shape" the reflections of the light: swaying flowers and hidden, fleeting tones. They point to the sensual, everyday elements of the cosmos, to growth, flowering, ripening. In their artificiality there lies a hint of transience. As "image", as arrangement, the installation is a still-life, a metaphor of the end, and by its permanence – as it were by its proviso as art – a "symbol" of the eternal rebirth. "Nature makes circles, even when I am not there," Eun Nim Ro wrote in 1984, referring to the constancy of beginning and end. The ego, one's own life, takes part in the process of this recognition of the eternal return.

To work in art always means for Eun Nim Ro a sounding out of the cosmic space which she, by "love, resistance and jealousy", sees mirrored in nature. The artist, like nature, again and again runs in the same orbit. That is why it is not at all surprising that she chose as title for the installation something already anchored in her œuvre: 'My Wings Are My Burden'.

Heinz Thiel

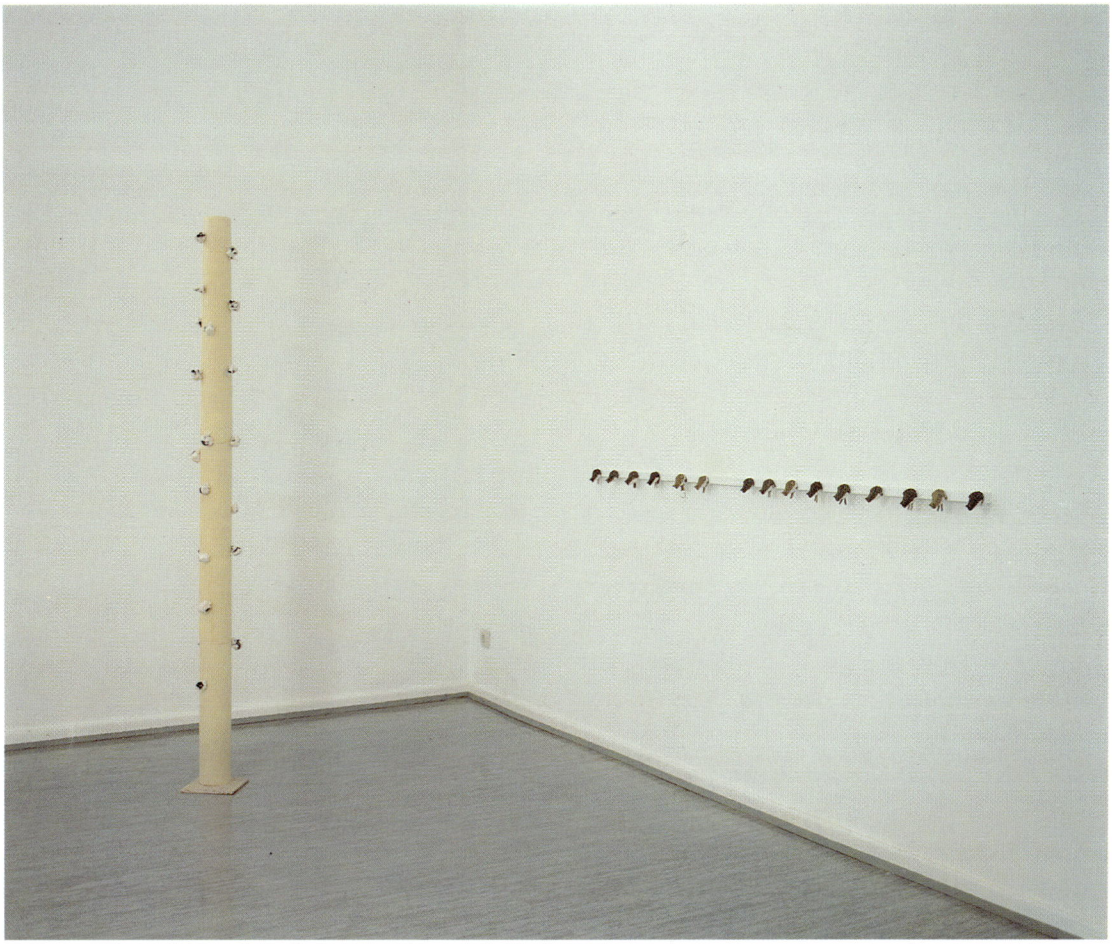

Eun Nim Ro: Meine Flügel sind meine Last, 1994. Rauminstallation. Ausschnitt. Reispapier, Karton. Höhe 200 cm, Breite 200 cm /
Eun Nim Ro: My Wings Are My Burden, 1994. Installation. Detail. Rice paper, cardboard. 200 cm high, 200 cm wide

James Rosenquist

1933 geboren in Grand Forks/North Dakota 1952–54 Kunststudium an der University of Minnesota und anschließend an der Art Students League Ausstellungen (Auswahl): 1962 Green Gallery, New York 1964 Galerie Ileana Sonnabend, Paris 1965 Leo Castelli Gallery, New York 1966 Kunsthalle Bern – Stedelijk Museum, Amsterdam 1972 Wallraf-Richartz-Museum, Köln 1974 The Mayor Gallery, London 1983 van Straaten Gallery, Chicago 1989 Leo Castelli Gallery, New York

1933 born in Grand Forks/North Dakota **1952–54** studies art at the University of Minnesota and then at the Art Students League **exhibitions (selection): 1962** Green Gallery, New York **1964** Galerie Ileana Sonnabend, Paris **1965** Leo Castelli Gallery, New York **1966** Kunsthalle Bern – Stedelijk Museum, Amsterdam **1972** Wallraf-Richartz-Museum, Cologne **1974** The Mayor Gallery, London **1983** van Straaten Gallery, Chicago **1989** Leo Castelli Gallery, New York

1986 bezog Tyler Graphics Ltd. sein neues Quartier in Mt. Kisco, New York, mit größerer Werkstatt und Galerie. Einen Monat vor der Eröffnung in der Kisco Avenue 250 schrieb Kenneth Tyler an Rosenquist. Er lud ihn ein, sich die neue Werkstatt anzusehen, und schlug eine Zusammenarbeit vor.

Bei ihrer ersten Besprechung erklärte Rosenquist Tyler, daß er Drucke mit derselben Spontaneität schaffen wolle, mit der er male. Tyler empfahl ihm, es mit Papierpulp zu versuchen, denn der handgeschöpfte Pulp ergebe eine dem gemalten Bild ähnliche Oberfläche. Zwei Wochen später besichtigte Rosenquist das Studio in der Kisco Avenue; nach dem Essen und einem Rundgang durch die Werkstatt wollte Tyler Rosenquists Wünsche hören. „Ich möchte Drucke machen, die so groß wie Gemälde sind“, antwortete Rosenquist. „O. K.“, sagte Tyler. „Ich mache Ihnen größere handgeschöpfte Papierbögen, als Sie jemals gesehen haben.“

Größe ist allerdings für Rosenquist kein Wert an sich. „Die Bilder müssen groß sein“, sagte er einmal, „nicht, weil viel darauf sein muß, sondern weil sie das Blickfeld bis zu den Rändern ausfüllen müssen, damit sie das Ich und das Ich-Bewußtsein relativieren.“ Von einer bestimmten Größe der Bilder an wird ihre Begrenzung nicht mehr wahrgenommen.

In 1986 Tyler Graphics Ltd. relocated to Mt. Kisco, New York in an expanded workshop facility and gallery. A month before the opening of 250 Kisco Avenue, Kenneth Tyler sent Rosenquist a note. It invited Rosenquist to visit the new workshop; it suggested a collaboration.

The first time they talked, Rosenquist told Tyler he wanted to make prints with the same spontaneity he made painting. Tyler suggested he try handmade paper pulp, explaining that the kind of surface paper pulp yielded came close to painting. Two weeks later, Rosenquist visited the Kisco Avenue studio; after lunch and a tour of the facilities, Tyler asked him what he wanted to do. "I want to make prints as big as paintings," Rosenquist answered. "O. K.," Tyler replied, "I'll make the biggest pieces of handmade paper you've ever seen."

However, the isolated fact of bigness is of little interest to Rosenquist. "The reason for bigness," Rosenquist has explained, "isn't largeness, it's to be engulfed by peripheral vision; it questions the self and questions self-conciousness." Big pictures cease to be discrete objects.

In May 1988, a year and a half after their first conversation, Rosenquist called Tyler to say that he was ready to work and that he wanted to make prints combining lithography with handmade paper

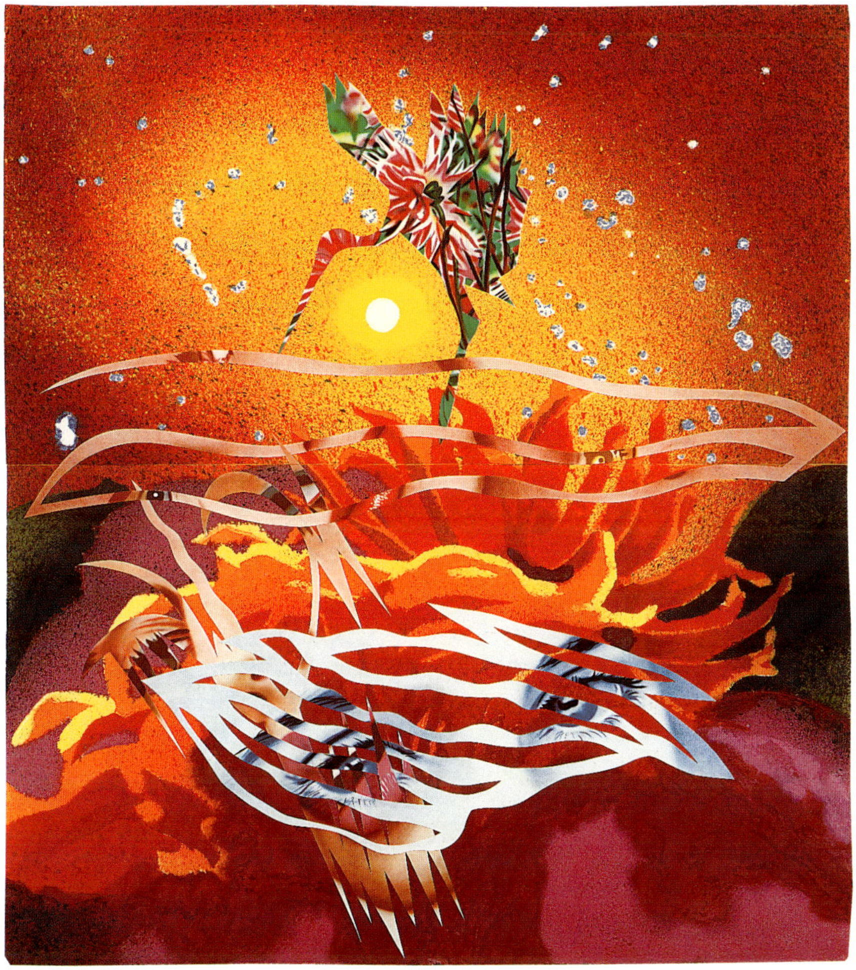

James Rosenquist: The Bird of Paradise Approaches the Hot Water Planet, 1989. Aus: Welcome to the Water Planet. Gefärbter und gepreßter Papierpulp, Lithographie, Collage. 2 Blätter. Gesamtgröße 246,4 x 214,6 cm. Auflage 28 / James Rosenquist: The Bird of Paradise Approaches the Hot Water Planet, 1989. From: Welcome to the Water Planet. Colored and pressed paper pulp, lithograph, collage. Two sheets. 246.4 x 214.6 cm total size. Edition of 28.

Im Mai 1988, anderthalb Jahre, nachdem sie zum erstem Mal darüber gesprochen hatten, rief Rosenquist bei Tyler an und erklärte, daß er nun soweit sei und mit der Arbeit beginnen wolle; es sollten Drucke werden, die lithographische Technik und die Arbeit mit Papierpulp verbänden. Letzten Endes sollten durch diese Technik Bilder entstehen, die beinah wie gemalt aussahen. Papierpulp würde als gemalter Grund fungieren, und die lithographischen Elemente, die darauf collagiert werden sollten, würden Vordergrund oder Figuren abgeben. Tyler brauchte Zeit, das vorzubereiten. Er sagte Rosenquist, daß es ein paar Monate dauern werde – im August sei er soweit.

Um Rosenquist das Versprochene zu liefern, mußte Tyler neue Vorrichtungen zum Papierschöpfen bauen. Er nahm mit Lee McDonald Kontakt auf, der mit Ausrüstungen zur Papierherstellung handelte, und stellte ihn als Berater an. Tyler hatte bei McDonald bereits eine 150 x 300 Zentimeter große stationäre Schöpfform in Auftrag gegeben. Er brauchte nun eine neue Anlage zum Absaugen und einen elektrischen Flaschenzug. Bis Tyler und McDonald mit den Umbau der Papierwerkstatt beendet hatten, war es September. Es hatte unvorhergesehene Schwierigkeiten gegeben, darunter die verspätete Lieferung der von Tyler konstruierten 1,50 mal 3 Meter großen kombinierten Litho- und Kupferstichpresse, die Rosenquist später „Double Trouble“ (Nichts als Ärger) taufte. Da er wußte, daß sie eine große Presse brauchten, bot Rosenquist seine eigene an, und Tyler schickte einen Lastwagen nach Florida, um sie zu holen.

Rosenquist war beeindruckt, als er das Studio in der Kisco Avenue betrat. „Ich kenne keinen anderen Laden auf der Welt, der so ehrfurchtgebietend aussieht wie der von Tyler.“

Vom September 1988 bis November 1989 arbeitete Rosenquist über 100 Tage in der Kisco Avenue 250. In jener Zeit schuf er zehn Papierpulpgemälde mit collagierten Lithographien. Dabei verarbeitete er mehr als 100 000 Liter Papierbrei, fertigte 70 Schablonen, mit denen 720 Blatt farbigen Büttenpapiers

pulp. In principle, the technique was meant to approximate painting. Paper pulp would function as a painted ground, and the lithographic elements, to be collaged onto the pulp, would act as foreground or figure. Tyler needed time to prepare. He told Rosenquist it would take a few months, that he'd be ready in August.

To accommodate Rosenquist, Tyler had to build a new papermaking system. He contacted Lee McDonald, who manufactured supplies for papermakers and hired him as a consultant. Tyler had already commissioned McDonald to build a 150 x 300 cm deckle box, a stationary mold to form paper. He was now going to need a new vacuum system and an overhead electrical hoist. By the time Tyler and McDonald finished revamping the papermaking studio, it was September. There had been unforeseen hitches, including the delay of the new five by ten foot combination litho and etching press Tyler designed and Rosenquist subsequently named “Double Trouble”. Knowing they'd need a large press, Rosenquist offered his own press, and Tyler sent a truck to Florida to pick it up.

As soon as he arrived at the Kisco Avenue studio, Rosenquist was impressed. “I don't know another outfit in the world as voracious as Tyler's.”

From September 1988 to November 1989, Rosenquist spent over 100 days at 250 Kisco Avenue. During that time, he created ten paper pulp images with collaged lithographs. In the process, he used 27 000 gallons of paper pulp; drew 70 stencils to create 720 sheets of handmade colored papers, one relief plate, and 44 separate lithograhic sections which utilized 139 colors. All images include printed elements; however, in their effect: in the saturation of their color, and in the size and scale achieved, they come closer to paintings than prints. They are most precisely described as paperworks with collaged lithographs. All images belong to an ongoing series ‘Welcome to the Water Planet’. In 1987, for an Atlanta commission, Rosenquist printed his first water planet picture. The title ‘Water Planet’ implies

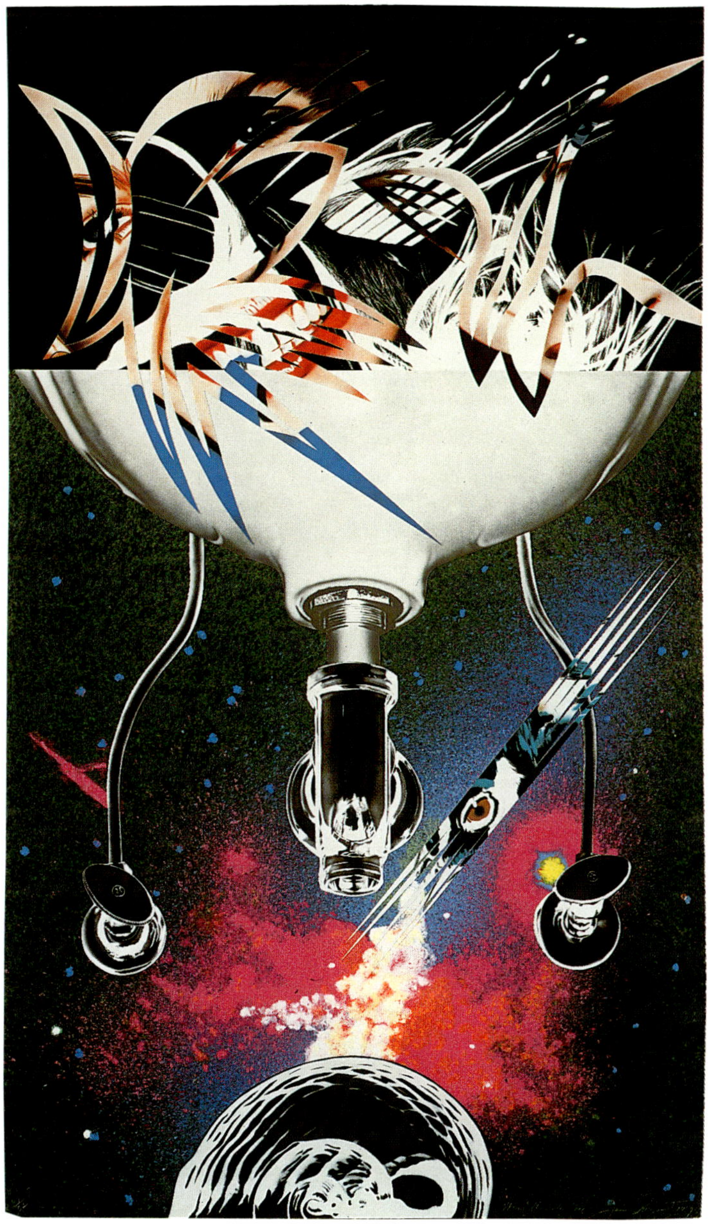

James Rosenquist: Where the Water Goes, 1989. Aus: Welcome to the Water Planet. Gefärbter und gepreßter Papierpulp, Lithographie, Collage. 261 x 147,3 cm. Auflage 32 / James Rosenquist: Where the Water Goes, 1989. From: Welcome to the Water Planet. Colored and pressed paper pulp, lithograph, collage. 261 x 147.3 cm. Edition of 32. © Tyler Graphics Ltd.

230

geschöpft wurden, eine Reliefplatte und 44 verschiedene Lithographievorlagen, die mit 139 Farben arbeiteten. Alle Bilder enthalten gedruckte Bestandteile; doch in ihrer Gesamtwirkung, in der Leuchtkraft der Farben, in Format und Maßstab ähneln sie Gemälden eher als Drucken. Am besten kann man sie als Papierarbeiten mit collagierten Lithographien beschreiben.

Alle diese Bilder gehören zu einer laufenden Serie mit dem Titel ‚Welcome to the Waterplanet'. Sein erstes Bild dieser Serie druckte Rosenquist 1987 als Auftragsarbeit für Atlanta. Der Titel ‚Wasserplanet' läßt an Science-fiction-Abenteuer denken, neue Welten, außerirdische Wesen. Doch der Wasserplanet ist ein uns wohlgesonnener Ort; kein fremder Planet, sondern die Erde, der einzige Himmelskörper, von dem man weiß, daß es hier Wasser gibt. Wie andere Arbeiten Rosenquists beinhalten auch die Wasserplaneten-Bilder ökologische Vorstellungen. Seit den frühen Werken, in denen er uns den Müll der Industriekultur vorführte, reflektieren Rosenquists Bilder das Schicksal von Mensch und Natur in einem Zeitalter, das von Reklame, Wissenschaft und Technik beherrscht ist. In der Serie ‚Welcome to the Water Planet' zeigt uns Rosenquist die Erde aus einer neuen Perspektive, vom Weltall aus gesehen, in einer Zeit, in der die Menschen über den Mond spaziert sind und die Erde umkreist haben. Es ist eine fruchtbare, üppige, bisweilen bedrohte Landschaft, ein Ort, wo die Zeit verstreicht und die Wissenschaft immer weiter voranschreitet.

Judith Goldmann: James Rosenquist. Welcome to the Water Planet, 1988–89. Tyler Graphics, Mount Kisco/New York 1989, S. 14, 15, 19

science fiction adventures, new territories, and alien creatures. The water planet, however, is a benevolent place; not a new planet at all, it is Earth, the only planet known to have water. Like other Rosenquist conceptions, the water planet embodies ecological ideas. Since early paintings in which he depicted the debris of a consumer culture, Rosenquist's images have reflected man's fate and nature's in an age determined by advertising, technology, and science. In the 'Welcome to the Water Planet' series, Rosenquist reveals earth from a new perspective, as seen from outer space, after men have walked on the moon and orbited the universe. It is a fertile, luscious, sometimes endangered landscape, a place where time passes and science advances.

Judith Goldmann: James Rosenquist. Welcome to the Water Planet, 1988–1989. Tyler Graphics, Mount Kisco/New York 1989, pp. 14, 15, 19

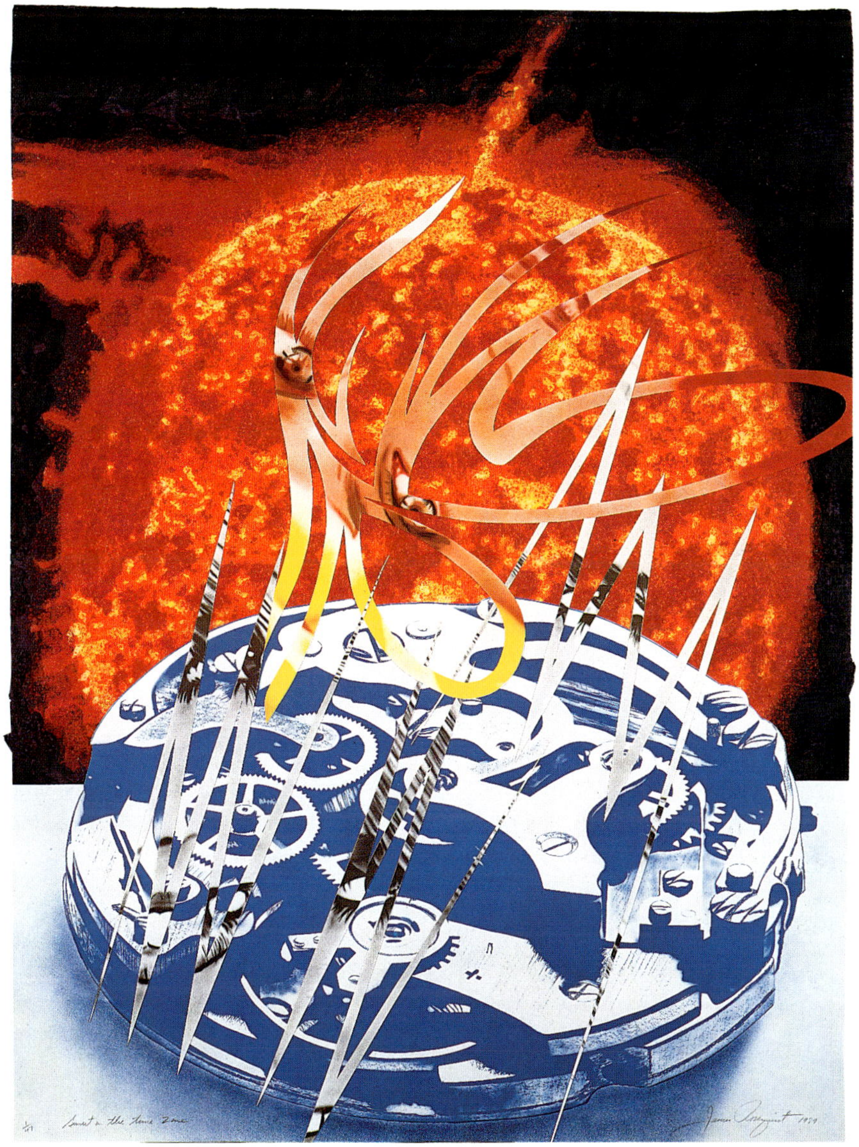

James Rosenquist: Sun Sets on the Time Zone, 1989. Aus: Welcome to the Water Planet. Gefärbter und gepreßter Papierpulp, Lithographie, Collage. 201,9 x 147,3 cm / James Rosenquist: Sun Sets on the Time Zone, 1989. From: Welcome to the Water Planet. Colored and pressed paper pulp, lithograph, collage. 201.9 x 147.3 cm. © Tyler Graphics Ltd.

Takako Saito

1929 geboren in Sabae-Shi/Japan, lebt in Düsseldorf 1963 Umzug nach New York, arbeitet zusammen mit George Maciunas, dem bedeutenden Organisator und Theoretiker von Fluxus 1968 Umzug nach Paris, danach nach Italien, Großbritannien und Deutschland Teilnahme und Organisation von Fluxusspielen in USA und Europa

1929 born in Sabae-Shi/Japan, lives in Düsseldorf **1963** moves to New York, works together with George Maciunas, the important organizer and theoretician of Fluxus **1968** moves to Paris, then to Italy, Great Britain and Germany – Participation and organisation of Fluxus plays in US and Europe

Den ersten Kontakt mit Papier hatte ich vor 27 Jahren, als ich in New York war. Ich konstruierte einen kleinen Würfel, ohne genau zu wissen, was ich damit wollte, und legte ihn auf den Tisch. Eines Tages ist er durch den Stoß meines Ellenbogens zufällig heruntergefallen. Der Würfel überraschte mich – er klang.

Viele Jahre später lernte ich, während ich Bücher machte, das Geräusch von Pergament kennen. Das Geräusch ist so, als wenn dürre Blätter angefaßt werden oder der Wind leise durch Blätter weht.

Das Geräusch des Cellophanpapiers ist besonders bemerkenswert. Mit diesem Geräusch wollte ich ein Konzert zusammen mit den Besuchern machen, was aber leider aus technischen Gründen nicht möglich war.

Danach hatte ich den Plan, in der Werkstatt ein großes Pergamentspiel im Raum zu gestalten. Die Besucher sollten hindurchgehen und damit spielen, wie sie wollten. Auch dieses Projekt konnte aus technischen Gründen nicht stattfinden .

Mein Traum, mit den Besuchern ein Konzert zu machen oder durch das Spielen der Besucher mit meiner Arbeit diese zu verändern, bleibt.

Takako Saito

I had my first contact with paper 27 years ago when I was in New York. I fashioned a small cube without knowing what I wanted to do with it and placed it on a table. One day, an unintentional blow of my elbow knocked it to the floor. The cube surprised me; it spoke.

Many years later while I was making books, I learned of the noise that parchment makes. The noise is like the touch of dry leaves or the wind blowing softly through the trees.

The noise of cellophane is special. With this noise I wanted to make a concert in cooperation with the visitors, but this unfortunately proved impossible for technical reasons.

Then I had a plan to install in the workshop a large parchment game in space. The visitors were supposed to walk through and play with it at will. This project also could not take place for technical reasons.

My dream still remains to make a concert with the spectators or to have them change my work by playing with it.

Takako Saito

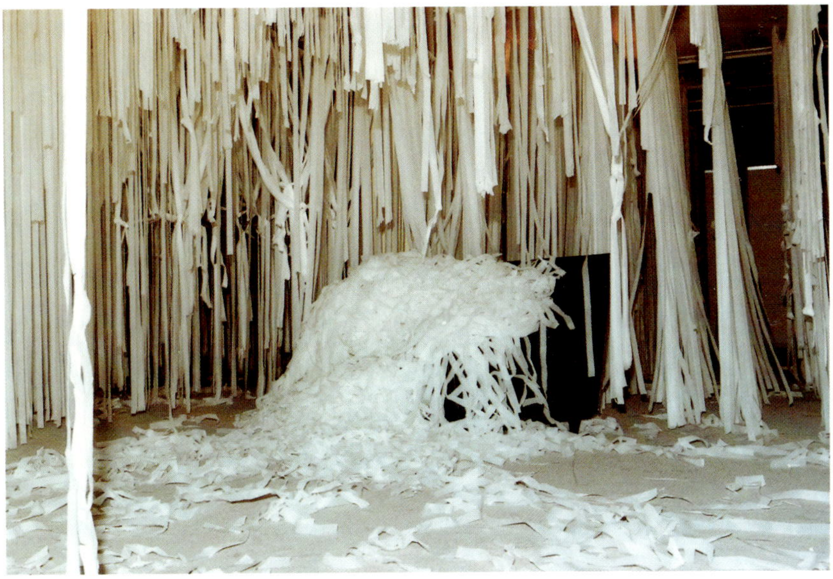

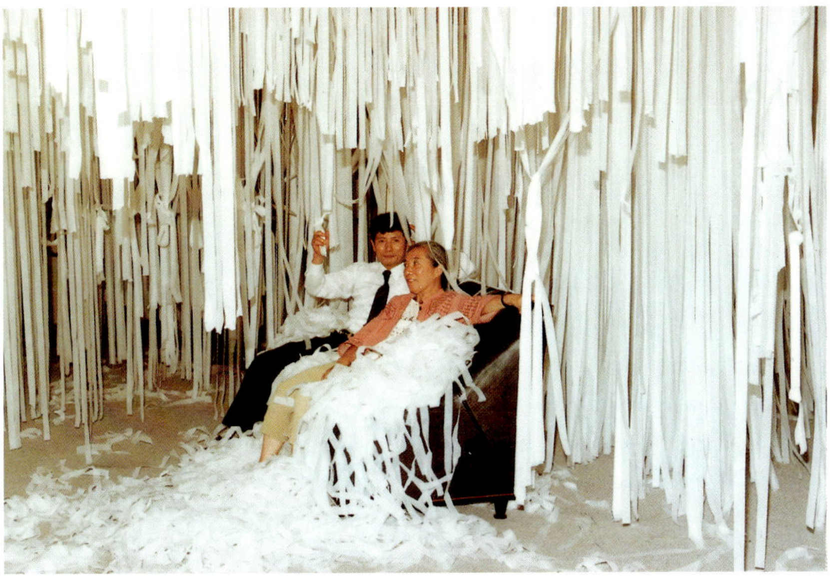

Takako Saito: Papierinstallationen während der Ausstellungen in Fukui/Japan, 1991 /
Takako Saito: Paper installations during the exhibitions in Fukui/Japan, 1991

Timm Ulrichs

1940 geboren in Berlin, lebt in Hannover 1956–59 Studium der Architektur an der Technischen Hochschule Hannover 1972 Berufung zum Professor an das Institut für Kunsterziehung, Münster, und der Kunstakademie Düsseldorf Ausstellungen (Auswahl): 1966 Galerie Patio, Frankfurt/M. 1969 Galerie Reckermann, Köln 1973 Kunsthalle Bielefeld 1974 Kunsthalle Bremen 1975 Kunstverein Hannover 1979 Kunstmuseum Hannover 1980 Städtische Galerie Lüdenscheid 1991/92 Kunsthalle Recklinghausen

1940 born in Berlin, lives in Hannover **1956-59** studies architecture at the Technische Hochschule Hannover **1972** appointed professor at the Institute for Art Education, Münster, of the Kunstakademie Düsseldorf **exhibitions (selection): 1966** Galerie Patio, Frankfurt/M. **1969** Galerie Reckermann, Cologne **1973** Kunsthalle Bielefeld **1974** Kunsthalle Bremen **1975** Kunstverein Hannover **1979** Kunstmuseum Hannover **1980** Städtische Galerie Lüdenscheid **1991/92** Kunsthalle Recklinghausen

Papier – von allen Seiten

Papier ist geduldig, wie man weiß; es kann sich nicht verwahren und wehren gegen all das, was zu Papier gebracht werden soll, ohne aber das zu bedruckende Papier wert zu sein. „Des vielen Büchermachens ist kein Ende“ (Prediger 12, 12), und dies offenbar nicht so sehr, weil man Bücher respektiert, sondern gerade weil man sie nicht respektiert. „Tout au monde existe pour aboutir dans un livre“ (Stéphane Mallarmé), alles, wirklich alles auf der Welt existiert, um in ein Buch zu münden – im guten als auch im bösen, wie ein einfacher Test beweist: „Wenn ein Buch und ein Kopf zusammenstoßen und es klingt hohl, ist das allemal im Buch?“ (Georg Christoph Lichtenberg). Wer ein weißes Blatt vor Augen hat, sollte – mit allem Respekt – bedenken, daß er nicht eine tote Fläche, ein totenbleiches oder leichenblasses Terrain vor sich hat, einen jungfräulichen „weißen Fleck“, den es mit Zeichen erst zu erschließen und zu besiedeln gilt, sondern stets schon geschichtsträchtigen Boden. Jedes, auch ein unbeschriebenes Blatt inkorporiert ganz allgemein die mehr als zweitausendjährige Entwicklungsgeschichte des Papiers und im besonderen seine eigene Herkunft von bestimmten Bäumen aus bestimmten Wäldern in be-

Paper – from all sides

Paper is patient, as the saying goes; it can't protest, can't defend itself against all that is put to paper without, however, it is being worth the paper it is to be printed on. “Of making books there is no end” (Ecclesiastes 12, 12), and this obviously not so much because books are respected, but exactly because they are not. “Tout au monde existe pour aboutir dans un livre” (Stéphane Mallarmé), everything, but everything in the world exists to end in a book – for better or for worse, as a simple test proves: “When a book and a head bang together and the sound is hollow, is this certainly in the book?” (Georg Christoph Lichtenberg). Whoever has a blank sheet of paper in front of his eyes should – with all respect – remember that it is not a dead surface, a deathly-white or corpse-white terrain that he finds before him, a virginal “white spot” that must be explored and colonized with signs, but that its ground is already historically charged. Each (also each blank) sheet incorporates quite generally the more than two-thousand year history of paper development and especially its own from certain trees in certain forests in certain countries, even if – cut up and parcelled out in standard dimensions, sorted according to type, made to order for certain

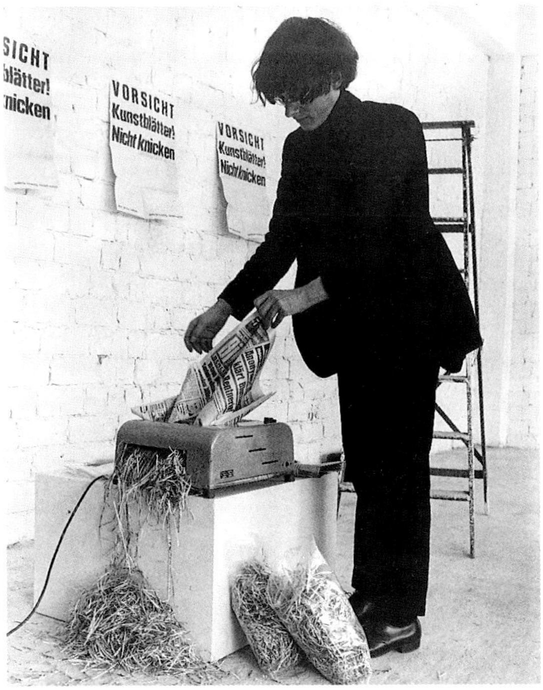

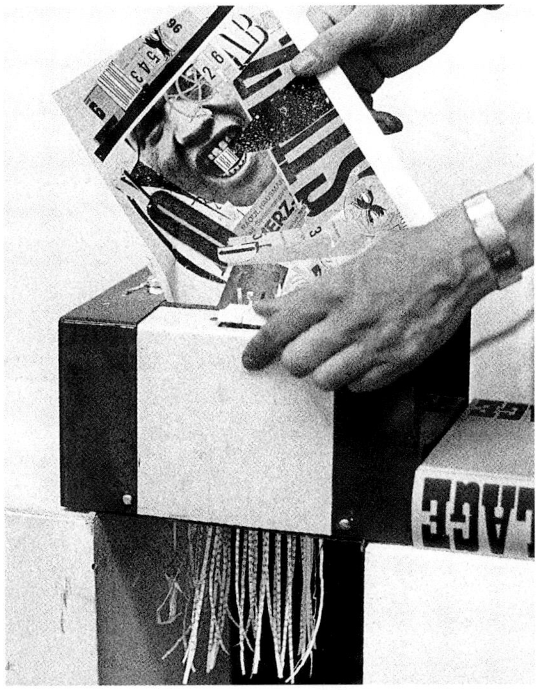

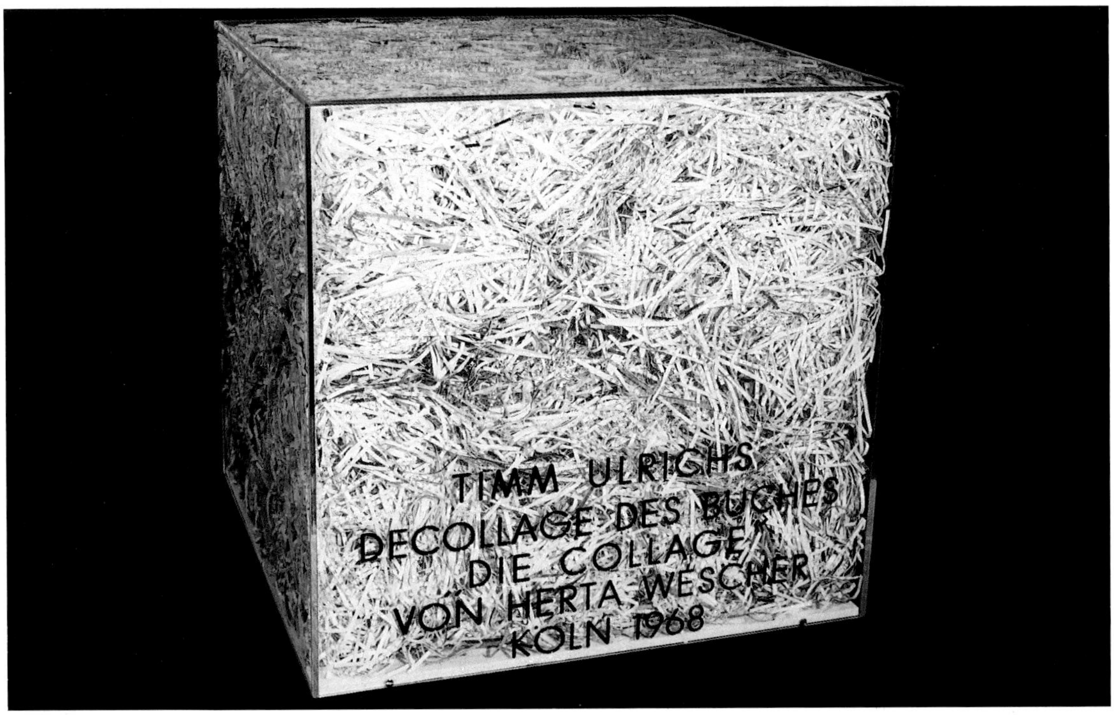

Abb. 1: Timm Ulrichs: Kulturbeutel. Destruktions-Aktions-Poesie mit einem Reißwolf und 100 Tageszeitungen, 1967. Galerie Ben Wargin, Berlin, 8. 5. 1967 / Ill. 1: Timm Ulrichs: Cultural Sack. Destruction-action-poetry with shredder and 100 newspapers, 1967. Gallery Ben Wargin, Berlin, 8 / 5 / 1967

Abb. 2 – 3: Timm Ulrichs: Décollage des Buches ‚Die Collage' von Herta Wescher, Köln 1968, durch einen Aktenvernichter und Sammlung der Papier-„Wolle" in einem Acrylglaskasten, 1967. 40 x 40 x 40 cm. Städtisches Museum Wiesbaden, 21. 9. 1971 / Ill. 2 – 3: Timm Ulrichs: Décollage of the book 'The Collage' by Herta Wescher, Cologne 1968, by a paper mangler followed by collection of paper "wool" in a glass case, 1967. 40 x 40 x 40 cm. Städtisches MuseumWiesbaden, 21 / 9 / 1971

stimmten Ländern, mag es auch, nach DIN-Formaten zurechtgestutzt und parzelliert, nach Arten sortiert und auf Funktionen hin getrimmt, ohne Individualität erscheinen. Doch jeder Bogen Papier und ein jedes Buch hat seine eigene Geschichte. Wer will, kann – ganz unabhängig von „Inhalten“ – am Rascheln des Papiers noch das Rauschen der Blätter der Wälder vernehmen, dem jenes entwuchs, ja im Papier überwintern gleichsam die Wälder, und man könnte geneigt sein, den Weg des Papiers wieder rückgängig zu machen und die papierenen Blätterwälder in die natürlichen Wälder zurückzuführen und am Ausgangsort zu kompostieren: Der „Anfänger“ beginnt mit Wellpappe und feinen Papieren wie Servietten, Pergamentpapier und leichtem Packpapier; der Fortgeschrittene verarbeitet Tageszeitungen, der Könner selbst Illustrierte. Rigoroser und radikaler ist gar Lichtenbergs Vorschlag: „Die Wälder werden immer kleiner, das Holz nimmt ab, was wollen wir anfangen? Oh, zu der Zeit, wenn die Wälder aufhören, können wir sicherlich so lange Bücher verbrennen, bis wieder neue aufgewachsen sind.“ Und im weiteren Nachdenken an Bücher, den Wald, seine Schonung und Schonungen – akut angesichts des drohenden Verlustes nicht nur der tropischen Regenwälder – macht derselbe Autor die Rechnung auf: „Acht Bände hat er geschrieben. Er hätte gewiß besser getan, er hätte acht Bäume gepflanzt oder acht Kinder gezeugt.“ Geschichtsgesättigt ist aber nicht nur der primäre Herstellungsprozeß des Papiers aus bearbeitetem Holz: 53 Prozent der Papiere und Pappen werden bereits nach Recycling-Verfahren aus Altpapier gewonnen, Papier also, das zuvor schon andere Botschaften getragen hat, gereist ist, von Hand zu Hand gewandert und gelesen, weggeworfen, wieder aufgehoben und wiederverwendet wurde: „Auch Bücher haben ihr Erlebtes, das ihnen nicht entzogen werden kann“, notierte Goethe in seinen ‚Maximen und Reflexionen‘.

Timm Ulrichs

functions – it seems to have no individuality. Yet every sheet of paper and each book has ist own tale to tell. Whoever wants to, can – quite apart from “contents” – hear in the rustle of the paper the rustle of the leaves in the forest where each one grew; for the woods hibernate, so to speak, in the paper and one is tempted to reverse the path the paper took and transport the forest of paper sheets back to the natural woods and make compost of them at their place of origin: The “beginner” begins with corrugated paper and fine papers like napkins, parchment and light wrapping paper; the more advanced uses newspaper, and the connoisseur what he has himself illustrated. The compost that arises is extremely fertile. Even more rigorous and radical is the suggestion Lichtenberg made: “The forests are getting smaller and smaller, the supply of wood is decreasing, what to do? Well, when the time comes and the forests cease, we can burn books instead for so long as it takes new ones to grow.” And thinking further along this line about books, the forest, its preservation and its seedling nurseries – critical in the face of the treatened loss not only of the tropical rain forests – the same author makes out the bill: “He wrote eight volumes. He would have done better had he planted eight trees or begot eight children.” It is not only the primary manufacture of paper from wood that alone has its past history: 53 % of the paper and cardboard are now recycled from wastepaper, i. e., paper that had already carried other messages, was shipped, gone from hand to hand and read, thrown away, picked up again and re-used: “Books too have their experience that cannot be taken from them,” Goethe noted in his ‘Maximen und Reflexionen’.

Timm Ulrichs

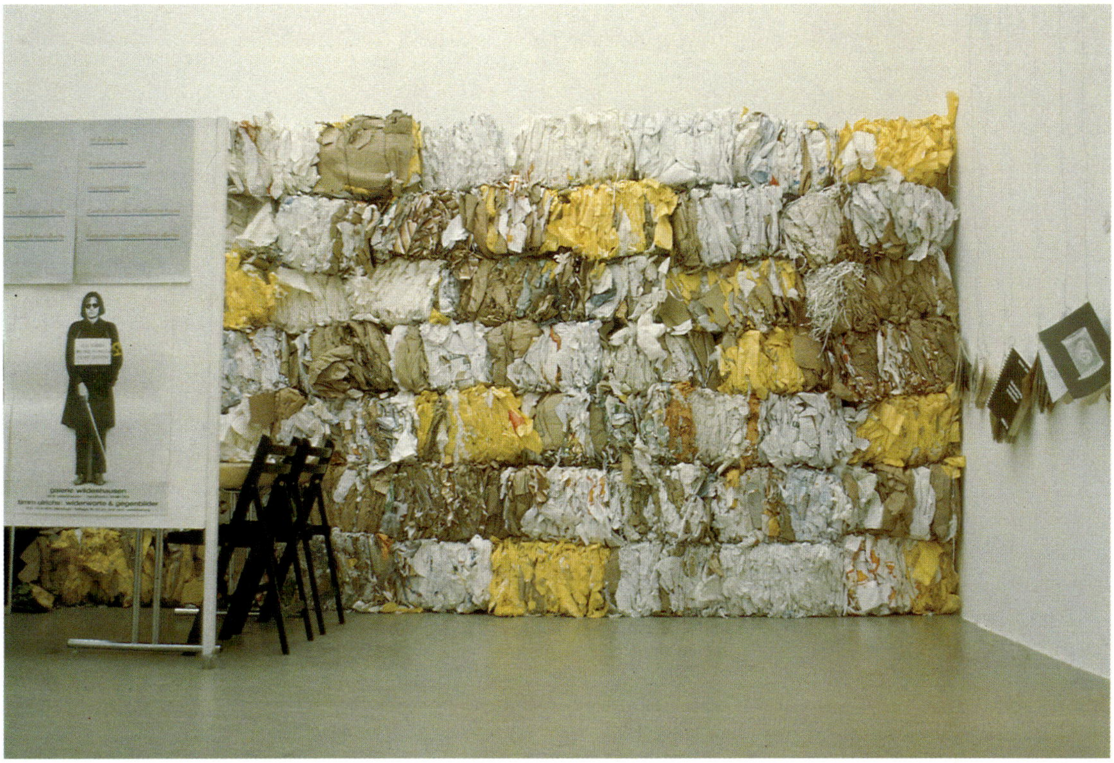

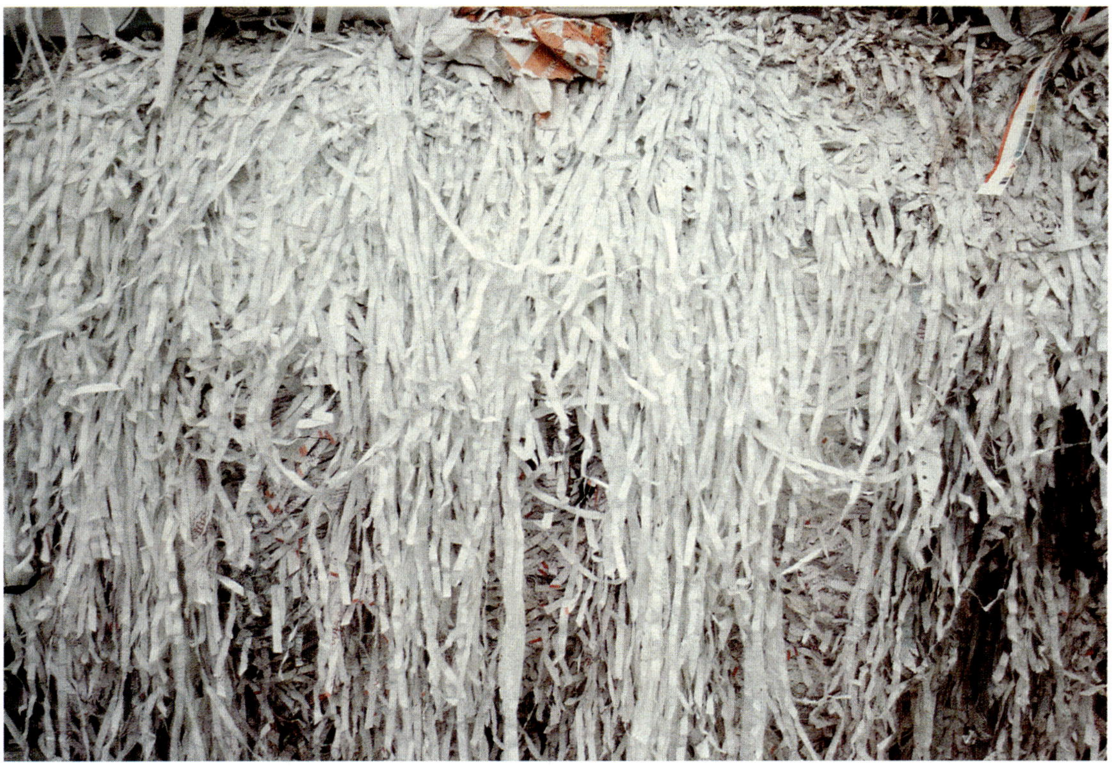

Timm Ulrichs: Bibliothek (babylonisch). Wand aus zerfaserten und gepreßten Altpapierballen. Ca. 250 x 450 x 50 cm. Kunstverein Hannover, November 1976 / Timm Ulrichs: Library (Babylonian). Wall from mangled and pressed waste paper, 1976. Ca. 250 x 450 x 50 cm. Kunstverein Hannover, November 1976

Andreas von Weizsäcker

1956 geboren in Essen, lebt in München 1980-84 Bildhauerstudium an der Akademie der Bildenden Künste, München 1985 Assistent am Lehrstuhl für freie Bildhauerei der Akademie der Bildenden Künste, München 1986 Lehrauftrag für freie Bildhauerei an der Akademie der Bildenden Künste, München Stipendien: 1988 DAAD Stipendium für die USA 1989 Stipendiat der Japan Foundation, Kyoto/Japan Ausstellungen (Auswahl): 1986 Galerie Go, Rehau 1987 Galerie Hennemann, Bonn 1988 Technisches Museum, Wien 1990 Galerie von der Milwe, Aachen 1991 Gallery William Jackson, London 1992 Galerie am Luxemburgplatz, Wiesbaden 1993 Flottmann-Hallen, Herne

1956 born in Essen, lives in Munich **1980–84** studies sculpture at the Akademie der Bildenden Künste, Munich **1985** teaching assistant for Sculpture at the Akademie der Bildenden Künste, Munich **1986** appointed to the chair for Sculpture at the Akademie der Bildenden Künste, Munich **grants: 1988** DAAD for US stay **1989** Japan Foundation, Kyoto/Japan **exhibitions (selection): 1986** Galerie Go, Rehau **1987** Galerie Hennemann, Bonn **1988** Technisches Museum, Vienna **1990** Galerie von der Milwe, Aix-la-Chapelle **1991** Gallery William Jackson, London **1992** Galerie am Luxemburgplatz, Wiesbaden **1993** Flottmann-Hallen, Herne

Nach dem Zusammenbruch des „Ostblocks“ verschwinden auch die sichtbaren Zeichen der Verherrlichung des Systems: die Denkmäler der von totalitären Systemen inthronisierten Heroen. Diese instrumentalisierte Form von Bildhauerei lagert inzwischen in den Depots verschiedener Museen, beispielsweise in Berlin, Dresden, Magdeburg.

Solch deponierte „Zeugen der Realität“ bilden die philosophische und künstlerische Basis der Rauminstallation ‚Gezeiten‘ des Andreas von Weizsäcker. Großfotos im Maßstab 1 zu 1 erwecken die Illusion des Lagers der Monumente. Auf dem Boden liegen Abformungen von Köpfen aus grauem Papierstoff. Fotos und Abformungen werden zum Träger von Erinnerung, zu Zeugen der Geschichte. Als Material für die „Erinnerungsträger“ wählte der Künstler das leicht zu zerstörende Papier als überzeugendes Medium von Endlichkeit. Seine „Form“-ulierung in Papier beinhaltet die Verwerfung instrumentalisierter Skulptur.

Der Titel ‚Gezeiten‘ bezieht sich auf fundamentale Vorgänge wie Ebbe und Flut in Verbindung mit der Frage, ob sich Geschichte wiederholt, und auf die

Following the breakdown of the east block, the visible signs that glorified the system have also disappeared: the monuments of the sculpture has been stored in the meantime in the depots of the different museums, e. g. in Berlin, Dresden, Magdeburg.

Such stockpiled “witnesses of reality” are the philosophic and artistic basis for the ‘Tides’ installation by Andreas von Weizsäcker. Large life-size photographs (1 to 1) create the illusion of a storehouse for monuments. On the ground lie heads cast from grey paperpulp. Photographs and moulds become conveyors of memory, witnesses to history. As material for the “memory conveyors” the artist has chosen the easily destroyed medium of paper as a convincing expression of infinity. His formulations in paper express the rejection of instrumentalized sculpture.

The title ‘Tides’ refers to the fundamental process of ebb and flow as it is associated with the question of whether history repeats itself and with cognizance of the fact that man does not learn from history. Despite this, Andreas von Weizsäcker undertakes the attempt to trace the future’s

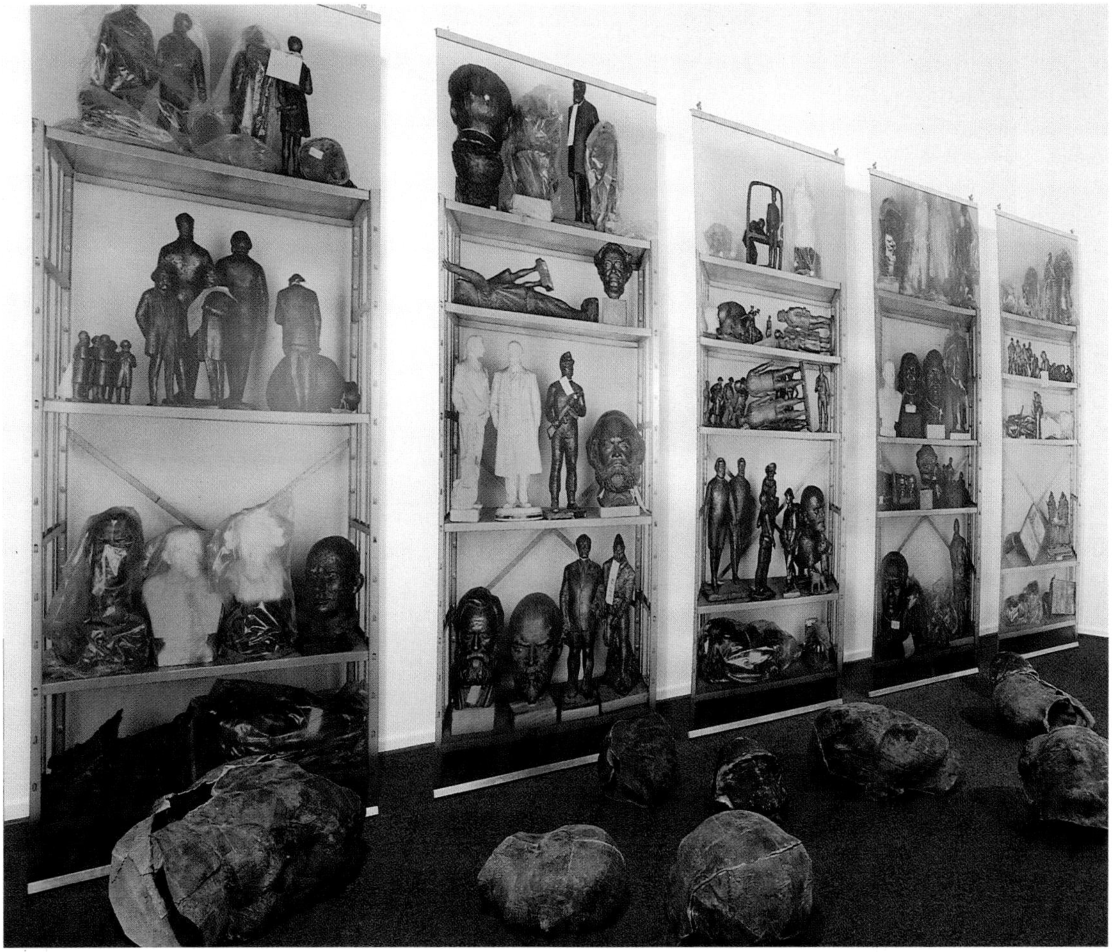

Andreas von Weizsäcker: Gezeiten, 1994. Installation mit Fotos und Papierabformungen. 400 x 630 x 250 cm /
Andreas von Weizsäcker: Tides, 1994. Installation. Photos and cast paper forms. 400 x 630 x 250 cm

Erkenntnis, daß Menschen aus der Geschichte nicht lernen. Dennoch unternimmt Andreas von Weizsäcker den Versuch, mit seinen verletzlichen Erinnerungsträgern der Zukunft verpflichtete Schlüssen nachzuspüren.
Thema von ‚Gezeiten' ist auch das Leben mit dem Zusammenbruch, Leben mit radikalen Veränderungen. Als Inspirationsquelle dienten Skizzen von Gericaults ‚Das Floß der Medusa' von 1818/19. Gericault zeichnete Köpfe ohne Rumpf, oft mehrere nebeneinander. Aus gezeichneter Physiognomie ist das grausige Geschehen erlesbar. Bei Andreas von Weizsäcker werden die Köpfe der Denkmäler zu Stellvertretern von Geschehen, von Geschichte.
Der Kopf als geistige Zentrale instrumentalisierter Aussage überführt er nun via Papier in eine Endlichkeitsform. Papierformungen von Köpfen werden zu Zeichen von Hoffnung.

Dank an:
Museum ‚Kloster unser Lieben Frauen', Magdeburg, Frau Dr. Hagedorn und Herrn Jens-Uwe Gellner; Militärhistorisches Museum, Dresden, Herrn Fregattenkapitän Heibei und Frau Karin Quaiser

obligatory conclusions with his vulnerable conveyors of memory.
The theme of 'Tides' is also living with breakdown, living with radical change. Sketches of Gericault's 'The Raft of the Medusa' from 1818/19 served as the source of his inspiration. Gericault had drawn heads without bodies, often several alongside each other. From this graphic rendition of physiognomy the terribly event became readable. In the case of Andreas von Weizsäcker, the heads of monuments become stand-ins for events, for history.
The head as spiritual center for instrumentalized proclamation is tranformed via paper into a finite form. The paper-cast heads become signs of hope.

Special thanks to:
Museum 'Kloster unser lieben Frauen', Magdeburg, Ms. Dr. Hagedorn and Mr. Jens-Uwe Gellner, Militärhistorisches Museum, Dresden, Naval Commander Heibei and Ms. Karin Quaiser

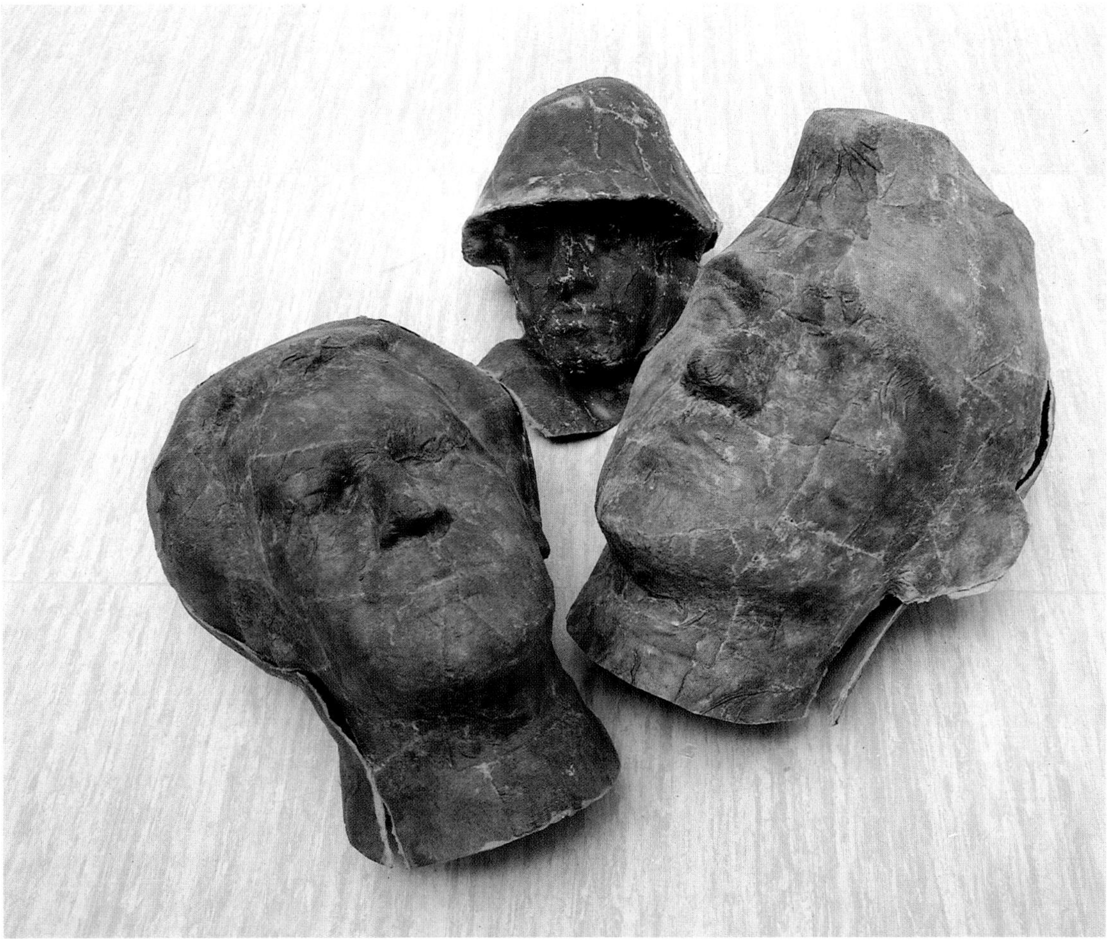

Andreas von Weizsäcker: Gezeiten, 1994. Installation mit Fotos und Papierabformungen (Ausschnitt). Gesamte Installation 400 x 630 x 250 cm / Andreas von Weizsäcker: Tides, 1994. Installation. Photos and casted paper forms (detail). Total installation 400 x 630 x 250 cm

Verzeichnis der Teilnehmer an Biennalen und Papierausstellungen seit 1981

Register of participants of Biennali and paper art exhibitions since 1981

Alpha 4 Performance 1988, 1992 Frederic Amat 1986 Elisabeth Ammon 1986, 1988 Pia Andersen 1990 Sascha Anderson 1990 Daniele Degli Angeli 1981 Suzanne Anker, 1986 Horst Antes 1986, 1988 Diana Arcadipone 1981, 1986 Marea Atkinson 1988 Bernard Aubertin 1990 John Babcock 1986 Frank Badur 1981, 1994 Jane Balsgaard 1986, 1988, 1992 Narcis Banchs I Valls 1986 Laurence Barker 1986, 1988 A. Harold Barreiro 1994 Eugenie Barron 1986 Randy Bass 1986 Barbara Isabella Bauer-Heusler 1992 Désirée Baumeister 1992 Ruth Bearsworth 1986 Helmut Becker 1986, 1988, 1992 Günther Beckers 1988 Curt Belshe 1990 Yeal Bentovim Burkes 1986 Bertholin 1981 Wolfgang Binding 1981 K. Reith Blake 1986 Hartmut Böhm 1981 Dominik Böhringer 1992 Fons Brasser 1981 Inger-Johanne Brautaset 1992 Stefanie Brüning 1988, 1992 Bettina Bürkle 1992 Ursula Buller 1992 Lore Burger 1990 Marnie Burns 1986, 1990 Marcelle Cahn 1981 Maria Lourdes Stamato de Camillis 1990 Vito Capone 1986, 1988 Béatrice de Caritat 1990 Anthony Caro 1986, 1994 Sotirakis Charalambou 1986 Sung Mook Cho 1988 Henning Christiansen 1990 Lori Christmastree 1986 Jan Cincera 1986 Kathryn Clark 1981, 1988 Kate Coolahan 1986 Boudewijn Corstiaensen 1986 Doru Covrig 1988 Tony Cragg 1994 Bernd-Rüdiger Damerow 1986 Pierre Daquin 1988 Sophie Dawson 1988, 1990 Claudia DeMonte 1992 Eddy Devolder 1986 Helmut Dirnaichner 1986 Cesar Domela 1981 Juan Downey 1990 André Drenth 1981 Felix Droese 1994 Pierre Duclou 1986 Michael Dudowitsch 1992 Torben Ebbesen 1988 Wolf Ebener 1981 Eve Eisenstadt 1981 Jo Enzweiler 1981 Leo Erb 1981, 1986 Bruno Erdmann 1981 Ingrid Evans 1986 Inge Evers 1986, 1988 Ruth Faerber 1986 Barbara Fahrner 1986 Carol S. Farrow 1986 Ken Feingold 1990 Christa Feuerberg 1990 Wolfgang Finck 1986 Joel Fisher 1981, 1986, 1994 Angelika Flaig 1992 Anne Flaten Pixley 1986 Morten Flyverbom 1990 Anita Ford 1986 A. Lynn Forgach 1986 Freddy Fraek 1988 Helen C. Frederick 1992 Jennie Frederick 1981, 1986 Antonio Freiles 1986 Helmut Frerick 1986 Frida 1981 Friedrich Friedl 1981 Bilgé Friedlaender 1992 Frank Gallo 1988 Tibor Gáyor 1981 Wilfried Gehring 1986 Nancy Genn 1986 John Gerard 1990 Michel Gérard 1986, 1988 Jorge Louis Giacosa 1990 Benjamin Gianni 1990 Leslie Gill 1990 Horst Gläsker 1994 Hermann Glöckner 1981 Hubertus Gojowczyk 1986, 1988 Maurizio Goldoni 1981 Kuno Gonschior 1994 Coco Gordon 1986, 1988 Gianni Gori 1981 Yvonne Goulbier 1990 Brian Paul McGrath 1990 Caroline Greenwald 1986, 1988 Katie MacGregor 1981 Joan M. Hall 1986, 1990 Gjertrud Hals 1990 Walter Samuel Hamady 1986 Ruth Handschin 1992 Axel Heibel 1981 Jean Heilbrunn 1988 Gottfried Helnwein 1992 Marilyn Helsenrott-Hochhauser

1986 Michelle Héon 1988 Ursula Herber 1986, 1988 Wolfgang Heuwinkel 1986, 1988 Charles Hilger 1990 Clinton Hill 1986 Claus Hildebrandt 1981 Jiří Hilmar 1981 David Hockney 1986 Lisa Hoever 1981 Beate Hoffmeister 1988 Cas Lesley Holmes 1986 Oskar Holweck 1981, 1988 Willem Honing 1986 Wen Yi Hou 1992 Guy Houdouin 1988, 1990 Douglass Morse Howell 1986 Lone Høyer Hansen 1992 Huang Yong Ping 1994 Marc ("M.F.A.„) Huber 1992 Hiltrud Huss 1992 Alfonso Hüppi 1981 James Hyde 1990 Kyoko Ibe 1988 Shoichi Ida 1986, 1988, 1990 Ritzi Jacobi 1986, 1988 Bertram Jesdinsky 1988 Françoise Jolivet 1992 Seop-Choi Jong 1986 Rolf Julius 1988 Kazou Kadonaga 1988 Liliane Karnouk 1986 Masaji Kashio 1988, 1990 Tatsuo Kawaguchi 1986, 1988 Reinhard Klessinger 1981 Jang-Sup Kim 1988 Yong-Hee Kim 1986 Yoshio Kitayama 1988 J. H. Kocman 1986 Reinhold Koehler 1981 Jiří Kolář 1981, 1988 Donna Koretsky 1988 Carla Kraayeveld 1986 K. Peter Kremer 1986 Maximilian Krips 1981 Lubomir Krupka 1986 Matthias Kunkler 1988 Harry van Kuyk 1981 Duck Jun Kwak 1990 Hugh Kyle 1986 Petra Landsknecht 1990 Marie Langlois 1988 Warja Lavater 1981, 1986 Rolf Laven 1992 Barbara Layne 1986 Isabelle Leduc 1988 Min-Joo Lee 1988 Thomas Leech 1992 Claude Lemaire 1986
Jean Le Noble 1986 Silke Leverkühne 1981 Golda Lewis 1986 Kathryn Lipke 1988, 1992 Lena Liv 1986, 1988, 1990 Sian Lloyd 1986 Julia Lohmann 1981 Helmut Löhr 1990 Christopher Lucas 1990 Winifred Ann Lutz 1986, 1988 Max H. Mahlmann 1981 Leopoldo Maler 1990 Wolfgang Mally 1981 Vincent Mangeat 1992 Fabian Marcaccio 1990 Sandra Marconato 1986 Cecile Massart 1986 Dóra Maurer 1981 Uwe Meier-Weitmar 1988 Marion Melody 1990 Walther Mertel 1988 Géza Mészáros 1986, 1988 Anne-Marie Milliot 1986 Milan Mölzer 1981 François Morellet 1981 Gilles Morissette 1986 Urbain Mulkers 1988 Carmen Müller 1986 Regi Müller 1988 Vik Muñiz 1990 Aurelia Muñoz 1986 Teresa Murak 1992 Ryozo Nachi 1981 Tomitao Nachi 1981 Irmari Nacht 1986 Hanjo Nagel 1992 Mitsushiro Nagatani 1988 Maurizio Nannucci 1981 Charles Nelly 1986 Yohei Nishimura 1988 Mogens Otto Nielsen 1990 Jean le Noble 1981 Kenneth Noland 1986 Koken Nomura 1992 Julie Norris 1986 Bob Nugent 1986, 1990 Nance O'Banion 1986 Hugh O'Donnel 1986 Hideyo Okuya 1992 Meret Oppenheim 1986 Maria Orzel-Hercka 1994 Yaeko Osono 1992 Papiertheater aus Köln 1992 Jean-Luc Parant 1994 Eun-Su Park 1992 Jacki Parry 1986 Gabriele Partisani 1981 Milko Pavlov 1994 A. R. Penck 1990, 1994 Norbert Walter Peters 1992 Finn Naur Petersen 1992 Claudine Péters-Ropsy 1986 Michael Petry 1986, 1994 Heinz-Dieter Pietsch 1986, 1988 Gudrun Piper 1981 Liliana Porter 1990 Chava Pressburger 1986 Otto Piene 1994 Dmitri A. Prigov 1994 Lise Prown 1990 Thomas P. Pupkiewicz 1986, 1988 Victoria Rabal I Merola 1986 Marylin Quint-Rose 1992 Pierre Racine 1992 Ted Ramsay 1990 Sigrid Redhardt 1981 Jane H. Reese 1986 Dorothea Reese-Heim 1986, 1988, 1992 Reviva Regev 1994 Maria Reuter 1981 Maureen Richardson 1986, 1990 Josef Anton Riedl 1988, 1990 Eun Nim Ro 1994 Mark Robbins 1990 Laurent Roberge 1988 Keith Roberts 1986 Osvaldo Romberg 1986, 1990 Roome and Starkey 1986 James Rosenquist 1994 Czashka Ross 1986, 1988 Otavio Roth 1986, 1988, 1992 Heidi Roulin-Kailasvuori 1986 Richard Royce 1986 Stephan Runge 1988 Paul Ryon 1986 Takako Saito 1994 Francisco Salazar 1981, 1986 Claire Jeanine Satin 1986, 1990 Annette Sauermann 1992 Antonio Scaccabarozzi 1981 Alan Scarritt 1990 Senga Kamor Maskentheater 1992 Barbara Scheck 1986 Hans Schmidt 1981 Joyce Schmidt 1986, 1988 Wolfgang Schmidt 1981 Carsten Schmidt-Olsen 1990 Inge Schmitt-Strassner 1986 Matthias Schneider-Hollek 1992 Jürgen Schön 1992 Helga Schröder 1986 Joshua Schreier 1981 H. A. Schult 1981 Annemarie Schulte-Wülwer 1986 Bernard Schultze 1981 Alison Margaret Scott 1986 Miloš Šejn 1986, 1992 Moon-Seup Shim 1988 Masaaki Shimuzu 1988 Steven Siegel 1992 Fred Siegenthaler 1981, 1986 Elisabeth Sinken 1986 Beatrix Sitter-Liver 1986 Andrew James Smith 1986 Leonardo Solaas 1992 Margarethe Sørensen 1988 Eileen Spikol 1992 Bonnie Stahlecker 1988 Karen

Stahlecker 1986, 1990, 1992 Antoni Starczewski 1981 Raphael M. Steinbach 1988 Ulunmichael Steinke 1981 Thomas Steudel 1992 Norbert Stockheim 1992 Yvonne Struys 1990 Elizabeth Stuart Smith 1986 Bernhard Stüber 1986 Hye-Joo Shu (Lee) 1988 Ilona Suonio 1988 Josephine Tabbert 1990 Yoichi Takada 1988, 1992 Heiko Tappenbeck 1981, 1988 Yoko Terauchi 1988 Nancy Thayer 1990 Theater für MICH 1990, 1992 Herbert Titz 1981 Zvi Tolkovsky 1981 Raymond D. Tomasso 1988 Eng Tow 1990 Shoei-Lin Tsay 1986 Tony Tsirantonakis 1990 Garner Tullis 1986 Silvie Turner 1981 Ian Tyson 1981, 1986 Timm Ulrichs 1981, 1994 Günter Umberg 1981 Susanne Ussing 1988 Kerry van der Meer 1986 Jean van Harlingen 1986 Auk van Wingerden 1988 Elisabeth Vary 1981, 1986 Lieve Verbeelen 1986 Burkhard Vernunft 1986 Anne Vilsbøll 1986 Bernie Vinzani 1981 René Vogelsinger 1981 Ulrich Wagner 1988, 1990 Therese Weber 1986, 1988, 1992 Martin Weimar 1986, 1988, 1990 Andreas von Weizsäcker 1986, 1988, 1994 Elke Werchan 1992 Jody Williams 1986 Jean Davey Winter 1986, 1990 Paul Wong 1988 Teruyoshi Yoshida 1992 Robert S. Zakanitch 1986 Markus Züricher 1981

Preise und Jury

Prizes and jury

Der Verband deutscher Papierfabriken (VdP) setzt regelmäßig für die Internationale Biennale der Papierkunst drei Preise aus. 1992 erhielt den
1. Preis: Annette Sauermann, Aachen
2. Preis: Karen Stahlecker, Anchorage/Alaska
3. Preis: Yaeko Osono, Reeßum

Der Jury zur Vergabe der Preise 1994 gehören an:
Bernard Ceysson, Direktor Musée d'Art Moderne La Terrasse, St. Etienne
Prof. Hilmar Hoffmann, Präsident des Goethe-Instituts
Dr. Dirk-Michael Barton, Geschäftsführung des Bundesverbandes Deutscher Zeitungsverleger
Eckhard Creutz, Stadtdirektor Düren
Dr. Peter Otzen, Geschäftsführendes Präsidialmitglied des Verbandes deutscher Papierfabriken
Dr. Dorothea Eimert, Direktorin Leopold-Hoesch-Museum und Papiermuseum Düren

Die drei Preise sind dotiert mit: 1. Preis: 10 000,– DM; zwei Preise je 5000,– DM

At the International Biennale of Paper Art, the Society of German Paper Factories (VdP) regularly awards three prizes. In 1992 the prize winners were:
1st prize: Annette Sauermann, Aix-la-Chapelle
2nd prize: Karen Stahlecker, Anchorage/Alaska
3rd prize: Yaeko Osono, Reeßum

The jury of the 1994 award prizes is as follows:
Bernard Ceysson, Director Musée d'Art Moderne La Terrasse, St. Etienne
Prof. Hilmar Hoffmann, President of the Goethe-Institut
Dr. Dirk-Michael Barton, Managing Director of the Bundesverband Deutscher Zeitungsverleger
Eckhard Creutz, Chief Executive of the City of Düren
Dr. Peter Otzen, Managing Director of the Verband deutscher Papierfabriken
Dr. Dorothea Eimert, Director of the Leopold Hoesch Museum and Paper Museum Düren

The three prizes are endowed as follows: 1st prize: DM 10 000,–; two prizes each: DM 5000,–.

Personenregister

 List of persons

Foto- und Copyrightnachweis

 Photo credits and copyrights

Copyrightnachweis Copyrights

ADAGP, Paris/VG BILD-KUNST, Bonn: Bernard Aubertin 53, Georges Braque 34, Jean Dubuffet 42, Antoni Tàpies 43
ARS, New York/VG BILD-KUNST, Bonn: Frank Stella 103
(c) Galerie Lelong Zürich Zurich: Eduardo Chillida 123
courtesy Krings-Ernst Gallery, Köln Cologne: Dmitri Prigov 127, 217
Printed and published by Gemini G.E.L., Los Angeles, © copyright Robert Rauschenberg/Gemini G.E.L. 1971 134
Printed and published by Gemini G.E.L., Los Angeles, © copyright Robert Rauschenberg/Gemini G.E.L. 1974 88
Printed and published by Gemini G.E.L., © copyright Anni Albers/Gemini G.E.L. 1978 67
© All rights reserved, The Metropolitan Museum of Art, New York. Robert Lehmann Collection 1975. (1975.1.736): Felix Vallotton 27
PRO LITTERIS, Zürich Zurich/VG BILD-KUNST, Bonn: Meret Oppenheim 116
SABAM, Brüssel, Brussels/VG BILD-KUNST, Bonn: Urbain Mulkers 112
SPADEM, Paris/VG BILD-KUNST, Bonn: Pablo Picasso 33, 35
SUCESSION Matisse, Paris/VG BILD-KUNST, Bonn: Henri Matisse 122
V.A.G.A., New York/VG BILD-KUNST, Bonn: Robert Motherwell, Kenneth Noland, Robert Rauschenberg, James Rosenquist
Printed and published by Tyler Graphics Ltd.: © copyright Anthony Caro/Tyler Graphics Ltd. 1982, 135 oben above, 136. Fotos photos: Steven Sloman
Printed and published by Tyler Graphics Ltd.: © copyright Anthony Caro/Tyler Graphics Ltd. 1993 167, 169. Fotos photos: Steven Sloman
Printed and published by Tyler Graphics Ltd.: © copyright David Hockney/Tyler Graphics Ltd. 1978 96/97. Foto photo: Steven Sloman
Printed and published by Tyler Graphics Ltd.: © copyright Ellsworth Kelly/Tyler Graphics Ltd. 1976 101. Foto photo: Steven Sloman
Printed and published by Tyler Graphics Ltd.: © copyright Robert Motherwell/Tyler Graphics Ltd. 1984 135 unten below. Foto photo: Steven Sloman
Printed and published by Tyler Graphics Ltd.: © copyright Kenneth Noland/Tyler Graphics Ltd. 1978 91, 92, 93. Fotos photos: Steven Sloman
Printed and published by Tyler Graphics Ltd.: © copyright James Rosenquist/Tyler Graphics Ltd. 1989 227, 229, 231. Fotos photos: Steven Sloman
Printed and published by Tyler Graphics Ltd.: © copyright Alan Shields/Tyler Graphics Ltd. 1984 104. Foto photo: Steven Sloman
Printed and published by Tyler Graphics Ltd.: © copyright Alan Shields/Tyler Graphics Ltd. 1985 105. Foto photo: Steven Sloman
Printed and published by Tyler Graphics Ltd.: © copyright Frank Stella/Tyler Graphics Ltd. 1975 103. Foto photo: Steven Sloman
VG BILD-KUNST, Bonn: Horst Antes 116, Joseph Beuys 16, Felix Droese 124, 125, 175, Wolfgang Finck 109, Axel Heibel 62, Jiři Hilmar 61, Bertram Jesdinsky 137, 138, Wolf Kahlen 71, Yaeko Osono 74, Annette Sauermann 141, Kurt Schwitters 36, Timm Ulrichs 76, 235, 237, Martin Weimar 75

Falls nicht anders angegeben, liegt das Copyright der Abbildungen bei den jeweiligen Künstlern. The authors are the copyright-holders if not mentioned otherwise.
Das Copyright der Texte liegt bei den Autoren. The authors are the copyright-holders of the texts.

Nachweis des Standortes Location

Collection Fondation Jean Dubuffet: Périgny-sur-Yerres 42
Colección Fundació Antoni Tàpies: Barcelona 43
Edition Gutsch, Berlin 163
Wolfgang Feelisch, Remscheid 16, 56 124, 139 oben above, 146, 147, 150
Folkwang Museum, Essen 35
Galerie Schoeller, Düsseldorf 53, 66
Galerie Wack, Kaiserslautern 57, 60 rechts right, 61 links left
John Gerard, Rheinbach-Hilberath 116 unten rechts below, right, 175
Günther-Peill-Stiftung, Düren 137
Josef Albers Museum Quadrat, Bottrop 39
Kröller-Müller-Museum, Otterlo 144
Leopold-Hoesch-Museum, Düren 29, 60, 116
Marilyn Pearl Gallery, New York 108
Märkisches Museum, Witten 114
Museum Ludwig, Köln Cologne 122, 132, 133
The Museum of Modern Art, New York. Geschenk des Künstlers. Gift of the artist. 33 rechts right
Musée d'Orsay, Paris 25
Axel-Hinrich und Christa Murken, Herzogenrath 63
National Gallery of Australia, Canberra 67
Sprengel Museum, Hannover 36
Springer & Winkler Galerie, Frankfurt/M. 129

Staatsgalerie Stuttgart, Das Archiv Sohm 72
Städtisches Museum Villa Zanders, Bergisch Gladbach 73
Ulmer Museum, Ulm. Dauerleihgabe des Landes Baden-Württemberg Permantent loan of the state of Baden-Württemberg 34
Washington University Gallery of Art, Saint Louis/Miss. 33 links left

Fotonachweis Photo credits

© John Babcock, Davenport/ Ca. 108 unten below
Berndt & Wolf Fotografie, Köln Cologne 127
© Josef Böhm, Stolberg 78, 81, 116 oben above + unten links below, left
C. Victor Dahmen, Köln Cologne 130
Edd Daniels, Hasselt, Belgien Belgium 112 unten below
Manfred Fischer, Düsseldorf 51 unten below
© Museum Folkwang, Essen 35
© Fondation Jean Dubuffet, Périgny-sur-Yerres 42
© Fundació Antoni Tàpies, Barcelona 43
Galerie Wack, Kaiserslautern 57, 60, 61 unten below
© Galerie Lelong Zürich Zurich 123
John Gerard 107, 116 unten rechts below, right
© Anne Gold, Aachen Aix-la-Chapelle 29 rechts right, 60, 74, 129 links left, 137, 141, 142 oben above, 143, 171, 173, 181, 183, 185, 187, 193, 199, 201, 203, 205, 213, 215, 219, 221, 223, 225, 239, 241
© Lindsay Green/Tyler Graphics Ltd., Mount Kisco/N. Y. 91, 95, 136
© Dieter Grundmann, Gelsenkirchen 61 oben above
© Gerhard Heisler, Saarbrücken 58
© Manfred Johannsen, Bonn 29 links left, 148
Uli Kreifels, Köln Cologne 195, 197
Krings-Ernst Galerie, Köln Cologne 138, 140, 217
The Metropolitan Museum of Art, New York 27
Christa Murken-Altrogge, Herzogenrath 63
Studio Müller + Schmitz, Remscheid 16, 56, 124, 139 oben above, 146, 147, 150
© Museum Folkwang, Essen 35
© The Museum of Modern Art, New York 33 rechts right
© National Gallery of Australia, Canberra 67
C. Omenetto – G. Agostini, Mailand Milan 111
Frank Paulin, Riverhead/N.Y. 79
Marilyn Pearl Gallery/New York 108 oben above
© Documentation photographique de la Réunion des Musées Nationaux, Paris 25
© Rheinisches Bildarchiv, Köln Cologne 122, 132, 133
Schmitz-Fabri, Rodenkirchen 64
Foto Siegel, Neu Ulm 34
© Steven Sloman/Gemini G.E.L., Los Angeles 88
© Steven Sloman/Tyler Graphics Ltd., Mount Kisco/N.Y. 92, 93, 96/97, 101, 103, 104, oben above, 105, 135
© Sprengel Museum, Hannover 36
© Staatsgalerie Stuttgart 72
Octavian Stacescu, Düsseldorf 51 oben above, 53, 66
Städtische Galerie Villa Zanders, Bergisch Gladbach 73
© Kenneth Tyler, Mount Kisco/N. Y. 87, 104
© Tyler Graphics Ltd., Mount Kisco/N. Y. 100
Foto photo: Umbo 39
© Elke Walford, Werkstatt Hamburger Kunsthalle 125
© Washington University Gallery of Art, Saint Louis/Miss. 33 links left
Edward Woodman, London 207, 209, 211
Horst Ziegenfusz, München Munich 114

Die übrigen Fotografien wurden von den Künstlern selbst erstellt. The other photographs were made by the artists.

Titelabbildung Illustration front cover:
Kenneth Noland: Diagonal Stripes TP VI-3
(aus dem ‚Handmade Paper Project'), 1978.
Gefärbter und gepreßter Papierpulp. 110 x 85 cm/
Kenneth Noland: Diagonal Stripes TP VI-3
(from the 'Handmade Paper Project'), 1978.
Colored and pressed paper pulp. 110 x 85 cm.
Printed and published by Tyler Graphics Ltd.

Foto photo: Steven Sloman

Die Deutsche Bibliothek – CIP-Einheitsaufnahme

Geschichte der Papierkunst: (Ausstellung 15. Juni – 25. September 1994) = History of paper art/ 5. Internationale Biennale der Papierkunst 1994. Leopold-Hoesch-Museum Düren. (Dorothea Eimert). – Köln: Wienand, 1994
ISBN 3-87909-358-X
NE: Eimert, Dorothea; Internationale Biennale der Papierkunst <5,1994, Düren>; Leopold-Hoesch-Museum <Düren>; History of paper art

Lektorat Editorship: Petra Kruse
Gestaltung Graphic design: Achim Seiffert, Köln Cologne
Übersetzungen Translations:
vom Deutschen ins Englische from German into English:
Jeanne Haunschild, Bonn
vom Englischen ins Deutsche from English into German:
Manfred Allié, Euskirchen (Rosenquist);
Cornell Hentze, Köln Cologne (Caro, Petry, Regev);
Petra Kruse, Köln Cologne (Prigov)
vom Französischen ins Deutsche from French into German:
Stefan Barmann, Köln Cologne
aus dem Israelischen ins Englische from Israelian into English:
Rela Mazali, Tel Aviv

Papier Paper:
Gedruckt auf printed on ikonorex special-matt Chlorfrei, weiß white 150 und and 300g/qm der ZANDERS Feinpapiere AG, Bergisch Gladbach und and Düren

Gesamtherstellung/General production:
Druck- & Verlagshaus Wienand, Köln Cologne

Printed in Germany

ISBN 3-87909-358-X